HISTORY OF THE GREAT WAR
SEABORNE TRADE
VOL. III

HISTORY OF THE GREAT WAR

BASED ON OFFICIAL DOCUMENTS

BY DIRECTION OF THE HISTORICAL SECTION OF THE
COMMITTEE OF IMPERIAL DEFENCE

SEABORNE TRADE

Vol. III

THE PERIOD OF UNRESTRICTED SUBMARINE WARFARE

BY
C. ERNEST FAYLE

The Naval & Military Press Ltd

Published by

The Naval & Military Press Ltd
Unit 10 Ridgewood Industrial Park,
Uckfield, East Sussex,
TN22 5QE England

Tel: +44 (0) 1825 749494
Fax: +44 (0) 1825 765701

www.naval-military-press.com
www.military-genealogy.com

In reprinting in facsimile from the original, any imperfections are inevitably reproduced and the quality may fall short of modern type and cartographic standards.

ADDENDA AND CORRIGENDA

VOLUME I

p. 104 (line 4 from bottom). For " July 29th," read " July 31st."

p. 127 (line 1). The D'IBERVILLE and the French destroyers were employed in the Java Sea during August, and did not take up their position in the Malacca Strait until after the arrival of the *Goldenfels* at Sabang (see p. 141).

p. 178 (line 18). For " the only German vessel," read " the only vessel under the German flag." There were certain German-owned ships under the Argentine flag which continued to ply (see Vol. II, p. 306 n.⁴).

p. 214 (lines 26–28). This account of the movements of the CHIKUMA is based on a telegram that was subsequently corrected. She actually left Colombo at 8.30 a.m. on September 30th, and by Captain Grant's direction proceeded towards Minikoi.

p. 325 (line 18). For " south-east," read " south-west."

(line 26). For " An hour or so later," read " Early next morning."

p. 426 (line 40). For *Marie Glasier*, read *Marie Glaeser*.

Maps. The position given in Map 9 for the capture of the *Semantha* is based on a report which subsequently proved to be incorrect. She was actually captured, as stated in the text, p. 377, in very nearly the same position as the *Highland Brae*. In the marginal references to Map 5, the captures in Area " D " should accordingly be attributed to the PRINZ EITEL FRIEDRICH alone.

ADDENDA AND CORRIGENDA

VOLUME II

p. 144. It should have been stated that the exercise of economic pressure during the earlier part of the war was under the general supervision of the Committee on Restriction of Enemy Supplies, appointed by the Admiralty in August 1914, "to examine and watch continually all means or routes by which supplies of food or raw material may reach Germany or Austria; to recommend by what methods, financial, commercial, diplomatic, military, they may be hampered and restricted, and, if possible, stopped." This Committee represented at first, only the Admiralty, Board of Trade, and Foreign Office. Representatives of the Committee of Imperial Defence, India Office, Colonial Office, Customs, War Office, and Trade Clearing House were subsequently added. A Restriction of Enemy Supplies Department, under the Foreign Office, was created in August 1916.

In September, 1915, the War Trade Advisory Committee was appointed, by a Treasury minute, "to advise on the restriction of enemy supplies; to co-ordinate the administration of the War Trade Department, the Contraband Committee, the Restriction of Enemy Supplies Committee, and the Committees for controlling the export of coal, cotton, rubber, and tin; and to advise the Cabinet on questions arising therefrom." In addition to representatives of the various bodies named in the terms of reference, and those represented on the old Restriction of Enemy Supplies Committee, it comprised representatives of the Ministry of Munitions, War Trade Statistical Department, Foreign Trade Department, Board of Agriculture and Fisheries, and Enemy Exports Committee.

To the Restriction of Enemy Supplies Committee and, later, to the War Trade Advisory Committee was mainly due the development of the system of agreements with neutral merchants, described in this and subsequent chapters, and of the "rationing policy" which became the basis of all measures of restriction in 1917.

p. 154. Add after first paragraph: "The extreme difficulty of obtaining conclusive evidence as to the enemy destination of particular cargoes, led to the proposal, originating in the Restriction of Enemy Supplies Committee, that the neutral States contiguous to Germany should be "rationed" on the basis of their normal domestic consumption, and that

ADDENDA AND CORRIGENDA

all imports in excess of this quantity should be cut off, by prohibition of export from the British Empire, and by the seizure of shipments from other sources. It appeared, however, to be very doubtful how far the Prize Courts would accept purely statistical evidence, and no general attempt at forcible rationing was made until a much later date." (See also p. 36 of Vol. III.)

p. 306 (n.[4]). For " Hamburg Amerika," read " Hamburg Süd Amerika."

p. 307 (n.[1], last line). For " 24 October," read " 29 October."

p. 376 (n.[1], last line). For " 1914," read " 1913."

p. 379 (line 5 from bottom). For " an Inter-departmental Committee under Sir H. Babington-Smith," read " a Committee under Lord Curzon of Kedleston " (see Vol. III, pp. 17 and 19).

The following figures should be corrected to bring them into line with those adopted in the tables to Vol. III, which are based on more recent information (see Vol. III, Appendix B: Note on Statistics):

p. 231 (last paragraph). For " 48,750,000," read " 45,042,000 " ; for " 56,000,000," read " 51,776,000 " ; for " over 300,000," read " 476,000 " ; for " nearly 25,000,000," read " 23,416,000."

p. 233 (line 29). For " over 25 per cent.," read " nearly 29 per cent." It was subsequently discovered that the tonnage deficit had been overestimated, owing to the omission of temporarily released ships from the tables supplied.

p. 295 (line 4). For " nearly 1,400,000," read " 1,237,000 " ; for " 370,000," read " 356,000."

p. 297 (lines 8 and 9). For " 7 per cent.," read " 6·4 per cent." ; for " 6 per cent.," read " 6·3 per cent."

p. 387 (lines 35–36). For " probably in the neighbourhood of 46,000,000 tons, about the same as in 1915," read " 44,282,000 tons, or within 5 per cent. of the total for 1915."

PREFACE

THIS volume, the third and last of the history of seaborne trade during the war, covers the period from the opening of the "unrestricted" submarine campaign to the Armistice.

During this period the process of economic pressure attained, on both sides, its maximum intensity. By the end of 1916 the war had become, to a great extent, a contest of endurance. The Central Powers were thrown back almost entirely on their own fast-dwindling resources. To the Allies the sea routes had hitherto been open; but the effects of the war on their export trade rendered the financing of future imports a problem of the gravest difficulty, and the progressive diminution of the available tonnage threatened to render it impossible at once to fulfil the demands of the fighting services, and to maintain the stream of supplies.

The story of the years 1917 and 1918 is the story of a great gamble. In deciding on unrestricted submarine warfare the German Government deliberately risked and actually brought about the intervention of the United States, by which, apart from its military results, the Allies' immediate financial problem was solved, and their grip tightened on every source of supplies yet remaining open to the Central Powers. The enemy staked everything on the chance that, before the exhaustion of Germany had reached the point of collapse, the destruction of Allied and neutral shipping would render Great Britain no longer able to feed her own people and, at the same time, perform her functions in the Alliance.

It has been the author's task to show how nearly this gamble succeeded. It has been his task also to show at how heavy a cost it was ultimately foiled.

In the spring and early summer of 1917, the submarines seemed not unlikely to exert a decisive influence on the course of the war. Their successes compelled recourse to the old method of protection by convoy. With the purely naval aspects of the convoy system this book is not concerned, save in so far as it records the effect of convoys in diminishing the tale of losses ; but the problem of adapting the system to the conditions of modern commerce was one of extraordinary difficulty, and the measures and organisation by which it was solved form by no means the least instructive, or least interesting chapter in the history of war-time trade.

Naval defence, however, was only one side of the great problem of supplies. Before the adoption of convoy, even before the outbreak of the unrestricted submarine campaign, the reduction in British tonnage and the reluctance of neutral ships to face the dangers of a voyage to Allied ports, had led to a redistribution of purchases, in which all ordinary commercial considerations were subordinated to the primary necessity of obtaining the maximum proportion of imports from the nearest sources of supply, and thus economising tonnage by concentrating it upon the shortest routes. This concentration it was never possible to relax. Although the monthly average of loss was far smaller in 1918 than in 1917, the strain on British shipping had been increased by the growth in Allied demands, and by the reactions of the Russian collapse. The great German offensive in France complicated, by carrying the tide of invasion further West, the problem of the French and Italian coal supply, and led to an increase in the American programme of trooping and military supplies which absorbed, not only all the tonnage that America could build, but a substantial proportion of the carrying power of British shipping. To the last, it continued to be a question not of maintaining " seaborne trade " in the ordinary sense of the term, but of straining every nerve to bring in the minimum supplies essential to the feeding of the Allied peoples and to the conduct of the war.

How far this situation could have been averted or alleviated by an earlier realisation of the danger, by maintaining the output of mercantile tonnage, by anti-submarine measures, by the earlier adoption of remedies for port congestion, by more careful adjustment of demands to resources ; how far it was relieved or accentuated by the measures actually adopted, history will decide, as the various factors fall into their proper perspective. These volumes have been written in the hope of contributing something towards the attainment of that perspective. Meanwhile, three things are clear: that the crisis of 1917–18 was the result of a cumulative deficit, dating back almost to the beginning of the war, in the carrying power available for commercial purposes; that in this crisis, rigid concentration of purchases and drastic restriction of non-essential imports proved the salvation of the Allies; and that the price paid has been heavy.

The full measure of that price cannot yet be estimated. Were this a general economic history of the war, it would be necessary to bring it down to date and to attempt a forecast of the future. It would be further necessary to attempt the extraordinarily difficult task of unravelling, in the economic situation of the world to-day, the factors arising respectively from the events of the war itself on the one hand, and from the Peace Treaties and events subsequent to the Armistice on the other. " The object of this book," however, as stated in the preface to Vol. I, " is to show how seaborne trade was affected during the war by naval operations and conditions having their origin in the naval situation." It has accordingly been thought wise to bring the narrative to a conclusion at the Armistice, and to limit the final summary to an analysis of the position in which the belligerents were left as an immediate result of the struggle, striving only to indicate such seeds of future weakness as can be traced directly to the effects of the war at sea.

In a friendly review of the second volume of this work, it was suggested that the absence of criticism was due to its " official " character. In justice to the Departments concerned, the Author wishes to say that no attempt has been made to fetter the expression of his opinion. He had to deal with many matters that are still the subject of acute controversy, on the basis of material much of which is not yet generally accessible. In these circumstances it seemed to him that he would perform the best service by telling, as clearly as he could, what was done, why it was done, and with what results; stating the grounds of any objections urged at the time, but abstaining, in general, from personal comment, and leaving the reader to draw his own conclusions. Whether this course be right or wrong, it is one for which he must accept full responsibility.

It seems desirable to repeat that this book makes no pretence of giving a complete account of the machinery for restriction of enemy trade. It deals with the effect of economic isolation on the Central Powers, and to make the results intelligible, it was necessary to give some account of the methods employed; but an exhaustive analysis of the intricate diplomatic and financial network woven round the enemy countries could only be made in a work devoted specifically to that side of the war organisation.[1]

A word may be added with regard to the statistical data. Any serious study of war-time trade must rest largely on a statistical basis; but the preparation of tables illustrating in detail the monthly fluctuations in the flow of trade, the entrances and clearances of ships under each flag, and the imports and exports of various classes of goods, would have added substantially to the bulk and cost of the book. Moreover, a great part of such tables would inevitably have been based on figures already published and easily accessible. The method adopted has been to give in the footnotes figures bearing on particular points in the text, and to confine other statistical material to a limited number of tables and diagrams that may assist in forming a bird's-eye view of the subject. In text, footnotes, and tables alike special attention has been paid to figures not elsewhere accessible, and those based on published material have been cut down to a minimum.

It will be observed that there is an entire absence of *pièces justificatives*. The documents consulted fall into two broad classes; those which are already accessible, to which reference is given in the notes, and those of which publication is at present withheld.

A large part of the preparatory work for this volume was done by Mrs. W. F. B. Scott, without whose industry and acumen in research, the task of dealing with so vast a mass of material would have been practically impossible. In this connection, too, the author desires to make grateful acknowledgment of the courtesy and assistance extended to him by the Admiralty, the Board of Trade, and the late Ministry of Shipping, and in particular of his obliga-

[1] The use of the word "blockade" to describe the machinery of economic pressure is technically incorrect, despite the creation of a "Ministry of Blockade." The possibility of misconception arising from the employment of the term has become increasingly clear since the second volume of this work was issued, and in the present volume it has been avoided throughout.

tions to Mr. L. F. Goldsmid, O.B.E., of the Ministry of Shipping, for his unfailing readiness to furnish material and clear up points of difficulty. To all those mentioned in the prefaces to the previous volumes his thanks are again due, especially to Sir Kenneth Anderson, Bart., K.C.M.G., Mr. A. F. Fawcus, Sir Lionel Fletcher, C.B.E., Sir Norman Hill, Bart., Mr. H. W. Macrosty, C.B.E., Admiral Sir Edmond J. W. Slade, K.C.I.E., K.C.V.O., and also to Mr. L. A. P. Warner (late Director, Port Branch, Ministry of Shipping), all of whom have been good enough to read the proofs, in whole or in part, for the purposes of revision, and to the staff of the Historical Section, who have given him loyal and untiring help.

One name remains to be mentioned. How much the author owes to the encouragement and advice of the late Sir Julian Corbett, under whom it was his great privilege to work as a member of the Historical Section, he can never adequately express.

C. ERNEST FAYLE.

CONTENTS

CHAPTER I

THE MINISTRY OF SHIPPING, DECEMBER 1916—APRIL 1917

The shipping problem, freights, supplies, administration—Powers of the Shipping Controller—His staff and its growth—Tonnage Priority Committee—Transfer of Transport Department to Ministry of Shipping—Position of Port and Transit Committee—Relations between Shipping Controller and Board of Trade—Refrigerated Shipping Committee—Organisation of Ministry of Shipping in April 1917 . . pp. 1-16

CHAPTER II

THE TONNAGE PROBLEM, JANUARY 1917

The question of import restrictions—Shortage of space for Munitions—Prospective tonnage shortage—Interdepartmental Committee on Import Restrictions—Commitments of Transport Department—Shipment of Australian wheat suspended—Demands of France and Italy—Inter-Allied Chartering Committee—The Greek Ship Scheme—Allocations of neutral tonnage—Breakdown of Freight Limitation Scheme—Activity of submarines and raiders—Allied Naval Conference—Further demands of Allies—The White Sea Programme—Sources of tonnage . pp. 17-34

CHAPTER III

UNRESTRICTED SUBMARINE WARFARE AND ITS EFFECTS ON NEUTRALS, FEBRUARY—MARCH 1917

Internal condition of Germany—Shortage of materials, coal, and food—German Government decide on unrestricted submarine warfare—Barred Zones declared—Neutral protests—Suspension of neutral sailings—Steps taken to meet the emergency—The "ship-for-ship" policy—British relations with Northern neutrals—Activity of Norwegian shipping—Danish produce-ships—Friction between Britain and Holland—Friction with Spain—Ore and fruit—Great decline in neutral entrances and clearances—Effect on French and Italian coal supply—Losses of neutrals—United States declares war on Germany . . . pp. 35-55

CHAPTER IV

GROWING SHORTAGE OF TONNAGE, IMPORT RESTRICTIONS, FEBRUARY—MARCH 1917

German hopes and their justification—Losses of shipping—Increased War Risk premiums—Tonnage deficit—Report on Import Restrictions—Principles and difficulties—Analysis of the restrictions—Effect on national life—Comparison with conditions in Germany—Reduction of German flour ration—German metal shortage—Work of Tonnage Priority Committee—Large deficit—Liner Requisition Scheme—Proposed restriction of re-exports—Condition of the ports—News of raiders—Mines in the Indian Ocean—WOLF, MOEWE, and SEEADLER—Destruction of the LEOPARD . . . . pp. 56–73

CHAPTER V

SHIPBUILDING AND SHIP PURCHASE, JANUARY—MARCH 1917

Continued decline in output—State shipbuilding programme—The " Standard " ship—Shortage of labour and steel—Increase in repair work—Prospective output—Oversea Ship Purchase—United States seizes German shipping—Germans damage the ships—China seizes German shipping—Prospects of tonnage supply . . . . pp. 74–84

CHAPTER VI

THE DARKEST HOUR, APRIL 1917

Slight improvement in situation—Effect of import restrictions—Prospective tonnage deficit—Proposals of Ministry of Shipping—Great increase in submarine activity—Heavy losses in areas of approach—Further rise in War Risk premiums—Three months' losses—Acceleration in rate of loss—Prospective import deficit—Neutral and Allied shipping—Losses of defensively armed merchantmen—Convoy proposals—Difficulties of convoy—French coal trade convoys—Scandinavian Convoy
pp. 85–100

CHAPTER VII

EFFORTS AT REPLACEMENT, MARCH—MAY 1917

Further seizures of enemy tonnage—Little immediately available—Progress of ship purchase—American shipbuilding programme—Controversies as to standard types—Acute shortage of steel—Acceleration of Repairs—Control of shipbuilding transferred to Admiralty   pp. 101–108

CHAPTER VIII

THE LINER REQUISITION SCHEME, FEBRUARY—JULY 1917

Difficulties of liner requisition — Outlines of the scheme — Special difficulties of North Atlantic trade—Negotiations with the lines—Scheme brought into operation subject to terms to be agreed—The Liner Requisitioning Committee—Services adjusted solely to import requirements—The Atlantic concentration—Import Priority Lists—Effect on exports—Special provision for Indian trade—Textile Exports Committee—Priority Lists and services in the various trades—Extent of Atlantic concentration . . . . pp. 109–127

CHAPTER IX

THE INTRODUCTION OF CONVOY, MAY—AUGUST 1917

Number of voyages to be protected—Report of Convoy Committee—Experimental convoys—Continued heavy losses in approach areas—Beginnings of North Atlantic Convoy—Extension of the system—Its success—Submarines in mid-Atlantic—Dakar and Sierra Leone Convoys—Reorganisation of homeward convoys in North Atlantic—Introduction of outward convoys—Career of the WOLF—Wreck of the SEEADLER—Pro-

CONTENTS xiii

gress of liner requisition negotiations—Modification of State Insurance Scheme—Convoy losses . . . . . . pp. 128-147

CHAPTER X

THE NEUTRAL TONNAGE AGREEMENTS, APRIL—JULY 1917

Neutral losses—Ship-for-ship policy, bunker pressure, and requisitioning—Negotiations for Tonnage Agreement with Norway—Kogrund Agreement with Sweden—Failure of tonnage negotiations with Spain—Tonnage Agreement concluded with Denmark—Conclusion of the Norwegian Agreement—Survey of the position as regards neutral tonnage pp. 148-157

CHAPTER XI

CARRYING POWER AND IMPORTS, FEBRUARY—JULY 1917

Six months' losses—Net reduction in tonnage available—Execution of White Sea Programme—Demands of Allies and Services—Conditions at the ports—Ministry of Shipping Port and Home Trade Branches—Work of Transport Workers' Battalions—Improvement in port conditions—Effect of Import Restrictions—Ministry of Shipping organisation in America—Entrances and Imports—Cereals—Meat and insulated shipping—Materials—Cotton Control Board—Oil-fuel crisis—Carriage of oil in double bottoms—Exports and re-exports—Situation in Germany—Value of Roumanian supplies—Acute shortage of food and materials—Deterioration of transport system—Oil supplies . . . . pp. 158-181

CHAPTER XII

CONVOYS AND TURN-ROUND, AUGUST—NOVEMBER 1917

Reduction in losses following adoption of convoy—Heavy losses in Mediterranean—Through Mediterranean Convoys—Gain in carrying power by reversion to Suez route—Local convoys in Mediterranean—Surface attack on Scandinavian Convoy—Losses by areas since introduction of convoy—Effect of convoy system on turn-round—Increased length of round voyage in Atlantic trade—Entrances and imports—Anxiety as to meat supply—Supplies of raw materials—Prospective deficit for 1918—Necessity of accelerating turn-round—Establishment of Liverpool Convoy Committee—Work of Port and Transit Committee—Increased use of West Coast ports—Further reduction in losses . . . pp. 182-203

CHAPTER XIII

THE PROGRESS OF REPLACEMENT, MAY—NOVEMBER 1917

Organisation of Navy Controller's Department—New programme—Steel and labour shortage—Shipyard extensions—The National Yards—Modifications of standard types—Standard tankers—American building programme—United States requisition British ships building in American yards—Utilisation of enemy tonnage—Supply of neutral tonnage
pp. 204-219

CHAPTER XIV

THE SYSTEM OF EMBARGOES, JULY—NOVEMBER 1917

Struggle for Danish produce—Embargo on shipments of fodder and fertilisers to Denmark—The United States and the neutrals—American export and bunker restrictions—British Agreement with United States regarding Norwegian tonnage—General embargo on exports to Northern neutrals—German exports to neutrals—Oil and coal shortage in Germany—Effect of embargoes in restricting enemy supplies—Effect in reducing task of Navy—Northern Patrol withdrawn . . . pp. 220-234

CHAPTER XV
THE INTER-ALLIED PROGRAMME, NOVEMBER—DECEMBER 1917

Bad harvests in France and Italy—World shortage of cereals—Existing Inter-Allied purchase and tonnage organisations—Russian Revolution and the White Sea Programme—Inter-Allied Food Agreement of November 3rd—Allied Conference in Paris—Tonnage situation and import requirements—Extent of the deficit—American trooping—Appeal to the United States for tonnage—Inter-Allied control of tonnage and imports decided on . . . . pp. 235-246

CHAPTER XVI
TONNAGE AND LOSSES, NOVEMBER 1917—JANUARY 1918

Working of Atlantic concentration—By-products problem in meat trade—*China Mutual* v. *Maclay*—Effects of decision on Liner Requisition Scheme—Heads of Arrangement signed—Inshore activity of submarines—Mediterranean losses—Reorganisation of Scandinavian Convoy—Shipbuilding output—Cumulative deficit—Employment of Allied and neutral shipping—Agreement with United States as to neutral shipping—Effect of the embargoes—*Modus vivendi* with Sweden—Negotiations with Holland . . . . pp. 247-266

CHAPTER XVII
DIMINISHING IMPORTS, AUGUST 1917—JANUARY 1918

Reduction in ballast voyages—Entrances and imports—Effect of import restrictions—Supplies of food and materials—Insulated tonnage and Allied meat supplies—Decrease in exports—Restriction of re-exports—Redirection of export trade—French and Italian imports—Financial situation of Allies. . . . . pp. 267-280

CHAPTER XVIII
INTENSIFIED ATLANTIC CONCENTRATION, FEBRUARY—MARCH 1918

Second Import Restrictions Committee—Big prospective deficit—Cereal programme—Block in American ports—Stock position—Meat programme—By-products—Increase of tonnage in North Atlantic—Submarine activity in Mediterranean and Home Waters—WOLF arrives at Kiel—Her career—Submarines off Azores—Rio Convoy—Appointment of Lord Pirrie as Controller-General of Merchant Shipbuilding—Revised proposals as to Dutch tonnage . . . . pp. 281-292

CHAPTER XIX
THE ALLIED MARITIME TRANSPORT COUNCIL, FEBRUARY—MARCH 1918

Organisation of Council and Executive—Relations with other Inter-Allied bodies—Joint import deficiency—United States tonnage absorbed

CONTENTS

by military programme—Italian Coal Programme—Requisition of Dutch shipping—Effects of German offensive on tonnage position—French and Italian coal supplies—American trooping—Tonnage economies—Provisional Inter-Allied Programme—Transport Council recommend revision of programmes—Inter-Allied chartering—The Neutral Pool pp. 293-306

CHAPTER XX
IMPROVEMENTS IN SHIPPING ORGANISATION, MARCH—JULY 1918

Rio Convoy for Plate grain trade—New arrangements in Home Waters—Blocking of Zeebrugge and Ostend—Effect on losses—Improved organisation in Mediterranean—Rearrangement of North Atlantic Convoys—Work of Liverpool Convoy Committee—New York Convoy Committee—Improved turn-round—Fall in cotton imports—Cereal diversions to France and Italy—Sacrifice made by Great Britain—Bunker difficulties, especially in connection with Rio Convoy—Redistribution of insulated tonnage—Australasian meat shut out—Development of Ship Management Branch—Employment of Neutral Pool . . . . pp. 307-331

CHAPTER XXI
DISTRIBUTION AND CARRYING POWER, FEBRUARY—JULY 1918

Labour difficulties at ports—Deterioration of rolling stock—Limited possibilities of diversion—Transport Battalions on rail and canal service—Diversions from rail to water—Work of Home Trade Branch—Home Trade Transport Control Committee—Avoidance of unnecessary haulage—Good effect of penalty rents—The glut of bacon—General position—Entrances and imports—Importance of improved turn-round pp. 332-346

CHAPTER XXII
REACTIONS OF THE RUSSIAN COLLAPSE, JANUARY—JULY 1918

Economic factors of Russian débâcle—German-Ukranian Agreement—Exaggerated optimism in Germany—Austria saved by Ukranian supplies—Finance and transport difficulties—Failure of Roumanian harvest—Breakdown of German moral—Effects of embargoes on northern neutrals—Norwegian-American Agreement—Agreement with Sweden—Intensified Economic Pressure—Escape of British ships from Russia—Requisition of Russian shipping—General effects of Russian defection . pp. 347-362

CHAPTER XXIII
TROOPING AND IMPORTS, JULY—AUGUST 1918

Continued reduction of losses—Submarines on American coast—Reduced losses in ore trade—Improved shipbuilding output—The tonnage position—Proportion of ships under repair—Increase in American trooping—The Import Programme Committees—Cereals—Coal—New services for Allies—British contribution to pool of tonnage—Allied Import Programmes—United States require assistance in military supply

pp. 363-380

CHAPTER XXIV

MUNITIONS TAKE PRECEDENCE OF FOOD, AUGUST—SEPTEMBER 1918

Effect of American demands—Tonnage economies—Labour troubles at ports—Entrances and imports—Ore—Cereals—American trooping and meat supplies—Continued rise in cost of living—Allied import programmes —Priority for munitions—Food supplies to be cut down and stocks reduced . . . . pp. 381-393

CHAPTER XXV

THE LAST PHASE, SEPTEMBER—NOVEMBER 1918

Tonnage economies—Improved turn-round in North Atlantic—Dwindling losses—Mines on American coast—Allied offensive on land—Critical economic condition of Central Powers—Disappointment of hopes from Ukraine—Effect of Bulgarian collapse—Oil famine in Germany—Deterioration of railways, mines, and industries—Shortage of military material—Reactions of economic conditions and military events—Famine, disease, and disintegration in Austria—Failure of submarine campaign—Anxieties of Allied Governments—Tonnage and requirements—The Armistice
pp. 394-410

CHAPTER XXVI

AFTER THE ARMISTICE

Position of Allies at Armistice—British supplies of food and materials—Diminishing exports—Position of France and Italy—Future prospects—Contrast with Central Powers—Decontrol of shipping—Tonnage shortage —Acquisition of enemy shipping—Delay in delivery of German ships—Provisioning of Germany—Tonnage and financial difficulties pp. 411-423

CHAPTER XXVII

THE LEGACY OF THE WAR

Effects of economic pressure in Germany—Food supplies and production —Industries and transport—Finance—Mortality and disease—Capacity for recuperation—Economic chaos in Austria and Russia—How far affected by war at sea—Condition of Belgium and France—Necessity for distinguishing between effects of invasion and effects of war at sea—Condition of Italy—Condition of Great Britain—Shipping and shipbuilding—Food supplies—Industries — Ports and railways—Exports—Redirection of Trade—Finance—Loss of markets—World conditions—Conclusions
pp 424-458

APPENDIX A: POWERS OF THE SHIPPING CONTROLLER . . . . . . pp. 459-461

APPENDIX B: NOTE ON STATISTICS . . pp. 462-463

APPENDIX C: TABLES . . . . . pp. 464-483

INDEX . . . . pp. 485-501

LIST OF DIAGRAMS AND MAP

MAP

THE ATLANTIC OCEAN AND EUROPEAN WATERS, SHOWING "BARRED ZONES."

IN SEPARATE VOLUME

STATISTICAL DIAGRAMS

DIAGRAMS SHOWING VOLUME AND DIRECTION OF TRADE
1913–18

1. NET TONNAGE OF VESSELS ENTERED WITH CARGOES AT PORTS IN THE UNITED KINGDOM, DISTINGUISHING BRITISH AND FOREIGN, in SIX-MONTHLY PERIODS.
2. NET TONNAGE OF VESSELS CLEARED WITH CARGOES AT PORTS IN THE UNITED KINGDOM, DISTINGUISHING BRITISH AND FOREIGN, IN SIX-MONTHLY PERIODS.
3. NET TONNAGE OF VESSELS ENGAGED IN THE COASTING TRADE THAT ARRIVED WITH CARGOES AT PORTS IN THE UNITED KINGDOM, IN SIX-MONTHLY PERIODS.
   N.B.—THE FIGURES OF ARRIVALS AND DEPARTURES ARE APPROXIMATELY THE SAME. FOREIGN TONNAGE IS NEGLIGIBLE AND THEREFORE NOT DISTINGUISHED.
4. ANNUAL VOLUME OF IMPORTS, DISTINGUISHING FOODSTUFFS.
5. TOTAL VOLUME OF IMPORTS, IN SIX-MONTHLY PERIODS.
6. DIAGRAM SHOWING IMPORTS FROM UNITED STATES AND CANADA, AND FROM FRANCE, ITALY, AND RUSSIA, RESPECTIVELY, AS A PROPORTION OF THE TOTAL IMPORT VALUES.
7. DIAGRAM SHOWING EXPORTS TO UNITED STATES AND CANADA, AND TO FRANCE, ITALY, AND RUSSIA, RESPECTIVELY, AS A PROPORTION OF THE TOTAL EXPORT VALUES.
8. IMPORTS OF WHEAT AND FLOUR, IN EQUIVALENT WEIGHTS OF GRAIN, DISTINGUISHING IMPORTS FROM NORTH AMERICA.
9. TOTAL IMPORTS OF IRON ORE, QUARTERLY.
10. IMPORTS OF IRON ORE, SHOWING SOURCES.
11. EXPORTS OF COAL, COKE, AND MANUFACTURED FUEL, DISTINGUISHING CHIEF MARKETS.

LIST OF DIAGRAMS

DIAGRAMS ILLUSTRATING UNRESTRICTED SUBMARINE CAMPAIGN

12. Tonnage sunk and damaged by Enemy Action, February 1917–October 1918.

13. Monthly Record for Period of Unrestricted Submarine Warfare, showing Total Tonnage of all Nationalities lost through Enemy Action, and Number of Ships that sailed in Ocean Convoys.

14. British and Foreign Steamers of 500 Tons Gross and upward sunk by Submarines: to illustrate Effects of Convoy System.

SEABORNE TRADE

CHAPTER I

THE MINISTRY OF SHIPPING

DECEMBER 1916—APRIL 1917

IN December 1916, when Mr. Lloyd George, the new Prime Minister, announced the appointment of Sir Joseph Maclay as Shipping Controller, the problem of tonnage was acute. The renewed outburst of submarine activity in the autumn of 1916 and the necessity of replacing, by imports from Australia, much of the wheat hitherto drawn from nearer sources, had more than neutralised the economies effected by the Shipping Control Committee, the Ship Licensing Committee, the Port and Transit Executive Committee, and the Transport Department of the Admiralty during the earlier months of that year. The available tonnage under the British and Allied flags had been seriously diminished, and not only had neutral losses been far heavier than in any previous period of the war, but neutral shipowners displayed an increasing tendency to withdraw altogether from Allied trade.

The results were clearly seen in all the three main aspects of the tonnage problem, the problem of freights, the problem of supplies, and the problem of administration. Intimately connected as they were, there had always been a tendency to regard these aspects separately, and considerations of finance, considerations of supply, and considerations of administrative convenience each played a prominent part in the development of the policy adopted by the new Government and embodied in the Ministry of Shipping.

It was the rapid and continuous rise in freights which, in 1915, had first drawn public attention to the existence of a tonnage problem, and an exaggerated notion of the influence of freights on prices had played a predominant part in creating the demand for State control of shipping in its commercial employment. It was to a great extent by the desire to keep down the cost of transport that the earlier attempts at control had been inspired; but this end had only partially been attained, and though the various schemes of freight limitation applied during 1916 had, in more than one instance, accentuated the major problem of tonnage and supplies, the sharp rise in both wholesale and retail prices during the last quarter of 1916 had intensified the demand for more general and drastic restrictions.

Apart from the actual effect of freights on prices, there was a strong feeling in the country that the accumulation of large profits by private firms and individuals as a direct result of war conditions was contrary to public policy and the principle of "equality of sacrifice." This feeling found expression in the limitation of profits in "controlled establishments" under the Munition of War Acts, and in the imposition of the Excess Profits Tax. It was partly satisfied, as regards the shipping industry, by the application of that tax to shipowners' profits, and by the requisitioning of ships at Blue Book rates for the carriage of essential imports such as wheat, meat, and sugar; but there was still a strong current of opinion directed towards more general limitation of shipowners' profits or even their total elimination. The Labour Party, who had joined the new, as they had the old, Coalition, were generally in favour of out-and-out nationalisation of shipping as a first step in the State ownership of Industry, and others, who were opposed to permanent nationalisation, were yet desirous that, for the duration of the war, all ships should be run on Government account, the owners receiving either a fixed flat rate of remuneration or some such guarantee of the average pre-bellum profits as had been accorded to the railways.

To any general scheme of freight limitation there were two obvious objections. In the first place, shipping was an international business. Every attempt to limit the profits of neutral shipping was inevitably followed by an exodus from neutral and Allied trade which, in practice, bunker pressure had proved only partially able to counteract. If British ships were carrying cargoes at artificially lowered rates, neutral tonnage would, as surely, be driven away into trades where there was no such artificial competition. In the second place, a flat rate of remuneration would not only remove an incentive to effort, but impair the feeling of personal responsibility on the part of all concerned in the running of the ships, and destroy those automatic, instantaneous checks on laxity and inefficiency which ensured the ships being run to the best advantage. Both these reasons made it very difficult to guarantee that any nominal scheme of limitation would produce a corresponding effect on " real " freights and prices. If tonnage was driven out of a trade, the inevitable result was a shortage of supplies, the effect of which must be felt either through an increase in the price of the commodity affected, or through the reactions on other trades, from which shipping was withdrawn to fill the gap. If the employment of requisitioned or controlled shipping, by a Department or an Ally, resulted in waste of tonnage or in port congestion, reducing the number of voyages annually made, the actual proportionate cost of transport might be increased, even though the shipowner were receiving Blue Book rates or their equivalent.

Behind these objections lay one still more fundamental. In so far as the maintenance of supplies depended on the activities of private traders buying from the most convenient source of supply those commodities for which there was a demand, it was absolutely necessary to preserve the freedom of the freight markets, since only by the offer of competitive freights could such traders make known the extent and importance of the demands they served. Only if the State were prepared to dictate, without regard to the ordinary processes of trade, the nature of the cargoes to be carried, could it safely destroy this index to commercial requirements.

This responsibility the Government had been unwilling to accept. They had long resisted even the proposal repeatedly made by the shipowners themselves, that they should prohibit the import of non-essential commodities, in order to relieve the pressure on the available carrying power and ensure space for the carriage of necessaries. In practice, however, a large proportion of the annual import now consisted of goods selected by the State, owing to the great increase in the volume of cargoes actually purchased on Government account, for the carriage of which requisitioned tonnage or requisitioned space was allocated.

To some extent this increase in Government imports probably reflected a general tendency, which had grown up during the war, towards extending the scope of Governmental activities; but it had also other, more tangible causes. In part it was due, undoubtedly, to the increasing demand for war material and to the desire to obtain complete control of supplies that might be required for war purposes, or which it was essential to prevent reaching Germany through neutral ports. Of still greater immediate importance was the decline in British purchasing power abroad, arising from the reduction in the export trade, and the consequent necessity of purchasing on the credit of the State, both for the supply of Great Britain and for fulfilling the requirements of the Allies. It was this wide extension of Government buying which, more than anything else, facilitated the extension of State control over shipping.

From the first the new Government was definitely committed, largely for political reasons, to the policy of controlling freights and profits, but the exact basis to be adopted, especially in respect of the liner companies, remained for some months a subject of discussion. In the meanwhile, on February 12th, 1917, the Government instructed the Controller "That the Shipping Control Committee should extend the requisitioning of tonnage at Blue Book rates so as to make it general and as nearly as possible universal, and that the cases to which requisitioning did not apply were to be justified only by exceptional circumstances."

The great difficulty in carrying out this decision lay in its application to the liner trades. By far the greater number of tramp steamers not employed for war purposes were already carrying Government cargoes at Blue Book rates. The chief exceptions were ships trading for the Allies, mostly at Limitation rates. The majority of these remained free throughout the war, the Government preferring to leave the business of management to the owners and derive revenue from them by taxation. There were also a few ships to which a varying degree of freedom had been promised in recoupment of "acceleration costs," [1] or of expenses incurred in escaping from the Baltic.[2] Subject to these and a few other unimportant restrictions, the remaining tramps were speedily brought under requisition, and the practice of "temporary release" [3] was gradually discontinued.

[1] See Vol. II, p. 236.   [2] Ibid., p. 335.   [3] Ibid., pp. 52–3.

On the other hand, comparatively few liners had yet been requisitioned except for war purposes, and the problem of liner requisition presented peculiar difficulties. When the State took up a steamer either for war service or to carry a full cargo on Government account, it assumed, in practice, the position of an ordinary time charterer; that is to say, it paid a fixed hire for the use of the vessel, and all it had to do, in order to obtain full benefit from its temporary ownership, was to ensure prompt loading and discharge, in which it could, if it chose, obtain the assistance of skilled business men, accustomed to getting the most out of time charters. The liner, on the other hand, was a general carrier, whose business it was to accept all cargo as it came forward from the shippers, either in large or in small parcels. For carrying on such a business effectively, a free freight market and an extensive commercial organisation were essential. Hence, while many liners had been requisitioned for war purposes, and a large proportion of the cargo space in free liners had been hired at Blue Book rates for the carriage of Government imports, no attempt had yet been made to control directly the great liner trades. On the other hand, the pool of tramp tonnage was already practically exhausted, and towards the end of 1916 it became evident that the Transport Department would be unable to fulfil their commitments towards the British and Allied Governments without making large drafts on the liner fleets.

A further complication, arising from the extreme shortage of tonnage, was the necessity of drawing the largest possible proportion of supplies from the nearest sources, irrespective of all financial and commercial considerations. In view of the exhaustion of British credit in North America it was as yet uncertain how far such a policy was feasible; but its desirability became every day more obvious, and in the view of the Transport Department it involved a tightening up of the control of shipping, in order that ships might be directed into new channels of trade more rapidly than they would be attracted by the changed direction of the demand, and more especially, a redistribution of liner services without regard to the goodwill and trade connections of the lines.

Some further centralisation of control was, indeed, desirable in the interests of administrative efficiency. The Shipping Control Committee, which exercised a general supervision over the whole field, the Admiralty Transport Department and its Advisory Committee, the Board of Trade, the Ship Licensing Committee, the Port and Transit Executive Committee, the unofficial Bunker Committee, the Coal Exports Committee, and the various local committees established under the Coal Freight Limitation Scheme, were all dealing with shipping problems. The creation of the Shipping Control Committee in January 1916 had gone far to secure co-ordination of effort, its decisions and recommendations had generally been supported by the Cabinet, and it had done its work well; but the problem of adjusting the conflicting demands of the Departments, the Allies, and private importers, to a supply of tonnage which every month became more obviously inadequate, demanded fuller executive powers than the Shipping Control Committee possessed. What was needed was a Department of State strong enough to adjudicate upon the competing demands of the Departments employing requisitioned tonnage, and to see that the best use was made of the shipping employed by the State as a whole. In November 1916 the Transport Advisory Committee had urged on the Government the necessity of investing the Shipping Control Committee or some other central authority with the fullest powers to survey the tonnage situation as a whole, and to transfer any ship from the service on which it was running to such other service as might seem expedient. The appointment of the Shipping Controller was a response to this demand as much as to the demand for control of freights and profits.

The actual powers and functions of the Controller were defined by the New Ministers and Secretaries Act, 1916,[1] as follows :

"It shall be the duty of the Shipping Controller to control and regulate any shipping available for the needs of the country in such manner as to make the best use thereof, having regard to the circumstances of the time, and to take such steps as he thinks best for providing and maintaining an efficient supply of shipping, and for these purposes he shall have such powers or duties of any Government department or authority, whether conferred by statute or otherwise, as His Majesty may by Order in Council transfer to him, or authorise him to exercise or

[1] 6 and 7 Geo 5, Ch. 68.

perform concurrently with or in consultation with the Government department or authority concerned, and also such further powers as may be conferred on him by regulations under the Defence of the Realm Consolidation Act, 1914, and regulations may be made under that Act accordingly."

This, though wide, was somewhat vague, and the Controller himself was instructed to report, after investigating the situation, as to the precise scope which should be assigned to the Ministry of Shipping. On January 12th, 1917, he submitted a Memorandum in which he outlined the work of the Ministry as including the direction of merchant shipbuilding; the exercise of the powers hitherto exercised by the Director of Transports with regard to the allocation of tonnage and the running of ships in commercial employment; licensing of voyages; control of port and transit facilities; chartering of neutral vessels; enquiry into the employment of ships allocated to Government service; consideration of questions relating to shipowners' profits; and co-operation with the Board of Trade in the administration of the Merchant Shipping Acts, consideration of questions affecting war risk insurance, requisitioning of insulated space, and similar matters.

This Memorandum was approved in principle by the Government, but the exact extent of the Controller's powers was not immediately settled. It was not until June 28th that the issue of Regulation No. 39BBB under the Defence of the Realm Acts defined the Controller's powers with regard to the requisition and direction of shipping, the control of shipbuilding and other matters, and it was subsequently found that amendments and extensions of this regulation were necessary, in order to cover more completely the field over which, in practice, he exercised jurisdiction. Meanwhile he acted under the general powers conferred on him by the New Ministers and Secretaries Act, and there was little disposition on the part of those concerned to question his authority.[1]

Partly as a result of the initial uncertainty as to the Controller's powers, and partly owing to the administrative work involved, the new Ministry itself was of slow evolution. The Act had given it legal sanction; it was not to be brought into effective existence by the stroke of

[1] For the powers conferred on the Controller under the regulations, see Appendix "A."

a pen. Even after the main lines of its organisation had been settled, new branches and sections were frequently added to meet changes in the tonnage situation, or to provide for extensions of the Controller's activities. Like the less formal machinery from which it developed, the Ministry of Shipping was gradually built up in response to the fluctuating requirements of the war.

The original appointments consisted only of the Controller himself and his Parliamentary Secretary; but from the date of his appointment, Sir Joseph Maclay took over from Lord Curzon the Chairmanship of the Shipping Control Committee, and Sir Leo Chiozza Money also attended its meetings. The Shipping Control Committee was thus brought within the organisation of the Ministry, and provided the Controller with a " Head Quarters Staff " for the discussion of broad questions of policy, though the responsibility for all decisions was transferred from the Committee to the Controller himself.

The Controller, however, had been entrusted with the direction not only of shipping but of shipbuilding, and in view of the great programme of construction and purchase on which the Government had embarked,[1] he felt the need of an equally strong and representative body to advise him on this side of his work. Accordingly, after a conference with representatives of the shipbuilding and marine engineering industries, he formed during December 1916, the Merchant Shipbuilding Advisory Committee to assist him in formulating his policy with regard to shipbuilding in general and the standard ship programme in particular. For executive purposes he collected a small staff which was placed under Mr. C. J. O. Sanders (lent by the Marine Department of the Board of Trade), as Director of Shipbuilding Work. This staff comprised Mr. W. S. Abell, Chief Surveyor to Lloyds Register, who now became Technical Adviser to the Shipping Controller, two or three surveyors, and a few clerks and typists. The acquisition of ships from abroad, whether second-hand or new, was entrusted to Mr. John Esplen, as Director of Overseas Ship Purchase.

Considering that the Controller was now solely responsible for the carrying out of the shipbuilding programme, the types of standard ships, the placing of orders at home and abroad, and the allocation of materials to such vessels

[1] See Vol. II, p. 379.

as were still building on private account, the organisation thus created was sufficiently modest. On the other hand the Controller was able to rely on the co-operation of the great Classification Societies, Lloyds Register, the Bureau Veritas, and the British Corporation, and on the services of their surveyors. He could rely also on the willing co-operation of the shipbuilders themselves through their representatives on the Advisory Committee.[1]

The shipbuilding side of the Controller's functions was thus provided for; it remained to provide an administrative staff for the Shipping Control itself. In January 1917 Mr. John Anderson was transferred from the National Health Insurance Committee to be Secretary to the Shipping Control Committee, in succession to Captain Clement Jones, who had resumed duty with the Army. Mr. Anderson brought with him two secretaries as the nucleus of a staff, and though nominally acting as Secretary to the Shipping Control Committee only, his real position was from the first that of Secretary to the Ministry of Shipping. As such it was formally recognised early in 1917. Later in January, when it had been definitely decided that Ship Licensing should be brought under the direct supervision of the Controller, Mr. Thomas Lodge, Secretary of the Ship Licensing Committee, was transferred to the Ministry as Assistant to Mr. Anderson, and the work of the Licensing Committee was brought under the direction of the Ministry.

Meanwhile it had become necessary to establish some machinery for dealing with the shipping side of the proposed import restrictions.[2] It was now obvious that the tonnage situation rendered it imperative not only to prohibit unessential imports, but to make drastic cuts in those normally regarded as essential. It was necessary, not only to lay down a definite programme of restrictions, but to establish a regular order of priority as between the demands of the various Departments and the commercial requirements of the country as represented by the Board

---

[1] Mr. Sanders and Mr. Abell were both members of the Advisory Committee. The other members were Mr. G. T. Carter (Cammell Laird & Co.), Chairman; Mr. F. N. Henderson (D. & W. Henderson & Co., Glasgow), Mr. James Marr (J. L. T. Thompson & Sons, Sunderland), Mr. A. C. Kerr (Hawthorn Leslie & Co., Newcastle), Mr. W. Rowan Thompson (David Rowan & Co., Glasgow), Mr. A. K. Duncan (Secretary, Shipbuilding Employers' Federation).

[2] See Vol. II, p. 37?.

of Trade. Hitherto such questions had been decided by the Admiralty Transport Department under the general supervision of the Shipping Control Committee; but the much larger reductions now contemplated called for fuller and more detailed investigation, and for this purpose the Controller decided to appoint an interdepartmental committee upon which all the supply departments, as well as the Ministry of Shipping, should be represented. To this Committee each department was to present a periodical statement of its requirements, and after examining these statements, the Committee was to draw up a monthly priority list, so framed as to bring the total demand for carrying power within the capacity of the tonnage available. Known as the Tonnage Priority Committee, this new body included representatives of the Admiralty, War Office, Board of Trade, Ministry of Food, Ministry of Munitions, Colonial Office, India Office, Treasury, and Timber Supply Department, and of the Commission Internationale de Ravitaillement, representing the requirements of the Allies. Its Chairman was Sir Leo Chiozza Money, Parliamentary Secretary to the Ministry of Shipping, and Mr. H. A. de Montmorency, of the Ministry of Shipping, acted as Secretary.

In order to provide the Tonnage Priority Committee with the data necessary for its work, the Statistical Branch of the Ministry of Shipping, with Sir Alfred Watson and Mr. W. P. Elderton as Statistical Advisers, was formed in the same month. The duty of this Branch was to collect statistical data as to the import requirements of the United Kingdom and the Allies, and as to the tonnage available, to forecast the prospective carrying power of the available tonnage at future periods and under various circumstances, and to prepare from time to time statements by which both the Shipping Controller and the Tonnage Priority Committee might be guided in the allocation of tonnage.

There remained the enormously important question of the relations between the Shipping Controller and the Admiralty Transport Department. This was a problem of great difficulty. On the one hand the Admiralty were directly responsible for the control of ships engaged on naval and military services, and for the appointment and direction of the Naval Transport Officers by whom the work of those ships was supervised. On the other hand,

RELATIONS WITH THE ADMIRALTY

the Commercial Branch and Collier Section of the Department were now responsible between them for providing tonnage for all imports of wheat and sugar, for a great part of the imports of ore, nitrate, and many other commodities, and for the guaranteed supplies of coal to the Allies. In other words, the Department had ceased to be concerned solely with naval and military services, and controlled the tonnage by which a great part of the trade of the country was carried on. The strain on the Department had been heavy even with the assistance of the Advisory Committee, but that Committee no longer existed, its members having resigned their position on the appointment of the Controller, in whom they recognised the central authority for which they had pleaded.

The dilemma was a real one. It was impossible for the Admiralty to relinquish their control over transport movements and ships requisitioned for naval and military purposes. It was impossible for the Controller to discharge his functions unless he had power to allocate tonnage to the different services, and effective control over the tonnage allocated. It was impossible to split the Department, in view of the constant interchange of ships between the various services, naval, military, and commercial.

It was not until February 9th that the question was finally decided by the Government. The solution arrived at preserved the integrity of the Transport Department, but assigned to it a dual capacity. In respect of all purely naval matters, such as the appointment of naval transport officers, the engagement of crews of Royal Fleet Auxiliaries, and the running of purely naval and military services, the Director of Transports was to remain responsible to the Admiralty. In all other matters he was to be responsible to the Controller. The Controller was not to intervene directly in the employment of vessels allocated for naval and military purposes, but he was to have the right of enquiring into the manner of such employment, and of making representations to the Admiralty or the Cabinet in the interests of tonnage economy.

In accordance with this decision the entire staff of the Transport Department was transferred, on February 20th, to the Ministry of Shipping, of which it became an integral part. Mr. Graeme Thomson retained his office with the amended title, Director of Transports and Shipping, and the general organisation of his department remained unchanged.

Theoretically the arrangement was open to objection. The dual responsibility of the Director of Transports and Shipping placed him in a position which might easily have become one of considerable delicacy, and no less delicate was the position of the Secretary, as permanent head of a department the greater part of whose executive staff took its orders from an official of co-ordinate rank. In practice, however, the machinery worked smoothly from the first, without any trace either of friction or inefficiency arising from the anomalous nature of its organisation.

Hitherto the small personnel by which the work of the Ministry had been carried on had been housed, first in the Admiralty Arch and subsequently in the Cunard Offices in Cockspur Street. In those offices by February 1917 were established the Controller, the Secretary, and the Assistant Secretary. There the small executive staff entrusted with the supervision of shipbuilding were hard at work on the "standard" programme. There, too, were held the meetings of the Shipping Control, Ship Licensing, and Merchant Shipbuilding Advisory Committees, as well as those of the Tonnage Priority Committee, whose complement, the Statistical Branch, was in course of formation. Just over the way, in the Admiralty Arch, was the Director of Transports with his steadily increasing staff, with whom the Controller and the Shipping Control Committee were in constant communication.

On the merging of the two bodies it became necessary, or at any rate highly desirable, to bring them under the same roof, and early in March the whole staff of the Ministry of Shipping, as then constituted, was moved, with one or two minor exceptions, into the new buildings which had been erected in St. James's Park. Into these new buildings also came the Port and Transit Executive Committee.

This Committee, which had been appointed at the joint instance of the Admiralty, War Office, and Board of Trade, had hitherto sat at Admiralty House for convenience of communication with the Admiralty and the Transport Department, but was also closely linked with the Board of Trade as the supreme authority over ports and harbours. The control of port and transit facilities had been included by the Controller among the matters which he considered should be brought within the scope of the Ministry of Shipping; but the work of the Committee was highly specialised, and though it profoundly affected all shipping problems, was not exclusively concerned with shipping. It was not, therefore, decided to transfer the Committee to the new Ministry, and it retained its independent existence; but in order to facilitate communication and co-operation, it was now brought under the same roof. At a later date (May 1917) a Port Branch of the Ministry was created to act as a more definite link between the Ministry and the Committee.[1]

The Controller had also specified, as matters which should come within his jurisdiction, co-operation with the Board of Trade in the administration of the Merchant Shipping Acts, war risk insurance, and the requisitioning of insulated space. The question of war risks insurance stood over for some months, no change being made in the existing organisation, and such matters as the adjustment of load line regulations to war conditions were dealt with by direct co-operation between the Controller and the Board of Trade.[2] The control of insulated tonnage presented a rather more difficult problem.

The requisitioning of insulated space, it will be remembered, had been carried out, not through the Transport Department but by the Board of Trade direct, as a corollary to their acceptance of responsibility for the meat supply of the Armies.[3] The control of insulated tonnage and the control of the imports of frozen meat were, in fact, so closely connected that the functions exercised by the meat department of the Board of Trade could hardly be divided; yet it was evident that in the exercise of these functions they might be brought into conflict with the Ministry of Shipping. The Board's requisition applied only to the insulated space in a ship, on her homeward voyage; it could be exercised only for the carriage of refrigerated produce; it gave no power to dictate outwards cargo, or even homewards cargo in non-insulated space. According to the strict letter of the Requisitioning

[1] In June 1917, by an amendment to Regulation 39C under the Defence of the Realm Acts, directions issued by the Committee were made "subject to any instructions of the Shipping Controller."

[2] The enclosing of upper deck space, by direction of the Controller, to increase the carrying capacity of the ship, was dealt with by Defence of the Realm Regulation 39E, issued February 6th, 1917.

[3] See Vol. II, pp. 79–86.

Proclamations there was no power to divert a ship from the Australasian to the Plate trade or *vice versâ*, although several ships had, by agreement, been so diverted by the Board. On the other hand, the Shipping Controller was charged with the supervision of tonnage in the general interests of the country as a whole, and it was essential to the performance of his duties that he should be able to requisition any ship as a whole and to put her into any trade he should think fit, without being fettered by any limitation either as regards route or cargo.

Thanks to the cordial relations which, from the first, existed between the two departments, no cause of friction arose; but experience soon showed the desirability of some definite machinery of co-operation, and on the initiative of Sir Lionel Fletcher of the Ministry of Shipping and Mr. H. W. Macrosty of the Board of Trade a conference was held on March 26th, 1917, between representatives of the Ministry, the Board, and the two Refrigerated Tonnage Committees. The result of this conference was the establishment of a joint Shipping Committee which, without formal appointment or terms of reference, met weekly to consider matters of common interest, especially the transfer of steamers from the Australasian to the Plate or North American Routes. At an early date representatives of the War Office and Ministry of Food were added to the Committee, and its activities were gradually extended to embrace the general supervision of insulated shipping, including the obtaining of statements of requirements from the War Office, Ministry of Food, and the French and Italian Governments, and the preparation of programmes to meet those requirements.[1]

In the same month, March 1917, another new Branch was added to the Ministry. Its original purpose was to supervise the running of prize and detained steamers.

---

[1] Members of the Committee:

War Office.—Lt.-Col. Sir Thomas Robinson, K.C.M.G., Chairman.
Ministry of Shipping.—Commander Sir Lionel Fletcher, R.N.R., Vice-Chairman.
Board of Trade.—Mr. H. W. Macrosty, Secretary.
Ministry of Food.—Capt. F. B. Elliot.
Australasian Refrigerated Tonnage Committee.—Mr. F. White.
Plate Refrigerated Tonnage Committee.—Mr. S. H. Kaye.

Expert assistants drawn from the Departments were subsequently added to assist the Departmental representatives in regard to detailed work, and other representatives of the Departments attended from time to time as substitutes or for consultation.

While the employment of these ships was determined by Requisitioning Branch, the work of management in the strict sense of the term, including such matters as outfit, repairs, stores, victualling, and wages, had been entrusted by the Director of Transports to various shipowners. It was now desired to re-allocate the vessels in such a way as to ensure that each manager should handle only steamers of a type to which he was accustomed in his ordinary business, and this work was entrusted to Mr. Ernest Glover, a member of the late Advisory Committee to the Transport Department. For the first nine months or so of its existence the new Branch was known simply as Mr. Glover's Branch; but it will be convenient to refer to it as Ship Management Branch, the name it subsequently received. Its scope was speedily extended to cover the appointment and supervision of managers for ships built on Government account or purchased abroad, and other vessels in the direct employment of the Shipping Controller, as distinct from requisitioned ships, whose management was left in their owners' hands.

By April 1917 the organisation of the Ministry was as follows: At its head stood the Controller, invested with sole executive authority and responsibility, but assisted in the consideration of broad general questions of policy by the Shipping Control Committee, the Shipbuilding Advisory Committee, and the Tonnage Priority Committee, and represented in the House of Commons by the Parliamentary Secretary. On its administrative side the Ministry was divided into three departments. The Department of the Director of Transports and Shipping comprised the Executive Branches of the old Admiralty Transport Department—Naval Sea Transport, Military Sea Transport, Technical, Requisitioning, and Commercial—transferred *en bloc* to the Ministry. The Secretary's Department included the Ship Management and Statistical Branches, a Ship Licensing Branch to which the Ship Licensing Committee was attached, and an Establishment Branch formed round the nucleus of the old Branch of that name taken over from the Transport Department. The Department of the Accountant-General, or Financial Branch, was similarly formed round the old Transport Department Finance Branch, on the creation, on April 1st, of a separate Ministry of Shipping vote. Independent of the Ministry, but housed in the same building and working in close co-operation, was the Port and Transit Executive Committee, while the joint Shipping Committee for insulated tonnage secured co-operation between the Ministry and the Board of Trade in its own special sphere. Other branches and sections were added from time to time as necessity arose, but before dealing with these later developments it is necessary to trace the progress of events by which the work of the Ministry and the tonnage problem as a whole were profoundly affected.

CHAPTER II

THE TONNAGE PROBLEM
JANUARY 1917

THE outstanding feature in the situation at the date of the Shipping Controller's appointment was the admitted inability of the carrying power available to bring in, during 1917, as large a volume of imports as had been maintained since the outbreak of war. The efforts hitherto made to bring about a more stable equilibrium between the demand for tonnage and the supply had been directed almost exclusively towards increasing the supply, and though these efforts had been crowned with a large amount of success, they had toiled hopelessly in the rear of the rising curve of destruction and the increasing requirements of the essential services. By December 1916 it had become evident that, if sufficient tonnage for the essential services were to be obtained, it would be necessary not only to take all possible measures to increase the supply but to reduce the demand by the elimination of non-essential imports, and on December 21st a Committee under the Chairmanship of Lord Curzon of Kedleston, a member of the War Cabinet, was appointed "to consider and report on the question of the restriction of imports." [1]

So early as October 1915, the Liverpool Steam Ship Owners' Association had urged the prohibition of non-essential imports as not only the most effective method of reducing freights, by equalising supply and demand, but as the only practicable method of securing that, if the total tonnage available were inadequate to the carriage of the cargoes on offer, the goods actually carried should be those really required under war conditions, and the goods shut

[1] The other members of the Committee were: Dr. Addison, Minister of Munitions; Sir Albert Stanley, President of the Board of Trade; Sir Joseph Maclay, Shipping Controller; Sir Maurice de Bunsen, Foreign Office; Mr. S. H. Lever, Treasury; Sir Norman Hill, Port and Transit Executive Committee.

out, those which could best be spared. For the shipowners themselves to discriminate between the goods presented to them for carriage was altogether impossible. Apart from the freight test, they had no adequate criterion by which to judge the relative importance of the competing demands, nor could they, in their position of common carriers, have exercised such discrimination without serious friction, not only with their shippers, but with foreign Governments. For the same reasons, drastic restriction of imports had subsequently been strongly advocated by the Ship Licensing Committee, the Port and Transit Executive Committee, and the Shipping Control Committee; but up to the end of 1916 little had been done.

There were indeed many objections to the deliberate restriction or prohibition of imports. It presented serious administrative difficulties; it involved serious interference with British trade and industry, and the possibility of friction with countries whose products were excluded. It was no light matter to prohibit the importation from the British Dominions or Allied countries, of goods on the export of which their financial strength in great measure depended; nor could the Government lightly run the risk of friction with neutrals who might retaliate by placing an embargo on essential supplies. Thus it was that, in the spring of 1916, the Board of Trade had refused to agree to prohibitions exceeding four million tons per annum, and that the restrictions then imposed had been whittled away by the grant of licences to less than half that figure. Since then a considerable number of other articles had been added to the list, but it had been necessary to make many concessions in the interests of British industries or of Allied exporters, and the total effect of the restrictions fell far short of what was now necessary.

Even during 1916 the effect of the unrestricted competition for carrying power had been most unhappy. Although from 20 to 30 per cent. of the liner space in the North Atlantic trade was definitely allocated to munitions in addition to the proportion of space reserved for wheat, the Ministry of Munitions were unable to obtain space for the whole of their purchases, while a good deal of general cargo of a non-essential character was still coming forward.[1]

Moreover, the pressure on tonnage and ports of a volume

[1] See Vol. II, pp. 260–1.

of trade which, in the existing conditions, they were unable to handle, had prevented even the limited carrying power available from being used to its full capacity. The North American ports had been choked by the arrival of goods for shipment in far greater volume than could be lifted ; the efforts of the Port and Transit Committee to avoid congestion at British ports had been in large measure defeated.

By December 1916 the position had been greatly aggravated by the effects of the extended submarine campaign and the diversion of wheat ships to Australia. The estimate obtained by the Shipping Control Committee from Sir Norman Hill allowed for a probable reduction of the entrances of British shipping during 1917—through losses, deviation, and other effects of the war, such as the shortage of efficient firemen and seamen—amounting to 10 per cent. on the 1916 figures, and for a shrinkage of neutral entrances by 25 per cent., involving a reduction of 500,000 tons a month, or 6,000,000 tons a year on the 1916 imports. Without committing themselves to the endorsement of these figures, the Board of Trade concurred in the necessity for restricting substantially the import of non-essentials, and on January 8th, 1917, Lord Curzon's Committee on Restriction of Imports decided to appoint an Interdepartmental Committee, composed of representatives of the Departments affected, with instructions to draw up detailed alternative programmes providing respectively for the restriction of imports by 250,000 and 500,000 tons per month. This Committee was placed under the chairmanship of Sir Henry Babington Smith, K.C.B., C.S.I.[1]

The task imposed on Sir Henry Babington Smith's Committee was a heavy one ; but the problem of import restriction was in some respects easier of solution than when it was first propounded during the winter of 1915–16. Not only had the Government greatly extended its control over British shipping, it had itself become an importer

[1] Other members: Mr. W. H. Beveridge, C.B., Ministry of Food ; Mr. C. T. Davis, C.M.G., Colonial Office ; Mr. R. E. Enthoven, C.I.E., Board of Trade ; Mr. C. W. Fielding, Ministry of Munitions ; Mr. H. Fountain, C.B., C.M.G., Board of Trade ; Sir Norman Hill, Port and Transit Committee ; Mr. L. J. Kershaw, C.I.E., India Office ; Mr. J. M. Keynes, Treasury ; Sir Leo Chiozza Money, M.P., Ministry of Shipping ; Mr. J. A. Salter, Admiralty ; Sir H. Llewellyn Smith, K.C.B., Board of Trade ; Mr. Græme Thomson, C.B., Admiralty ; Hon. C. H. Tufton, C.M.G., Foreign Office ; Mr. W. F. Wintour, C.B., C.M.G., War Office ; Mr. E. H. S. Marker, Board of Trade, Secretary.

on a very large scale. Wheat, munitions, and other commodities on Government account made up a large proportion of British imports, and many commodities, such as ore, wool, and cotton, which were not imported by the Government direct, were subject in varying degree to its control. Moreover, the proportion of labour, plant, and capital specifically directed to production for war purposes was continually on the increase. In these circumstances both the administrative difficulties and the probable dislocation of trade and industry involved in restriction of imports, became less formidable, while the increasing commitments undertaken on behalf of the Allies, rendered it easier to obtain the assent of the Allied Governments to restrictions on their trade. Above all, the acuteness of the tonnage crisis was now so obvious that the necessity for facing the difficulties and taking the risk could no longer be denied.

With the appointment of the Babington Smith Committee and, almost immediately afterwards, the Tonnage Priority Committee, the policy of adjusting the demands for tonnage to the available supply took definite shape, but to work out and apply so drastic a programme of restrictions necessarily took time, and meanwhile the Transport Department were at their wits' end to procure ships. Their commitments had been heavily increased during the last few weeks of 1916. Large new demands for the transport of railway material to France, increased pressure of munition demands on liner space, a renewal of the Italian coal crisis, urgent demands for early shipments of wheat and maize, had all to be met at the same time.

For the moment, it was the wheat supply of the United Kingdom and the Allies which presented the most urgent problem, especially the provision of tonnage for the purchases effected or negotiated in Australia during the autumn and winter of 1916.[1] The first Australian contract for 500,000 tons was definitely signed on January 11th, 1917, at which date the earlier shipments under the contract were already coming forward. Completion of the second contract for 3,000,000 tons was delayed by prolonged negotiations with regard to the centralised control of freight, including liner space, insisted on by the British Government. Not only did the Commonwealth Government desire to retain the control of loading operations,

[1] See Vol. II, pp. 339–43.

and the right to arrange further c.i.f. shipments to the European Allies, they wished also to reserve the available liner space for shipments of surplus wheat outside the contract. To none of these conditions could the British Government agree, and after much discussion, all points were settled in their favour: c.i.f. shipments were discontinued, the liner space was made available for the contract wheat, and the sole agency was entrusted to Messrs. Paxton, representing the Royal Commission on Wheat Supplies, and Messrs. Wills, representing the Ministry of Shipping. These firms were also represented on the Commonwealth Shipping Board formed to superintend the operations. On these terms the 8,000,000 tons contract was signed in February 1917; but by that time the whole situation had radically changed.

In entering into negotiations for the purchase of the Australian surplus, the Government had been guided by the reports received as to the comparative failure of the North American harvests; but so early as December 1916 it had been necessary to modify the programme of Australian shipments by diverting tonnage to North America, in order to avert a wheat crisis in the United Kingdom in the early months of 1917, before the Australian exports could arrive. By January it had become clear that the North American harvest, though much inferior to that of 1915, had been underestimated by the experts. Much more wheat had come into sight than was anticipated, and what was equally important, the Treasury had been able to overcome the difficulty of the exchanges and to arrange for the financing of increased shipments from the States. On the other hand the gravity of the tonnage crisis had become more and more apparent. To continue to send large numbers of ships to Australia for wheat which could be brought from North America in about one-third of the time, or by one-third of the tonnage, was simply impossible, and while the Government had no intention of repudiating its liabilities under the 8,000,000 ton contract, it was obvious that the lifting of the Australian wheat must be postponed. By the beginning of February the Australian Wheat Programme had been practically given up. Ships sufficient to lift the original 500,000 ton contract and about 300,000 tons of the second had already been directed to Australian ports, but no more could, for the time being, be sent; the Wheat Commission were buying heavily in the United States and Canada, and every available vessel was being crowded on to the North Atlantic tracks.

Hardly less important than the provision of tonnage for wheat was the maintenance of the French and Italian coal supply. Owing mainly to the shortage of neutral shipping, neither France nor Italy had received during the last few weeks of 1916 anything like the amount which they put forward as representing their minimum requirements, and on January 4th the French Government asked for a special shipment of a million tons to make up the leeway. To grant this was impossible in view of the tonnage shortage; but it was of the first importance to maintain shipments at the highest possible level, and even more important was it to do something for Italy, where stocks were running dangerously low. On December 27th, 1916, the Admiralty had agreed to provide an extra 180,000 tons during the next few months as an emergency measure, on the understanding that all colliers, British, Allied, or neutral, were used for return cargoes of ore, and that any British requisitioned tonnage employed should be considered as on account of the coal compensation due under the coal-ore agreement. This, however, was at best a temporary palliative. The real crux of the Italian position lay in the falling away of neutral clearances for the Italian ports, and the problem of the Italian coal supply was closely bound up with the general question of retaining neutral tonnage in Allied trades.

While it was hoped that the arrangements being made for the insurance of neutrals against war risks would do something to check the withdrawal of neutral shipping, the heavy losses suffered by such shipping, especially in the coal and ore traffic, and the attraction of high freights and safe employment in distant waters, combined to render its retention a matter of doubt and difficulty. It was, therefore, of the utmost importance to secure as many ships as possible on time-charter terms which would permit their employment in essential services. The Clémentel Agreement of December 3rd, 1916, had provided that all chartering of neutral steamers should be centralised in an Inter-Allied Bureau to be established in London, and no time had been lost in giving effect to this decision. On January 6th, 1917, a definite agreement was concluded between France, Italy, and Great Britain providing for the creation of a Central Bureau for the chartering and allocation of neutral tonnage. It was further agreed that each of the three Governments should prohibit the chartering of any non-national vessel except through the medium of the Bureau.

This agreement was followed, on January 7th, by the issue of Regulation 39D under the Defence of the Realm Acts, which prohibited any firm or individual from entering into negotiations for the charter, whether by time or voyage, of any non-British ship for the carriage of goods to or from any port in British or Allied territories, or for the purchase from abroad on c.i.f. terms of any goods exceeding 1,000 tons weight, without the consent of the Board of Trade.[1] Similar orders were issued in France and Italy.

The powers thus conferred on the Board of Trade were delegated in practice to the Inter-Allied Chartering Committee, called into being under the Agreement of January 6th, which held its first meeting on the 15th of the same month. It consisted of representatives of France, Italy, and Great Britain, under the chairmanship of Mr. C. Hipwood of the Board of Trade. Its principal functions were to formulate the general policy of the Allies on matters concerning neutral shipping and to allocate as between the several Allied Governments and the Wheat Executive—whose demands it was from the outset decided to treat separately—such tonnage as could be procured.

The administrative side of the work arising out of the Chartering Agreement, comprising the scrutiny of tonnage on offer and the supervision of the arrangements to be made for chartering and management, was delegated to a small business organisation in the City known as the Inter-Allied Chartering Executive. This organisation was under the direction of Mr. O. G. Holmden, by whom centralised chartering had been originally suggested to the Board of Trade in 1916.[2] All vessels taken up on time-charter, with the exception of a number of ships which, with the prior consent of the Executive, were fixed direct to the French Ministry of Transports, were chartered to Messrs. Furness, Withy & Co., who sub-chartered them to firms nominated by the several Govern-

---

[1] In January 1918, this regulation was amended by the substitution of the Shipping Controller for the Board of Trade.
[2] See Vol. II, p. 323.

ments, or by the Wheat Executive, in proportions determined by the Chartering Committee. The usual address commission of 2½ per cent. was payable to the Chartering Executive to cover administrative expenses.[1]

Tonnage allocated to France was managed by a Chartering Bureau formed by the French Ministry of Transports. The general management of steamers sub-chartered to nominees of the British and Italian Governments or of the Wheat Executive was entrusted to Messrs. Furness, Withy & Co., and by the end of the first month of the Committee's activities, the number of ships chartered was increasing so rapidly that it became necessary to call in sub-managers to assist that firm in their task.

This sudden influx of tonnage was due mainly to a new development in the treatment of Greek shipping. Owing to the exceptional risks to which shipping engaged in the trade of the Eastern Mediterranean was exposed, and also to the unstable political position in Greece itself, Greek shipping had for some time been singled out for specially stringent treatment at the hands of the British authorities. Since July 1916 it had been the practice to allow bunkers to Greek ships only if they were employed in approved trades, or, with the consent of the British Legation at Athens, were engaged in the carriage of essential supplies to Greece. By the end of the year it had become apparent that bunker pressure, unless reinforced by some further measure of control, would fail to keep Greek tonnage in Allied trades. The pull of other employment was at least as strong in respect of Greek as in respect of Scandinavian shipping, the dependence of Greece on British exports was much less marked, and as the majority of Greek shipowners were single ship companies, the Bunker Regulations lost much of the deterrent effect arising from the threat to "black-list" the whole of an owner's fleet in the event of breach of the regulations by any of his vessels. Accordingly in December 1916, all Greek ships in any port under British control were detained until they were time-chartered to the British Government, on terms to be disclosed to their owners. In the following month the Greek Ship Scheme was initiated, under which all Greek ships, except those requisitioned by the Greek Government with the approval of the British Legation, were fixed on time-

---

[1] Of this commission ¼ per cent. was offered to Messrs. Furness, Withy & Co., but was declined, the firm giving its services free of charge.

charter to Messrs. Furness, Withy & Co. for the duration of the war and up to six months afterwards. The rates of hire were considerably lower than those offered by the Chartering Executive for other neutral tonnage, ranging from 30s. to 35s. per ton dead-weight as against 47s. 6d. to 52s. 6d. paid for Norwegian ships. In addition, each owner had to lodge a bond with the British Government for the due fulfilment of the charter-party. In return for the acceptance of these terms, the British Government guaranteed the liability of the charterers in regard to the war risks insurance of the steamers, and gave the Greek owners certain valuable assurances of a semi-political nature. It was provided, for instance, that in the event of a war between Royalist Greece and Great Britain, ships chartered under the scheme should not be liable to capture or detention by the Allies, and that the transfer of the vessels to the Greek Provisional Government would be recognised, the charters remaining valid.[1] In view of these concessions, Greek shipowners in general proved willing to accept the scheme, the general supervision and working of which was entrusted to a body known as the Greek Ship Committee.[2] So rapidly was the scheme put into operation that out of 48 steamers chartered by the Inter-Allied Executive during January, no fewer than 34 were Greek.

Although the powers entrusted to the Chartering Committee under Regulation 39D extended to all charters, of whatever description, and to all ships, irrespective of size and class, direct chartering by the Executive was confined almost, if not entirely, to time-chartering, and at first to steamers of over 1,000 tons deadweight. At the first meeting of the Committee it was decided that there should be no general interference for the present with the employment of sailing vessels, steamers under 1,000 tons deadweight, or steamers employed in the short sea trades, such vessels being permitted to continue their employment on a voyage basis, provided each fixture was made at approved rates and reported to the Executive. It was subsequently agreed that the time-charters of vessels already in French or Italian service might, for the time being, be continued,

---

[1] The Greek Provisional Government, at Salonika, had declared war on Germany on November 23rd, 1916.
[2] This body worked under the auspices of the Foreign Office until November 1917, when it was transferred to the Ministry of Shipping.

provided each fixture was reported and the rate approved, and that direct time-charters of vessels engaged in the Pacific trades should also be permitted, without further obligation than that of reporting the fixtures.

The chief administrative problem to be faced by the Committee at the outset was that of adjusting its relations with the extensive machinery for the control of chartering set up under the Coal Freights Limitation Scheme. This, however, was quickly solved on common-sense lines. In view of its powers and the task entrusted to it, the Committee could not well disavow responsibility for so important a branch of the employment of neutral shipping. On the other hand it was obviously undesirable to lose the advantage of the experience already gained by the local organisations, nor was it possible without serious disadvantages, to centralise in London the whole business of neutral chartering. It was accordingly arranged that all voyage-charters in the French and Italian coal trades should be completed without reference to the Chartering Executive, provided the approval of the Local Coal Committees had been obtained. These committees were informed of the rates fixed by the Chartering Executive and were themselves responsible for seeing that no ships were fixed except at approved rates, and that all fixtures were reported to the Executive. In the same way, and for the same reasons, it was decided that the Chartering Department of the Ministry of Munitions should continue to fix steamers for the ore traffic.[1]

In allocating the steamers time-chartered by the Inter-Allied Executive itself, the Chartering Committee adopted provisionally the principle that the larger vessels, to a total of about 80 per cent. of the aggregate dead-weight tonnage, should be allotted to the Wheat Executive for the service of the joint Allied programme, and that the remainder should be divided between France and Italy in approximately equal proportions. Although the British representatives recorded their right to claim a share of the tonnage if and when required, they were content for the time being to forgo their claim. So long as the tonnage available for the Allies continued to be inadequate, it was

---

[1] On April 1st the Chartering Department of the Ministry of Munitions was transferred to the Ministry of Shipping, and Mr. G. C. Welborn became Official Ore Broker in place of Mr. T. Woodward Owen. He was responsible to Mr. W. A. Stewart, Head of the Minerals Section, Commercial Services Branch.

ALLOCATION OF NEUTRAL SHIPS

indeed obvious that the inevitable result of allocating to Great Britain a share of the neutral tonnage obtained by the Committee would be further demands by France and Italy for British requisitioned ships. Apart, therefore, from participation in the service of ships allocated to the Wheat Executive, the only direct assistance rendered by the Committee to Great Britain was the allocation of a few ships, from March onwards, to the supply of the coaling depôts abroad.

In order to provide a pool of tonnage from which emergency demands could be met, it was decided that all steamers over 5,000 tons dead-weight, up to a maximum of 50, should come up for re-allocation on the completion of each voyage. For the time being, practically all such vessels secured were allocated to the Wheat Executive and were allowed to remain in that employment.

It was, of course, essential to the success of the scheme that outside competition for neutral shipping should be reduced to a minimum, and early steps were taken by the British Government to ensure that the chief possible European competitors, the Swiss Government and the Commission for Belgian Relief, should refrain from competitive offers for tonnage available to the Committee. With the Swiss Government an agreement was effected in March by which they agreed to charter only such ships as could be guaranteed rapid discharge at Cette and Marseilles, and to consult the Inter-Allied Committee in chartering vessels for their requirements, which the Committee estimated at 10 steamers a month. Such ships were obtained chiefly from Spanish owners, unwilling to charter to the Committee itself. The Commission for Belgian Relief chartered on a voyage basis, mainly from neutral owners who were averse to accepting the risks of Allied trade.

So far as Europe was concerned the Inter-Allied Committee had thus succeeded in practically eliminating competition. With America, so long as the United States remained neutral, no arrangement was possible, and the danger of neutral shipping escaping into the safe and lucrative employment afforded by American trade continued to form a serious weakness in the whole machinery of centralised chartering, bunker control, and freight limitation.

It was not long before the question of approved rates in

the French and Italian coal trade became urgent. Owing to the increased cost of war risks insurance and the artificially lowered rates on return cargoes of ore, many neutral shipowners were actually sustaining heavy losses, and it was now almost impossible to obtain tonnage, especially for the Mediterranean, at the rates fixed under the Limitation Scheme. The Local Coal Committees were accordingly informed on January 27th that the Chartering Executive had decided to increase the limitation rates for neutral shipping by 20 per cent. in respect of voyages to French Channel and Atlantic ports, and by 50 per cent. for voyages to Italian and French Mediterranean ports. This order, which came into operation on January 29th, marks the virtual abandonment of the Coal Freight Limitation Scheme so far as neutral steamers were concerned. For a long time it had been evident that even the utmost rigour of bunker pressure was insufficient to retain neutral shipping in a dangerous trade artificially rendered unremunerative. While the guaranteed supplies to France and Italy, and the additional Italian supplies for transport of which the Admiralty from time to time accepted responsibility, put a heavy strain on British tonnage, the total effective deliveries to those countries showed an increasing monthly deficit due to neutral withdrawals, and desirable as it was to keep down the cost of transport, it was now evident that considerations of freight must give way to considerations of supply. The increases announced on January 29th were only the first step in a series of modifications which eventually, at any rate so far as the Mediterranean was concerned, approximated neutral coal freights very closely to the market level.

Meanwhile the enemy were busy, and it was especially against the vessels taking coal to France and Italy or returning with ore and pitwood to British ports that the attack of the submarines was directed. In the Bay of Biscay, off Ushant, and off the north-western coast of Spain, the number of casualties was unusually large, and the total destruction of neutral tonnage during January was greater than in any previous month of the war. Including vessels sunk by mines or by surface raiders, the losses of neutral shipping amounted to 125,000 tons, of British to 154,000, and of shipping under other Allied flags to 88,000.

Of surface raiders there were now three operating on the trade routes. The MOEWE, under the enterprising command of Count zu Dohna-Schlodien, had again made her presence felt in the Atlantic in December 1916, and among half a score of prizes during that month had made one of peculiar importance. This was the British steamer *Yarrowdale*, bound from New York to Italy with munitions. So valuable was her cargo that for once the Germans decided to take the risk of sending her into port, and favoured by the long nights and stormy weather, the prize crew succeeded in eluding the British patrols and reaching Swinemunde.

By the end of the first week in January the MOEWE had run down the North Atlantic, and in company with a captured collier, the *St. Theodore*, armed with one or two small guns, was operating north-west of Pernambuco. Shipping, however, was well scattered, in consequence of a general warning sent out by the Admiralty on December 8th, and few prizes were made.

Meanwhile another raider, the SEEADLER, had got to work. She was originally the *Pass of Balmaha*, an American sailing vessel captured by a German submarine in the North Sea in August 1915. The Germans had fitted her with an auxiliary motor, giving her a speed of 12 knots, but her chief feature was the wide radius given her by her sail power, and she was destined for a lengthy cruise. Steering wide into the Atlantic, she captured two steamers during January, south of the Azores, and then proceeded to the first part of her real mission, an attack on the South Atlantic sailing trade.

For the third raider, the WOLF, a bolder programme had been drawn up. It was her mission to disturb the security enjoyed by British trade in Eastern waters since the destruction of the EMDEN. Before the war she was the Hansa liner *Wachtfels* of 5,809 tons and 10 knots speed. She had now received not only an armament of guns and torpedo tubes but the equipment of a minelayer. She was too slow for successful raiding in the Atlantic, but her size enabled her to carry a large coal supply, and her orders were to avoid the Atlantic tracks and pass unperceived into the Indian Ocean, where she was to lay mines off the focal points of British trade.

Nothing was known as yet of the WOLF or SEEADLER,

but the arrival of the Japanese steamer *Hudson Maru* at Pernambuco, on January 16th, with 287 prisoners taken from 6 ships sunk between the Azores and the Brazilian coast, had supplemented the previous intelligence with regard to the activities of the MOEWE. It was, however, on the destruction wrought by the enemy submarines and the shortage of tonnage arising therefrom that attention was chiefly concentrated, and on January 23rd and 24th, an Allied Naval Conference was held in London to discuss ways and means of dealing with the situation. At this Conference considerable discussion took place as to the best means of protecting merchantmen in the Mediterranean. The problem of defending trade in that sea was complicated by the fact that it was cut up into ten different zones, for which the British, French, and Italian fleets were respectively responsible. It was agreed by all three Admiralties that in the Western Basin the coastal route should be utilised as much as possible, but with regard to shipping in the Eastern Basin there was a wide difference of opinion. The French held to the system of patrolled routes, frequently changed; the British favoured a system of dispersal of trade, with trawlers working in pairs or threes in different parts of each zone. It was eventually agreed that the French system should be adopted in all zones for traffic to and from Salonika and the Ægean, and that the British system should be given a trial for traffic between Cape Bon and Port Said. Arrangements were also made for giving further protection to a drifter barrage which had been instituted by the British in the Straits of Otranto.

Outside the Mediterranean, it was agreed that the British Admiralty should supply a dozen armed trawlers to reinforce the French patrols off Ushant, for the protection of the inshore route which the French had established between Belle Île and Cherbourg. The greater part of the time of the Conference was devoted, however, to other than purely naval questions.

Both the French and Italian delegates represented in the strongest terms the needs of their countries with regard to carrying power. The French representatives stated that four-fifths of their shipping was already under control and that the greater part of the remainder was employed in the carriage of Government purchases. One-fifth of the total tonnage was required for the service of the Salonika force alone, and in order to fulfil the requirements of the army, the colonial services had been so drastically reduced that France was almost cut off from her more distant possessions. The import of wood-pulp had been prohibited; all metals and wood were to be brought under control; restrictions had been imposed on imports, consumption, lighting, and heating; the milling of grain was regulated. In spite of all these measures, they were unable to obtain fulfilment of their needs. The shipments of coal from the United Kingdom showed a deficit for the last four months of 1,400,000 tons; factories were stopping, and the Paris-Lyons-Marseilles Railway had only a week's supply in hand. The munition works were short of steel, iron, and copper; 230,000 tons of pig iron were awaiting shipment in the United States.

The Italian representatives painted a still blacker picture. They stated that the coal shortage was so acute as to threaten the paralysis of military operations, owing to lack of munitions and transport, and that despite the prohibition of luxury imports, they were unable to fulfil their minimum requirements for grain, meat, and sugar. Two meatless days a week were in force, the manufacture of confectionery was prohibited, and the people were subsisting on black bread.

Translated into terms of tonnage, the additional assistance for which Italy was now asking came to something like 50 ships of 5,000 tons average capacity for cereals, and 90 for coal, together with 35 other colliers for 3 months to make good the deficiency already existing. In addition to these specific requirements, the Italian representatives proposed that the employment of all Allied tonnage should be reviewed and that as a result, " the whole tonnage belonging to the Allies or controlled by them " should be redistributed " in proportion with their respective needs, and in such manner as to ensure equal powers of resistance to all nations engaged in the war; " that any eventual deficit of carrying power should be calculated; and that steps should be taken by the regulation of consumption, and if necessary by immediate rationing, to allocate equally as between the Allies, the burden of such deficit.

These proposals went, in the opinion of the French and British representatives, beyond the scope of a purely

Naval Conference, and they could only promise to bring them to the notice of their respective Cabinets. Two resolutions of great importance were, however, unanimously passed. Of these, the first emphasised the paramount importance of restricting non-essential imports in all Allied countries, the second called for the establishment of a standing International Shipping Committee, for the purpose of exchanging information as to the employment of the shipping controlled by the several Allies, and of considering and arranging with the Allied Governments the adoption of co-operative programmes or other measures for the economy of carrying power. On their part, the British Admiralty promised to do their best to supply France and Italy with additional steel for the completion of the few merchant steamers under construction in those countries, and to do what was possible to relieve the Italian coal crisis.

These great new Allied demands came at an unfortunate time. About a fortnight before the Naval Conference was held, Requisitioning Branch had reported that when the demands of the Wheat Executive had been satisfied, and a little extra tonnage had been found for Italian coal, practically every tramp which could load before the end of February would be under requisition, with the exception of those exempted at the request of the Allied or Dominion Governments, and a few others already engaged in essential trades. In fact, although no fewer than 100 tramps had been taken up during the last few weeks, the Branch had come to the end of their resources, and over their future arrangements hung the shadow of the White Sea Programme.

Although a small winter programme to the ice-free port of Murmansk had been sanctioned and was being carried out, this went only a very little way towards the fulfilment of Russian requirements. The Russian Government were placing very heavy orders abroad, and appeared to find some difficulty in realising that there was not an unlimited supply of British tonnage for the transport of the goods. To comply with all their demands was impossible, but in view of Russia's dependence on oversea supplies for the means of continued resistance, it was essential to do all that could be done, and the White Sea summer programme, as contemplated, involved lifting a quarter of a million tons more than had been carried in

1916. Nearly the whole of this increase was to fall on British shipping.[1]

The total amount to be lifted by British ships was 1,880,000 tons. For this purpose it was calculated that 368 separate voyages would be required, and after allowing for repeated voyages, a maximum of 246 ships would be on service at the height of the season.

The outlook for the future was thus still more unpromising than the existing situation, for few of the ships now engaged in essential services were likely to be released before the White Sea Programme began, and even without taking into account any fresh demands by France or Italy, the tonnage deficit in the spring would be dangerously large. It was true that the Government had now embarked on extensive programmes of shipbuilding and ship purchase, but neither of these could be expected to affect the situation in time to give substantial relief.

In these circumstances, Requisitioning Branch proposed to meet the crisis by taking further space on the Australian liners for the carriage of wheat, and by diverting some thirty vessels, principally liners, from distant routes and the inter-foreign trade. They proposed also to draw on the vessels engaged in the China coasting services for service in the Persian Gulf, for the purpose of releasing ocean-going ships. The Shipping Control Committee had already been instructed further to comb out the ships permanently trading abroad, and during January it was decided to request the Dominion Governments to investigate the employment of vessels engaged in their local and coasting trade with the object of releasing, if possible, vessels suit-

[1] Comparison of White Sea Programme 1917 with total carried in 1916.

	Carried 1916.		Programme 1917.	
	In British s.s. 1,000 tons.	Total. 1,000 tons.	In British s.s. 1,000 tons.	Total. 1,000 tons.
From United Kingdom	580	790	500	600
,, ,, ,, coal	760	1,010	600	1,000
,, France	225	310	320	480
,, U.S.A.	85	360	460	640
	1,650	2,470	1,880	2,720

Certain cargoes carried from miscellaneous ports in 1916 have been included under United Kingdom.

able for ocean traffic. The employment of shipping in War Office service had already been reported on by Mr. F. W. Lewis to the Shipping Control Committee, in accordance with the instructions given by the late Government. His report was very favourable to the work done by the Transport Department, but contained a number of suggestions whereby further economies might be effected, and many of these had already been carried out.

In these ways it was hoped to tide over the emergency, but the full extent of the crisis was not yet apparent. Before anything of importance could be done to relieve the situation as it appeared in January 1917, the war at sea had taken a new turn which threatened to increase still further the deficit of British tonnage and to neutralise all the efforts of the Inter-Allied Chartering Committee to secure the services of neutral shipping.

CHAPTER III

UNRESTRICTED SUBMARINE WARFARE AND ITS EFFECTS ON NEUTRALS

FEBRUARY—MARCH 1917

THE rejection by the Allies of the tentative peace proposals put forward by the German Government in December 1916 strengthened the hands of that party in Germany which had long chafed against the restrictions on submarine warfare imposed in consequence of the American protests.[1] Those restrictions were already wearing thin. Not only did the Germans claim to treat defensively armed merchantmen as cruisers, but during the last quarter of 1916 there were several instances of unarmed vessels, both British and neutral, being sunk without warning. On the whole, however, the Germans still professed and to some extent observed, a certain respect for their own Prize Regulations, especially in dealing with neutral ships.

Even within these limitations the submarines had achieved remarkable success, and there were many in Germany who believed that a vigorous campaign, waged without any respect for the considerations by which they had hitherto been guided, might prove not only destructive but decisive. They were well aware of the effect which the heavy losses inflicted during the last three months of 1916 had produced on neutrals, and they believed that it might be possible, by the threat of unrestricted sinkings, to paralyse entirely the activity of neutral shipping in the trade of Great Britain and her Allies, and at the same time to inflict such losses on British and Allied shipping as would render it impossible, without neutral assistance, to maintain the essential services.

To take this course was, indeed, to court complications

[1] Unrestricted submarine warfare had been rejected in August 1916 only on account of possible complications with neutrals for which Germany was then unprepared. See General Ludendorff, *My War Memories* (English ed.), pp. 243, 312–5.

with neutral Powers, especially with the United States, but a situation had been reached in which the possibility of success appeared to outweigh the risks to be run. The internal condition of the Central Powers was well-nigh desperate.

All through the year 1916 the Allied machinery of economic pressure had been steadily increasing in efficiency. The Orders in Council of March 30th and July 7th had removed many of the difficulties experienced in proving hostile destination of contraband goods.[1] The adoption of the "rationing" principle by the Ministry of Blockade had substituted the statistical for the evidential method as the basis of all action in restriction of enemy supplies.[2]

This principle, it will be remembered, implied that the imports of all neutral States contiguous to Germany should be restricted to such quantities of each commodity as could be shown, by reference to peace statistics, to be necessary for their normal domestic consumption. When first proposed, in the spring of 1915, in the Restriction of Enemy Supplies Committee,[3] it had been rejected as a basis for forcible interference with neutral trade, on the ground that the Prize Court was unlikely to accept purely statistical evidence as sufficient ground for condemnation of cargoes. These doubts were confirmed by the judgment in the case of the Norwegian steamer *Kim*, delivered in September 1915, and so late as December of that year, a majority of the War Trade Advisory Committee had reported against the possibility of applying the principle by Order in Council, on the ground that neutral Powers would never consent to so drastic an interference with their trade.

Many agreements with neutral countries had, however, been concluded on a rationing basis even before the appointment of the Ministry of Blockade,[4] and in April 1916, the Ministry appointed a small Rationing Committee to prepare the way for a general enforcement of the policy. In the same month the judgment in the *Baron Sternblad* laid down that statistical evidence, while not affording grounds for condemnation, might afford such prima facie

---

[1] Vol. II, pp. 306-8.   [2] *Ibid.*, p. 301.
[3] There is a clear enunciation of the principle in a Memorandum by Sir Leo Chiozza Money, then a member of the Committee, dated April 25th, 1915.
[4] Vol. II, p. 154, etc.

evidence of enemy destination as to justify seizure and detention of a cargo, and defeat any claim for damages by the neutral consignee. By August 1st the necessary statistical machinery was in working order, and during the latter half of 1916, the statistics of neutral trade were scrutinised with increasing severity, and all surplus imports were cut off either by agreement or by embargo. The enforcement of a rationing policy was now much easier than in the early days of the war, owing to the friction between the United States and Germany arising out of the submarine campaign, and the hold obtained by the Allies over the European neutrals through bunker and insurance agreements. By the beginning of 1917 it had become clear to the Central Powers that practically the whole of the small but valuable supplies of foodstuffs and materials formerly received from oversea, through neutral ports, must be finally written off.

Further, the fish and agricultural agreements, concluded by Great Britain during the latter part of 1916 with Holland and Norway, had deprived the Central Powers of a considerable proportion of the food supplies hitherto furnished by the contiguous neutrals from their own domestic produce. Worst of all, the cumulative effect on the productivity of Germany herself, of a long-continued stoppage of imported fodder and fertilisers, had now made itself felt with terrible severity.

The sufferings of the "turnip winter" were telling heavily upon both the physical and moral powers of resistance of their peoples. For the future the outlook was quite as black. Even the scanty and deleterious diet provided by the reduced rations was secured only by mortgaging the future. In order to provide for the mass of the urban population food barely sufficient to preserve life, it had been necessary to divert cereals, potatoes, and turnips from fodder to human consumption to an extent which had disastrous results. The enormous consumption of turnips for human food necessitated by the failure of the potato crop reacted on the supply of milk and butter.[1] Although the stock of horned cattle showed no appreciable diminution in numbers, the average slaughter weight had fallen from 250 kg. before the war to 210 kg. in the last three months of 1916. On the other hand, while the

[1] According to Herr Batocki, the Food Controller, 1 cwt. of turnips produced 15 litres of milk.

slaughter weight of pigs had been maintained, the numbers had fallen from 25,700,000 to 17,000,000.[1]

Any hope of substantial immediate relief from the occupation of Roumania had already become extremely doubtful, and to add to the difficulty of the situation the bargaining power of Germany in contiguous neutral countries was declining, owing to the reduction of coal exports through transport difficulties. To Sweden only 175,000 tons were shipped in December 1916, against 586,000 tons in May, and with the suspension of navigation on the Rhine through ice, the exports to Holland fell off so gravely that, in February 1917, the Dutch Government were compelled to take special steps for the collection of railway wagons in order to assure the supply. Iron and steel exports, too, were practically at a standstill, owing to the demands of the war industries.

The transport difficulties which hampered the export of coal, were equally serious in their effects on its internal distribution, and the coal famine was severely felt by the ill-fed people. Warm clothing, too, was becoming scarce. The stocks of textile materials—now incapable of replenishment—were too small to allow of manufacture for civilian use; permits for the purchase of clothing could only be obtained with difficulty; the sale of old clothes was strictly regulated; the use of paper yarn for apparel had already begun. In Austria-Hungary matters were still worse, and the coal famine, in particular, was acute, involving the most drastic restrictions on heating, lighting, and tramway traffic.

It was the food-shortage which was the dominant preoccupation of the enemy Governments and peoples. The prospects for the 1917 harvest were poor. Cereal supplies in Germany were threatened by the loss of artificial fertilisers; the all-important potato crop, by a shortage of seed potatoes. It appeared probable that the harvest would be both late and bad, and meanwhile it was a question whether the available foodstuffs could be made to hold out until it was gathered. Even if this could be done by drastic rationing, some strong stimulus in the shape of new hopes of a speedy and decisive victory was required in order to steel the nation to endurance. This stimulus it was hoped to provide by the promise of reducing

[1] Cmd. 280, pp. 24–5.

Great Britain, by relentless submarine warfare, to a peace of starvation.

The rejection of the German peace proposals not only emphasised the gravity of the position but afforded, in the German view, an opportunity of deprecating neutral indignation by representing the attitude of the Allied Governments as the real obstacle to peace. Accordingly, on January 31st, the German Ambassador in Washington presented to the United States State Department a Note complaining that "In brutal contempt of international law, the group of Powers led by England not only curtail the legitimate trade of their opponents, but they also, by ruthless pressure, compel neutral countries either to altogether forgo every trade not agreeable to the Entente Powers, or to limit it according to their arbitrary decrees." Since the English Government insisted "upon continuing its war of starvation, which does not at all affect the military power of its opponents, but compels women and children, the sick and the aged, to suffer for their country pains and privations which endanger the vitality of the nation," the German Government announced that it was "compelled to continue the fight for existence, again forced upon it, with the full employment of all the weapons which are at its disposal," not only in fulfilment of its duty to its own people but for the general benefit of mankind, to shorten the war and "to prevent further misery and unavoidable sacrifice of human life."

What the German Government meant by "the full employment of all the weapons which are at its disposal" was explained by a memorandum accompanying the Note. The effect of this memorandum was to establish " barred zones " round Great Britain, France, Italy, and in the Eastern Mediterranean, within which all navigation was prohibited, and all ships, British, Allied, or neutral, encountered by a German submarine after February 1st were liable to be sunk without warning.

Around the British Isles the barred zone covered the whole of the English Channel and the western half of the North Sea. A passage of twenty sea miles in breadth along the Dutch coast was left free to enable neutral steamers from the Dutch ports to pass into the eastern area of the North Sea, whence another narrow passage was left free along the Norwegian coast. North of the Shetlands the barred zone extended to a point three miles south of the Faroes, and all down the western coasts of Scotland, Ireland, England, and France it extended far into the Atlantic. In the Bay of Biscay only a narrow passage of twenty miles was left along the northern coast of Spain to provide entrance to and egress from the Spanish ports.[1]

In the Mediterranean the barred zone covered a strip sixty sea miles in width along the North African coast, beginning at the Algerian frontier, and the whole sea east of a line drawn southward from a point east of Cette, with the exception of a safety lane, twenty miles in breadth, leading to Greek territorial waters.[2] Access to Cette was permitted out of consideration for Switzerland, for whom that port was now to be the sole outlet.

It was stated in the Memorandum that the instructions given to German submarines provided that neutral ships on their way towards ports within the barred zones, which had already closely approached the zones, should be spared "during a sufficiently long period," but the German Government strongly advised that all available means should be used to communicate with them and order their return. Ships already in ports within the zones could leave them " with the same safety."

Similar Notes were presented at the same time to the other neutral Governments, but to the United States one humiliating concession was specially offered. If the American Government would consent to limit their trade with the United Kingdom to one passenger steamer each way weekly, such ships would be allowed to pass on condition that they arrived at and departed from Falmouth only, sailed on stated days, bore distinctive marks, followed a course laid down by the German Government, and were guaranteed by the United States to carry no contraband according to the German list.

It can hardly be believed that even the German Government expected such a proposal, made to a proud and powerful nation, to be taken seriously. If they did, they were speedily undeceived. Anxious as were the American Government to preserve an honourable neutrality, the situation had long been strained. Successive incidents arising out of the German submarine campaign had produced a tension which it wanted little to snap. Even the

---

[1] See Map.   [2] See Map.

final step had not been unanticipated, as from the moment it became evident that the German peace proposals were likely to prove abortive, the possibility of the German Government withdrawing their undertaking of May 1916, had to be regarded as possible. There had thus been ample time for the United States Government to consider their attitude in face of such a contingency, and no time was now lost in defining their position. On February 3rd President Wilson announced to Congress that diplomatic relations with Germany had been severed, and on the same day the German Ambassador, Count von Bernstorff, received his passports. The President was still not without hope that the Germans might refrain from putting their threat into effect and that actual hostilities might be avoided, but he stated that if American ships and American lives should in fact be sacrificed, he should ask Congress for authority to use any means that might be necessary for the protection of American traffic.

No other neutral Power went so far, at this time, as the severance of relations; indeed the northern European neutrals could hardly have done so without exposing themselves to the fate of Belgium; but strong protests were delivered by Norway, Sweden, and Denmark, who presented a joint Note; by Holland, Spain, Switzerland, Brazil, Chile, Peru, Argentina, Uruguay, Bolivia, Panama, Cuba, and China. In the Dutch and Scandinavian Notes particular stress was laid on the threat to neutral ships sailing from and to neutral ports. To Holland this threat was specially serious, since the barred zone in the Mediterranean blocked the passage between Port Said and the safety channel from Gibraltar to Greece, thus cutting off Holland from her East Indian possessions. Great stress, too, was laid on the illegality of a blockade which extended to seas far distant from the enemy coasts, and by its very nature could not possibly be " effective " according to the recognised laws of war.

It remained to be seen whether the German blockade, ineffective in law, would prove effective in practice. At first the signs were favourable to the Germans. British and Allied shipowners made little or no alterations in their sailings, but it appeared as if the suspension of neutral traffic would be so wide and general that a great part of the end aimed at by the enemy would be achieved. In America the International Mercantile Marine Company postponed all sailings indefinitely, the Standard Oil Company and other shipowners recalled by wireless vessels bound to the danger zones, and during the first nineteen days of February only five American freighters sailed for barred ports.[1]

The effect on the European neutrals varied in intensity and duration with the geographical and political situation of the countries affected, but everywhere it was serious. Even before the announcement of unrestricted submarine warfare neutral shipowners were showing, as we have seen, a tendency to withdraw from British and Allied trade, and this new and immeasurable extension of the risk was more than most of them would face. British, Allied, and neutral ports were alike crowded with vessels detained on their owners' instructions, and for the moment it looked as if that part of Allied trade which was carried on under neutral flags would come practically to a standstill, save in so far as it was carried in vessels on time-charter to the Allies. Some even of these vessels refused to sail, and for a few weeks the paralysis of neutral shipping was general.

The crisis was acute, but it was not altogether unexpected, and provision had been made to meet it. In London, as in Washington, the probability of Germany's embarking on an unrestricted submarine campaign had been known to the Authorities before the Barred Zone declaration was actually issued, and the measures to be taken in the event of such a contingency had been considered by the Bunker Committee and the Trade Division of the Admiralty. A Memorandum embodying their suggestions was, in fact, ready for presentation to the Government on February 1st, and was circulated on the following day.

As a first step the Government gave instructions on February 1st that all neutral vessels, to the number of some 600, in the ports of the United Kingdom, should be provisionally detained, pending some assurance against the general laying up or withdrawal of neutral shipping trading with or for the Allies. Harsh as this measure may appear, it must be remembered that, for a long time, neutral countries had been receiving supplies and bunker facilities under agreements which involved the employment of their shipping in British and Allied trade, and it was of vital importance to secure that such agreements, whether

---

[1] *The European War, New York Times Current History*, vol. x, p. 980.

express or implied, should continue to be carried out despite the new German threat.

On the following day, February 2nd, the Customs were instructed to release the American, Spanish, and South American ships, of which there were comparatively few, together with a Swedish steamer on which the members of the Swedish Mission had arranged to return. On the 3rd, the matter was again before the Government, who decided as a general policy to continue the detention of neutral shipping, and to entrust its execution to a small Interdepartmental Committee which had just been formed under the Ministry of Blockade, to deal with the question of British ships held up in the Baltic, and any other shipping questions involving Foreign Office action.[1]

A wide discretion was given to the Committee to release such ships and on such terms as they might consider desirable, but for general guidance in questions of detention and release they were referred to the Trade Division Memorandum.

In accordance with the suggestions of that Memorandum all ships in United Kingdom ports on February 1st, which had called voluntarily for examination, were released at an early date, with the exception of those carrying grain and fertilisers to Denmark and Holland, which it was decided to retain until some assurance had been received as to the receipt of supplies from those countries. The treatment accorded to vessels calling for examination after that date varied widely, according to the relations existing with the countries under whose flag they sailed.

Of other ships in United Kingdom ports on February 1st, those on time-charter to the Allies or trading between Allied countries were generally released on an undertaking being given that they would not be diverted to a neutral port to be laid up, and such vessels for the most part continued to run in their accustomed trades. Ships bound for a neutral port, on the other hand, were only allowed to proceed if fixed to return with an approved cargo to a British or Allied port. If an approved cargo was not available, the usual penalty trips with coal to

---

[1] The original members of the Neutral Tonnage Committee were: Commander Fisher of the Admiralty; Mr. C. Hipwood, Board of Trade; Mr. H. Knatchbull-Hugessen, Foreign Office. Mr. Thomas Royden of the Shipping Control Committee was added on February 2nd, and Mr. Leverton Harris of the Ministry of Blockade was subsequently appointed Chairman, with instructions to report daily to Lord Robert Cecil.

France were exacted. The same principle was applied to ships arriving after February 1st, and any ship arriving in ballast or with unapproved cargo, and desiring to load coal for Scandinavia or Holland, was required to undertake a duty voyage before loading for her own country. Further, in order to guard against the danger of general laying up, clearance was only granted to Dutch and Scandinavian vessels bound for ports in their own country, whether in port on February 1st or arriving subsequently, on the arrival at a British port of a similar vessel under the same flag. In the Scandinavian trade the British Consuls were instructed to report by telegraph the departure of each vessel for the United Kingdom, and the nature of the cargo carried, in order that arrangements might be made for the release, without delay, of a suitable vessel in return. This principle, known as the " ship-for-ship " policy, was the main basis of all subsequent negotiations with Holland and the Scandinavian States, and was relaxed or tightened according to the results achieved.

Neutral shipping in British ports abroad was also detained under instructions sent out through the Colonial Office and India Office on February 5th, but at the end of a week, all vessels permanently employed outside Atlantic and European waters were unconditionally released. Other vessels were ordered to proceed to Suez or Cape Town for further instructions, and were generally allowed to proceed to their destinations on a written undertaking by the master that they would not be diverted to a neutral port to lay up. The Allied Governments, too, were informed of the policy adopted with regard to neutral shipping, and co-operated to some extent in its enforcement.

It was necessary, at the same time, to make arrangements for the continued interception of German supplies. It was at once made clear that the German declaration would not be accepted as involving any relaxation of the examination service, and in order to deter neutral vessels from attempting any breach of their agreements as to calling at British ports, an Order in Council was issued on February 16th providing that all goods of enemy origin or destination should be liable to condemnation, and that any ship carrying such goods should also be liable to condemnation in default of calling voluntarily for examination. Further, any vessel bound to or from a neutral port affording means of access to enemy territory and not calling at a British or Allied port, should be deemed to be carrying enemy goods until the contrary was proved, and should be brought in for examination and, if necessary, adjudication.[1] In order, however, to enable neutrals to comply with the regulations without unnecessary risk, it was arranged that an examination service should be instituted at Halifax, Gibraltar, Alexandria, and other ports outside the danger zone. The privilege of calling for examination at these ports was granted only to ships whose owners undertook to conform to regulations in force as to the carriage of coal to the Atlantic bunker depôts, and not to lay up vessels hitherto engaged in Allied trades. It was further required that all cargoes should be covered by letters of assurance under the Navicert system, or approved under the system of advance bookings in the South American trade.[2] Special courses laid down by the Admiralty were communicated confidentially to the masters and owners of vessels complying with these conditions.

Such were the measures devised for dealing with the situation created by Germany's unprecedented attack on neutral trade. The application of such measures, as already mentioned, varied greatly as between flag and flag. To apply them to American shipping was neither possible nor desirable, and both the situation and the attitude of the European neutrals forbade any hard-and-fast adherence to a general rule.

With Holland relations were already severely strained. Early in January the Dutch Government introduced legislation giving power to requisition 75 per cent. of the space of the principal liner companies in order to safeguard the maintenance of the grain supplies.[3] Uncertain as to how far this action would affect the continuance of the services performed by the Dutch lines in return for bunker supplies, the British authorities decided to extend the application of the North Sea Freight Regulations to Dutch ships as from January 25th, a proceeding which led to many protests. A further source of friction was provided by the refusal of the Dutch Government to furnish information as to the carrying out of the Agricultural Agreement. Pending a satisfactory settlement of this question,

---

[1] Supplement to the *London Gazette* of 20 February, 1917.
[2] See Vol. II, p. 304.
[3] Law of 10 February, 1917 (J.O. No. 211).

Dutch ships loaded with fodder and fertilisers for Holland were now detained, and the ship-for-ship policy was strictly applied in the traffic between Holland and the United Kingdom.

Relations with Denmark were little more satisfactory. Early in January the Danish Government had issued an order prohibiting the time-charter of Danish vessels to foreigners without the consent of the Ministry of Commerce. The ostensible purpose of this order was to enable the Government to withdraw ships from distant trades to meet a threatened shortage of tonnage for Danish requirements. Its issue at a time when the Allies, through the medium of the Inter-Allied Chartering Committee, were initiating time-chartering operations on an extensive scale, gave rise to considerable anxiety. Accordingly, negotiations were opened in London at the end of January, with representatives of the Danish shipowners, for the conclusion of a comprehensive agreement with regard to the employment of Danish tonnage. At the outbreak of the unrestricted submarine campaign these negotiations were abandoned. Danish sailings to the United Kingdom were cancelled, and some owners even threatened to lay up their ships for the duration of the war. The ship-for-ship policy was accordingly enforced, and Danish vessels laden with fodder and fertilisers were held up, on calling for examination, till some satisfactory guarantee for the continuance of shipments from Denmark should be received.

A similar policy was adopted with regard to Sweden, with whom relations at the beginning of 1917 were strained almost to the breaking point. The persistent refusal of the Swedish authorities to curtail their exports to Germany had resulted in the imposition of a long list of embargoes on commodities of prime importance to Sweden. The detention of British and Allied vessels in the Baltic consequent upon the mining of the Kogrund Passage was a further source of friction. A Swedish Mission to London had proved abortive, and it was hardly surprising that immediately on the issue of the German declaration, Swedish shipowners engaged in trade with or for the Allies proceeded to lay up their vessels. In reply, the British Government not only applied the ship-for-ship principle with the utmost rigour, but held up all Swedish ships calling for examination, and excluded Swedish shipowners from "Halifax privileges" pending a satisfactory settlement of the Kogrund dispute.

In striking contrast to the friction which had arisen with so many neutrals, British relations with Norway were on a friendly footing. The dispute which had arisen during the winter of 1916 with regard to the carrying out of the Fish Agreement had now been settled, and since they had been able to obtain assistance from the British Government in the insurance of their vessels, Norwegian shipowners had shown little reluctance to run the risks inseparable from British and Allied trade. Nor were they now long deterred from their accustomed activities even by the additional perils with which neutral shipping was now threatened. By February 23rd, 18 Norwegian steamers had left Norway for the United Kingdom; by March 10th, 35 more; by March 20th, 76 had arrived from Scandinavia or Iceland since February 20th.

It was evident that compulsion was unnecessary, and on March 13th the British Minister at Christiania was informed that clearance would be granted to Norwegian ships, subject to the North Sea Freight Regulations, without waiting for the arrival of a corresponding vessel. The Customs were instructed to grant clearances, without reference to London, to ships owned by companies who undertook to continue their sailings and to furnish bi-weekly information as to the position of their ships; vessels calling for examination were allowed to proceed without delay provided their cargoes were in order; and instructions were given that Norwegian ships should be cleared at British ports abroad without any restriction other than the obligation to call at some British port on their way to their destination.

In view of the marked predominance of the Norwegian over other neutral flags in the general carrying trade, it was a matter for extreme satisfaction that methods of compulsion, involving endless possibilities of friction, could be laid aside in respect of Norwegian ships. It was evident that the dependence of Norway on British coal, and the interest of Norwegian shipowners in procuring cargoes for their large surplus tonnage, rendered them genuinely anxious to employ their vessels in the service of the Allies, with whom their country was on friendly terms. In these circumstances, the British Government were hopeful of obtaining even an increased proportion of

Norwegian tonnage, and negotiations were accordingly opened with the Norwegian Government and the Shipowners' Association, for an agreement whereby all Norwegian shipping not required for the trade of Norway herself should, so far as possible, be employed in Allied interests, in return for a guarantee of the Norwegian coal supply. These overtures were favourably received by the Norwegian Authorities, and the discussions proceeded in an amicable spirit which gave good hopes of ultimate success.

Meanwhile the application of the ship-for-ship policy to other neutrals was continued with varying success. As regards Denmark the situation was complicated by the prolonged diplomatic dispute over the disposal of agricultural produce. Although the great commercial associations were honourably anxious to fulfil the agreements under which Danish supplies of fodder and fertilisers were allowed to go forward, the Danish farmers were naturally tempted to dispose of their produce in the highest market, and the result was that, during 1916, Germany received three times as much butter, eleven times as much pork and bacon, and nearly twenty times as many eggs as before the war, while shipments to Great Britain were largely reduced. On the outbreak of the unrestricted submarine campaign the Germans threatened to cut off Danish exports to the United Kingdom altogether, and the geographical position of the Danish ports gave reality to the threat. The British Government replied, as we have seen, by detaining all ships with fodder and fertilisers bound for Denmark until assurance was received that the Agricultural Agreement would be satisfactorily carried out. The Germans then offered to allow three produce ships a week to sail to Aberdeen and return with coal, an arrangement which the British Government did not regard as satisfactory. Direct sailings being very dangerous, the Danes now tried to send the ships viâ Bergen, but on arrival at Bergen the crews refused to proceed. By this time the situation had become very strained, and in the first week of March the British authorities, fearing that the shortage of feeding-stuffs would cause abnormal slaughterings of livestock and a resultant increase of exports to Germany, temporarily relaxed the embargo. This concession did something to ease the strain, and by the middle of the month shipments of produce viâ Bergen had been resumed and fodder ships were allowed to go forward freely. The suspension of Danish sailings had not, however, been confined to ships loaded with produce. Colliers and even ships chartered to the Allies also refused to move, and it became necessary to take drastic steps in order to terminate the deadlock. The refusal of Danish ships to carry out their charters was not approved by the representatives of the leading Danish shipowners with whom the negotiations for a tonnage agreement had been opened, and with their consent, about a dozen Danish steamers were requisitioned during March in British and Allied ports, on terms which provided for the payment of hire, redelivery in good condition after the war, and compensation in the event of loss. The vessels were then armed and placed under the British flag, special bunker facilities were granted to the non-requisitioned portion of the owners' fleets, and permission was given for a number of Danish colliers to arrive in ballast to load coal, without the enforcement of a penalty trip.

Despite this strong hint as to the consequences of laying up, and although some of the leading Danish shipowners were willing to take advantage of the British insurance proposals, very few Danish ships had arrived at ports in the United Kingdom up to the end of March, and except that a number of produce steamers were known to be on passage, the position was still unsatisfactory. Swedish owners were even more obdurate. Between February 20th and March 20th only two ships from Sweden arrived in the United Kingdom under the national flag, and the embargo on Swedish shipping continued, in consequence, to be rigorously maintained.

It was in Holland, however, that the difficulties of the situation were most cruelly felt. On the one hand the country depended largely on foreign trade for its prosperity and even for the food supply of its people. On the other hand, its situation exposed it in an especial degree to German pressure. All Dutch sailings to the United Kingdom were at once suspended on receipt of the German declaration, and any hope of a revival of trade received a severe set-back on February 22nd, when eight Dutch steamers, with an aggregate tonnage of about 40,000 gross, were captured and sunk off the Scillies. Seven of these vessels had been released from Falmouth at the request of the Dutch Government, who had received assurances that they should be allowed to sail in safety, and four of the seven were homeward bound with cargoes of foodstuffs. The German Government alleged that only a conditional promise of safety had been given for February 22nd, as submarines already at sea might not have received instructions, and that the absolute safe conduct was valid only for March 17th. Notwithstanding this, they made offers of compensation which the Dutch Government refused to consider as satisfactory.

Alarmed by this incident, Dutch owners refused the offer of insurance facilities in Great Britain, on the ground that it would afford the enemy an additional inducement to sink their ships, and only a very few Dutch ships ventured across with margarine and agricultural produce. As the ship-for-ship principle was rigidly enforced, return sailings from the United Kingdom were practically suspended, except for a few British ships carrying materials for the margarine factories. The export of British coal to Holland was at a complete standstill, but since the Dutch requirements could still be satisfied in part by imports from Germany, this was, perhaps, a less severe blow than the continued detention of Dutch vessels laden with cereals and fertilisers. By the latter part of March the position as regards the Agricultural Agreement had been cleared up by the receipt of satisfactory information as to the disposal of Dutch produce, and fodder ships were gradually released in consequence. A new cause of friction, however, had arisen through the refusal of the Dutch authorities to allow the British steamer *Princess Melita* to enter a Dutch port, on account of her defensive armament, an attitude which led, for a time, to the refusal of all facilities to Dutch ships. So severe was the effect in Holland of the continued suspension of traffic that it became necessary to reduce the bread ration as from April 2nd, on account of the shortage of grain; but despite the pressure thus exercised, there was no sign of any general resumption of Dutch sailings in British and Allied trade.

By this time, too, serious difficulties had arisen with Spain. Even in December and January, before the outbreak of unrestricted submarine warfare, Spanish entrances had shown a marked decline. Towards the end of 1916 the Coal Exports Committee, seeking to make a larger proportion of the tonnage in the ore trade available for the carriage of coal to France and Italy, endeavoured to make the licensing of coal for export to Spain conditional on its shipment in Spanish bottoms, thus releasing Scandinavian tonnage for French service. This attempt met with little success; the high war risk premiums in war-zone trade, and the delays caused by discharge of ore cargoes alike tended to drive Spanish shipping out of the traffic. The great increase of risk consequent on the new extension of the submarine campaign naturally accentuated the reluctance of owners to send ships to British ports. Serious trouble, fomented by German agents, was experienced with Spanish seamen, and firms under contract to carry ore to the United Kingdom, refused to carry out their obligations, on the plea of *force majeure*. A large proportion of the sailings were suspended, and Spanish importers of coal entered into negotiations for the purchase of extensive supplies from the United States.

To make matters worse, the Spanish Government, faced with a prospective shortage of tonnage both for the import of coal and for the export of fruit, issued two decrees, one of which stipulated that 10 per cent. of the space in outward bound oreships loading at or near a fruit port should be reserved for the carriage of fruit, and the other provided that all ships arriving at a Spanish port to load ore must bring coal to the proportion of 33 per cent. of the ore they proposed to lift. The objection to the first-mentioned decree lay not so much in the shutting out of ore as in the waste of time involved by the double loading. The second, or 33 per cent. order, constituted a serious menace to the French and Italian coal trade. It meant that ships which, in the ordinary course of events, would have discharged coal cargoes in a French bay or a Mediterranean port, returning with ore to the United Kingdom, had now to discharge a considerable proportion of their coal cargoes at a Spanish port, in return for permission to load ore.

Owing to the vital importance of her ore exports, Spain was in too strong a position to permit the application of the ship-for-ship principle or similar measures to her shipping. All that could be done was to open negotiations with the Spanish Government for a general agreement with regard to trade and shipping, a game in which the Spaniards held most of the trump cards. Meanwhile very few Spanish ships came forward with ore cargoes—not a single Spanish ship arrived at a British port during the first three weeks of March—and the hope of obtaining any relief to the French coal trade had to be indefinitely postponed.

This was the more serious, inasmuch as the French and Italian coal trades were already feeling the effect of the unrestricted submarine campaign. Losses in the coal and ore traffic were heavy, and still more serious was the effect of the paralysis of neutral shipping in reducing the tonnage available. During the two months February and March, the aggregate net tonnage of Scandinavian, Dutch, and Spanish shipping entered at British ports with cargoes from all countries was far less than in the single month of January, and only about one quarter of what it had been in the corresponding months of 1916. The clearances were almost as unsatisfactory. But for the enterprise and courage displayed by the Norwegian shipowners and seamen the comparison would have been far more unfavourable; indeed it was only under the Norwegian flag that any considerable volume of trade continued to be carried (see tables opposite).

The effect of this decline on the coal supply of the Allies may be gauged by the fact that during 1916 44 per cent. of the tonnage cleared under the Scandinavian, Dutch, and Spanish flags was for France, Italy, or the Mediterranean bunker depôts. The crisis was indeed acute. Even the provision of facilities in London for insurance against war risks and the increased freight rates offered on January 29th were insufficient to retain neutral tonnage in the vital trades, and on February 12th the Inter-Allied Chartering Committee announced that the limitation coal freights to French Mediterranean and Italian ports would be increased by 12s. per ton in addition to the 50 per cent. advance previously granted. At the same time the 20 per cent. advance on rates to Channel and Bay ports was raised to 50 per cent. Ore freights also were substantially increased.

Even at the greatly increased rates now offered neutral shipping was very difficult to obtain, especially for the Mediterranean. From the first it had proved practically impossible to fix an equivalent time-charter rate for the Mediterranean trade, and by this time the whole limitation scheme was practically a dead letter so far as that sea was concerned. By the end of February the Inter-Allied Chartering Committee had come to the conclusion that no maximum freight rates should be allowed to stand in

DECLINE IN NEUTRAL TRAFFIC

ENTRANCES 1,000 TONS NET

1916.	Norwegian.	Swedish.	Danish.	Dutch.	Spanish.	Total.
January . . .	203	84	64	104	90	545
February . . .	224	94	62	89	85	554
March . . .	234	115	66	87	93	595
Total, February March	458	209	128	176	178	1,149
1917. January . . .	201	96	67	51	56	471
February . . .	112	17	8	7	24	168
March . . .	97	11	6	10	7	131
Total, February March	209	28	14	17	31	299

CLEARANCES 1,000 TONS NET

1916.	Norwegian.	Swedish.	Danish.	Dutch.	Spanish.	Total.
January . . .	536	125	177	146	126	1,110
February . . .	526	157	196	125	98	1,102
March . . .	627	159	205	110	90	1,191
Total, February March	1,153	316	401	235	188	2,293
1917. January . . .	398	125	125	115	69	832
February . . .	216	22	17	26	27	308
March . . .	298	14	8	13	19	352
Total, February March	514	36	25	39	46	660

the way of securing ships for Allied services, whether in the coal or other trades, and whether on time or voyage charter. The Executive were accordingly instructed that, while refusing to accept ships from individual owners at exorbitant rates, they might give whatever rates proved to be necessary in order to persuade neutral shipping as a whole to accept Allied charters. On March 14th the Central Coal Committee were informed of this decision, but it was intimated that British and Allied shipping would still be bound by the original scheduled rates for voyage-charters, and equivalent time-charter rates. Even for neutral shipping the amended schedule rates remained nominally in force, and were taken as a basis of calculation, though as regards Mediterranean voyages particularly, they were not allowed to fetter the discretion of the Inter-Allied Executive.

Notwithstanding the increased freights paid to neutrals and the large amount of British requisitioned tonnage employed in the service, the supply of coal to France and Italy continued to give cause for anxiety. The deliveries to France during the first nine weeks of 1917 fell short by 39 per cent. of the French requirements, and Italy was in yet graver plight. Although the Admiralty loyally fulfilled and more than fulfilled their obligations for the shipment of coal in requisitioned tonnage, including compensation under the coal-ore agreement, the total export fell 58 per cent. short of the Italian demands. Some of the leeway was made up in March, when the shipments to both France and Italy reached a high figure, but, as a result of the withdrawal of neutral shipping, the strain on British tonnage was serious. Even to fulfil the Admiralty obligations to Italy it had been necessary to ship coal in liners diverted from the Cape to the Mediterranean route, thus increasing the submarine risk and shutting out cargo for Indian ports.

In view of the extreme shortage of neutral tonnage, the employment even of steamers under 1,000 tons dead-weight had now become a matter of importance, especially as such steamers could usefully be employed in the cross-Channel coal traffic. The Inter-Allied Chartering Committee accordingly decided on March 3rd to extend their operations to steamers between 500 and 1,000 tons dead-weight, and the necessary order, prohibiting private chartering, was issued on March 13th.

That the hesitation of neutrals to engage in traffic in the barred zones was not without justification, was proved by the increase in the number of casualties under neutral flags. In January 125,000 tons of neutral shipping had been destroyed, 25 per cent. more than in any previous month of the war. In February, despite the great diminution in sailings, the losses rose to 186,000, and in March, when Norwegian shipping was again moving freely,

UNITED STATES DECLARES WAR

to 161,000 tons.[1] Norway alone lost 165,000 tons during the two months. Swedish, Danish, and Spanish losses were comparatively light owing to the laying up of so many ships, but Holland, as we have seen, lost 40,000 tons in a single day, and American losses amounted to 25,000 tons.

So general was the hold-up of American shipping following on the break with Germany, that on February 26th President Wilson requested Congress to empower him to arm American merchantmen in order to enable trade to be carried on. A Bill for this purpose was at once introduced, but owing to the obstructive tactics of a small group in the Senate, it failed to pass before the end of the session on March 4th. In the meantime public opinion in the United States had been deeply stirred by the torpedoing of the Cunard liner *Laconia* on February 25th, by which twelve lives were lost, including two American citizens. On March 9th the President issued a Proclamation calling Congress in extra session, and on the 12th he gave formal notice that he should proceed by virtue of his presidential powers to arm American vessels traversing the war zone. The work was at once put in hand and American freighters prepared to resume their sailings. But before any armed American steamer could enter the war zone or Congress could meet, the United States vessel *Vigilancia* had been torpedoed without warning on March 16th, and fifteen members of her crew were lost. On March 21st the tanker *Healdton*, bound for Rotterdam, was sunk without warning in the North Sea, with the loss of seven lives. The cup was now full. On April 2nd the President addressed Congress in extraordinary session and asked them to recognise the existence of a state of war. On April 6th the United States declared war on Germany.

[1] The proportion of these losses caused by submarines was for January 111,000 tons, February 131,000, March 144,000.

CHAPTER IV

GROWING SHORTAGE OF TONNAGE—IMPORT RESTRICTIONS

FEBRUARY—MARCH 1917

IN deciding on the unrestricted submarine campaign, the rulers of Germany were engaging in a conscious gamble for high stakes. They were perfectly aware that war with the United States was a probable consequence; but they hoped that, long before the Americans could so mobilise their resources as to render them effective in the military sphere, the submarines would have starved the European Allies into submission.

This hope was not altogether unreasonable. The immediate paralysis of neutral shipping brought about by the announcement of the barred zones, went a long way towards its fulfilment, and the first results of the intensified attack on British shipping were almost equally promising. The greatest amount of British tonnage hitherto lost in any one month was 182,000 tons in December 1916; the greatest amount sunk by submarines alone was 147,000 in October of the same year. In February 1917 the total losses rose to 313,000 tons, of which the submarines claimed 256,000. In March the figures rose still further, to 353,000 tons and 284,000 tons respectively.[1] Including Allied and neutral ships, the reduction of the world's tonnage by war causes during the two months amounted to over 1,100,000 tons.

So heavy were the monetary losses that it became necessary once more to raise the premiums for insurance against war risks under the State Scheme, and on March 19th an increase was announced in both the hull and the cargo rates. For cargoes shipped in vessels sailing after April

---

[1] The figures for total losses and ships sunk by submarines are given separately, in order to show the effects of "unrestricted" sinkings; but many casualties were also due to mines laid by submarine mine-layers. The total is swelled, however, during these two months by the activities of the surface raiders.

30th, the rate was to be 3 per cent., for hulls the new rate, which came into operation at once, was 1½ per cent. for a single voyage, 3 per cent. for a round voyage, or a 91 days' time policy.[1] This was the highest premium which had yet been charged for hull insurance at any period of the war, but vexatious as was the additional burden thus placed on British trade, it was a very small matter compared with the reduction of carrying power.

The effect of such losses as were suffered in February and March, coupled with the wholesale diversion or laying up of neutral tonnage, was, of course, to accentuate in the gravest possible manner the difficulties with which the Transport Department, now transferred to the Ministry of Shipping, were already wrestling. The new programme of ship purchase and accelerated construction could bring little relief to the situation. During January the Shipping Controller had estimated for a home output of about 100,000 tons a month for the year 1917[2]; but this was only one-third of the rate of loss, and even this proved impossible of attainment. Bad weather, insufficiency of labour, and above all shortage of material impeded the execution of the programme, and the ocean-going tonnage actually rendered available during February and March, including vessels transferred from foreign flags or otherwise acquired, as well as new ships brought into service, amounted only to 150,000 tons, as against war and marine losses amounting to nearly 650,000. Large contracts had, it is true, been placed in the United States and Japan, but it must be several months before the effect of these contracts could be felt and since the Admiralty held out no hope of diminution in the rate of loss, the immediate prospect was of a net monthly wastage perhaps twice as great as the average gross loss during 1916.

In these circumstances there could no longer be the slightest doubt that the imports brought in during 1917 would fall short by several million tons of the figure attained in the previous year, and the only question was how far the supply of food and war material could be safeguarded by throwing the burden of the reduction on non-essentials. It will be remembered that Sir Henry Babington Smith's Interdepartmental Committee had been instructed to prepare alternative programmes, based respectively on reductions of 250,000 and 500,000 tons

[1] Cmd. 98. [2] See Chapter V, *post*.

per month, and on February 10th they duly presented a report in which such programmes were worked out in detail. Four days later this Report was forwarded to the Government by the Curzon Committee, with an emphatic recommendation of the larger, or 500,000 ton programme, as the lowest which could be expected appreciably to relieve the situation. On February 16th this programme, with one or two modifications of detail, received the approval of the War Cabinet.

In framing their programme, the Babington Smith Committee had been guided by two main considerations —economy of tonnage and the condition of the exchanges. Economy of tonnage involved the exclusion, so far as possible, of bulky and especially of heavy commodities, and of those imported from the most distant countries. Considerations of exchange suggested the exclusion, even when the space occupied was comparatively small, of articles of high value in proportion to bulk, and of goods imported from countries where the exchange problem was acute. Both considerations of exchange and considerations of public policy and sentiment suggested that, if any restrictions were to be imposed, the import of luxuries should be prohibited.

The application of these principles was, of course, limited by the necessity of admitting all articles, whatever their bulk, cost, or source, indispensable for the conduct of the war or the maintenance of a minimum standard of life for the civil population. It was necessary also, both for exchange purposes and in order to avoid creating widespread unemployment and distress, to import so far as possible, the raw materials of the great staple industries, especially those prominent in the export trade. Further, there were political considerations which gravely complicated the problem. Not only was it necessary to pay some regard to the interests of the Dominions and the Allies, but where imports were allowed from Allied countries, it was difficult to maintain a prohibition against the products of neutral countries enjoying the benefit of " most favoured nation " treaties. In some directions the hands of the Government were further tied by commercial agreements effected for the purpose of restricting enemy trade, and many neutral countries who might feel themselves aggrieved either in respect of their treaty rights or on more general grounds, were in a position

IMPORT RESTRICTIONS ADOPTED

to back their protests by effective pressure. Some of them were able to retaliate by laying embargoes on articles of primary importance for war purposes; others, if export to the United Kingdom were stopped, could divert the current of trade to enemy markets.

As finally drafted by the Committee and approved by the Government, the programme represented an inevitable compromise between tonnage, exchange, and political considerations; but the urgent necessity of securing for essential supplies the limited carrying power available was, throughout, the predominant factor. The restrictions proposed fell under six principal headings.

In the first place, the existing prohibitions and restrictions were greatly extended. By far the most important of the restrictions imposed in 1916 was that on the import of paper and paper-making materials. These imports had already been cut down to about two-thirds of the 1913 figures, but were still over a million and a quarter tons, and it was decided that they should now be further reduced by one half to 640,000 tons, giving a saving of 53,000 tons a month. The importation of paper hangings, printed posters, and other coated papers, as well as books, newspapers, and periodicals, except for single copies sent through the post, was prohibited altogether, and the burden of the remaining reductions was distributed between the printing and packing trades in consultation with representatives of the industries affected. With a view to diminishing the burden on trade, immediate steps were taken to enforce economy in the consumption of paper by Government Departments and to organise the collection of waste paper for repulping.

Among other articles previously restricted, the imports of stones and slates, hardwoods and furniture woods, had been greatly curtailed as a result of war conditions, even before the original restrictions were imposed. They were now, however, singled out for further cuts. Tobacco, too, had been placed on the prohibited list, but so freely had licences been granted that the imports for 1916—76,000 tons—were actually higher than for the last year of peace. As ample stocks were in hand, it was now possible to effect a drastic reduction. Other prohibitions, such as those on sheet, window, and plate glass, and glass table ware, had only been recently imposed, and were expected to yield a substantial saving during 1917, and there were many minor prohibitions in the application of which it was hoped to effect a greater stringency. Altogether a saving of about 30,000 tons a month on the 1916 imports was expected from miscellaneous existing prohibitions, bringing up the total under this head to 83,000 tons monthly.

The second category comprised all timber other than hardwoods, and this, from the bulk of the imports, was the most important of all. In 1913 the imports had amounted to over 11,000,000 tons, and though greatly reduced through the closing of the Baltic route from Russia, they were still well over 6,000,000 tons in 1916. Here was the possibility of the greatest saving, and by economies in use, by increase in home production, especially of pit-props, by further cutting for military purposes in France, and by drawing on stocks, it was hoped to reduce the imports during 1916 by an average of 200,000 tons a month, 40 per cent. of the whole saving contemplated under the programme. To secure this, it was decided to appoint a single authority, under the War Office, to control the purchase and supply of timber for all Government Departments, the licensing of imports and utilisation of existing stocks, and the development of home supplies. Sir J. Bampfylde Fuller was accordingly appointed Director of Timber Supplies, and took over the functions of the Home Grown Timber Committee and other existing authorities. Immediate steps were taken to restrict the use of timber and wood in building and otherwise for Government, domestic, and industrial purposes; application was made to the French Government to permit unrestricted cutting in the forests nearest the front, and steps were taken to increase the supply of labour for cutting both at home and in France.[1]

In the third category came various classes of food and

---

[1] The stocks in hand amounted to about eight months' supply. The savings it was hoped to effect were as follows:

Excess of 1916 imports and home production over requirements for 1916	550,000 tons.
Increase in military supplies from French forests	250,000 ,,
Increase of production in United Kingdom for military purposes	300,000 ,,
Increased production of pit-props in United Kingdom	300,000 ,,
Supplies drawn from stocks (one quarter of stocks)	750,000 ,,
Economies in use (say, 5 per cent. of estimated requirements)	220,000 ,,
	2,370,000 tons.

(say, 200,000 per month)

feeding stuffs. Imports of raw fruit and vegetables, the nutritive value of which was small compared with their bulk, were drastically restricted. With the exception of lemons, the import of all raw fruit was prohibited, and it was decided to license at most 50 per cent. of the 1916 imports.[1] Imports of onions and tomatoes were similarly cut down. In this way it was hoped to save between 50,000 and 60,000 tons a month.

About 30,000 tons a month was to be saved on luxury foods and drinks. Mineral waters, cocoa preparations, and confectionery were to be wholly excluded, and the import of all other articles of food containing sugar was prohibited. It was decided, however, to license imports of canned fruits up to 50 per cent. of the 1916 imports, as their total exclusion would have borne hardly on the poorer classes of the population. Imports of canned salmon, which had risen greatly during the war, were to be restricted. Imports of tea were to be cut down, not by reducing consumption, but by drawing on stocks and further restriction of re-exports. In view of the large stocks in hand, imports of coffee were to be wholly excluded, those of cocoa largely cut down. For the same reason, imports of rum were to be excluded, and those of wine and brandy reduced to one half the level of 1913.[2]

In cereals and feeding stuffs the only large saving possible was in brewing materials. Brewing had already been restricted under the Output of Beer Restriction Act, and a further cut was now proposed which would bring down the output to about 10,000,000, barrels as compared with 35,000,000 barrels before the war. The combined effect of these restrictions was expected to show a monthly saving of some 48,000 tons in barley, brewer's sugar, etc. A further saving of 5,000 tons was hoped for from the replacement of corn and grain offals by other feeding stuffs possessing greater nutritive value in proportion to weight, and of soya beans by oil seeds drawn from nearer sources.

In the fourth category, comprising raw materials, few

---

[1] Oranges, grapes, bananas, and onions were to be cut down by 75 per cent., tomatoes by 66 and nuts by 50 per cent. All other fruits were to be entirely excluded. It was understood that the 75 per cent. reductions left a margin for bargaining and adjustment, and that not more than a 50 per cent. reduction might be possible.

[2] Stocks. Tea, 4½ months' supply; cocoa, 1 year; coffee, 5 years; wine (in bond), 8 months; brandy, 2 years; rum, 4 years.

reductions were possible, but by drawing on stocks and restricting re-exports it was hoped to cut down the imports of jute by over 50 per cent., and leather for non-military purposes was also to be restricted. In this category the savings were estimated at 15,000 tons a month.

Restrictions on the import of manufactured goods, of which a long list was scheduled, were in many instances imposed for exchange reasons as much as, or more than, for the purpose of tonnage economy, but the total saving was expected to amount to 10,000 tons a month.[1] With re-exports, the sixth category, there was little interference other than that involved in the import restrictions themselves. A large proportion of re-exports went to Allied countries, and in many instances there would be little or no economy of tonnage in direct shipment. Other re-export trades were of special importance to the exchanges. There was, however, an increasing tendency to ship supplies direct to the Allied countries wherever possible, and many re-exports were already restricted under recent decisions, with a view to the conservation of stocks or increasing the stringency of economic pressure on the Central Powers. Altogether a saving of about 10,000 tons a month was looked for under this head.[2]

The total saving looked for under all six categories was from 448,000 to 458,000 tons a month, leaving a balance of from 42,000 to 52,000 tons, in order to make up the proposed 500,000. In respect of this deficit the Food Controller and the Board of Agriculture were to consider what reductions could be made in imports of food and

---

[1] In point of bulk the most important goods affected were glass bottles, painters' colours and pigments, and Italian marble. Glass bottles were to be cut down by 50 and painters' colours by 33 per cent. Italian marble (hitherto licensed up to 50 per cent. of the 1915 import) was to be wholly excluded. Among the most important articles restricted mainly for exchange purposes were the following (the figures show the value of imports in 1916 in thousands of £): Silk manufactures (12,879); cotton hosiery, gloves, and lace (4,669); embroidery and needlework (3,248); apparel and hats (1,038); straw plait (1,008); feathers and down (827); typewriters and parts (665); manufactures of skins and furs (530); leather gloves (507); fancy goods (452); artificial flowers (473); sewing-machines and parts (413).

[2] The chief direct restriction was on the re-export of Egyptian cotton to the United States. This was estimated at 2,500 tons a month, and the restriction had the advantage of releasing space in Mediterranean tonnage for lifting ore, while the cotton could still go to America in ships which would otherwise have sailed in ballast from the Eastern Mediterranean.

feeding stuffs, in default of possible further savings on timber.[1]

This deficit was liable, however, to be increased by concessions in licensing. In respect of many important items in the programme much work was left for diplomacy before the restrictions could be made effective. Australia, South Africa, and Canada were deeply interested in the fruit trade; Canada in her exports of canned salmon; India in shipments of tea and jute. Neither France, Italy, nor Japan could hear without alarm that the imports of silk manufactures were to be cut down to 20 per cent., and of straw plait to 50 per cent. of the 1916 figures. Cotton hosiery, gloves, hats, apparel, flowers both natural and artificial, and fancy goods were among articles the import of which from Allied countries was now to be restricted. In all these and in many other instances it was necessary to communicate with the Governments concerned and convince them of the necessity of the measure, before the prohibitions could be put in force. Nor was it likely that neutral countries, such as Spain, in a position to retaliate, would accept the restrictions on fruit and other valuable trades, without an effort at bargaining.

It was obvious, too, that restrictions on so large a scale must involve a very serious interference with national life and habits. While many of the articles to be excluded were luxuries in the full sense of the word, there were others which had come, by long usage, to be regarded as necessaries of normal existence, and so drastic a reduction of supplies involved a severe strain upon the spirit and

[1]
			Monthly saving
I. Articles already restricted:			
Paper and paper-making materials		53,000	
Other articles		30,000	
			83,000
II. Timber			200,000
III. Food and feeding stuffs			130,000
		to	140,000
IV. Raw materials			15,000
V. Manufactures			10,000
VI. Re-exports			10,000
			448,000
		to	458,000
Increased saving on timber or reduction of food and feeding stuffs			42,000
		to	52,000
			500,000

temper of the people, and this was likely to be aggravated by unemployment and financial loss arising from the interference with established trades. The immense decrease in timber imports involved the practical cessation of private building, already severely restricted in the interests of the Ministry of Munitions. The restrictions on paints and pigments rendered it necessary to release tenants and landlords during the war from all covenants requiring the painting of houses at specified periods. The reduction in imports of paper and paper-making materials involved drastic interference with the use of posters, tradesmen's price lists, and advertising circulars. The restrictions on fruit and other foodstuffs rendered it necessary, in order to guard against speculation, to consider a further extension of the rationing and price-fixing system which had already been applied to many of the staple foodstuffs.

In the aggregate these difficulties formed no light obstacle, but with the available carrying power barely sufficient for the transport of indispensable necessaries, it was a choice between inconvenience and disaster. There could be no wavering, and on February 28rd the Prime Minister made a general announcement, in the House of Commons, of the policy decided upon.[1] Immediate steps were taken to obtain the consent of the Dominions and the foreign Governments affected, and on March 31st the long list of prohibitions appeared in the *Gazette*.

Whatever inconvenience the restrictions might cause, their interference with the normal life of the people and the normal course of business was a very light burden compared with that under which the enemy peoples had long been staggering, and which was continually becoming heavier. On March 27th it was announced that the ordinary German flour ration would be reduced, as from April 15th, from 200 to 170 grammes per head per day, and that the permitted consumption of self-producers and the supplementary rations for those engaged in heavy labour would also be reduced by 25 per cent. By way of compensation the meat ration was raised from 250 to 500 grammes per week, and it was hoped to maintain in full the weekly ration of 5 lb. of potatoes, which had recently not been reached. The promise of additional meat was, however, of little value to the poorer classes, who were

[1] *Hansard*, vol. xc, No. 11, col. 1585.

SITUATION IN GERMANY

more and more unable to pay even the controlled prices. A large proportion of the urban poor were existing mainly on a diet of black bread and turnips, and even for the rich, who were willing to pay fabulous sums to procure a more varied and palatable diet, such luxuries as milk and coffee were hardly obtainable. Even skim milk was only obtainable in Berlin by families with children between the ages of 6 and 10, at the rate of 1 litre a week irrespective of the number of children. Real coffee had practically disappeared, and coffee substitutes were severely rationed.

To add to the suffering caused by lack of food, the soap shortage had now reached a point involving actual danger to health. Not only was the supply insufficient to go round, so that it was extremely difficult to get body-linen washed, but the use of war-soap often proved directly injurious to the skin, and even royal princesses were driven to write to their relatives in neutral countries begging for a few cakes.

Meanwhile the shortage of metals continued to inspire the German Authorities to more and more drastic measures of requisition. All church bells, with a few exceptions, were being seized to be melted down for copper, and during March it became necessary to provide for the requisitioning of aluminium utensils, which had hitherto escaped seizure.

In comparison with the burden of insufficient food, insufficient fuel, and insufficient clothing laid on the Germans, the sacrifices now asked from the British people were light, and the feverish anxiety displayed by the German Government with regard to the stocks of essential war materials contrasted strongly with the unlimited supplies which had hitherto been received in Great Britain, and which the new restrictions on unessential imports were intended to ensure.

Far-reaching as were the measures adopted, it was already doubtful whether they went far enough to meet the requirements of the situation which had now arisen. Sir Norman Hill's estimate, on which the 500,000 ton programme was based, had been made two months before the announcement of unrestricted submarine warfare, and it looked as though the diminution in entrances, especially of neutral shipping, would be much greater than he had assumed. In a memorandum laid before the Shipping Control Committee on February 20th, the Statistical Branch of the Ministry of Shipping estimated the probable reduction in imports during 1917 at 8,000,000 tons, or 660,000 tons a month, and as the curve of destruction continued to rise, it appeared that even this might be unduly optimistic.

Meanwhile the Tonnage Priority Committee had got to work on their task of adjusting the demands of the Departments to the tonnage available. At their first meeting, held on February 14th, they settled, on the basis of a memorandum prepared by the Chairman, Sir Leo Chiozza Money, the procedure to be adopted. Each of the importing Departments was to draw up a statement of its estimated monthly requirements for six months ahead, including not only articles imported by itself on Government account, but all imports in which it had a predominant interest. Thus the Ministry of Munitions budgeted not only for direct Government purchases of arms and munitions, but for all imports of iron ore and other materials used in the munitions factories. For imports in which no Government Department was directly interested, the Board of Trade was responsible. The statements prepared by all Departments were to show, in respect of each commodity, not only the amounts required, but the country of origin, and the existing stocks held in this country, whether by the Department itself or by private traders.

The preparation of these statements took time, and when received, it was necessary for them to be analysed and collated by the Statistical Branch of the Ministry of Shipping, for the purpose of preparing a balance sheet of requirements and carrying power; but by March 21st Statistical Branch were able to draft a balance sheet and present it to the Committee for examination at their second meeting, held on that date. It was not encouraging reading. For the five months April to August inclusive, the minimum demands put forward by the Department[1] averaged about 4,260,000 tons a month, a good deal above the average monthly imports for 1916. The shipping available, as calculated by the Branch, might be expected to carry an average of 2,870,000 tons monthly, or about two-thirds of the total. In view of the admitted necessity for large reductions, it was waste of time to discuss a

[1] The original intention was that the programme should embrace the six months March–August, but it proved impossible to obtain the Departmental statements in time to affect the March imports.

programme based on an actual increase of imports, and the various statements were accordingly referred back to the Departments concerned, in order that they might go through them with Statistical Branch, and endeavour to bring them more nearly within the bounds of possibility.

Since neither the new Import Restrictions nor the work of the Tonnage Priority Committee could affect the situation before April, at the earliest, and the programme of ship purchase and construction showed no signs of yielding, in the immediate future, a surplus over losses, or even of making good those losses themselves, Requisitioning Branch were left, for the time being, to struggle as best they might with the problem of providing for the essential services from an inadequate and wasting supply of tonnage.

In one respect only did their position show any signs of improvement. Since the pool of available tonnage had been practically exhausted, it was obvious that any further tonnage for the essential services must be obtained from the liner fleets, and this was entirely in accordance with the policy of the Government, who, in instructing the Shipping Controller that the application of requisitioning should be made " general and as nearly as possible universal," certainly contemplated its extension to the liner trades. Liner requisition and the diversion of liners from their accustomed services was, however, a complex and difficult operation, the effective carrying out of which depended to a large extent on the co-operation of the liner companies themselves. Even before the adoption by the Government of the policy of universal requisition, those responsible for the supply of tonnage for essential services had recognised the necessity of drawing on the liner fleets; but the method by which this was to be effected was not so easily decided. In February, however, Sir Kenneth Anderson and Sir Lionel Fletcher, who had now placed their extensive knowledge and experience of the liner trades at the service of the Ministry of Shipping,[1] submitted a joint memorandum on " the possibility of greater economy in the administration of liner programmes so as to release a proportion for intermittent or continuous service of a more urgent character than their own regular trade," and postulating as " an essential condition pre-

[1] Sir Kenneth Anderson had been a member of the Shipping Control Committee since the autumn of 1916.

cedent to securing the most effective use of tonnage" that "all liner tonnage must be made equally available for any employment," by Government requisition, giving equality of reward under all conditions of employment. For this purpose they sketched out an organisation the main feature of which was that the management of the ships should remain in the hands of the Liner Companies, who would run them as for themselves, but on Government account, under the direction of a Committee representing both the Shipping Controller and the owners, absolute power to divert or transfer tonnage being vested in the Controller or his representatives.

On the basis of this memorandum, the Ministry of Shipping worked out, during the early months of 1917, the machinery of what became known as "The Liner Requisition Scheme." The letter of requisition was actually sent to the lines comprised in the Australasian Conference on February 28th, and those to the other trades followed in rapid succession, the more distant trades receiving first attention. By the end of March the requisitioning letter had been sent to most of the lines engaged in the direct United Kingdom trades, as well as to some whose ships were employed on the cross-routes. It was not until months later that the negotiations with the Liner Companies were finally completed and the scheme brought into full working order; but by the end of March the diversion of some 400,000 tons of liner tonnage to the Atlantic, chiefly from the Australasian and Eastern trades, had been arranged to take place by the end of April, and the Ministry of Shipping was endeavouring to arrange still further transfers.[1]

As against this economy of liner tonnage, Requisitioning Branch were faced by the facts that the obligations for the supply of coal to Italy in requisitioned tonnage had been increased; that the requirements of the Ministry of Munitions were constantly expanding; that it was proposed to increase the imports of nitrate from 20,000 to 50,000 tons a month; that about 100 vessels had been added since August 1916 to those on naval service, largely as a result of the MOEWE's operations in the Atlantic; and that the increase in the White Sea Programme as compared with 1916, was estimated to involve the loss of carrying power for 500,000 tons of British imports. They

[1] For details of the scheme, see Chapter VIII, *post.*

A CUMULATIVE DEFICIT

were faced also with a great increase in the wastage of tonnage through war losses. Although 200 extra vessels had been requisitioned between January 1st and March 20th, they calculated that by the end of May they would be short to the extent of 159 ships of average size for the fulfilment of demands for which they were responsible, and that by the end of August this deficit would have been increased to 392. They urged, therefore, the necessity for considering still further restriction of unessential imports, the transfer of further liner tonnage to the essential trades, a revision of the munitions and nitrate programmes, a careful comb-out of ships on naval and military service or employed in the coasting and interforeign trades, and an appeal to the Dominions and Allies for the release of vessels reserved for their service.

Considerable stress was laid by the Branch on the restriction of the re-export trade, not only on account of the tonnage economy involved, but for the purpose of avoiding the double risk of transit traffic as compared with direct shipment. In spite of the extended range of submarine attack, exemplified in the last quarter of 1916 by operations off the American coast and the Atlantic islands, the greatest weight of the unrestricted campaign fell on the crowded waters of the European terminals, and the losses in the English Channel, Irish Sea, and Bristol Channel, as well as in the approaches south of Ireland, were exceptionally heavy.[1]

About the same time that Requisitioning Branch suggested, with special reference to the danger in these waters, the restriction of the re-export trade, the Trade Division of the Admiralty put forward the suggestion that, in order to minimise the exposure of shipping in Home Waters, greater use might be made of ports on the north-west, west, and south coasts of Ireland. On this proposal the Port and Transit Executive Committee reported unfavourably, after inspection of the ports by Commander Underwood, R.N.V.R., on the grounds of the very limited capacity of the Irish ports and railways to deal with a greatly increased trade, the necessity of double handling,

---

[1] In February 46 British and foreign steamships of 500 tons gross and upwards were sunk in the English Channel, Irish Sea, and Bristol Channel, and 29 in the Fastnet and Scilly approaches. In March the numbers were, respectively, 56 and 28. The total losses of such ships for the two months were, respectively, 138 and 164.

the dangers of the cross-Channel Service, and the difficulties which would arise on the English and Scotch railways in distributing the diverted cargoes. They were of opinion, however, that greater use might be made of the Irish ports for direct import into Ireland itself, thus avoiding the double risk involved in transhipment, and they suggested that the dangers of the English Channel might be avoided to some extent by making greater use of ports on the south-west and south coasts of Great Britain, and of the Clyde ports. The whole question of alternative ports was, at this time, continually under discussion, and on March 21st the War Cabinet appointed a Committee, under the Chairmanship of Lord St. Davids, to consider the possibilities of port development in Scotland and Ireland for the importation of wheat. This Committee reported on April 19th, but the possibilities of development disclosed were not great and no important action followed.

Apart from this question of alternative ports, the old problem of congestion continued to give constant trouble, and was aggravated by the dislocation arising from the detention or diversion of shipping through fear of submarine attack. Although the measures taken or brought about by the Port and Transit Committee, especially the creation of the Transport Workers' Battalions, the pooling of railway trucks, and the imposition of penal rents, had done much to improve the situation, it was calculated by the Shipping Controller that the loss of carrying power through port delays was still equivalent to the shutting out of from four to five million tons of imports in the year. The shortage of railway trucks had again become a grave factor, and the reduction in railway labour through recruiting had an equally serious effect. Impressed by the representations of the Shipping Controller, based on a memorandum on the importance of railway facilities submitted by the Port and Transit Committee, the Government decided on January 31st to appoint a special Committee, under Mr. Percy Illingworth, to investigate the possibility of accelerating the turn-round of ships, more especially with regard to the improvement of railway facilities. As a result of the investigations of this Committee, on which the Port and Transit Committee were represented, the Government decided on February 19th to prohibit the export of railway wagons except under licence, and to empower the Board of Trade to enable the Railway Companies to load empty privately owned wagons on the return journey. They further instructed the Illingworth Committee to confer with the Director of National Service and the War Office on the question of canal, railway, and cartage labour.

At the same time the Government urged strongly on the War Office the necessity of bringing up the Transport Workers' Battalions to the full strength of 10,000 men authorised in December 1916. With every month that went by, the value of this central, mobile, reserve of labour became more apparent, but at the end of February the actual strength was still about 3,000 short of that authorised by the Army Council.

Meanwhile, every problem connected with the maintenance of seaborne trade continued to be overshadowed by the alarming increase in the ratio of loss. It was not only the unrestricted submarine campaign and the mine-laying by submarines in European waters which caused anxiety; the security of the ocean trade-routes was again in grave danger. On March 20th the arrival of the French barque *Cambronne* at Rio de Janeiro gave the first definite intelligence of the SEEADLER's activity. The *Cambronne* was one of a dozen British and Allied vessels captured by that raider since the beginning of January, and though eight of them were sailing vessels, most of these had valuable cargoes of grain or nitrate.

It was now known that at least two raiders, the MOEWE and SEEADLER, had penetrated into the South Atlantic. Nor was this all. On January 26th the first indication of a new danger had been given by the blowing up of a steamer off Dassen Island, near Cape Town. During February a second ship was destroyed in the same area, and yet a third was severely damaged by striking a mine off Cape Agulhas to the south. In the same month two steamers were sunk by mines within a dozen miles of Colombo, and during March another was damaged in the Gulf of Aden.

Insignificant as was the loss, compared with the destruction wrought in home waters, these incidents were in the highest degree disturbing. The disasters in Indian waters were at first attributed to internal explosions caused by anarchist activities, but precautionary sweeping off Colombo soon revealed the real danger, and the news that mines had been widely scattered at the focal points of the Indian, Australian, and South African trade opened up alarming new possibilities of mischief. The danger zone became world-wide, and a serious blow was struck at confidence in the safety of the Eastern tracks.

It is now known that all these disasters were the work of the WOLF. That elusive raider had laid the Cape of Good Hope minefields during January, and then struck across the Indian Ocean to Colombo and Bombay, off which ports more mines were laid. From the Indian coast she proceeded towards Aden, capturing on the way the s.s. *Turitella*, to which a number of her mines were transferred. The prize was then sent off, under the name of the ILTIS, to lay a minefield in the Gulf. This she did, but the prize crew never rejoined the WOLF. Meeting a British warship from whom they were unable to escape, they scuttled their ship and gave themselves up as prisoners.

On the failure of the ILTIS to rejoin, the WOLF, which had meanwhile captured and sunk a second steamer, turned eastwards across the Indian Ocean. Minelaying rather than raiding was her real game, and though she captured another prize or two, she avoided the steamer tracks, and the end of March found her heading for the Pacific, with the object of laying mines off the Australian and New Zealand coasts.

Meanwhile the MOEWE had brought her second cruise to an end. After coaling from the *St. Theodore* early in February, she worked her way down the Brazilian coast, making two or three further prizes, but by this time every British cruiser in the South Atlantic was on the alert, and after a narrow escape from the EDINBURGH CASTLE, Count zu Dohna-Schlodien decided to run for home. On March 22nd the MOEWE arrived at Kiel, having made half a dozen further prizes on her homeward voyage, among them the New Zealand Shipping Company's *Otaki*, which was only captured after a sharp engagement. It is noteworthy that no fewer than ten of the ships captured by the MOEWE on her second cruise were defensively armed; but the armament which often sufficed to beat off a submarine was of little use against so formidable an antagonist.

In all the MOEWE accounted, during her second cruise, for 122,000 tons of shipping, of which 112,000 tons were British, a record comparing very favourably either with that of the EMDEN and KARLSRUHE earlier in the war, or with those of individual submarines. The Germans, however, continued to concentrate their efforts on the submarine campaign, and only one surface raider was sent to sea during the first three months of 1917. This was the MOEWE's prize, the *Yarrowdale*, renamed LEOPARD, armed, and disguised as a Norwegian merchantman. Like the GREIF, she failed to elude the patrols and was destroyed at the outset of her career, being sunk on March 16th by the ACHILLES and the Armed Boarding Steamer DUNDEE.

CHAPTER V

SHIPBUILDING AND SHIP PURCHASE

JANUARY—MARCH 1917

IN view of the great increase in the rate of loss consequent on the outbreak of unrestricted submarine warfare, the new programmes of shipbuilding and ship purchase on which the Government had embarked, acquired additional importance. If the shortage of tonnage were not to become an immediate and vital danger, it was essential that the rate of replacement should be increased.

During 1916 the total output of naval and mercantile tonnage had been 1,878,000 tons gross, as against an average of 2,199,000 for the three years immediately preceding the war.[1] But whereas 1,808,000 tons of the antebellum output consisted of merchant shipping, the merchant tonnage completed in 1916 amounted only to 539,000 tons, or about 48 per cent. of the tonnage lost during the year by war causes alone. The rate of loss was now very much higher than in 1916, and it was evident that the peace output must be at least equalled if the losses now being sustained were to be made good; that it must be considerably surpassed if any relief to the tonnage situation were to be obtained from new construction.

The shipping in course of construction at the end of 1916 comprised nearly 500 vessels with an aggregate tonnage of over 1,800,000 gross, but the majority of these ships were progressing very slowly towards completion. Only on those ships certified for priority by the issue of Munitions Certificates was any work being done, and even this work was hampered by difficulties as to acceleration costs, shortage of labour, and, above all, shortage of steel. In issuing certificates, special regard was paid to the value of the ship under war conditions. The building

[1] In arriving at these figures 1 ton displacement (warships) is taken as the equivalent of 2 tons gross.

of big liners, other than those equipped with insulated space for the carriage of meat, had been brought practically to a standstill, and every effort was concentrated on the production of handy cargo boats, which gave the largest immediate return in carrying power for the labour and material employed.

This principle had been carried still further at the end of 1916, when the Government decided on a programme of State shipbuilding. Their decision was based mainly on the hope of overcoming in this way the difficulties in allocating steel and labour as between naval and mercantile construction, but it was hoped also, by assuming responsibility for the design of new ships, to increase the rate of output by concentrating on the production of a limited number of standard types.

Standardisation, both of hulls and engines, was not unknown before the war, and during 1916 the construction of standard ships had been extensively advocated as the most effective method of relieving the tonnage situation. The advantages of further standardisation of engines was generally admitted, as delays to ships in the water while their own engines were completed accounted for much of the falling off in output, but on the standardisation of hulls opinion was divided.

On the one hand it was claimed that general standardisation would enable fuller advantage to be taken of the limited plate rolling facilities, by reducing the number of different scantlings in the designs and enabling larger parcels of material to be rolled to one pattern. Further, interchangeability of parts would enable hull as well as engine materials to be delivered to the first builder requiring them. On the other hand it was urged that the majority of builders were already in the habit of producing " repeat ships " to standard designs of their own, which probably differed little more than the standard types must themselves differ in order to provide ships of the sizes required, and that the theoretical advantages of general standardisation were outweighed by the incalculable advantage of working to specifications with which the employees were thoroughly familiar.

After full consideration, the Shipping Controller, on the advice of the Merchant Shipbuilding Advisory Committee, decided at the end of December 1916, " to proceed at once with an extensive building programme of cargo ships of simple design and as far as possible of standard types with respect to both engines and hull," and by January 10th complete specifications of the first standard type were ready. By the end of February four types had been approved, and to these it was proposed for the time being to confine the programme.

The two principal types, known as " A " and " B," were both 400-foot freighters of 5,080 tons gross ; but whereas " A " was a single-decked steamer of 8,175 tons dead-weight capacity, " B " had two decks, with a consequent reduction in capacity of 100 tons. The third type, " C," was a smaller vessel with a length of 331 feet, a gross tonnage of 3,000, and a dead-weight capacity of 5,050 tons. A still smaller ship, type " D," of 285 feet length, 2,300 tons gross, and 2,980 dead-weight, was produced, mainly in response to Admiralty demands for vessels of this size for naval employment. No further variety was, for the time, attempted. One vessel of a fifth type " E," of 4,400 tons gross and 7,020 dead-weight, was ordered during the spring, but she was not a great success, and only five ships were ever built to the design.

In all five types the simplification of design was carried to such a length that the number of steel sections required in construction was reduced to 8 or 10 as compared with 30 to 40 normally used in ships of the same size. Further, only two types of engine were required for the five designs. All were single-screw ships, and the sea speed originally proposed for all five types was 10 knots, but in view of the heavy losses suffered by steamers of low speed during December and January this was raised in February, when the designs were finally approved, to $11\frac{1}{2}$ knots. All the ships embodied the latest anti-submarine safety devices suggested by the Admiralty, so far as these could be adopted without unduly restricting their capacity as cargo-carriers.

On the decision to build standard ships for Government account, the issue of Munitions Certificates for the fulfilment of private orders was completely suspended, and work on vessels already certified was allowed to proceed only when, in the judgment of the Controller, the ships were of a type suitable to meet war emergencies, and could be completed within six to eight months. In respect of such vessels, and of such vessels alone, the Shipping Controller continued for the time being the policy initiated by the

Transport Department in 1916, of allowing owners to repay themselves for the enhanced cost of construction by one or two free voyages, before the ships became subject to requisition at Blue Book rates.

To decide on a shipbuilding policy was one thing; to execute it was another. The dominant factors, as in 1916, were labour and steel. Although the War Committee had decided in the autumn of 1916 that skilled workers should be released from the Army for the shipyards and engineering shops, it had not proved easy either to trace them or to obtain their release. Of 6,470 for whom applications had been made by the middle of November only 3,816 had been obtained; 721 had been refused release, and the remainder were still being traced. At the date of Sir Joseph Maclay's appointment little hope was entertained of obtaining any further men from the Army, but it was decided that immediate steps should be taken to prevent further depletion of the labour force, and in January 1917 all men employed in shipbuilding and marine engineering shops prior to March 29th were definitely exempted from military service.

Meanwhile it was hoped to obtain an increased output per man employed by introducing the principle of payment by results, either on the " piecework " or the " premium bonus " system. One great object of State shipbuilding was to remove all suspicion of private " profiteering " and convince the workers that the construction of merchant ships was as surely " war work " as the execution of Admiralty orders, and it was hoped that this would remove any objections to the general application of the principle, which had already been accepted by one or two of the Unions concerned with very promising results. Negotiations were accordingly opened with all Trade Unions in the shipbuilding and marine engineering industries, and the question of dilution of labour on a large scale was also raised, but little progress was made in either respect.

The opposition both to dilution and to payment by results was based not only on the industrial objections, practical as well as theoretical, which had led to the adoption of the Trade Union Rules, but also on the position arising from the shortage of steel. So long as the supply of shipbuilding material remained at the current level it appeared probable that acceleration of production in the shipyards themselves would lead to periods of widespread unemployment, without really increasing the annual output. The shortage of steel was, indeed, even more acute than the shortage of labour. Although the amount allowed to be used for commercial work had been cut down to an extent which had the most serious effects on the export trade, the demands of the armies for shell-steel, railway and constructional material were so great, that even in face of the tonnage crisis existing at the beginning of 1917, it proved impossible to increase to any great extent the admittedly inadequate allocation for shipbuilding purposes, and of the restricted supplies obtained by the yards a large proportion was definitely earmarked for naval construction.

An additional drain upon the scanty supply, both of labour and steel, was the immense amount of repair work to be executed. In addition to the large number of vessels damaged by mine, torpedo, or gun-fire, the number of minor marine casualties, such as engine-room breakdowns, was continually on the increase. The Mercantile Marine had been drained of a large proportion of its best officers, engineers, firemen, and seamen by the vast development of the Royal Navy and the Auxiliary Patrol, and though the spirit displayed by the men procured as substitutes was wholly admirable, they inevitably lacked the skill and experience of those whom they replaced. The coal available was often inferior, owing to the Admiralty demands on the better qualities. The shortage of tonnage and the demands of the Admiralty on dry dock accommodation prevented the usual periodical overhaul and refit from being carried out. The exigencies of the war frequently required vessels to be employed in trades to which they were not accustomed, and for which they were not suited. Such conditions naturally bore fruit in a heavy crop of accidents. Many of these were of a minor character which could speedily be set right, but others, occasioned by collisions or strandings, were of a more serious nature, and with the intensification of the submarine campaign came a great increase in war casualties which often required several weeks to make good.[1]

Repairs as well as construction had now been brought

---

[1] On January 31st shipping to the extent of 131,000 tons (s.s. of 1,600 tons gross and upwards) was undergoing serious repairs; by February 28th the figure had risen to 330,000.

within the province of the Controller, and not even the urgency of the new shipbuilding programme could be allowed to interfere with them. The relief afforded to the tonnage situation by the speedy repair of injuries, especially those of a minor character, gave a far higher immediate return for the labour and material employed than new construction, and for this reason it was given a definite priority.

In these circumstances the largest output for which the Shipping Controller could venture to hope was 1,200,000 tons gross to be completed in the course of the year, an amount insufficient even to make good the current rate of loss, without doing anything to relieve the existing shortage, or making any provision for further demands by the Allies consequent on the depletion of their own tonnage, or for the replacement of neutral ships withdrawn from Allied trade. It was hoped, however, to supplement the limited resources of the British programme by large purchases from abroad.

From the European neutrals little or no new tonnage could be obtained. Their output was comparatively small, and their yards were fully employed in making good their own losses. It might be possible, by the offer of high prices, to obtain a considerable amount of second-hand tonnage from owners who were unwilling to face the increasing risks to neutral shipping, but few of such ships were of a size suitable for ocean voyages. Further, the prices demanded were out of all proportion to the value of the ships, and as a general rule the Shipping Controller and the Director of Overseas Ship Purchase were averse to buying vessels the services of which could be obtained for the Allies on time-charter. Such purchases as were made were confined to ships which, for one reason or another, could not otherwise be forced or induced to accept Allied employment.

The attitude of France and Italy was rather different. Many of the neutral vessels obtainable, though unfitted for ocean voyages, were suitable for the French and Italian coal trade, or for coasting and local service in the Mediterranean and elsewhere. Merchant shipbuilding in France and Italy was practically at a standstill,[1] and the Govern-

---

[1] France had 8 steamers under construction; Italy had laid down 3 or 4, but expected to be able to build 10 or 12 if materials could be supplied, They would, however, take 18 months to complete.

ments of both countries were anxious to increase the tonnage under their direct control. For these reasons both the French and Italian Governments, but especially the French, bought a considerable quantity of second-hand shipping from European neutrals at the end of 1916 and the beginning of 1917, with the result of forcing up still higher the prices demanded, and complicating the task of the Inter-Allied Chartering Committee in arranging an equitable distribution of neutral tonnage and restricting the rise in freights.

On the formation of the Inter-Allied Chartering Committee in January 1917, the British Government proposed that the purchase as well as the chartering of ships should be brought under joint control, but owing to the opposition of France the matter had, for the time, to be dropped. By Regulation 39cc under the Defence of the Realm Acts, issued on February 16th, all British subjects were prohibited from buying any ship without permission from the Shipping Controller, and while no obstacle was placed in the way of transfers of British ships from one British subject to another, the acquisition of tonnage from abroad was confined to the Director of Overseas Ship Purchase. This regulation, however, in the absence of Allied co-operation, had little effect in checking the inflation of values.

Outside Europe two important sources of new shipping were available—Japan and the United States. The American output before the war averaged only 173,000 tons gross, and in 1915 it sank to 155,000 tons,[1] but during 1916 the capacity of the yards had been greatly extended. The war had reduced the British tonnage available for American trade and put a complete stop to the German services. This shortage of tonnage and the consequent rise in freights led to a strong demand from American shipowners, and the activity of the yards was further stimulated by the placing of large contracts by Norwegian and other neutral firms, unable to obtain fulfilment of their requirements in the United Kingdom or Germany. As a result of this demand, many new shipbuilding corporations were founded, and those already established increased their yards and plant.[2] In Japan, too, the war had produced

---

[1] These figures are exclusive of ships launched on the Great Lakes.
[2] The output of ocean-going tonnage in 1916 was 286,000 dead-weight (say, 174,000 tons gross), but a much larger amount was under construction at the end of the year.

a boom in shipping. As British ships were gradually withdrawn from distant waters, the trade of the Pacific and Indian Oceans fell largely into Japanese hands, and the Japanese shipyards were now capable of responding freely to the demand for tonnage.

It was in Japan that the British Government's first orders for new construction were placed in December 1916. Acting through the agency of Messrs. Furness, Withy & Co. they secured for delivery at various dates from March to August 1917, seven steamers then on the slips, with an average tonnage of about 6,000 gross. An option was also secured on five other vessels of the same average size, for delivery at later dates.

Towards the end of December Mr. James Esplen, brother of the Director of Overseas Ship Purchase, was sent out to make enquiries as to the capacity of the American and Canadian yards, and at the end of January 1917 he was formally appointed Technical Adviser to the Shipping Controller in the United States and Canada, for the purpose of obtaining estimates and supervising the work of construction. In this work he was assisted by Superintendents sent out to direct, under his supervision, the building of groups of from six to eight ships.[1] In Canada all contracts were placed through the Imperial Munitions Board at Ottawa, but in the United States it was impossible for the British Government to purchase ships direct without raising questions of neutrality, and all contracts, whether for new construction or ships already on the stocks, were placed in the name of the Cunard S.S. Co., whose New York representative, Mr. Ashley Sparkes, was in close and constant touch with Mr. Esplen.

So actively was the work of placing orders carried on, and so great was now the capacity of the American yards that, by the end of March "Cunard" contracts had been signed for over 700,000 tons dead-weight.[2] This included a number of ships already in course of construction, of which a few had already received American registry, while others were laid down to the orders of Norwegian firms from whom they were now purchased. In addition, considerable orders had been placed with Canadian yards.

[1] These Superintendents were sent out by the Managers appointed by Ship Management Branch for the purchased ships.
[2] For definition of dead-weight see Vol. I, p. 6, n. 4. In dealing with large figures 3 tons dead-weight may be taken to equal 2 tons gross, though the proportion varies greatly in individual ships.

Down to this time, no objection had been raised in the United States to the British acquisition of the ships. On February 12th a Proclamation was issued by the President forbidding the sale or charter to a foreigner of any vessel registered in the United States, except with the consent of the United States Shipping Board, which had just been constituted, by virtue of an Act of September 1916, to promote the interests of the American Mercantile Marine.[1] It was not, however, anticipated that there would be any difficulty in procuring that consent in respect of the few vessels acquired that were already on the American register.

Apart from new construction at home and abroad and the acquisition of second-hand neutral tonnage, there was one possible source of supply which held out more hope of immediate relief to the situation than any other measure that could be taken. The German and Austrian steamers laid up in the ports of North and South America, Spain, the Canaries, and the Far East, amounted at this time to over a million and three-quarter tons gross, and if any large proportion of these could be brought into service, the relief would be immediate and substantial. It was not at all likely that any of those in Spanish or Dutch East Indian ports could be procured on terms allowing of their employment in Allied interests, but it was in North and South American harbours that the bulk of the tonnage lay, and this, with smaller blocks in Chinese ports and at Bangkok, it might be possible to obtain.

In the earlier stages of the war all proposals for acquisition of these ships had been negatived on the ground of the financial relief which would be afforded to the Central Powers, to whom it was of special importance to stabilise their exchanges in the United States and the Latin Republics, and for the same reason the British Government had refused its consent to all proposals for purchase of those in United States ports by the Americans themselves.[2] In the beginning of 1916, however, when the shortage of tonnage became a vital issue, the attitude of the Government changed, and they agreed to recognise the transfer of immobilised enemy shipping to neutral firms, on condition that they should be resold to British subjects, or chartered to them for use in approved trades, and further that they should not be retransferred to their German owners after

---

[1] W. C. Mattox, *Building the Emergency Fleet*, Cleveland, 1920.
[2] See Vol. I, p. 111.

the war. Negotiations on these lines proceeded during 1916, but with little success, as the Germans refused to sell without a guarantee that the ships should not be employed in Allied interests.

These negotiations were now renewed with energy, and it was hoped that the sufferings of neutrals at the hands of the German submarines would induce them to take steps, by requisitioning the vessels sheltering in their ports, to restore the depleted supply of tonnage. Unhappily, the Germans fully realised the possible consequences of their own actions, and on February 1st, the day after the announcement of the unrestricted submarine campaign, the crews of German ships in North American harbours received orders to disable their vessels. In anticipation of such action the American Government placed armed guards on the ships and wharves and took other measures to secure the safety of the ships, but almost everywhere they were too late to prevent much injury being done. In New York the engines of all ships except the *Vaterland* were so effectively damaged as to necessitate repairs estimated to require from six to eight months' work. At Honolulu the boilers of ten steamers were burned out, and though the damage in most other districts was less serious, many of the ports were so remote from repair facilities that there was no hope of the ships being available for many months.[1]

Warned by this example, the Chinese Government, which broke off diplomatic relations with Germany on March 14th, moved so promptly in taking possession of the German steamers in their ports that the crews were surprised and overpowered before any harm had been inflicted. The ships so seized were, however, neither numerous nor large.[2]

Thus the prospect of obtaining any considerable immediate relief by bringing immobilised German shipping into service was small, and though shipbuilding in the United Kingdom had been speeded up to some extent, it still lagged very far behind the rate of destruction. The

[1] The German shipping seized by the United States comprised between 80 and 90 steamers, with an aggregate tonnage of about 600,000 gross. This includes vessels in the harbours of Hawaii and the Philippines.

[2] The German steamers seized by China numbered ten, with an aggregate tonnage of 21,000 gross. Three Austrian steamers, with an aggregate tonnage of 15,000, were also seized on or prior to the declaration of war against Germany and Austria, on August 14th.

output of completed tonnage for the March quarter was 246,000 tons, a considerable improvement on anything attained in 1916, but about 18 per cent. below the average rate of construction contemplated by the Controller, which was itself altogether insufficient to replace losses at the current rate. Nor was the outlook for the future much brighter. The deficit was attributed mainly to bad weather conditions, shortage of labour, and dearth of material, and only in respect of the first of these factors was there any immediate prospect of improvement. It was hoped, however, that the introduction of standard designs would increase the rate of output. Meanwhile, the first of the steamers ordered in Japan, a big freighter of 12,500 tons dead-weight capacity, had been delivered by the builders, and others were approaching completion; the American and Canadian shipyards were busily employed in fulfilling orders placed by the Director of Overseas Ship Purchase, and during the second half of the year it was anticipated that the ship purchase programme would to a large extent make good the deficit arising from the inadequacy of the British output.

CHAPTER VI

THE DARKEST HOUR
APRIL 1917

WHATEVER success might attend the Shipping Controller's endeavours to speed up construction at home and to acquire new tonnage from abroad, there could be little hope of making good in this way the discrepancy between the supply of tonnage and the demand for carrying power. The most that could be expected was that the progressive depletion of the available pool of shipping might be checked by effective replacement of future losses. Moreover, it must be some months at least before the new programmes of construction and purchase bore fruit in any large deliveries of completed vessels, and meanwhile the rate of loss increased to such a frightful extent that it became a question whether either the output of standard ships or deliveries under the "Cunard" contracts could affect the situation in time to prevent a complete breakdown in the supply services of the Allies. It was no longer a question of whether losses could be ultimately replaced, but whether they could be checked or countered before they involved utter disaster.

During the first fortnight of April the situation was, if anything, a little easier. The gross loss of British ocean-going tonnage was almost identical with the average rate for the three months January to March inclusive, and was thus appreciably below the highest level to which it had risen. On the other hand, the acquisitions of new tonnage showed a considerable increase. Further, the effects of the diversion of wheat ships from Australia to North America, and of other steps taken to reduce the length of voyages, were visible in the entrances of British shipping, which were practically up to the level of 1916. Foreign entrances showed a reduction of over 50 per cent., but both Norwegian and Danish vessels were now coming forward more freely, and the total decline, serious as it was, was smaller than in March.

The restriction of imports, too, was already beginning to affect the distribution of available carrying power between essential and non-essential commodities. The total imports for March as shown in the Board of Trade returns, from which it must be remembered certain important Government purchases were excluded, were about a million tons, or 30 per cent. less than in March 1916 ; but whereas the imports of those commodities on which restrictions had been placed were down by over 50 per cent., the decline in unrestricted imports was only 23 per cent. Timber, paper and paper-making materials, and fruit showed specially heavy reductions. These were no doubt due in part to the withdrawal of neutral tonnage, which specially affected the timber and wood-pulp trades, but it was evident that the effort made to discriminate between essential and non-essential cargoes was already producing important results, and still further success was anticipated in April, especially as the home production of pit-wood and the cutting of Army timber in France were developing more rapidly than the Import Restrictions Committee had dared to hope.

In the development of the war there were also encouraging features. Chief among these was, of course, the entry of America into the war. Apart from any naval or military assistance that might be received from the United States, the intervention of America was of incalculable importance in regard to the problem of supplies. It was now evident that the available tonnage could be rendered adequate only by confining purchases, so far as possible, to the nearest sources, at whatever cost in adverse exchanges and severance of trade connections. Yet it had been more than doubtful whether British credit in the United States could much longer be stretched to cover the vast requirements of Great Britain and her Allies. With America an Ally, it was possible to obtain credits from the American Government, and by mortgaging the future, to pull through the immediate crisis.

In other directions there were also favourable developments. The prospect of American assistance which had been clearly foreshadowed by President Wilson's attitude towards the German declaration of unrestricted submarine warfare, had been counter-balanced during March by the Russian

Revolution, but by the middle of April it was clear that the Provisional Government had every intention of carrying on the war with energy, and it was not considered necessary to make any change in the White Sea Programme. Further, the action of the United States was followed, on April 9th by Brazil breaking off diplomatic relations with Germany, as a sequel to the torpedoing of the Brazilian steamer *Parana* in the English Channel on April 4th, and though the Brazilian Government did not yet see fit to proceed to a declaration of war, their attitude aroused hopes of securing for the use of the Allies the large block of German tonnage lying in Brazilian ports. On April 17th, too, the Allied forces in the Mediterranean were joined by two Japanese destroyer flotillas, a most welcome reinforcement, in view of the difficulty of dealing with submarines in that sea.

Nevertheless the situation was still full of danger. In a memorandum presented to the Government on April 16th, the Ministry of Shipping estimated the deficit in ships necessary for the fulfilment of Government requirements, after allowing for the effect of all measures yet taken, at 132 vessels by the end of May, and 310 by the end of August. These figures represented a slight improvement on the estimate made by Requisitioning Branch in March, but they were sufficiently serious in view of the difficulties to be encountered in making good the deficit.

Of 3,325 British steamers of 1,600 tons gross and upwards (excluding tankers and prizes), 1,897 were, on March 31st, already under full requisition or definitely allotted to the Allies ; 85 were repairing or completing, and 188 were Colonial registered vessels in the service of the Dominions and Colonies. This left 138 tramps and 1,017 liners not already in full Government service, to constitute the pool of available tonnage. Practically the whole of the tramps were already employed in essential services, and though the process of bringing them under requisition at Blue Book rates continued in accordance with the general policy of the Government, there was little hope that any of them could be diverted to make good the deficit. Of the liners, 299 were employed in distant waters, and represented vessels left there after more than a year's continuous pressure, as unsuitable for general ocean trading, or employed in services essential to some portion of the Empire. The remainder, 718 ships, of which 255 were in the North Atlantic, were engaged in the trade of the United Kingdom itself. On the North Atlantic liners 80 to 85 per cent. of the space was definitely allocated to wheat and munitions, the insulated space on the Plate and Australian liners was requisitioned for meat, and in all the trades a large amount of space was occupied by Government imports. In the remainder had to be carried—since practically all tramps were on full Government service—all imports for which the Government had not assumed full responsibility, including raw materials, such as cotton, of vital importance both for war and industrial purposes. Taking together the liner space and such part of the fully requisitioned tonnage as was allocated to the carriage of Government imports, such as wheat, ore, and sugar, the available carrying power was admittedly insufficient to carry even those commodities which the Import Restrictions Committee had regarded as essential.

So grave was the deficiency that, when the Tonnage Priority Committee met again on April 25th, it was found that even the revised estimate now presented by the Departments greatly exceeded the capacity of the tonnage in sight, and it became necessary for the Committee to suggest still further reductions. The two chief problems were wheat and munitions. The Ministry of Food were aiming not only at making good a deficit of 235,000 tons in March arrivals of wheat, but at building up stocks to the equivalent of thirteen weeks' supplies, as against the ten weeks' basis on which the Ministry of Shipping were working in their allocation of tonnage. The Ministry of Munitions desired to increase the imports of iron ore to 735,000 tons a month, 650,000 from the Bay and Mediterranean and 85,000 from Narvik, as against a total average of 583,000 in 1916. Eventually the Ministry of Food agreed to accept the ten weeks' basis for stocks, and the Ministry of Munitions to a reduction of 20 per cent. on their whole programme; but even so, the demands for tonnage far exceeded the capacity of the available shipping.

It was during the summer months, when the White Sea Programme was in full swing, that the strain was expected to be greatest, and in their Memorandum of April 16th, the Ministry of Shipping suggested that during these months the shipments of munitions from America should be reduced from 250,000 to 100,000 tons a month, and that a proposed increase in the imports of nitrate from 20,000 to 50,000 tons a month should be postponed till the autumn or winter. On the assumption that a large proportion of the munitions imports were not required for the current year's campaign, they pointed out that stocks could be built up during the autumn and winter months when some 250 vessels engaged in the White Sea Programme, and 75 sent to Australia for wheat, would again become available. By that time, too, it was hoped that the East African Campaign, which absorbed 25 vessels, would be completed, that many of the enemy ships in North American ports would be at work, and some of those in South America might also be available.

In addition to these proposals, the Ministry hoped for some relief through obtaining wheat from Russia which could be carried in ships returning from the White Sea, and for some reduction in the number of vessels allocated to sugar, timber, and miscellaneous services. Meanwhile, they were continuing the diversion of liners from the more distant routes to the North Atlantic, and had asked France for the return of 100 vessels, on condition that Great Britain and Russia should forgo their share of neutral tonnage time-chartered by the Inter-Allied Committee, and that any assistance to be given by American shipping should go to France.

In these ways the Ministry hoped to wipe off the deficit in vessels required for Government services, but in view of the uncertainty as to losses, delays arising from diversions, and other consequences of the submarine campaign, they suggested that a margin for contingencies should be provided by a reduction in the Russian programme. They urged also that further facilities should be given for increasing the rate of mercantile construction, for increasing the supply of skilled labour available for ship-repairing, and for further increasing the home output of timber. Still more strongly they urged that, with a view to the quickest possible turn-round in port, the Transport Workers' Battalions should be raised to 15,000 men, observing "It is clear that there is *no* work upon which the return per man has so high a value in increasing supplies."

How urgently necessary were all possible measures for increasing the supply of tonnage or reducing the demands upon it were soon to be proved. The balance provisionally estimated for by the Ministry of Shipping was never, in fact, attained. The project of securing a large quantity of wheat from Russia fell through, and though the Government agreed to the postponement of the increased nitrate programme, they were unable to sanction a reduction of more than 40,000 tons a month in the munitions shipments from North America. Thus the basis of the proposed reconciliation between demand and supply was, in a large measure, destroyed at the outset, and meanwhile a new and most alarming factor had entered into the calculation. Heavy as had been the losses during the first ten weeks of the unrestricted submarine campaign, they were far transcended by the havoc worked during the second half of April.

Both the number of the enemy's submarines and their individual endurance and sea-keeping power were now greater than at any previous period of the war, and since the United States had definitely entered the lists against them, the Germans were more than ever bent on making the most ruthless and energetic use of their chosen weapon, in the hope of forcing a speedy decision. From the Norwegian coast to Gibraltar, from Gibraltar to Port Said, the attack was persistent and formidable. In the Mediterranean fifty-six British and foreign steamers of 500 tons and upwards were sunk during the month, and at the western entrance to the Straits casualties were thickly clustered. Losses in the English Channel, the Irish Sea, and the Bristol and St. George's Channels were below the level of February or March; but neutral, especially Norwegian shipping, suffered severely on the passage from Norway to the Shetlands and down the east coast of Great Britain. It was, however, in the western approaches that the havoc was greatest.

The protective system adopted in these waters was based on the provision of patrolled inshore routes for vessels entering or leaving Home Waters on an ocean voyage. This system of protected concentration, combined with wide dispersal in mid-ocean, had been adopted off the south coast of Ireland in the summer of 1915, and, having given good results, had been gradually extended since that time. Since, however, the effect was to compel the submarines to operate further out from the coast, and they had shown themselves increasingly capable of doing so, it became necessary to bring in homeward-bound ships and disperse those outward bound on definite approach routes, also patrolled so far as the resources of the navy would allow. This system of approach routes, introduced in July 1916, had also been gradually extended, and there were now three great cones of approach within which the routes converged on Tory Island for vessels entering or leaving the Clyde or Liverpool (north-about), on the Fastnet for North Atlantic traffic to or from Liverpool (south-about), the Bristol Channel, and London or other East Coast ports, and on Scilly for ships engaged in Mediterranean or South Atlantic voyages.

The weakest point of the system was in the areas of concentration where the approach routes converged towards the protected inshore lanes. Great as was the development of the Auxiliary Patrol, great as was the energy displayed in naval construction, the number of fast, armed craft available, after providing for the needs of the Grand Fleet, the provision of escort for troop transports and supply ships, and the protection of the inshore tracks, was altogether inadequate to the provision of adequate patrols on the approach routes. During the last fortnight of April submarines were working on a line extending 150 miles north-west from Tory Island, in an area extending some 270 miles from the Fastnet, and on a radius of 150 to 200 miles from the Scillies. The danger area in each cone of approach covered from 10,000 to 15,000 square miles, and so thinly were the patrols scattered that the crews of many sunken vessels had pulled for a day or two days in their boats before they were sighted and picked up. In these circumstances the areas of concentration were, in the long run, little better than death-traps.

Until April 16th, the losses of British shipping, heavy as they were, showed no increase on the rate of the preceding months; but on the 17th the storm broke with terrible violence. On that day alone the submarines destroyed nearly 34,000 tons of British shipping, on the 19th the losses were over 32,000 tons, and for the second half of April the destruction by mine and submarine reached the appalling figures of nearly 400,000, bringing up the total for the month to 545,000 tons. The losses of Allied shipping amounted to 138,000 tons; those of neutrals to 191,000. In all the world's tonnage was reduced by 881,000 tons gross, of which 847,000 tons was accounted for by the submarines, and the rest by mines.[1]

[1] This total includes British fishing vessels

In the face of such staggering losses even the enhanced premiums announced in March were insufficient to ensure the solvency of the State Scheme, and on April 23rd the cargo rate was raised to 5 per cent., the maximum originally proposed under the scheme, and the hull rate to $2\frac{1}{2}$ per cent. for a single voyage, or 5 per cent. for a round voyage or ninety-one days' time policy.[1] This, however, though a serious addition to the burden laid on commerce by war conditions, was a small matter in comparison with the depletion of carrying power.

Alarming as they were, the figures quoted above fall short of showing the full extent of the danger, for it was on the most vital element of British shipping, the steamers of ocean-going size, 1,600 tons gross and upwards, that the greater part of the loss now fell. Of such ships 120 were sunk during April, accounting for over 90 per cent. of the British losses, and of these 53 were lost in the three great areas of concentration, 35 of them in the Fastnet area alone. Now that every effort was being made to bring the largest possible proportion of British shipping into the North Atlantic trade, such losses assumed a special and most sinister significance.

The full menace of the unrestricted submarine campaign could now be seen. It had raged for three months, and during those three months the world's tonnage had been reduced by over two million tons, of which nearly a million and a quarter were British. Nor was this all; over 270,000 tons of British, and nearly 50,000 tons of Allied and neutral shipping had been damaged, and with the shipyards already choked with repair work, the carrying power of a vessel seriously damaged might be lost for many weeks.

Compared with such losses, the acquisitions of shipping by new construction or transfer from foreign flags sank into insignificance. New ships of 1,600 tons gross or over, brought into service under the British flag, amounted for the three months to under 200,000 tons. About 60,000 tons had been obtained from other sources, but the net reduction in ocean-going tonnage, after allowing on the one hand for all gains and on the other for war and marine losses, was some 940,000 tons or about 5·66 per cent. of the total tonnage available (including tankers and prizes) on February 1st. In other words the wastage of ocean-going tonnage was at the rate of nearly 23 per cent. per annum.

[1] Cmd. 98.

A BLACK OUTLOOK

It was, however, the acceleration in the rate of loss during the second half of April which was the most alarming feature in the situation. While the ratio of war losses for the three months (without regard to replacements) was about 7 per cent., or 28 per cent. per annum, the losses suffered during the fortnight April 17th–30th inclusive were at the appalling rate of over 50 per cent. per annum on the available tonnage. On the basis of the same period, it was estimated that the risk to an individual steamer homeward bound from a port more distant than Gibraltar was about 2 in 11; to an outward-bound steamer, which could be more easily stayed or diverted, about 1 in 14. Her chances of leaving the United Kingdom on such a voyage and returning safely were only about 1 in 4.

It might be hoped, of course, that this black fortnight represented a supreme effort, and that so high a ratio of loss would not be maintained, but it was evident that the continuance of losses, even at the average for the three months which had elapsed since the opening of the unrestricted campaign, would soon bring the Germans within measurable distance of the decision on which they had staked so much. On April 17th, the very day on which the period of maximum loss began, the Statistical Branch of the Ministry of Shipping submitted a revised estimate, based on the expectation of future losses then entertained by the Admiralty, in which they calculated that the reduction in imports for the whole year would be nearly ten and a half million tons, or four and a half millions more than the Import Restrictions Committee had considered could be provided for by the elimination of non-essentials.

In this estimate the Statistical Branch allowed for entrances of foreign shipping to the extent of two-fifths those recorded in 1916. This agreed very closely with the actual entrances for the three months, which showed a decrease of over 57 per cent. By tonnage agreements and by the enforcement of the ship-for-ship policy, it might be hoped to stimulate the revival of neutral activity observable towards the end of March, but in accepting a probable permanent decrease of 60 per cent., Statistical Branch no doubt took into account the heavy losses which the more active neutrals were suffering. Norway alone had lost more than a quarter of a million tons since the proclamation of the barred zones, and though the losses of other neutral Powers had been restricted by the abstention of their shipowners from Allied trade, Denmark had lost 33,000 tons in April, and Greece 41,000.

Over Greek shipping, indeed, complete control had been obtained. By the end of April nearly 560,000 tons dead-weight (say, 370,000 gross) had been chartered to the Inter-Allied Chartering Committee under the Greek Ship Scheme, and practically the whole Greek mercantile marine suitable for ocean voyages was now running under Allied direction in the essential trades. As the majority of the vessels were suited to the carriage of wheat, coal, and ore, this was a substantial addition to the resources of the Allies; but Greek shipping was essentially a wasting asset, as losses among unarmed, low-powered steamers engaged in the most dangerous trades were certain to be heavy.

In addition to the Greek steamers the Inter-Allied Chartering Committee, which had now been brought under the ægis of the Ministry of Shipping, had procured on time-charter about 200,000 tons dead-weight of Norwegian shipping and a few Japanese steamers of medium size, but only one Swedish vessel had been fixed, and not one under the Danish, Dutch, or Spanish flag.[1]

In the direct trade between neutral countries and the United Kingdom and among the vessels which ran on voyage-charters in the coal and ore trades, much the same conditions obtained. Norwegian shipping, despite its heavy losses, continued to brave the dangers of the North Sea, and to play a considerable, though diminished, part in the vital Allied services, but the shipowners of the other European neutrals still held aloof from Allied trade. The Danish produce ships were coming forward under the combined influence of the ship-for-ship policy and the need of the Danes for coal, but few Spanish vessels arrived at British ports, the restricted traffic still maintained with Holland under cover of the light forces based on Harwich was carried mainly in British bottoms, communication with Sweden was almost cut off, and neutral

---

[1] Figures of I.A.C.C. charters represent tonnage time-chartered to the Executive. They exclude ships fixed on voyage-charter by the Local Coal Committees or Ministry of Munitions, and other vessels which, with the approval of the Committee, were chartered by Allied Authorities or firms otherwise than through the Executive itself. The figures are exclusive of renewals, but many of the vessels chartered may previously have traded in Allied interests on owners' account.

tonnage, other than Greek and Norwegian, was almost unprocurable for the Allied coal services. At the beginning of April the scheduled limitation rates for neutral vessels were again raised, to cover an increase in the war risks premiums, and in the Mediterranean trade the principle of limitation was finally abandoned, the local Committees being simply instructed to submit to the Inter-Allied Executive such offers as could be obtained. Even so, little tonnage was procurable.

It must be remembered that nearly all the ships chartered by the Inter-Allied Executive were employed for the benefit of France and Italy, and the difficulty of procuring an adequate supply of tonnage for the Allied services was so great that there was little prospect of any considerable portion of such further neutral shipping as might be procured, either by force or by inducement, being available for the import service of the United Kingdom. Further, it was extremely doubtful how far either force or inducement would be sufficient to overcome the terrorising effect of the unrestricted submarine campaign, while even if neutral shipowners were willing to accept charters, the tonnage at their disposal was being rapidly reduced.

Nor could any additional assistance in the carriage of British imports be looked for from shipping under Allied flags. France and Italy required for themselves the services of every ship on which they could lay their hands. French shipping was, indeed, taking a larger share in the coal traffic, where it assisted to make good neutral withdrawals, but few French ships brought cargoes to the United Kingdom, and the part of Italian shipping in the British import trade was confined almost entirely to the lifting of ore-cargoes under the Coal-Ore Agreement. This was, indeed, an appreciable help, for in March no less than 100,000 tons was carried in Italian bottoms, in addition to an equal amount lifted by British and neutral time-chartered steamers under Italian control. This, however, was the maximum which could be expected.

Russian shipping was almost all employed in the supply of Russia herself, and a large proportion of the ocean-going steamers which still flew the Belgian flag were required for the work of the Belgian Relief Commission. Both Japan and the United States, on the other hand, owned a considerable and expanding mercantile marine which had suffered little as yet from war casualties. From the entry of America into the war much was hoped, but it was too early as yet to say whether any large block of American tonnage would be available for the service of the Allies. To Japan a proposal had been made in February that she should requisition vessels for employment in the war-zone, but the Japanese Government had replied that they had, under the constitution, no power of general requisition, and though a few ships were fixed, as we have seen, with the Inter-Allied Executive, the majority of Japanese shipowners preferred safer and more remunerative employment in trades from which British ships had been withdrawn.

Thus, whether neutral or Allied shipping was considered, there was little reason to doubt the wisdom of the estimate by Statistical Branch. The main burden of maintaining the flow of foodstuffs and materials to the United Kingdom was likely to rest to a still greater extent than heretofore on British shipping, and that shipping was now subject to losses on a scale never before experienced.

A specially disquieting factor was the increasing ascendency of the submarine over the defensively armed merchantman. The proportion of such ships in the ocean trades had, indeed, been steadily growing: of the steamers attacked in October 1916, only half were provided with the means of defence; among those attacked in April 1917, seventeen out of every twenty were armed. On the other hand, not only were the submarines now definitely committed to a policy of ruthlessness which led to two-thirds of the vessels sunk in April being torpedoed without warning, but the more recent types were provided with an artillery armament superior to that of most merchant steamers. The consequence was that whereas 68 per cent. of the defensively armed ships attacked during the last three months of 1916 had escaped destruction, the proportion of escapes during the first three months of the unrestricted campaign sank to 49, and in April to 43 per cent. Whereas, in the earlier period, just over half the steamers of all classes attacked succeeded in reaching port, it had now to be reckoned that, in spite of the spread of defensive armament, only four steamers out of every ten attacked would escape destruction.

It was obvious that defensive armament, though it might mitigate the perils of a voyage, no longer afforded any reasonable prospect of keeping down the rate of loss to a bearable level, and the successes of the submarines in the areas of approach showed how little reliance could be placed on the routeing system adopted. If the enemy's hopes of bringing the Allies to their knees by the unrestricted submarine campaign were to be defeated, some more effective measure of trade protection was urgently required. In these circumstances it was natural that the old method of direct convoy, by which so large a proportion of British trade had been conducted during the wars of the sailing era, should again come up for consideration.

To direct convoy under modern conditions, there were many objections. Even in the era of sails, the delays inseparable from the system had often rendered it difficult to enforce the convoy regulations, as the owners and charterers of fast-sailing ships preferred to run the risks of an independent voyage, in order to forestall their competitors by placing their cargoes on the markets at the earliest possible date. For the bulk of the long-distance trades, however, convoy entailed no very serious delay; the ships made only one voyage in each year, and wind and weather considerations restricted their sailing dates within definite limits. Under steam, on the other hand, both the earning power and the national utility of a vessel depended on her making the greatest possible number of voyages in a given time, and the enormously increased volume of traffic could be carried only on the condition that the available shipping was used to its utmost capacity. With this the convoy system necessarily interfered. It must often involve an intermediate voyage from the port of loading to the port of concentration, or the rendezvous with the escort. It involved delays in port while the convoy was collecting, or while the escort was being awaited. It involved reducing the speed of the fastest ship in the convoy to that of the slowest, a very serious consideration in view of the great disparity between the sea-speeds of the various types of merchant steamers. Thus, for the majority of the ships to be escorted, convoy entailed both a longer stay in port and a longer passage than was usual under normal conditions.

Further, the conditions of modern commerce emphasised the importance of preserving the utmost possible regularity in the flow of trade. Both the berthing and the distributive facilities of the ports were based on the expectation of a steady stream of arrivals, and the experiences of the war had strikingly exemplified the danger of dislocation and congestion arising from the arrival of vessels in larger batches than those with which the ports were accustomed to deal.

In addition to these commercial objections, the Admiralty themselves entertained doubts both as to the possibilities of accurate station-keeping under steam, and as to their ability to provide escorts for such numerous convoys as would be necessary in order to maintain the flow of trade at anything approaching the normal volume. The result was that, on the outbreak of war, there was practically no mention of convoy either from the commercial or the naval side, and so long as the ratio of loss continued to be small in proportion either to the number of sailings or the total tonnage available, the question of adopting convoy was rarely, if ever, raised. Indeed, it is probable that, under the conditions prevailing during the first year, or even the first two years of war, the disadvantages inherent in the system would have resulted in a diminution of imports outweighing the gain derived from reduction of losses.

The conditions were now changed. Such losses as had been suffered since the extension of submarine activity in the autumn of 1916, and still more since the beginning of "unrestricted warfare," threatened to cut down the supply of available shipping to a point at which, however fully its carrying capacity were utilised, it would be unable to maintain the supply of essential imports. Moreover, the loss of time arising from detention in port when submarines were reported in the vicinity, and from deviations to avoid dangerous areas, had become so great that the adoption of convoy, permitting of fixed sailing dates and a direct route, might reasonably be expected to increase, or at any rate not to diminish the number of voyages made.

In these circumstances, the idea of resorting to mercantile convoy revived, and in February 1917 the Admiralty called a conference of ten masters in the port of London to consider the question. Their opinion was discouraging. They pointed out that a large proportion of the best officers and men in the merchant service had been absorbed into the auxiliary services and naval reserves, that merchant ships in general were badly equipped with the electric signalling apparatus for communication between bridge and engine room, necessary for the performance of complicated manœuvres, and that owing to the vast Admiralty demand for coal, they had frequently to be content with fuel of an inferior quality. They considered themselves, therefore, unable to guarantee the degree of accuracy in station-keeping requisite for the effective organisation of convoys.[1]

On the naval side an objection was made to increasing, by the adoption of convoy, the target offered to a single submarine; but the main difficulty was that the Admiralty believed themselves unable to provide a sufficient number of vessels suitable for escort. The needs of the Grand Fleet, the provision of escort for troops and stores to France, Salonika, Mesopotamia, and East Africa made so great a demand on the cruisers, destroyers, and light craft available that the Admiralty considered it altogether impossible to procure adequate forces for ocean convoy work.[2]

For the short sea traffic, such as the French coal trade and the Scandinavian trade, escort could more easily be provided, and was the more necessary inasmuch as the majority of the vessels employed were unarmed neutrals. In February 1917 the French coal trade was organised on a basis of daily convoys from four assembly ports—Southend for Boulogne and Calais, St. Helens for Havre, Portland for the Cherbourg area, and Penzance for Brest and ports south thereof. Convoys for the sailing traffic from the south-western ports were also provided. In the North Sea a system of " protected sailings " had been introduced towards the end of 1916 under which the routes given to shipping between Norway and the Shetlands were patrolled by the local forces of the Orkneys and Shetlands, with some assistance from the Grand Fleet. By April 1917 the protection thus given was found to be insufficient, and a direct daily convoy was established between Lerwick and the Norwegian coast, the protection being extended by the provision of destroyer escort for ships proceeding to or from Lerwick along the East Coast.[3] The few British ships still trading to Holland had been sailing in a loose convoy formation, under protection of the Harwich Force, since July 1916.

[1] *The Crisis of the Naval War*, by Viscount Jellicoe of Scapa, pp. 105-6.
[2] For the position as regards destroyers and patrol craft see Jellicoe, *op. cit.*, Chapter IV.   [3] See Jellicoe, *op. cit.*, pp. 119-22.

The results of the " controlled sailings " in the French coal trade were so satisfactory that, during April, the question of applying the convoy system to the ocean trades began to be pressed in several quarters. The Board of Admiralty were still of opinion that it was impossible to provide adequate escorts from the forces at their disposal, but they were hopeful of obtaining some help from the United States, and by the end of the month they had advanced to the position of contemplating the organisation of Atlantic convoys if and when a sufficient number of cruisers and destroyers should become available. Meanwhile, Commander R. G. H. Henderson, R.N., the officer responsible for the organisation of the French coal trade convoys, approached the Ministry of Shipping with the object of obtaining more exact information as to the number of vessels entering and leaving the country each week in the long-distance trades, with a view to ascertaining exactly what the strain of providing escort would be.

The unprecedented losses suffered during the last fortnight of April, especially in the approach areas, greatly strengthened the hands of those who advocated the general introduction of the convoy system, and by the end of April the question was under constant consideration by the Admiralty, the Ministry of Shipping, and the War Cabinet itself. In the meantime the system of approaches remained in force, but an effort was made to minimise its dangers by giving orders that the route directions at the port of departure abroad were to be varied every four days, in order to obtain the widest possible dispersal in the areas of concentration.

CHAPTER VII

EFFORTS AT REPLACEMENT

MARCH—MAY 1917

WITH so great an acceleration of the rate of loss as was witnessed in April, the provision of replacements by shipbuilding, by ship purchase, or by bringing immobilised enemy shipping into service, became more than ever a matter of vital urgency. Unhappily the progress effected in these directions went but a little way towards relieving the anxiety of those responsible for the supply of tonnage.

All Austrian, as well as German tonnage in American ports had now been seized,[1] and a few steamers lying in the harbours of Cuba and Panama were also requisitioned by those states, and subsequently handed over to the American Government.[2] In all, nearly 700,000 gross tons of enemy shipping was thus rendered available, but no effective steps had yet been taken to repair and refit the ships for service, and it was likely to be some months before any considerable relief was derived from this source.

In Brazil, where war had not yet been declared, though diplomatic relations had been broken off, no drastic step had yet been taken with regard to German shipping. The Brazilian Government were hampered by the fear of Germany repudiating a debt of between £6,000,000 and £7,000,000 in respect of Brazilian coffee seized at Hamburg on the outbreak of war, and for this reason refrained, even after the severance of relations, from requisitioning the German vessels. In spite of repeated warnings it was not until April 10th, the day after relations were broken off,

[1] The United States broke off diplomatic relations with Austria on April 8th, though war was not declared until the following December. The Austrian steamers seized numbered fourteen, with an aggregate gross tonnage of 66,500.

[2] Cuba and Panama declared war on Germany on April 7th. Four German ships were seized by Panama; five, and one Austrian, by Cuba. One or two German steamers were retained by Cuba for naval purposes.

EFFORTS AT REPLACEMENT

that they placed guards in the ships, and by that time damage had been done which was the more serious because the facilities for repairs were altogether inadequate.[1]

No other South American Government had yet gone the length of breaking off relations with Germany, but nearly all had strongly protested against the German Declaration of January 31st, and negotiations for the purchase of the German ships in their ports, or otherwise making them available for Allied service, continued to take place with Uruguay, Chile, and Peru, as well as with Brazil. Nothing as yet had come of these negotiations, but in Uruguay the Germans had become sufficiently alarmed by April 14th to disable the machinery of the ships laid up at Montevideo.[2]

Thus, the only enemy shipping immediately available was the small block of tonnage seized by China in March, and though the Chinese Government was ready enough to place ships in service, the conflicting claims of Great Britain, France, Italy, the United States, and Japan to a share of these thirteen steamers proved so difficult to reconcile, that not until the end of the year were they finally adjusted and the ships brought into service.

Meanwhile the British programme of ship purchase had been carried on with vigour. By the end of May the contracts signed or definitely closed by the Director of Overseas Ship Purchase comprised ships with an aggregate tonnage of about 1,440,000 dead-weight, or 960,000 gross, representing an expenditure of nearly £60,000,000. Of the total tonnage about 39 per cent. was for delivery in 1917, and about 41 per cent. for delivery during the first half of the following year.

Included in this total were 2 tankers and 5 other steamers acquired second-hand from neutral owners, and 10 barges each of 1,000 tons dead-weight capacity under construction in the United Kingdom. Of the new ships building or contracted for overseas 24, of about 220,000 tons dead-weight, were ordered in Japan, and 31, of 150,000 tons dead-weight, in Canada. The remainder, 171 steamers, including 8 tankers, with an aggregate dead-weight capacity of nearly 1,040,000 tons, were on order in the United States.[3] Negotiations had also been entered into for the construction in

---

[1] The German steamers in Brazilian ports numbered forty four, with an aggregate tonnage of 233,000 gross.
[2] Eight steamers of 42,658 tons gross.
[3] Two of these were wooden ships.

Canada of some 50 wooden steamers, but definite orders for these had not yet been placed.

It was unlikely, for the reasons already stated, that much additional tonnage for the United Kingdom could be obtained from European neutrals, but it might be possible to secure further ships for France and Italy, and by this time arrangements had been made to avoid further inflation of values by competition between the Allied Governments. The French had, indeed, so far gone back on their former attitude as to propose that any agreement for the allocation of tonnage jointly acquired by the Allies should be made retrospective and applied as from December 3rd, 1916, the date of the Clémentel Agreement. To this the British Government was unable to agree, but negotiations for joint action in the future went forward smoothly, and in May the Inter-Allied Ship Purchasing Committee was established under the Chairmanship of the Director of Overseas Ship Purchase, to centralise all purchases of neutral tonnage on the same principle as had already been applied to Inter-Allied chartering.

For the long-distance trades, it was only to Japan and North America that the new Committee could look with any confidence, and the utility of the Japanese yards was restricted both by the extremely high cost of construction and by shortage of steel.[1] More than ever, America was the main hope of the Allies, and the development of the situation in America was by no means favourable.

Towards the end of March an amendment to the American Shipping Laws was proposed, requiring all vessels building in the United States to remain under the American flag, and some anxiety was naturally felt in this country as to the effect of this proposal on the " Cunard " contracts. With the entry of America into the war, on April 6th, the situation became easier; but it was soon apparent that there was a strong party in the States who were determined on the retention of the ships. The American Shipping Board contemplated a programme of state construction, and on April 16th the United States Shipping Board Emergency Fleet Corporation was formed, under the law of September 1916, to carry out the work. It was hoped by the British Government that the almost inexhaustible

---

[1] The average cost of construction, exclusive of ships ordered in Japan, was just under £37 per ton dead-weight; for ships built in Japan it was about £45 16s. per ton.

capacity of the States for the production of steel would enable them, without interference with the " Cunard " contracts, to spare a considerable amount of steel for the British shipbuilding yards, and, in addition, to build on a scale permitting them, after fulfilment of their own requirements, to give large tonnage assistance to the Allies. On the other hand, the American Shipping Board found all the existing shipyards fully occupied with existing contracts, and were doubtful as to the possibility of building even the additional ships required by the United States themselves. In these circumstances it was certain that strong pressure would be put on the American Government to retain for the States the output of their own yards, the more so as the idea of regaining the place held by America in the carrying trade during the first half of the nineteenth century had taken a strong hold of the people. The departure of Mr. Balfour's Mission to the United States about the middle of April afforded an opportunity of discussing the matter direct with the American Government, but at the end of May the question was still unsettled.

Meanwhile the Shipping Controller was doing his best to accelerate the completion of ships under construction in the United Kingdom, and as fast as vessels were cleared off the slips, their place was taken by steamers of the new standard types.

His work was not allowed to proceed without distractions; the controversy that had raged over the question of standardisation was by no means silenced when the general principle was decided, it broke out anew over the design of the standard ships themselves. The idea of the " unsinkable " ship as an answer to the submarine obtained wide currency during the spring of 1917, and the standard designs were freely criticised on the ground of insufficient subdivision. In other quarters it was urged that the ships should be either much larger or much smaller than the main standard designs. If very large, they would be fast, and sufficiently few in number to be escorted individually through the danger zone; if very small, they would present a small target and could be built in numbers allowing of the widest possible dispersal.

To the Shipping Controller and his advisers, the " unsinkable ship " appeared to be a dream unlikely to be realised, and until it could be shown that something more than relative immunity would be obtained by minute subdivision, they declined to impair in this way the cargo-carrying capacity of the vessels. As to the proposed "mammoth" ships, a 14½-knot vessel of 40,000 tons dead-weight capacity, such as was suggested, would require as much steel as would suffice for the construction of eight standard ships; she would be able to use very few ports, and would take a month to load.[1] Further, she would take three times as long to build as an "A" or "B" freighter, and what was wanted was not tonnage on the stocks, however perfect the design, but tonnage on service. On the other hand, ships below 5,000 tons dead-weight were comparatively useless for ocean voyages, and even those of 5,000 tons gave, allowing for relatively smaller loss, an inferior return in cargo-carrying capacity for the labour and material expended. For these reasons they preferred to concentrate mainly on the 8,000 ton freighters of the "A" and "B" types, relegating even the 5,000 ton "C" class to a secondary place, and building nothing smaller except for special purposes.[2]

The question of speed was less easy to decide, and after the heavy losses in April there was considerable discussion as to the advisability of raising the speed of types "A" and "B" to 13 knots. The decisive factor was the time occupied in building. It was hoped that the average period of construction for these classes would not exceed six months; an increase of two knots in the speed would raise this period to eight months.[3] Thus for every four steamers of the existing types, only three 13-knot vessels could be built, and for any period down to the end of 1919,

[1] One "mammoth" was laid down at Belfast in April, but in August all work on her was stopped.
[2] The number of each type ordered to the end of May was as follows: "A" 39; "B" 69; "C" 20; "D" 20; "E" 1.
[3] The actual time occupied in building ships of the four main standard types, completed before the cessation of hostilities, was as follows:

Type.	Tons d.w.	Number completed to date of Armistice.	Number of days under construction.		
			Minimum.	Maximum.	Average.
"A"	8,175	16	195	356	270
"B"*	8,075	45	162	457	307
"C"	5,050	24	203	369	309
"D"	2,380	21	210	370	299

* Two decks.

These figures cannot, of course, be accepted as a fair criterion of the time required for the various types under favourable conditions, as they reflect the influence of adverse conditions affecting the whole shipbuilding output, and also, as between type and type, the relative urgency attached from time to time to the completion of particular ships.

it was calculated that adherence to the existing designs would give a greater importing power, even on the assumption of a much lower ratio of loss among the faster ships.

By the end of May, 148 standard vessels had been ordered, of which 132 had already been certified as war work. Only 45, however, with an aggregate tonnage of 220,000 gross, were actually under construction; for the others slips were not yet vacant. The total tonnage under construction comprised 368 steamers with an aggregate gross tonnage of 1,718,000. This total included 4 ice-breakers, 40 trawlers and drifters, 22 passenger and cargo liners, including cross-Channel steamers, 27 ships with insulated space for the carriage of meat and fruit, 11 tankers, and 265 ordinary freighters, of which 45, as we have seen, were of standard type.

In adjusting the programme of construction to the emergency needs arising from the war some progress had been made, but even now ships were only very slowly being cleared off the stocks. The shortage of labour and steel was as great as ever, and appeared likely to increase rather than to decrease. During April the average weekly allocations of steel amounted to 132,600 tons, of which only 24,400 tons, or under $18\frac{1}{2}$ per cent., could be allocated to shipbuilding.[1] But the activity of the enemy submarines had necessitated successive increases in the naval programme, and of this restricted supply not more than 13,000 tons was available for mercantile construction.

Meanwhile the rate of loss had risen, as we have seen, to a level which left the Shipping Controller's original building programme far behind, and on April 26th the Government, seriously alarmed, held a consultation with the Shipping Control Committee and the Merchant Shipbuilding Advisory Committee, to consider how the rate of output might be increased to something more nearly commensurate with the losses. The result was not encouraging. The figures submitted showed that for an output of 1,800,000 tons a year, or 50 per cent. above the Controller's

---

[1] Shipbuilding: Naval, Auxiliary and Merchant . 24,426 tons.
Shells, etc. : British . . . . . 31,948 ,,
  ,,   ,,   Allied . . . . . 11,094 ,,
War Office and Ministry of Munitions Construction,
  Railway Material, and General . . . 13,900 ,,
Export . . . . 6,573 ,,
Miscellaneous . . . . . . 43,751 ,,

132,592 tons.

original programme, it would be necessary to increase the weekly supply of steel from 13,000 to 22,000 tons, and to procure 35,000 additional skilled workers, or 44,000 unskilled. And even this would represent replacements at only about one-third of the current rate of loss.[1]

For the moment, 2,500 tons of steel a week was the largest addition it seemed possible to make, in view of the Admiralty and Ministry of Munitions demands; but it was hoped to obtain 3,000 tons more by the end of June, when the obligations to Italy undertaken in January had been finally discharged. There was also a prospect of further relief through the supply of American steel to France; but the total supplies in view fell far short of those required for such a programme as the situation demanded. The question of labour was equally difficult. The War Office declared it impossible to release any more men from the Army with the exception of a few hundred fitters, and all that could be done was to press on with negotiations for the adoption of payment by results, in the hope of increasing the output per man.

Meanwhile increased efforts were being made to deal promptly with repairs to damaged ships. The great increase in tonnage sunk had been accompanied by an equal increase in the number of ships which, though escaping destruction, suffered injury as the result of submarine attack, and on April 16th a conference took place between representatives of the Shipping Controller and the Admiralty, together with certain dockyard experts, as the result of which Dock Allotment Committees were formed in each dry-docking area, to allocate the accommodation among ships requiring repair. All arrangements made were to be reported to the Controller, and it was laid down as a principle that no vessel should be docked for repairs likely to take more than six weeks, without his express permission. Both warships and transports, however, took priority over merchant shipping in their claim on repair facilities, and the number of ships off service

[1] *Additional* steel and labour required:
For a programme of 1,600,000 tons: 7,000 tons steel weekly; 17,500 skilled or 22,000 unskilled workers.
For a programme of 1,800,000 tons: 9,000 tons steel weekly; 35,000 skilled or 44,000 unskilled workers.
For a programme of 3,000,000 tons: 19,000 tons steel weekly; 95,000 skilled or 120,000 unskilled workers.
The 3,000,000 ton programme would also require large additions to existing plant.

owing to injury continued to form a very serious factor in the tonnage situation.

In view of the difficulties presented by the shortage of steel and labour, the Controller might well be congratulated on the improvement in output secured in comparison with 1916; but only a small proportion of the losses sustained was being replaced, and early in May the Government decided on yet another change in the administrative control of shipbuilding. In the hope of solving once for all the problem presented by conflicting claims to labour and material, they revived as a separate office the old office of Navy Controller, which for many years had been combined with that of Third Sea Lord, and appointed Sir Eric Geddes to the post, with full control of the shipbuilding programmes for the Navy, the War Office (Inland Water Transport), and the Mercantile Marine. In this way it was hoped " to provide the Admiralty with an organisation comparable to that which has provided the Army with munitions . . . to develop and utilise to the best advantage the whole shipbuilding resources of the country." By the end of the month the entire organisation of shipbuilding and ship purchase had been transferred from the Ministry of Shipping to the Admiralty. In the meantime a great effort had been made to increase, by concentration on the shorter routes, the carrying power of the available tonnage.

CHAPTER VIII

THE LINER REQUISITION SCHEME
FEBRUARY—JULY 1917

THE gravest significance of the appalling losses suffered in the Fastnet area lay, as has been said, in the effort which was being made to divert tonnage from other routes into the North Atlantic trade. Of that effort the Liner Requisition Scheme was the pivot.

The genesis of the scheme may be traced back to the closing weeks of 1916, when the Transport Department, faced by the practical exhaustion of the pool of tramp tonnage, began to contemplate the necessity of making large drafts on the liner fleets, in order to procure sufficient shipping for the fulfilment of their commitments. All that was contemplated at first was the progressive direct requisition of ships, as and when required for the carriage of Government imports; but it soon became apparent that the application of this method to the liner services involved much greater difficulties and much greater inequalities than the requisitioning of tramps. Meanwhile the new Government had pledged itself publicly to bring the entire Mercantile Marine under requisition at Blue Book rates, irrespective of the character of the ships or the nature of their employment. Even so, the administrative difficulties of liner requisition might have caused some hesitation in the application of the principle, but for the decision to abandon the greater part of the Australian wheat programme and to divert tonnage, wherever possible, from the longer routes to the North Atlantic, a decision which inevitably involved serious derangement of the liner services. It was the coincidence of the tramp deficit, the general requisitioning decision, and the theory of Atlantic concentration, which emphasised the immediate urgency of the problem.

The difficulties of liner requisition arose from the

distinguishing characteristics of the liner trade: fixity and continuity of service, mixed cargoes, and passenger traffic. The management of a line of vessels running to a fixed schedule, and carrying on each voyage numerous passengers and a highly miscellaneous cargo collected from a large number of shippers and destined for a large number of consignees, involved a far more costly and extensive organisation than was required in the tramp trade. Not only was a large establishment necessary in the United Kingdom, but branch or agency offices, many of them on an imposing scale, were required at all ports of call or destination, and in shipping or commercial centres where passengers or cargo could be booked.

It was the fixity of the services and the cost of the management organisation which made either progressive requisition or redirection of sailings bear so much more hardly on the Liner Companies than on the tramp owner. The injury to a tramp owner whose ships were requisitioned was confined, broadly speaking, to the loss of profit arising from the inequality between Blue Book and market rates. Further, so long as requisitioning remained partial, he was free to fix the remainder of his fleet on the freight markets, in the most remunerative trade, at rates raised to an abnormal level largely through the effect of requisitioning on the supply of tonnage. The Liner Company was in a very different position. The injury suffered through the requisitioning of any substantial portion of its fleet extended beyond the immediate loss of profit to the loss of trade connections and goodwill, built up by many years of continuous and regular service. Owing to the necessity of preserving this goodwill so far as possible, as well as to the specialisation of type and demarcation of interests, characteristic of the trade, the line was, to a great extent, precluded from seeking employment for its free vessels in any but their accustomed service. Finally, however, its services were depleted by requisitioning, the costly management and agency organisation must still be maintained, lest trade connections and goodwill should disappear altogether.

Considerable drafts had already been made upon the liner fleets. In addition to the large, fast vessels commissioned as Armed Merchant Cruisers or Naval Auxiliaries, a large number of the lower-powered cargo steamers had been taken up as transports, or for the carriage of

ELEMENTS OF THE PROBLEM

Government imports, and by February 1917 about one-third of the total number of liners was under requisition. These, however, being requisitioned as required, had been taken in approximately equal numbers from the various services, and during the earlier stages of the war the lines had been able, to a great extent, to make good their losses by time-chartering. By one means or another the principal services were still adequately maintained. A large proportion of the space on most of the vessels was under requisition at Blue Book rates for the carriage of Government imports, but this seldom involved any serious interference with routeing, and the goodwill and connection of the lines was maintained, even though profits were limited. Moreover, the payment for requisitioned space was sufficient, when supplemented by the freight on private cargo, to leave a profit, after payment of establishment and overhead charges.

The situation was now changed. Since the extension of liner requisition was bound up with the scheme of concentration on the shorter routes, its incidence must inevitably be very unequal as between trade and trade, nor was there now any possibility of obtaining substitute tonnage for the vessels requisitioned. It was thus possible that the lines engaged in the long-distance services, such as the Australasian, might see their fleets reduced to a point at which the total earnings would be insufficient to pay the costs of their organisation; yet they could not break up this organisation without destroying their own trade connections and goodwill, and abandoning services essential, though on a reduced scale, to the supply of the country.

On these grounds it was argued that grave injustice could only be avoided by the general requisitioning of all liners, and by making some provision for the payment of establishment charges, without regard to the actual volume of trade maintained on each route. Further, apart from any political considerations which may have actuated the Government in declaring for universal requisition, there were now many, even among the ship-owners, who favoured this step for reasons of supply. It had now become necessary to disregard the economic considerations by which commerce is normally actuated. The purchase of supplies by the State, out of borrowed money, enabled all exchange considerations to be subordinated to the one purpose of drawing supplies, so far as possible, from the nearest source, and while some shipowners believed that shipping could safely be left to follow the redistribution of demand, others maintained that only by direct, centralised control, could the necessary flexibility of services be secured.

General requisition of the liner trades was, however, no simple matter. While the Blue Book rates were generally held to cover such duties of strict ship management as would devolve on owners under a time-charter, it was obvious that requisition of the liner services would be useless except on terms which gave to the Government the full benefit of the owners' organisation at home and abroad, the more so as, in respect of all cargo not on Government account, the ships would still be left in the position of common carriers, operating on ordinary commercial lines. This was an extension of their obligations which the Blue Book rates could not possibly be stretched to cover. The ships might be requisitioned; but their utilisation depended on the voluntary whole-hearted co-operation of the owners.

All these considerations had been fully reviewed by Sir Kenneth Anderson and Sir Lionel Fletcher in their original memorandum, and it was on their proposals that the requisitioning letter was based when, on February 28th, it was sent out to the lines in the Australian and New Zealand Conferences. In effect, the ships were requisitioned on terms to be subsequently arranged, and the shipowners were instructed to continue to run them as for themselves, though actually on account of the Government, on the understanding that provision would be made for meeting establishment charges.

Requisition was to take effect as from the first occasion of each vessel completing discharge in the United Kingdom, or if not trading to the United Kingdom, on a date to be communicated. As from that date, the owners were to credit the Government with the full gross earnings of the ship and debit net charges. They would themselves be credited with hire at Blue Book rates, subject to subsequent adjustment in respect of disbursements. In the meantime, they were authorised to incur and to debit the Government with all usual and necessary expenses, including payments to agents and the upkeep of branch offices abroad; but in order to allow the utmost flexibility of programmes, it was desired that a system of pooling agency interests should be devised, which would render it a matter of indifference to what port the ships were sent.

For general supervision of the trade, a Committee was to be nominated by the Controller from names submitted by the Chairman of the Conference, and this Committee was to include representatives of the Controller. Its task was to submit for the approval of the Controller a programme for the outward employment of the vessels, and to inform the Controller of any tonnage in excess of the outward requirements available for withdrawal to other trades. In the event of the Controller diverting tonnage from the trade, the Committee was to advise as to the consequent rearrangements of programme. In the same way, the homeward employment, loading programme, and movements of the steamers were to be placed by the Committee in the hands of central Committees of Agents in Australia and New Zealand.

Subject to the Controller's directions and the arrangement of programmes by the Committees, the owners were to retain and were expected to discharge the responsibility of management in the fullest sense of the term: " The general intention is in a word that you should run the steamers as for yourselves, though on account of the Government, who confidently look to you to conduct the business with as much zeal and care as if your own interests alone were still involved."

On March 5th a requisitioning letter in similar terms was sent to the lines comprised in the Indian and Far Eastern Conferences, and by the end of the month, as has been said, the majority of the lines engaged in the direct trade of the United Kingdom, and several of those running the most important services on the cross-routes, were brought under requisition. As the organisation in the Ministry of Shipping gradually developed, the remaining lines, including even the Indian and China coastal services, were brought into the scheme, and by the end of May only a very few local services in distant seas remained exempt from requisition.

There was, in general, little opposition to the scheme. On the financial side, the owners were already contributing to the State, in Income Tax and Excess Profits Duty, a very large proportion of their profits, and they were now much less interested in the retention of the remaining margin than in securing the maintenance of their organisations. They had been heavily hit by exclusion from the right shared by all other industries to a final settlement of Excess Profits under one account covering the war as a whole. They were thus unable to set off against profits earned in the earlier years of the war any losses now incurred through the increase of running expenses, or the extravagant cost of replacing lost tonnage. If, therefore, they were able to secure payment of their organisation charges and the recoupment of losses from war or marine risks, they were quite willing to accept the Blue Book rate of hire, or some approximate equivalent, as the financial basis of the new arrangement now proposed to them. Moreover, the lines were genuinely anxious to co-operate to the full in maintaining essential supplies, and the new scheme was generally accepted as an inevitable corollary of the concentration of purchases in near markets. The memorandum forming its basis had been discussed, before the requisitioning letters were sent out, with representatives of the liner interests, and the obligation to run the ships on Government account, with the same zeal and energy as displayed in private trade, was accepted as a necessity of the times. The points raised by the companies related to details of hire and accounting, and in particular to the payment to be made by the Government for the services of the liner organisations. This, the crux of the whole problem, had been left by the requisitioning letter for subsequent discussion, and the majority of the Conferences suggested that it should be met by a 10 per cent. commission on the gross earnings of the vessels.

In one quarter, however, and that a most important one, more serious difficulties arose. The North Atlantic Conference occupied a position widely different from that of most other trades. From those trades it was proposed to withdraw tonnage. On the North Atlantic tracks it was proposed to concentrate it, and it was necessary to make arrangements for the management of the diverted vessels. Further, the conditions of the trade itself presented important special features.

In the first place, the number of ships employed, and the number of voyages made during a given period by each ship, were greater than in any other trade. The

Committee established for the Australasian trade would control some 150 to 200 round voyages during the year, a number likely to be reduced by diversions. A similar Committee for the North Atlantic would control about 2,000 round voyages, irrespective of vessels to be brought in from other routes.[1]

Further, the North Atlantic trade was a " ferry service " in which the carrying power of the ships depended above all else on loading and discharging facilities, and the part played by the offices and agencies of the lines in the collection of cargoes was as important in securing a quick turn-round, as that of their pier, berth, and wharf establishments.

For these reasons the lines in the Atlantic Conference represented that to place in the hands of a Committee detailed control over the employment of the ships, or the use of the agencies and port facilities would hamper the work of the lines at every turn and lead, inevitably, to a serious waste of carrying power. While expressing themselves doubtful as to the legal validity of the proposal not only to requisition their ships, but " to commandeer the profit-earning powers of their organisations both here and abroad," and equally doubtful as to the effect on the utilisation of carrying power of running the ships on behalf of the Government instead of for individual profit and at individual risk, they were ready and willing to carry out the wishes of the Government, provided the conditions under which they were to work interfered as little as possible with the individual responsibility of the lines, on which, in their judgment, depended the possibility of using the ships to the greatest possible national advantage. They therefore submitted to the Controller, on March 31st, alternative Heads of Proposal for the management of ships in the North Atlantic trade, based primarily on the responsibility of the established lines.

It had always been recognised by the Controller that the special conditions in the North Atlantic would necessitate some modification of the machinery proposed to and accepted by the other trades, and on April 4th he wrote to Sir Alfred Booth, Chairman of the North Atlantic Conference, accepting the Heads of Proposal put forward by the lines as the basis of discussion, subject to certain modi-

[1] Australasian trade, about 70 liners, 2 to 3 round voyages a year; North Atlantic trade, about 250 liners, average 8 voyages a year each way.

fications, intended to define more clearly the rights of the Government. As thus modified, the Heads of Proposal provided that the whole carrying trade in British steamers between North America and the United Kingdom and Northern France, other than that carried in fully requisitioned ships, should be placed in the hands of scheduled firms and companies called " the Established Lines," and that, subject to the rights and instructions of the Government, each line should continue to manage its own business and run the vessels controlled by it with as much zeal, and should have the same discretion in such management, as if its own interests alone were involved. The vessels to be so managed by each Established Line would include (1) those owned or then managed or chartered by the line itself; (2) any vessels engaged in the regular liner trade voluntarily placed under its management by other owners; (3) any other vessels allotted to the line by a Committee to be formed for the purpose of allocating tonnage diverted to the trade.

The main principle contended for by the North Atlantic Conference, the substitution of the Established Lines for a Central Committee, as the authority responsible for the movements of the individual ships, had thus been conceded, but many points remained to be decided, both as to the arrangements for management of diverted vessels, and the financial adjustments to be made, especially with regard to organisation charges. For meeting these charges the North Atlantic, like other Conferences, proposed a commission on gross earnings, and the Ministry of Shipping were at first inclined to accept this proposal. Owing, however, to the wide variations in practice and conditions between trade and trade, it was found impossible to fix any rate adequate in all trades which would not have been excessive in many. Further, if payment were based on the volume of trade actually handled, it would be practically impossible to maintain for the benefit of the Government the organisations of heavily depleted trades. The Ministry therefore decided to fall back on the alternative method of paying, by reimbursement as a voyage charge, third party agency commissions, and the actual cost of maintaining proprietary offices. This principle was agreed between Sir Kenneth Anderson, who was conducting the negotiations on behalf of the Ministry of Shipping, and Sir Alfred Booth, at the end of April, but the exact definition of the charges to be allowed under this head involved lengthy negotiations.

It was very desirable, in order to avoid the possibility of friction, and to enable accounts to be readily adjusted, that a definite and comprehensive agreement should be arrived at. In all, over thirty Conferences were involved,[1] and in order to centralise and facilitate the negotiations, a Committee, consisting of the Chairman of the leading Conferences, was formed to conduct the negotiations on behalf of the lines. Of this Committee, Lord Inchcape was Chairman. Direct communications also continued to pass between the Ministry of Shipping and the North Atlantic Conference on points specially affecting the Atlantic trade. The Heads of Arrangement provisionally agreed between the North Atlantic Conference and the Ministry were taken as the basis of the agreement with all the lines, both for the sake of uniformity and because all the trades were interested in questions relating to the treatment of diverted vessels. In most of the other trades, however, the machinery of control by a Central Committee at home and Loading Committees abroad, was established on the lines of the requisitioning letter.

Although it was some months before the terms were finally settled, no time was lost in bringing the scheme into active operation. During March a Liner Requisitioning Section, under Sir Lionel Fletcher, was formed within the Ministry of Shipping Requisitioning Branch. This Section was responsible for all executive action in connection with the scheme, but the actual decisions, both on general policy and on points of detail, were in the hands of the Liner Requisitioning Committee, which was attached to the Section. The original members of this Committee, in addition to Sir Lionel Fletcher and Sir Kenneth Anderson, were Sir Frederick Lewis, Sir Aubrey Brocklebank, Mr. W. H. Tregoning, Mr. C. Reiss, and Mr. C. W. Warwick, each of whom undertook the general supervision of a group of trades, while broad matters of policy, such as the transfer of ships from one trade to another, were decided by the Committee as a whole. Sir Kenneth Anderson, as a member of the Shipping Control Committee,

---

[1] The number of lines in each Conference varied from 29 in the North Atlantic to 2, or even a single line, in some of the cross-trades. In a few trades, where no Conference existed, a Conference Committee was specially formed for the purpose of the scheme.

exercised a general supervision over the working of the scheme, for which he was directly responsible to the Controller.[1]

As an additional check on the running of the vessels, the licensing system was retained in operation, general licences being issued as need arose, on the instructions of the Liner Requisitioning Committee. The main object, however, in retaining the system, was to facilitate the process of decontrol after the war. It was anticipated that the relaxation, like the imposition of control, would proceed by gradual stages, and for this reason it was desirable to keep the licensing machinery in continuous operation.

In April the North Atlantic Allocation Committee was formed by the North Atlantic Conference to deal with diverted tonnage,[2] and by the end of that month Conference Committees and Loading Committees had been formed for most of the direct long-distance trades. Pending completion of the negotiations, the lines continued to run their ships " as for themselves though actually on account of the Government," subject to subsequent adjustment of financial questions.

The main basis of the scheme was the readjustment of the liner services in accordance with import requirements, on the understanding that only such essential imports should be drawn from the more distant sources as could not readily be procured nearer home. This principle had been adopted, in practice, when the first diversions from the more distant trades were made at the beginning of the year. As the tale of losses increased during the spring, its urgency became more and more evident, and the intervention of America, by placing almost unlimited dollar credits at the disposal of the Allies, provided the necessary financial basis. It was strongly pressed by the Ministry of Shipping and was also favoured by the Admiralty,

---

[1] During the course of the war, Sir Frederick Lewis retired from the Committee, and Mr. W. P. Tyser and Captain A. Stuart Black were added to it.

[2] It was a term of the Heads of Arrangement agreed with the Ministry that lines whose ships were diverted to the North Atlantic should have the option of consigning such vessels to any Established Line chosen by them. All ships brought into the trade, other than such "self-consigned vessels," were allotted by the Allocation Committee, in the light of the tonnage already running under the control of each Established Line, and its capacity for undertaking additional responsibility. Ships diverted to the Atlantic prior to the formation of the Liverpool Allocation Committee were allotted by the Controller.

more particularly on the ground that it would facilitate the introduction of a convoy system in the ocean trades. During May it was considered in great detail by a special committee under Lord Jellicoe, on which the Admiralty, Ministry of Shipping, Board of Trade, and Ministry of Munitions were represented, and on May 17th the War Cabinet decided definitely that the purchasing Departments should at once take the necessary steps to procure all further supplies so far as possible from North America, and to reduce their commitments in other markets to the lowest possible level.

This decision involved, of course, a concentration both of liners and of fully requisitioned tramps on the Atlantic tracks. The extent to which it could be carried out was limited by the necessity, under war conditions, of imports which North America could not provide either at all or in the requisite quantities; by the receiving capacity of the West Coast ports; by the suitability of ships for North Atlantic voyages; and by the importance for exchange, political, or other reasons, of maintaining outward services and cross-services, of which it was desirable to take advantage for imports. Both tramps and liners had, however, been diverted to the Atlantic in increasing numbers since the beginning of the year, and as the arrangements of the buying departments were perfected, the tendency to concentration continually increased.

For the purpose of applying the principle to the liner trades, Commercial Services Branch drew up a monthly priority programme for the various trades, indicating the quantity of each essential commodity to be lifted. In theory, these programmes were based on the decisions of the Tonnage Priority Committee, but in order to avoid delays the Branch acted, in practice, mainly on direct communication with the Allies and Departments, who were able, almost invariably, to put their requirements at a lower figure than that stated by them to the Priority Committee. The monthly quantities to be lifted in each trade were communicated to the Conferences, and the Conference Committees then arranged, through the Loading Committees abroad, the programme of loading ports, and the allocation of the cargoes to be lifted among the vessels available.[1]

[1] The Loading Committees were composed of the owners' representatives abroad, whether officials of the various companies or members of

All proposals that the Branch should themselves issue directions with regard to the loading of individual cargoes were steadfastly resisted by those responsible for its operations, as they held that the best results could be obtained only by leaving the lines as much freedom and responsibility as possible.

The general supervision of this work was in the hands of the Liner Requisition Committee, who maintained a running forecast of tonnage available in each trade, and were responsible for diverting any tonnage in excess of that required for the priority programme drawn up by Commercial Services Branch. It was, however, impossible to secure a mathematically accurate balance between shipping and cargoes in any particular trade, and when a ship had loaded her prescribed priority cargo, she was instructed to fill up with private cargo, other than prohibited goods, at the highest rate of freight obtainable.[1]

As regards outward cargoes, the position was the exact reverse of that in the import trade. While the tonnage left in each trade was regulated by the priority import programme drawn up by Commercial Services Branch, the export programme depended entirely on the tonnage available, and it was obvious that a rearrangement of services based wholly on the principle of obtaining the maximum proportion of imports from the nearest sources must inevitably tend to produce an excess of outwards tonnage on the shorter routes, with a corresponding increase in the number of ballast voyages, and a shortage of tonnage for exports in the long-distance trades. This, from the point of view of the Ministry of Shipping, was a matter of indifference, but to the Treasury, already at their wits' end to finance Government purchases, it might well be a vital matter. Their views were accordingly sought, and on March 14th a Conference took place between the two Departments, at which the whole effect of the scheme, on its financial side, was thoroughly explored. It appeared that the Treasury were willing to face the reduction of the services to China and Japan, valuable as those markets were to the textile industries of the country. The Indian trade was another matter. Not only was India the greatest

agency houses. In the Australasian trade, the Sub-Committees formed for supervision of the insulated traffic (see Vol. II, p. 83), acted as Loading Committees for the purposes of the Liner Requisition Scheme.

[1] This private cargo, as well as the priority cargo, was, of course, for Government account.

market for British manufactures; Indian exports to the United States—then still neutral—were large and valuable, and the British Government were able to take advantage, as part of the Indian Loan, of the credits with which India was thus provided in New York. Since exchange difficulties in North America could not well be more acute, the Treasury could not, without the gravest anxiety, face the loss of this assistance. It was agreed, therefore, that both outwards tonnage to India and tonnage on the cross-route between India and the States, should be interfered with as little as possible. It was agreed, further, that the Liner Requisition Committee should endeavour, in arranging cross voyages, to give a preference to ships carrying goods from any part of the Empire to the United States, over ships engaged in carrying American exports. They were also to bear in mind the desirability of maintaining the flow of exports to Java and the Plate, in order to pay for the heavy imports from those countries.

In no other respects were considerations of exchange allowed to interfere with the working of the principle of concentration. Some regard, indeed, had to be paid to the essential requirements of the Oversea Dominions; but only in respect of those trades for which the Treasury had specially pleaded were ships retained in the service for the purpose of adjusting the balance of trade. It is probable, however, that no great reduction in the volume of exports can be attributed directly to the effects of liner requisition. The mischief that might have followed the rearrangement of services had already been effected by the redirection of national effort. Owing to the increasing absorption of labour and materials by the war industries, the tonnage required for priority imports in any trade was usually more than sufficient to lift the outward cargoes available, and though an Export Priority Committee was formed, its decisions had little effect on the working of the scheme.[1] It was only in the textile trades that the diversions produced any serious shortage of outwards tonnage, and to meet the difficulties in these trades, the Textile Exports Committee, composed of trade representatives, was formed by the Ministry of Shipping and

---

[1] General instructions were given to the lines, for exchange reasons, to give a preference to goods of high value. Exports to Australia were ultimately controlled, in large measure, by priority certificates issued by the Commonwealth Government

Board of Trade. The task of this Committee was two-fold, to ration the available space amongst shippers, and to prevent congestion in the loading ports, by preventing any goods from going forward until licensed for shipment.

The concession with regard to the Indian services could the more easily be granted, inasmuch as there was a long list of priority cargo to be lifted at Indian ports.[1] Even after the entry of the United States into the war, when the difficulty of financing exports was overcome by the grant of large credits by the American Government, the Indian services were maintained at a fairly high level, and were frequently supplemented by the diversion of South African liners. The list of priority cargo from South Africa was small,[2] but it was necessary to keep sufficient tonnage in the trade to supply the essential demands of the Union,[3] and the surplus vessels were either sent on to Australia for trooping, or despatched to Indian ports to load a homewards cargo. On the voyage between South Africa and India, the cargo liners frequently carried coal from Durban to the bunker depôt at Colombo.

It was from the Australasian and Far Eastern services that the first large diversions were made. The Far Eastern Priority List comprised little beyond tin and rubber from the Malay Peninsula, beans from China and Japan, and hemp from the Philippines,[4] and required no very large volume of shipping for its carriage. Considerable reductions in the services were made at an early stage and the trade was marked out for still more drastic treatment if need arose. In the Australasian trade the Priority List was far more important. Wool, both for the United Kingdom and the Allies, and lead were by far the most important items as regards bulk; but copper and jams were also important and there was a long list of sundries, including hides, tallow, and other meat products.[5] The

[1] The first Priority Lists for India and Ceylon, and Rangoon (May 1917), amounted to 140,000 tons. Manganese, rice, oil-seeds, tea, sandbags, and jute were the bulkiest items. Others of special war importance were magnesite, saltpetre, and chrome ore.

[2] The South and East African Priority List varied, in 1917, from 12,000 to 15,000 tons. The only large items were wattle bark, copper, and chrome ore. Hemp, guncotton, and asbestos were also of some importance.

[3] Owing to the opposition of the Dutch element in the population, the South African Government were never able to enforce an import priority list.

[4] It never exceeded 20,000 tons at its highest point.

[5] The May list amounted to nearly 50,000 tons, exclusive of meat and wheat. It should be observed that some of the most important items

determining factor in the allocation of tonnage was, however, the provision of insulated space for refrigerated produce, and this led to the retention in the trade of shipping with a greater amount of ordinary cargo space than was required for lifting the priority items. The lines were accordingly instructed to fill up this surplus space with wheat and flour.[1]

So far as possible, however, it was desired to draw meat from the Plate rather than from Australia, on account of the shorter voyage involved, and as there was a shortage of tonnage for April and May loadings at Plate ports the Liner Requisitioning Committee agreed, early in the spring, to divert five liners from the Australasian trades, in addition to three already arranged. At the end of May, owing to the desire of the Ministry of Food to build up wheat stocks, a further draft was made on the Australasian trade, in order to provide additional tonnage for cereals from North America. The insulated space on these diverted vessels was used for lifting bacon, fish, and dairy produce, and a quantity of Canadian beef purchased by the Ministry.[2]

In this way the Australasian services had been seriously depleted by the summer of 1917. For the moment, however, the dislocation was not severely felt, as the Australian meat output was still affected by the drought of 1914-15, so much so that meat for the supply of the armies in the Eastern Mediterranean had to be brought almost entirely from the Plate.

In order to obtain the fullest use of the tonnage that remained, by giving a quicker turn round, the steamers were ordered to load at one port only in Australia, and at two or three at most in New Zealand; cargo lying at open roadsteads in New Zealand was railed to the main ports, and a small steamer belonging to the Union S.S. Co. of

in the priority lists, from the military point of view, such as wolfram and molybdenite from Australia, had no real bearing on the tonnage situation, owing to the very small size of the total output. They could be carried by the most attenuated service, so long as it was sufficient to maintain regular communication.

[1] Thus, while the priority cargo to be lifted in Australia during the summer of 1917 averaged 50,000 tons a month; the provision of insulated tonnage to lift some 30,000 tons of refrigerated produce, had the result of making about 75,000 dead-weight tons monthly available for non-refrigerated cargo. The balance of 25,000 tons monthly was used for wheat and flour.

[2] All purchases in North America were made by the Ministry of Food, not by the Board of Trade.

New Zealand was specially told off to act as a port-to-port ferry and to carry cheese to Australian ports for shipment.[1]

In the South American trade also, the question of refrigerated tonnage was the determining factor. The Priority Cargo List from Brazil was small, for imports of coffee were now restricted, and rubber, the most important Brazilian product, occupied little space. From the Plate there was a larger list, including preserved meats, quebracho extract for the War Office, and hides; but this was less important than the shipments of refrigerated meat, and grain, which lay outside its scope.[2] The insulated tonnage in the trade was increased, as we have seen, by diversions from Australasia, and the lines were instructed to fill up with wheat all ordinary cargo space not required for priority commodities. What wheat would be available was, at first, somewhat doubtful, as on March 26th the Argentine Government issued a decree forbidding export, on the ground that stocks were running low, and it became necessary for the Ministry of Shipping to divert requisitioned tramps on their way to the Plate. On April 23rd, however, an agreement was signed by which the President consented to allow the export of 180,000 tons of wheat and 20,000 tons of flour, on condition of obtaining, if necessary, an equivalent amount of sowing wheat from Australia, later in the year.[3]

The Plate services were thus maintained, for the sake of the meat cargoes, at a higher level than was necessary to meet export requirements, and many ships went out in ballast. Others were employed to carry cargoes of coal to the South American bunker depôts, thus relieving the strain on fully requisitioned tonnage. With the services to the west coast of South America there was little interference, as they were no greater than was required to lift the priority cargoes of nitrates, sugar, copper and other metals, cotton, and borate of lime.[4] The greater part of the nitrate imports, however, were still brought by fully requisitioned tramps.

Of the other direct services, the South African, as we

[1] In all matters relating to insulated ships the Liner Requisitioning Committee acted on the advice of the Joint Committee on Refrigerated Tonnage set up by the Ministry of Shipping and the Board of Trade.
[2] The Brazilian Priority List during the summer of 1917 averaged about 6,000 tons; the Plate list varied from 12,000 to 25,000.
[3] This option was not exercised.
[4] Total about 25,000 tons.

have seen, was regulated by the import requirements of the Union, and was used on the homeward voyage to supplement Indian and Australian tonnage. From the West African service few ships were withdrawn subsequently to the diversions made at the beginning of the year, when the Atlantic concentration was first decided on. The tonnage in the trade was, indeed, barely adequate to the demands of the Ministry of Munitions for oil-seeds and of the Ministry of Food for margarine materials.[1]

Nearer home, the liner trade to Spain, Portugal, and the Mediterranean was run under two Conference Committees, one for the Egyptian trade and the other, specially formed for the purpose, covering trade with the Iberian Peninsula and the Western Mediterranean. In these trades the main controlling factor was the demand for outward space, to relieve fully requisitioned tonnage in the supply of Italy and the Mediterranean bunker depôts with coal. The ships employed were not, generally speaking, of a size and type suitable for diversion to the North Atlantic, and as the Mediterranean coal crisis had now become permanent there was little interference with the sailings. A large Mediterranean Priority List was, however, drawn up to regulate the homeward cargoes.[2] Cotton, cotton seeds, and onions from Egypt, sulphur from Italy, phosphate from Tunis, lead and onions from Spain, were the largest items; but no assistance was given by the liners in lifting the ore imports, for the carriage of which they were ill-suited.

To the cross-trades no hard and fast rule could be applied. The first concern of the Ministry of Shipping was the restriction of tonnage on these routes to the barest minimum; and with this object the Ministry did its utmost to persuade the Dominion Governments to restrict as much as possible the import of non-essential commodities. In practice, however, it was necessary also to show some regard for the trade interests of the United States, and occasionally, for the essential requirements of neutrals from whom valuable supplies were received. The services between India and the United States were maintained, as we have seen, for reasons of exchange; those from the United States to South and West Africa and

---

[1] The priority cargo list at this period amounted to about 40,000 tons, almost entirely made up of kernels, ground-nuts, and palm-oil.
[2] About 70,000 tons.

Australasia were regulated by the import requirements of the British Dominions concerned ; in West Africa specially for food ; in South Africa and Australasia for oil, mining, and agricultural machinery. Between India and South and East Africa, it was necessary to run sufficient ships to maintain the food supply of the native Indian population, and some provision had to be made for the export of gunnies from India to South America, in order that the benefit of the Argentine harvests and the Chilian nitrate output might be secured for the Allies.

The cross-trade most drastically treated was that between North and South America. With the exception of Messrs. Lamport & Holt's triangular service, practically all British ships were withdrawn from this trade during the first two or three months of 1917. In order to keep their goodwill alive the companies concerned were permitted to keep up an attenuated service with chartered neutrals, which were brought under the control of the Liner Requisition Committee.

With the exception of insulated vessels diverted to the Plate, practically all the ships withdrawn from the long-distance and cross-routes were put into the North Atlantic trade, and by July 31st, one-third of the total number of liners on the Register of the United Kingdom, exclusive of those on full requisition, were in the North Atlantic. On the other hand, the proportion employed in services other than that of the United Kingdom, had fallen from one-third to under one-quarter, and the Far Eastern and Australian services had also been seriously cut down.[1]

[1] Figures from Requisitioning Branch Returns, exclusive of ships on Colonial Register trading abroad. The details are as follows :

	January 31st.		July 31st.	
	No.	Percentage.	No.	Percentage.
*U.K.—N. America	246	22·1	306	33·8
U.K.—Plate and Brazil	80	7·2	61	6·7
„ India	114	10·2	96	10·6
„ Far East and Australasia	147	13·2	100	11·0
Other U.K. Services	172	15·4	140	15·5
Non-U.K. Services, including local coastal services in Indian, China and Australian Seas, etc..	355	31·9	203	22·4
	1,114	100·0	906	100·0

* These figures include a few ships proceeding to Australia, etc., viâ Panama.

With reference to the large proportion employed on non-United Kingdom

ROUTES AND PROGRAMMES

Included in the figures for North America are ships employed in the direct West Indian services. These, though brought under the Liner Requisition Scheme in April, were subject to little interference. A priority programme, in which sugar, asphalt, and cocoa were the main items, was drawn up in June,[1] but the main reason for abstention from interference was that many of the vessels loaded homewards at Gulf ports and could be regarded as running in the strictly North American trade.

For this trade Commercial Services Branch drew up no priority list, but the liners continued to carry wheat and munitions to a total of 85 per cent. of their space, leaving only 15 per cent. for private cargo.[2] With the actual running of the services there was little interference. The ships diverted from other trades were either " consigned " by their owners, or allotted by the Allocation Committee to one or other of the Established Lines, and by these lines the tonnage, whether original or diverted, continued to be managed at their own discretion, with the sole object of developing the maximum carrying power. An altogether new feature had, however, been introduced into the trade by the adoption of the convoy system.

services in January, it must be remembered that practically the whole of these services were in Empire interests and could only be further restricted under pressure of the gravest emergency. It should be remembered, too, that about one-third of the liner tonnage was on full requisition and many of the ships requisitioned had been withdrawn from these trades. Further, the ships abroad included a large number of small vessels employed in local services, and altogether unsuitable for ocean trade. The proportion of the *gross tonnage* in the North Atlantic in July was 40 per cent. of the whole.

[1] About 12,000 tons.
[2] In this space, however, bacon, hams, and lard were required to be carried up to a total of 4 per cent. of the total dead-weight capacity.

CHAPTER IX

THE INTRODUCTION OF CONVOY

MAY—AUGUST 1917

DURING the whole month of May the enquiry into the naval possibilities of applying the convoy system to the ocean trades went on without interruption. The essential preliminary to any effective scheme of convoy organisation was accurate information as to the number of vessels trading on each route, and this was already provided by the Ministry of Shipping's Card Index. For a general estimate as to the total number of ships requiring escort during any given period, no detailed investigation was necessary. The actual number of ocean-going ships afloat had again and again been impressed on the Government and the Admiralty by the various shipping authorities and the shipowners themselves, and the average number of voyages made annually by each ship was equally well known. Unfortunately, these facts were not appreciated. A weekly return of losses and sailings was published by the Admiralty, and with a view to the effect in enemy and neutral countries, the figures were swollen by the inclusion of cross-Channel steamers, coasters, and short-sea traders, many of whom made more than one port in a day, and the allowance to be made for this factor seems to have been very imperfectly apprehended. The actual number of British ocean-going steamers that arrived weekly from transatlantic ports, and ports east or south of Gibraltar, would have been only about 100, even if all vessels had arrived safely, and the departures were on the same scale. Including ships from all countries, the inward voyages were about 120 to 140 each week.[1]

On the other hand, the Admiralty return, based on the

---

[1] Cf. Sir J. A. Salter, *Allied Shipping Control*, 1921, p. 123. In times of peace the inward voyages of British ships of 1,600 tons gross and upwards from all countries averaged under 200 a week.

THE CONVOY COMMITTEE

arrivals and departures of ships of 300 tons gross and upwards, showed a weekly average of 2,500 to 2,600 each way. Whether or no these figures actually deceived those responsible for their publication, the fact remains that there was a general tendency both to underestimate the ratio of loss in the ocean-trades and greatly to exaggerate the number of vessels that would require escort under a system of ocean convoy.

The investigations made by Commander Henderson at the Ministry of Shipping had the effect of calling attention to the true facts, and during May the possibility and necessity of ocean convoy found strong advocates not only among the shipowners but in the Ministry of Shipping and the Admiralty itself. Further, the arrival of a division of American destroyers at Queenstown gave hopes of American co-operation. There was still considerable difference of opinion both as to the number of vessels which could be handled in a single convoy, and as to the strength of the escort it was necessary to provide; but early in May it was decided to test the possibilities of the system by running two experimental convoys from Gibraltar and Newport News respectively. The Gibraltar convoy, of seventeen vessels, sailed on May 10th and arrived without loss. The Hampton Roads convoy sailed on May 24th and consisted of twelve ships.

In the meantime, on May 17th, the Admiralty appointed a committee to draw up a general scheme of convoy organisation for the ocean trades.[1] In anticipation of the adoption of the system, the Card Index at the Ministry had been revised and extended so as to enable prompt and accurate information to be given as to the ships in any port, or on any route, at a given date, and measures were also taken to obtain more accurate information as to the actual sea speed of ships, under existing conditions.

On June 6th the Convoy Committee presented its report. In this document full advantage was taken of Commander Henderson's experience and investigations, and the Ministry of Shipping had been consulted, through Mr. Norman Leslie, as to the directions in which convoys were required. The report contemplated the establishment of

---

[1] Jellicoe, *The Crisis of the Naval War*, p. 132. The members of the Committee were: Captain H. W. Longden, R.N., Fleet-Paymaster H. W. E. Manisty, R.N., Commander J. S. Wilde, R.N., Lieutenant G. E. Burton, R.N., and Mr. Norman A. Leslie, representing the Ministry of Shipping.

convoys for homeward-bound shipping from Gibraltar for the Mediterranean and through Mediterranean trade; from Dakar for ships from South America, from Africa, or from Australia and the East viâ the Cape; from Hampton Roads for the Panama Canal, Gulf and Caribbean traffic, and for ships loaded in United States Atlantic ports up to and including Philadelphia and Baltimore; from New York for vessels from American and Canadian ports north of Baltimore. It was proposed also to run outward convoys, with Milford, Lamlash, and Falmouth as the ports of concentration. The idea was that cruisers should be provided as ocean escort to bring the homeward-bound convoys to a rendezvous 300 or 400 miles from land, where a destroyer escort would meet them and bring them in. The outward convoys were to be escorted by destroyers to a similar distance from the coast, and then dispersed to their destinations. To ensure the shipowners' co-operation, the scheme for Atlantic convoys was laid by the Ministry of Shipping before the Atlantic Conference, Commander Henderson being in attendance to explain its details, and steps were taken to work out the necessary arrangements for co-operation between the Navy and the Mercantile Marine, and to provide such additional signalling gear, etc., as was required for the steamers.

Two days after the report was presented, the experimental convoy from Hampton Roads arrived. No loss had been suffered whilst in convoy, but two vessels had dropped out through inability to keep up the required speed, and one of these was torpedoed and sunk; the other arrived safely five days after the convoy.

From the reports of the officers commanding the experimental convoys, it appeared that the station-keeping had been good; indeed, Captain Whitehead of the ROXBURGH, who brought over the Hampton Roads convoy, was confident that the number of vessels could safely be greatly increased. It appeared, therefore, that the difficulty of providing escorts was the only remaining obstacle to the general adoption of the system.

Meanwhile the necessity for better protective methods had been emphasised by continued heavy losses, especially on the approach routes. The destruction of British shipping during May was, indeed, below the high-water mark of April, but it amounted to 350,000 tons, and the losses of Allied and neutral shipping were in proportion. Owing, probably, to the effect of the order for varying the approach routes every four days, casualties in the areas of concentration were less numerous than in the previous month, but 25 steamers of 1,600 tons gross or upwards were destroyed in those areas, and 15 more on the coastal routes.

In view of the motives that lay behind the Atlantic concentration, these losses were of the gravest significance. Granted that, by drawing from North America supplies formerly procured from more distant sources, the annual carrying power of the available shipping could be greatly increased, it was very doubtful whether the war could be brought to an end before the depletion of tonnage had reached a point at which, even with the maximum economy in its employment, it would be incapable of fulfilling its essential tasks. Involving, as it did, an attempt to maintain the volume of supplies by drawing in ships from the cross-routes and increasing the frequency of voyages to and from the United Kingdom, the Atlantic concentration had become a desperate gamble with the fast-diminishing reserve of carrying power, on which the Allies depended alike for the sustenance of their armies and peoples, and for the means of continued resistance.

It was obvious in fact that, in default of a substantial reduction in the rate of loss, the Allies were playing a losing game at sea, and everything appeared to hinge on the possibility of establishing an effective convoy system. On June 8th, two days after presentation of the Convoy Committee's report, the First Sea Lord reported to the War Cabinet the success of the two experimental convoys, and stated that the convoy organisation was now nearly complete and that the Admiralty hoped to start weekly convoys of oilers and provision ships in the immediate future. On June 14th Admiral Jellicoe formally approved the report of the Convoy Committee. The first experimental convoy from Hampton Roads was followed by four others during June, and on July 2nd a regular four-day series from that point was inaugurated. On July 10th the first convoy of another series left Sydney, Cape Breton. The Admiralty, however, were still of the opinion that, owing to the shortage of patrol craft, it would be impossible to provide adequate escort for any large proportion of the Atlantic trade.

How urgently such protection was required was shown

by the June losses, which amounted to nearly 420,000 tons. Though considerably smaller than the April total, this figure was about 70,000 tons greater than that for May, and it brought up the total losses since the outbreak of the unrestricted submarine campaign to 1,980,000 tons, an average of nearly 400,000 tons a month. Nearly the whole of the losses during May and June were inflicted by the submarines, and such losses fell with special severity on steamers of ocean-going size. Moreover, the tonnage under repair rose steadily, owing both to the increasing number of ships damaged by torpedo or gunfire, and to the wear and tear of war conditions. On January 31st the tonnage of steamers of 1,600 tons gross and upwards undergoing serious repairs was 181,000; at the end of April it was 262,000; at the end of June 454,000.

This could not go on. Excluding ships completing or under repair, and allowing on the one hand for war and marine losses, and on the other for all gains by new construction or transfer, the available ocean-going shipping had been reduced, since February 1st, by more than one-tenth, giving an annual rate of depletion of about 25 per cent. At this rate the margin of safety would soon disappear beyond all possibility of recovery by accelerated construction or economy in employment. The question of protection had become an over-mastering preoccupation before which all other problems paled.

On July 10th the War Cabinet met to discuss the situation. They had before them a strong memorandum by Sir Norman Hill, calling attention to the losses in the areas of concentration during April and May, and pointing out that those areas had become simple death traps, and that the last reserves of ocean-carrying power were fast being used up. They had before them, also, reports showing that on the previous day, July 9th, 22,000 tons of shipping had been destroyed. On the other hand they had a memorandum by the First Sea Lord, emphasising the strain on the available destroyers and patrol craft, and stating bluntly that it was impossible to procure sufficient ships of this description either to patrol adequately the whole of the areas of approach, or to provide escort on the scale which the Admiralty considered necessary for safety.

Strongly impressed both by the urgency and the difficulty of the problem, the Government resolved to in-

FURTHER INVESTIGATIONS

vestigate the question personally in conjunction with the Admiralty, the Shipping Controller, and representative shipowners. The result of their decision was a series of meetings on July 12th, 13th, and 20th, at which the whole problem of the submarine menace was discussed with the First Sea Lord, Admiral Duff (Assistant Chief of the Naval Staff), Captain Webb (Director of the Trade Division), Commander Henderson, the Shipping Controller, Lord Inchcape, Sir Norman Hill, and Sir John Ellerman.

At these meetings the shipowners naturally refrained from advocating any specific method of protection; but they were clear that, unless the losses in the areas of approach could speedily be reduced, a complete breakdown must follow. After the first meeting on July 12th, they visited the Admiralty, when Admiral Jellicoe stated that, provided eleven American destroyers continued to be available, there was a sufficient force to provide four escorts every eight days, and on the following day Sir Norman Hill suggested that, if that were really all that could be done, such ships only should continue to run as could be given the fair measure of safety provided by such escorts, and that the remainder (about one-half) should be placed in reserve, or utilised on other and safer trade routes. This suggestion approximated closely to one previously made by Sir Leo Chiozza Money, Parliamentary Secretary to the Ministry of Shipping, and the Shipping Controller was instructed to investigate the possibility of such action. On July 20th, however, he reported that, in view of the minimum demands of the Departments and the Allies for supplies essential to the continued prosecution of the war, the formation of a reserve, by cutting down the number of ships in active employment, was altogether out of the question.

Meanwhile the Admiralty had been considering, in conjunction with the shipowners' representatives, the possibility of extending the convoy system. It appeared from the earlier discussions that they still greatly overestimated the number of weekly sailings of ocean-going ships for which escort would be required, and it was suggested that, by employing rather smaller escorts than they had previously considered, and by using trawlers as escorts for slow steamers, protection could be provided for the greater proportion of the steamers under 14 knots in the Atlantic trade. On this basis the Admiralty reconsidered the application of the forces at their disposal, and by July 20th Admiral Duff was able to announce that four homeward convoys were already running regularly, and that it was hoped shortly to have eight convoys every eight days. He could not, at present, contemplate provision for outward convoys, but this was regarded as less important, owing to the greater facility with which outward sailings could be controlled.

On August 2nd, as the result of a suggestion made at the meeting on July 20th, a conference was held at the Admiralty with representatives of the Chamber of Shipping, mercantile masters, and marine superintendents at the ports, for the purpose of discussing the necessary co-operation between the Admiralty and the Mercantile Marine. At this conference the First Sea Lord stated that it had been found impossible to provide a sufficient number of convoys to allow the inclusion of ships over 12 knots. Apart from the shortage of destroyers, the provision of ocean escort was proving a great difficulty, and it was suggested by the shipowners' representatives that this might be overcome, for the faster ships, by giving one vessel in each convoy additional armament, sufficient to enable her to act as escort for the ocean passage.

By this time regular homeward convoys were actually running from four points, giving a total of six sailings every eight days. The first regular convoys from Hampton Roads and Sydney, Cape Breton, sailed, as we have seen, on July 2nd and 10th respectively; on July 14th the New York convoy was inaugurated; on the 26th the first regular convoy left Gibraltar. All these, with the exception of that from Sydney, were among those proposed by the Convoy Committee. The Sydney convoy was an addition to the scheme. The St. Lawrence was now open, and the Admiralty considered that the risks through fog, involved in the original proposal for combining the New York and Canadian trade at Louisburg, at Sydney, or at sea, were sufficiently great to justify a separate convoy for Canadian shipping.

So far as homeward convoys were concerned, the greater part of the scheme embodied in the Convoy Committee's Report was now covered, only the Daker Convoy for the Cape and South Atlantic trade remaining to be established. On the other hand, no escort had yet been provided for the outward trade.

Of the convoys already working, those from Hampton Roads and Gibraltar were scheduled to sail every four, and the remainder every eight days. Both the method of protection and the grouping of the ships followed closely the lines of the report.[1] From each starting point the convoys ran alternately to West Coast and to Channel and East Coast ports in the United Kingdom, thus avoiding the necessity of splitting the destroyer escort, at the cost of some delay to merchantmen in awaiting their appropriate convoy. In order to minimise these delays it was at first arranged that all ships with cargoes of wheat, sugar, timber, or fuel oil should sail in the earliest convoy they could catch, receiving their destination orders from the destroyer escort. Later, when the winter gales rendered the transmission of orders by the destroyers a dangerous business, it was arranged that the Port Convoy Officers in America should cable lists of probable starters a few days before the sailing of a convoy, in order that destination orders might be cabled from Great Britain. In the event of a ship sailing before these orders were received, they were communicated by wireless from the American port to the cruiser escort. It was not, however, for British trade alone that protection was required, and the system was extended, from the first, to cover the passage of French imports. Ships bound to northern French ports were brought on by the East Coast Convoys; those bound to Bay ports were detached on approaching Home Waters, to be brought in by French escort.

For all the North Atlantic convoys the speed was fixed at 8 knots, and no vessels of over 12 knots speed were included, as it was considered that the diminution of risk to such ships would not compensate the delays entailed. Ships of less than 8 knots speed, which were excluded in order to avoid too great a lengthening of the voyage for faster vessels, sailed individually on special routes indicated by the Admiralty. To the Gibraltar Convoy, however, including as it did a large proportion of low-powered vessels in the coal and ore traffic, a speed of 7 knots only was assigned. This rendered the convoy of little use to the through traffic, but the greater part of that traffic had long been diverted to the Cape Route, and it was

---

[1] For details of the protective system, of the internal organisation of convoys, the training courses established for masters, etc., the reader is referred to *Naval Operations* and *The Merchant Navy*.

mainly for the ore trade and homeward-bound colliers and supply ships that protection was required. In all the convoys Allied and neutral vessels bound to British or French northern or Bay ports were included, and the size of each convoy varied at first from about 10 to 20 ships. Experience proved, however, that this number could be safely exceeded, and it was thus possible to bring under escort a much larger number of vessels than at first contemplated.

The whole system demanded, of course, the most careful organisation. At the Ministry of Shipping a Convoy Section was created, under Mr. Norman Leslie, to act as a clearing house for all information with regard to prospective shipping movements, and the destination, speed, cargo, and bunkers of vessels requiring escort. At the Admiralty, the working of the system was placed under the Assistant Chief of the Naval Staff, Rear-Admiral A. L. Duff, to whom Commander Henderson acted as Naval Assistant. For the detail work a Convoy Section was gradually built up under Fleet-Paymaster Manisty, a member of the original Convoy Committee, who was appointed, on June 25th, Organising Manager of Convoys. He was responsible to the Assistant Chief of the Naval Staff, at first directly, and later, from the end of September, through the Director of Mercantile Movements (Captain Frederic A. Whitehead), and his task included the arrangement of all programmes for the assembly, sailing, and dispersal of convoys, the allocation of escorts, and the general executive authority over the whole system. He co-operated also with the officer in charge of the Chart Room, in assigning routes and rendezvous, and arranging for any diversions necessitated by information as to enemy movements.

From the first, the Convoy Sections of the Admiralty and the Ministry of Shipping were in close and constant touch; but no less important was the co-operation, both ashore and afloat, between the Navy and the Mercantile Marine itself. Ships had to be fitted with additional signalling gear and engine-room telegraphs, masters, officers, and crews trained in station-keeping and anti-submarine methods; the experience of the earlier convoys had to be analysed and digested by the Navy and the Merchant Service alike. In this work the great shipowners' organisations rendered invaluable service, both in hastening all necessary additions to the equipment of the ships, and in sifting and forwarding suggestions for improvements in organisation. At the end of the war a generous tribute was paid by the Admiralty both to the support received from the owners and to the zeal and intelligence displayed by the officers and men of the Mercantile Marine in the discharge of their new duties. Nor will the Merchant Service easily forget its debt to those by whom the convoys were organised and to the escorts on whose sleepless vigilance the success of the whole system depended.

From the first the success of the convoys was unmistakable. The losses of British shipping in July amounted to over 360,000 tons; but out of twelve convoys, comprising 205 ships, which had arrived at British ports up to August 4th, two vessels only had been torpedoed. One of these was an oil-tanker which, though severely damaged, ultimately reached port, the other was a wheat-laden vessel from Montreal, which had parted company in a fog. One ship also had been sunk by collision.

With such results to encourage them, the Admiralty made great efforts to increase the number of destroyers, sloops, P-boats, and trawlers available for escort duty. With some reluctance they had agreed to risking the provision of trawler escort only (stiffened by one destroyer) for the slow Gibraltar convoy, and the experiment was fully justified by results. For the American convoys, sloops and destroyers were drawn from the flotillas and patrols, and even from the Grand Fleet. Ocean escort was provided by the cruisers of the old North American Squadron, which had been set free by the entry of the United States into the war, and by Armed Merchant Cruisers withdrawn from the Northern Patrol, whose work had been greatly lightened by the network of agreements and embargoes on which, for the most part, the restriction of enemy supplies now rested. Ocean escort for the New York convoy was usually provided by the United States Navy. Further, the suggestion of using merchantmen themselves as escorts had been anticipated by Admiral Duff, who had been collecting, since May, a stock of 6-inch guns for this purpose. These guns were mounted on selected vessels which, though loading cargoes and navigated by their own masters, were placed under the White Ensign as " Commissioned Escort Steamers," and provided with naval ratings to fight their guns. For the ocean escort of the Gibraltar convoy, a Q-ship or an American Revenue Cutter was commonly held sufficient.

By one means or another sufficient force was collected to enable the Admiralty, during August, not only to complete and extend the original scheme of homeward convoys, but to furnish escort for outward sailings.

The importance of giving effect to the proposal for a convoy from Dakar for the South American, Cape, and West African trade, had been emphasised by the appearance of a new danger in mid-Atlantic. On one or two occasions during the latter part of 1916 submarines had made their appearance so far to the westward as Madeira; but for the ordinary submarine, even of recent type, such an extension of her range of action was exceptional, and she could not hope to operate for more than a few days in such distant waters. The Germans, however, had now converted the commercial submarine *Deutschland* and her sisters into fighting craft, and were building others of the same type. These "submarine-cruisers," as they were called, could carry stores sufficient for a cruise of 150 days, and enabled the enemy to strike effectively in waters to which they had hitherto paid only a flying visit. During June the *Deutschland*, now known as U 155, made her appearance off the West African coast, where she sank two or three ships. On July 4th, she bombarded Ponta Delagada in the Azores, and during July and August she cruised in mid-Atlantic, sinking in the course of ninety days' active operations, 10 steamers and 7 sailing vessels —British, Allied, and neutral—with an aggregate tonnage of nearly 52,000 gross. Among these vessels were some homeward-bound from the Plate with grain cargoes, which were steering wide of the tracks in order to escape danger, and it was evident that, unless the Plate traffic could be brought into the convoy organisation, the losses were likely to be heavy.

Fortunately it proved possible to provide the necessary escort, and on August 22nd the first convoy sailed from Dakar. The original intention was that this convoy should run once every four days, with a speed of 8 knots, but even before the first convoy sailed this arrangement had been modified. It had by now become evident that speed, unless it approached 20 knots, gave little protection against the most recent type of submarine. At the same time, the disadvantage of grouping together ships of widely different speed was fully recognised, both by the Admiralty and by the Ministry of Shipping. Convoy had hitherto been confined to ships of 12 knots and under; but the inclusion of even 12-knot steamers in an 8-knot convoy involved a serious waste of carrying power, and during August arrangements were made both for providing escort to the faster cargo liners which had previously sailed unaccompanied, and for separating the original 8-knot convoys into groups of more approximately equal speed. This scheme involved considerable rearrangement of sailings, as well as of convoy organisation, but so early as August 10th the proposals relating to the liners of 13 knots and over had been approved by Sir Alfred Booth on behalf of the North Atlantic Conference. In the Dakar Convoy, too, the need of separate provision for the faster ships was manifest.

The shipping for which Dakar was a focal point was of a very miscellaneous character, ranging from the Java sugar tramps to the South American and Australasian liners, and it was impossible to combine the various types in one convoy without serious sacrifice of speed. The interval for the Dakar Convoy, which retained a group speed of 8 knots, was accordingly altered from 4 to 8 days, and a second 8-day convoy, with a group speed of 10 knots, was started for the faster ships, who were ordered to assemble at Sierra Leone for the purpose of picking up their ocean escort.

Owing to the large number of trades represented, neither the Dakar Convoy, which averaged ten to a dozen ships, nor the Sierra Leone Convoy of from six to eight vessels, could well be run to a schedule providing, as in the North Atlantic, for regular alternate sailings to East and West Coast ports. It was necessary to bring on together all ships collected at Dakar or Sierra Leone by the sailing date, and split them on their arrival in Home Waters. The Admiralty made, accordingly, special arrangements for reinforcing the escort at the point of separation.

It was on August 11th that the first convoy sailed from Sierra Leone, and during the succeeding fortnight, the revised scheme for the North Atlantic trade was brought into operation. Its basis, as regards the faster cargo liners, was the inclusion of such vessels in the Canadian troop convoys which sailed at irregular intervals from Halifax to Liverpool. These convoys were now fixed to run on a regular schedule, with a sailing every eight days, to include both transports and merchantmen. The chief difficulty arose from the impossibility of making this a " mixed " convoy on the Dakar model, to be separated to East and West Coast ports on arrival in Home Waters. This was overcome by making arrangements with the Atlantic Conference for the faster ships in the London trade to be transferred to Liverpool or other West Coast ports, and replaced by slower ships from the Liverpool services. The minimum speed for the new convoy was fixed at $12\frac{1}{2}$ knots, and it included all liners of this speed and upwards, with the exception of those fast enough to be risked in independent sailings. The first regular convoy left Halifax on September 5th, and consisted of 5 Canadian troopships and 7 merchantmen.

The regrouping of the 8–12-knot vessels was also effected at the beginning of September. Its basis was the alteration of the New York Convoy from a speed of 8 knots to a speed of 10 knots, and from an interval of 8 days to one of 4. At the same time, the sailings of the Hampton Roads Convoy were reduced from one in 4 days to one in 8. The New York Convoy, which still sailed alternately for East and West Coast ports, now included all steamers of 10 knots and upwards which were not good enough for Halifax, or were compelled to come to the East Coast, while the Hampton Roads and Cape Breton Convoys absorbed the slower ships previously sailing from New York. The net result of this rearrangement was that, instead of four 8-knot convoys from North American ports in every eight days, there were now one of $12\frac{1}{2}$, two of 10, and two of 8-knots speed.

The main basis of the North American convoy organisation was now speed rather than trade, and the geographical limits of the original convoys were considerably relaxed. Thus an 11-knot steamer from the Gulf, arriving at Newport News for bunkers, would be sent to New York, to join the 10-knot convoy, unless the date of her arrival synchronised so closely with that of an 8-knot convoy from Hampton Roads that the advantage of an earlier sailing date outweighed the loss of speed involved.

At least equally important with the development of the homeward convoy system was the provision of escort for the outward trade. Finding the attack on a convoy little to their liking, the submarines, now that so large a part of the homeward traffic was adequately protected, were turning their attention to the outward sailings, and the percentage of loss rose among outward-bound vessels as steadily as it fell among those homeward-bound. In response to this new danger, outward convoys were introduced about the middle of August. For these the organisation sketched out in the Convoy Committee's report was modified, in accordance with the experience gained, and for the purpose of synchronising the sailings with the arrival of inward convoys, so that the destroyer escorts which had taken out outward-bound vessels might bring in a homeward convoy.

For vessels from Channel and East Coast ports, wherever bound, the ports of assembly were Falmouth and Devonport. The Devonport Convoy, which sailed about three times in eight days, took the faster ships and had a speed of 10 knots; from Falmouth one $7\frac{1}{2}$-knot convoy sailed in every eight days for the slower vessels.

Outward-bound ships from the West Coast ports assembled at Milford, Queenstown, or Lamlash, from each of which one convoy sailed every eight days. That from Milford, with a speed of $7\frac{1}{2}$ knots, took the slower ships south-bound to the Mediterranean and other destinations. Faster ships from the Bristol Channel bound for America or the South Atlantic, south-about, made their rendezvous at Queenstown. Ships from Liverpool and Glasgow for America or the South Atlantic, proceeded north-about in an 8-knot convoy from Lamlash. The faster liners continued to run independently, whether north- or south-about.

Thus, by September 1917, the convoy system was in full swing. The sailings escorted averaged about 120–130 each way in eight days, and covered the greater part of the shipping on the direct Atlantic trades, or between Gibraltar and the United Kingdom, other than those steamers which were fast enough to dispense with escort. The French coal trade, the North Sea traffic, and the few ships still maintaining communication with Holland were separately provided for.[1]

The only ocean tracks of importance leading through the danger zones, on which convoy was not provided,

[1] From June 1917 the Dutch convoy proceeded in close formation, at uniform speed.

were those between North and South America and the Mediterranean, and between the Cape and South America, and Dakar. The whole traffic of the Mediterranean, through or local, was still destitute of escort while within the Mediterranean itself.[1] This was a big exception, but it was the security of the North Atlantic which was the point of primary importance, and this, in large measure, had been attained. Outward-bound ships were still exposed to attack in the waters immediately surrounding the British Isles, on their way to the port of assembly; but for the greater part of the passage through the danger zone, and above all, in the approach areas, the great majority of ships in the Atlantic trade had adequate protection.

Meanwhile unpleasant evidence had come to hand that the outer seas were still insecure. During May, June, July, and August, seven large steamers, of which five were British,[2] were sunk or damaged by mines off Cape Town, Cape Agulhas, and Bombay. The new menace thus revealed was indeed alarming. It was evident that in spite of sweeping operations, the minefields laid by the unknown raider in Eastern waters were still dangerous; nor was this the full extent of the mischief, for on July 6th the *Cumberland*, of 9,471 tons, owned by the Federal Steam Navigation Company, was blown up off Gabo Island on the Australian coast, and on September 18th the sinking of the Commonwealth and Dominion Liner *Port Kembla*, off Cape Farewell, New Zealand, gave further proof of the wide extent of the danger.

All this was the work of the WOLF, whose extraordinary cruise was still uncompleted. We last saw her in March, heading across the Indian Ocean for the Pacific. On March 30th she was 410 miles west by south from Cape Leeuwin, where she captured and sank a small sailing vessel, and for some little time she cruised between Tasmania and New Zealand, on the look-out for meat ships and colliers bound to Panama or South America.[3] Finding nothing, she proceeded to New Zealand, where she laid two minefields, one at the western entrance to Cook Straits, the channel between the two islands, and the other

---

[1] Except for tankers and other ships with individual escort.
[2] The exceptions were a Spanish steamer sunk off the Cape and a Japanese steamer mined off Bombay.
[3] "The Cruise of the Wolf," *Journal of the Royal United Services Institution*, February 1922. Translated from *Rivista Marittima*, July 1921.

off the north-eastern extremity of North Island, on the track between Auckland and Sydney. It was the Cook Strait minefield, on the track from Wellington, which proved fatal to the *Port Kembla* ; the other field had to wait a little longer for a victim.

From New Zealand the WOLF proceeded to the Kermadic Group to effect engine repairs. Here, by means of a seaplane carried on board, she captured the *Wairuna*, of the Union S.S. Co. of New Zealand, on June 2nd, and took from her a large quantity of coal. Returning to Australian and Tasmanian waters, she laid the minefield by which the *Cumberland* was destroyed, and then proceeded on her return to the Indian Ocean, by way of the Fiji and Solomon Islands and the Dutch East Indies. Three little American sailing vessels and a small Australian steamer were captured on the way, and some time was spent in transferring stores ; but by September she was back in the Indian Ocean. By this time all her mines were expended, and she accordingly made the best of her way back to the Atlantic, capturing on her way a Japanese liner. Her cruise in Eastern and Pacific waters had been equally daring and fortunate. More than once she had escaped detection and destruction by a hair's breadth; but her temerity had been well rewarded ; for though the minefields she had sown at the focal points of Eastern and Australasian trade were, in general, quickly discovered and swept, stray mines frequently escaped detection, and for months after they were originally laid they continued to cause occasional casualties. Although neither the WOLF's own prizes nor the victims of her minefields were very numerous compared with the wholesale destruction of shipping by submarines in Home Waters, they were mostly liners of considerable size, and both the *Cumberland* and the *Port Kembla* were insulated vessels, the *Cumberland* in particular having a very large meat-carrying capacity.

The WOLF was not the only raider in the Pacific during the summer of 1917. The SEEADLER had made her way round the Horn during the spring, and after cruising up the Chilian Coast, struck out for Christmas Island, and proceeded to cruise among the archipelagoes. She was not, however, capable of much mischief, as she avoided the steamer tracks, and after capturing three little American sailing vessels engaged in local trading, she was wrecked among the Society Islands on August 2nd, leaving the

WOLF the only surface raider still at sea. During the SEEADLER's whole career she had captured only 4 steamers (3 British and 1 French), with an aggregate tonnage of 12,000 gross, and 12 sailing vessels of which only 3 were British, with an aggregate tonnage of nearly 18,000.[1] It was a creditable record for a ship of her class, but had little significance in relation to the volume of Allied trade.

Operations in distant seas had, in fact, become a minor, almost a negligible factor in the war against commerce. Had these operations been so multiplied as to compel an extensive diversion of defensive force from the main theatre, they might, indeed, have aided powerfully the submarine attack; but the risks involved in running the gauntlet in the North Sea appear to have acted as a sufficient deterrent. Confined as they were to the activities of two or three stray raiders, such operations could no longer affect sensibly the issue of the conflict. That issue remained to be fought out by the submarines and the convoys which they had called into existence.

The efficiency of the convoy system, as now organised, depended largely on the concentration of shipping on the Atlantic tracks, and that concentration was maintained or accentuated all through the summer of 1917. The Liner Requisition Scheme had been in effective operation since May, and though its formal basis was even yet undetermined, the prolonged negotiations between the Ministry of Shipping and the Liner Conferences were far advanced towards conclusion. The broad principles of the scheme had, indeed, been laid down during the spring; but the adjustment of details was a lengthy and troublesome matter. The financial terms of the proposed " Heads of Arrangement " in particular were as intricate as they were important, especially those relating to the payment to be made in respect of establishment and agency services, including the use of accommodation provided in premises belonging to the Established Lines. Other difficulties arose in connection with the payment of part hire on vessels laid up through marine risks attributable to war conditions. Careful provision had to be made for the adjustment of accounting and other interests between the owners of diverted vessels and the Established Line to whom they were consigned, with a view to maintaining unimpaired

[1] These figures include one small French sailing vessel captured by the SEEADLER's crew after the wreck.

the goodwill and business of each line. By the beginning of August, however, all questions of importance had been satisfactorily settled, with the exception of those relating to War Risks Insurance.

It was a term of the arrangement that the State, which now received the whole earnings of the lines, should take over, as part of the disbursements debited, the full war risks on each vessel. There were, however, difficulties in the way. On the one hand, the shipowners, who had since 1916 been insuring on their own account the difference between the actual current value of entered vessels and the amount insurable under the State Scheme, were unwilling to accept an undertaking by the Government to pay, as for fully requisitioned ships, the *ascertained value* of ships lost by war perils, as an equivalent of the definite values for which they had hitherto been insured. On the other hand, the Government desired to retain the machinery of the War Risks Associations for the adjustment of claims and administration of the scheme. Further, there was a difficulty in adjusting the incidence of calls made by the War Risks Associations, for the purpose of meeting claims in excess of the proportion of premiums received by them under the scheme.

It was finally arranged with the Ministry of Shipping that both the original War Risks Associations and the Excess Values Associations should continue to insure entered vessels, but that as from August 20th, 1917, the whole of these insurances should be reinsured by the State at the full rate of premium received by the Associations. The State thus accepted full liability both for the original entered values of the ships and for the excess values subsequently insured, receiving in return the whole premium on either class of risks. The maximum insurable value in respect of all vessels under the Liner Requisition Scheme was to be fixed by agreement between the Shipping Controller and the Committees of the War Risks Associations, or failing such agreement, by the Shipping Controller ; but inasmuch as the final decision was thus left to the Controller, the owners were given the option, after a loss, of claiming either under the policy, or for the ascertained value at the date of loss. In the latter event, the State, while paying the ascertained value, received the amount due under the policy.

In respect of the period up to August 19th, during which

the ships were still insured on the old basis, the owners were to be entitled to debit all premiums actually paid in respect of voyages on Government account (including an apportionment of premiums under time policies) and a proportion of calls made by the Associations from February 20th to August 19th, both inclusive, based on the proportion of the deficiency under the Government and Excess Value Insurance Schemes attributable to each ship from the date of her entry into Government Service.

This matter being settled, a meeting of the drafting Committee of Chairmen was held on August 22nd, by whom the Heads of Arrangement were finally approved. Formal approval by the Controller followed, and nothing now remained but to agree the valuation of each ship for war risks purposes, settle the form of Auditors' Certificate for voyage accounts, and obtain the signatures of the lines to the Heads of Arrangement.[1]

It will be observed that the new arrangements between the State and the War Risks Associations, while they arose out of the liner requisition negotiations, covered all entered vessels, whether they came under the scheme or no.[2] The State assumed full liability in respect of all such vessels and received all premiums in respect of them. On the date, August 25th, when the new arrangements came into operation, a new scale of premiums also came into effect. For a ninety-one-day time-policy—the form under which practically all liners were insured—the premium was raised from 5 to 9 per cent. For voyage premiums, a schedule of differential rates was introduced, varying with the estimated risk on each route. At the same time, the Board of Trade arranged for the " free " ships running in the French coal trade to be taken out of the Associations, and insured by the State War Risks Office direct, for French account. They also agreed to give much needed assistance to the coasting traffic, by reinsuring 70 per cent. of the

---

[1] Although the Committee of Chairmen acted, in the negotiations, for the lines as a whole, they had no legal power to bind them, and it was necessary for the Heads of Arrangement to be signed separately by each of the Established Lines, who were the responsible parties under the terms of the scheme.

[2] Apart from ships under Liner Requisition, only the few ships that, for one reason or another, remained "free" were affected by the change. Throughout the war the State assumed full responsibility for war risks on fully requisitioned ships; no premiums were paid, and compensation, in the event of loss, was based on the value at the date of loss, as ascertained by agreement or arbitration.

values on a number of small coasting and short-sea traders which, while entered in two Mutual War Risks Associations of their own, were not entered in either of the three " Approved Associations." [1]

The big rise in time premiums now announced reflected, of course, the heavy losses incurred during the spring and summer. There was already a deficit on hull insurance involving a heavy State liability, and though the introduction of the convoy system gave good hopes of a reduction in the rate of loss, it was too early as yet for the effects of that system to be accurately estimated. The majority of the convoys had been running for too short a time to have much influence on the August losses of British shipping, which were nearly as large as in the previous month.[2]

So far as the convoys themselves were concerned, the results to date had been eminently satisfactory. Out of nearly 600 vessels convoyed homewards during July and August, only three were torpedoed in convoy, and one of these was saved. Six others, that had parted company through lack of speed, stress of weather, or mischance, were also torpedoed, and one or two sunk by marine risk, including a steamer in one of the earliest Gibraltar convoys, which had the unusual experience of colliding with an enemy submarine.

Of about 200 steamers which had sailed in outward convoys, three only had been lost. Of these three, two were in the first Lamlash convoy. Owing to the defences of that port being incomplete, this convoy started from Buncrana, and was attacked by two submarines while forming up outside the harbour.

These results were very encouraging. Now that the defences of Lamlash were completed, there was no fear of a repetition of the Buncrana episode, and with greater experience there was every hope that the losses in homeward convoys arising from bad station-keeping or parting company would be gradually eliminated. It was already apparent that the risk to a ship actually in convoy was comparatively small, and it appeared that an effective reply to the submarine attack had at last been found.

[1] Cmd. 98. *Annual Report of Liverpool and London War Risks Insurance Association*, 1919.
[2] 330,000 tons gross.

CHAPTER X

THE NEUTRAL TONNAGE AGREEMENTS
APRIL—JULY 1917

THE unrestricted submarine campaign had presented, from the first, two main problems, that of providing direct protection for ships sailing to or from British and Allied ports, and that of inducing neutral shipping to brave the perils of the barred zones. The problem of defence had been solved in large measure, so far as it concerned the trade of the United Kingdom and Northern France, by the introduction of the Atlantic convoy system. This was not without its bearing also upon the attitude of neutral shipping, for neutral as well as Allied vessels in the Atlantic trades were admitted to the benefits of escort, but the problem of neutral shipping was complicated by the exceptionally heavy risks attaching to the short-distance trades for which the services of neutrals were mainly required, by friction arising out of the blockade regulations, and by the possibilities of direct German pressure on the neutral Governments concerned. Moreover, while British and Allied ships could be kept, by requisition or licence, in the trades deemed most important, there were open to neutral shipowners safe and lucrative fields for the employment of their vessels outside the war zone; and even before the German declaration of February 1st added so greatly to the dangers of war-zone trade, the utmost rigours of bunker pressure had proved barely sufficient to retain neutral shipping in trades where not only was the danger great, but freights had been forced down by the action of the Allied Governments.

By April, as we have already seen, Norwegian and, to a smaller extent, Danish shipping had recovered from the paralysis produced by the announcement of the unrestricted submarine campaign. Full control, too, had been obtained over the majority of ships under the Greek flag; but the enterprise of Danish shipowners was mainly confined to the direct trade with the United Kingdom, and Swedish, Dutch, and Spanish shipowners were almost universally holding back from any form of Allied employment. Nor was the destruction of 191,000 tons of neutral shipping during April likely to produce greater alacrity on their part in the acceptance of Allied charters.

The special dangers to which neutral shipping was exposed had been reduced, during March and April, by the introduction of " controlled sailings " in the French coal trade, and of the Scandinavian Convoy. The organisation of that convoy presented considerable difficulties, owing to the fact that the majority of the vessels were neutrals, and included a large proportion of low-powered steamers, many of them of considerable age. Station-keeping was always indifferent, especially at night, and the convoys were apt to be widely scattered by dawn.[1] Casualties, in consequence, were more numerous than in the majority of the Atlantic convoys; but there was no doubt that the risks of the passage were, to some extent, reduced.

In the French coal trade, the success of the convoys was, from the first, remarkable. As the majority of the ships were slow, the protection provided was, in the main, only trawler escort; but this in itself enabled a larger number of escorting vessels to be provided. Thanks to admirable organisation, the fact that the greater part of the short passage could be traversed at night, and the comparative immunity conferred by shallow draught, the percentage of loss was extraordinarily small. From March to the end of August only 14 vessels were lost, as against a total of 8,825 voyages successfully made in convoy.[2]

The coal-trade convoys, however, provided no protection for ships bound to, or returning from Bay ports south of Brest, or for those engaged in the still more dangerous Mediterranean trade. It was not until the end of July that the institution of the Gibraltar Convoy enabled escort to be given to returning colliers; not until August that the outward convoys were established for the southbound traffic. In the meantime the losses were heavy.

Apart from the courage and enterprise displayed by the Norwegians, the attitude of neutrals in the spring of 1917 gave little hope of any general resumption of sailings

---

[1] Jellicoe, *The Crisis of the Naval War*, pp. 110, 123, 143.
[2] *Ibid.*, pp. 110, 119-20, 143.

to Allied ports. The ship-for-ship policy had been applied with some success, but both that policy and bunker pressure appeared to have reached the limit of their effectiveness, and the only hope of procuring any substantial addition to the neutral tonnage under Allied control lay in direct requisition, or in the conclusion of comprehensive tonnage agreements with neutral Governments or shipowners. Direct requisition had already been applied, with the consent of the Danish shipowners' representatives, to vessels under the Danish flag, and the number so acquired ultimately rose to 24, with an aggregate gross tonnage of about 36,000. No further step in this direction was taken until May, when 11 Dutch steamers, with an aggregate tonnage of 40,000 gross, were requisitioned. These vessels, however, though sailing under the Dutch flag, were owned by companies almost the whole capital of which was held in the United Kingdom, and their seizure was justified by the British Government, not only under the law of angary, but on the ground that the British interests affected could only be adequately protected by bringing the ships under the British flag in order that they might be armed for self-defence.[1]

It was for many reasons neither desirable nor practicable to extend the practice of requisitioning, save as a last resort, to neutral shipping in general; nor could such measures prevent the laying up of ships not actually in an Allied port. Far better results were promised by the conclusion of amicable agreements, where any chance of arranging them existed.

We have seen that, so early as March, tentative suggestions for a coal and tonnage agreement with Norway had been put forward, and had been favourably received. There were, indeed, strong reasons on both sides for coming to some definite arrangement. Although the Norwegian shipowners had shown great determination in running their vessels, it was doubtful how long they could continue to face the terrible losses of war-zone trade. Although trade between the United Kingdom and Norway had hitherto been kept on foot, it was only at a very high cost. Sawn

---

[1] *Correspondence with the Netherlands Government regarding the Requisitioning of British-owned Ships under Neutral Flags* [Cd. 8986], 1918. The companies affected were the Furness Scheepvaart en Agentur Maatschappij, in whom Messrs. Furness, Withy & Co. held a controlling interest, and the Nederlandsche Stoomvaart Maatschappij "Oceaan," in which a controlling interest was held by Messrs. Alfred Holt.

timber freights had risen to £22 per standard as against a normal peace rate of about 22s., and freight on wood pulp, normally about 10s. per ton, was now in the neighbourhood of £10. Outward coal freights rose in proportion, and the consequences were serious to both countries. The combination of prohibitive freights and steady depletion of the available tonnage threatened a complete breakdown of intercourse, while Norwegian tonnage for the still more important French and Italian coal trade and for the carriage of ore from Spain, was increasingly difficult to procure.

In these circumstances the Foreign Office, during April, opened definite negotiations through Sir M. Findlay, H.M. Minister at Christiania, with the Norwegian Shipowners' Association (Norges Rederforbund) and the Norwegian Victualling Commission (Norges Proviantingsdirektorat), with the object of concluding a comprehensive agreement for the employment of Norwegian tonnage in Allied interests, in return for British co-operation in maintaining the coal supply of Norway.

These negotiations were not finally concluded until July. Meanwhile the proposals for a Danish tonnage agreement were revived, and owing to the urgent need of Denmark not only for British coal, but for a guarantee of her supplies of fodder and fertilisers, the new negotiations, backed as they were by the restrictive measures taken in February, made rapid progress.

As regards Holland and Sweden the situation was much less satisfactory. Dutch shipowners still preferred to lay up their ships rather than to allow them to be employed in Allied trade, and though agricultural produce continued to come forward from Holland, it was mainly in British bottoms. In all dealings with Sweden, the hands of the British Government were tied by the importance of preserving the overland transit route to Russia, and still more by the dependence of the Ministry of Munitions on Swedish ore and on supplies of manufactured products such as ball-bearings. In the circumstances, requisitioning was impossible, and the most that could be done was to continue the strict application of the ship-for-ship policy in Anglo-Swedish traffic, and the embargo on Swedish shipping calling at British ports or intercepted by the patrols. These measures had little effect in inducing Swedish shipping to move. Direct traffic between Great Britain and Sweden was almost at a standstill, and hardly any Swedish tonnage was procurable for Allied services. Moreover, as the Swedish Government stubbornly refused to enter into or permit any negotiations involving restrictions on the employment of Swedish shipping, all hope of alleviating the situation by the conclusion of a tonnage agreement had to be abandoned.

Sweden, however, was feeling acutely the loss of British coal, which was the more serious inasmuch as German shipments during the first three months of 1917 had fallen short by 80 per cent. of the 1916 figures. Equally serious was the situation caused by the detention of her cereal and other imports from overseas, and though no progress could be made in negotiations for Swedish tonnage, the lever thus provided was turned to account in procuring the release of British and Allied vessels held up in the Baltic by the mining of the Kogrund Passage. The Swedish Ministry responsible for this step fell from power in April, and the new Government, though little more inclined than their predecessors to make concessions with regard to Swedish shipping, were less hostile in their general attitude towards the Allies. Hence, in order to end a situation fast becoming intolerable, they were willing to come to terms on the Kogrund dispute. By an exchange of notes on May 8th, it was agreed that the Swedish Government would facilitate the passage of British and Allied vessels in the Baltic through the mined channel, and would guarantee them protection against attack while in Swedish territorial waters, in return for the release of 14 Swedish steamers held up in British ports, and permission for 19 other Swedish ships, with cereal cargoes, to proceed by the North-about Route after calling at Halifax. Arrangements were at once made by the Ministry of Shipping for bringing out the Baltic vessels, and it was understood that the specified Swedish ships would be released as and when the escaped steamers arrived.[1]

Meanwhile the negotiations with the Spanish Government had broken down. A convention providing for

[1] The arrangements for the escape of ships in the Baltic were concluded through the same Anglo-Swedish Syndicate as had acted in 1916. The ships began to move in June, and by the end of August the majority of them had come out. Fifteen, which had reached a Swedish port in 1916, came out at their own risk and expense, and were granted freedom from requisition, subject to direction as to trade and freights. The remainder were requisitioned in the Baltic, the Ministry taking all risks and bearing all expenses. A few Belgian steamers were also brought out. Whenever possible, cargoes, mostly of sawn timber, were procured for the ships.

permission to time-charter Spanish shipping up to a total of 400,000 tons dead-weight, in return for coal export and bunker concessions, was actually signed on April 12th, but a week later the Romanones Cabinet fell, and their successors refused to ratify the convention. All that could be done, in the circumstances, was to make the best arrangements possible with individual shipowners. During May agreements were concluded by the Cunard Company, acting for the Ministry of Shipping, with three of the chief Spanish shipping companies, by which the owners agreed to keep a specified number of steamers running continuously in the ore trade, in return for certain facilities in obtaining coal export licences from the United Kingdom or the United States. Although the number of ships affected was not large—17 vessels then running and 2 others to be added on completion—the fact that they were to be continuously employed in a service of vital importance gave the agreements considerable significance.

The negotiations with Denmark had a more fortunate issue. By an agreement concluded in June, it was provided that the British Government should license the export of coal to Denmark in Danish ships, at the rate of 100,000 tons a month, free of any return cargo conditions. In return for this concession, the Danes agreed that 200,000 tons dead-weight of Danish shipping, including the vessels already requisitioned, should be time-chartered to (or requisitioned by) the British Government at a rate of 45s. per ton, the charterers undertaking war risks insurance. No Danish ships were to be laid up without the consent of the British Government, and all vessels outside the 200,000 tons, not engaged in the trade of Denmark, Iceland, and the Faroe Islands, were to be employed in trades approved by the Inter-Allied Chartering Executive.

This was a substantial gain, but still more important was the result of the negotiations with Norway, which had gone forward amicably all through May and June. By the end of July a complete agreement had been arrived at on all points, and the result was a genuine triumph for British diplomacy.

The original proposals had been for the employment of the bulk of Norwegian tonnage in Allied interests, in return for a guarantee of coal export licences; but owing to the intensification of the submarine campaign, it became evident at an early date that a mere guarantee of export licenses would be far from providing adequately for the Norwegian supplies. No fewer than 27 Norwegian steamers were sunk by submarines in the North Sea during March, 19 in April, and 10 in May. The institution of the Lerwick Convoy went a long way in reducing the risk; but it was evident that, so long as a large proportion of the Anglo-Norwegian traffic was carried on by unarmed steamers, the risk must always be considerable. Not only the Norwegian coal supply but the vital Narvik ore trade was affected, and both parties were profoundly interested in providing a remedy. It was accordingly provided that the British Government should have the right to requisition or time-charter all Norwegian vessels previously engaged in the North Sea trade, with the exception of the regular cargo liners, and should replace them by defensively armed British ships of equivalent capacity. The British Government further undertook to license coal exports to Norway up to a maximum of 250,000 tons a month,[1] and to carry the coal exported on a cost basis, calculated on the rate of hire paid for the requisitioned Norwegian vessels, and the actual cost of running the substituted ships. The hire for Norwegian ships requisitioned or time-chartered was to be 35*s*. per deadweight ton per month for steamers over 1,000 tons deadweight, and 45*s*. for smaller ships, war risks to be borne by the British Government.

Ships requisitioned or time-chartered under this substitution scheme were, of course, available for war-zone trade, and if requisitioned, as the majority of them were, were armed and run under the British flag. But it was a further term of the agreement that all other Norwegian ships not now required for the necessary service of Norway herself[2] should, on completion of their current charters, be offered to the Inter-Allied Chartering Committee on terms equivalent to the 35*s*. requisition rate.

By the end of July the total tonnage of all nationalities time-chartered to the Inter-Allied Committee was roughly 930,000 dead-weight, of which about 585,000 tons was Greek. Greek shipping was no longer neutral; for, follow-

---

[1] This was a maximum figure never actually approached. The real limit was the cargo capacity of the shipping employed.
[2] There were certain other small exceptions, such as whalers, fruit steamers, and other vessels of special construction; but special terms were subsequently arranged for some of these, which the Chartering Committee were anxious to secure.

ing the abdication of King Constantine on June 12th, a new Government had been formed, with M. Venizelos at its head, and on June 27th Greece declared war on Germany, Austria, Turkey, and Bulgaria. This change of status made, however, no effective difference to the working of the Greek Ship Scheme. The new Government agreed that all Greek steamers over 1,000 tons gross, with the exception of 15, should be time-chartered to the Inter-Allied Committee, and that those under that tonnage should be controlled by the French Naval Authorities, and save in so far as they were required for the Greek coasting trade, should be employed on Allied service in the Mediterranean. In return, the British Government undertook, through the Wheat Executive, the supply of Greece with cereals, and it was estimated that the 15 ocean-going steamers excluded from the agreement would suffice for the supply of the country with other necessary imports. Additional assistance in the carriage of cereals and other commodities was occasionally given by the release for single voyages of steamers allocated to France, Italy, or the Wheat Executive.

Apart from Greek shipping, the bulk of the time-chartered tonnage was still Norwegian. Since the end of April, no further Japanese vessels had been fixed, all further negotiations for the employment of Japanese tonnage being left to the United States Government; no Spanish shipowner could be induced to accept a charter, and the fixture of vessels under the Swedish, Dutch, and Danish flags numbered little more than a dozen all told. The Anglo-Danish agreement was, however, gradually bringing forward Danish steamers in rather greater numbers, and a few charters of Swedish vessels bore witness to the easing of the situation by the conclusion of the Kogrund Agreement.

Of Norway's steam tonnage about one-half was now employed in Anglo-Norwegian trade or in the interests of the Allies, and it must be remembered that most of the ships carrying coal to Norway returned with Narvik ore or other cargoes of importance to Great Britain. Of Danish tonnage, about one-quarter was indexed as trading with or for the Allies, but this included a number of colliers permitted to arrive in ballast in order to load coal for Denmark. In the essential Allied services Danish shipping counted as yet for very little; but as fast as ships came forward under the agreement, they were placed in the French coal trade, to which they were peculiarly suited. Deliveries, however, were slow. Shipping under the Swedish, Dutch, and Spanish flags was of little account. More than a quarter of the steam tonnage of Sweden was actually laid up, and the participation of Swedish ships in Allied trade was confined mainly to the direct traffic between their own country and the United Kingdom. In this they became rather more active during the summer, as a result of Sweden's need for coal and the application of the ship-for-ship policy. Dutch shipowners still stood aloof, and though negotiations for a commercial agreement had been reopened by the Spanish Government, no tonnage concessions had yet been obtained, and the obnoxious "38 per cent." and "10 per cent." orders continued to hamper the ore traffic.

Taking Scandinavian, Dutch, and Spanish shipping together, the entrances with cargoes at ports in the United Kingdom during July, amounted to 200,000 tons net, as against 725,000 tons in the previous year, a decline of 72 per cent. The clearances were 456,000 tons as against 1,082,000, a decline of nearly 58 per cent. For the whole period of six months since the proclamation of the barred zone the decreases work out at 71 per cent. and 64 per cent. respectively. Bad as these figures were, they would have been far worse but for the enterprise and determination displayed by Norwegian shipping, which accounted in July for more than half the entrances and nearly three-quarters of the clearances.

With the conclusion of the Norwegian and Danish agreements and the improvement, slight as it was, in relations with Sweden, an increase might reasonably be expected, not only in the entrances and clearances at British ports, but in the number of ships ready to accept a time-charter from the Inter-Allied Executive. Much, however, depended on the prospects of American co-operation. A very large block of neutral tonnage was employed in American waters, in the trade between North and South America, or in the Pacific, and the whole of the vessels so employed could obtain bunkers at depôts in the United States territory. The combined effect of intensified submarine warfare and freight limitation schemes had led to many neutral steamers endeavouring, during the winter of 1916, to escape into the American trades, and the counter-measures taken by the Bunker Committee had produced considerable irritation in the United States. On the entry of America into the war, it was hoped that the United States would co-operate, both as regards bunker control and centralised chartering, with the European Allies. Without such co-operation it was, indeed, impossible to render the control of neutral shipping completely effective, or even to enforce the provisions of the tonnage agreements, so far as they affected ships previously trading in American interests. So far, however, no organisation for the control of chartering had been established in the United States, and it was not until July 14th that the American Government took power to control the export of coal from the States.

CHAPTER XI

CARRYING POWER AND IMPORTS
FEBRUARY—JULY 1917

THE spring of 1917 had been, beyond all comparison, the most critical period for Allied commerce since the initial dislocation caused by the war was overcome. The summer months witnessed the turn of the tide. By the introduction of the ocean convoy system in July, and its extension during August to cover outward sailings and the balance of homeward sailings in the Atlantic trades, a check had been administered to the submarines which, though its full effect could not yet be seen, could reasonably be relied upon to prevent a repetition of such losses as were suffered at the outset of the unrestricted campaign. By the tonnage agreements with Norway and Denmark, the paralysing effect of that campaign on neutral shipping in Allied services was, to some extent, countered.

The turn, however, had come only just in time: indeed, it was impossible as yet to assert with certainty that it had not come too late. During the first six months of unrestricted submarine warfare—February to July inclusive—2,350,000 tons of British shipping had been lost through war casualties, besides about 1,500,000 tons of shipping under Allied and neutral flags. By far the heaviest sufferer other than Great Britain was Norway, with 440,000 tons. France and Italy had each lost over 200,000, Greece and the United States over 100,000 tons.[1] The fleets of the remaining Powers had suffered less, either because they were relatively insignificant in size, or because they took little part in the trade of the barred zones. The total reduction in the world's tonnage exceeded 3,850,000 tons.

Even these figures fail altogether to convey the total

---

[1] France, 220,000; Italy, 208,000; Greece, 152,000; United States, 109,000.

HEAVY NET LOSSES

effect of the unrestricted submarine campaign on the supply of carrying power. Many ships injured by torpedo, gunfire, or mine were yet brought to port. In Great Britain alone the ocean-going tonnage under repair had risen, as we have seen, to over 400,000 tons, and the total was still going up.[1] Still more important was the reduction in the number of voyages, due to delays and deviation arising directly from the submarine menace. The introduction of the convoy system promised to reduce, in large measure, the necessity for direct official detention of shipping; but in its initial stages, it added appreciably both to the time spent by ships in port, and to the length of the sea passage, owing to the necessity of waiting for escort or steaming to a port of assembly, and the reduction in the speed of the faster ships. Finally, as regards the carrying power available for British and Allied trade, there was the withdrawal or diversion of neutral shipping, which the ship-for-ship policy and tonnage agreements had only partially overcome.

British shipbuilding, as has been seen, had failed altogether to keep pace with the rate of loss, and it was already becoming doubtful whether delivery of the vessels building in American yards would ever be obtained. Allowing on the one hand for war and marine casualties, and on the other hand for new construction, ships purchased abroad, requisitioned neutrals, and a few ships which had already escaped from the Baltic under the Kogrund Agreement, the grand total of ocean-going shipping had been reduced from 3,731 steamers of 1,600 tons gross and upwards on January 31st to 3,344 on July 31st, and from 16,600,000 tons gross to 15,200,000. Thus the reduction in numbers amounted to over 10 per cent., and in tonnage to over 8 per cent. These figures, however, include ships completing or under repair, and if such be excluded, the reduction in available tonnage works out at nearly 12 per cent.[2]

A net loss at the rate of 20 per cent. per annum, though it was a long way below the high-water mark reached in April, was ruinously heavy. There was, indeed, every reason to believe that the ratio would be permanently reduced by the introduction of the convoy system; but

---

[1] In August it reached 537,000.
[2] These figures include tankers, prizes, and some vessels on Colonial Register.

the real gravity of the position lay in the fact that, even before February 1st, the available tonnage had been unequal to the demands upon it. We have seen that, so early as March Requisitioning Branch were calculating on a serious deficiency of tonnage during the summer months, and that during April the Tonnage Priority Committee were obliged to press both the Ministry of Food and the Ministry of Munitions for a reduction of their demands. In May, when the Committee met again to discuss the programme for the summer months, there was again a heavy deficiency to be adjusted. Throughout the summer the shipping available fell far short of the demands of the Departments, and it was continually necessary to revise the import programmes.

In one respect the strain on tonnage had been somewhat eased. The Russian Revolution had not led to a suspension of the White Sea programme, as the Russian Provisional Government had announced its intention of carrying on the war with vigour; but the situation was so uncertain that the British Government were anxious to minimise the tonnage risked in the White Sea service, and gave instructions towards the end of April that some part of the allocations for the Russian programme should be postponed until the situation cleared. To postpone the programme altogether was impossible if the Russian res'stance was to be sustained, and from April onwards the number of ships on White Sea service steadily increased; but the tonnage employed was decidedly below the original estimate, and rather less than was allocated in the previous year. To the Vladivostok service no requisitioned tonnage was allocated this year, arrangements being made instead to load Russian Government cargo on the Conference liners, up to 80 per cent. of their capacity.

In the actual employment of the vessels considerable economies were effected. For the 1917 season the Ministry of Shipping took over the organisation of the Russian Government Committee's Transportation Department, and by improvements in organisation and the elimination of much paper work hitherto required, succeeded in securing a more rapid despatch, the average rate of loading for general cargo rising from 390 to 597 B/L tons a day. Messrs. Mathwins continued to look after the coal shipments, but during May the control of thirty Russian colliers hitherto in the hands of the Russian Government

Committee was transferred to the Ministry of Shipping, who appointed the Ellerman-Wilson Line as managers. Thanks to these arrangements, it became possible to effect a reduction in the number of requisitioned steamers allocated to the service without reducing, to a dangerous extent, the volume of supplies.

Even with a reduction in the number of ships allocated, the strain of the White Sea Programme was too heavy to be borne, in the conditions which prevailed, without a grave effect on British imports. We have seen that, in their Memorandum of April 16th, the Ministry of Shipping stated they were asking France for the return of a hundred requisitioned ships, on condition that Great Britain and Russia should forgo their claim to tonnage chartered by the Inter-Allied Committee. The possibility of such revision of allocations had been provided for by the Clémentel Agreement, and the claim was pressed, with the result that about fifty steamers of an average size of 4,500 tons dead-weight, or their equivalent, were actually withdrawn during May and June, the withdrawal of the remainder being postponed until July and August in deference to French representations.

An additional reason for this withdrawal was the crisis in the Italian coal supply produced by the continued withdrawal of neutral shipping. Great efforts were being made to wipe off the deficit, and a means of economising tonnage and minimising risk had been found in the despatch of colliers to Blaye, a French port on the Gironde, whence the cargoes could be forwarded to Italy by rail. Blaye, however, could not, in the spring of 1917, handle more than about 50,000 tons a month, though this amount was doubled or trebled at a later period, and the bulk of the cargoes had to go to the Mediterranean. Exposed to attack, as they were, throughout the whole length of the route, the losses among the colliers were heavy, and during May it was decided that the shipment of coal to Italy from the United States should no longer be discouraged, the lesser risk providing compensation for the longer voyage, while neutral tonnage could more readily be obtained.

In addition to coal, a large amount of assistance had to be given in the carriage of Italian wheat, and despite the rapid reduction of British tonnage, the proportion in Italian service was fairly steadily maintained during the first half of 1917. The combined steel and oat service to France and Italy ran on the same lines as in the previous year, the total shipments averaging about 120,000 tons a month. Including ships directed to Allied ports by the Wheat Executive, and allowing for ships loading outwards for the Allies and homewards for the United Kingdom, the total of British ocean-going shipping on Allied service during the first half of 1917 amounted to over 12 per cent. of the available tonnage other than oil-tankers not available for ordinary cargoes.[1] In addition, a large number of British steamers under 1,600 tons gross were employed in the French coal trade.

Tonnage in the employment of the Army and Navy rose considerably at the beginning of the year. The demands of the Salonika expedition were heavy; the operations in Mesopotamia, and the requirements of the East African campaign, which was proving very troublesome, were on the increase. The strain of the Mesopotamian operations was increased by the very indifferent berthing facilities in the Persian Gulf, and the provision of bunkers for shipping on the East African coast was also a source of continual anxiety, as it caused long delays to colliers. In March 1917, Salonika, Egypt, Mesopotamia, and East Africa accounted between them for 335 ships of 1,600 tons gross and upwards, and so severe was the strain, both on tonnage and escort, that the question of abandoning some or all of these distant expeditions had to be taken seriously into consideration.

This, fortunately, proved to be unnecessary, owing to the check given to the submarine campaign by the introduction of convoy. Meanwhile, considerable economies had been effected. Cross-Channel transport had been greatly improved as a result of the investigations made at the close of the previous year, the reorganisation of the transport arrangements in France under Sir Eric Geddes,[2] and the development of a cross-Channel railway ferry service. By July 1917 the rate of discharge of cargo at the Northern French ports was nearly twice as great as at the end of 1916, though the tonnage employed had not increased. In January sanction was obtained for a general increase of 20 per cent. in the number of men carried on

---

[1] In March the total was 1,939,000 tons, 13·2 per cent. of the whole; in June 1,692,000 tons, 12·4 per cent. Available tonnage includes prizes, but excludes ships repairing or completing.

[2] See Vol. II, pp. 374-5.

British transports. The overland route to Salonika, through Italy, was developed; bunkering arrangements were overhauled. By one means or another the ocean-going tonnage in naval and military service, excluding oilers, was cut down from just under 4,000,000 tons in February to 3,400,000 in July. Even so, it still amounted to more than a quarter of the total.

To the shipping available for the trade of the United Kingdom considerable additions had been made by withdrawals from the inter-foreign and Dominion services, as well as through the economies effected by the Admiralty and War Office; but so heavy had been the losses that, against a total of over 7,400,000 tons in January, there was available in June only 6,600,000 and in July only 6,425,000 tons.

The carrying power of the available tonnage had, however, been considerably increased by the redistribution of trade, and the concentration of both tramp and liner tonnage on the shorter routes. This had not yet been in progress long enough for its effects to be fully manifest, and against those effects must be set the increased delays caused by the intensified submarine menace; but they were already visible, especially in the very heavy arrivals of grain from North America during June and July, and it was mainly thanks to this rearrangement of services that the shrinkage in imports fell short of the reduction of tonnage.

Much also was due to the work of the Port and Transit Committee in keeping the ports free from the worst phases of congestion. Their greatest difficulty arose, of course, from the strain imposed on the West Coast ports, not only by the Atlantic concentration, but by the routeing of vessels to such ports in order to minimise submarine risk. Owing to the very heavy losses in the Channel there was, naturally, a strong desire to use the West Coast ports up to the utmost limit of their capacity. The question was brought into special prominence by the sinking of several large liners bound for London, which had been torpedoed on their way up Channel, after calling, to land passengers or for Admiralty instructions, at a south-western port, and constant pressure was brought to bear for the diversion of such ships from the London trade. The problem, however, was not an easy one, nor was it simply a matter of the convenience of shipowners and importers. The

West Coast ports had only a limited margin of importing power. Any large increase in the demands upon them would entail the provision of increased accommodation and equipment, and of housing for the labour transferred. In view of the immense demands now being made by the fighting services and the Ministry of Munitions on manpower and plant, the extent to which labour and material could be allocated to port development was strictly limited. Moreover, the real governing factor was not the receiving capacity of the ports, but their power of distributing the cargoes received to those who were to use them.[1] This power was already strained, owing to the military demands on railways and road transport, and the effects of recruiting. In June 1917 it was calculated that, owing to the immense increase in military and munitions traffic, the total demand on the carrying power of the railways was over 30 per cent. greater than in time of peace. Here again, every proposal for the construction of new lines or the replacement of rolling-stock worn out by the abnormal traffic, had to be considered in the light of the competing military demands on the resources of the country. In this connection, too, it must be remembered that the demands of the Armies in France, and of France herself, on engines and rolling stock were continually increasing and were only met with the greatest difficulty.

The difficulties of diversion may be illustrated by the fact that, of 27,000 tons of cargo discharged at Plymouth in the early summer of 1917, by six ships originally bound for London, only 7,000 tons was ever forwarded to London, and even this caused a block which resulted in holding up temporarily 14,000 trucks. The remainder of the cargoes was accordingly distributed in the West. The actual average time occupied in the discharge of the ships at Plymouth was three weeks, as against a normal seven days in London.

Increased distribution by coaster would not, in itself, have solved the problem of eliminating submarine risk, though it might have reduced it by multiplying the number and diminishing the size of targets in the most dangerous areas. Whether desirable or no, it was impossible. The combined effect of requisitioning, losses, and the restriction of railway rates, had gradually reduced the general coasting trade until, in the first six months of 1917, the tonnage

[1] Cf. Vol. II, Chapter IV.

arrived and departed with cargoes was 16 per cent. less than in the same period of the previous year, and considerably less than half of what it had been in 1913. Movements between Great Britain and Ireland, on the other hand, were comparatively stable, owing to the amount of military traffic involved. To assist in the maintenance of this traffic Mr. H. F. Burgess was appointed, in June, Director of Cross-Channel Services, for the purpose of co-ordinating the arrangements for the handling of traffic at the Irish ports. In the same month a Home Trade Branch, under Mr. A. H. Read, was formed in the Ministry of Shipping, and entrusted with the control both of cross-Channel and coasting traffic.

It was the question of distribution which, above all else, restricted the diversion of trade from the East to the West Coast; but the Wheat Commission and other importing departments naturally gave the West Coast ports as much preference as was possible. Although the total volume of traffic at the majority of the ports fell off with the decrease in entrances, the proportion of imports handled on the West Coast steadily increased, and the actual volume was quite as great as the ports, with their depleted resources, could readily handle. The difficulties were increased by the fact that, owing both to the large-scale operations of the Departments, and to the effect of deviations and routeing, ships tended to arrive in large batches and at irregular intervals.

Despite these difficulties, the condition of the ports during the first half of 1917 showed a distinct improvement. The two main objects which the Port and Transit Committee had sought—pooling of railway wagons and adequate development of the Transport Workers' Battalions—had now been achieved. The wagons and sheets owned by the companies had been pooled during 1916, and as we have seen, powers had now been taken for the compulsory pooling of privately owned trucks. Great assistance also, in the co-ordination of port and railway organisation had been received from a Joint Committee, consisting of the Railway Executive Committee and representatives of all Government Departments and Committees interested in transport. This Committee, which held its first meeting on March 21st, enabled transit problems to be considered as a whole with greater clearness than had yet been obtainable, and greatly facilitated the adjustment of departmental demands to the facilities available.

Meanwhile the Illingworth Committee [1] had appointed a travelling sub-committee to visit the ports, and as a result of the reports received, put forward, in July, a proposal that they, the Illingworth Committee, should be kept in being as an advisory body on both port and railway problems, with a right of direct reference to the Government. This proposal was strongly opposed by the Shipping Controller, on the ground that the information obtained by the visiting sub-committee had only confirmed the importance of questions with which the Port and Transit Committee was already dealing, and that nothing but confusion could arise from an unnecessary multiplication of authorities. As a result of his representations, the Government ultimately decided to reject the proposal, and the Illingworth Committee ceased to exist.

With regard to the supply of labour, the proposal made by the Shipping Controller in April for bringing up the strength of the Transport Workers' Battalions to 15,000 men had not yet been adopted, but during February the authorised strength was increased from 10,000 to 10,930. By the middle of April that strength had been raised, and though it was not quite maintained, the actual strength during this period was always well over 10,000. The average number of men daily employed in actual work at the ports rose from 2,131 in January to 4,702 in April, and 5,760 in June. By July 31st the number of days' work performed since the raising of the first battalion had reached 944,436. When not at work, the men were engaged in the completion of their military training, and their progress as soldiers gave complete satisfaction to the inspecting officers.

In two respects the work of the battalions proved particularly valuable. They were of the greatest assistance in the discharge of heavy cargoes, such as ore, which had been giving great trouble owing to the enlistment of the strongest dock workers, and they were invaluable at the smaller ports, where the local labour supply was quite unable to deal with any sudden rush of shipping. Thanks mainly to the work done by men of the battalions and to the improved supply of railway trucks, the average rate of ore discharge at Glasgow rose steadily from 572 tons

[1] See p. 70, *supra*.

a day in January to 1,204 tons in April, while during March and April the average discharge of ore cargoes in all ports (including Sundays, holidays, and days of arrival and departure) was at the high daily rate of 963 tons. Further efforts to speed up discharge were made at various ports during the following months by the provision of additional mechanical appliances, by speeding up acceptance of ore at the works, and by the formation, when necessary, of dumps at the docks. As regards the smaller ports, men of the battalions were working during July at thirty-three of such ports, and gave great assistance both in dealing with commercial cargoes and in military transport.

So successful had the scheme proved that, during April, arrangements were made, in consultation with the Railway Executive Committee and the National Union of Railwaymen, for extending the scope of the battalions to railway work, and in the following month application for assistance was received from the Canal Commission. Such extensions of the scope of the battalions had not yet, however, progressed beyond the experimental stage.

Many suggestions had been made that the receiving capacity of the West Coast ports should be increased by continuous night and day work on a system of shifts, and during May the Port and Transit Committee made enquiries on the subject. All the port authorities, however, were unanimously of the opinion that, except for coal, the proposition was impracticable; that a full day and half a night was the utmost attainable; and that even this could not be maintained throughout the week. Wherever possible, however, steps were taken to increase the capacity of the ports, by providing additional accommodation and equipment, and the situation at Liverpool, in particular, was considerably eased by an extensive use of motor lorries for the removal of goods.

The net result of all the efforts that had been made was illustrated by the fact that in June 1917, only four vessels (all at Newcastle) were waiting for berths at the eleven great ports, as against a total of fifty-two in November 1915, when the Port and Transit Committee were first appointed; there was a shortage of railway wagons at one port only (Newcastle) as against nine in November 1915; and the movements on the railways were reported as normal or satisfactory at nine ports instead of three.

The only real cause of anxiety was the pressure of the immense shipments of wheat and flour which were now coming forward from North America. On this point the Committee were in close touch with the Royal Commission on Wheat Supplies, whom they pressed to stow back the grain inland, as far as possible, in order to release the storage accommodation at the ports to deal with incoming cargoes.

Throughout all this period the Port and Transit Committee had maintained close touch with the Ministry of Shipping. Though not brought within the organisation of the Ministry, they sat in the same building, and the fact that the Director of Transport and Shipping was a member of the Committee further assisted the co-ordination of effort. Some more formal machinery of co-operation was, however, felt to be desirable, and at the end of May a Port Branch was formed within the Ministry for the special purpose of liaison with the Committee and the Railway Executive. The Director of this Branch was Mr. L. A. P. Warner, Deputy General Manager of the Mersey Docks and Harbour Board, who had previously served on the staff of the London & North-Western Railway and thus combined dock and railway experience. The Branch, whose staff, at its maximum, numbered only six, worked chiefly through and with the Port and Transit Committee, which retained its independent status, and proved a valuable assistant in obtaining priority for labour and material required in connection with the extension of port facilities, especially at the West Coast ports, and in adjusting the routeing of vessels, in convoy or otherwise, to the capacity of the ports.

On the other side of the Atlantic also, the conditions at the ports had given rise to considerable anxiety, though the trouble there was not so much actual congestion as lack of co-ordination between the authorities responsible respectively for the rail and sea transport of Government-owned goods. Prior to 1916 there had been no direct official supervision of shipments from North America, with the exception of those to Russia, which were looked after by a New York branch of the Russian Purchases Committee under Mr. T. S. Catto. For all British Government purchases in the United States, Messrs. Lunham and Moore acted as forwarding agents, while in Canada, the whole supervision of transport services was conducted through the organisation of the Canadian Pacific Railway Company. As regards Canada these arrangements worked well, but in the United States difficulties arose early in 1916, owing to the wide extension of Government control over both imports and shipping. On many occasions requisitioned space had to be abandoned at the last moment, owing to the non-arrival of cargo, and the North Atlantic lines urged the necessity of setting up some official organisation to do the work of the commercial machinery that had been displaced. In March 1916 the Ministry of Munitions accordingly appointed Mr. E. J. Kerr, of the Pennsylvania Railway, to supervise the rail transport of munitions shipments, and in the following July the Transport Department sent out Lieutenant Connop Guthrie and Lieutenant M. Faulknor, R.N.V.R., to open an office in New York. Under their supervision, the shipment of general Government cargoes, the bulk of which had previously been shipped from New York, was widely decentralised, and a much closer adjustment attained between the arrival of Government goods at the various ports and the requisitioned space available.

On the appointment of the Shipping Controller, the New York Office of the Transport Department was transferred to the Ministry of Shipping, for whom the Canadian Pacific Railway continued to act as representatives in Canada.[1] The New York organisation consisted at this time of two main departments, one of which allocated shipments to requisitioned space in the liners, while the other superintended the loading of all tramps consigned to Messrs. Furness, Withy & Co. In addition, there was Mr. Catto's Russian forwarding department, which also came under the aegis of the Ministry. In February 1917 a Grain Traffic Department was established, to superintend the movement of cereals by rail, in conjunction with the American Wheat Export Company,[2] agents for the Royal

[1] No change in the Canadian organisation was made until July 1918, when the Shipping Controller appointed Sir Arthur Harris as his official representative. The Canadian Pacific Railway, however, continued to provide offices and staff.

[2] This Company was incorporated under American law with a monopoly of all cereal exports to the Allies. The Wheat Export Company of Canada was a similar organisation. In India and Australia the purchases were effected through Wheat Commissioners, co-ordinating the work of various controlled firms. In addition the Wheat Section appointed shipping agents in the various exporting and Allied countries, to superintend the arrangements for loading, despatch, and discharge. In Italy, where the

Commission on Wheat Supplies, and other departments were subsequently added to cope with the extension of Government imports.

Throughout the first half of 1917, however, the control of munitions movements on the United States railways remained in the hands, not of the Ministry of Shipping, but of the Ministry of Munitions, and this division of responsibility led to a certain amount of confusion which adversely affected the grain shipments from American ports. The Government accordingly decided in May 1917 that the Shipping Controller's New York office should take over the Munitions Traffic Department and assume sole responsibility for all railway movements of Government-owned goods. This decision was carried into effect in August, and contributed materially to an improvement in the situation which was the more important now that tonnage was being concentrated on the North Atlantic tracks.

In addition to the Atlantic concentration and the steps taken to clear the ports, there was a third factor which had considerable effect in off-setting the decrease in available tonnage. This was the restriction of imports. The primary object of the import restrictions was, of course, to secure that, when carrying power was inadequate, it should be essential commodities that were carried and non-essentials that were shut out; but the effect of restricting drastically the imports of bulky materials, such as timber, led also to an actual substantial increase in the weight-carrying power of the ships. In a comparison of the imports for May with those of January, it was estimated that, while the ship-carrying power as shown by the entrances was smaller by 10 per cent., there was an increase of 4 per cent. in the weight of the cargoes carried, the chief decreases being in timber, cotton and jute, and miscellaneous foodstuffs, while the most notable increases were in wheat and flour, and iron ore.

For the six months ending July—that is to say, the first six months of unrestricted submarine warfare—the entrances of British shipping showed a decrease of under 5·5 per cent. on the previous half year. That the decrease in entrances was so much smaller than might have been expected from the reduction in tonnage was due mainly

conditions of discharge were generally bad, the Cunard Company acted as central agents, under the supervision of a special representative of the Ministry of Shipping at Rome.

—if not entirely—to shorter voyages and quicker turn-round. For the month of July itself, when the full effects of the reorganisation of sailings became visible, the British entrances were greater by 4 per cent. than in July 1916. The entrances of foreign shipping, on the other hand, declined during the six months by no less than 53 per cent., and the total reduction in carrying power, as shown by the entrances, was over 20 per cent. on the previous six months, and nearly 22 per cent. on the corresponding period of 1916.

The weight of imports, as shown by the Board of Trade Returns, was 15·5 per cent. less than in the preceding half year, and 21·4 per cent. less than in 1916. Those returns, however, did not until July, when the system was revised, include imports, other than food, on Government account. If these imports, chiefly munitions and oil fuel, are included, and an allowance made for similar imports during 1916, the decrease on the preceding six months was only about 8·8 per cent., and on the six months ending July 1916, 13·9 per cent. When compared with the falling off in entrances, these figures give satisfactory evidence of the increase in effective carrying power of the shipping remaining available.

A large proportion of the decrease in imports, as compared with the corresponding period of 1916, fell on commodities the shipments of which had been deliberately restricted. Thus, the reduction in timber, including pit-props, was very nearly 2,000,000, or five-sixths of the contemplated saving for a whole year. This reduction was no doubt due in part to the laying up of neutral shipping in the North Sea, but that it was unnecessary to replace by British tonnage the neutral ships withdrawn, or to obtain substituted supplies from elsewhere, was due to the effect of the restrictions, and the efforts, made in conjunction therewith, to economise consumption and stimulate cutting at home and in France.[1] In paper and paper-making materials the reduction was 400,000 tons; in barley, 180,000; in raw fruit, 160,000; in jute, 45,000. In stones and slates, tobacco, onions, tomatoes, tea, wines and spirits, and many minor commodities, there were smaller, but still appreciable, savings.

---

[1] During May and June a proposal was under consideration for bringing over timber from Sweden in rafts; but it came to nothing, owing to the shortage of tugs and the difficulty of providing protection.

On the other hand, the imports of wheat and flour were greater by 450,000 tons. During the early months of 1917 the level of imports from North America had been comparatively low, owing to the diversion of shipping from the North Atlantic to Australia and elsewhere towards the end of 1916, and this drop in imports from the United States and Canada was only partially compensated by shipments received from Australia and the Plate; but from May onwards the arrivals from North America steadily increased, and as considerable amounts were also received from Australia, the imports during June and July were abnormally heavy, especially in July, when the total from all sources reached the very high figure of 875,000 tons. For the whole six months the receipts from North America showed a slight decrease on the previous year, balanced by a large increase from other sources; but practically the whole of the shipments arranged from Australia and the Plate had now been received, and it was almost entirely to North America that the Wheat Commission were looking for British imports during the new cereal year.

Most food imports, so far as they were not affected by the restrictions, were, on the whole, well maintained. The imports of oats and maize were large, a much greater proportion of the maize now coming from the United States. The decrease in arrivals of Scandinavian produce was made good by larger imports of butter from Australia, by heavy deliveries of cheese and condensed milk under the Dutch Agricultural Agreement, and by extensive purchases of cheese made in Canada by the Board of Trade. There was, however, a shortage of cheese for civilian requirements, owing to the building up of army stocks. The Norwegian Agreement secured the fish supply. On the other hand, two very important items, meat and sugar, showed a considerable decline.

Imports of dead meat of all kinds, including bacon and hams, were lower by 9 per cent. than in the corresponding period of 1916, and were 11 per cent. below those for the six months ending January 1917. If refrigerated beef and mutton alone be considered, the decline is still more marked, amounting to 12 per cent. on the 1916 figures, and 20 per cent. on the preceding six months'. The sources of supply had been extended by arrangements for the shipment of Patagonian mutton and lamb, by the lease to the British and Argentine Meat Company of a meat works at Rio de Janeiro, and by a considerable development of exports from South Africa.[1] The greater part of the South African meat was, however, sent to Egypt for the use of the armies in the Eastern theatre. There had been considerable difficulty in providing sufficient tonnage for the Plate and Brazilian exports, and though this had been met, as we have seen, by diversions from the Australasian trade, the diverted ships had only been on service for the latter part of the six months.

The main factor in the reduction of imports was, however, the submarine campaign. There was little doubt that the meat-carrying liners were specially signalled out for attack, and their losses had been very heavy. During the six months February to July inclusive no fewer than twenty-three insulated ships, with an aggregate meat capacity of 48,600 tons, had been sunk,[2] and five others, with a capacity of 13,700 tons, seriously damaged. Further, the carrying power of the ships had been reduced by the effect of delays and deviations imposed for considerations of safety. The Australasian liners, owing to the number of troops carried, were specially subject to delays, arising from putting in to Falmouth or Devonport for orders or to discharge troops. One large liner was actually unloaded at Devonport, and the cargo railed to London.

Apart from the actual reduction in imports caused by these delays and losses, the army requirements were increasing, and the War Office were making great efforts to build up stocks, which had fallen dangerously low. This, of course, accentuated the shortage in civilian supplies; but so serious was the position as regards army stocks that, in March the Government appointed a Committee under the Board of Agriculture to consider the question of drawing on home-grown meat for part of the military supplies.

Imports of sugar also fell away. The decrease on the previous six months was over 10 per cent., and on 1916, no less than 28 per cent. This was due directly to shortage

---

[1] A proposal to develop an export from Colombia broke down, owing to the inability of the syndicate concerned to arrange satisfactory terms with the Colombian Government.

[2] Two of these were sunk by mines laid by the WOLF, one by the MOEWE, and the remainder by submarines. The figures are exclusive of ships on Admiralty service.

of tonnage, and could be met only by more drastic rationing.

Among imports other than food, there were few heavy decreases, except in respect of articles affected by the Import Restrictions which, in addition to the savings already referred to, had a great effect on the figures for miscellaneous manufactures and commodities for re-export. The supply of wool was well maintained, and the vital imports of iron ore were remarkably good, considering how severely the traffic had suffered from losses and the withdrawal of neutral shipping. They amounted to 3,200,000 tons, which was less by 400,000 tons than in the corresponding period of 1916, but practically equal to the imports for the six months ending January 1917. The chief falling off was not in the imports from Spain and the Mediterranean, where the decrease in neutral tonnage had been made good, to a large extent, by increased allocation of British requisitioned steamers and by the services of Italian shipping under the Coal-Ore Agreement, but in the imports from Narvik, which showed a sad decline owing to the effects of the submarine campaign on North Sea traffic.

In striking contrast to the imports of iron and wool, those of cotton, the third, and in commercial importance the first, of the staple raw materials, were less by 190,000 tons than in the corresponding period of 1916. Although cotton was not used for war purposes to anything like the same extent as iron, or even wool, the commercial interests affected were so vast, and the difficulty of finding alternative employment for the workers so great, that the Imports Restrictions Committee had hesitated to interfere with the shipments, beyond placing a limit on re-exports. During the summer, however, the proportion of space occupied on the Atlantic liners by wheat and munitions was so large as to restrict greatly the space available for cotton, and in the existing shortage of tonnage it was impossible to allocate or release space sufficient to bring in anything like the normal import. It was still possible to import the quantities required for war purposes, and for the reduced export trade ; but it was evident that domestic consumption must be cut down, with the probable result of a large number of work-people being thrown out of employment or placed on short time. In view of the importance of the industry, it was essential that steps should be taken to regulate and as far as possible to equalise, the incidence of the reduction, and in June 1917 a Cotton Control Board was set up for this purpose. With the exception of Mr. H. D. Henderson, the Secretary, who represented the Board of Trade, the members of this Board were all men engaged in the industry as employers or operatives, and as restrictions became more and more drastic, it proved remarkably successful in averting the financial disasters and wide-spread distress which would otherwise have been inevitable.[1]

Imports on Government account, excluded from the trade returns prior to July, rose from 254,000 tons in January to 402,000 tons in June, and averaged about 330,000 tons a month during the first half of 1917. These imports included certain cargoes of munitions and munitions material, some shipments of timber on War Office account, nitrate for munitions purposes, and oil fuel for naval use. Space for munitions shipments was secured by the liner allocations and by the restriction of unessential imports. A proposed increase of the nitrate imports had, as we have seen, been postponed. Oil fuel was, in point of bulk, by far the most important of these items, but, owing to its shipment in specially constructed vessels, it did not compete with the imports of other commodities, nor did it suffer from their competition.

The oil-fuel situation was, nevertheless, one of the gravest anxieties of the Government. Like the meat-carrying liners, oil tankers were specially hunted by the submarines, and their peculiar build rendered them easy of identification. The losses were heavy, and owing to the difficulties which beset the shipbuilding programme, replacement was slow. Thanks to the special priority given to oil-carrying vessels, the total available tanker tonnage was tolerably well maintained; but this was not enough. The construction of oil-burning ships for the Navy had, even before the war, outstripped the construction of oil-carriers, and the great majority of the naval vessels completed under the war programme used oil fuel.

It had always been the desire of the Admiralty to hold stocks ashore and afloat equivalent to a six months' supply, but this had proved impossible from the first, and

[1] For a full account of the Board's operations, see *The Cotton Control Board*, by H. D. Henderson, 1922.

by June 1st, 1917, the total stocks amounted only to 750,000 tons, or a little under three months' supply at the then rate of consumption. What was more serious, there seemed little hope that, in face of the continued heavy losses and the increasing demands of the Fleet, even that reserve could be maintained. On the entry of the United States into the war, the Admiralty had hoped to obtain assistance from the large fleet of tankers under the American flag, but it was some months before the American Government took power to requisition shipping, and American owners were averse to the dangers of the war zone. Yet unless something could be done to increase the supply of fuel—it was useless to think of reducing the consumption—it was probable that, by the end of the year, the reserves would be exhausted.

So critical was the position that it was necessary to adopt drastic remedies, and during June it was decided, mainly on the initiative of Mr. B. A. Kemball-Cook, Director of Naval Sea Transport, Ministry of Shipping, to fit a number of liners in the North Atlantic trade for the carriage of oil fuel in the double bottoms of their ballast tanks. The expedient was not one which could be lightly adopted, since it involved a reduction in the dead-weight capacity of the vessels for ordinary cargo; but the crisis was too grave for hesitation. Even at the risk of shutting out wheat and munitions, the vital supply of oil fuel must be maintained. Operations were started at once both in the United Kingdom and in the United States, and by July 3rd shipments were commenced. The system was speedily extended to tramps, and the fitting of additional ships went forward as rapidly as possible during the summer months. The work to be done was not, fortunately, very extensive, and the average delay to each vessel fitted was only two and a half days. It was the shutting out of ordinary imports that was the real price paid. Meanwhile the introduction of the convoy system promised greatly to reduce the rate of loss, and a special programme of accelerated tanker construction had been put in operation.[1]

As regards the export trade, the Liner Requisition Scheme, that part of the Atlantic concentration by which it was chiefly affected, had not yet been in progress long enough for its effects to be very visible, but there was a slight general falling off, cloaked by the rise in values,

[1] See Chapter XIII, *post*.

OIL IN DOUBLE BOTTOMS

which was mainly attributable to increasing diversion of labour and materials to war purposes. From May onwards, too, the figures of re-exports showed clearly the effect of the import restrictions. Inasmuch as the total value of imports continued to increase, while that of exports remained stationary, the adverse trade balance was piling up to an alarming extent; but this was of less immediate consequence now that the United States had become associated with the Allies, and there was a prospect of obtaining extensive credits in the principal source of supply. As yet, however, the amount of assistance which could be looked for from the American Government was uncertain, and the problem of exchange continued to harass the Treasury in connection with all extensive operations of the importing departments.

Notwithstanding all such anxieties, and those arising from the inadequacy of the oil fuel, meat, and sugar stocks, and from poor harvests in France and Italy,[1] the general economic situation was better than in the spring. It was the frightful increase in the rate of loss at sea which had been, all this time, the over-mastering preoccupation and which lay at the root of almost all other problems, and if this rate had not yet been very substantially reduced, the successful introduction of convoy gave good hopes for the future.

For Germany, too, the immediate economic crisis was over. By drastic rationing, and at the cost of terrible suffering, the critical months preceding the gathering of the 1917 harvest had been bridged, and though a heavy price had to be paid in the weakening of both moral and physical stamina, it was once more possible for the Government to hold out hopes of a sufficiency of food, including supplies from Roumania, to enable the war to be prolonged until it was ended by a smashing military victory, or by the good work of the submarines, which was exaggerated with calculated mendacity.[2]

It was in May that the arrivals of grain from Roumania first began to affect the situation, and though the supplies

---

[1] See Chapter XV, *post*.
[2] For the six months, February to July inclusive, the figures of gross tonnage, British, Allied, and neutral, which the Germans claimed to have sunk, showed an exaggeration of over 40 per cent. This may be partly accounted for by ships torpedoed, which subsequently reached port; but the exaggeration, which steadily increased from now onwards, was too great to exclude the supposition of deliberate falsehood.

received fell far short of expectations, there can be little doubt that the Roumanian grain played a very large part in enabling both Germany and Austria to struggle on to the harvest.[1] By July 21st it was considered safe to increase the German flour ration, as from the middle of August, from 170 to 220 grammes a day, and to make a similar increase in the allowance to self-suppliers, though the supplementary rations were still maintained at their reduced level. On the other hand, the meat supply gave increased anxiety. In June it had been necessary to resort to the slaughter of milch cows in order to maintain the ration, and from August 15th, when the increased flour ration came into force, the issue of meat was again reduced to 250 grammes a week.

The increased supplies of grain had come only just in time. In May even the rations of first-line troops had been reduced to the equivalent of about three-fifths the amount received by British soldiers. During June food riots, involving serious damage to munition factories, were reported from many industrial centres in Germany, and the friction and discontent arising from the contrast between the free living of the producers and the starvation ration of the urban population, had become very bitter; nor had the Government proved able, despite all its efforts, to secure equality of distribution, or to check the growth of illicit trading.

Even now, the outlook was by no means hopeful. The rations were but just sufficient to keep body and soul together, and provided no surplus to make good the decrease in weight and stamina caused by the sufferings of the winter and spring.[2] There was direct evidence that the physical deterioration of the workers had begun to affect the output in the mines and factories. Diseases

[1] According to the *Kölnische Zeitung* of January 30th, 1918, the total amount of grain received by Germany and Austria from Roumania during 1917 was 1,386,000 metric tons. From current reports, about 540,000 tons was received by Austria and 250,000 tons by Germany up to the middle of July.

On August 16th General Höfer, the President of the Austrian Food Office, stated, in a speech at Salzburg, that since April Austria had been living mainly on supplies from Roumania.

[2] The average value in calories of the daily ration during the year 1917–18 was 1,510 calories per head. The ration maintained by the Belgian Relief Commission for a population mostly abstaining from heavy labour during the German occupation, was 2,067 calories per head. Moreover, the German ration was particularly deficient in protein, and above all in fats. Cmd. 280.

GERMAN FOOD SUPPLIES

attributable to insufficient nourishment were rife, and while the birth rate continued to fall even more rapidly than could be accounted for by the number of men under arms, the death rate continued to rise. Nor was there much prospect of improvement in the situation, unless new sources of supply could be found. The harvest was again indifferent, and even if sufficient cereals to maintain the bread ration were forthcoming, it must be maintained at the expense of fodder, with the effect of still further deterioration of the live stock.

It was, as of old, the deficiency in fats which was the most important factor in the shortage, and in this respect the position was growing steadily worse.[1] It was for fats especially that the Germans depended on imports from contiguous neutrals, and thanks to the effect of the Dutch and Danish Agricultural Agreements, and the Norwegian Fish Agreement, the food imports from contiguous neutrals during the June quarter were again very small. They were, however, slightly greater than for the previous three months, owing to the difficulty of transporting Dutch and Danish produce to Great Britain, and the slaughter of cattle in Denmark which followed the stoppage of fodder imports. On the other hand, steps were being taken by the Allies which were to reduce effectively even the meagre supplies still received.[2]

So long as actual starvation could be averted the Governments of the Central Powers might be expected to spur their people indefinitely to resistance. Shortage of war material was another matter, and here the loss of imports was acutely felt. The application of the rationing system to neutral imports not only reduced almost to nothing the leakage of overseas products to Germany, but reacted on the export of goods produced in the neutral countries themselves, a larger proportion of such goods being now required for home consumption. The agreements made by the British Government with neutral producers further restricted the traffic. Very little copper was now reaching Germany, either from Norway or Sweden, and during May a fire at the Kristiansand refinery cut off her only considerable outside source of nickel supplies.[3]

---

[1] See Vol. II, pp. 163, 309-10, 404.   [2] See Chapter XIV, *post*.
[3] By an agreement made in August, production at this refinery was suspended until January 1918, in which month the Norwegian Government requisitioned the works and stocks.

In their urgent need of metals the German Government were now requisitioning or making provision for the collection of door-plates, window fastenings, buttons, and toy soldiers. The scarcity of copper, nickel, and manganese had at last begun to show its effect in the quality of munitions production, though the deterioration in quality was not, as yet, considerable, and the actual output was threatened by the extreme scarcity of the metals, such as wolfram and molybdenum, used in making high-speed machine tools. How acute that scarcity had become may be illustrated by the fact that the price of wolfram had risen by 4,000 per cent. On the condition of the rolling stock the lack of hardening metals had a more pronounced effect. So early as the end of March 8,000 engines were said to be awaiting repairs at Essen alone, and the steady deterioration of transport through the use of inferior materials for construction and repairs, and the acute shortage of proper lubricants, immensely complicated the problem of food and fuel supply.

Of textiles and leather practically no stocks were now available for civilian use. Even the dead were buried in paper yarn, and the war boots, of leather sutstitutes with wooden soles, were a constant source of complaint. The Armies, however, were still tolerably well supplied. More important was the shortage of rubber, for which no adequate substitute had been found, and on July 26th an order was issued for the requisitioning of all rubber tyres and billiard table cushions not already surrendered.

In one respect only had the position appreciably improved. The breach made in the Allied cordon by the conquest of Roumania was as important in the supply of oil as in the supply of grain. By May the damage done to the Roumanian wells had been sufficiently made good for a little oil to come forward, though no lubricating oils had yet been received. By July the average output had risen to 1,470 tons a day. Although less than half of the normal output before the war, this was a substantial relief to a situation fast becoming desperate.

The overwhelming of Roumania had been, indeed, a cruel blow to the Allied cause. Just when the slow process of economic pressure was beginning to exert its maximum effect, it had opened up a new source of supply which, while insufficient to save the German people from acute suffering and their Government from acute anxiety, had, in respect of two vital commodities, made just the difference between shortage and collapse. By the autumn of 1917, the war, on its economic side, had become once more a race between the submarine and the exhaustion of German resources ; but while the pressure on Germany was, as we shall see, to grow steadily in stringency through American support, the activities of the submarine were now met by a new and effective defence.

CHAPTER XII

CONVOYS AND TURN-ROUND
AUGUST—NOVEMBER 1917

By the beginning of September, as we have seen, the convoy system had been extended to cover the greater part of the sailings on the Atlantic tracks, and in the figures of loss for that month—the first complete month during which both inward and outward convoys had been running—the good effects of the system were plainly to be seen. The destruction of British tonnage was still far too great to be regarded with indifference—it amounted to just under 200,000 tons—but it was 40 per cent. less than in August, and only about one-half the monthly average since the inception of the unrestricted submarine campaign. The losses of Allied and neutral shipping were also on the down grade.

How greatly this reduction in the average risk was due to convoy is clear from an analysis of the areas in which the losses occurred. In June, the last month prior to the first beginnings of regular convoy, 173 British and foreign steamers of 500 tons gross and upwards were sunk by submarines. Of these 54 were sunk in the Fastnet, Scilly, and Tory Island Approaches, and 32 in the Bay of Biscay or between Corunna and Dakar; making a total of 86 in the areas chiefly affected by the introduction of the Atlantic and Gibraltar convoys. In September, out of 87 casualties, only 7 took place in the Approaches, 7 in the Bay, and 10 between Corunna and Dakar; a total of 24. For the first time, not a single ship was sunk in the Fastnet Approach, and the only areas returning more than a dozen casualties were the English Channel, where ships collecting or dispersing were exposed to attack as well as the cross-Channel traffic, and the Mediterranean, where the convoy system had not yet been introduced.

The question of Mediterranean convoys had, however,

been under discussion for some time. The system of patrolled routes had proved thoroughly unsatisfactory, and the division of the sea into various zones under the control of the British, French, and Italians respectively, added to the difficulty of protecting traffic. In April, when the German submarines made their great effort, they sank no fewer than 56 British and foreign steamers of 500 tons and upwards in the Mediterranean, and in May and June the losses were 36 and 30 respectively. During July, August, and September, they fell to an average of 19 a month; but this was due in part to a diminution in the volume of traffic consequent on the severity of the previous losses. A primary cause of this diminution was the delay caused by night sailings and the detention of ships to await escort from one patrolled area to another. From Malta to Port Said the passage not uncommonly occupied 30 to 32 days, and the movements of the inter-Mediterranean trade were similarly affected. Further, the confidence even of British masters had been badly shaken, and there was a tendency to prolong the time spent in harbour on minor repairs.

The importance of the through route had, of course, been greatly decreased by the diversion of Far Eastern and Australian shipping, but the large naval and military forces employed in the Eastern theatres of war made the Gibraltar–Port Said Passage a matter of vital concern, and the coal supply of Italy, Algeria, and Southern France, together with the return ore traffic from North African and Southern Spanish ports, was of first-class importance both from its size and its character. About 180 steamers a month with coal and stores followed the route to the Gulf of Lyons and Genoa alone, and the total number of steamers passing into the Mediterranean from the West averaged about 13 a day, or 400 a month. From the East there was a considerable traffic in grain and fodder; for the South of France, Italy, and the Allied forces in the Balkans were now being fed, as far as possible, from Asia and Australia, in order to secure economical use of tonnage, and reserve the North Atlantic supplies for Northern France and the United Kingdom.

Admiral Wemyss, who came home from Egypt in July, prior to taking up the duties of British Commander-in-Chief at Malta, had run on his own initiative since May, a restricted system of commercial convoy between Malta and Port Said; but no attempt had yet been made to tackle the problem of a general convoy system, either for the through or the inter-Mediterranean trade. The shortage of patrol craft was here, as elsewhere, a serious obstacle, and the main energies of the Naval Authorities were concentrated on the completion of the net barrage across the Straits of Otranto, with the object of stopping the exit of submarines from their bases in the Adriatic.

Both Admiral Wemyss and Admiral Calthorpe, who eventually took up the Mediterranean command, were anxious for the convoy system to be tried, and as the result of a visit to the Ministry of Shipping by Lieutenant-Commander Godfrey, an officer on Admiral Wemyss' Staff, the Ministry produced the outline of a suggested plan for inter-Mediterranean convoys, and sent out with Admiral Calthorpe a nucleus staff for the creation of a Card Index, similar to that kept at the Ministry, but to deal solely with inter-Mediterranean movements.[1] At a Conference with the Ministry on August 14th, the First Sea Lord stated that the forces available were not yet sufficient to carry out the system they desired, but Admiral Calthorpe was instructed to investigate its possibilities, in the light of the information furnished by the new Intelligence Section at Malta, as to the incidence of traffic.

During September, "Shipping Control Officers" were appointed to various Mediterranean ports to furnish Malta with information, expedite the turn-round of vessels, and collect them for escort, and in October Admiral Calthorpe cabled that he was ready to start five-day convoys: Alexandria–Bizerta, Malta–Milo, and Milo–Alexandria. Simultaneously, the French put into operation a convoy system between Marseilles and Bizerta. Meanwhile the long-discussed Through Mediterranean Convoy had come into being.

The strongest argument for this convoy was that it would allow the use of the Suez Route by Indian and Far Eastern shipping. The diversion of this shipping to the long route viâ the Cape had undoubtedly reduced losses, but at the expense of a serious prolongation of the round voyage. It was not only that the distance to be travelled was much greater (for the Indian ships, about 11,800 miles

---

[1] The Intelligence Section at Malta was furnished by the main Section in London with advance particulars of all ships bound to the Mediterranean.

THROUGH MEDITERRANEAN CONVOYS

as against 7,900); there was also the question of bunkering at South African ports. Owing to the addition of the diverted traffic to the volume of trade to be handled, and the cumulative effect of the strain on the railways from the coalfields, the condition of these ports was now even worse than in 1916,[1] and the delays caused by waiting for bunkers formed an important factor in the length of the voyage. As a result of these delays, coupled with the longer sea passage, the Indian liners were now making only two voyages in the year, and the resulting loss of carrying power was very serious. Indeed, it was calculated that, if the Suez Route could be reopened, the whole priority cargo from India and the Far East could be carried by a fleet of 90 steamers instead of about 130 actually employed,[2] thus setting free 40 liners for work in the North Atlantic or elsewhere.

About the middle of September Admiral Calthorpe cabled that he was in a position to take care of a through convoy, provided it was not run at a shorter interval than ten days. This was accepted by the Ministry of Shipping; indeed they were prepared to go still further in easing the strain on escort, by accepting a sixteen-day interval, which they considered not too long to allow time for turn-round and provide an adequate number of ships for each convoy. The speed was fixed at 10 knots, and the original intention was that the convoys should start alternately from Liverpool, and from Devonport for the London trade. In practice, however, it was found that there were about three times as many ships sailing from Liverpool as from London, and that the only practicable course was always to start the convoy from Liverpool. The London ships went out with the ordinary Devonport convoy, and after its dispersal, steamed south to Gibraltar, where they joined the Mediterranean Convoy on its arrival.

On October 3rd the first outward convoy sailed from Liverpool. While it was loading, orders were sent to India and China that all vessels of 10 knots actual sea-speed and over were to come home viâ the Suez Canal. The port of assembly was to be Perim, in order to give the ships some practice in station-keeping while coming up the Red Sea; but later, when all steamers in the trade had gained experience in convoy organisation, this arrangement was altered and the vessels proceeded independently

[1] See Vol. II, p. 368. [2] This forecast proved to be correct.

to the Canal. The homeward convoys were to be mixed; that is to say, they comprised ships both for East and West Coast ports.

Inasmuch as these convoys were in the danger zone the whole way between Home Waters and Port Said, they retained their full escort throughout. The escort which took the outward convoy as far as Bizerta met the westbound convoy at that port and brought it home, while the outward convoy proceeded under escort of the force which had accompanied the homeward-bound ships from Port Said.[1]

In October, when Admiral Calthorpe's message announcing the establishment of the Alexandria–Bizerta convoy was received, the Admiralty sent out orders that slow steamers in the East, such as the Java sugar ships, were to come home viâ the Canal, as well as the faster liners. These slow steamers were incorporated in the ordinary five-day convoys from Alexandria; but from Bizerta to Gibraltar they proceeded without escort, by the coastal route. On arriving at the Straits, they came on with the ordinary Gibraltar convoy.

It was some time, of course, before the ships that were in the Far East when orders were sent out could reach the Canal; indeed, it was not until November 16th that the first convoy was ready to start for the United Kingdom from Port Said. In the meantime the first outward convoy had passed through the Mediterranean. Its experience was not altogether encouraging, for on October 19th the *Pera*, of 7,685 tons, was torpedoed and sunk about 100 miles from Crete, and on the following day the *Collegian*, of 7,520 tons, was sunk 100 miles from Alexandria. The loss of two big ships out of eleven which had started in company was something of a shock; but with additional experience and improved organisation it was hoped to reduce the risk, and the advantages of using the Suez Route were too great to be lightly thrown away.

In another direction the convoy system was called upon, during October, to face a new form of attack. It had always been recognised by the Admiralty that the Scandinavian Convoy was exposed not only to submarines

---

[1] In June of 1918 this arrangement was altered, the escort being provided by patrol gunboats, which took the outward convoy right through to Port Said. The result of this reorganisation was an average gain of two days on the outward passage. The homeward voyage remained at about the same length.

but to surface raiders. To guard against this danger by direct escort was impossible, without undue dispersal of force; but the constant activity of Grand Fleet forces to the southward of the convoy route gave a large measure of safety. The route passed, however, within 350 miles of Horn Reef, and the greater part of this distance could, in winter, be covered by fast ships during the hours of darkness. It was not until October 17th, some six months after the establishment of the Scandinavian Convoy, that the first surface attack was made; but at daybreak of that day a convoy of 12 steamers (two British, one Belgian, and nine neutral) under escort of the destroyers MARY ROSE and STRONGBOW, and two trawlers, was attacked by a German light cruiser force. The odds were overwhelming, both the destroyers were sunk, and of the whole convoy, only the British and Belgian ships escaped. As a result of this attack, it was decided to increase the size and decrease the frequency of the convoys, in order to facilitate their protection; but owing to the difficulty of collecting additional forces it was some weeks before the scheme could be carried out.

Apart from these incidents, the working of the convoy system during October, though not unattended with loss, was highly successful. It is true that the total losses of British shipping rose to 276,000 tons—80,000 more than in the previous month—but even this total was considerably less than in any other month since the outbreak of the unrestricted submarine campaign. Moreover, it was due mainly to very heavy losses in the Mediterranean, where the local convoy system had hardly begun, and in the inshore waters, where the submarines were now concentrating their attack on the coasting trade and on ships dispersing from a homeward-bound convoy, or on their way to ports of assembly. The total number of British and foreign steamers of 500 tons and upwards sunk by submarines during the month was 121. Of these 35 were sunk in the Mediterranean, 23 in the Channel, 16 in the Bristol Channel and Irish Sea, and 17 in the North Sea. In the three great Approaches there were only 4 casualties.

By this time the Ocean Convoy System had been in more or less full operation for about three months.[1] During those three months the total war losses of British shipping had been 800,000 tons, against 1,185,000 tons in the

[1] Outward convoys were only started towards the end of August.

previous quarter, and 1,200,000 tons in the three months ending April 1917. The total reduction of the world's tonnage had been 1,800,000 tons against 1,800,000, and 2,000,000 in the two previous quarters.[1] The reduction of risk was thus considerable; but the rate of loss was still dangerously high. On the other hand, it had to be considered that the convoy system in the Atlantic had only reached its full development at the beginning of September, and that it was only now being extended to the Mediterranean trade. How great its influence had been we have seen in the analysis of the monthly losses by areas, and when the three months are taken together, the results are even more striking.

By far the most significant feature is the reduction of losses in the Fastnet, Scilly, and Tory Island Approaches. During the three months ending April 30th, 127 British and foreign steamers of 500 tons and upwards were sunk in these areas, being 24·1 per cent. of the total casualties. For the three months ending July the figures were 118 ships sunk, 25·3 per cent. In the October quarter only 26 ships were sunk, and the percentage to total losses was 7·6.

In the Bay of Biscay the losses were reduced, owing to the effect of the Gibraltar, Dakar, Sierra Leone, and Outward convoys, from 53 in the July to 28 in the October quarter. In the Corunna–Dakar area, however, and in mid-Atlantic, west of the Bay, 38 vessels were destroyed as against 37 in the July quarter, and the proportion rose from 7·9 to 11·0 per cent. This was due mainly to the operations of submarine cruisers in the neighbourhood of the Azores against vessels, chiefly Allied and neutral, not included in the convoyed trades. In the Mediterranean, North Sea, English Channel, Bristol Channel, and Irish Sea, and off the west coast of Ireland, the losses suffered in each area, during August, September, and October, bore a higher relation to the total loss than in the July quarter; but this was due not so much to any actual increase in the number of ships sunk as to the great decrease of losses in the Approach areas. Indeed, it was only in the Mediterranean and North Sea, on the cross-tracks in mid-Atlantic, and in inshore waters, that the submarines could now look for any substantial success.

[1] The fact that the decrease in losses was proportionately greater in respect of world tonnage was due to the laying up of neutral shipping.

LOSSES REDUCED ALL ROUND

Tried by the percentage of losses to sailings, the convoy system had more than justified itself. From the institution of the Atlantic convoys in July, to October 27th, 1,500 ships had arrived safely in convoys from North America, Dakar, Sierra Leone, and Gibraltar, against 24 which had been sunk; since the middle of August over 1,000 vessels in outward convoy had been escorted through the danger zone, with a loss of 6.

The short-distance convoys, which had now been running for six months, had proved equally successful. In the Scandinavian Convoy some 5,700 voyages had been made, with a loss of 1·29 per cent. In the French coal trade the results had been astounding; for though some 12,450 voyages had been made during the six months, only a score of vessels had been lost, giving a ratio of sinkings to sailings of 0·16 per cent.

Thus, while the rate of loss was still too high to be contemplated with equanimity, there was every reason to hope that, as the convoy system was gradually extended to cover a larger and larger proportion of the sailings, and as the organisation of the system itself was gradually improved, there would be a progressive diminution in the losses suffered.

These results not only confirmed beyond cavil the foresight of those who had first urged the feasibility and necessity of ocean convoy, but reflected the highest credit on all concerned with the working of the system. It is mainly with the results that we are here concerned; but it is impossible to record what was achieved without paying the tribute due to those by whom it was accomplished—to the masters, officers, and crews of the Mercantile Marine, who adapted themselves with surprising rapidity to the new conditions; to the officers and crews of the escorts, on whom, owing to the paucity of reliefs, the system threw an almost intolerable strain; to those at the Admiralty, entrusted with the onerous task of adjusting the forces available for escort to the sailings required, synchronising the inward and outward sailings, and routeing the convoys; to the Ministry of Shipping and to the shipowners themselves, by whom the commercial requirements of the country had to be fulfilled under conditions so far removed from those of ordinary trade.

There was still, however, much to be done in adjusting

the requirements of defence to the conditions necessary for maintaining supplies, for the introduction of Atlantic convoys, while it had preserved many ships from destruction, had seriously reduced the carrying power of the whole tonnage in the trade, by increasing the length and decreasing the frequency of voyages. This was a grave matter, since it neutralised to a great extent the advantages obtained by concentrating shipping on the shorter routes.

The two great factors tending to increase the length of the round voyage were, of course, the time spent in steaming to a rendezvous or port of assembly, or in awaiting the sailing date from such port, and the reduction in the speed of the faster ships due to their being grouped in the same convoy with slower vessels. To this must be added the choking of the ports caused by the arrival of ships in comparatively large batches instead of in a steady daily stream, and by the tendency to force East Coast cargoes through West Coast ports, in order to diminish the submarine risk. On the other side of the Atlantic there was a similar tendency to congestion at the ports of assembly. Against the effect of these factors was to be set the fact that ships sailing in convoy avoided the risk of detention when submarines were reported in the neighbourhood of a port, and when at sea, were able to follow a comparatively direct route.

In the net result arising on balance from the operation of these conflicting factors, there was a considerable variation between route and route, and trade and trade. The average delay to vessels in the Gibraltar Convoy was two days, and this was made good, generally speaking, by the more direct route, as the deviations under independent sailings from Gibraltar had been very extensive. In order to minimise delays to the invaluable ore cargoes, it was arranged that ore steamers should sail in the first convoy leaving Gibraltar after their arrival, irrespective of their Bill of Lading destination, orders being given through the escort, as to the port to which they were to proceed.[1] There were, however, certain ships carrying ore of special qualities to which this procedure could not be applied, and such ships were detained at Gibraltar, by telegraphic

---

[1] It will be remembered that the Gibraltar Convoys sailed alternately to the East and West Coast.

instructions, for their appropriate convoy. Such delays, however, were not sufficient to overbalance the advantage of the direct route.

For meat-ships, coming home in the Dakar or Sierra Leone Convoys, the system frequently involved a prolongation of the voyage, through the time spent at the port of assembly, awaiting escort; but on the whole the Dakar Convoy appears to have been a time-saver, at any rate for the slower steamers, such as those with sugar from Java. The time spent by such ships awaiting convoy was no longer than that previously spent in port, and the length of the actual passage was slightly shortened.[1] For the sugar ships from Cuba, on the other hand, which joined the Hampton Roads Convoy, the length of the voyage was considerably increased.[2]

In the North Atlantic trade as a whole, the general tendency in the autumn of 1917 was for the round voyage of slow ships to occupy from 15 to 30 per cent. longer than they did even in 1916, when independent sailings were so gravely interfered with by war conditions.[3] For the vessels of higher speed, such as those now included in the Halifax Convoy, the figures varied greatly according to the fortune of the vessel in arriving at the port of assembly on or near

---

[1] The average time for six typical sugar steamers from Java sailing independently in 1915–16, from arrival at Dakar to arrival in the United Kingdom, was $3\frac{1}{4}$ days in port, 24 days at sea; total $27\frac{1}{4}$ days. The average for six representative sailings under convoy was $3\frac{1}{4}$ days in port, $21\frac{3}{4}$ days at sea; total $25\frac{1}{4}$ days.

[2] Twelve representative independent sailings (1915–16) show, from the date of leaving Cuba, an average of $27\frac{7}{12}$ days at sea, $1\frac{1}{4}$ in port; total $28\frac{11}{12}$. Twelve sailings under convoy (1917–18) give an average of $32\frac{1}{12}$ days at sea, $5\frac{5}{12}$ days in port; total $37\frac{1}{2}$.

[3] Average length of time occupied by a $10\frac{1}{2}$-knot cargo carrier on the round voyage:

	Under Peace Conditions. 1913.	Under War Conditions. 1916.	Under Convoy. Autumn 1917	Percentage Increase.		
				1916 on 1913.	1917 on 1916.	1917 on 1913.
	Days.	Days.	Days.			
St. John, N.B..	40	46	53	15·5	15·2	32·5
Philadelphia	43	47	58	9·3	23·4	34·9
New York	42	45	52	7·1	15·5	23·8
Boston	43	44	50	2·3	13·6	16·3
Baltimore	43	48	63	11·6	31·2	46·5
Gulf Ports	58	60	71	3·4	18·3	22·4
Savannah	45	50	60	11·1	20·0	33·3

a sailing date, but only for the fastest ships did the results approximate to the 1916 standard.[1]

The effect of this increase in the length of the North Atlantic voyage was to discount, to an alarming extent, the advantages derived from the concentration of shipping on the shorter routes. The liner tonnage entered in the Liverpool and London War Risks Association, representing practically the whole of the liner tonnage in the North Atlantic trading with London, Liverpool, Glasgow, and Bristol, with the exception of the Furness, Withy and Wilson fleets, had risen from 124 steamers of 590,000 net tons in September and October 1916, to 192 ships of 870,000 tons net in the same months of 1917, an increase of 46·6 per cent. This, on the basis of the average round voyage in 1916, should have involved an increase of 3,000,000 tons a year in carrying power. But the average round voyage for ships in the North Atlantic trade, other than those from Gulf ports, had risen by 28 per cent. for ships of 12 knots and under, and by 20 per cent. for ships over 12 knots. The net result for the whole trade was an increase in the round voyage of 25 per cent.[2] Thus the average liner was making only six round voyages in the year instead of eight, and the actual increase in carrying power was only 600,000 tons, or one-fifth of what it would otherwise have been. The requisitioned tramp tonnage in the Atlantic trade was similarly affected, and the total entrances of British shipping from the United States and British North America, during the autumn of 1917 were rather below than above the 1916 level.

The total ocean-going British tonnage available for the trade of the United Kingdom in the autumn of 1917 [3] was about 6,000,000 tons gross, as compared with 7,000,000 in February and about 6,500,000 during the summer months, the net loss after allowing for replacements having fallen more heavily on such tonnage than on that in the employment of the Army, Navy, and Allies. This pro-

[1] Shortest and longest time occupied on a round voyage, in the New York trade, by a vessel of 18 knots :

	Under Peace Conditions. 1913.	Under War Conditions. 1916.	Under Convoy. Autumn 1917.
Shortest	27 days	35 days	36 days
Longest	34 ,,	52 ,,	52 ,,

[2] The increase on time in port alone was 14 per cent., in the time spent at sea 35 per cent.

[3] September figures.

gressive reduction should, probably, have been fully made good by the concentration of shipping on the shorter routes, but the actual entrances with cargoes of British shipping from all countries during the three months August, September, October, compared more unfavourably with the figures for the previous year than in either of the two preceding quarters.[1]

Owing to the still greater decrease in foreign entrances, which were now only about two-fifths of those recorded in 1916, the diminution in imports during the three months was heavy, amounting to about 12·7 per cent. on the previous quarter, and 20 per cent. on the corresponding period of 1916.[2] The cereal stock position was not, however, unsatisfactory. Very heavy shipments of wheat and flour from North America during the summer months had removed the anxiety felt during the spring, and it was calculated that by the end of November the stocks would be equal to twenty-two weeks' supply. The oat stocks were also much better than in 1916.

In other respects the position was not so good. The meat supply in particular caused great anxiety. Imports, indeed, were better than in the first half of the year, for the diversion of shipping from the Australasian to the Plate Route was beginning to tell, and considerable quantities of American and Canadian beef were coming forward in the liners diverted to the North Atlantic. The convoy system, too, had reduced the rate of loss, and a few new steamers had come on service. As against this the tendency to concentrate shipping on the West Coast ports caused considerable difficulties. The Refrigerated Shipping Committee did their best so to distribute the ships as to prevent congestion. They used Manchester as much as possible, as a safety valve for Liverpool, and made additional use of Glasgow, Barry, and Avonmouth. The extent to which new ports could be used depended, however, on the cold storage available and the facilities for rail transit to con-

[1] Entrances of British ships with cargoes at ports in the United Kingdom (in 1,000 tons net):

3 months ending	1916	1917
April	4,537	4,438
July	5,358	5,129
October	5,224	4,744

[2] Allowing for estimated Government imports prior to July 1917, including oil-fuel.

suming centres. In 1913, London and Liverpool had each handled over 37 per cent. of the total weight of meat imported into the United Kingdom, and there were no other ports anything like so well suited to deal with the traffic. Southampton, with just under 5 per cent. of the total imports, had stood next to London and Liverpool before the war, and there large cold stores were available; but Southampton was a military port, and to make full use of its facilities necessitated very close co-ordination with the Admiralty and most careful watching.[1]

Bunkering was another source of anxiety. Owing to the congestion on the railways, and the decline in coasting traffic, little coal for bunkers could be brought from the North. Bunkering was therefore concentrated as much as possible in South Wales, and even the steamers of H. and W. Nelson's Highland Line, whose headquarters were in London, were sent round to Swansea to coal. Apart from delays so occasioned, ships bunkering in South Wales were always liable to be held up by congestion of the ports through the number of ships arriving to coal, or through shortage of bunker coal, arising from Admiralty demands.

By close co-operation between the Refrigerated Tonnage Committee, the Ministry of Shipping, the Admiralty, and the Port and Transit Committee, all these difficulties were gradually overcome; the routeing of shipping was adjusted to the capacity of the ports, and a reasonable degree of

[1] Meat imports in 1,000 tons (including bacon and hams and all kinds of meat—fresh, refrigerated, or preserved—except game and poultry):

	1913.	1914.	1915.	1916.	1917.	1918.
London	436	477	553	486	366	450
Liverpool	436	408	473	476	391	512
Southampton	58	42	21	37	36	46
Hull	37	41	54	45	42	29
Glasgow	30	24	29	32	38	64
Bristol (including Avonmouth)	11	13	23	21	34	63
Cardiff (including Barry)	5	2	7	2	8	28
Manchester	4	19	8	12	20	45

The 1918 figures are given, as the tendency to greater use of the West Coast ports developed during the latter part of 1917, and is not fully shown in the figures for that year. The important point in the table is, of course, not the total figures for each port (which depended largely on the total imports), but the ratio between port and port.

MEAT IMPORTS AND STOCKS

priority in bunkering was accorded to meat ships, even to the extent of drawing, when necessary, on Admiralty stocks. Imports improved, and by October the beef stocks were equal to six weeks' supply, about twice as much as at the same period of 1916; but the slaughter of home-grown cattle for Army consumption had begun on September 1st, and in anticipation of price-fixing by the Food Controller, heavy slaughtering of both cattle and sheep for civilian consumption took place during the autumn, and was accentuated by the high price of feeding stuffs. As a result of this depletion of home stocks, it was anticipated that there would be a serious shortage of civilian supplies in the spring of 1918, and ration cards had already been introduced. Bacon stocks, too, were very short, and the Ministry of Food was buying heavily, in order to restore the balance.

There were now two Departments, the Board of Trade and the Ministry of Food, buying refrigerated produce, and during September the Food Controller, who had recently set up, in co-operation with the Food Ministers of other Allied countries, an Inter-Allied Meat and Fats Executive for joint purchase and allocation, suggested that the whole supply of meat and other refrigerated produce, both for civilian and military requirements, should be transferred to him, together with the control of insulated tonnage. After some discussion with the Army Council and Ministry of Shipping it was decided by the War Cabinet that no change was desirable which might break the continuity of an organisation that had given admirable results. It was arranged, therefore, that the Board of Trade should continue to be responsible for Army supplies, and for all meat purchases in South America, Australasia, and South Africa. The Ministry of Food was responsible for civilian supplies, and for purchases of meat in North America. North American meat for Army consumption, and other meat for civilian supplies, was to be obtained by the Department responsible for supply from the Department responsible for purchase. The Ministry of Food was made solely responsible for the purchase of fish, cheese, and butter, whether for civilian or military requirements, and the Board of Trade staff engaged on that work was to be transferred. Finally, a representative of the Ministry of Food was appointed to the Refrigerated Shipping Committee, and Sir Thomas

Robinson, with Mr. Macrosty as assistant, was appointed to represent the Board of Trade on the Meats and Fats Executive.

Thanks to heavy imports arranged by the Board of Trade from New Zealand and Canada, the stocks of cheese were now ample. Butter and margarine, on the other hand, were very short, owing to the interruption of trade with Scandinavia and Holland, for which the imports of colonial butter no longer afforded adequate compensation. Of sugar, too, there was only two months' supply, and it had already been decided that rationing must be brought into operation on January 1st.

As regards raw materials, the stocks of paper, pulp, and timber had been cut down, of set purpose, under the import restrictions. Pit wood stocks were light, but three-quarters of the supply was now derived from home cutting. Of sawn softwoods there were five months' supply. Stocks of wool, flax, hemp, and jute were all adequate, but those of American cotton were down to six weeks' supply, one-third of the normal. The position was serious, for the industry was already living on its stocks, owing to the inadequacy of the monthly imports, and at the beginning of September the Cotton Control Board were obliged to cut down production in the spinning mills using American cotton by 30 per cent. Of the total output, as thus restricted, about two-thirds was exported, and nearly one-sixth was required for war purposes. Thus only about one-sixth was available for domestic consumption.

The chief cause of anxiety, however, was the shortage of mineral oils. There was only two months' supply of motor spirit (only 13 per cent. of which was now released for private consumption), and one month's supply of kerosene. The oil-fuel crisis, on the other hand, had been somewhat relieved by the use of double bottoms for carriage of oil. By November 9th, no fewer than 443 steamers had been fitted for this purpose, and 320,000 tons had been actually loaded, of which 243,000 tons had arrived. Thanks to the efficacy of the convoys, only 4,500 tons had been lost on passage, leaving about 72,000 tons still afloat. Nevertheless, this expedient, while it was already estimated to give results equivalent to the continuous employment of fifteen additional tankers, was at best a regrettable necessity, for it had the very serious effect of shutting out an equivalent quantity of other

AN ALARMING FORECAST

imports, and thus still further reducing the carrying power of ships in the Atlantic trade.

It was, indeed, the prospective rather than the actual import position which gave the chief cause for alarm. During August, the Statistical Department of the Ministry of Shipping had worked out a provisional estimate of the probable imports for 1918, on the basis of continued losses from enemy action at the rate of 375,000 tons a month. On this basis they estimated that the imports in 1918, exclusive of full cargoes of oil fuel and munitions carried in requisitioned ships, would be less by 8,500,000 tons than in 1917. In October they prepared a further and more elaborate estimate, based on the actual figures of imports for the nine months to September inclusive, and assuming the rate of loss through enemy action at 325,000 tons a month (approximately the September figures).[1] In this estimate allowance was made on the one hand for the effects of the Atlantic concentration, and on the other for the increase in length of the round voyage due to convoys and for the effect of carriage of oil in double bottoms. The new forecast was no more consoling than the old. The Statistical Department now estimated the total imports of all kinds during 1918 at 7,330,000 tons less than in 1917; but in this estimate a large increase in the supply of oil-fuel for the Navy was set against a decrease of all other imports. The reduction in those imports recorded in the Board of Trade returns prior to June 1917—that is to say, all articles other than oil-fuel and certain munitions cargoes—was estimated at 8,426,000 tons: a reduction (on their calculations) of 26 per cent. on 1917, and about 44½ per cent. on 1916.

In view of the drastic restriction of non-essential imports already in force, and the grave danger of any large further reduction in the imports of essentials, this forecast was most disquieting. The prospects of obtaining additional tonnage, not allowed for in the estimates, were small, and in view of the extent to which the theory of concentration had already been pushed, it was doubtful whether much more could be accomplished in that respect. The one hope of alleviating the situation appeared to lie in reducing the duration of the round voyage, and thus adding to the number of voyages that could be made by each ship.

[1] This forecast of losses fortunately proved to be overestimated. On the other hand, the replacements fell considerably short of expectations.

This, certainly, was the view of the shipowners themselves, and the Liverpool Steam Ship Owners' Association, who were primarily concerned in the Atlantic trade, had been pressing strongly, since the conference at the Admiralty on August 2nd, for a reorganisation of the convoy system, permitting a reduction in the average length of voyages. It was true that, on the time-basis of remuneration now universally applied, the number of voyages made no financial difference to the shipowner, but as they pointed out, it might make to the nation all the difference between reasonable plenty and starvation. For this reason they were extremely anxious that closer touch should be established between those responsible for the naval control of the convoys, and the liner organisations by which so large a proportion of the North Atlantic trade was run.

In response to their representations, Captain R. G. H. Henderson, of the Admiralty War Staff, who, as will be remembered, had been closely connected with the original introduction of the convoy system, was sent to Liverpool, in November, to investigate the conditions. On his arrival Captain Henderson attended a general meeting of the Liverpool Steam Ship Owners' Association, called to discuss the situation, and subsequently conducted a minute and careful enquiry into the whole working of the system as it affected the port, including the grouping of ships, the organisation of sailings, and berthing and bunkering arrangements, all of which were exhaustively discussed with representatives of the lines.

As a result of this enquiry and of subsequent correspondence between the Association, the Admiralty, and the Ministry of Shipping, a meeting of the North Atlantic Lines was held on November 29th, at which it was decided to form a Convoy Committee, under the Chairmanship of Mr. T. Harrison Hughes, to deal with all questions relating to the working of the system at Liverpool. By this Committee a scheme was worked out, and subsequently accepted by the Admiralty, on the following lines:

A return was prepared by each of the Established Lines, and sent in to the Secretary of the Convoy Committee, showing in respect of each vessel under their control, the then actual sea-speed, in ballast and down to marks; approximate cargo capacity, dead-weight and measurement; armament, and other relevant particulars. From these returns the Secretary prepared for the Admiralty a general return, and a summary showing the vessels included in the general return, classified according to their actual sea-speed. Similar returns were subsequently sent in by the lines on the first day of each month, beginning January 1st, 1918, and dealt with in the same way.

The Admiralty, on their part, agreed to notify to the Secretary of the Convoy Committee, as soon as possible after the sailing of each home-bound convoy, the probable date of the ships' arrival in the Mersey. This information was at once passed on by the Secretary to the lines, who were required to complete the form in which it was contained by a statement showing the probable date on which each vessel would be ready to sail on her next outward voyage. In respect of each ship they were to give alternative dates, allowing respectively for normal and forced turn-round, together with particulars of any special considerations likely to delay or expedite the process. From these returns a second general return was prepared and forwarded to the Admiralty, for guidance in fixing the most convenient date for outward-bound convoys, from the point of view of obtaining the earliest possible return voyage. The date and port of assembly of such convoys, when fixed, were notified by the Admiralty to the Secretary of the Convoy Committee, who passed on the information to the lines.

In order to keep the closest possible touch, the Admiralty appointed a Port Convoy Officer at Liverpool to act as the channel of communication.

By the Port and Transit Executive Committee [1] also, the effects of the convoy system were being watched with grave anxiety. The satisfactory situation attained in the ports during the summer of 1917 had not been altogether maintained. During August, heavy arrivals of grain caused difficulties with regard to storage and handling at Liverpool, London, and Bristol, and by September the storage space in all the larger ports was very full. In Liverpool alone there were 99,000 tons of grain, and the stocks of grain and general produce were occupying the greater part of the space usually used for the storage of cotton. The main difficulty was the slow removal of

---

[1] Lord Inchcape had resigned the Chairmanship of this Committee in July, owing to pressure of other work. He was succeeded by Sir Norman Hill.

Government goods after discharge, and the tendency to use the transit sheds as warehouses for such imports. The majority of the smaller ports were also very full, and great difficulty was anticipated in dealing with the autumn arrivals. The Committee accordingly called a meeting of representatives of the Wheat and Sugar Commissions, the Army Contracts Department, the War Office Wool Department, and the Cotton Control Committee, to discuss means of clearing the ports, and accelerating turn-round. As a result of this meeting, it was agreed that the Wheat Commission should endeavour to procure more space in general warehouses, in order to clear the transit sheds, and that the Sugar Commission and Army Contracts Department should endeavour to make more use of East Coast ports, particularly those on the Humber. Extended use of motor haulage and other questions were also discussed.

During August, the Committee sustained a severe loss in the resignation of Mr. Harry Gosling, at the instance of his Executive. His withdrawal was based on the opinion of the Transport Workers' Federation, that the transport resources of the nation were not being used to the best advantage, that the labour supply at the ports was being dangerously depleted, and that the Transport Workers' Battalions were being introduced without sufficient care to organise first the civilian labour. At the same time, all Labour representatives were withdrawn from the local committees.

In Mr. Gosling's view, the difficulties which had arisen were due mainly to the separation of function of the Co-ordination Committees, the Port Labour Committees set up by the Board of Trade, and the local committees established by the Port and Transit Committee in connection with the Transport Workers' Battalions. In this view the Port and Transit Committee concurred, and after some negotiation with the Federation and the Board of Trade, the whole organisation was readjusted on the following lines : the Port Labour Committees and local Port and Transit Committees were to continue responsible respectively to the Board of Trade and the Central Port and Transit Committee ; but the members of each local Port and Transit Committee were to be *ex-officio* members of the Port Labour Committee for their centre. The Co-ordination Committees at Liverpool, Glasgow, and Bristol were merged in the respective local Port and Transit Committee. In the event of any difference as to exemptions between a Port Labour Committee and the local Port and Transit Committee, the question was to be decided by the Board of Trade, after consultation with Sir Norman Hill and Mr. Gosling. The representation of Labour on the Central Port and Transit Committee was strengthened. On the completion of this scheme the Labour representatives on the local committees were invited to resume their membership, which they did without exception, and Mr. Gosling also resumed his seat on the Central Committee.[1]

It was a tribute to the tact and care with which the Transport Workers' Battalions were employed, and the excellent relations existing between the Port and Transit Committee and organised Labour, that during the interregnum between Mr. Gosling's resignation in August, and the reconstitution of the organisation towards the end of October, the scheme continued to work without friction, although the number daily employed at the ports had risen to about 7,000 in August and September, and 7,400 in October.

It was in October that the effect of the convoy system on the condition of the Western ports began to attract the serious attention of the Committee. In that month a Committee under Colonel Pringle, R.E., was appointed by the Board of Trade to enquire into the possibility of arranging for the supply of London and the East Coast through the Western ports should the Channel become impossible for merchant vessels. On this Committee the Port and Transit Committee were represented.

In view of the very heavy losses in the Channel during the autumn the advisability of using the West Coast ports to the utmost of their capacity was obvious, and Liverpool especially was marked out as the recipient of an increasing proportion of the traffic by its position as the headquarters

---

[1] Labour representation on the Port and Transit Executive Committee now consisted of Messrs. Harry Gosling, James Sexton, Ben Tillett, and Ernest Bevin (with Mr. Robert Williams as alternate to either), representing the Transport Workers' Federation, and Mr. J. H. Thomas (with Mr. C. T. Cramp as an alternative), representing the National Union of Railwaymen.

Other additions to the Committee, representing various Departments and interests, were made from time to time, and in August Paymaster-Lieutenant-Commander H. B. Tuffill, R.D., R.N.R., succeeded Sir Frederick Dumayne as Secretary.

of the trade with North America, whence an ever-increasing proportion of the imports was drawn, and as the most convenient port for the disembarkation of American troops, who were now arriving in considerable numbers. Thus, though the number of convoys sailing to East and West Coast ports was approximately equal, the tendency was for the West Coast convoys to absorb a larger and larger proportion of the ships. The grain position both there and at other ports was now easier, as with ample stocks in hand, cargoes were being diverted to France and Italy, who were in urgent need of wheat. Nevertheless, the re-routeing of vessels involved serious difficulties, as the railways already showed signs of breaking down under the heavy strain imposed upon them by increased haulage, coupled with shortage of wagons and sheets, and lack of repairing facilities.[1] The Committee continued, therefore, to urge that, so far as possible, cargoes should be routed to the natural port of distribution for the area in which they were to be consumed, and that, in any event, sufficient trade should be directed to the East Coast ports to enable them to keep their labour together and preserve their importing power.

The two closely allied questions of turn-round under convoy conditions, and the capacity of the ports to which the majority of ships were now being routed, constituted at this time the most serious problem in connection with oversea supplies. The success of the convoy system in reducing loss was clearly manifest, despite an untoward incident in the Mediterranean.

The first west-bound Through Mediterranean Convoy, like the first outward convoy, was attended by ill-fortune. Consisting of six ships only, it sailed from Port Said on November 16th. It was persistently attacked, and lost the *Clan Mac Corquodale* off Crete, the *Kohistan* off Malta, and the *Karema* in the neighbourhood of Cape de Gata, Algeria. So lamentable an experience led to a proposal for a reversion to the Cape Route, but by the end of the month the second, third, and fourth outward convoys, comprising a total of twenty-two ships, had arrived at Port Said without loss, and both the Admiralty and Ministry of Shipping were confident that, with increasing experience, losses could be kept within narrow limits. The arrangements for the second homeward convoy were

[1] In November, 23,000 trucks were under repair.

LOSSES FURTHER REDUCED

accordingly allowed to go on, and on December 3rd this convoy, consisting of fourteen ships, sailed from Port Said.[1]

Apart from this incident, the working of the convoy system during November was very successful, so far as concerned the diminution of risk, and the losses of British shipping during the month—174,000 tons—were decidedly the lowest recorded since the outbreak of the unrestricted submarine campaign. Those of foreign shipping—115,000 tons—showed a similar reduction. Not a single steamer of 500 tons and upwards was sunk in the Approaches, and the greatest number of casualties were reported, as in the previous month, from the Channel and Mediterranean.

[1] The homeward convoys were always rather larger than the outward, as they comprised a proportion of vessels which had gone out by the Cape Route.

CHAPTER XIII

THE PROGRESS OF REPLACEMENT
MAY—NOVEMBER 1917

WELCOME as was the diminution in losses brought about by the introduction of convoy, the destruction of British shipping was still proceeding at a rate considerably in excess of the replacements. In spite of all the efforts made, in spite of the new machinery set up to control construction, shipbuilding in the United Kingdom was still quite unable to keep up with the rate of loss, to say nothing of making good the deficit of previous months, and the programme of oversea ship purchase had received its death-blow, so far as the main source of supply was concerned.

On the appointment of Sir Eric Geddes as Controller of the Navy, in May 1917, the new branch of the Admiralty thus created was organised in three departments, each under the direction of a Deputy Controller. These three departments were Armament Production, Warship Construction, and Auxiliary Shipbuilding. The first and second were purely naval, the third embraced not only the construction of naval auxiliaries proper, but merchant shipbuilding. It was placed under the direction of Major-General C. S. Collard, R.E., who had no experience of shipbuilding, but had gained a reputation as an organiser, in connection with the development of the port of Richborough. As expert advisers he had the Merchant Shipbuilding Council, formed by additions to the Merchant Shipbuilding Advisory Committee, and the whole administrative staff—numbering about thirty—which the Shipping Controller had collected, was transferred to the new department. The control now exercised, however, was much more direct and detailed than that exercised by the Shipping Controller, who had trusted much to the co-operation of the great classification societies, and the Marine Department of the Board of Trade. One result of the change of administration was, therefore, a great expansion of the staff, which ultimately swelled to about 600 persons, grouped under thirteen Directorates—Merchant Shipbuilding, Auxiliary Vessels, Designs, Ship Repairs, Extensions, Supplies, Engineering Work, Ships' Engines, Oversea Ship Purchase, Concrete Construction, Medical and Sanitary, Information, and Labour. The Director of Merchant Shipbuilding was Lieutenant-Colonel Lithgow, M.C., of Russell & Co., Port Glasgow; Mr. John Esplen retained his position as Director of Oversea Ship Purchase.

Connection between the new Department and the Ministry of Shipping was maintained by investing the Navy Controller with *ex-officio* membership of the Shipping Control Committee, and in theory the Shipping Controller remained responsible for approving the design of standard types, and deciding the ratio in which the output contemplated by the Navy Controller should be divided among those types.

By July 5th the Navy Controller had worked out his programme.[1] The mark at which he aimed was a total naval and mercantile output, in completed ships, at the rate of 4,600,000 tons gross per annum. Of this total the proportion of merchant shipping was to be 3,100,000 tons. This was the ultimate aim; it involved a rate of production twice as great as that of the record peace year, 1913, and it was not expected that it could be at once attained. Sir Eric Geddes hoped, however, for an output of 1,190,000 tons during the last seven months of 1917 which, with 376,000 tons completed to the end of May, would give a total output for the year of 1,566,000, 30 per cent. above the Shipping Controller's estimate. In 1918 the output anticipated was 2,300,000, the monthly figures rising gradually throughout the year until, at the end of 1918, they reached the equivalent of 3,000,000 tons per annum.

Had such a programme been embarked upon in the earlier days of the war, or had the supply of steel and labour for mercantile shipbuilding been so jealously guarded that the private shipowners were able to obtain delivery of the ships for which they were ready and eager to contract, the tonnage crisis of 1916 might have been averted, and even the blows inflicted by the submarines

---

[1] Shortly after this date Sir Eric Geddes succeeded Sir Edward Carson as First Lord of the Admiralty, and Sir Alan Anderson became Navy Controller.

in the early months of 1917 might have been borne without fear of immediate disaster. Unhappily neither the length of the war nor the extent of the submarine danger had been foreseen, and the enormous expansion of the Army forced upon Great Britain by events in France and Flanders, had been achieved at the expense of the vital industries of the country. At the time of the great munitions crisis in the spring of 1916, the economic resources of the country still possessed some degree of elasticity, and the demands of the Armies had been met by a vast redirection of the national energies. It was now suggested by the Navy Controller that the time had come for a similar readjustment of the national resources to meet the danger created by the submarine campaign; but such a readjustment was not easily to be effected now that so large a proportion of the labour and material available was absorbed by the demands of the Armies themselves, and the fulfilment of the commitments undertaken on their behalf, or on that of the Allies, by the Ministry of Munitions. The control of shipbuilding had been transferred from the Ministry of Shipping to the Admiralty in the hope of increasing output by facilitating allocation of labour and material between naval and mercantile construction; but the real problem was that presented by the insufficiency of the total supply, and this remained to be solved.

In order to realise the estimate of 1,190,000 tons for the seven months June to December 1917, it was necessary that the total allocation of steel for shipbuilding, naval and mercantile, should be increased at once from 24,000 to 30,000 tons a week; in order to attain an output at the rate of 3,000,000 tons per annum by the end of 1918, it would have to be raised ultimately to 53,000 tons a week.[1] Further, the full programme required that the labour

[1]
	Tons.
Warship and dockyard requirements	8,000
Auxiliary vessels	4,307
Merchant and auxiliary repairs	3,170
Merchant shipbuilding	36,667
Constructional steel for new yards	1,000
	53,144

This represented a larger demand than was contemplated in April for a 3,000,000-ton programme (see note on p. 107); but repair work and naval construction were both on the increase.

employed in the shipyards and marine engineering shops should be increased, by the summer of 1918, by 80,000 physically fit men, 12,500 of whom must be skilled workers.

For the moment, it was still the supply of steel which dominated the situation. Although the allocation during May showed a still larger increase than had been anticipated, the improvement was not sustained. So far from the summer months bringing further relief, the average deliveries for June, July, and August were slightly below the April level, and mainly as a result of this deficit the output of completed merchant shipping for the September quarter was only 248,000 tons gross, as against an estimate of 420,000. In September, for the first time, the deliveries of steel rose to the programme level of 80,000 tons a week, and in October 146,000 tons of shipping were completed. The estimate for October, however, had been 210,000 tons, and by October 31st there was a total cumulative deficit of 233,000 tons on the Navy Controller's 1917 programme.

Moreover, although the weekly deliveries of steel during October again reached the 80,000-ton level, the immediate effect of the improvement in the steel position was to bring to a head the problem of shipyard labour, which had hitherto taken second place. So long as the supply of steel was inadequate for fulfilment of the programme, the question of providing additional labour was a secondary matter; when the steel became obtainable, it was urgently necessary that the labour available should be sufficient to turn the supply of material to account.

It will be remembered that, at the beginning of the year, all men employed in the shipyards and marine engineering works prior to March 29th, were exempted from military service. The Navy Controller desired this exemption to be made permanent and absolute for all men at any time in such employment, but in face of strong War Office opposition, the Government felt it impossible to do more than extend the exemption to all men so employed on or before July 15th. It had proved equally impossible to make any substantial progress in the release of skilled workers who had joined the colours earlier in the war. This was a very serious matter, as if large numbers of unskilled workers were to be added to the staff of the yards, it was urgently necessary that they should be leavened by an increased number of skilled and experienced men.

The dilemma was a real one. The developments of the war on land and the wastage of the armies in the field involved a continual and pressing demand on the manpower of the country; but, largely owing to the sudden and unexpected nature of the initial military expansion, and the consequent failure to foresee its consequences, the progress of recruiting reacted disastrously on services which were as essential to the maintenance of the military effort as to the feeding of the civil population and the financing of the war. It was exactly the same dilemma as had been presented by the recruiting of transport workers, and the proposal was actually made that it should be solved on the lines of the Transport Workers' Battalions, since, especially at the North Eastern ports, the working of a double-shift system would be greatly facilitated by the employment of men enlisted for home defence. This suggestion, however, was not adopted.

It was the question of skilled labour which was the pivot of the problem. In November 1917, the Navy Controller reported that, now the supply of steel had been brought up to the level of his demands, it was essential that the supply of labour should be increased. In order to bring the total labour force up to the peace level 20,000 additional workers were required, and since an ultimate output was now aimed at, much in advance of the peace figures, it was essential not only to provide these workers, but to press to the utmost schemes for the adoption of pneumatic riveting, payment by results, and the dilution of skilled by female and unskilled labour. All these schemes had already been the subject of negotiation, but little or no progress had been made, and the principal Trade Unions concerned now declared definitely that they would maintain their opposition until all skilled workers in the forces, overseas and home, or on the sick list, were returned to their former employment. In view of the difficulty of tracing and bringing home individual men, especially from the more distant theatres of war, this was not a demand with which it was easy to comply, and the attitude of the Unions was probably coloured by the industrial friction which, at this time, had reached an acute stage in some of the chief shipbuilding centres. It was unquestionable, however, that the enrollment of a great force of unskilled labour would be useless unless a strong nucleus of skilled workers could be provided, and the Navy Controller accordingly pressed the Government for the immediate release (transference to the Army Reserve) of 20,000 skilled workers. This, however, was no easy matter in view of the many conflicting demands on the man-power of the country, and it was some weeks before the Government arrived at a decision.

There was, indeed, one important potential source of labour which had not yet been tapped. The idea of using German prisoners of war in the shipyards had for a long time been under discussion, and now that adequate steel supplies were at last available, the Admiralty were extremely anxious to obtain sanction for this step. It was generally recognised, however, that prisoner-of-war labour under military discipline could not be utilised in the ordinary shipyards alongside British labour, and for this reason, a project for the establishment of National Shipyards, contained in Sir Eric Geddes's July report, came into new prominence.

The ultimate 3,000,000-ton programme contemplated in that report obviously involved an extension of the existing shipbuilding facilities of the country. Such an extension was, indeed, most desirable, and so early as April, the Shipping Controller had circularised the shipbuilders, urging them to extend their slips and plant. In view of a possible post-bellum slump, the extent to which builders could afford to sink their capital in such developments was limited, and in July it was decided to permit grants-in-aid to be made in respect of approved schemes. Munitions certificates were issued for the work, and many extensions, with or without financial assistance from the State, were put in hand.[1]

The extent to which the private shipyards could be profitably developed depended, however, on the supply of labour, and as has been seen, prisoner-of-war labour could not be used in such yards. General Collard, who had already established a yard at Richborough for the construction of small craft, proposed that National Yards

---

[1] By the end of the war over 300 schemes of extension and improvement to existing shipyards and marine engineering works had been sanctioned, of which two-thirds received a grant. These schemes included the construction of 80 new slips and the lengthening of 19 existing slips. Of these, 32 and 11, respectively, had been completed by the cessation of hostilities. The total grants amounted to about £2,400,000.

should now be established for the utilisation of German labour, in the building of Fabricated Ships from parts made in bridgebuilding and constructional engineering works, which could easily be assembled by unskilled workers. The site chosen was the Bristol Channel, where large constructional steel works were available, and it was proposed to build yards at Chepstow, Beachley, and Portbury, with a total of forty-one slips, including seven taken over from Messrs. Finch & Co., who had established a yard at Chepstow in 1916.

This scheme received the approval of the Government on August 9th, and the preliminary work at Chepstow was begun in September. In the hope that the supply of steel for the future was assured, General Collard was now exceedingly anxious to push ahead with the National Yards, in order that the prisoner-of-war labour might be utilised ; but it was obviously necessary that the supply of material to existing shipyards capable of turning it to immediate account should be fully safeguarded, and during October a deputation of shipbuilders, headed by Sir George Carter, obtained from the Prime Minister a guarantee that the supply of steel and labour (other than German) to existing yards, whether for shipbuilding or extensions, should receive a definite priority, up to the full limit of their capacity. They further strongly advised the Government, before committing themselves too deeply to the scheme for National Yards, to consult the Trade Unions affected, and obtain an agreement with them as to the employment of the skilled nucleus who would be necessary to leaven the mass of German labour.[1]

This priority to the existing yards was a matter of the first importance. The necessary preliminary work on the National Yards embraced, not only the erection of slips and plant, but a vast amount of constructional work on roads, railways, water supply, electric power, and housing, and even under the most favourable conditions, General Collard estimated that it would take six or seven months before the yards could be in working order, and that the earliest date by which ships could be launched was November 1918. Should the war last well into 1919 the

---

[1] They also pointed out that the establishment of a shipbuilding yard in a repairing centre must inevitably lead to friction, unless the matter was previously discussed with the Unions, as repairers' wages were on a higher scale than builders'.

output of the National Yards would be available; but the immediate problem was to make good the current losses by which the tonnage under the British flag was being steadily and rapidly depleted.

For the replacement of those current losses it was to the existing yards alone that it was possible to look, and apart from ships with insulated space, and cargo vessels in an advanced stage of construction, it was upon the standard shipbuilding programme that the energies of the yards were now concentrated. Yet, though the first standard steamer, an " A " type freighter, *War Shamrock*, was delivered by Messrs. Harland & Wolff in August, only five standard vessels had been delivered by the end of October.

By this time, too, the programme had been complicated by the introduction of important variations on the standard types. Of the five original types, " E " had now been practically dropped, and no further orders were at present being placed for " C " and " D " ships, as it was considered that the number of these smaller classes already laid down or arranged for, would be sufficient. Only the big " A " and " B " freighters were being ordered. It had, however, become necessary to make certain additions to the list. In July, a body of representative liner owners, headed by Lord Inchcape, made strong representations to the Admiralty and the Shipping Controller as to the necessity of making some provision for the replacement of liner tonnage. The losses of the big lines were very heavy; they were no longer permitted to place orders on their own account, and the standard ships were suited neither as regards speed nor construction for the liner trades.

This contention was admitted to be reasonable. Apart from the desirability of considering the position of British shipping in international competition after the war, a larger and faster type of ship had great advantages even for war purposes, and it was desirable that some at least of the vessels produced should comply with the requirements of the liner trades, even at some sacrifice of deadweight capacity. Two new types of standard vessels, " F " and " G," were accordingly sanctioned in August 1917. Of these " F " was an ordinary freighter, of similar construction to " B," but with a speed of 12 knots, and a dead-weight capacity of 10,795 tons, on a gross tonnage of 6,440. The other new type " G " was of more elaborate design, having the general characteristics of the cargo liner, with a length of 450 feet, a gross tonnage of 8,000 tons, 10,800 tons dead-weight capacity, twin screws, and a speed of 13 knots.

Both the " F " and " G " types required engines of different design from the two sets which sufficed types " A " to " E," and neither could be produced so quickly as was possible, under favourable conditions, with the earlier designs, but on the average the loss of time was small. More serious in its effect on output was an alteration in the programme necessitated by the oil-fuel crisis. In order to make good the deficiency in tanker tonnage, it was decided in August that nineteen vessels of the " A " type, ordered for delivery in or before March 1918, should be converted into tankers, and that four specially designed tankers of standard type should be laid down each month.

The new tanker type "ZO" was of the same dimensions as " A " and had the same engines and speed, with a gross tonnage of 5,800, and a dead-weight capacity of 8,000 tons. The converted vessels, known as "AO," had a gross tonnage of 5,250, and a dead-weight capacity of 7,885. On the average the construction of the " Z " tankers occupied about forty days longer than that of the " A " type freighters; but only about a week longer than those of type " B." The effect of converting the " A " freighters to "AO" tankers was much more serious, as it involved an average delay of nearly five months in the delivery of the ships.[1]

The proportion in which orders were to be divided among the various standard types was settled in August as follows:

Freighters	type " A "	. . . .	7
,,	,, " B "	. . . .	10
,,	,, " F "	. . . .	5
,,	,, " G "	. . . .	5
Tankers	,, " ZO "	. . . .	4
Converted tankers	,, " AO "	. . . .	4

This gave a monthly programme of thirty-five ships, but

[1] No ship of type " F " was completed before the termination of hostilities, and only one type " G." This vessel took 344 days to build. The times for the tankers were as follows:

	Minimum Days.	Maximum Days.	Average Days.
" ZO "	267	386	314
" AO "	212	585	411

Compare note, p. 105, *supra.*

in practice it proved impossible to lay down ships at this rate; nor were the proportions thus indicated adhered to with any precision. The bulk of the effort, however, continued to be directed to the production of the "A" and "B" freighters and to tankers, either of the "ZO," or converted type.[1]

There were thus three main factors—shortage of steel, shortage of labour, and conversion of freighters to oilers—which tended to retard the shipbuilding output, and of these only the first had been, partially and temporarily, overcome. Not only was the effect on the current completions very serious, but by November it had become necessary to revise drastically the estimate for 1918. It was still hoped to work up, by the end of that year, to a rate of production equal to 3,000,000 tons per annum, but the actual tonnage to be completed during 1918 was now placed at 1,800,000 instead of 2,300,000 tons. On this estimate the output of the British yards would be equivalent to little over two-thirds of the losses in ocean-going steamers alone, at the average rate for the three months, September, October, and November 1917, when losses were at their lowest since the outbreak of the unrestricted submarine campaign. Thus, so far from making good the havoc wrought in 1917, there would still be a cumulative deficit. The prospect of an eventual output at the rate of 3,000,000 tons a year was cheering in relation to the recovery of the mercantile marine after the war; but it was evident the war might be won or lost before its effects could be felt.

This reduction in the prospective programme was the more serious inasmuch as all hope of making good the deficit by oversea purchase had been finally extinguished.

Throughout June and July 1917, the fate of the "Cunard" contracts was trembling in the balance. In pressing for delivery of the vessels the British Government

[1] Certain further variations from standard types were sanctioned during the last quarter of the year. A shelter deck vessel of 5,680 tons gross and 9,000 dead-weight, and three 'tween deck vessels of 4,600 gross and 7,520 dead-weight were building in October, and were sanctioned by the Shipping Controller during December. At a later date sanction was given for the construction of similar vessels up to a dozen of each type. They were known as "F¹" and "J" respectively. Official designs for five types of small coasters, "CS," were approved in October; and for type "H," an improved edition of "D," in December. Of these new types, "F¹" took the same engines as "F"; "J" took the same engines as "A" and "B"; "H" had a separate set. No ships of any of these types were completed till late in 1918.

were on strong ground, as they were able to point to the fact that down to the end of 1916 the fullest possible facilities, subject to British requirements, had been given for the completion and transfer of ships ordered by Allied subjects, and even ships ordered by neutrals prior to the Transfer Restriction Regulations, had been allowed to be delivered on completion, subject to an agreement for time-charter to the British Government for the duration of the war, at specially reduced rates.[1]

The precedent created by their own action towards Allied shipbuilding was strongly emphasised by the British Government, who laid stress also on the urgent need of the European Allies for tonnage. It was, indeed, the war employment of the ships rather than their ultimate ownership with which they were mainly concerned, and they were prepared, if necessary, to consent to their retransfer after the war, or even to their immediate transfer to the American flag, provided they could be obtained for employment in the war zone.

Mr. Balfour, with most of the members of his Mission, returned from the States at the end of May, but a few days after his arrival, Mr. Thomas Royden and Mr. J. A. Salter arrived at Washington for the purpose of discussing co-operation in shipping matters, and during June they were able to obtain a personal interview with the President, and to state fully the British case from the point of view of the Ministry of Shipping.

During all this time a heated controversy was raging in the United States as to the policy to be followed in the American shipbuilding programme. It was stated at the time that the existing shipyards were full up with work, and unwilling or unable to do anything considerable in the way of extending their plant or accelerating output. In these circumstances Mr. Denman, the Chairman of the Shipping Board, proposed to meet the emergency by a vast programme of wooden steamship construction, and this policy was enthusiastically taken up in the Western States, where a great amount of timber was available, and by a considerable section of the press. On the other hand, General Goethals, Manager of the Emergency Fleet Cor-

---

[1] More recently a stipulation had been made that such vessels should, for defensive purposes, remain under the British flag for the duration of the war, a guarantee being given that they should be transferred after the termination of hostilities.

poration, was convinced that, by working double shifts, the extension of existing plant, and the laying down of new yards, a large programme of steel construction could be carried out. Meanwhile a large number of firms had been instructed to build slips for the construction of wooden vessels, but few definite contracts had been placed. On the other hand, Mr. Denman had refused to sanction contracts into which General Goethals was anxious to enter, on the ground of the prohibitive height to which the price of steel had risen.[1] Indeed, it was not until July that the powers of the Shipping Board were finally defined. By an Urgent Deficiencies Act, approved on June 15th, the President had been authorised to requisition, construct, and operate ships, and these powers he delegated by an Executive Order, dated July 11th, to the Emergency Fleet Corporation, which was empowered to acquire vessels already constructed, and to operate, manage, and dispose of ships to be acquired by the United States.[2]

Towards the end of July the strained situation thus created came to an end. General Goethals resigned, and the President himself requested the resignation of Mr. Denman. Mr. Edward N. Hurley thereupon became Chairman of the Shipping Board, and Admiral Capps Manager of the Emergency Fleet Corporation. As Mr. Denman was known to be strongly in favour of requisitioning the ships building under the " Cunard " contracts, the Ministry of Shipping were hopeful that the change in administration might lead to Great Britain obtaining delivery of the vessels. An order had, however, already been drawn up, though not yet issued, requisitioning all steel ships of 2,500 tons dead-weight or over, under construction for private owners of any nationality, on the plea that only by State organisation could the rate of construction be sufficiently accelerated. This Order was adopted by the new authorities, who, indeed, extended its scope to include all vessels contracted for as well as those under construction. On August 3rd the Requisitioning Order was issued.[3]

In demanding the requisitioning of the ships building for foreign owners a large section of the American press and public were, no doubt, thinking of the re-establishment of the American mercantile marine, as well as of the emergency necessities of the war. One main reason for

[1] Mattox, *Building the Emergency Fleet*, pp. 17–25.
[2] *Ibid.*, pp. 6–7.   [3] *Ibid.*, pp. 26, 33–6.

requisition, however, was the desire to clear the slips of vessels under construction, in order to make way for a new " standard " programme, and for some little time hopes were held out to the British Government that, on payment of acceleration costs, they might yet receive delivery of the ships they had ordered. A few of those first completed were actually handed over, making, with some half-dozen ships delivered before the date of the order, a total of thirteen steamers with an aggregate dead-weight capacity of 78,800 tons. In October, however, the Shipping Board announced definitely that no further transfers would be permitted, and the remaining vessels building or contracted for had to be written off, so far as the British balance sheet of tonnage was concerned.

This was a heavy blow. The steamers thus taken over by America amounted to 158 of 960,800 dead-weight tons (say, 640,000 gross), and the possibility of placing future orders was also negatived.[1] In view of the restricted capacity of the Japanese and Canadian yards, it became evident that, great as were the difficulties of construction in Great Britain, it was to her own efforts that, in the main, she must look for making good her losses.

Under the Canadian contracts only three small steamers had yet been delivered, and few others were due until the summer of 1918 [2]; but good progress had been made in Japan, where a number of the ships purchased were in an advanced state of construction when the contract was closed. The first two Japanese-built steamers, *War King* and *War Queen*, arrived during July, bringing on their maiden voyages 20,000 tons of wheat from Australia, and by the end of October twelve large ships, with an aggregate capacity of 87,600 tons, had been delivered by the Japanese builders.

Meanwhile some progress had been made in the work of bringing the immobilised German tonnage into service. Although the United States had declared war on April 6th, it was not until June 20th that a Presidential Order was issued, empowering the Shipping Board to take over,

---

[1] The ships taken over by the United States included eight tankers building for the British Admiralty. Full compensation was eventually paid by the United States for all expenses incurred in connection with the uncompleted contracts.

[2] In addition to the ships built in Canada, a few Canadian steamers running on the Great Lakes were transferred to ocean employment; the owners undertaking the necessary structural alterations on condition of a period of exemption from requisition.

repair, and operate the German vessels in American ports, and owing to the injuries inflicted by the German crews, many of the ships were still in the repairers' hands at the end of October. Several, however, which had escaped serious injury, were already on service. On the other hand, there appeared to be little prospect of obtaining any part of this tonnage for the use of the European Allies. The whole, so far as could be seen, was likely to be absorbed by the trooping and other requirements of the United States themselves.

In Brazil the situation had been changed by the declaration of war on October 26th. The Brazilian Government had now requisitioned the German ships in their ports, and there was a prospect of their being repaired and brought into service. The process of repair was, however, likely to be lengthy. Negotiations for the use of German tonnage in the ports of other South American countries were still proceeding, but without, as yet, any tangible result. The severance of relations with Germany by Uruguay and Peru had, however, been accompanied by seizure of the German vessels in their harbours, and though the engines of all these vessels had been seriously damaged, there appeared to be some hope that they might ultimately become available.[1]

In Asia, the ships seized by China were still the subject of negotiations between the Allied Powers. A small further supply of tonnage had, however, come into sight through the action of the Siamese Government, who, on July 22nd, declared war against Germany and Austria, seized the German steamers at Bangkok, which were found to be in good condition, and brought them before a Prize Court.[2]

The one really satisfactory feature in the situation was the acquisition of neutral tonnage under the Danish and Norwegian Agreements. By October 12th about 116,000 tons dead-weight of Danish shipping had been time-chartered under the scheme, which with 62,000 tons previously requisitioned, and 11,000 tons trading for the Allies in European waters on voyage-charter, very nearly made up the stipulated 200,000 dead-weight tons. One serious point of contention had, however, arisen. The

[1] The Uruguayan Government severed relations with Germany on October 7th. They had previously, on September 15th, seized the German ships at Monte Video, 8 s.s. of 42,658 tons gross. Peru severed relations on October 5th. The German ships then seized were 6 s.s. of 34,697 tons.
[2] 9 s.s. 19,252 G.T.

British Government interpreted the agreement as providing that the full total of 200,000 tons dead-weight should be *maintained* in Allied service; that is to say, that vessels lost in such service should be replaced by other Danish ships. This claim the Danes persistently denied, and the losses were not, in fact, replaced, with the result that this block of Danish tonnage had to be regarded as a wasting asset. Its utility was further limited by a decision, reached after much negotiation, that no ships secured under the Agreement should be forced to trade in the Mediterranean.

In the carrying out of the still more important Norwegian Agreement, no serious dispute arose. It comprised, as will be remembered, two main provisions: one for the replacement of Norwegian ships in the North Sea by British vessels; the other for the charter to the Inter-Allied Committee of all other Norwegian tonnage not required for the import service of Norway.

Replacement of the Norwegian tonnage in the North Sea began during August, and by the end of that month about 50,000 tons of Norwegian shipping had been handed over and replaced. By the beginning of November it had grown to nearly 130,000 tons, of which 90,000 tons was requisitioned, and nearly 40,000 tons time-chartered by the British Government. The ships requisitioned were, of course, placed under the British flag, and about one-third of this tonnage consisted of steamers of 1,600 tons gross and upwards. But though they went to swell the total of British tonnage these vessels did not, in fact, represent a net addition to the available carrying power, as equivalent British tonnage had to be provided, under the agreement, for the carriage of coal to Norway. At the same time, the replacement scheme was not only of benefit to Norway, by securing a guarantee of her coal supply, but secured substantial advantages to the Allies. It was necessary that the Norwegian coal supply should be maintained, and the heavy losses in that trade were a factor limiting the Norwegian tonnage available for Allied employment. It was far better that the coal should be carried by armed British ships, among whom losses were likely to be smaller, and that the Norwegian steamers should be available for Allied service elsewhere, as armed vessels under the British flag. Further, the substitution of British for Norwegian tonnage not only facilitated the organisation of the Scandinavian convoy but diminished the number of ships risked in this dangerous trade, since the same amount of coal could be carried by a smaller amount of tonnage than was required when the work had to be done by Norwegian ships subject to the restrictions of the North Sea Freight Scheme.[1] For the purpose of the scheme, all arrangements, both for the carriage of coal and for the return cargoes of essential imports from Norway, were concentrated in a specially created Norwegian section of the Ministry of Shipping under Mr. T. E. Ruddock of Newcastle-on-Tyne, formerly coal adviser to His Majesty's Government in Scandinavia. Messrs. Ellerman, Wilson & Co. were appointed as chief agents in Christiania, both for the discharge of outward and the collection of homeward cargoes, and the staffs of the British Consulates in Norway were strengthened by the addition of commercial men, to assist in the working of the scheme. From the first, all efforts were concentrated on obtaining the quickest possible turn-round, and though these were at first partially defeated by congestion arising from the convoy arrangements, the difficulties were subsequently overcome, and a substantial tonnage economy effected.

Meanwhile the charter to the Inter-Allied Committee of Norwegian ships outside the North Sea trade went rapidly forward. During August, September, and October over 100,000 dead-weight tons were fixed by the Executive direct. In October alone the fixtures exceeded 55,000 tons, and other ships were being fixed as fast as their current charters expired. Nearly 900,000 tons dead-weight (say, 600,000 gross) of Norwegian shipping, other than requisitioned vessels, was now running in Allied services, either on time-charter to the Executive, or on voyage-charter in the coal and ore trades, and the only serious uncertainty related to a large block of tonnage on charter to American citizens, but under obligation to offer to the Inter-Allied Executive on termination of their existing engagements.[2]

[1] See Vol. II, pp. 279-80, 359-60.
[2] For the purpose of securing co-ordination between the various departments concerned with neutral shipping, especially with regard to Tonnage Agreements and other matters affecting Foreign Office interests, the Neutral Tonnage Conference was formed in September 1917. This was an interdepartmental committee meeting two or three times a week at the Ministry of Shipping, and consisted of representatives of that Ministry, the Foreign Office, the Admiralty (Trade Division), and the Inter-Allied Chartering Executive

CHAPTER XIV

THE SYSTEM OF EMBARGOES
JULY—NOVEMBER 1917

In the relations between the Allies and neutral States during the spring and summer of 1917 tonnage considerations were inextricably entangled with the restriction of enemy trade. The network of agreements created during 1915 and 1916 had for its main object the restriction of enemy supplies; but the coal export and bunker regulations had been used from an early date for forcing neutral tonnage into Allied employment, and the agreements entered into by neutral shipowners, in order to avoid delay at the ports of examination, contained provisions for space to be offered to the Allies as well as guarantees against engaging in enemy trade.

The outbreak of the unrestricted submarine campaign at the beginning of 1917, and the consequent paralysis of neutral shipping, brought the tonnage aspect of the question into greatly increased prominence, and it was to securing control of tonnage that the Danish and Norwegian agreements were directed; but the importance of restricting enemy supplies could never for a moment be overlooked. More and more was the struggle becoming a war of attrition; indeed, the violence of the new submarine attack, and its initial success, threatened to convert it into a race with starvation on either side. Thus, side by side with the measures taken to acquire control of neutral tonnage, there went on an intensification of economic pressure, in which the association of the United States with the European Allies was of immense assistance.

Through the application of the rationing system to neutral imports, leakage to the Central Powers of commodities received by contiguous neutral countries from overseas had been reduced almost to nothing. There was still, no doubt, a little smuggling, especially of commodities of small bulk and high value, but the supplies received by the enemy from sources outside Europe were so small as to be almost insignificant, and the most important aspect of the blockade was now the stoppage of supplies produced in the contiguous neutral countries themselves, especially those produced by the aid of imports, such as fodder and fertilisers, which the Allies had allowed to pass. These supplies had, indeed, been considerably restricted, but they had a value out of all proportion to their bulk, in view of the fact that they consisted mainly of the fatty foods which were the enemy's greatest need, and it was, therefore, a matter of real importance to reduce them still further and, if possible, to stop them altogether.

The question of products dependent on imports from abroad came to a head, as regards Denmark, in the summer of 1916. The resumption of sailings by the Danish produce ships had not by any means put an end to the difficulties with regard to the distribution of Danish foodstuffs. As the shortage of food in Germany became more and more pronounced, the prices offered for meat, bacon, and dairy produce rose higher and higher. Despite this temptation, the Danes loyally endeavoured to fulfil their undertakings to Great Britain, but on the resumption of traffic they found the British market well stocked with colonial butter, and it became necessary for the Food Controller to take this butter off the market, in order to enable the Danish produce to be sold. Even then, the prices realised in Great Britain were lower than those obtainable, not only in Germany, but in Norway; partly because, owing to long delays caused by the submarine danger, much of the Danish produce arrived in very poor condition.

In the face both of these difficulties and of the submarine danger itself, the Danes persevered in their efforts. Despite the interruption of traffic during February, British imports of bacon and butter from Denmark, during the first five months of 1917, were little below those of the previous year, and during April and May only 12 per cent. of the total output of bacon went to Germany. There were other items, however, such as live cattle, eggs, and milk, of which the exports to Germany were on the increase, and in view of the difficulties of taking delivery of Danish produce, it was not easy to see how this leakage was to be stopped. Moreover, Germany was exercising increased pressure. Two produce ships were sunk and several others were captured and taken into Swinemünde. The Danes replied by threatening to stop all exports to Germany; but this was met by something very closely approaching an open threat of invasion, and it was obvious that the Danish Government could not maintain their attitude.

The Ministry of Blockade had watched the course of events with great anxiety. Meat, eggs, milk, and butter were now so scarce in Germany, that the interception of even the smallest addition to the enemy's supplies was worth some sacrifice. Further, the export of horses from Denmark was of military importance to the enemy, who had obtained a considerable temporary increase in the numbers exported as the price of allowing produce ships to proceed as far as Bergen unmolested. Fresh negotiations with Denmark during June were unproductive, and in view of the practical impossibility of imposing a rigid check on the distribution of Danish produce, the Government decided upon a complete reversal of their previous policy.

Hitherto that policy had been to maintain the output of Danish bacon and dairy produce at its maximum, by allowing free importation of fodder and fertilisers, which had even been excepted from the rationing agreements. This policy was based on a desire to preserve the output available for purchase by Great Britain, no less than on the difficulty of justifying drastic interference with the leading Danish industry. There was also a fear that any stoppage of the fodder imports would lead to panic slaughtering, with the result of large exports of meat and pig products to the Central Powers, a point of great importance so long as a speedy termination of the war was expected. It was doubtful, however, whether the Danish food supplies were not now of greater importance to Germany than to Great Britain. For Germany they were irreplaceable; whereas Great Britain could look to the United States for increased shipments of bacon, and the importance of Danish butter was reduced both by the possibility of substituting colonial produce, and by the progress made in the home manufacture of margarine. Moreover, the necessity of reducing consumption by rationing had already been accepted. On the other hand, the entry of the United States into the war enormously increased the pressure which could be exerted by the Allies, and the exercise of such pressure was justified by

DANISH IMPORTS HELD UP

the fact that, owing to the action of the submarines and the German threat of invasion, Denmark could hardly be regarded as a free agent in the negotiation or execution of agreements.

In these circumstances, the British Government decided to aim at a reduction of the Danish output to a minimum, by cutting off the supply of fodder and fertilisers. This involved writing off the imports of dairy produce from Denmark, but it would lead, if successful, to a practical stoppage of all such supplies to the enemy, whereas the agreements had aimed only at limiting those supplies to a definite figure.

In pursuance of this policy the Government began, in the summer of 1917, to hold up all shipments of fodder, fertilisers, oils, fats, margarine materials, and soya beans. At the same time they requested the American Government to prohibit the export of fodder to Denmark. They agreed, however, to soften the blow financially, by taking over all commitments abroad into which the Danes had already entered.

This was only the beginning of a very wide extension of the machinery of economic pressure. The United States Government had, by this time, created its own organisation for the control of exports, and was prepared to use it for far more drastic restriction of neutral trade than had been possible while the chief source of supplies remained outside the circle of belligerents. Rigorously as the rationing principle had been applied since the creation of the Ministry of Blockade, some small proportion of the supplies received by neutrals from overseas was, undoubtedly, still re-exported to the Central Powers. Further, in the various agreements entered into with neutral Governments or producers, it had frequently been necessary to provide specifically for a division between the Allies and Central Powers of the home products of neutral countries. What the American Government now aimed at was to obtain from neutral States, in return for their rationed imports, definite guarantees, not only against re-export to the Central Powers, but against the export to the enemy of any part of their own output.

The first step was taken on July 9th, when an order was issued, prohibiting the export from the United States, except under licence, of coal, foodstuffs, steel, and other essential products. The avowed object of this order was the conservation of stocks for domestic use. On August 27th, however, it was followed by a Presidential Proclamation placing all exports to European neutrals under the control of the Export Council, and many neutral ships laden with grain, fodder, and similar cargoes were detained in American ports.

On September 16th the Exports Administrative Board issued a " Conservation List " of commodities, of which it was announced that practically no shipments to neutral countries would, for the time being, be licensed. This list included wheat, flour, sugar, steel, iron, and explosive materials, and the embargo applied equally to all neutral States. With regard to other exports, a list of some 600 articles was published on October 2nd, the export of which, without licence, was permitted to all countries except Holland and Scandinavia. Against Norway, Sweden, Denmark, and Holland the embargo was complete, and extended to all classes of goods.[1]

Simultaneously with the imposition of the embargoes, the American Government took steps, for the first time, to provide for a complete control of bunkering at American ports. This was a development of the highest importance in the evolution of the machinery for dealing both with the tonnage problem and with the restriction of enemy trade. By the summer of 1917 the Inter-Allied arrangements for bunker control and centralised chartering had been carried to as high a pitch as was practicable without the active co-operation of the United States ; but the absence of any corresponding organisation on the other side of the Atlantic opened a gap which it was impossible to close, and which went a long way to neutralise the effect of the measures taken by the European Allies. In September, however, the United States Shipping Board set up a Chartering Committee to centralise all private chartering for American trades, and to deal with all questions relating to neutral tonnage. This step was followed, on October 4th, by an order establishing a comprehensive control of bunkering at American ports.

The American Bunker Regulations were avowedly aimed directly at the Northern neutrals—Holland and the Scandinavian States—in support of the embargo on exports to

[1] Despite their more sweeping character, the policy underlying these measures was, of course, precisely similar to that which had, from the first, governed the British export restrictions (see Vol. I, p. 187).

those countries. The combined effect of the prohibition of exports and the withholding of bunkers, was to produce a complete temporary paralysis of Dutch and Scandinavian shipping in the Transatlantic trade. No fewer than 136 steamers, with an aggregate gross tonnage of 750,000, were held up in American ports, including 50 Dutch vessels which had loaded wheat in August, 53 Norwegians, and 33 Danish and Swedish steamers.[1]

With the establishment of a Chartering Committee and the issue of Bunker Regulations by the United States Government, the prospect of effective co-operation was brought much nearer, and the British Government hoped, at first, that the United States would nominate representatives on the Inter-Allied Chartering Committee, and participate fully in the existing arrangements for the chartering and allocation of neutral tonnage. This proposal, however, was rejected by the Shipping Board, on the ground that it was impracticable to centralise all chartering in London. In face of their refusal, it became necessary to accept a division of control, and to concentrate on an attempt to obtain unity of policy. This was not altogether easy. While the European Allies were in full accord with the American policy of putting the utmost possible pressure on neutrals, with a view to the prevention of trade with Germany, the need of tonnage was a predominant factor in their calculations, and they could not view without apprehension the immobilisation of shipping which might directly or indirectly do something to relieve the shortage. Moreover, the American Bunker Regulations rendered the grant of bunkers in American ports conditional on the loading of a return cargo to the United States, and this regulation was enforced not only on neutral ships trading on owners' account but also, in some instances at least, on vessels running on time-charter for the Allies. The American rule, based on the necessity of compelling ships receiving bunkers to return to American jurisdiction, was framed on the analogy of the British regulations, and reflected the natural anxiety of the American people to obtain a sufficiency of tonnage for their expanding trade. On the other hand, it appeared likely to deflect tonnage from war-zone services, vitally essential to the continuance of the struggle by the European Allies, to American services, for which, putting them at their highest, no such urgency

[1] *New York Times, Current History, The European War,* xiii. 241.

could be claimed. Further, it threatened interference with the employment of vessels whose services had been obtained for the Allies only in return for heavy and specific obligations undertaken by the British Government. In particular, it was essential that some definite understanding should be arrived at with regard to the numerous Norwegian vessels on charter to American citizens, but under an obligation to offer to the Inter-Allied Committee.[1]

As the result of communications between the two Governments, conditions of co-operation were formulated during October, which dealt with the questions at issue on a comprehensive basis. It was agreed that, so far as possible, all neutral ships were to be time-chartered (or requisitioned) on terms permitting of their employment without geographical restriction, and that such vessels should be allocated in the proportion of one quarter each to the United States, France, Italy, and the United Kingdom.[2] Vessels that could only be time-chartered on a basis excluding war-zone trade, were to be equally divided between the United States and the United Kingdom (acting for the Inter-Allied Committee), and used in services of war importance in such a way as to release corresponding national tonnage for war-zone trade. All voyage-charters were to be subject to the approval of the Shipping Board, or of the British Government, such approval only to be given to charters at standard rates, for voyages of war importance. Finally, full information of all fixtures was to be exchanged between the Shipping Board and the Inter-Allied Committee.

Meanwhile, the European Allies had made the necessary arrangements for co-operating in the general embargo on exports to Scandinavia and Holland; though not without some anxiety on the part of the British Government as to its possible effect, in the event of failure to arrive at an agreement with the neutral Governments concerned, on the supply of the Allies, the tonnage situation, and the supply to Germany of neutral products covered by existing agreements. On October 2nd an Order in Council appeared in the *London Gazette*, prohibiting all exports

[1] In November 1917 the Norwegian shipping recorded as trading in American seas amounted to 162 steamers of 398,000 tons gross. Not all these were on American charter, but all were liable to be affected by the American bunker regulations.

[2] The British share of all tonnage obtained was, in fact, placed at the disposal of Italy.

to Holland and Scandinavia. Similar action was taken by France and Italy. At the same time the British Government gave notice to terminate the majority of the Norwegian Agreements, the provisions of which might conflict with the new policy.

To apply this policy without restrictions was, for Great Britain, impossible. It would have been madness to denounce the tonnage agreements with Norway and Denmark, by which such substantial advantages were secured to the Allies, and so long as they remained in force it was necessary to fulfil the obligations which had been accepted with regard to the coal supply of those countries. Further, there were certain imports of vital importance for war purposes which could be drawn only from Scandinavia, and for which it was necessary to pay, and even after the imposition of the embargoes, agricultural and dairy produce continued to be received, though on a reduced scale, from Denmark and Holland, and could not be relinquished without setting free those products for export to Germany.

For these reasons it was necessary to license considerable shipments of coal to Norway, Sweden, and Denmark, and even to Holland a few cargoes were despatched. In return, the colliers, and the few regular liners which were still running, brought ore from Narvik; such quantities of timber, wood-pulp, and paper from Norway and Sweden as were still permitted under the Import Restrictions Scheme; carbide and pyrites from Norway; other munitions requirements from Sweden; and fish purchased under the Norwegian Agreement. From Denmark came large quantities of eggs, but little bacon or butter, owing to the heavy slaughtering which followed the embargo on fodder. From Holland came condensed milk, cheese, and margarine.

The vital imports and the continued services of Norwegian and Danish shipping were thus secured, and everything else, including all exchange considerations, could be sacrificed in the hope of tightening the blockade. From the end of October onwards, the exports to Holland and Scandinavia of yarns, textiles, hardware, and manufactured goods generally, came practically to an end. Month after month the export returns showed either a complete blank or figures so small as to be negligible.

In the United States, where there were no similar

import interests to be considered, the embargo on all exports to the Northern neutrals was absolute, save that, at an early stage in the negotiations which followed its imposition, the American Government licensed the export to Norway of six months' supply of cereals. There were, indeed, good reasons for not pushing Norway to extremities. The attitude of the Norwegians to the Allies had always been friendly, a large proportion of Norwegian tonnage was in Allied or American service, and the agreements entered into with the British Government had, on the whole, been well kept. Norwegian exports to the Central Powers were confined by this time mainly to a few metallurgical and chemical products such as pyrites, chrome ore, synthetic nitrates, carbide, and ferro-silicon. The military importance of these products even in small quantities was, indeed, very great, and the enemy were correspondingly eager to obtain them, as shown by the fact that they were offering up to 10,000 marks per ton for ferro-chrome containing less than 60 per cent. of chromium; but there were good hopes of coming to an amicable arrangement, and it was deemed unwise to run the risk of alienating Norway by stopping completely her cereal supplies.

Negotiations with Sweden, Denmark, and Holland presented much greater difficulties. The outstanding points of dispute with Holland were two. First came the permission by the Dutch Government of unneutral traffic on the Dutch railways in metals for military use, and sand and gravel for concrete construction on the German front.[1] Against this traffic the British Government had strongly, but vainly protested, and their attitude was now firmly backed by the United States. Secondly, trouble had arisen over the export of potatoes to Germany in breach of the Agricultural Agreement, and this Agreement itself, to which the American Government were not a party, permitted the export to the Central Powers of a certain amount of agricultural and dairy produce. The German Government were now negotiating for the balance of foodstuffs not covered by the Agreement; in return for which, and for credits in Holland, they were willing to guarantee the supply of 200,000 tons of German coal a month (as against a previous average of about half that amount),

[1] See Parl. Papers, Misc., No. 17 (1917), Cmd. 8693, and Misc. No. 2 (1918), Cmd. 8915.

and an additional 50,000 tons from Belgium. This arrangement the United States refused to recognise, and as the Dutch would give way neither on this point nor on the sand and gravel traffic, the deadlock was complete, and the embargo was rigidly enforced.

The attitude of Denmark was equally stiff. The great difficulty here arose in respect of the export of horses and live cattle, and the embargoes already imposed on fodder and fertilisers were so drastic that it was difficult to devise a further turn of the screw, sufficient to counteract the pressure Germany was in a position to exercise.

As regards Sweden, the dominant factor was the question of iron ore. Not only was the ore itself of enormous value to the enemy; its free importation enabled the Germans to economise man-power by retaining in the army men who must otherwise have been sent back to the mines, and its distribution by German and Swedish coasters in the Baltic relieved the overworked and fast deteriorating transport organisation of the strain which must have been imposed upon it, had all the ore used in the munitions industries been carried by rail from the Rhine Provinces, the occupied territories, and Silesia. The American Government believed, not without reason, that a complete stoppage of the Swedish export would finally break the enemy's power of resistance, and they pressed for nothing less; but the Swedes replied that they would rather forgo all imports from the United States. Indeed, the shipments of ore increased rather than diminished, as the Germans were making desperate efforts to build up their stocks, so that even in the event of Sweden giving way, their supplies might be secured.

The Germans, of course, were not slow to seize the opportunity presented by the embargoes, of strengthening their position by agreements with the neutral States; but their bargaining powers were now very restricted. Their stocks of raw materials were too scanty to permit much manufacture for export. Textile stocks were insufficient even for internal supply, and the output of the metallurgical industries was almost all required for war purposes. For the year ending June 30th, 1917, only 6 per cent. of the output of the Steel Works Union had been exported, as against 13 per cent. in the previous twelve months, and though efforts were made during the last quarter of 1917 to increase the exports to Sweden and

Holland, the result was not great, as coal and transport difficulties continued to restrict the total output.

On the announcement of the embargoes, the Germans went so far as to offer even cereals and potatoes to neutrals; but as regards cereals the offer was delusive, and only a small quantity of potatoes of very inferior quality was ultimately exported. A more useful lever was provided by the export of oil. The clearing of the Roumanian wells had proceeded with vigour, and by the end of the year, the output was up to 3,000 tons a day, or more. On the other hand, the Galician output was falling, stocks were nearly exhausted, and after providing for Austro-Hungarian consumption, less was left for German requirements. The increased supplies from Roumania were all absorbed by the expanding demands of the war industries, the submarines, and the flying service, and though military supplies were still maintained, the restrictions on civilian lighting and heating were very drastic both in Germany and Austria, and added greatly to the hardships endured by the people; while the all-important question of lubricants continued to cause the gravest anxiety to those responsible for the transport services. Yet so great was the German need for neutral products that fuel-oil, and even lubricating oil, was still exported in small quantities, to maintain the fish supply from Denmark, and to pay for other imports.

Coal exports, too, continued, despite the internal shortage which not only led to the most drastic restrictions on civilian consumption, but had begun to affect the output even of factories engaged in the war industries. This shortage was due in part to a reduction of output, arising from the substitution of prisoners of war and other unskilled labour for skilled workers, and from the reduction in physical efficiency due to mal-nutrition; but its main cause was the extreme difficulty of transport. Not only had trucks, locomotives, and rolling stock seriously deteriorated, owing to lack of lubricants and facilities for repairs, but the very successes of the German Armies had increased the strain, by lengthening the lines of communication, especially in the east, and thus rendering necessary the despatch of many thousand trucks to the occupied territories. In face of these difficulties, the supply of coal to neutrals, important as it was, could only be maintained on a very limited scale. For the months of May, June, and July 1917, the exports to Sweden had averaged only 180,000 tons a month, as against an average of about 500,000 tons in the same period of 1916. During the second half of the year great efforts were made to increase the shipments, but with indifferent success; indeed, the previous level was barely maintained. The agreed export to Switzerland, 200,000 tons a month, could not be sustained—in November the total was 35 per cent. short of that amount—and the ability of the Germans to fulfil the new guarantee given to Holland was very doubtful.

This restriction of exports naturally affected the exchanges, and the decline in the value of the mark was further accentuated by the effect of the Allies' financial offensive. The operation of the Black Lists,[1] and the entry of the United States into the war, had greatly restricted Germany's credit facilities, and in particular had cut off entirely the dollar-credits in the United States and South America, hitherto employed for the purchase of neutral European currencies. Moreover, the German holdings of Swiss and Scandinavian securities had, for the most part, been disposed of by the spring of 1917. By June 30th the value of the mark in the capitals of contiguous neutral countries stood at a discount varying from 41 to 47 per cent., and by the end of September it had fallen to less than half its nominal value in Stockholm, and little above half in other centres. The depreciation of the Austrian krone was still more pronounced. Towards the end of the year, however, there was a strong reaction in favour of both Vienna and Berlin. This was due in part to an increased export of luxury goods and other commodities requiring small expenditure of labour and material but commanding a high price in countries deprived of their usual supplies from the Allies and the United States, and in part to credits negotiated by the German Government. The main cause, however, was the enhanced military credit of the Central Powers, due to the Austrian victory at Caporetto, and the situation in Russia, where the Bolshevik Revolution held out hopes of a separate peace, which would open a yet wider gap in the blockade than that caused by the downfall of Roumania.[2]

The extent to which the Central Powers could benefit

[1] See Vol. II, pp. 305–6.
[2] See note on following page.

by this somewhat speculative appreciation in the value of their currencies, was limited by the surplus commodities available in neutral countries. These were not great. The first effect of the embargo on Danish fodder imports was heavy slaughtering of cattle, and more especially of pigs, in Denmark; but little of the bacon and lard produced reached the enemy. The greater part was reserved for domestic consumption, and of the rest most went to Sweden, where the long-continued restriction of imports, dating back to the autumn of 1916, had produced an acute food shortage. In fact, the immediate effect of the general embargo on the distribution of Danish produce as a whole, was not to increase the German supplies, but to divert at least a portion of those supplies to Scandinavian use. The

NOTE—

RATES ON BERLIN PER 100 MARKS

	Normal.	June 30th, 1917.	Sept. 29th, 1917.	Dec. 31st, 1917.
Sweden (kronor)	88·88	47·00	40·25	60·00
Norway (kroner)	88·88	48·62	44·62	60·37
Denmark (kroner)	88·88	50·00	44·75	64·00
Holland (gulden)	59·26	34·75	32·90	45·25
Switzerland (francs)	123·45	69·12½	65·00	85·50

RATES ON VIENNA PER 100 KRONEN

	Normal.	June 30th, 1917.	Sept. 29th, 1917.	Dec. 31st, 1917.
Sweden (kronor)	75·61	30·00	25·50	37·50
Denmark (kroner)	75·61	33·00	28·50	40·00
Holland (gulden)	50·41	21·90	20·87	27·30
Switzerland (francs)	105·01	42·80	41·50	52·50
Germany (marks)	85·06	64·25	64·25	64·25

PERCENTAGE DISCOUNT

	On Mark.		On Krone.	
	Sept. 29th, 1917.	Dec. 31st, 1917.	Sept. 29th, 1917.	Dec. 31st, 1917.
Sweden	54·71	32·50	66·27	50·40
Norway	49·80	32·08	—	—
Denmark	49·64	28·00	62·31	47·10
Holland	44·48	23·64	58·60	45·84
Switzerland	47·37	30·74	60·48	50·00
Germany	—	—	24·47	24·47

effect on exports of Dutch produce was very similar. This was a serious matter for the enemy, in view of his grave deficiency in fats. In Vienna, even during the late summer of 1917, queues of would-be purchasers stood all through the night outside the shops where fats were sold, and many of them, after their long vigil, went away empty-handed. In Germany a further reduction of the fat ration was announced during December, to take effect on January 1st, 1918. The shortage was accentuated by the decrease in the fish supply arising from the Norwegian Agreement, and from the laying up of the Dutch fishing-fleet.[1] Only a very small proportion of the Norwegian catch was now available for Germany, and the Dutch fishermen had practically suspended operations, owing to fear of the German submarines, fear of seizure by British patrols, and the dearth of fishing requisites caused by the embargoes. Taken as a whole the food imports of Germany from contiguous neutral countries fell in nutritive value from 382 milliards of calories during the second quarter of 1917 to 314 in the third quarter, and 279 in the fourth, as against 840 milliards in the first three months of 1916.

Thus, apart from any restrictions which might ultimately be secured by negotiation, the effect of the embargoes in reducing the productivity of contiguous neutrals had already begun to be felt by the enemy. Nor was this the only benefit derived from them. They had the effect of lightening greatly the task of the patrols. With all traffic at a standstill between Scandinavia and Holland and the United States, the volume of shipping on the North-about route sank rapidly to a small fraction of the previous total. During the second quarter of 1917, the total number of neutral vessels reported sailing into or out of the North Sea was 611. From July onwards, the figures sank rapidly in consequence of the widespread laying up of neutral shipping and the numerous detentions in American ports. For the September quarter the total was 346, and during the last three months of 1917 only 162 neutral vessels passed into or out of the North Sea.

Ever since the beginning of 1916 the Northern examination service had depended on the agreements with neutral shipowners as much as on the interception of shipping by the patrols. By the end of that year the proportion of

[1] In all, the German imports of fish during 1917 amounted to 160,000 tons, as against 360,000 in 1913, and probably about 400,000 tons in 1916.

ships calling voluntarily had risen to 75 per cent., and during the three months ending June 1917, 545 ships, or 89 per cent., had called for examination, as against 57 intercepted by the patrols, and 9 which evaded them. The institution of the embargoes tended to increase the proportion, as the majority of the ships that continued to sail were either regular liners owned by companies with whom agreements had been made, or vessels sailing as the result of special concessions. Thus, of the 162 vessels which passed in or out during the last three months of 1917, only 11, of which 3 were intercepted, disregarded the obligation to call at a British port.[1]

Thanks to the increase in ships calling voluntarily, it had already been possible to withdraw many armed merchant cruisers from the Northern Patrol for service as ocean escorts to the convoys. It had now become doubtful whether, seeing that the supply of nearly all commodities likely to be re-exported to the Central Powers was firmly controlled at the source, the interception of one or two suspicious vessels a month was worth the expenditure and risk of the force still devoted to that purpose. The Admiralty accordingly decided during December, to withdraw the Northern Patrol entirely and break up the 10th Cruiser Squadron for convoy or other service, leaving the cordon to be maintained by the light forces attached to the Grand Fleet, and still more effectively by the embargoes and agreements.

The immediate effect of the general embargo was thus both to increase the stringency of the economic pressure and to diminish the strain of enforcing it. Its ultimate effect depended upon the length of time during which the Northern neutrals could continue to dispense with imports from the United States and the United Kingdom.

[1] Ships calling voluntarily include those taking advantage of " Halifax Privileges " (see p. 45, *supra*).

CHAPTER XV

THE INTER-ALLIED PROGRAMME
NOVEMBER—DECEMBER 1917

IN many respects the shipping and economic situation in the autumn of 1917 was favourable to the Allies. The introduction of convoy had, for the first time since the development of the intensified submarine campaign, administered a distinct check to the destruction of tonnage; the cumulative effects of the economic offensive were telling slowly but surely on the enemy's power of resistance; the co-operation of the United States was making itself felt, both in facilitating the supply of the Allies, and in increasing the stringency of economic pressure on the Central Powers. All, however, was not well. Once more the beginning of a new cereal year was marked by a crisis in the organisation of supplies; but this time it was chiefly the position of France and Italy which gave rise to anxiety.

The harvest in both those countries had been poor. In France only 85 per cent. of the preceding year's acreage had been sown with wheat, and in both France and Italy the crops had suffered severely from climatic conditions. It was already evident that their import demands, both for breadstuffs and for fodder, would be largely in excess of the 1916 figures, and that a heavy additional strain would thus be thrown on the depleted tonnage available.

Further, the general outlook as regards the supply of cereals was unsatisfactory. All over the world the wheat harvest had been decidedly below the average, and this was only imperfectly compensated by good crops of oats and maize in the principal producing centres. So far as breadstuffs were concerned, it appeared likely that there would be a substantial deficit in the total supply to be adjusted among the Allies.

The emergence of this crisis gave a strong stimulus to the movement for closer and more scientific co-operation between the Allies in the organisation of tonnage and supplies. We have seen that, so early as January 1917, the Allied Naval Conference had put forward a proposal for the establishment of an Inter-Allied Shipping Committee, to consider as a whole the adjustment of the available tonnage to the essential requirements of the various States. Such a Committee was in fact formed during that month, and it was hoped at the time that it might ultimately provide the machinery for the preparation of import programmes for the Allies as a whole, on the lines of those prepared by the Tonnage Priority Committee for the United Kingdom, and of joint shipping programmes for fulfilment of the requirements so indicated. The time, however, was not yet ripe for such an innovation. The Committee had no executive staff, and its members lacked the Ministerial or official status needed to ensure compliance with their recommendations. Despite urgent representations by the British representative, the Committee never even succeeded in obtaining from France and Italy a full statement as to the employment of their national tonnage, on the lines of that provided by the British Card Index,[1] and in May 1917 the Inter-Allied Shipping Committee came to an end, having accomplished little of importance.

As between Great Britain and France, shipping relations continued to be governed mainly by the provisions of the Clémentel Agreement of December 1916 ; though it became necessary, as we have seen, to withdraw from French service a portion of the tonnage left at her disposal under that agreement. As regards Italy, the chief new development was the increasing employment of British requisitioned tonnage in the Italian coal trade, to take the place of neutral shipping withdrawn from the Mediterranean. The Wheat Commission continued to buy for the Allies as a whole, and the Wheat Section of the Ministry of Shipping assisted in the transport of supplies allocated by the Wheat Executive to France and Italy ;[2] the Board of Trade and the Refrigerated Tonnage Committee looked after the French and Italian meat supply ; and the special steel and oat service carried about 100,000 tons a month

---

[1] This Index had been extended in October 1916 to neutral, and in January 1917 to Allied shipping, so far as the information could be obtained.

[2] Subject, as regards tonnage for France, to the provisions of the Clémentel Agreement.

of metal, grain, and sundries, to French and Italian ports.[1] In October a new direct service was started by the Ministry of Shipping for the supply of shell steel from the United States to France. For this service, the object of which was to save transhipment at British ports, the Ministry allocated a number of fully requisitioned tramps, which were supplemented by liner parcels, and by occasional parcels carried in vessels on Wheat Executive or other service. The shipments, superintended by the Ministry's New York office, averaged some 30,000 tons a month.

In addition to the various special services and the tonnage, whether requisitioned or time-chartered, placed unreservedly at the disposal of the Allies, the Buying Departments and the Ministry of Shipping continued to effect many miscellaneous purchases and fixtures on French or Italian account; but there was as yet no central authority charged with the general adjustment of tonnage to the requirements of the Allies as a whole.

In respect of the acquisition of neutral tonnage, whether by purchase or charter, greater progress had been made. The Inter-Allied Ship Purchase Committee had been unable to do much to relieve the situation, as little tonnage was on offer, and that only at prohibitive prices; but the Inter-Allied Chartering Committee, as we have seen, had been active throughout the year in the fixing and allocation of neutral ships.

Somewhat outside the operation of the various bodies and services already referred to, lay the question of assistance to Russia, which was governed, as formerly, mainly by the capacity of the White Sea ports and their distributive organisation, to deal with supplies. The question was now, however, gravely complicated by political developments. All through the summer the situation in Russia had been such as to arouse grave fears for the future. The Kerensky Government showed every desire to carry on the war with vigour, and obtained substantial initial successes; but during July and August a strong Austro-German counter-offensive cleared Galicia, and by September the Russian resistance was beginning to crumble. The causes which had produced the original revolution were, in fact, still at work, and were too strong to be controlled. Of the physical factors, by far the most

[1] From May onwards a number of ships on this service were run direct to Salonika, with fodder for the Balkan forces.

important was the breakdown of internal transport. The strain put on the imperfectly organised transport system by mobilisation and war movements was very great, and it was greatly aggravated by the suspension of imports through the Baltic and Black Sea. Archangel, as we have seen, was neither able to receive nor to distribute more than a fraction of the normal imports, and under war conditions the transport of food from the producing to the industrial areas, and of coal from the Donetz minefields, presented almost insuperable difficulties. As a natural consequence, there were acute local shortages both of food and materials, and by July 1917 the cost of living had increased about 500 per cent. on 1915, and was more than double even what it was in 1916.[1] The effect was not only to arouse intense local hostility to the export of wheat from Archangel to France, but to weaken the authority of the Government, and to produce strong " stop-the-war " demonstrations. The Kerensky Government was now threatened at once by the plots of counter-revolutionaries and the activities of extremists, and with divided forces and a discontented and dispirited people, could oppose but a feeble barrier to the German onslaught. Riga fell on September 3rd. On the 8th a revolt broke out under General Korniloff, the Commander-in-Chief. By the 14th this was suppressed, and on the 15th, in an effort to rally their people, the Provisional Government proclaimed a Republic ; but it was evident that their position was extremely insecure.

So long as a flicker of resistance could be kept alive, it was impossible, in honour and in prudence, for the Western Powers to desert their Ally. On October 3rd the last steamer sailed from Great Britain for the White Sea, but a winter programme to Murmansk was, at that date, still contemplated. It was considered essential, however, in view of the political conditions, to accelerate as much as possible the discharge of vessels at Archangel, in order that both the British and Russian tonnage employed should be cleared before the freezing of the White Sea.

On the whole the discharge at Archangel had, as a result of improved arrangements effected through Commodore Bevan, been better than in 1916. The daily rate for coal cargoes went up from 250/300 tons to 350, and the discharge of general cargo averaged 307 tons a day,

[1] Private letter dated July 18th, 1917.

THE SUPPLY OF RUSSIA 239

and would have been still more rapid had it not been necessary, for reasons of safety, to discharge explosives in the river, instead of alongside the quays. At Kem and the Murman ports, where 210,000 tons of coal were discharged, the average rate was as high as 402 tons a day.

The total coal shipments, roughly 1,000,000 tons, were up to the level of 1916, but the grand total of all cargoes shipped under the White Sea summer programme was less by 16 per cent. than in that year. It amounted to just over 2,000,000 tons, of which about 300,000 tons was from the United States, and 240,000 tons from France. Three-quarters of the whole was carried in British, and about one-fifth in Russian shipping. The rest was carried mainly in French and American steamers, very little neutral tonnage being employed. Altogether 420 voyages were involved, as against 620 in 1916, the average individual cargo rising from 4,000 to nearly 5,000 B/L tons. The losses from war and marine risks combined amounted to about 13 per cent. on the total number of round voyages; but many of the casualties occurred on the return voyage, and the loss of outward cargo was under 8 per cent. These losses were considerably heavier than in the previous year, owing to a sustained and vigorous attack by submarines on the Archangel route.

To Vladivostok about 440,000 tons of cargo was shipped, of which 150,000 tons was carried in British vessels. This was only about one-third of the original programme; but the port was extremely congested throughout the year, and about half-way through the season the Ministry of Shipping were obliged to withdraw tonnage from the trade, as it was evident that the further accumulation of cargo at the port would be sheer waste of effort, owing to the inability of the Siberian Railway to handle the traffic.

It was just at the point when the White Sea Programme was on the verge of completion that the final crash came. On November 8th the Bolshevik *coup d'état* in Petrograd hurled the Kerensky Government from power, and on the 21st the new Government opened negotiations for an armistice with the Central Powers. It was clear that, so far from undertaking a winter programme to Murmansk, the one thing essential was to bring away such ships as were still at Archangel before they could fall into the hands of the Bolsheviks. Archangel was still held by adherents of the Kerensky Government, and all ships

British or Russian, were hastily despatched without even waiting to complete discharge. At the same time all further shipments to Vladivostok were stopped.

Russia had now to be written off, either as an asset or a liability; but the situation arising from the food crisis in France and Italy had to be met, and during November a big stride forward was made in the development of Inter-Allied organisation.

The basis of this new development was an agreement with regard to food tonnage arrived at, on November 3rd, between the British, French, and Italian Governments. This agreement, after reciting the existence of a tonnage shortage due to the failure of the French and Italian harvests, the effects of submarine warfare, and other causes, provided that the three Governments were prepared to accept the responsibility of providing the tonnage required for the carriage of food " proportionately to their respective means of transport," with or without the help of the United States. They further agreed that they would proceed forthwith to examine the tonnage requirements for other purposes.

The interpretation of this agreement was not altogether clear. On the face of it, it appeared to suggest that the tonnage required for the food import programmes of all three countries should be provided by Great Britain, France, and Italy, respectively, in exact mathematical proportion to the total tonnage under each flag available for commercial services, without any examination of the services in which that tonnage was already engaged, or of the need for imports other than food. Apart from this impossible interpretation, it could only mean that the food programmes of each country should be considered in common, and tonnage under each flag allocated thereto after joint examination of all the demands on that tonnage. On this interpretation it came very near to the pooling of all available tonnage, for all purposes, which had been proposed by the Italian representatives at the Allied Naval Conference in January.

Since the date of that Conference, however, the situation had undergone a considerable change. In all three countries Government control over both shipping and imports had been greatly extended. Almost all ships had been brought under some form of requisition, import restrictions had been introduced or extended, and the greater part of the imports admitted were either directly for Government account, or were under Government control. In the United Kingdom the monthly programmes of the Tonnage Priority Committee were supplemented by the monthly Priority Lists sent to the Conferences under the Liner Requisition Scheme, and in view of the alarming estimate prepared by the Statistical Branch of the Ministry of Shipping, the Government, on November 6th, appointed a new Imports Restriction Committee, to adjust the 1918 demands to the estimated available carrying power. In France, a standing Committee under the chairmanship of M. Clémentel was similarly responsible for the 1918 programme.

In these circumstances, it was decided to interpret the Agreement of November 3rd as implying a detailed examination of all Allied demands on tonnage, and the creation of a permanent organisation, with executive powers, to frame joint import programmes for the Allies as a whole and allocate tonnage for their fulfilment. At a meeting during the second week of November, between Mr. John Anderson (Secretary to the Ministry of Shipping), Mr. J. A. Salter (Director of Requisitioning), Sir Percy Bates (Director of Commercial Services), and M. Jean Monnet, French representative on the Commission Internationale de Ravitaillement, the plan of such an organisation was worked out in detail. This plan was subsequently discussed and accepted in principle by the British Government, and by Colonel House's Mission, together with Mr. Bainbridge Colby, a member of the American Shipping Board, on behalf of the United States. It was then embodied in a Memorandum by Mr. Salter, on behalf of the Ministry of Shipping, which was taken as the basis of discussion by an Allied Conference in Paris, November 29th to December 3rd, at which representatives of Great Britain, France, Italy, Russia, the United States, Belgium, Japan, Portugal, Roumania, Serbia, Greece, Brazil, and Cuba were present.

The situation with which the Conference had to deal was serious, disclosing on the part of all the European Allies, a deficit of carrying power as compared with importing requirements. The failure of the French and Italian harvests involved an addition of over 2,000,000 tons to the cereal programmes, equivalent to the continuous service of about 750,000 dead-weight tons of shipping, which the French and Italian Governments looked to Great Britain to provide. But even apart from these additional cereal requirements, the tonnage in French and Italian service, including British and neutral as well as national vessels, had been so gravely reduced by war losses as to be altogether unable to provide during 1918 for maintaining imports on the 1917 scale, which was assumed to be an irreducible minimum. On this basis the French deficit was estimated at 750,000 dead-weight tons of shipping, and the Italian at 500,000, making a total of 1,250,000 tons dead-weight, irrespective of the additional cereal requirements.

To provide tonnage on such a scale was clearly beyond the power of Great Britain, who was already providing the Allies with some 3,000,000 dead-weight tons of ocean-going shipping (of which France and Italy together had more than two-thirds), in addition to liner services and cargoes carried on the outward voyages, by vessels returning with imports to the United Kingdom. Even if no additional tonnage were allocated to the Allies, it had been estimated by the Statistical Branch of the Ministry of Shipping that the imports, exclusive of oil-fuel, would fall in 1918 from 34,000,000 to 28,000,000 tons. Yet the 1917 imports already represented a reduction of about 37 per cent. on the 1913 figures. Of the 34,000,000 tons imported in 1917, food, munitions, and munitions materials such as ore accounted for 26,000,000, leaving only 8,000,000, as compared with 36,000,000 before the war, for miscellaneous materials and manufactures. The supply of cotton, the raw material of the greatest British industry, had been so greatly reduced that in some branches of the trade the output had been cut down by 40 per cent.; many other industries had been subject to still more drastic interference; and even the food supplies had been severely restricted. In order to maintain supplies at this reduced level, export and shipping interests of great importance had been ruthlessly sacrificed, by the concentration of tonnage on the shorter routes; and now a further reduction of 6,000,000 tons was in contemplation.

Could the tonnage in Allied services be withdrawn, British imports could, indeed, be kept up to the 1917 level; but far from this, it was evident that the failure of the cereal harvests at least must be made good, and the British Authorities were prepared to increase their import deficit by 2,000,000 tons for this purpose. Beyond this they could not go ; and to avert a joint decrease of 3,750,000 tons in the French and Italian import programmes, they suggested that the United States should provide the necessary 1,250,000 tons dead-weight, 500,000 tons at once, and the balance so soon as the development of the American shipbuilding programme permitted. They asked further for immediate assistance in the supply of oil-fuel for the British Navy. The deficiency of tanker tonnage, partly caused by the requisition of British tankers building in the States, already compelled Great Britain to import about 100,000 tons of oil a month in double bottoms, thus shutting out other imports, and it was hoped that the United States might be able to spare at once 100,000 dead-weight tons of tanker tonnage, and another 200,000 tons in the near future.

This question of American assistance was the uncertain factor in the calculation. The ocean-going tonnage under the American flag amounted to about 3,600,000 tons deadweight, of which tankers accounted for over 1,000,000. Of the 2,600,000 ordinary tonnage, 1,000,000 was in naval or military employment, and 800,000 tons was either allotted to the service of the European Allies, or trading on private account in the war zone. The balance of about 800,000 tons was, on the latest American estimate, inadequate to the fulfilment of American requirements for essential imports from countries outside the war zone ; but a large block of neutral tonnage was trading in American waters, and the neutral vessels lying idle in American ports, as a result of the embargoes, might also be rendered available. Japanese tonnage, too, could give large assistance.

Estimating the further movements of American troops to France at 400,000 by the end of April 1918, and 800,000 by September 30th, it was calculated that the United States could scarcely do more than provide about 500,000 dead-weight tons for immediate Allied employment. The prospect of obtaining the full 1,250,000 tons necessary to make good the French and Italian deficits, depended on the possibility of curtailing American import requirements, the extent to which additional use could be made of Japanese and neutral tonnage, and the progress of the American shipbuilding programme.

This programme, according to the latest estimates, stood at about 5,000,000 to 6,000,000 tons dead-weight per annum, including 900,000 tons ordered by the British Government, and taken over under the Requisitioning Order. Great as this effort was, the Allied representatives considered it insufficient in view of the tonnage situation and the slow progress of shipbuilding in Great Britain. They urged, therefore, that it should be increased to 9,000,000 tons.

This was the situation presented to the Special Committee for Maritime Transport and General Imports of the Paris Conference, and after a further examination of the tonnage position, it was unanimously agreed by the representatives of the United States, Great Britain, France, and Italy that a statement should be forwarded to the American Government in the name of the Conference, setting out, on these lines, the needs of the European Allies. That is to say, the United States were urged, in addition to the provision of tanker tonnage, to supplement the assistance given to France and Italy by Great Britain by providing 500,000 tons dead-weight in the immediate future, and to raise this figure, as soon as possible, to an average of at least 1,250,000 tons. For this purpose it was suggested that the American shipbuilding programme should be raised to 9,000,000 tons dead-weight per annum, and that steps should be taken to economise shipping by restricting import requirements, and to make the greatest possible use of Japanese and neutral shipping.

It remained to provide the requisite machinery of Inter-Allied co-operation. On this point the Conference agreed with a decision previously arrived at in the course of the discussion in London, that the creation of an International Board, with complete executive power over a common pool of tonnage, was undesirable, if not impracticable. It would be extremely difficult for any nation, especially for either of the great ship-owning Powers—Great Britain and the United States—to delegate to a representative on an International Board absolute power to dispose of its tonnage, and if it was necessary for each representative to refer important questions to his Government, prompt and decisive action would be impossible. Further, it was impossible to centralise in one body and in one place complete control over the whole of Allied and American shipping; or to create any central body sufficiently in touch with shipping problems and at the same time authorised to make reductions in supply programmes.

It was obvious that the main basis of Inter-Allied co-operation in the allocation of tonnage must rest on a previous examination and adjustment of the import programmes of each country, in the way already adopted in respect of wheat. Inter-Allied Executives on the model of the Wheat Executive were already being formed for sugar, for meat and fats, and for oil-seeds. It was now agreed that the same principle should be extended to cover, so far as possible, the whole of the main requirements of the European Allies for food, for munitions, and for raw materials. In the meantime it was agreed that the United States, France, Italy, and Great Britain should all tabulate and communicate to each other a statement showing in detail, both their import requirements in each class, and the tonnage, actual or prospective, under their control. The requirements so shown were then to be classified as regards source of supply, etc., and adjusted to secure first, a reasonably uniform standard of adequacy, as between classes of commodities, and as between countries, and secondly, an equilibrium between the total import programmes and the total carrying power available. In other words, any deficit in the total import programmes, caused by the inadequacy of the total carrying power, was to be adjusted, as between the various countries, according to common estimate of their essential needs.

On the basis of the joint programme so determined, and revised from time to time in the light of losses, war developments, and other factors, the general allocation of tonnage was to be worked out; but it was an essential feature of the scheme that, subject to such periodical reallocation, each nation should continue to manage and supervise the tonnage under its control. That is to say, the allocation of, for instance, additional British or American tonnage to the import service of France, would not remove such vessels from the control of the Ministry of Shipping or the United States Shipping Board.

A further very important resolution provided that, " the neutral or interned tonnage obtained through any channel and by whatever country shall be used in such a way as to increase by an equal extent the tonnage in direct war services, the extra tonnage being allotted so far as practicable to the most urgent war needs of any of the Allies." The exact method of allocation was left to be worked out later; but the importance of the provision lay in its recognition of the principle that the urgency of war needs was to be the criterion of allocation, irrespective of the method by which the tonnage was acquired.

Resolutions were also passed as to the importance of bringing into war service all possible tonnage, such as the German ships in South American ports, and as to the control of imports, for the purpose of securing that the commodities carried by ships allocated to any State, should consist solely of those essential war requirements for which the tonnage had been allotted. The most important step, however, apart from the laying down of the broad general principles above recited, was the provision made for carrying into effect the adjustment of tonnage to programmes, which was the main object of the scheme.

It was clear that the supervision of the scheme—the examination and revision of import programmes, and allocation of tonnage in accordance with proved requirements—could be carried out only by a body able to meet at frequent intervals, and possessing a permanent statistical and administrative staff, to supply or analyse the necessary information, and see to the execution of the decisions arrived at. It was clear also that, since the representatives of the various States were not to be delegates, they must be of ministerial rank and able to speak for, and with the authority of, their respective Governments. It was accordingly agreed that Great Britain, France, and Italy should each appoint one or two Ministers, and the United States one or two special delegates, who should be responsible to their respective Governments for the execution of the agreements arrived at, and should meet from time to time, either on their own motion or at the request of the Executive Departments. It was further agreed that the appropriate Ministers, and the representatives of the United States, should at once take steps to establish the permanent office and staff necessary for this purpose.

The establishment of this machinery and the preparation of the necessary statements of tonnage and requirements were, of course, a matter of time, and it was not until March 1918 that the Allied Maritime Transport Council, as the new authority was called, held its first meeting; but the general lines of Inter-Allied co-operation had now been clearly and finally laid down. From the date of the Paris Resolutions the conception of a joint import programme for the European Allies, as the basis of tonnage allocation, coloured all consideration of the problem of supplies.

CHAPTER XVI

TONNAGE AND LOSSES
NOVEMBER 1917—JANUARY 1918

IMMENSE as was the importance of the Paris Resolutions, they left the shipping situation, for the time being, very uncertain. While it was clear that the joint import programmes for 1918 would involve a demand on the part of France and Italy for large additional assistance, the extent of that demand could not be accurately measured until detailed programmes had been prepared, and examined by the new Inter-Allied Council which it had been decided to create ; nor was it possible to say how far Great Britain would be called upon to make good the deficit in Allied tonnage until a definite reply had been received to the request for assistance addressed to the American Government. The one tangible factor was the obligation which lay on Great Britain under the Agreement of November 3rd, to make good, independently of any help received from the United States, the deficiency in the food supply of the Allies caused by the failure of the French and Italian harvests, and this obligation was estimated, as we have seen, to involve the carriage of an additional 2,000,000 tons of cereals, or the continuous employment in Allied service of 750,000 tons dead-weight (say, 500,000 tons gross) of ocean-going shipping.

In the meantime the situation continued to be dominated on the one hand by the losing race between replacements and losses, on the other by the effects of the Atlantic concentration. Of that concentration the main basis was the Liner Requisition Scheme, coupled with the cereal programme. Since the abandonment, at the very beginning of 1917, of the attempt to lift the Australian wheat surplus, tramp tonnage in the ocean trades had been, so far as British imports were concerned, almost entirely restricted to the North Atlantic tracks. With the exception of sugar from Java and Mauritius, and nitrates from Chile, the indispensable imports which it was still necessary to bring from the more distant sources, were mostly covered by the liner priority programmes, and made little demand on tramp tonnage.

These priority lists, varied from time to time according to requirements, were on the whole closely adhered to ; but it was occasionally necessary to make concessions, in order to clear accumulations of cargo which impeded the shipment of more important commodities. Thus, in October, licence was given for excess shipments of hides from Rio de Janeiro, as the accumulations threatened a stoppage of the meat works.

This question of the by-products of the meat factories, such as hides and tallow, caused continual difficulties both in South America and in Australia and New Zealand, especially towards the end of the year. Tinned meats were another source of trouble. These meats, which did not require insulated space for their carriage, fell outside the province of the Refrigerated Shipping Committee and were included in the ordinary priority programmes ; but the space available under those programmes was frequently inadequate. In South America, large purchases were made both for War Office account and for French and civilian consumption, especially in October when, owing to strikes, no wheat was available for the liners. In Australia, on the other hand, the accumulations were considerable, until arrangements could be made for the Army supplies in Egypt to be drawn from this source, so that they could be brought forward by meat ships running to Port Said.

The necessity for such occasional adjustments was an accepted feature of the scheme and had no appreciable effect on its general working. In the general policy underlying the scheme there was neither change nor wavering. During the autumn, indeed, there was a tendency for liner tonnage to flow back, to some extent, from the North Atlantic to the trades whence it had been diverted. This was due in part to a falling off in the grain shipments from North America, but its main cause was the withdrawal of ships ill-suited to withstand the stress of winter voyages in the North Atlantic. As a result of these withdrawals there was, during the winter, an appreciable increase of tonnage in the Indian trade and some measure of recovery in Australasian traffic and that of three or four of the cross-routes. Far Eastern services, on the other hand, were still further cut down. By November, this reaction from the spring and summer concentration had spent its force, and at no time did the number of liners in the North Atlantic fall much below 30 per cent. of the total, as against 22 per cent. in January.

All this time the liner companies were running their vessels under direction of the Liner Requisitioning Committee, on the basis of the requisitioning letters and the Heads of Arrangement drawn up by the Committee of Conference Chairmen in negotiation with the Ministry of Shipping, but though the scheme had been in full operation since the spring of 1917, it was not until the very end of the year that the Heads of Arrangement were finally agreed, or the scheme itself placed on a definite and unquestionable basis. It will be remembered that the drafting Committee of Chairmen had approved the " Heads of Arrangement " on August 22nd, and the Shipping Controller's formal approval having been obtained, nothing further remained but to obtain the approval and signature of the individual lines. Before this could be done, however, a new development had arisen which struck at the validity of the whole scheme.

On October 18th a full meeting of the Conference Chairmen was held at which it was agreed, Mr. R. D. Holt dissenting, to recommend the various lines to accept the proposals, subject to the settlement of one small outstanding point with regard to victualling charges. On November 1st a meeting of the Established Lines in the North Atlantic trade agreed to accept the proposals and to sign the " Heads of Arrangement " so soon as the values of their vessels for War Risk Insurance had been proved.[1] The other lines, with one exception, took similar action.

The one exception was the China Mutual Steam Navigation Co., and the reason for Mr. R. D. Holt's dissent from the resolution passed by the Chairmen was that an action brought by his line against the Shipping Controller for the purpose of testing the validity of liner requisition, was pending in the courts. Judgment in this action was pro-

---

[1] In communicating their decision to the Ministry of Shipping, the North Atlantic lines desired to place on record that, while willing to meet the wishes of the Government, they were still doubtful as to the legality of its action in requisitioning their vessels for commercial trading, and were apprehensive as to the effects of the scheme and of the prohibition of private shipbuilding, on the future of British shipping.

nounced by Mr. Justice Bailhache on November 15th. The plaintiffs' case rested on the contention that the requisitioning letter purported to requisition not only the ships owned by the line but the services of the owners and their staff; that this requisitioning of services was without legal or constitutional warrant; and that as the requisitioning letter must be read as a whole, its whole operation became null and void. On each of these points the Judge decided in their favour, and the effect of his decision was to invalidate all action taken or to be taken under the scheme.[1]

In these circumstances it appeared that it would be necessary for the Ministry of Shipping to approach Parliament for the purpose of obtaining legal sanction for their proceedings; but the liner companies had, in fact, no intention of taking advantage of this decision. The action had been brought as a test case to establish the legal position, and that being done, the China Mutual Co. at once agreed to waive their rights under the judgment and co-operate voluntarily in the working of the scheme. The same attitude was adopted by all the other lines; but in order to regularise the position the Ministry of Shipping sent to each line on November 17th a letter formally requisitioning their ships " on the basis of Blue Book rates and conditions, subject to any agreed modifications," and requesting the formal assurance of the lines that they would co-operate in the management of the vessels, on the terms of the Heads of Arrangement. This assurance was willingly given by all the lines, and the Heads of Arrangement were signed by each line as soon as the values of their ships for war risk purposes were proved.

The conclusion of these prolonged negotiations was the more important inasmuch as everything pointed to a yet more drastic diversion of shipping from the longer to the shorter routes during the forthcoming season. Meanwhile the defensive system by which this concentration was covered continued, in the main, to give satisfactory results, as did the short-sea convoys in European waters. In the Mediterranean, however, the protection given to trade was still very imperfect, and though the Mediterranean traffic was far less important to Great Britain than that with

---

[1] *China Mutual* v. *Maclay*, 34 *Times Law Reports*, pp. 81–5. A similar action entered by the British South American Steam Navigation Company was subsequently withdrawn.

North America, it was of such vital importance to the Allies, especially to Italy, that the general situation could not be considered satisfactory so long as submarine activity within the Straits remained unchecked. Further, while the Atlantic convoy system gave a measure of protection to the ocean voyage, even greater than its advocates had dared to hope, the insufficiency of the available forces to provide protection right up to and from the ports of arrival and departure, left a chink in the armour, and the enemy was now modifying his tactics so as to take full advantage of this defect.

In November, as will be remembered, the destruction both of British and of the world's tonnage fell to the lowest point yet reached since the outbreak of the unrestricted submarine campaign. In December the losses of British shipping rose to over 250,000 tons gross, and including Allied and neutral tonnage, the total casualties reached the formidable figure of 400,000 tons. For this increase heavy losses in the Channel and Mediterranean were mainly responsible, and in January, when British losses fell again to 180,000 and world losses to just over 300,000 tons, these two areas accounted between them for 53 out of 87 British and foreign steamers of 500 tons gross and upwards sunk by submarine attack. There were also, during January, 14 casualties in the Irish Sea and Bristol Channel, leaving only 20 for all other areas together.

Outside the Mediterranean the submarines were, in fact, concentrating more and more on the inshore attack. Operations against steamers sailing in organised convoy had proved risky and unremunerative, and the only chance of making an effective impression on the volume of trade was to put forward a special effort in those waters where ships could be attacked after they had parted from their escort or before they had picked it up. During the first three months of unrestricted submarine warfare only 20·4 per cent. of the losses in European waters (excluding the Mediterranean) were due to attacks made within ten miles of land ; exactly half the casualties occurred outside the fifty-mile limit. Now, for the three months November to January inclusive, only 1·7 per cent. of the successful attacks took place more than fifty miles from land, and 62·8 of the losses were incurred within ten miles from shore.

So persistent was the inshore activity of the submarines that it became necessary to abandon altogether the outward convoy from Queenstown, as vessels on their way to that port were particularly exposed to attack on their way down the Irish Sea. Accordingly, from January 8th, 1918, the faster Bristol Channel ships, which had hitherto made Queenstown their port of assembly, were merged in the slow Milford Convoy. The loss of speed was regrettable, but it was more than compensated by the advantage of escort from so early a period of the voyage. Ships bound from London or the East Coast were, however, still exposed to attack on their way to the ports of assembly at Devonport and Falmouth, and those from the Mersey or the Clyde on their way to Lamlash.

In the Mediterranean the disasters to the initial through convoys had not been repeated, though the sixth outward convoy lost the *City of Lucknow* on December 21st. The traffic of the Mediterranean itself, however, had suffered very severely. The system of local convoys established in October, covered only a small portion of the traffic, and the gap left in the system by the absence of convoy between Bizerta and Gibraltar involved heavy risks to the Java sugar ships and other slow steamers from the East which had come on with the local convoy from Alexandria to Bizerta, and caused great delay, through the adoption of the coastal route. In consequence of increased submarine activity on this route during December, a four-day convoy between Bizerta and Gibraltar was started on January 1st, 1918. This was a distinct gain both in time and safety to the Egyptian and slow through traffic; but a great part of the trade of the Mediterranean itself, including the all-important traffic to the Gulf of Lyons and Italian ports, was still outside the system. The losses of Greek and Italian, as well as of British shipping, were heavy, and much of the loss fell on the Italian coal trade, which could ill bear any addition to its difficulties. About the middle of December 1917 it was calculated that 40 per cent. of the total losses in all areas were colliers, and as the voyage to Italian ports was much the most dangerous undertaken by vessels of this class, the French Government were urged to increase as much as possible the transport of coal to Italy by rail and coaster, in order to allow a reduction in the number of ships exposed to this risk.

In the French cross-Channel coal trade the losses, thanks to the system of daily convoys, were still very small in comparison with the number of sailings; but the other

SCANDINAVIAN CONVOY REORGANISED 253

principal short-sea convoy—the Scandinavian—had again been hard hit by a surface attack. On this occasion the convoy consisted of one British and five neutral steamers, which were eastward-bound under escort of the destroyers PARTRIDGE and PELLEW and four armed trawlers when, on December 12th, they were attacked by four German destroyers, with the result that the whole convoy and escort were sunk with the exception of the PELLEW, disabled.

The whole question of the reorganisation of the Scandinavian convoy had been under consideration ever since the previous surface attack on October 17th, and on December 10th, only two days before the second attack, a conference had assembled at Scapa for the purpose of working out a scheme. It was not, however, naval considerations only that rendered a reorganisation desirable. The great prolongation of the route involved in the necessity of touching at Lerwick both on the outward and homeward voyage had very seriously affected the running of the North Sea trade and brought about grave congestion of the terminal ports. The combined effect of the longer voyage and port delays was of special importance in relation to the shipments of ore from Narvik to Great Britain, which fell during 1917 to 268,000 tons as against 866,000 in the previous year and 467,000 in 1915.[1] Great difficulties, too, were experienced in maintaining the supply of coal to Norway under the tonnage agreement.

As a basis for reorganisation, the Ministry of Shipping prepared statistics showing the volume of Scandinavian traffic from and to the various ports in the United Kingdom, both on the East and the West Coast. It was in the West Coast traffic that the delays had been most serious, the maximum of delay being represented by a steamer which took no less than forty-five days on the passage from Christiania to Liverpool, and the Norwegian Section of the Ministry now proposed to eliminate so far as possible voyages to and from West Coast ports, and replace them by a more extensive use of ports on the Humber, Tyne, and East Coast of Scotland.

The amount of traffic to be redirected was considerable, the most important feature being the demands of the soap and allied trades in Lancashire for box boards and

[1] The total imports of ore from Norway and Sweden amounted in 1917 to 307,000 tons, as against 1,031,000 in 1916.

wood pulp. From a conference between trade representatives and the Port and Transit Executive Committee on January 8th, it appeared that about 15,000 standards (50,000 tons) of box boards, and 20,000 tons of pulp annually landed at Garston would now require to be imported through the Humber ports, and it was obvious that the effect of throwing this additional traffic on to the already overburdened Lancashire and Yorkshire railway system would be very serious. The Port and Transit Committee accordingly took the matter up, both with the Railway Executive Committee and the Canal Control Committee, promising to give whatever assistance was possible with regard to labour, from the Transport Workers' Battalions, and they were eventually able to arrange for a large part of the traffic to be forwarded from Hull by canal.

Apart from the saving in time, which was very considerable, this elimination of West Coast voyages exactly suited the Admiralty, who were now desirous of running the Scandinavian Convoy from the Firth of Forth, and on January 20th the new scheme came into effect. Under this scheme the convoys assembled at Methil in the Firth of Forth and were thence escorted direct to Norwegian waters. In order to enable the Grand Fleet to provide covering forces against surface attack, the convoys were run every third day,[1] instead of daily as hitherto, so as to avoid having two convoys at sea at the same time, the size of each convoy being correspondingly increased. The result of this change was not only to provide increased protection, but greatly to accelerate turn-round. Whereas the average length of the voyage from the Tyne to Christiania under the old system had been ten to twelve days, as compared with three days for a direct voyage under peace conditions,[2] ships fortunate enough to arrive at Methil on a sailing date could now complete the passage in five or six.

In view of the continual extension and improvement of the convoy system, both in the ocean and short-sea trades, and of the increasing smoothness with which that system worked, as the result of experience in station-keeping and zigzagging, it might well be hoped that the downward tendency of the curve of loss, checked as it had been in

---

[1] Shortly altered to every fourth day.
[2] For an ordinary tramp steamer of $8\frac{1}{2}$ to 9 knots.

December, would be continued and accentuated in 1918. It was necessary, indeed, that it should be, if the shortage of tonnage were not to become absolutely disastrous. By January 31st, 1918, the unrestricted submarine campaign had raged for just twelve months, and during that period the world's shipping had been reduced, through war casualties, by nearly 6,200,000 tons gross, of which 3,750,000 tons was British. In ocean-going steamers on the register of the United Kingdom alone, the losses amounted to about 3,500,000 tons, or more than 20 per cent. of the tonnage available in January 1917. Nor was this all: during the same period about 1,175,000 gross tons of shipping of which 925,000 tons was British had been damaged by enemy action, and the majority of ships so damaged were out of service for a period of from four to six months. Marine casualties, too, had tended to increase, and in the last week of January 1918 the total of British shipping in the repairers' hands amounted to 1,500,000 tons gross, a third of which was in dry dock for serious repairs.

With such losses the programme of new construction was utterly unable to cope; nay, as we have seen, it was unable even to keep up with the current rate of loss, greatly as that rate had been reduced since the summer of 1917. The total output of mercantile tonnage in British yards, during the calendar year 1917, was 1,163,000 tons gross, practically as much as the Shipping Controller had ventured to hope for in February, but short by 400,000 tons of the Admiralty programme.[1] Taking into account naval construction, the 1917 output as a whole was well above that of the record year 1913; but the merchant tonnage launched was still 30 per cent. below the average of the last three years of peace. Moreover, the peace standard had become totally inapplicable. In face of losses amounting to 3,750,000 tons, an output of under 1,250,000 was profoundly unsatisfactory.[2]

Nor was the outlook for the future much more promising. Although excellent records had been obtained in the construction of a few standard ships, only about a dozen standard freighters and oilers had been completed by

[1] These figures refer to completions. The launchings comprised 399 vessels with an aggregate tonnage of 1,208,000 tons; 447 vessels were laid down, with an aggregate tonnage of 1,263,000 gross.
[2] The new ships actually brought into service during the year amounted to just under 1,000,000 tons.

December 31st, 1917, and though 51 per cent. of the vessels on the stocks were of standard type, only 10 per cent. of those launched and completing were standard vessels. It was evident both that the clearing of the slips for standard vessels would take longer than had been anticipated, and that the time required, in existing conditions, for construction of the standard types themselves had been considerably underestimated.

It was the supply of labour which was now the greatest difficulty, and in the hope of overcoming this obstacle, the Government gave instructions that the 20,000 skilled workers for whom the Navy Controller had asked, should be released from the colours. The Army Council directed, however, that all shipyard workers and marine engineers in the Home Forces should be released before those serving overseas were called upon, and pending the release of the last man at home no machinery for bringing back skilled workers from abroad was set in motion. Meanwhile a strike broke out in the principal shipbuilding districts, owing to differences arising in connection with the $12\frac{1}{2}$ per cent. time-workers' bonus introduced by the Ministry of Munitions; the tonnage completed in January dropped to 58,000 gross, and the realisation of even the revised programme of 1,800,000 tons for 1918 seemed very doubtful.

Home construction, it is true, was supplemented by purchases from abroad; but here too the disappointment had been bitter. Of tonnage built overseas the Navy Controller had hoped for 327,000 tons during the second half of 1917, and a further 592,000 tons early in 1918. Since his estimate was made the whole situation had been changed by the American Requisitioning Order. Thanks mainly to the good work of the Japanese shipyards, a total of about 170,000 gross tons of oversea shipping, including second-hand neutrals, had been delivered during 1917; but the Japanese shipbuilders were now running short of steel, and unless they were able to procure large supplies from the United States, could not maintain their output. The Americans, however, were unlikely to spare steel for Japan, in view of their own shipbuilding programme. In these circumstances Canada was practically the only effective source of new tonnage, and many further contracts had been placed in the Dominion both for steel and wooden steamers; but large deliveries from Canada were not to be expected before the late summer or autumn of 1918. For the first half of that year at least, the bulk of the replacement tonnage must be provided by the inadequate British programme, and there was every prospect of a steady cumulative increase in the tonnage deficit.

In addition to purchased vessels there had been, of course, a considerable addition to the available tonnage under the British flag through the requisitioning of neutrals and the escape of ships from the Baltic; but valuable as was every ship, such additions were but a small compensation for the excess of war and marine losses over new construction. The fact remained that, at the end of January 1917, the Requisitioning Branch return showed a total of 3,731 ocean-going steamers of 16,591,000 tons gross available for war or trade; on January 31st, 1918, 3,153 steamers of 14,547,000 tons. In numbers the net decrease was 15·5; in tonnage 12·3 per cent.[1] As compared with July 1914, the ocean-going tonnage under the British flag showed a decline of nearly 18 per cent.

Allied shipping also had suffered heavily. Since the inception of the unrestricted submarine campaign, France and Italy had each lost about 400,000 tons gross. Their total losses since July 1914 (about 700,000 tons under each flag), far exceeded the tonnage acquired by new construction, purchase, or capture. In ocean-going steam tonnage, France was poorer by about one-eighth, and Italy by more than one-fifth, than at the outbreak of war.

With diminishing tonnage and increasing requirements, both France and Italy were driven, as we have seen, to lean more and more heavily for support on British shipping. The assistance that they themselves could give in the carriage of British imports, was small. Although the number of French steamers in the cross-Channel coal traffic increased during 1917, as the result of neutral withdrawals, fewer French ships brought cargo to British ports. The arrivals of Italian steamers with ore cargoes fell away during the winter months, owing to the strain on Italian tonnage created by the cereal deficit.

With the exception of Greece, the remaining European Allies counted for little in the tonnage balance sheet. Russian shipping—more than half of which was locked up

---

[1] The relatively greater decrease in numbers was due to the greater risk run by low-powered ships. These figures include ships under repair.

in the Baltic and Black Sea—had at no time in the war been of much importance outside the trade of the White Sea and Vladivostok, and the remaining Belgian tonnage was chiefly employed in the service of the Relief Commission. Greek shipping, indeed, was almost entirely under the control of the Inter-Allied Chartering Committee, but, owing to its employment in the French and Italian coal trade, the losses had been heavy; many ships had been sold earlier in the war, and there were now only about 70 steamers of 1,600 tons gross and upwards under the Greek flag, as against about 250 in 1914.

In striking contrast to the heavy net losses suffered by the European Allies, the United States and Japan had lost little and built much, and their mercantile fleets were now far larger than at the outbreak of war. Their shipping, however, took little part in the supply either of the United Kingdom, or of France and Italy. To Japan, the withdrawal of British ships from the Pacific and Far Eastern tracks had presented an opportunity which absorbed all her energies, and American shipowners were no less busy in filling the gap left by the disappearance of the German flag from the seas and the concentration of British tonnage on war services. The steam tonnage under the United States flag (exclusive of vessels on the Great Lakes) had risen through new construction and the seizure of enemy ships,[1] from about 2,000,000 to well over 3,500,000 tons gross, and thanks in large measure to the requisition of steamers building for British account, it was still rapidly expanding. Nevertheless, the entrances and clearances of American shipping at British ports were lower than before the war. It was hoped, indeed, that during 1918 the United States would be able to relieve Great Britain of some part of the burden imposed by the demands of the Allies, but even if steps were taken to divert tonnage from the less essential trades, it had to be remembered that the transport and supply of the American troops were likely to require an increasing proportion of the national shipping.

[1] Of the enemy steamers seized by the United States, 83 were shown as trading in the Ministry of Shipping's return for January 1918; 15 others, more seriously damaged or seized at ports remote from repair facilities, were still in the repairers' hands. Of those already brought into service, about 50 were running to France, Italy, or Great Britain, mainly on American trooping service; the remainder were mostly employed in American or Eastern waters.

AN UNSATISFACTORY POSITION

From the various minor States who had entered the war during 1917, little aid was to be expected, save in so far as they could make available the enemy steamers seized in their ports. Negotiations with regard to those seized by Brazil had been left by the British Government to the United States, who, in turn, handed over the matter to the French, and during December an agreement covering 30 of the ships was arrived at between the French and Brazilian Governments. Meanwhile the ships came very slowly into service. The Brazilian Government had refused an offer to tow the ships to a United States port for repairs, and by January 31st, 1918, only 17 out of 44 were actually on service, mostly in Brazilian coasting or Inter-American trade. The ships seized by Uruguay and Peru were so badly damaged that none of them had yet come on service,[1] but the British Government had given permission for a British firm to undertake the repair of those at Monte Video, and, with the consent of the United States, was negotiating with the Uruguayan Government for their use. Meanwhile the long wrangle over the ships seized by China and Siam had at last been concluded, and on December 21st charters were signed by which 9 of those in Chinese ports and 7 of those at Bangkok were brought into the service of the Allies and the United States, China retaining 4 and Siam 2 vessels.

As regards the Allied and Associated Powers, the position at the beginning of 1918 was thus wholly unsatisfactory. France and Italy, with their mercantile fleets depleted by losses they had no means of replacing, were making greater and greater demands on British shipping, which was itself rapidly diminishing. The United States and Japan contributed little to the pool of tonnage available for the supply of the European Allies; the Minor Powers had little to contribute.

Had the paralysis of neutral shipping which followed the institution of the barred zones, continued throughout the year, the machinery of supply must have broken down altogether. But though this disaster had been averted by the tonnage agreements with Norway and Denmark, and the other measures taken to obtain control over neutral shipping, the total amount of such shipping avail-

[1] Negotiations with Peru were left to the United States, but no agreement was concluded till September 1918, and even then the ships had not been repaired.

able for Allied services was still far smaller than in 1916. The Norwegian Agreement was, indeed, a factor of prime importance, in view of the part played by Norwegian ships in the general carrying trade ; but the losses of Norwegian shipping had been heavier, in proportion, than those of British shipping itself, and its power to assist in the supply of the Allies had been correspondingly reduced. Norway had lost, during the twelve months of unrestricted submarine warfare, over 600,000 tons of shipping. Her total losses since the outbreak of war were over 1,000,000 tons, many ships building in the United States had been requisitioned, and she had available, on February 28th, only 323 steamers of 1,600 tons and up, as against 378 in July 1914.[1] The losses of other neutrals had been far lighter ; but it was only by extreme pressure, and except as regards Denmark, in small numbers, that their ships could be made available for British or Allied trade.

The total number of Greek and neutral steamers chartered to the Inter-Allied Executive up to January 31st was 362, with an aggregate tonnage of over 1,250,000 dead-weight (say, 850,000 gross).[2] Of these steamers 125 were Greek, 173 Norwegian, and 31 Danish. The remaining 23 were made up of Swedish, Japanese, and Dutch. Apart from a few ships employed in the carriage of coal from the United Kingdom to the bunker depôts, the whole of this tonnage had been divided between France, Italy, and the Wheat Executive, roughly in the proportion of 8 : 8 : 7.[3] The needs of Greece and of the Commission for Belgian Relief, so far as not otherwise provided for, had been met by occasional single voyages. The majority of the ships running under the approval of the Chartering Committee, though not directly fixed by the Executive, were also in the service of France and Italy, and the share of neutral shipping in the British import trade was now confined mainly to a proportion of Wheat Executive voyages, the Scandinavian traffic, and the ore lifted by returning colliers.

It was only in the direct Scandinavian traffic, stimulated by the application of the ship-for-ship policy and the

[1] It must be remembered that between 20 and 30 steamers of 1,600 gross tons and upwards were now running under the British flag, under the North Sea substitution scheme.

[2] These figures relate to fixtures and take no account of subsequent losses.

[3] This ratio relates to tonnage, not to numbers. The majority of the smaller ships were put into the cross-Channel coal trade.

need of the Swedes for coal, that Swedish shipping took any prominent part in the supply of Great Britain or the Allies,[1] and Dutch tonnage was withdrawn almost entirely from Allied service. Many Swedish and a still larger number of Dutch vessels were laid up as a result of unwillingness to accept Allied charters, or of the American and British embargoes. The remainder, so far as not required for the national import service, was mostly employed, outside the war zone, in American or Eastern waters, where also a large block of Norwegian and Danish shipping was still trading.[2]

Thus the prospect of obtaining any increase in the neutral shipping available for the service of Great Britain and the Allies, depended mainly on the co-operation of the United States. Meanwhile it had become necessary to revise, in the light of the Paris Resolutions, the agree-

[1] Six small steamers under the Swedish flag, but owned wholly or mainly in the United Kingdom, were requisitioned during the autumn of 1917. Their aggregate tonnage was only 7,500 gross.

[2] Employment of Dutch and Scandinavian steam shipping as shown in a Return for January 31st, 1918 (in 1,000 tons gross):

	Norwegian.	Swedish.	Danish.	Dutch.
* National trade with U.K.	43	162	89	56
Other U.K. trades, not with European Allies	75	3	11	3
† Allied services in war zone	547	35	102	4
Belgian relief	33	36	—	23
National import, colonial, and coasting trade	135	130	74	§ 535
Other neutral trades	4	2	13	4
‡ Trading in American and Eastern seas	543	121	248	453
Trading with or seized by Germany	15	63	11	6
Laid up	28	109	13	103
Employment unknown	29	97	26	37
New vessels, repairing, etc.	15	9	8	41
Total	1,467	767	595	1,265

* Many of the Danish colliers came to U.K. ports in ballast. The figures appear to include some Dutch and Swedish ships detained in U.K. ports.

† Includes national traffic with France, Italy, etc., traffic between U.K. and Allies, and between Allies and overseas.

‡ Includes ships running to Dominion ports from ports outside the war zone.

§ In addition to the Dutch tonnage shown as laid up, nearly 400,000 tons was detained in Dutch or United States ports as a result of the American embargoes.

ment with regard to neutral tonnage, arrived at in October between the British and American Governments. The principal question involved was the allocation of the tonnage comprised in the Anglo-Norwegian Agreement, to which the United States became a party in November. This question was settled in January 1918, on the basis that all Norwegian ships chartered to American citizens prior to November 23rd, 1917, should be taken over by the Shipping Board; that ships chartered prior to that date by the Inter-Allied Chartering Committee should remain under their control; and that the balance of Norwegian tonnage remaining to be secured under the Agreement should be equally divided between the Shipping Board and the Inter-Allied Committee. The net effect of this arrangement was to give the United States control of about 450,000 gross tons of Norwegian shipping, and to leave about 700,000 tons under the control of the Inter-Allied Committee.[1] This was, of course, exclusive of ships requisitioned under the North Sea substitution scheme. The total tonnage of such vessels now running under the British flag, after deduction of losses, was about 140,000 gross; but as an equivalent block of British shipping had been diverted to the North Sea, for the carriage of Norwegian coal, the Norwegian ships were not taken into account in considering the question of Inter-Allied allocation.[2]

It was understood by the British Government, though not expressly stipulated, that a similar principle would be applied in the allocation of any further neutral tonnage under other flags, control of which might be obtained by Great Britain or the United States. The chief sources from which such additional tonnage might be expected

---

[1] Chartered to U.S. prior to November 23rd, 1917: 234,617 tons net; say, 376,000 gross, 564,000 dead-weight.
Chartered to I.A.C.C. prior to November 23rd, 1917: 389,260 tons net; say, 622,000 gross, 933,000 dead-weight.
Balance to be chartered, 92,180 net; say, 147,000 gross, 220,000 dead-weight.
U.S.: 376,000 gross + 74,000, share of balance = 450,000 gross.
I.A.C.C.: 622,000 gross + 74,000, share of balance = 696,000 gross.
The ships under control of the Inter-Allied Chartering Committee include those running on approved charters, as well as those time-chartered by the Executive direct. Ships employed in Belgian relief were excluded from the arrangement.

[2] Owing to economies effected in the service, the British tonnage carrying coal to Norway was always, after the first few months, rather less than the Norwegian tonnage transferred.

were Dutch and Swedish shipping; but the negotiations for Dutch and Swedish tonnage were still hampered by disputes relating to blockade questions. With Spain there were no such complications; but any immediate hope of a tonnage agreement had been definitely abandoned. After long negotiations a commercial agreement was concluded, in December, between the British and Spanish Governments; but that agreement contained no tonnage provisions. Its chief importance was derived from the fact that it removed the most serious of the restrictions on the ore traffic. In return for a modification of the restrictions on imports of Spanish fruit, bunker concessions, and a guarantee for the licensing of coal exports in Spanish ships, which were to be permitted to arrive in ballast for the purpose, the Spanish Government agreed specifically to repeal the Order obliging ore steamers to bring to a Spanish port coal to the amount of one-third of the ore they proposed to lift. This was a distinct gain, though the ore trade was still hampered by the reservation of 10 per cent. of the space on ore steamers for the carriage of fruit.[1] It proved impossible, however, to arrange for any definite allocation of tonnage to Allied services. Unlike the Northern neutrals, Spain had not a mercantile marine fully adequate to the carriage of her own trade, and the shortage of shipping obliged the Spanish Government, at the beginning of 1918, to issue a decree requisitioning tonnage for use in the essential trades.

The vital importance of Spanish ore to the Allies prevented the application to Spain of any method of pressure so drastic as the general embargo on exports to the Northern neutrals; but on those States the stoppage of supplies was now beginning to tell heavily. Although the general embargo had only been in force since October 1917, their imports had been grievously curtailed for many months prior to that date, through the British embargoes on shipments of particular commodities, and the effects on oversea communications of the submarine campaign and the retaliatory measures adopted by the Allies. During the calendar year 1917, the Scandinavian States and Holland, taken as a whole, had received little over one-third of their normal supply of foodstuffs, raw materials other than coal,

---

[1] The allocation of 10 per cent. space to fruit was estimated to shut out 20 per cent. of a dead-weight ore cargo. A proposal to increase this proportion to 33 per cent. dead-weight was successfully resisted.

and manufactured goods.[1] They were now almost entirely deprived of imports.

In Sweden the situation was fast becoming unbearable. Ever since the autumn of 1916 the majority of the more important Swedish imports had been drastically restricted, and stocks were already low when the general embargo was imposed. The home production of food had been seriously curtailed by the earlier embargoes on fodder,[2] and by the winter of 1917 the food crisis, aggravated by a bad harvest, was really acute. Hardly less serious were the effects of the coal shortage. Shipments of coal and coke from Great Britain had amounted during 1917 to a little over 600,000 tons, under 40 per cent. of the rigorously restricted exports for 1916, and about one-eighth of the 1918 figures. From Germany, too, the supply had been greatly reduced, and now that winter had come, it was absolutely necessary to make some attempt to relieve the rigour of the fuel situation.

A Swedish Mission was accordingly despatched to London with instructions to make concessions to the Associated Governments in return for the promise of coal and food. So divergent were the views of the two parties that, even now, no definite agreement could, for the time being, be reached, the question of ore shipments to Germany remaining an insuperable obstacle; but by the end of January 1918 a *modus vivendi* was arrived at, which did something to ease the strain. It was agreed that, pending the conclusion of a definite agreement, at least 100,000 tons deadweight of the Swedish shipping lying idle in British, French,

---

[1] Imports into Scandinavia and Holland from all sources other than Germany, exclusive of coal (in 1,000 tons):

	Average Import, 1911–13, less Exports.	1916.	1917.
Corn and Grain	4,891	4,252	1,768
Other Foodstuffs	763	792	310
Oils, Fats, and Gums	895	997	397
Textiles and Manufactures thereof	217	235	106
Metals and Manufactures thereof	1,119	299	201
Other principal articles	904	860	307
	8,789	7,435	3,089

From *Statistics of Imports into Scandinavia and Holland* [Cd. 8989], 1918.

[2] The total imports of fodder in 1917 were only 46,000 tons, as against a normal net import of nearly 300,000.

and Italian ports should be chartered for a period of three months for employment in the war zone, and that ships laid up in American ports might be chartered for four months for voyages outside the war zone. It was further provided that all tonnage then trading in Allied interests should continue in such employment, that ships might be chartered by the Belgian Relief Commission without the imposition of any conditions, and that the Swedish Government should place no restrictions on the offer to the Allies of ships lying idle in Swedish ports and not required for national trade. In return the British Government agreed to license for export an increased quantity of coal, and permission was given for the import of sufficient foodstuffs to stave off starvation.

By Holland, negotiations with the Associated Powers were opened in November 1917. The state of the Netherlands was little better than that of Sweden. Only about 40 per cent. of the normal net import of fodder had been received during 1917, and not a ton was now coming forward. Normally over 500,000 tons of fertilisers were imported; now every source of supply was stopped. The progress of the margarine industry in Great Britain, coupled with the rationing of the product, had permitted the stoppage of all shipments to Holland of oil-seeds, kernels, and other margarine materials. Coal shipments from Great Britain had amounted during 1917 to 380,000 tons only as against 1,350,000 tons in 1916, and an average of over 2,000,000 before the war; nor was much reliance to be placed upon the German supplies.

The Dutch representatives had thus strong motives for coming to an agreement, and by January 4th, 1918, the discussions had made sufficient progress to enable the British Government to put forward definite proposals for a tonnage agreement. These proposals included the time-charter to the British and American Governments of 600,000 dead-weight tons of Dutch shipping, and provisions for the employment of the remainder in such a way as to serve Allied as well as national interests. In view, however, of the special difficulties inherent in the situation of the Netherlands, it was considered necessary to offer an express stipulation that no Dutch steamer, even when time-chartered to the Allies, should be employed in war-zone trade without the owner's consent. The intention was to use the tonnage obtained in essential trades outside the war zone, in such a way as to release British, American, or Norwegian tonnage for war-zone service.

Pending a definite decision by the Dutch Government on these proposals, their representative in London accepted provisionally a *modus vivendi* by which, in return for coal and cereals, a large part of the Dutch shipping in American ports was to be chartered to the American Government for one round voyage outside the war zone, or for Belgian Relief, or on service for the Swiss Government in discharge of Allied obligations. It was further provided that, on the departure from an American port for Holland of a steamer in Belgian Relief service, a corresponding vessel should leave Holland for the United States.

This arrangement was never carried into effect, owing to a German threat to torpedo at sight any Dutch vessel leaving for the States, and to differences which arose with the owners of vessels lying in American ports; nor was any definite reply received to the proposals for a general tonnage agreement. The embargoes, therefore, remained in full force.

As regards neutral tonnage, therefore, the prospect of obtaining any large additions to that already in Allied service remained doubtful, and in view of the inadequacy of the British shipbuilding output to replace losses, the prospect of making good the anticipated tonnage deficit in 1918 depended mainly on the possibility of American assistance. All that could be done meanwhile, was to strive in every possible way to increase the effective carrying power of the ships actually available, and to adjust the import programmes in such a manner that as little as possible of the burden of the deficit should fall on the essential services. Before tracing the measures taken to this end, it is necessary to examine the effect on imports of the conditions existing during the second half of 1917.

CHAPTER XVII

DIMINISHING IMPORTS
AUGUST 1917—JANUARY 1918

SETTING aside for the moment measures such as the development of the convoy system in the Mediterranean and the appointment of the Liverpool Convoy Committee, the effect of which had not yet become fully apparent, the conditions under which British trade had been carried on during the six months ending January 1918—the seventh half-year of war—may be summarised as follows.

The adoption of the convoy system had materially reduced losses both in the ocean and short-sea trades; but the rate of loss still exceeded, by a considerable margin, the rate of replacement. A considerably larger amount of neutral tonnage was now running on Allied charter than during the spring of 1917, but the reluctance of neutral shipowners, other than Norwegian, to send their vessels to British ports was still very marked, and Norwegian shipping, though active, was rapidly diminishing. Thus, month by month, the total available tonnage dwindled. On the other hand, the proportion of ships and cargoes which sailed for British ports but failed to reach their destination was steadily reduced, and as the submarine attack was now directed more especially against outward-bound and coasting traffic, the percentage of imports sent to the bottom diminished, probably, faster than the total loss of shipping. In the utilisation of the shipping available the dominant factor was the Atlantic concentration; but the effects of this concentration were neutralised, in large measure, by the increased average length of the round voyage in the North Atlantic, and by the use of double bottoms for the import of oil, which shut out, at the end of the year, about 80,000 tons of other imports monthly. On the other hand, considerable progress had been made in the elimination of ballast voyages inwards. In respect of foreign steamers, the percentage of such voyages was higher than before the war, owing to the use of neutral and Allied tonnage for the coal supply of France and Italy, without regard to purely British interests. For the same reason there was an increase in the proportion of ballast voyages made by the smaller British steamers, and the total percentage of vessels entering in ballast steadily increased throughout the war; but ballast voyages by the larger steamers were now comparatively rare, owing to the restriction of the cross-trades. Thus, the total percentage of *tonnage* entering in ballast was decidedly on the decrease.[1] Further, apart from the problems presented by the routeing of ships under convoy, the position at the majority of the ports was better than in 1916, and enabled quicker turn-round to be given.

There was thus a complex of factors tending on the one hand to increase and on the other to reduce the effective carrying power of the tonnage available; but, while the balance of these factors was probably on the side of improvement, any such gain was more than off-set by the steady reduction of that tonnage itself. The total entrances with cargoes of both British and foreign shipping during the six months compared badly either with the figures of the previous half-year or with those for the six months ending January 1917.[2]

[1] PERCENTAGE OF STEAMERS AND TONNAGE ENTERED IN BALLAST AT PORTS IN THE UNITED KINGDOM

	British.		Foreign.		Total.	
	s.s.	Net tonnage.	s.s.	Net tonnage.	s.s.	Net tonnage.
1913	33	30	45	53	39	40
1914	35	28	47	55	40	40
1915	37	20	55	58	48	37
1916	43	22	58	61	52	40
1917	47	18	70	61	53	31

[2] ENTRANCES WITH CARGOES AT PORTS IN THE UNITED KINGDOM (1,000 TONS NET)

Six months ending	British.	Foreign.	Total.	Ratio.
January 1917	10,146	4,603	14,753	100·0
July 1917	9,584	2,154	11,738	79·6
January 1918	9,059	1,943	11,002	74·7

The decrease in foreign entrances is partly accounted for by the replacement of Norwegian by British tonnage in the Scandinavian trade, and the transfer to the British flag of the Norwegian ships withdrawn. But for this, the decrease in British entrances would have been still greater than it actually was.

A BIG REDUCTION

The weight of imports, allowing for the estimated weight of Government cargoes not included in the Trade Returns before July, compared more favourably with the last corresponding period than the entrances would indicate; but the actual decrease was heavy, and but for the large imports of oil-fuel on Admiralty account, it would have been heavier still.[1] For the complete calendar year 1917 the estimated weight of imports was about 37,000,000 tons, a decrease of 8,000,000 tons or more on 1916.

That this diminution in the volume of imports was not disastrous in its effects on the food supply of the country and the supply of materials required for war purposes, was due to the fact that the principle of excluding unessential imports, and thus preserving for essentials the full advantage of the carrying power available had at last been adopted. Thanks to the work of the Import Restrictions Committee, supplemented by that of the Tonnage Priority Committee and the monthly priority programmes under the Liner Requisition scheme, the supply of vital commodities had been fairly well maintained, and the bulk of the reduction fell on those which, however valuable, could be dispensed with under war conditions.

No less than 4,000,000 tons—one half of the total decrease—was accounted for by the diminution in imports of wood, timber, paper, and paper-making materials (mainly wood-pulp). Imports of pit-props alone had dropped by 1,000,000 tons, a decrease of 50 per cent., the loss being made good, as we have seen, by increased home cutting. Of the total imports 70 per cent. came from France —mostly in returning colliers. Shipments from Spain were discontinued, the space being left free for ore, and owing to the longer voyage, no further use was made of the Canadian and Newfoundland supplies. In sawn and planed timber the decrease was still greater, from nearly 3,700,000 to 1,700,000 tons, and here, too, tonnage

[1]

Six months ending	Estimated weight of all Imports in 1,000 tons.	Ratio.
January 1917	21,378	100·0
July 1917	19,497	91·2
January 1918	17,111	80·0

Excluding oil-fuel the ratio is 100·0 ; 89·7 ; 74·4.

economies were effected in purchase, the decrease falling most heavily on supplies from the more distant sources.[1]

Restrictions on brewing, and the greater use of more concentrated feeding-stuffs were mainly responsible for a very considerable saving on barley, corn offals, etc., and the prohibition of re-exports had the effect of cutting down imports of rice, jute, and other products. Of the other restrictions some proved impossible to enforce, at any rate in their entirety, either, as in respect of Spanish fruit, on account of political pressure, or for other reasons; but the net effect of the minor restrictions in making room for more important products was very considerable.[2]

Another restriction voluntarily accepted was that on raw cotton. From August 1917 onwards, space for the

---

[1] IMPORTS OF SAWN, SPLIT, PLANED, AND DRESSED TIMBER, IN 1,000 LOADS

	1916.	1917.
Scandinavia	1,965	1,073
Russia	640	295
North America	1,062	318

[2] The following table shows in 1,000 tons the actual, as compared with the contemplated, saving in certain directions:

	Imports.		Greatest contemplated saving.	Actual saving.
	1916.	1917.		
Wood and timber, other than hardwoods	6,228	2,802	2,400	3,426
Hardwoods	90	72	*	18
Paper and paper-making materials	1,282	586	644	696
Stones, slates, and marble	231	163	*	68
Barley	791	457	*	334
Corn and grain offals	189	72	*	117
Soya beans	65	25	*	40
Raw fruit (other than limes and lemons), tomatoes, and onions	956	434	743	523
Luxury food and drink, including tea, coffee, cocoa, wine, etc.	549	302	346	247
Tobacco	75	22	*	53
Rice	433	324	*	109
Jute	238	110	144	128
Hides and leather, boots and shoes	132	114	36	18
Glass, sheet, plate and table	65	11	50	54
Glass bottles	84	23	42	61
Colours and pigments	61	31	20	30

* Not separately distinguished.

There was also a saving of about £10,000,000 on miscellaneous imports, chiefly manufactures, for which weights were not given. As values were steadily rising, this must represent a considerable diminution in bulk.

permitted imports had been allocated among the importers, at fixed rates, by Commercial Services Branch, in consultation with the Board of Trade and the Liverpool Cotton Association. In deciding on the monthly import the Board had been guided mainly by the requirements of the war industries and the export trade, and the output for domestic consumption had been drastically curtailed. Imports from all sources amounted to 725,000 tons, against 969,000 in the previous year, and in view of the continued depletion of stocks the Cotton Control Board, in November, further reduced the output of spinning mills using American cotton to 60 per cent. of the normal. In the following month they decided that only 70 per cent. of the machinery in the weaving sheds should be run.[1]

Among the chief non-restricted imports adversely affected by the tonnage shortage were sugar, which fell away by 145,000 tons, margarine, lard, and manufactured iron and steel.[2] It was, however, the imports of iron ore that showed most plainly the effects of the unrestricted submarine campaign. Shipments from Spain and the Mediterranean were, indeed, very nearly as large as in 1916, for the withdrawal of neutral tonnage had been made good by increased employment of British requisitioned ships, and by the assistance received from Italy under the coal-ore agreement. Moreover, the Norwegian and Danish tonnage agreements had brought a good deal of neutral tonnage into the trade during the latter part of the year. On the other hand, the risks of the North Sea passage had brought about a decline of no less than 70 per cent. in the shipments of Scandinavian ore. In the aggregate, the imports of ore from all sources were less than in 1916 by nearly 750,000 tons.[3]

To the cereal position reference has already been made.[4] For the whole year the imports of wheat and flour, in teims of wheat,[5] were 5,596,000 tons, as against 5,714,000 in 1916; but owing to an increase in the home harvest, as a result of steps taken to stimulate production, the total supplies were a little above the 1916 level. Imports

---

[1] Henderson, *The Cotton Control Board.*
[2] The reduction in imports of iron and steel manufactures was, to a great extent, due to the expansion of the munitions industries in Great Britain, which enabled the shipments from North America to be reduced.
[3] See footnote on the next page.
[4] See pp. 193, 241-2, *supra.*
[5] Taking 7 tons flour = 10 tons wheat.

of oats were almost exactly the same as in 1916, but the home harvest was more abundant by nearly 20 per cent. This increase in the total supply of oats was of great importance in view of the demand for military fodder, the more so as maize imports were lighter by 450,000 tons than in the previous year. For all cereals North America remained by far the most important source of supply. Owing to the early shipments under the abandoned Australian wheat programme, the proportion of wheat and flour derived from the United States and Canada fell from 87 to 80 per cent., but in the supply of oats and even of maize North America was now gradually taking the place of the Plate. So far as possible, all other sources of cereal supply were left to the Allies. By the end of the year, there was a distinct tendency to increase the imports of rolled oats maize meal, and other farinaceous preparations providing, in small space, a substitute for grain.

Thanks to the transfer of Australasian liners to the Plate tracks, the steps taken to accelerate turn-round, and the reduction of losses, the deficit in the meat supplies during the first half of 1917 had been to a great extent wiped out during the latter part of the year. The reduction in the rate of loss bore eloquent testimony to the value of convoy. From August 1917 to January 1918 inclusive the number of meat-carrying liners sunk or damaged by enemy action was only 16, as against 28 during the previous

Footnote [3] from previous page.

IMPORTS OF IRON ORE
(In 1,000 tons)

	1916.	1917.
From Spain and the Mediterranean	5,843	5,811
,, Scandinavia	1,031	307
,, Other Countries	60	72
	6,934	6,190

ENTRANCES FROM SPAIN AND ALGERIA
(1,000 tons net)

	1916.	1917.
British	1,565	1,894
Spanish	916	216
Norwegian	441	309
Swedish	109	14
Danish	139	50
Dutch	33	1
Greek	120	94
Italian	90	219

These figures, of course, include ships not in the ore trade; but the comparison is instructive.

HEAVY LOSSES OF MEAT SHIPS

six months.[1] Moreover, more than half of these casualties occurred in August and September, when the convoy system was in its infancy and afforded little protection to meat ships.

For the calendar year 1917, the losses of insulated shipping amounted to 37 steamers sunk, with a total capacity of 82,000 tons of meat. In addition, one steamer was very badly damaged, and only a small proportion of her insulated space was reinstated. The annual importing power of these ships, assuming them to have continued in the trades in which they were running at the time of their loss, was about 230,000 tons. A French steamer with a capacity of 1,200 tons (4,800 annual) was lost by marine risk, and two Italian steamers were damaged by the enemy. One of these, torpedoed towards the end of the year, was not repaired during the war.

As against this loss 13 new steamers were put into service, 4 in the Plate, and 9 in the Australasian trade. Their total capacity was about 43,500 tons, and their annual importing power in their respective trades about 114,000. Three of these steamers, however, were not ready until the very end of the year, and did not in fact begin trading till 1918. It must be remembered, too, that the damaged ships took many weeks to repair.[2]

[1] The losses for the six months ending January 1918, include the *Port Kembla*, sunk by the New Zealand minefield. The ships sunk or damaged by submarines were thus 15 as against 25 in the six months ending July 1917.

[2] The following table shows the tonnage actually on service in the various trades, exclusive of ships damaged and still under repair, and of new ships not actually on service:

	End 1916.		End 1917.	
	s.s.	Tons meat capacity.	s.s.	Tons meat capacity.
Australasian service	113	280,200	86	223,700
Plate service	55	148,800	47	128,300
North American service	—	—	11	21,600
Minor services	7	15,500	15	31,500
	175	444,500	159	405,100
French and Italian insulated tonnage	19	37,900	17	33,200

Broadly speaking, ships in the Australasian trade performed two voyages in the year; those in the Plate trade four. The figures for North America exclude insulated space in the ordinary liners.

In spite of these heavy losses, and of the manifold difficulties by which the trade was hampered, the shipments of meat to the Allies for 1917 delivery amounted to 957,000 tons, and were practically equal to those for the preceding year—a striking testimony to the work of the Board of Trade Meat Department and the Refrigerated Shipping Committee. Of this total, rather over 46,000 tons was lost *en route*, the percentage of loss working out at 4·8.[1]

Despite the diversion of shipping from the Australasian to the South American trade, shipments from Australasia were practically level with those of 1916, the effects of the drought having at last worn off, so that full cargoes could be obtained at Australian ports. The depleted tonnage in the trade was insufficient, however, to lift the whole New Zealand output, and nearly 15,000 tons of beef and 52,000 tons of mutton and lamb were left in New Zealand at the end of the year.[2] Supplies from the Plate fell away by 10 per cent., owing to the diversion of ships to South Africa for the Egyptian service, and to the effect of railway strikes in Argentina during the last three months of the year. Some compensation was found, however, in increased shipments from Brazil. From North America the shipments were rather larger than in 1916; but a much greater proportion came from Canada, as the poor quality of the United States beef led to reduction of purchases.

Of the total meat delivered about 440,000 tons were landed in the United Kingdom, and 290,000 tons (of which 113,000 were for British Army supplies) in France; 98,000 tons were landed in Italy, and the same amount in Egypt and Salonika. These shipments to the Eastern Mediterranean were a source of great trouble to the Refrigerated Shipping Committee, owing to the delays in unloading at Port Said, and the necessity of arranging cargoes from the Plate, Brazil, South Africa, China, and Madagascar, arising from the interference of the drought with Australian exports. By the autumn, however, the recovery of Australian exports enabled most of the minor sources to be dispensed with, about half the supply coming from Australia and the balance from the Plate and South Africa.

[1] The majority of the casualties occurred on outward voyages.
[2] In arranging the shipping programmes a preference was given, for reasons of army supply, to the beef-producing countries.

MEAT SUPPLIES AND STOCKS

Re-exports from the United Kingdom, which had amounted to 21,000 tons in 1916, were reduced in 1917 to 1,000 tons only, a very welcome economy in carrying power and risk.

In the distribution of the supplies received, the main feature was again the growth of the military demand. Over 400,000 tons went to the British armies, and about 325,000 to the French and Italians, leaving for the supply of British civilians only 180,000 tons, a decrease of 30 per cent. on the previous year. Even allowing for the increased numbers receiving army rations, the reduction in civilian supplies was very serious, and it was accentuated by the slaughter of home-grown cattle for army consumption.[1] Rationing was strict, and civilian stocks of imported meat had fallen during 1917 to 17,400 tons on December 31st, as against 27,000 on January 1st. On the other hand, the troops had received their full rations throughout the year, and the army stocks in the United Kingdom and Egypt had been raised from 25,200 tons in January to 54,500 tons in December. Both the French and Italian supplies fell considerably short of the quantities guaranteed under the agreements, mainly owing to delays and deviations for reasons of safety; but the actual deliveries to France were little less than in 1916, and those to Italy rather greater.[2]

Having regard to the violence of the attack on British trade, the frightful losses of shipping, and the heavy burden of the Allied supply services, the general record for the year was surprisingly good. Dilution of the loaf, rationing of meat and sugar, meatless days, unemployment in the cotton industry, the interference of import restrictions with many branches of industrial activity and domestic consumption, prices which, despite Government control of freights and products, continued to rise rapidly throughout the year—all these things bore witness to the severity of the strain; but the strain had been met. The supply of munitions, of materials required for war purposes, and of the essential foodstuffs, had been, on the whole, adequately maintained. It was evident, however, that any such further reductions in imports as were contemplated at the Paris Conference must involve grave risks. The margin of non-essential imports was now

---

[1] From September 1st to December 15th, 76,186 cattle were bought and slaughtered, yielding 20,577 tons of fresh meat for the army at home.
[2] See footnote on the next page.

small, and big further cuts could be made only at the expense of munitions or food.

The exports of British products and manufactures were, in value, slightly larger than in 1916, but owing to a heavy falling off in re-exports, the total values were just under those for that year. Values, however, provided a very imperfect criterion of the situation, as prices had risen rapidly throughout the year. The volume of almost every class of export showed a decided drop.

Such a drop had been accepted as a necessary corollary of the reorganisation of the liner services in the interest of the import trade, and a large part of the all-round decrease in exports to Australia and New Zealand may fairly be attributed to the withdrawal of shipping from the

Footnote ² from previous page.

SOURCES OF MEAT SUPPLY 1917
(In 1,000 tons)

	Beef.	Mutton.	Total.
Plate and Patagonia	456·0	56·5	512·5
Australia	105·5	32·3	137·8
New Zealand	38·1	65·8	103·9
Canada	66·3	—	66·3
United States	52·2	0·4	52·6
South Africa	15·1	—	15·1
Brazil	51·4	—	51·4
Venezuela	4·6	—	4·6
Madagascar	6·1	—	6·1
China	7·1	—	7·1
	802·4	155·0	957·4

DISTRIBUTION OF SUPPLIES 1917
(In 1,000 tons)

	Beef.	Mutton.	Total.
British Army	330·7	75·0	405·7
British Civilians	117·9	61·8	179·7
French Army	217·1	12·9	230·0
Italian Army	95·6	—	95·6
Total received	761·3	149·7	911·0
Losses *en route*	41·1	5·3	46·4
Total shipments	802·4	155·0	957·4

Of the French supplies 74·6 per cent., and of the Italian 61·8 per cent., were carried in British ships.

Compare tables for 1916, Vol. II, p. 371.

Australasian services. On the other hand, the reduction in shipments to the Far East was not, generally speaking, in excess of that experienced in other directions, and outward tonnage to India was generally sufficient for the reduced demands of Indian buyers. On the whole, it would appear that the redistribution of the liner services was not, as yet, responsible for a large proportion of the general decline.

The export of coal to countries other than France, Russia, and Italy, was regulated mainly by the necessities of bunker supply, and by the obligations incurred under tonnage agreements,[1] and apart from coal the provision of tonnage was still a minor factor in the export trade. Had it been possible for production for export to be maintained at anything like the normal level, the lack of shipping to maintain the volume of exports would have made itself severely felt; but it was not so possible. Not only was the total labour force available continually depleted by the calling up, under the Military Service Acts, of men for whom the new female and other labour introduced into industry provided only a partial replacement, but the percentage of industrial workers engaged on Government work had increased by July 1917 to 55·3, and the total percentage engaged directly or indirectly on war services was probably considerably higher. The claims of munitions production and military supply on material were at least as great as the demands of those services on manpower. Further, while the export trade was not directly affected by the shortage of tonnage, it was indirectly affected to a great extent through the import restrictions, which fell heavily on many of the raw materials required in the export trade, and were directly aimed at reduction of the re-export traffic. Finally, the restriction of traffic with the Northern neutrals, arising out of blockade and tonnage disputes, as well as the submarine campaign, and culminating in the general embargo at the end of the year, affected all classes of exports to Scandinavia and Holland.

The effect of import restrictions on re-exports was very marked during the second half of 1917, and the totals for the year showed a big drop in most of the bulkier commodities. Among those specially affected by the restric-

[1] There was thus an increase of exports to French West Africa (for Dakar), to Tunis (for Bizerta), to Canada (for Halifax), to Sierra Leone, British South Africa, Singapore, the Azores, and the Mediterranean depôts; but a heavy decrease in shipments to almost all other countries, with the exception of the principal Allies.

tions were rice, tea, coffee, cocoa, cotton, jute, timber, hides and leather. The total decrease in re-exports of these articles amounted in the aggregate to over 300,000 tons.[1] Marked decreases were also recorded in respect of maize, oil-seeds,[2] iron and steel manufactures, bark and tanning extracts, rosin, hemp, lead, gums, spices, and many other products, and the total decrease in re-exports was in the neighbourhood of 500,000 tons.

This reduction in re-exports, however disadvantageous its effect on the exchanges, was a great benefit from the point of view of tonnage economy, since space was saved both on the inward and the outward voyage. Even when the necessities of the Allies compelled tonnage to be allocated for the carriage direct to their ports of commodities formerly re-exported from the United Kingdom, there was a clear gain in shorter voyages, the avoidance of double handling, and the minimising of war risks.

In the exports of British produce and manufactures, the most conspicuous decline, in point of volume, was in manufactures of iron and steel, paper, and manures. Iron and steel exports, of course, were specially affected by the competition of the war industries, and those of paper by the restrictions on imports of wood pulp. The decrease in exports of manures was largely due to the tendency to draw sugar from nearer sources, which cut down the shipments of fertilisers to Java from 83,000 to 6,000 tons. Of the textile industries, the woollen trade was still flourishing, and the reduction in imports of raw cotton and consequent rise in prices had not yet greatly affected the exports of piece goods. Shipments of jute manufactures were also well maintained, owing mainly to the large demand from North America for gunny bags to be used in making up the harvests; but linen exports fell off considerably, owing to increased army demands.[3]

[1] The diminution in cotton re-exports was chiefly in Egyptian cotton to the United States. The decrease in timber was due, partly to the restrictions on the import of hard woods, and partly to increased cutting in France.

[2] Largely due to the smaller dependence now placed on Dutch margarine.

[3] **Exports of Piece Goods**
(In 1,000,000 yards)

	1915.	1916.	1917.
Cotton	4,748	5,254	4,978
Woollen and worsted	148	184	166
Jute	109	120	126
Linen	129	144	103

In miscellaneous manufactures, owing to the diversion of labour, there was a big falling off.

The redirection of the export trade, so marked in 1915 and 1916, was accentuated in 1917. Of the total value of exports and re-exports, no less than 35·6 per cent. went to France, Italy, and Russia. Yet neither their increased share of British trade, nor the assistance so freely given by British shipping in the carriage of supplies from other countries, availed to maintain French and Italian imports at the level of the previous year. Excluding oil-fuel, French imports in 1917 amounted to 32,200,000 tons, of which 17,000,000 tons consisted of coal and coke. This was a decrease in total imports of nearly 7,000,000 tons, or 17 per cent., as compared with 1916, and of over 11,000,000 tons, or 26 per cent., as compared with 1913.[1] Even the coal imports were less by 5,500,000 tons than in the year preceding the war, the increased shipments from Great Britain having failed to make good the loss of the German and Belgian supplies. Of 15,000,000 tons of commodities other than coal imported in 1917, cereals and pulses for human or animal consumption accounted for 3,200,000, meat, sugar, oils and fats and other foodstuffs for 2,700,000. Imports of munitions, of ores and metal manufactures, of nitrates, chemicals, and tanning substances, all of which were required mainly for army purposes, amounted to nearly 7,000,000, leaving less than 2,500,000 tons for all other commodities whatsoever. It was thus evident that there was little or no margin for saving to set off against the expected cereal deficit, which could only be made good by the allocation of additional tonnage.

Italy was in still worse case. The total imports, 11,100,000 tons, were less by 4,400,000, or 28 per cent., than in 1916, less by nearly 7,000,000, or 38 per cent., than in 1913; but nearly the whole of this decrease was represented by diminished imports of coal, and the situation created by the exhaustion of the accumulated stocks was such as to render it indispensable that the imports for 1918 should be on a considerably larger scale than in the previous year. In 1917 they had just exceeded 5,000,000 tons, and of the remaining imports 1,750,000 were munitions, metals, or chemicals, 2,400,000 cereals and about 500,000 other foodstuffs. As the demands of the munition factories were not likely to be less in 1918 than in 1917,

[1] Special commerce.

and the deficit in the harvest had to be made good by increased imports of cereals, the outlook was not hopeful.

On the financial side, all the Allies were in the same boat. The value of British exports and re-exports together was only 56 per cent. of the import values; neither France nor Italy paid by exports for a quarter of the imports received. Now that the United States had come into the war, this adverse balance was, however, of less immediate importance. Its effect on the future prosperity of the three countries might be serious; but for the moment the almost unlimited credit facilities granted by the United States sufficed to ensure the financing of imports. The question of transport was now, more than ever, the supreme problem.

CHAPTER XVIII

INTENSIFIED ATLANTIC CONCENTRATION
FEBRUARY—MARCH 1918

THE first step towards the solution of the tonnage problem during 1918 was the preparation by each Allied Government of a detailed statement of its import requirements. The second step was the revision of the import programme in the light of the available tonnage. These measures, as we have seen, had been decided on at the Paris Conference; but in Great Britain the necessity of further import restrictions had been accepted before that conference met, and so early as November 6th, 1917, the Government appointed a small Committee, under the chairmanship of Lord Milner, to consider the direction in which further restrictions were possible.[1]

As the basis of their calculations, the Committee had before them a memorandum by the Ministry of Shipping, estimating the probable reduction in British imports, other than oil-fuel, during 1918 at 8,000,000 tons.[2] In view, however, of a more reassuring estimate of prospective losses, submitted by the Admiralty, the Committee decided to accept 6,000,000 tons as the total of the cuts to be made. This agreed closely with an estimate made by the Chairman of the Tonnage Priority Committee on November 20th, which showed a prospective loss in carrying power of just over 6,000,000 tons (including oil-fuel), and a deficiency on departmental demands as then

---

[1] Members of the Committee: Lord Milner (subsequently Lord Curzon), Member of the War Cabinet, Chairman; Lord Rhondda, Food Controller; Mr. Walter Long, Secretary of State for the Colonies; Mr. Winston Churchill, Minister of Munitions; Sir Albert Stanley, President of the Board of Trade; Sir Joseph Maclay, Shipping Controller; Captain Clement Jones, Secretary.

[2] This estimate was based on the assumption that it would be necessary to carry for France and Italy an additional 2,000,000 tons of cereals.

furnished to the Tonnage Priority Committee, amounting to 5,600,000 tons.[1]

There was now little room for further economy in the imports formerly regarded as non-essential, and apart from a further reduction of 1,000,000 tons in the imports of timber the cuts proposed by the Committee in an interim report dated December 12th, fell mainly on the requirements of the Food Controller and the Ministry of Munitions. The total cuts proposed amounted to 5,500,000 tons; but the Ministry of Shipping pointed out that, as a large proportion of the commodities affected had been drawn from the nearer sources of supply, the full shipping value of the cuts would not be obtained. The Committee accordingly presented, on February 11th, a report showing further reductions amounting to 2,000,000 tons. Thus it was now proposed to reduce the imports for 1918, other than oil-fuel, to 7,500,000 tons below the level of 1917, and even then no allowance had been made for additional use of British tonnage in the transport of American troops. Fortunately, the event proved that the deficit had been overestimated; but the fact that such reductions were ever contemplated is eloquent as to the gravity of the shipping crisis at the beginning of 1918.

It was obvious, of course, that all estimates must be of a more or less tentative character, until a more precise statement could be obtained as to the amount of extra assistance required by the Allies, and the aid, if any, which could be rendered by the United States. In the meantime, apart from any further improvement in the submarine situation, much might be done to reduce the prospective deficit by still further concentration of shipping on the shorter routes, and the programmes of all Departments were carefully revised with a view to effecting purchases in the nearest markets.

As regards tonnage, the cereal programme was by far the most important item, and this programme was dominated mainly by the desire to lift every available ton from North America. No less than 2,500,000 tons of wheat purchased in Australia during 1917 remained unshipped, and the Commonwealth Government were now pressing, on financial grounds, for purchase of the 1917–18 crop; but though this suggestion was, at the time, entertained, in order to complete the Allies' control of the

[1] On a similar assumption.

world's wheat supply, there was no intention of allocating British tonnage to lift wheat from so distant a source. It was hoped, indeed, that the purchase of the wheat might be used as a lever to obtain for war-zone trade a number of Australian registered steamers and prizes under the control of the Commonwealth Government.[1]

The Wheat Executive had already entered into negotiations for the purchase of the entire Argentine surplus; but this was intended mainly for the supply of France and Italy, to whom also the greater part of the Indian export was to be shipped. For British imports, the Executive looked almost entirely to North America. Apart from the actual length of the voyages involved, this arrangement greatly facilitated the adjustments rendered necessary by the agreement of November 3rd, 1917. Down to that date each of the Allied countries had, in the main, executed its own programme with the tonnage under its control, including British and neutral shipping on Allied charter; but under the November agreement it became incumbent on Great Britain to make good, with British tonnage, all deficiencies in French and Italian imports, and this could only be done conveniently by the diversion of fully requisitioned tramps. It was therefore additionally desirable to draw the largest possible proportion of British imports from North America, as by further diversions under the Liner Requisition Scheme, it was possible to carry the bulk of such imports in liner tonnage, thus setting free tramps for France and Italy.

In the shipment of the North American wheat a great economy of space was effected, by increasing to a very large extent the proportion taken in the form of flour.[2] On the other hand, the American wheat harvests were below the average, and it was anticipated that the use of other cereals for dilution of the loaf would result in a decrease of carrying power, owing to their lower average of extraction. Whether such other cereals would be forthcoming was, indeed, doubtful, as during February a report came from the United States that the quality of the maize crop was the worst on record, the greater part being wet and unfit for export. Further, shipments of grain

---

[1] Ships on Colonial Register could be requisitioned by the Shipping Controller only with the consent of the Dominion or Colonial Government concerned.

[2] This, of course, involved sacrificing the by-products.

at American ports were held up very seriously during December, January, and February. As a combined result of congestion on the American railways, caused by grain and munitions traffic, of an unusually severe winter, and an acute shortage of bunker coal (itself mainly due to railway congestion), there was extreme difficulty in clearing ships during those months, and by January over 100 British and Allied steamers were held up, awaiting bunkers, in New York alone. It actually proved necessary to send out coal cargoes from the United Kingdom to release some of the ships. Other cargoes were sent to Canada, where conditions were very similar.[1]

Meanwhile the consumption of breadstuffs in the United Kingdom was increasing, owing to the shortage of meat and sugar for civilian consumption, and the French and Italian deficiencies had also to be made good. Hence, although railway strikes, attributed in part at least to German influence, had again broken out in Argentina, rendering shipments uncertain, it became necessary to send out a large number of ships to the Plate for March and April loadings. Even if the Plate shipments were effected, the Royal Wheat Commission calculated that, by May 1st the stocks of wheat and substitute breadstuffs, apart from those held on the farms in the United Kingdom, would be reduced to about four weeks' supply. Stocks of oats, which were not included in the Wheat Commission's calculations, were more satisfactory, but no provision had yet been made for 1918 imports, and in view of the large demand for military fodder, and the restrictions now imposed on the feeding of barley to animals, the position was serious.

By the beginning of March the situation was a little better. The rate of extraction was now 92 per cent., and though this, together with the use of diluents, rendered the bread less palatable, it economised wheat. The consumption of bread, too, was going down, and import prospects were improving. The United States Authorities had succeeded in relieving the congestion on the railways, and though industrial conditions in Argentina were still unstable, the wheat shipments from the Plate

[1] The coal sent to Canada was carried by steamers which would otherwise have gone out in ballast. A further cause of dislocation in the Canadian services during December 1917 was the great munitions explosion at Halifax, which interfered with bunkering and necessitated the diversion of steamers to St. John (N.B.), Portland (Maine), and Boston.

were now considered to be assured. Further, in view of the very low rate of loss among grain cargoes since the convoy system had been firmly established, the Wheat Commission felt justified in revising their estimate of future losses.[1] They now hoped for eight weeks' stocks on May 1st.

By intensifying the concentration of liner tonnage in the North Atlantic, the cereal programme reacted inevitably upon the meat imports. The Board of Trade purchases for army supplies were still confined almost entirely to South America and Australasia, for the quality of the North American beef was below War Office standard. The Ministry of Food, however, were buying largely in the United States and Canada for civilian supplies, and were confident of their ability to fill the insulated space in diverted tonnage. Both for the execution of the cereal and munitions programmes and for the transport of American troops, it was desired to increase as much as possible the liner tonnage on the North American tracks, and it was accordingly decided by a conference at the Ministry of Shipping, on January 16th, that the provision of sufficient tonnage to lift all possible meat from the United States and Canada should be a first charge on the pool of insulated shipping. Subject to this, all possible meat was to be lifted from South America, and only the balance of shipping then remaining was to be left in the Australasian trade. Egypt, Salonika, Basra, and Malta, which were fed from Port Said, were to draw their supplies so far as possible from Australasia, supplementary cargoes being shipped from South Africa and the Plate. Towards the end of 1917, when ample supplies once more became available in Australia, the Refrigerated Shipping Committee had laid the foundations of a regular Australasian–Egyptian service, and this was now in full working order. Its advantages over the previous supply arrangements were considerable. Not only was Australia the nearest source to Egypt, but the establishment of the regular service enabled Australian and New Zealand stocks to be cleared more rapidly than if they had all been shipped to the United Kingdom. The gain in turn-round was great and the ships avoided Mediterranean risk. In addition

---

[1] They had estimated losses at 10 per cent. In May 1917 the actual losses had been 7 per cent. From September 1917 to the beginning of March 1918, they were 2·4 per cent.

to refrigerated meat they carried tinned meats, rabbits, and cheese to Egypt for War Office account, horses from Australia to India, wool for transhipment to Italy at Port Said, and on their return voyage, army stores from Egypt to the Near East.

Despite the relief thus afforded to Australia, the diversion of tonnage to the North Atlantic and South America left shipping very short in the Australasian trade, especially as the Food Controller had bought up the whole exportable surplus of butter and cheese. As this was now the main source of dairy produce, while North American beef, though rejected by the Army, could be placed on the market for civilian consumption, the Food Controller claimed a priority for butter and cheese shipments. Thus, although Australian fruit was altogether excluded, it became necessary to economise tonnage in every possible way, and as the result of successful experiments, instructions were given in February that sheep carcasses from New Zealand should be cut across and telescoped in order to save space. Rabbits also were " hook skinned " with a saving of some 30 per cent. in bulk. For by-products such as hides and tallow very little space was available, and the accumulations became very large. They were equally troublesome at the Plate, where the cereal programme threatened to shut out the by-products altogether, and in February the meat companies were considering giving notice to terminate their contracts; but the ordinary liner priority list was modified to include large quantities of hides, tallow, and tinned meats, and the situation was temporarily eased.[1] The ordinary Plate priority list was, in fact, practically cancelled for the time being, and the Plate Conference were instructed to load meat products and whale oil up to any available amount, and complete with cereals.

As a result both of the lines on which the meat and cereal programmes were now laid down, and of the general instructions to concentrate purchases more rigorously on the nearer markets, the tonnage in both the North Atlantic and the South Atlantic trade went up with a bound at the

[1] The trouble with regard to tinned meats arose from the fact that the meat companies had to buy their cattle in mobs, select the better animals for freezing, and convert the others into tinned meats. When these meats, and such by-products as hides and tallow, could not be shipped, the result was not only financial loss, but the smothering of the works with accumulations for which no storage space was available.

beginning of 1918. On January 1st the liner tonnage in the North Atlantic trade, including chartered neutrals and tramps loading on berth under control of the lines, amounted to 2,300,000 tons gross; by March 1st this figure had grown to 2,580,000, and by April 1st to 2,775,000 tons. In the River Plate and Brazilian trade, the tonnage rose from 660,000 to 830,000 and then to 890,000 tons.[1] In order to provide this additional tonnage, the Australasian and Far Eastern services were further reduced, a big cut was temporarily made in the Indian tonnage, and additional ships were withdrawn from several of the crossroutes. It was decided also to draw in all meat ships on the China service.

Hitherto no official loading programmes had been drawn up for the liners in the North Atlantic trade. Even before the application of the Liner Requisition Scheme, these ships were carrying 85 per cent. food and munitions, and for administrative purposes in the Ministry of Shipping they had come under Military, not Commercial Services Branch.[2] In December 1917, however, they were transferred to Commercial Services. No priority list was drawn up, but the North Atlantic Committee, representing all the lines in the Conference, undertook to draw up in advance a monthly programme of ships due to load in United States and Canadian ports, for the purpose of facilitating diversions and adjustments in respect of Government shipments. These monthly programmes, after approval by Commercial Services Branch, were cabled to the Ministry's representatives in New York and Canada, who arranged, in co-operation with the agents of the lines, the routeing of cargoes to the ports of shipment, in accordance with the tonnage allocation.

Such were the measures taken, during the opening months of 1918, to meet, so far as it could be met by the redistribution of British tonnage, the situation created by the Inter-Allied tonnage deficit. Meanwhile the available total of that tonnage was still being, month by month,

[1] North Atlantic figures are for ships loading for United Kingdom or Northern France, and are exclusive of the West Indian trade. The highest figure reached in 1917 was 2,500,000 tons on October 1st. Plate figures include ships loading for Egypt, France, or Italy. The Plate trade had been steady during 1917, at about 650,000 tons.

[2] This was purely a matter of administrative convenience. The organisation of Commercial Services Branch was not yet sufficiently developed to undertake the direction of all services, and this trade was left to Military Branch, as requiring comparatively little commercial supervision.

reduced. The losses during February—British 227,000 tons, total 319,000 tons gross—were only slightly above those of the previous month; but they presented disquieting features. The greater number of the casualties were still confined to the Mediterranean and the waters immediately surrounding the British Isles. In the Mediterranean, the chief gap in the local defensive system had been closed by the institution of a four-day convoy between Gibraltar and Genoa, but the initial results were not entirely satisfactory, and in March orders were given to revert to the Spanish coastal route. Still more disconcerting was the development of the attack in Home Waters. In addition to 20 British and foreign steamers of 500 tons gross and upwards sunk in the English Channel, no fewer than 24 were lost, during February, in the Irish Sea and Bristol Channel. Early in March a determined attack on the North Channel traffic led the Admiralty to abandon that Channel entirely for the moonlight period towards the end of the month, and bring in all West Coast convoys south-about. The traffic between Great Britain and Ireland was also gravely impeded, and the London and North-Western Railway were compelled to abandon their all-night services, as navigation lights were prohibited and the risk of collision proved prohibitively great.

This intensified submarine activity on the inshore tracks was fast becoming a serious menace. Not only was the peril great to ships on their way to Buncrana or Milford to pick up their outward escort, but the presence of submarines off the Isle of Man, Lundy, Anglesea, and the estuary of the Mersey, constituted a grave threat to that regularity of sailings which was essential to the smooth working of the system, and towards which the Liverpool Convoy Committee were working, in conjunction with the Admiralty and the Ministry of Shipping. It threatened also the coasting and Irish traffic which the Home Trade Branch of the Ministry of Shipping was endeavouring to organise and foster, with the object of easing as much as possible the strain on the railways. Although a report presented by the Traffic Diversion Committee on March 18th disposed finally of any idea that in existing circumstances London could be fed wholly through the West Coast ports, the western ports were still receiving an abnormal proportion of the traffic, partly through the desire of the Admiralty to avoid the risks of the passage up-Channel, and partly for convenience of convoy organisation. This increase in the Irish Sea and Bristol Channel sinkings threatened both to neutralise all attempts to facilitate distribution by coaster from the western ports, and to destroy the comparative safety of the ocean traffic to those ports themselves.[1]

On the other hand the outer seas were once more clear of raiders. The WOLF, on her return to the Atlantic in the autumn of 1917, had no such organisation for supply as would enable her to operate effectively against commerce. Her main task, indeed, was accomplished when her minefields were laid. On her way round the Cape and up the Atlantic she captured two neutral steamers[2] and a couple of sailing vessels, one American and one French, but she indulged in no systematic cruising. Her main object was to reach home. Passing round the North of Scotland, she crowned her astonishing career by a safe run across the North Sea, and on February 17th she arrived at Kiel, after a cruise of 451 days and 64,000 miles. By this time the minefields she had laid had mostly been swept up, but not before they had wrought further damage. Indeed, it was not until August 1918 that they claimed their last victim.[3] The WOLF's mission had, indeed, been well fulfilled; by direct capture or through the minefields she had laid, she accounted in all for 120,000 tons of shipping, of which three-quarters was British. In addition, six British steamers, aggregating 37,500 tons, were damaged by her mines.[4] It was an aggravation of her success that the majority of the ships sunk by the minefields were liners of from 5,000 to 9,000 tons. Small as was the total, compared with the havoc wrought by the submarines, it was considerable in itself, and the psychological effect of her operations in waters so long undisturbed

---

[1] For further particulars relating to the ports and the coasting trade at this period, see Chapter XXI, *post*.

[2] One of these, the Spanish *Igotz Mendi*, accompanied the WOLF as a prison ship. She was stranded on the Danish coast while running the blockade, and was subsequently refloated and returned to her owners.

[3] In addition to ships already mentioned, the minefields accounted for the following steamers:
 November 1917, 1 sunk off Bombay.
 January 1918, 1 damaged off the Arabian coast.
 February 1918, 2 sunk off Colombo.
 June 1918, 1 sunk off the northern point of New Zealand.
 August 1918, 1 damaged in the Indian Ocean.

[4] Captured: 8 steamers and 6 sailing vessels (5 s.s., 1 s.v. British). Sunk by mines: 13 steamers (11 British).

by the appearance of an enemy, was no less important. Had her exploits been repeated, had the peace of the outer seas been disturbed simultaneously by other WOLFS and other SEEADLERS, the necessity of hunting down the raiders and providing protection for the more distant tracks, must have caused a dispersal of both naval force and collier tonnage in the last degree distracting at a time when tonnage was desperately short and when the Admiralty were straining every nerve to scrape together ocean escort for the Atlantic convoys. Her cruise, however, was isolated, and was not repeated.

Apart from surface raiders, there was now, however, a serious menace to shipping in the South Atlantic from the large-type submarines operating in the neighbourhood of the Azores, and when negotiations were opened for the purchase of the Argentine wheat crop, arrangements were simultaneously made for running a new convoy from Rio to give the maximum protection to the Plate trade.[1] By March, when shipments were well under way, these arrangements had been completed and a sufficient stock of coal accumulated at Rio, to bunker vessels for a non-stop run to the United Kingdom, or to Gibraltar for France and Italy. The first Rio Convoy sailed, accordingly, on March 13th.[2]

The security thus attained in the South Atlantic and the outer seas was some compensation for the heavy losses in Home Waters; but the total loss was still far above the rate of replacement. Indeed, the February output of new tonnage in British yards was only 100,000 tons, or less than half the tonnage sunk, and the shipbuilding programme was falling more and more into arrears. In the hope of expediting construction the War Cabinet decided on another administrative change. Down to December 1916, mercantile construction had been left to private enterprise, under the general supervision of the Board of Trade, but subject to the prior claims of the Admiralty and Ministry of Munitions on steel and labour. In that

[1] In November 1917 the Germans had formally declared the existence of a barred zone round the Azores, at the same time extending the existing Atlantic zone. On January 11th, 1918, they announced an eastward extension of the Azores zone, and the establishment of a new zone stretching from Dakar to the Cape Verdes. These announcements, however, were of no practical significance, as the submarines had already sunk ships in these areas, and at no time confined their operations within the limits of the zones.

[2] See Chapter XX, *post*.

month the responsibility for the new State programme and for shipbuilding generally had been vested in the Shipping Controller. In May 1917 it was transferred to the Navy Controller. Now it was decided to entrust the whole responsibility to a leader of the industry itself, and on March 20th Sir Eric Geddes, the First Lord of the Admiralty, announced in the House of Commons, the appointment of the Rt. Hon. Lord Pirrie, K.P., P.C., head of the great firm of Harland & Wolff, as Controller-General of Merchant Shipbuilding. As such, he was directly responsible to the First Lord; but it was a term of the arrangement that, on all questions affecting his special task, the Controller-General should have the right of direct access to the Prime Minister and the War Cabinet.

In view of the continued wide discrepancy between losses and replacements, and the existence of an admitted, though as yet unascertained deficit in carrying power for the 1918 import programmes of the Allies, the acquisition of neutral shipping became more than ever important. Some progress had been made in January by the conclusion of the *modus vivendi* with Sweden; but the negotiations with Holland had hitherto come to nothing, and by the beginning of March, the development of the tonnage situation led to an important change in the attitude of the Allies towards Dutch shipping. The original proposals of January 4th, 1918, were for the employment of Dutch steamers outside the war zone, to release Allied and Norwegian ships for war-zone trade. The American Shipping Mission which arrived in London during the winter of 1917 had, however, urged from the first the importance of obtaining Dutch tonnage free of restrictions as to employment, and by March 1918 it had become evident that the requirements of the Allies were too pressing for the substitution scheme, with its inevitable delays, to afford adequate relief. Since the proposals had never been accepted, they were in no way binding on the Allies, and on March 8th the British Minister at The Hague was instructed to inform the Dutch Government that the restrictions on the employment of ships could no longer be accepted without serious derangement of the Allied programmes, and to propose that the Dutch tonnage to be chartered to the Allies should be freed from all such restrictions, in return for a guarantee as to the replacement of losses after the war, and assistance in securing wheat for the supply of Holland. An answer to this new proposal was requested by March 18th.

Before the expiration of this time-limit, not only the allocation of neutral tonnage but the whole problem of adjusting the import programmes of the European Allies to their available shipping resources had passed into the hands of a new authority.

CHAPTER XIX

THE ALLIED MARITIME TRANSPORT COUNCIL
FEBRUARY—MARCH 1918

ON February 15th, 1918, a meeting of the representatives of France, Italy, Great Britain, and the United States was held at the Foreign Office, to make arrangements for the establishment of the Inter-Allied authority to whom the execution of the Paris Resolutions was to be entrusted.[1] At this meeting the general lines of procedure were laid down, and preliminary steps taken to provide the new body with a permanent staff to supply the requisite executive machinery. On March 11th–14th, the Allied Maritime Transport Council held its first session at Lancaster House.

In conformity with the agreement arrived at in Paris, the representatives of Great Britain, France, and Italy were Ministers, able to speak with the authority of their respective Governments. The United States, though associated with the European Powers for the purposes of the war, was not technically a member of the Alliance, and the American representative, who was not of Ministerial rank, was unable to the same degree to bind his Government. His presence, however, ensured a large measure of American co-operation, and on the executive organisation of the Council the United States was equally represented with the three European Powers.[2]

---

[1] See p. 246, *supra*.
[2] The original members of the Council were:
Great Britain: Lord Robert Cecil (Minister of Blockade), Sir Joseph Maclay, Bart. (Shipping Controller).
France: M. Loucheur (Minister of Munitions), M. Clémentel (Minister of Commerce and Shipping).
Italy: Signor Crespi, Onorevole Salvatore Orlando.
United States: Hon. Raymond B. Stevens.
Secretary to the Council: Mr. J. A. Salter (Director of Ship Requisitioning, Ministry of Shipping).
In May 1918, Signor Villa replaced Signor Orlando; and in July the

That organisation comprised, in the first place, a Main Executive Committee, with three international Sub-Committees, Tonnage, Imports, and Statistical, and a non-national secretariat; in the second place, four National Divisions whose work was co-ordinated by the Main Committee and Sub-Committees. The object of this arrangement was to avoid the creation of a large new organisation over-lapping the existing national organisations. The four National Divisions, though all housed at Lancaster House,[1] were in close touch with their respective national Executives, and the British Division was, in practice, little differentiated from the Ministry of Shipping. Each Division remained responsible to its own Government for the consideration of national requirements [2]; but their work was co-ordinated for the purpose of dealing with Inter-Allied problems, by the fact that the Heads of these Divisions formed the Main Executive Committee, known as the Allied Maritime Transport Executive. The whole organisation was further linked to the work of the Council itself, by the fact that the Secretary to the Council was Head of the British Division and Chairman of the Executive.[3]

The object of the Council, as laid down by the Paris Conference, was not, as will be remembered, to frame import programmes for the countries represented, but to examine in the light of the available tonnage the programmes prepared by the national authorities, and to

Hon. George Rublee was appointed as a second representative of the United States.

The chair was taken at each session by the senior Minister of the country in which the meeting was held. Expert and official representatives of each country also attended the sessions of the Council to give evidence or advice on particular questions.

[1] The Secretariat and the American Division were located in Lancaster House from the first. The French and Italian Divisions (already in London) were transferred to that building in July.

[2] The American Division was directly responsible to the American Delegate, who worked in the same building; the three other Divisions were responsible to their national representatives on the Council. Each Division had its own secretarial staff for purposes of confidential correspondence and separate communication with its own Government. The Central Secretariat was composed of members of all four nationalities, who were required to divest themselves of any national point of view, acting in a secretarial capacity for the Executive as a whole.

[3] The members of the Executive were: Mr. J. A. Salter (Great Britain), M. Jean Monnet (France), Professor Attolico, C.B. (Italy), Hon. G. Rublee (United States).

The term "Allied Maritime Transport Executive" was also applied, for convenience, to the whole administrative organisation.

ORGANISING JOINT PURCHASES

adjust, both as between countries and as between commodities, the reductions necessitated by any deficit in carrying power. The preparation of a draft import programme for each country was a national responsibility; but considerable progress had already been made in the development of joint purchase and, in respect of certain commodities, joint programmes, and there were already in existence Inter-Allied authorities for dealing with some of the most important imports.

To begin with, the Inter-Allied Council on War Purchases and Finance was concerned with the financing of purchases in America, and the Commission Internationale de Ravitaillement with the placing of French and Italian orders in the United Kingdom, and the work of both bodies provided considerable opportunities for joint discussion and adjustment of programmes. The actual preparation of joint programmes had only been undertaken, however, in respect of particular commodities, the most important of which were cereals and meat.

The combined purchase of all classes of cereals for the European Allies, and their allocation, when purchased, to the respective countries, was now in the hands of the Wheat Executive, acting through the Royal Commission on Wheat Supplies. A Meat and Fats Executive on similar lines had been set up in August 1917; but it will be remembered that the supply of frozen meat to the armies, and the purchase of all such meat from sources other than North America, remained in the hands of the Board of Trade Meat Department, who were, however, represented on the Executive. The supply of meat to the Allies was regulated by definite agreements; but the governing factor in the whole supply and distribution of refrigerated produce was now, as always, the insulated space available on the various routes.

Other Executives already formed covered the purchase and distribution of sugar, oil-seeds, and nitrates; but of these three, only the Nitrate Executive was actually at work. The preparation of a nitrate programme was, however, inseparable in practice from the consideration of the general munitions programme of each country, for a great part of which nitrates formed the basis. The question of oil-seeds, too, cut across all three of the main categories of imports, as they were required for food (margarine), munitions (glycerine), and civil industry (soap). As regards sugar, centralised purchase had been in operation since October 1916, when the French and Italian Governments agreed to effect all purchases through the Royal Commission on Sugar Supplies; but nothing in the way of a definite joint programme had yet been attempted.

There was also in existence a Petroleum Conference; but no regular joint programme had yet been drawn up. So far as the oil could be imported in tanker tonnage, unavailable for general imports, the question of petroleum stood rather outside the main tonnage problem; but so long as the use of double bottoms in ordinary cargo steamers continued, the competition of oil with other commodities remained a very important factor in the consideration of the tonnage balance sheet.

With all these bodies it was necessary for the Council to establish a liaison; but this was necessarily a matter of time, especially in view of the fact that several of the Import Executives were as yet only in process of formation. For the moment, the Council were obliged to depend mainly on their own resources and on the information already collected by their staff.

Their primary task, on which all others depended, was the preparation of a tonnage balance sheet for 1918, and the adjustment of the joint import programme to the estimate of available carrying power. A British programme had already been prepared, showing a reduction of 4,000,000 tons on the import for 1917; but detailed particulars of tonnage under the control of France and Italy had not been obtained in time for examination before the meeting of the Council, nor had the French and Italian import programmes yet been revised in the light of the tonnage situation. On the basis of such information as was already available, the total deficit in carrying power for the import services of the European Allies was estimated at 2,200,000 tons dead-weight of shipping, equivalent on voyages of average length to 10,000,000 tons of imports in the year. Such estimate, however, was subject to revision of programmes and to the possibility of American assistance or the acquisition of additional interned or neutral tonnage, such as the German ships in South American ports, and Dutch or Swedish vessels detained under the embargoes. From the United States, however, came a serious note of warning. It will be remembered that, at the Paris Conference, an appeal had been made to the American Government to provide in the immediate future at least 500,000 tons deadweight, and to raise this figure, as soon as possible, to an average of 1,250,000 tons. The development of the military situation had led, however, to a large increase in the demand made upon the United States for military assistance, and the American representative now stated that the military programme as adopted by the Supreme War Council and agreed by the United States Government, was likely to absorb all surplus American tonnage existing and building, and all additional neutral tonnage which might be brought under American control.

Until full particulars of the Allies' tonnage and import programmes had been received and analysed, and the question of American assistance definitely settled, it was impossible for the Council to make much headway with the general problem of adjusting imports and carrying power. They decided, therefore, to accept provisionally the figure of 10,000,000 tons as representing the joint import deficiency, and to defer further consideration of the question to a meeting in four or five weeks' time, when it was hoped the examination of programmes would have been completed by the Executive.

In the meantime the most urgent question was that of the Italian coal supply. Throughout 1917 the imports into Italy from all sources had averaged only about 400,000 tons a month, less than half the normal import, and only about two-thirds the minimum requirements of the country under war conditions. To make good the deficiency the Italians had been obliged to draw on reserve stocks, which were now practically exhausted. It was thus absolutely necessary that the imports should be immediately and substantially increased, at least up to a point which would prevent dislocation of transport and munitions production. The Italian coal trade was, however, always one of the most difficult to keep supplied with tonnage. The effect of the intensified submarine attack, following on that of freight limitation schemes, had driven neutrals out of the trade. Italian tonnage, depleted by heavy losses, could take but a small share of the work, and though the Ministry of Shipping could use freely its power to direct British ships to Italian ports, it was extremely difficult, in the existing shortage, to find sufficient steamers of the type required, especially for a trade in which the rate of loss was abnormally heavy.

Despite all difficulties, however, the task had to be attempted, and even before the meeting of the Council, the British, French, and Italian officials had been engaged in the solution of the problem, and had taken executive action for relief of the situation. Their plans, with some modifications, were confirmed and adopted by the Council, and provided for bringing up the total supply to 600,000 tons a month—which the Council agreed to represent Italy's minimum requirements—without exposing the whole of the additional shipping to Mediterranean risk. The use of Blaye had already saved from that risk a portion of the tonnage employed; but it was now proposed not only to use the railways from the Gironde for the transport of British coal, but to draw a large proportion of the Italian supplies from the southern French coalfields. The provisional programme agreed upon comprised a monthly supply of 360,000 tons of British and 240,000 tons of French coal. Of the British exports, 150,000 tons were to be shipped direct to Italian ports, 100,000 tons to Blaye, and 110,000 tons to Rochefort or the Gironde. Thus the total amount to be drawn from French coalfields or shipped to French ports, would be 450,000 tons, of which it was anticipated that 270,000 would be railed to Italy direct, and 180,000 tons to Marseilles or other French Mediterranean ports, for transport by coaster. It was suggested, however, that economy in tonnage would be effected and a smaller strain on railway transport involved, if the whole supply other than that shipped by the long sea route or to Blaye, were drawn from the French coalfields, France receiving compensation in additional cross-Channel shipments for the 110,000 tons supplied beyond her original quota.

This scheme had the very great advantage of both economising tonnage and minimising submarine risk, but the shipping problem still presented serious difficulties. It was decided by the Council that, in view of the importance of maintaining the strategic coal reserves in France, it would be necessary, at any rate for the present, to replace by British coal the whole of the 350,000 tons to be supplied by France.[1] By drastic combing out of the coasting trade it was hoped to find tonnage for the

[1] Original quota 240,000 tons plus 110,000 to be supplied from French coalfields instead of through Rochefort or Gironde.

carriage of 150,000 tons, but the remaining 200,000 could only be shipped by sending Atlantic vessels to a French port with a coal cargo, before entering on their Atlantic voyage, and this delay involved an estimated loss of 70,000 tons of imports from the United States.

On this basis the programme was ultimately approved; but the period for replacement was extended to six weeks, and the whole arrangement was made conditional upon Dutch tonnage in American ports being rendered speedily available, to compensate for the loss of Atlantic imports through diversion. For this purpose the Council recommended that, whatever might be ultimately decided as to the possibility of tonnage assistance from the United States, at least one-half the Dutch tonnage in American ports should be allocated, when acquired, for one voyage in the import service of the European Allies.

This recommendation was based not so much on the expectation of an agreement with the Dutch Government, as on the decision of the Associated Governments to requisition the shipping in question, in the event of the negotiations breaking down. Within a week of the day on which the first session broke up, their forecast was justified. On March 18th the time-limit for a reply to the amended proposals expired without any satisfactory reply having been received. The Germans were now threatening, in the event of compliance with the Allied demands, to torpedo all Dutch vessels at sight, irrespective of their employment, and in these circumstances, the Dutch Government refused their consent to any tonnage agreement except on terms prohibiting the use of the ships for the carriage of "war material." In view of the wide field now covered by that term, acceptance of this qualification would have deprived the acquisition of the ships of most of its value. The negotiations had, in fact, hopelessly broken down, and on March 21st the Associated Governments intimated their intention to requisition all Dutch ships in their ports, with the exception of tankers and steamers under 500 tons net. Immediate steps were taken to carry out this decision, and by the end of the month nearly 680,000 tons dead-weight (say, 450,000 gross) of Dutch shipping had been seized; 553,000 in American and 124,000 in British ports.[1]

---

[1] *Correspondence with the Netherlands Government respecting the Requisitioning of Dutch Ships by the Associated Governments* (Cmd. 9025), 1918.

This was undoubtedly an extreme step. It amounted to the forcible seizure of over one-third of the tonnage belonging to a neutral country. The Associated Governments were justified, however, not only by the law of angary and by the existence of grievances against the Dutch Government in respect of the sand and gravel traffic and other questions, but by the fact that the failure of the negotiations for an amicable agreement was notoriously due to German pressure. While over a million tons of river and canal craft under the Dutch flag were employed in German trade, the ocean-going shipping of Holland was withdrawn from Allied and American employment as a result of the German threats, and requisition was not adopted until every other method of bringing it into service had failed.

Both to the Dutch shipowners and the Dutch people the requisitioning of the ships was, in fact, a benefit rather than an injury. In accordance with a recommendation of the Allied Maritime Transport Council, the terms conceded under requisition were substantially as generous as those proposed in the suggested agreement. The provisions as to rate of hire and replacement of losses afforded the shipowners a good return from vessels which had been idle, many of them for long periods, as the result of the embargoes and bunker restrictions. Special concessions were now granted as to the bunkering of Dutch steamers, and a specific guarantee was given that no Dutch ship leaving port after March 21st would be requisitioned on any pretence. Most important of all, the proposed arrangements for the supply of cereals to Holland were strictly carried out, and wheat to the amount of 50,000 tons in North American and 50,000 tons in South American ports, was placed at the disposal of the Dutch Government, despite the continuance of the general embargo.[1]

The Dutch tonnage on which the Transport Council had counted was thus obtained; but their recommendation as to its employment could not be carried out. With Russia out of the war and Italy staggering under the defeat of Caporetto, the Germans were now free to concentrate for a great offensive against the French and British. On March 21st, the very day on which notice of requisition was given, the storm burst in the West. By the end of the month the British armies had been driven back across

[1] Cmd. 9025.

the Somme battlefields, and a new attack had broken out on the Lys. On April 12th, Field-Marshal Haig issued his celebrated Order of the Day in which he described the British Army as fighting " with its back to the wall," and from now onwards all other considerations were dominated by the military situation. The American trooping programme assumed an aspect of new urgency and the Supreme War Council decided that all Dutch shipping in American ports should be used, in the first place, for this purpose. Efforts were made by the Inter-Allied Transport Executive to obtain at least the 70,000 tons dead-weight which would give compensation for the loss of Atlantic imports arising from the Italian coal arrangements; but even this proved to be impossible.

Those arrangements, nevertheless, went forward; but with some important modifications. The recall of British troops from Italy interfered seriously with the movement of French coal by rail, and the available supply of French coal itself fell short of the estimate, owing to the advance of the Germans to within a short distance of the Amiens–Montdidier line, which impeded the railing of coal from the mines. No less than 100,000 tons of British coal destined for Gibraltar and the Mediterranean was accordingly diverted to Italy. This necessitated sending British and French Atlantic liners with coal to Gibraltar in replacement, and involved a great increase in the proportion of the total supply sent by the long sea route, with a consequent loss of tonnage economy; but it enabled the total supply promised to be made good.

In addition to complicating the Italian coal problem, the German advance reacted very seriously on the supply of France herself. The normal output of the Pas de Calais mines was from 900,000 to 1,000,000 tons a month, of which about a quarter was consumed locally or by the British armies, and about three-quarters railed to the south. It now appeared that the movement of nearly the whole of this three-quarters might be stopped. The actual output had suffered, and was likely to suffer still further, as a result of the German advance; and even if the output could be maintained, the railing of coal to the south had become almost impossible, owing to the necessity of keeping the railways clear for the transport of troops and supplies. It was, indeed, calculated that, after allowing for increased raisings in the central and southern coalfields, and economies in control, some 400,000 to 450,000 tons additional imports from Great Britain would be necessary in order to make good the deficit.

Graver still were the effects of the German offensive on the general tonnage situation. The new American trooping programme approved by the Supreme War Council was likely to absorb not only the Dutch vessels seized in United States ports but, according to the estimate of the American Government, all tonnage under the American flag or under American control, whether existing, under construction, or to be acquired, with the exception of ships already employed in the service of the European Allies or needed for the indispensable imports of the United States.

Thus, by April 23rd, when the Allied Maritime Transport Council met in Paris for their second session, the situation had altered decidedly for the worse. On the one hand, the prospect of assistance by the United States in the import programme of the European Allies had vanished; on the other hand, the strain on tonnage represented by the French and Italian coal supply had increased.

Against this had to be put the effect of certain adjustments effected by the Executive since the first meeting of the Council. Some economy had been effected in the coaling of French ships in the Eastern Mediterranean. Six fast Italian passenger liners of small cargo capacity had been diverted to American trooping and replaced by more suitable British tonnage in the Italian import service. Negotiations had been opened for the use of a number of large French passenger vessels for American trooping as soon as certain troop movements from North Africa were completed. The total effect of these and other economies was, however, small in comparison with the total tonnage deficit.

That deficit had now been more exactly ascertained. Since the first meeting of the Council, the administrative staff had been able to obtain and analyse detailed statements of import requirements and available tonnage put forward by the British, French, and Italian Governments, and to prepare a provisional balance sheet. It was not cheering reading. The British programme contemplated a reduction of over 4,000,000 tons on the imports for 1914. The French estimated their requirements at about 1,000,000 tons in excess of their 1917 imports, savings in certain directions being swamped by increased requirements for cereals and coal. Italy, owing to the failure of the harvests and the exhaustion of the coal stocks, required an increase in imports of over 6,000,000 tons. The total of the three programmes amounted to 80,000,000 tons, an excess of 3,000,000 on the preceding year. The available tonnage, after allowance for ships in naval and military employment, or unsuitable, or unavailable for import work, would carry 71,500,000 tons, leaving a deficit of 8,500,000.

This deficit was, indeed, somewhat smaller than that originally contemplated (10,000,000 tons); but in view of the fact that no assistance from America could now be relied on, this was small consolation. Eight and a half million tons of imports represented, on voyages of average length, the continuous employment of about 1,900,000 dead-weight steam tonnage, and it was impossible to see where this tonnage was to be obtained. After deducting tonnage in naval and military service, ships under repair, and ships unsuitable or unavailable for import work, the total of British ocean-going tonnage amounted to 10,000,000 tons dead-weight, of which about a quarter was already allocated to the Allies, and this proportion could hardly be exceeded without serious results on the British import programme. The majority of the neutral steamers under control of the Inter-Allied Chartering Executive were already in French or Italian service, and no considerable source of additional tonnage was in sight. The British output of new shipping was inadequate even to replace British losses. Every prospect of acquiring additional carrying power was blocked by the American trooping programme, and the equilibrium between tonnage and imports could be restored only by cutting down the import programmes, or by more economical employment of the ships available.

The problem was further complicated by new demands put forward at the meeting of the Council. The Commission for Belgian Relief had hitherto been able to fulfil its requirements with shipping under the Belgian flag and chartered neutrals, including a number of Swedish and other vessels which were unwilling to accept ordinary war-zone charters. By now, however, the control of neutral tonnage by Great Britain and the United States had become so complete that it was almost impossible to effect fixtures on the open market, and there was already a serious shortage of breadstuffs. The Commission were accordingly obliged to appeal to the Council for direct assistance.

France also put forward immediate claims additional to the supplementary tonnage for cereals, which had already been taken into account. These claims included the coal needed to replace the output of the Pas de Calais mines, and a number of miscellaneous items (locomotives and rolling stock, nitrate, barbed wire, and explosives) aggregating 85,000 tons a month. From Italy, too, came urgent representations that, in addition to maintaining the monthly coal shipments at the 600,000-ton level, it was essential to build up a military strategic reserve of fuel. The accumulated stocks had been exhausted during 1917, and though the new import programme was sufficient to meet the essential normal requirements, it allowed no margin for emergencies.

Although the granting of these new demands could only increase the already formidable deficit, they were too important to be ignored. Belgian relief had been acknowledged by the Paris Conference in December to possess a moral claim to priority over all other Allied imports, and the Council accordingly decided that, subject to the approval of the Associated Governments, all articles required for the revictualling of the occupied districts in Belgium and Northern France should be included, with priority, in the programme of the Wheat Executive, and that the Transport Executive should be directed to arrange the supplementary tonnage required. The question of the Italian coal reserve, and the French demands for rolling stock and munitions, of which no previous notice had been given, were referred to the Executive for consideration.

With regard to the French coal supply the most that could be done was to examine the situation as closely as possible, and arrange the shipments so as to secure the maximum economy in both sea and railway transport. The governing factor was no longer solely the tonnage available or the capacity of the French ports. To these had now been added a falling off in the British output, due to further recruiting of miners as a consequence of the military situation. Even before the new French demands had been put forward, it had proved impossible to maintain, in practice, the programme figure of 1,740,000 tons a month adopted in March. Steps were being taken to divert further tonnage into the traffic from the general Anglo-French trade and from British coasting, but the maximum export was still problematical. The Italian coal shipments, on the other hand, represented a minimum below which it was impossible to fall without grave risks, and it was decided to maintain the 600,000 level, though the disorganisation of the French railways rendered it probable that an increasing proportion of the coal would have to be sent by the long sea route.

There remained the primary problem of the general tonnage deficit. In view of the impossibility of obtaining any large block of additional tonnage, the existence of this deficit was accepted, and the Council directed their attention mainly to securing that its incidence should be so regulated as to safeguard supplies of urgent military or national importance. For this purpose, they recommended to the Associated Governments that a further drastic revision of the several import programmes should be undertaken, and that the necessary instructions to this end should be given to the appropriate national and Allied bodies. These bodies, however, did not yet cover the whole field, and the Council strongly recommended that Inter-Allied Executives or Programme Committees should be appointed to deal with all commodities not covered by existing Executives. At the same time, the Council arranged for close co-operation, through the Secretariats, with the Inter-Allied Council on War Purchase and Finance.

On the tonnage side of the problem, the Council instructed the Executive to examine closely the employment of all ships hitherto regarded as unsuitable or unavailable for import work, and requested the Allied naval and military authorities to make a similar examination into the tonnage under their control. They also represented strongly the importance of obtaining such additional tanker tonnage as would enable the supply of oil-fuel to be maintained without using the double bottoms of ships available for the carriage of other imports.

As regards neutral tonnage, since there was little probability of many additional steamers being obtained, the main object of the Council was to ensure the utmost flexibility of employment. For this purpose the Inter-Allied Chartering Committee was brought under the direct control of the Council, to whom they were made responsible for the allocation of the vessels. Pending a definite agreement, it was decided that all future timecharters should be signed, in equal proportions, by firms nominated by the British, French, and Italian Governments; but in accordance with the Paris resolutions, the actual employment of the vessels was to be decided by the relative urgency of war needs and not on an arithmetical basis. It was decided, therefore, that all ships so time-chartered should be relet to the Inter-Allied Committee, acting for the Council, and employed under the immediate direction of the Council. Although all ships were to be chartered, so far as possible, on a time basis, the allocation to a particular service was to be for a round voyage only, or for three months in the short voyage trades, after which the steamer was to come up for reallocation. Similarly, all steamers of over 1,000 tons dead-weight allocated by the Inter-Allied Committee since February 15th, 1917, and all steamers under 1,000 tons allocated since May 9th, 1917, were to come up for reallocation on the completion of their existing engagements.[1] There would thus be formed, gradually, a pool of neutral tonnage under the direct control of the Council, which would be available for meeting emergency demands from any source, or for the adjustment of the import programmes.[2]

[1] The total allocations of time-chartered steamers made by the Inter-Allied Chartering Committee to the end of March 1918, were as follows:

	Fixtures. Tons dead-weight.		Allocations. Tons dead-weight.
Greek	585,477	France	431,137
Norwegian	568,931	Italy	430,251
Swedish	29,530	Wheat Executive	363,063
Danish	74,338	Great Britain (chiefly for supply of coaling depôts)	58,125
Dutch	7,855	United States	5,900
Japanese	34,300	Unallocated	11,955
Total	1,300,431	Total	1,300,431

These figures exclude ships running on voyage-charter under approval of the Committee, and take no account of losses.

[2] For a detailed account of the formation and proceedings of the Inter-Allied Maritime Transport Council and Executive, see Sir J. A. Salter, *Allied Shipping Control*.

CHAPTER XX

IMPROVEMENTS IN SHIPPING ORGANISATION

MARCH—JULY 1918

GREAT as had been the importance of the Atlantic convoy system in 1917, it was evident that its successful operation in 1918 would be yet more vital to the cause of the Allies. The magnitude of the tonnage deficit, as revealed at the sessions of the Allied Maritime Transport Council, emphasised at once the need for still closer concentration on the shorter routes, and the danger arising from losses even on the reduced scale of the winter months. In order to secure the supply of essential foodstuffs and essential materials in quantities sufficient to satisfy even the bare minimum requirements of the Allies, it was necessary that every available ship should be utilised to the fullest advantage, and that a period should be put to the progressive depletion of the available shipping. The German spring offensive, by leading to a vast increase in the American military programme, emphasised still further the need for concentration and the need for protection.

On the whole, the experience of 1917 had proved beyond cavil the success of the protective system adopted during the summer; but in that system there were, at the beginning of 1918, three weak points. In the first place, the development of submarine activity in Home Waters—the English Channel, the Irish Sea, and its approaches—threatened to neutralise in large measure the comparative immunity now attained on the ocean tracks. In the second place, the operations of the new large-type submarines in mid-Atlantic had created a new danger area to which particular significance was given by the necessity of lifting additional grain cargoes from the Plate. Finally, conditions in the Mediterranean were still unsatisfactory, and affected both the vital Italian coal trade, and the slower through traffic which came on in local convoy from Port Said.

The necessity for providing additional protection for the Plate trade had been realised as soon as negotiations began for the purchase of the Argentine grain surplus. The extended range of the German submarines rendered it unsafe to entrust the protection of this trade, as heretofore, to the Dakar Convoy, as the ships were now liable to attack on their way to that port of assembly. A direct non-stop convoy from Rio was accordingly started on March 13th. This convoy was, at first, intended only for the slower ships, and owing to the number of old and slow steamers, especially Italian, employed in the grain traffic, its speed was fixed at 7 knots.[1] The interval between convoy and convoy was fixed at six to eight days, but in practice eight days was usually adopted. In order to economise ocean escort, arrangements were made for the Rio Convoy to meet that from Dakar at sea. The joint fleet then proceeded homewards under protection of the Rio escort, while the Dakar cruiser returned to bring out the next convoy from that port or Sierra Leone.

This arrangement was rendered possible, without involving a fleet of unwieldy size, by a reduction in the size of the Dakar Convoy. Now that the local convoy system in the Mediterranean had been developed, ships from Mauritius and East Africa, as well as from the Far East, were instructed to use the Canal route. Australasian steamers with sufficient bunker capacity for the Pacific voyage were ordered home viâ Panama, and practically the only vessels now assembling at Dakar were those from West, South, and South-East Africa.

Plate steamers of 10 knots and upwards were, at first, still directed to Sierra Leone, as their speed was considered to be sufficient protection; but about the middle of April, when the experiment of meeting at sea had proved successful, a separate fast convoy was started from Rio and worked in with the Sierra Leone Convoy, in the same way as the slow convoy was worked in with that from Dakar. Ships bound to the Mediterranean were picked up by the cruisers, based on Gibraltar, which took out the Mediterranean–United States traffic clear of the Straits.

The value of these convoys was soon proved. The Germans, as had been anticipated, were aware of the Allies'

[1] The average voyage from Rio was thirty-two days.

NEW CONVOYS STARTED

wheat purchases from Argentina, and during March they sent out two large submarines to attack the homeward-bound grain ships. So efficient, however, was the protection provided that, during the whole period for which the Rio Convoys were run, only two vessels, one British and one French, were lost by enemy action, neither of them in the new danger area.[1] Once only did the cruiser escort sight a submarine, and on that occasion the enemy did not venture within range.

Practically the whole ocean-going trade of the Allies was now covered, and losses on the ocean routes continued to be small. It remained to strengthen the defence in the terminal waters. As a result of the attack on the North Channel during March, all homeward-bound convoys had been brought in south-about, and the destroyer escorts had accompanied the ships right up the Irish Sea. Advantage was taken of the presence of these destroyers to send out two convoys from Liverpool direct, on March 21st and 24th, with escort from the Mersey instead of from Milford or Lamlash. The experiment proved successful, and a new regular outward convoy was accordingly started from Liverpool towards the end of March. This Liverpool Convoy sailed south-about every eight days, with a speed of 10 to $11\frac{1}{2}$ knots, an average of eight or nine ships being comprised in each convoy. Protection was thus given to the faster ships which had previously sailed independently on their outward voyages. The slower ships still assembled at Milford or Lamlash; but the faster ships were now protected from the first hour of their outward voyage, and the escorts of homeward-bound convoys continued to bring them further in than during 1917.

The result of these new arrangements was to increase considerably the protection afforded to shipping in the Irish Sea and its approaches; but even more important in its effect on the safety of shipping in Home Waters was an offensive stroke carried out on the Belgian coast. On April 23rd the harbours of both Zeebrugge and Ostend were blocked by the sinking of old British cruisers across the entrance channel. At Zeebrugge the success was complete; at Ostend a narrow passage was left, but this was closed by the sinking of the VINDICTIVE on May 9th. The dash and heroism displayed in these blocking raids

[1] Both these casualties occurred in May; one in Home Waters, and one in the Gibraltar area.

have given them an honourable place in British naval tradition; their results in the protection of British commerce were no less noteworthy. It was on these ports that the Germans had based the coastal submarines which had wrought so much havoc in the English Channel, and by the blocking of these bases the attack on the Channel traffic was deprived of most of its terrors. From November 1917 to April 1918 inclusive, an average of twenty-six British and foreign steamers of 500 tons gross and upwards were sunk by submarines in the English Channel, over a quarter of the total casualties during that period. In May, 1918, only four ships were lost in the area.

No such striking success was to be recorded in the Mediterranean: indeed, April 1918 was a black month in the history of the Through Convoys. Those convoys had been adopted in the face of considerable opposition, and this opposition had been revived by their disastrous early experiences. Although the later convoys had been much more successful, the loss of one or two vessels at the end of 1917 and the beginning of 1918, led to renewed criticism and a proposal to revert to the Cape Route. Sir Aubrey Brocklebank, however, who was responsible for Indian priority cargo, stated that it would be impossible to lift the monthly requirements if steamers had to follow the longer route, and the convoys went on without noteworthy incident until the sailing of the ninth Homeward Convoy from Port Said, on April 4th. That convoy consisted of 21 steamers, and so vigorously was it attacked that, by the time it reached Gibraltar, it had lost three ships sunk and two damaged. Again it was proposed to abandon the route; but this was now clearly impossible. No fewer than 130 steamers would have been required on the Cape Route to lift the priority cargo which 90 could bring through the Canal, and now that every possible liner was wanted in the Atlantic for American trooping, it was impossible to think of returning vessels to the Eastern trade. The convoys accordingly went on, and it was hoped that improved organisation and a mine barrage to be laid across the Straits of Otranto would give security against the repetition of heavy losses.

Meanwhile the system of local convoys was being developed. Although the Gibraltar–Genoa Convoy had been abandoned during March, in favour of the Spanish

MEDITERRANEAN REFORMS

Coastal Route, it was found that even the use of territorial waters gave no immunity from attack. The convoys were accordingly resumed, and from April onwards proved successful in diminishing the rate of loss.

Great efforts, too, were made to prevent delays to Mediterranean shipping. Reports received from representatives sent out by the Ministry of Shipping had shown that there was no adequate organisation to replace the commercial machinery which universal requisitioning had thrown out of gear. Many ships were now running to ports where their owners had no regular agents; many owners did not even know where their ships were. The Principal Naval Transport Officers were concerned only with fully requisitioned British ships, and there was little co-ordination of their work with that of the Patrol Commanders and Shipping Control Officers. The bunker ports, especially Gibraltar, were congested. Bunkering and repairs consumed an undue period, and with delays awaiting orders and delays awaiting escort, seriously affected the flow of trade.

As a result of these reports, and of a visit to Italy and Malta by Sir Eric Geddes (First Lord of the Admiralty) and Captain Henderson, Mr. Oswald Sanderson was sent out by the Ministry of Shipping in April, to exercise a general supervision over the commercial side of convoy, and to arrange for fuller co-operation between the naval and shipping authorities. At the same time representatives of the Ministry, with a right of direct communication with the Controller, were appointed to Malta, Port Said, Genoa, and Gibraltar. As a result of these appointments, a great improvement took place from May onwards. A complete list of Agents was drawn up and issued to every ship, a bunkering scheme was devised which relieved the strain on Gibraltar, and much was done to synchronise convoys and sailings. This last measure was considerably assisted, during April, by an alteration of the Alexandria–Bizerta Convoy from a five-day to a four-day basis, so as to fit in with the system between Bizerta and Gibraltar.

Thanks to these measures and other improvements in the naval organisation of convoys in the Mediterranean, the delays incidental to the system were so greatly reduced that, in May 1918, the voyages under convoy were very considerably shorter than in the summer of 1917, when the " patrolled route " system was in vogue. As compared with June and July of that year the reduction in the passage between Gibraltar and Malta was five days; between Gibraltar and Egypt, six days; between Gibraltar and Salonika, two days. Similar improvements were effected in the other trades, and if Mediterranean losses were still considerably heavier than in other areas, the general outlook was brighter than it had been for a long time.

Thus, of the three weak points in the convoy system of protection two—the mid-Atlantic area and Home Waters —had been, to a great extent, made good by May 1918, and the third—the Mediterranean—was in a fair way to improvement. In addition, it was anticipated that the activity of the submarines as a whole would be restricted during April by the Northern Barrage, a deep mine-field to be laid by the British and American fleets between the Orkneys and the Norwegian coast. The laying of this field had already been begun, and while it could not be expected that it would, at first at any rate, be impenetrable, it was likely to make the work of the submarines increasingly risky and increasingly wearing.

It was well that it should be so, for, in addition to the Allied import programmes, the American military programme was now in full swing, both to France direct and to the United Kingdom. Despite the utilisation of the interned German and requisitioned Dutch steamers, the rate at which troops were poured across the Atlantic far exceeded the capacity of the available American tonnage, and though troops landed in France direct were mostly carried under the national flag, nearly all those brought to British ports came in British shipping. This, of course, profoundly affected the whole organisation of shipping in the North Atlantic. The troop convoys run at irregular intervals by the Americans themselves did not, indeed, affect the Allied shipping programmes, except in so far as they absorbed tonnage which might otherwise have been available to assist the Allies; nor was the import trade much affected by the commissioning as troopers of the *Mauretania* and *Aquitania.* These vessels—together with the *Olympic* and the ex-German *Vaterland*—ran independently, trusting to their speed and armament for protection on the ocean voyage and to special destroyer escort in the danger zone. The bulk of the work had to be done, however, so far as troops landed in the United Kingdom were concerned, by ordinary liners engaged in the Atlantic trade. This not only decreased the cargo-carrying power of the vessels concerned, but involved an important rearrangement of the North Atlantic convoys.

For trooping purposes it was essential to provide fast vessels, both in order to land the greatest possible number of men in a given time, and in order to minimise the risk. The first thing, therefore, was to obtain the requisite number of fast steamers; the second to group them so as to take full advantage of their speed. The fast liner tonnage in the North Atlantic had already been considerably increased during the early months of 1918 by diversions from Australia and elsewhere; but the supply of ships suitable for use as troopers was still insufficient. An elaborate system of transfers was accordingly carried out, ships of $11\frac{1}{2}$ to 12 knots being diverted from the Plate and other routes to the North Atlantic and replaced, when necessary, by slower vessels from the North Atlantic trade.

As regards the grouping of the ships, the guiding principle was to load and run from New York—the chief port of embarkation for American troops—every steamer capable of maintaining 13 knots at sea in ordinary fair Atlantic weather, and 14 knots for a spurt through the danger zone. For this purpose, the original fast convoy from Halifax was transferred to New York, and all ships of the requisite speed running to any other port were incorporated in this convoy, which ran, as before, to West Coast ports only, at an eight-day interval. At the same time the West Coast sailings of the old $9\frac{1}{2}$-knot convoy from New York were stopped, and this convoy sailed, thenceforth, every eight days, to East Coast ports only. In place of the old West Coast sailings from New York, a second mixed troop and cargo convoy was started from Halifax, with a speed of $11\frac{1}{2}$ knots, for ships not quite good enough for the 13-knot fast convoy. Of the ships included in the new Halifax Convoy, it was expected that about one-half would load in New York, and the remainder would serve Boston, Portland, St. John, Halifax, and (on the opening of the St. Lawrence) Montreal. The interval was fixed at eight days, and the convoys sailed alternately to East and West Coast ports. For this there were two reasons. In the first place, so large a proportion of the liners diverted to the North Atlantic were meat-carrying vessels, that Liverpool would have been quite unable to store or distribute their refrigerated cargo, had West Coast sailings only been provided. In the second place, the East Coast sailings of the Hampton Roads and Sydney (C.B.) Convoys had been swelled to an unwieldy size [1] by the growth of the American cargo traffic to France, and it was desirable to divert a portion of this traffic to the liner sailings, so as to reduce the number of tramps in these slow convoys.

In view of their importance in the trooping programme, the East Coast sailings of the new Halifax Convoys were accompanied by their destroyer escorts right up the Channel to Dover, and advantage was taken of this fact to protect the ships from the same point on their return journey. For this purpose a new outward convoy was started from Southend, sailing every sixteen days, and consisting of ships which had come in with the previous East Coast Convoy from Halifax. These vessels proceeded in company to Dover, where they picked up the destroyers which had brought in, on the previous day, a new Halifax Convoy. To ensure the readiness of these vessels, as well as to obtain better despatch with those sent to Devonport for assembly, a port Convoy Officer was appointed at London, and a little later, a London Convoy Committee was successfully established,[2] under the chairmanship of Mr. J. Herbert Scrutton, Vice-President of the Chamber of Shipping, on the lines of that already existing at Liverpool.

The first of the New York fast convoys sailed on April 9th; the first of the new Halifax convoys on May 11th. Meanwhile a fresh convoy had been started under American or French escort, but organised by the Convoy Section of the British Admiralty, for protection of the American store ships running direct to Bay ports. The speed of this convoy was fixed at $9\frac{1}{2}$ knots, and it ran, at first, at somewhat irregular intervals about twice a month. Thus by May 1918 there were six distinct convoys running from North American ports and covering, between them, practically the whole of the North Atlantic trade.[3]

This reorganisation of the system entailed heavy work, both for the Ministry of Shipping, who were responsible for the transfer of the vessels, and for the Convoy Section of the Admiralty, by whom the actual arrangements for the new convoys had to be made. Its success depended, obviously, on exact knowledge as to the actual sea-going speed of the

---

[1] They had gone up on occasion to as many as 44 or 45 steamers.
[2] In August 1918.   [3] See footnote on following page.

steamers to be grouped together, and on the greatest possible regularity of sailing; especially in respect of the fast troop and cargo convoys to Liverpool, which had to be synchronised with the new outward convoy from that port, in order that the destroyers which had brought in the homeward trade might sail, on the following day, with the outward traffic. But for the creation of the Liverpool Convoy Committee at the end of 1917, the task would have been impossible, and it was due to the close co-operation between that Committee, the Admiralty, and the Ministry of Shipping, that it was now successfully accomplished. Thanks to this co-operation it was now possible for the Established Lines to bring the full driving power of their organisations to bear on the ships run by them, whether belonging to their own fleets or brought in from other routes, and the results achieved were in the highest degree creditable to all concerned. Yet even now, the task was one that tried to the full the resources of the port, and at times between 4,000 and 5,000 men of the

[3] The following table shows the effect of the reorganisation:

NORTH ATLANTIC HOMEWARD CONVOYS, FEBRUARY AND MARCH 1918

From	To	Speed.	Interval.	Average number of ships.
Hampton Roads	E. and W. Coast alternately	8 knots	8 days	20
Sydney (Cape Breton)	,, ,, ,, ,,	8 ,,	8 ,,	19
New York	,, ,, ,, ,,	9½ ,,	4 ,,	21
Halifax	W. Coast only	12½ ,,	8 ,,	8

5 convoys, about 89 sailings every 8 days.

NORTH ATLANTIC HOMEWARD CONVOYS, JUNE AND JULY 1918

From	To	Speed.	Interval.	Average number of ships.
Hampton Roads	E. and W. Coast alternately	8 knots	8 days	27
Sydney (Cape Breton)	,, ,, ,, ,,	8 ,,	,,	25
New York	E. Coast only	9½ ,,	,,	21
New York	W. ,, ,,	13 ,,	,,	14
Halifax	E. and W. Coast alternately	11¼ ,,	,,	12

5 convoys, about 99 sailings every 8 days.

Also American New York Convoy to Bay ports twice a month. The size of these convoys varied from 8 to 25 ships.

Transport Workers' Battalions had to be brought in, in order to avoid a dislocation of the sailing dates.

The general principle on which the Convoy Committee worked was that it was for the Ministry of Shipping to determine what services should be run, and for the Admiralty to decide on convoy arrangements; but that the responsibility of selecting the most suitable tonnage for each service and working that tonnage to its utmost capacity, must be accepted by the Established Lines themselves. For this reason the Committee left to each individual line full responsibility for the working of the vessels it owned or controlled, subject always to the directions of the Admiralty or the Shipping Controller. They arranged, however, for the lines to pool port facilities, berths, labour, and dry docks, so that each vessel might receive the quickest possible turn-round. Further, the monthly book of North Atlantic tonnage, prepared by the Committee, furnished exact and up-to-date information as to the sea-going speed and troop-carrying capacity of the ships, and thus afforded a reliable basis for the convoy groupings. What was even more important, the arrangements made between the Committee and the Admiralty for exchange of information as to probable arrival and sailing dates, and of ships in readiness, were of incalculable assistance in synchronising inward and outward convoys, and avoiding delays through any vessel missing a sailing date.

At the beginning of April the Committee were informed that the object of the new fast convoy to be established between New York and Liverpool, was to land, if possible, about 140,000 American troops a month at that port, and that, for this purpose, about 60 steamers of 13 knots and upwards would be allocated to the convoy. On this basis the Committee estimated that it would be necessary to secure a turn-round in Liverpool of 10 days, and a round voyage of 40 days for the ships sailing in the convoy. As the fast steamers had taken anything up to 52 days on the round voyage in the autumn of 1917, this was a big improvement at which to aim; but the Committee were confident that it could be achieved, and so well did they work that the 40 days' turn-round soon became the general rule.[1]

---

[1] For the whole period during which the fast convoy was based on New York, 77 per cent. of the round voyages were accomplished in 40 days or under.

They were assisted in their efforts by the fact that a similar organisation was now in existence on the other side. So early as January 15th, the Ministry of Shipping resolved to inform their New York office of what was being done at Liverpool, and to suggest similar action. On March 4th the New York Convoy Committee held its first meeting, under the Chairmanship of Sir Connop Guthrie, Ministry of Shipping (subsequently succeeded by Lieutenant M. Faulkner, R.N.V.R., also of the Ministry). The other members were all representatives of lines in the Atlantic trade.

Sub-committees composed of representative agents of the Established Lines were formed at New York and at every other American Atlantic and Gulf port. Working in close touch with the Ministry of Shipping, the Committee were able to effect a very considerable speed-up in the turn-round of steamers, by obtaining preference in cargo delivery and loading arrangements for such vessels as needed the greatest effort to enable them to make a sailing date. They also took up, in co-operation with the Ministry of Shipping in London, the question of diverting liners from East to West Coast ports and *vice versa*, to enable them to catch an earlier convoy than if they had to await one sailing for the coast to which they were originally destined. On this point, however, the Liverpool Committee called attention to the fact that almost the greatest difficulty they had to cope with was the question of distribution from the ports, and that far more time might be lost through congesting a particular port, or its railway communications, than could be saved by the catching of an earlier convoy. They asked, therefore, that no steamer running in an Established Line should be diverted without previous communication with them, the diversions of all other steamers being arranged direct with the Ministry in London.

The establishment of the New York Convoy Committee was not the only important development in the organisation of the Ministry of Shipping's New York office during the early months of 1918. Throughout the previous year, the work of that office had been steadily increasing both in extent and in importance. In addition to the ordinary routine work of supervising shipments and movements, large questions of policy had constantly to be threshed out with the American authorities, in conjunction with the British Embassy and the British War Mission. In these discussions Sir Thomas Royden, when in America, acted as special representative of the Shipping Controller, and his position as a member of the Shipping Control Committee, together with his high standing in American shipping and official circles, enabled him to contribute powerfully to their solution.

In January 1918 Sir Percy Bates, Director of Commercial Services, visited the United States for the purpose of looking into the Ministry's American organisation, and in April the Director of Transports, Mr. Graeme Thomson, himself went over in connection with the accelerated trooping programme. As a result of these visits the whole organisation was thoroughly overhauled. During February an American Shipping Control Committee was formed to act as an Executive for the Shipping Board, and Sir Connop Guthrie was invited to join that Committee as representative of the Shipping Controller. As this work absorbed his whole time, it became necessary to provide a new head for the British Ministry of Shipping in New York, and Mr. T. Ashley Sparkes was accordingly appointed Director-General, with Mr. William Boyd as deputy. As finally reconstituted in May 1918, the organisation under Mr. Sparkes' control comprised thirteen departments under Directors chosen for their experience in the various branches of the work, with branch offices at Baltimore, Boston, Brunswick, Chicago, Galveston, Newport News, New Orleans, and Savannah, connected by private telegraph lines with New York. A department at Washington under Sir Thomas Royden (when in America) and Captain T. Fisher, R.N.; handled questions of policy which required to be taken up with the Shipping Board, direct or through the Embassy.

The reorganisation of the Atlantic convoys was thus accompanied by a development of the machinery of control, on both sides of the Atlantic, and a general speeding-up in turn-round, that went a long way to make good not only the loss of annual cargo-carrying power involved in the increased trooping programme, but the reduction in ordinary cargo capacity occasioned by the carriage of oil in double bottoms. The time spent in port, both by liners and tramps, in loading, discharging, or awaiting convoy, was steadily reduced on both sides of the Atlantic, and the new grouping of the ships, by ensuring closer approximation between the speed of vessels included in the same convoy, had the effect of reducing the time spent on passage by the faster ships. Down to the end of 1917, the increase in annual carrying power derived from concentration on the shorter routes, had been largely neutralised by the delays incidental to the convoy system ; but those delays had now been so far minimised that the intensified concentration represented a clear gain in importing power.

This improvement had not come before it was badly needed. Even with intensified concentration and quicker turn-round, the available tonnage was only just equal to the fulfilment of essential requirements.

Apart from American trooping, the governing factor in the employment of shipping at this period was the Inter-Allied cereal programme. So completely were the Atlantic loadings dominated by wheat and munitions, and so serious was the effect produced on imports by American trooping and the carriage of oil in double bottoms, that it was still impossible to allocate adequate space for cotton, and on March 18th the Cotton Control Board were obliged to restrict the working of machinery to 50 per cent. in the mills using American cotton and 80 per cent. in those using the Egyptian product. Later, on June 10th, they reduced the weekly working hours for even this percentage of the machines from $55\frac{1}{2}$ to 40.[1] The result was, of course, a further rise in the price of the manufactured article, which reacted unfavourably on exports.

When the premier British industry was thus hardly treated, it may be imagined that others, of less importance, suffered even more heavily. Broadly speaking, the most that was aimed at, was to maintain the supply of essential foodstuffs, and the requirements of the fighting forces and the war industries. Even this was no easy matter, in view of the needs of France and Italy for grain. The obligations imposed on Great Britain under the Agreement of November 1917 were heavy, and during April and May alone 480,000 tons of cereals in British ships were diverted to France and Italy, over and above the quantities carried in British ships previously time-chartered to those countries. As a result of these diversions British imports of wheat and flour fell considerably below the level of the previous year, though about 40 per cent. of the total import was now taken in the form of flour, with a great economy in

[1] Henderson, *The Cotton Control Board*.

space. Imports of oats, maize, and barley were still further reduced, but increased quantities of rice were brought from India as liner priority cargo, and there was an increasing import of concentrated farinaceous foods and other substitutes or diluents.

How heavy was the sacrifice imposed on Great Britain may be seen by comparing the 480,000 tons of cereals diverted during April and May with the actual British imports of wheat and flour for those months, which amounted to 930,000 tons. Even if the weight of all cereals is taken, whether imported for human consumption, animal feeding-stuffs, or industrial use, the amount diverted was over one-fifth of that received in the United Kingdom. But these figures minimise the sacrifice ; for owing to the comparative poverty of the North American harvest, and to the strain of the military programmes on shipping, British imports were destined to decline, while the diversions under the November agreement increased. Nor was this all. As the diversions could most easily be effected in tramp tonnage, the supply of Great Britain fell more completely into the hands of the liners, and the result was very greatly to increase the difficulty of distribution. While Liverpool was full of grain, so great a milling centre as Hull was often on the brink of starvation.

Both the diverted purchases and the ordinary cereal import programmes were now under the control of the Wheat Executive, and all additional tonnage for French and Italian imports from North and South America was provided by the Wheat Section of the Ministry of Shipping. Tonnage from India was arranged by Military Branch. The special combined steel and oat service came to an end in April. This service had given considerable trouble since the establishment of the convoy system. In order to avoid delays through waiting for the appropriate convoys, it was early arranged that the ships, when loaded, should always sail with the next convoy, receiving their final instructions as to destination on approaching European waters. Now, however, that the whole cereal programme of the Allies was in the hands of the Wheat Executive, and Great Britain had undertaken to make good any deficiencies in the French and Italian imports, this separate service was no longer necessary, and it was merged in the general programme.

CEREAL PROGRAMME 321

In the arrangement of the respective import programmes from the various sources, the lines previously laid down were closely adhered to. Great Britain relied mainly on North America, with supplementary shipments from the Plate. France drew more than two-thirds of her cereal imports from North America, but imported also considerable quantities from India, as well as from Argentina. For Italy, India was the chief source of supply, followed closely by North America, and at a longer distance by the Plate. From Australia all grain shipments had ceased, with the exception of a little wheat lifted by the liners left in the trade.

We have seen, however, that, owing to short shipments from North America, it had been necessary, early in the year, to send out additional ships to the Plate for March and April loadings. As the season progressed it became more and more evident that a serious deficiency in the North American shipments must be allowed for, and that the supply of Great Britain and the Allies could only be secured, and the French and Italian deficits made good, by drawing largely on the Argentine surplus. On April 15th the Plate Conference were instructed that, between April 20th and May 15th, at least ten of the smaller liners should load entirely with cereals, disregarding the ordinary priority cargo. Two days later, 13,000 tons of linseed was added to the priority list, as this made for economical loading in combination with the cereals ; but apart from refrigerated cargo, grain was now the most prominent consideration even in the liner trade, and the stream of tramps to French, Italian, and British ports was larger than it had been since the early days of the war. From May onwards the arrivals of wheat from Argentina at British ports were heavy, and in the cereal supply of the Allies as a whole the Plate usurped the leading position hitherto held by North America.

It was this increase in the cereal imports from the Plate which gave peculiar importance to the Rio convoys, and the remarkable success of these convoys was one of the most decisive checks administered to the German hopes of starving out the Allies. They were not, however, arranged without great difficulty, especially with regard to bunker supplies.

The whole question of bunkering had, for a long time, given much trouble. The coal output was falling as the result of increased recruiting of miners, and labour troubles in South Wales. The demands of France and Italy became more and more insistent. Collier tonnage was short. The combined effect of coal and tonnage shortage rendered it impossible to maintain a steady and adequate flow of fuel to the bunker depôts abroad, and constant adjustments were necessary. Apart from the falling off in British exports, it was frequently impossible to procure shipping for the supply of the depôts from the nearest sources abroad. Thus in January 1918 it was necessary to despatch colliers to Colombo from South Africa, during a period of acute tonnage shortage at the Indian coal ports.

Moreover, owing to the redistribution of trade, and the necessity of routeing ships to avoid submarine danger zones, it had become necessary to concentrate much of the bunkering abroad at ports ill-equipped to handle so large a volume of traffic as that with which they were now required to deal. In the South Atlantic, for instance, the extended range of the German submarines compelled the disuse of the Atlantic Islands as bunker depôts, and the concentration of bunkering at Dakar and Sierra Leone, the ports of assembly for the homeward convoys, and this necessitated the transfer of lighters and equipment from the disused island depôts.

To complicate the problem still further, it was necessary for vessels passing through the danger zone to be supplied with fuel giving the minimum of smoke, and this involved the allocation to all depôts where such vessels were bunkered, of a certain proportion of the best quality coal. Further, there was a tendency on the part of masters of requisitioned steamers to overestimate their requirements, and ship a safety margin greater than they would have allowed themselves when running on owners' account. Under convoy this was easier to control, but early in 1918, it became necessary, in order to conserve cargo-carrying capacity, to issue stringent regulations against the loading of more bunker coal than was absolutely required for the homeward voyage.

By this time the Admiralty and Ministry of Shipping had become responsible for a large proportion of the bunkering arrangements abroad. All fully requisitioned ships, and in many ports also those on liner requisition, were supplied from Admiralty stocks, for the replenishment of which the

Department of Naval Stores was responsible. Coal for the replenishment of these stocks was carried in requisitioned tonnage, and towards the end of 1916, the Transport Department made arrangements to obtain from each Executive Branch a monthly statement of the prospective bunker requirements of requisitioned ships on each route, to guide Collier Section in the allocation of tonnage. In the spring of 1917, the Shipping and Coal Co-ordinating Committee [1] was formed to facilitate further the adjustment of competing demands both on coal and on collier tonnage, and during that year a system was inaugurated by which the various departments of the Ministry of Shipping submitted a weekly list showing the bunker requirements of requisitioned vessels, on receipt of which the Naval Stores Department indented on the Ministry for the collier tonnage required to maintain the necessary stocks. The Department further instituted pooling arrangements among the bunkering firms at Gibraltar, the Red Sea ports, Colombo, and the South African ports, which greatly facilitated prompt bunkering and economical use of the commercial supplies available. Even with improved organisation, however, the supply of bunkers presented a difficult and complex problem, and nowhere were the difficulties greater than at South American ports.

It must be remembered that it was a cardinal principle of the Rio convoys that the ships should be fully bunkered for a direct run home, without calling at any intermediate port. This was no light matter, for the British coal exports to Brazil, Argentina, and Uruguay now amounted only to a small fraction of the normal supply, and though these countries were now drawing large supplies from the United States, their needs were not fully met. Towards the end of 1917, indeed, the Argentine Government imposed severe restrictions on the bunkering of vessels, as stocks had fallen so low as to threaten the stoppage of railways and factories. The severance of relations between Uruguay and Germany did something to relieve the position, as the Uruguayan Government placed no restrictions on bunkering at Montevideo, and it became

[1] This Committee comprised representatives of the Admiralty (Trade Division, Director of Navy Contracts, and Director of Naval Stores), the Ministry of Shipping (Naval Sea Transport Branch, Collier Section, Liner Requisition Section, and Ship Licensing Committee), the Coal Mines Department, Coal Export Committee, and the Inter-Allied Chartering Committee.

possible to transfer the bunkering of wheat ships to that port; but the accumulation of adequate stocks was no easy matter. It was rendered more difficult by the hold-up at American ports during the winter, which caused a temporary falling off in the exports from the United States to all South American countries. Nor was this all. Considerable supplies hitherto drawn from South Africa for the South American railways and bunker depôts, were suspended, at the beginning of 1918, owing to the washing-out of the South African railways by floods. All the main sources of supply were, in some way or other, affected, and it was only with the greatest difficulty that the Admiralty were able to build up the stocks necessary for the convoys. By March, however, export from the United States was resumed, and during April arrangements were concerted, through the Allied Maritime Transport Executive, for co-ordinating the coal exports to South America, in such a way as to involve the least possible strain on tonnage. The principle was that the United States should supply the whole requirements of Brazil and such portion of the Argentine and Uruguayan demand as could be carried in the shipping required for United States imports from those countries, the balance being supplied from the United Kingdom or South Africa, in ships going out to lift grain cargoes from the Plate. Further, all American export licences were to be granted to the British Government or its nominees, thus ensuring control over the cargoes and their allocation by the Consular Officers at South American ports to the bunkering of vessels on Allied services, and the meat works and railways in which the Allies were interested.

On the West Coast of South America also, there was an acute coal shortage during the spring of 1918; but this was met, to some extent, by cargoes brought from Hampton Roads in requisitioned tramps going out to load nitrate at Chilean ports. Although a certain amount of nitrate was loaded by the liners as priority cargo, the bulk of the shipments was lifted by tramp tonnage, and as the increased requirements of the Ministry of Munitions had brought them up to an average of over 70,000 tons a month, it was of the first importance to economise time and space in the service. For this reason, when not required to carry out coal from Hampton Roads, the ships were sent to Colon in ballast, as the saving in time was held to outweigh the extra cost of bunkering at that port. On their homeward voyage also, the ships followed the Panama route, and in 1918 the practice was adopted of bunkering the ships only as far as Colon, where they filled up with fuel for the passage to the United Kingdom. In this way it was possible to load on each ship one or two hundred tons of nitrate that would have been shut out had the vessel been bunkered in a Chilean port for the whole of the homeward run.

In addition to the saving in time effected by sending the vessels out, when possible, direct to Colon, a considerable acceleration of loading was brought about by authorising Messrs. Anthony Gibbs & Co., who acted as Chilean agents for the Ministry of Shipping, to pay despatch money in respect of cargoes loaded under the prescribed time. The average rate of loading increased from under 500 to over 1,000 tons a day, and the total effect of the various improvements in the service was to bring down the average round voyage from 120 to 103 days. From May onwards the steamers of the Pacific Steam Navigation Company's local line were pressed into the service, landing their cargoes at Colon for transhipment. In addition a number of time-chartered Norwegian steamers were put on by the Ministry of Shipping to carry nitrate cargoes to New York for account of the United States Government or the Imperial Munitions Board of Canada.

Following, as they did, the Panama Route, the nitrate steamers went up to join the Hampton Roads Convoys for the passage through the war zone, and it was thus unnecessary to provide for them in the organisation of the Rio convoys, which were restricted to East Coast shipping. The slower of those convoys, indeed, consisted almost entirely of grain ships; the faster convoy subsequently added, derived its chief importance from the preponderant position of the Plate trade in the meat supply of the Allies.

The question of insulated tonnage had always been a disturbing factor in the problem of liner concentration. In January, as we have seen, the principle had been definitely laid down that meat, like other products, should be drawn, in strict order of geographical priority, from the nearest sources available; but it was by no means easy to square the demands for North Atlantic tonnage with the maximum economy in the use of insulated space and the demand for refrigerated produce. With the growth of American trooping, not only were further steamers from the Australasian trade diverted to the North Atlantic, but it became necessary to divert also the fastest steamers then in the South American trade, including a number of the South American lines themselves, or Australasian liners previously transferred to the Plate service. These were replaced, in order to maintain the supply of meat from the Plate, by slower vessels previously diverted to the North Atlantic or left in the Australasian service, and by vessels withdrawn from the minor services. These diversions could only be arranged as ships came off their current voyages, and the task of effecting them without interfering with the Army supplies, taxed the powers of the Refrigerated Shipping Committee to the full.

In June 1918 there were in the North Atlantic no fewer than 32 insulated steamers diverted from the Australasian service, and 5 from the Plate and China trades. The capacity of these steamers in American beef, which gave very good stowage, was about 95,000 tons. Including the meat capacity of the ordinary liners and 3 converted fruit boats, the insulated space in the North Atlantic had a capacity of 115,000 tons, or over 75,000 tons a month. To fill this space economically was not easy, as the Food Controller's purchases of meat did not exceed 36,000 tons of meat a month, and a large part of his other purchases of foodstuffs, such as bacon and lard, did not require insulated space. Such space was used, however, for a certain amount of lightly cured bacon, and poultry. The difficulty was increased by the fact that the frozen meat trade in the States, developed as a war emergency, was largely of a make-shift character. Deliveries at the ports were slow, and much of the meat had to be refrozen on board the ships, owing to the inability of the converted chilling plants at the works to maintain a sufficiently low temperature for freezing. Further, it was by no means easy to dispose of the meat when shipped. The Armies would not eat it unless compelled, and the effect of putting it on the British market was a fall in civilian consumption.

In the River Plate trade—the main source of Army supplies—there were now 46 steamers belonging to the South American lines, including those withdrawn from other services, and 28 Australasian steamers. Including other diversions, and the French and Italian steamers, the total was 91 steamers, with an aggregate capacity of 237,000 tons of meat or 59,000 tons a month. This was an increase of over 50 per cent. on the tonnage working at the beginning of the year, and as the by-products problem was now giving less trouble, the demands for the carriage of meat were adequately met, and the Argentine butter export was also lifted at the rate of 1,000 tons a month.

For all this, however, the Australasian services had to pay. At the end of March 40 insulated steamers, excluding Commonwealth prizes, were running between Australasia and the United Kingdom; at the end of June only 23. There were 11 others running to Egypt; but the total quantity these 34 ships could lift monthly did not exceed 18,000 tons. The result was that 30,000 tons of meat were awaiting shipment in Australia, and 140,000 tons in New Zealand. About 14,000 tons of Australian rabbits, and 33,000 tons of cheese and butter, mostly in New Zealand, had also been shut out.

These accumulations of cheese were a source of great anxiety to the Ministry of Food, as stocks at home were running low; but to the Australasian Governments the most serious matter was their inability to dispose of the meat itself. One-third of the Queensland freezing works were closed, and works in New Zealand were also closing down. In New Zealand the financial position had caused trouble early in 1917, and in June of that year the Board of Trade agreed to take over the storage charges and fire insurance (after four months) of meat awaiting shipment. By 1918 the position had become so serious as to interfere with the flotation of a New Zealand War Loan, and on May 28th the Treasury agreed to advance £3,000,000, or approximately 90 per cent. on the value of the meat in store.

At such high cost was the concentration of shipping on the North and South Atlantic tracks secured; but there was no wavering in the application of the principle. Owing to the falling off in North American wheat exports, there was a slight reduction of the liner tonnage in the North American trade, which amounted in July to 2,680,000 tons gross; but in the Plate and Brazilian trade the tonnage had increased by that month to 1,175,000 tons, nearly 300,000 tons more than in April. Including the West Indian and Amazon trade, over 4,000,000 tons, or

56 per cent. of the tonnage under control of the Liner Requisition Committee [1] was now in the North or South Atlantic.

For the management of the liners so as to obtain the utmost development of their carrying capacity, the Established Lines themselves were responsible, in co-operation with the Conference and Loading Committees, and under the supervision of the Liner Requisitioning Committee. In the running of the fully requisitioned tramps, mostly employed in the Plate and North American grain trade, or on the short-distance routes to Scandinavia, France, and the Mediterranean, a change of considerable importance had been made during the spring of 1918. It will be remembered that the Ship Management Branch of the Ministry of Shipping had been created in March 1917 mainly for the purpose of appointing new managers for the Prize Steamers running on Government account, with special regard to their type and the trades in which they were engaged. The next duty of the Branch was to appoint managers for the standard steamers under construction in the United Kingdom and for steamers built overseas to the orders of the Director of Oversea Ship Purchase, or bought by him second-hand. Later came the requisitioned neutrals, especially the Norwegians transferred under the Norwegian Agreement, and the Dutch ships seized in March 1918. There were also under the Branch a few British steamers which had been demised to the Government for special services, or in special circumstances—such as the calling up for military service of an owner who had no partner—which prevented the owner from fulfilling his responsibilities to the Ministry of Shipping.

In appointing managers for all these ships, the main consideration was to allot each vessel to a manager accustomed to handling vessels of the same type; but subject to this, the Branch endeavoured, so far as possible, to allocate ships to owners who had lost their steamers through war losses or requisition (but not through the sale of their fleets), and to whom the management remuneration was therefore of importance. This remuneration was on a fixed basis; but a percentage of earnings was also allowed, when the ships were employed at ordinary commercial rates for the carriage of non-Government cargo. In return

[1] Including chartered neutrals allocated to Established Lines.

for this remuneration the managers undertook, under supervision of the Branch, all the ordinary duties of management with regard to manning, storing, and provisioning the vessels, and were generally responsible for their seaworthiness, and fitness for employment. The nature of the employment, however, was still determined by Requisitioning Branch.

By the spring of 1918 a large number of managers had been appointed, each looking after a small group of Government-owned ships or requisitioned neutrals; but the Branch had as yet no general responsibility with regard to the bulk of British requisitioned vessels. At this time, however, the Shipping Controller decided that it was desirable to establish closer supervision over the running of steamers on requisition than could be obtained through the Executive Branches responsible for their employment. He formed, accordingly, a new Division of Ship Management Branch for the special purpose of watching the employment of steamers under the control of the Executive Branches, for the purpose of securing full cargoes, quick turn-round, and generally the maximum utilisation of carrying capacity, and to deal with all questions of bunkering, ballast, repairs, and dry-docking.[1] For this purpose twenty experienced shipowners were brought into the Ministry, each undertaking the supervision of about 100 steamers. Hospital and troop ships, oilers, cross-Channel steamers, ships employed in the Indian, Persian Gulf, and East African services, and steamers under 1,600 tons gross were excluded; but the great bulk of the fully requisitioned ships was now directly supervised by the Branch.

This extension of the functions of Ship Management Branch was of considerable importance in relation to the carrying capacity of the vessels. Not only did it provide, to some extent, a substitute for the direct control by the shipowner, which requisition had removed; but it enabled the actual allocation of the ships between the various services to be more closely watched, with a view to utilising each type of steamer to the best advantage. Although Ship Management Branch were not directly responsible for allocation, their representations carried too much weight to be neglected.

[1] Questions relating to wages of officers and crews were dealt with through the National Maritime Board, established in November 1917.

For the management of chartered, as distinct from requisitioned, neutrals, Ship Management Branch were not directly responsible, as it was the duty of the neutral owners to provide for their running. No managers were, therefore, appointed, but a special Section was established in the Branch to exercise a general supervision over the employment and running of the ships, and the observance of the terms contained in the various charters and agreements under which they were acquired.

The majority of the neutral steamers on time-charter were, however, in the service of France and Italy. It will be remembered that the actual chartering of all ships for the Inter-Allied Chartering Executive was done by Messrs. Furness, Withy & Co. This firm also exercised a general supervision over the running of all ships allocated to the British or Italian Government, or the Wheat Executive, while the French share of the tonnage was managed by a French Government Bureau. By the end of 1917 Messrs. Furness, Withy & Co. had no fewer than 470 neutral steamers on their hands, and were compelled to call in sub-managers to relieve them of a portion of the work. It was accordingly arranged that the Inter-Allied Chartering Executive itself should take over the management of all ships to be chartered in the future, as well as of ships allocated to the Italian Government.

The most important question with regard to these neutral steamers was, however, that of allocation, and this, as we have seen, had been dealt with by the Allied Maritime Transport Council at their meeting in April. The outstanding feature of the arrangement then arrived at, was the formation, from ships coming up for reallocation, of a pool of tonnage to be allocated directly, voyage by voyage, by the Council itself. The general lines on which such pool tonnage was to be employed were laid down, in the following month, by the Allied Maritime Transport Executive. Steamers of 1,700 tons dead-weight or under were allocated to the French coal trade. Those between 1,700 and 3,000 tons loaded coal cargoes for the Bay ports, or for Blaye on Italian account, and returned with ore from Northern Spain. Those between 3,000 and 4,500 dead-weight loaded coal outwards to Italy, and ore from the Mediterranean on their homeward voyage. Steamers above 4,500 tons passed into the Wheat Executive service, after completing a coal voyage to Italian ports. The great advantage of the Neutral Pool, however, was the power given to the Allied Maritime Transport Council to divert into any service where tonnage was urgently required, a body of tonnage which started, in May, at 60,000 tons dead-weight, but increased rapidly and automatically, as old charters ran off and ships came up for reallocation.

The spring and early summer of 1918 thus witnessed, in almost every direction, not only a substantial increase in the degree of protection afforded to shipping against submarine attack, but a distinct advance in the economical utilisation of carrying power. Concentration of tonnage on the shorter routes was carried to still further lengths; the delays incidental to the convoy system were minimised, both in the Atlantic and in the Mediterranean; the running of requisitioned tramps was brought under stricter supervision; and greater elasticity was attained in the use of neutral tonnage.[1]

[1] On the financial side of shipping control, the early months of 1918 were marked by an important modification of the Blue Book rates. With a few exceptions, liner rates had remained unchanged since they were originally fixed by the Arbitration Board, and tramp rates had not been altered since the Agreement of March 1915. As the result of an investigation by accountants appointed by the Ministry of Shipping and the Chamber of Shipping respectively, it was now proved that, owing to the great increase in working costs, the owners of some requisitioned ships were incurring an actual loss, and in many other instances the margin of profit was insignificant. New tramp rates were accordingly fixed, to take effect as from March 1st, 1918. These rates were intended to give an average return of approximately 10 per cent. on *ante-bellum* first costs, taking running expenses as on January 1st, 1918.

CHAPTER XXI

DISTRIBUTION AND CARRYING POWER
FEBRUARY—JULY 1918

QUITE as important as the organisation of shipping, in its relation to the fulfilment of the import programme and the progress of American trooping, was the question of internal distribution of imported cargoes. The annual carrying power of the ships depended on the speed with which they could be turned round, and the speed with which they could be turned round depended on the distributive capacity of the ports. In its turn the distributive capacity of the ports depended mainly on the supply of labour and the railway facilities available, and the capacity of the railways, turned on prompt instructions as to the ultimate destination of the goods—instructions which it was often difficult to obtain in respect of Government imports, especially of rationed commodities.

The supply of labour had been to a great extent secured by the general exemptions granted to transport workers and the creation of the Transport Workers' Battalions; but the military developments on the Continent led to more men being continually called up, even from reserved occupations, for service with the Colours, and to the growth of recruiting for such auxiliary services as the Inland Water Transport. Thus the Port and Transit Executive Committee, on whom the Ministry of National Service had been represented since November 1917, were continually called upon to exercise their utmost vigilance in the protection of dock workers, lightermen, and others engaged in the work of distribution, in order that, while every possible man was spared for the Army, this essential work should not be crippled for lack of man-power.

In March 1918 they had to intervene, also, to prevent the recruiting of shipyard labour from dock workers and even from the Transport Workers' Battalions. This question raised in an acute form the relation between the distributive and importing services, for it was obviously useless to provide additional tonnage by measures which must seriously reduce the annual carrying power of the ships already available.

That men could still be spared for the Army without utter dislocation was due mainly to the growth of the Transport Workers' Battalions, which were maintained at or very near their authorised strength of 10,000 to 11,000 men, and were available to meet any sudden emergency. In December 1917 men of the battalions were employed in forty-six ports, and during the first three months of 1918 the average number actually engaged in transport work averaged well over 8,000. Their relations with civilian labour continued to be excellent. In November 1917, to remove the last trace of suspicion as to their employment in strike-breaking, the refusal of civilian labour to work was deleted from the clause in the Port and Transport Committee's pamphlet defining " shortage " of labour, and this concession removed the last elements of opposition in certain districts. Where essential traffic was actually held up by strikes, men of the battalions were still employed, but such instances were few. Although disputes relating to wages, hours, and conditions were rather frequent during the first half of 1918, the influence of the Transport Workers' Federation, who co-operated cordially with the Committee, was generally sufficient to ensure the continuance of work pending a settlement.

Some part of such discontent as existed arose from the conditions, directly arising out of the war, under which the arduous duties of transport workers had to be performed. So early as December 1917, the Port and Transit Committee took up with the Liquor Control Board the question of enabling night workers at Liverpool, more especially the night coal workers engaged in bunkering, to obtain refreshment outside the licensed hours. In order to ensure the readiness of vessels to sail in convoy, it was frequently necessary for these men to work right through the night, with an interval for refreshment between 10 and 11 p.m. In view of the enormous importance of regularity in sailing dates, the Committee pressed strongly for an exception to be made in their favour, but the Control Board were unwilling to grant the concession, and in February 1918 the matter was dropped, only to arise in an acute form at a later date. The Committee were, however, successful in February, in arranging with the Ministry of Food for the issue of extra rations to men who had worked a full day in the ports and were then required to put in more than four hours of overtime work. In March also the Ministry agreed to include all transport workers in the class of " very heavy industrial workers " entitled to the maximum supplementary ration.

It was, however, the conditions on the railways, rather than those in the ports themselves, which gave the chief grounds for anxiety. A large percentage of trained railway workers, including enginemen and guards, had been called to the Colours, and the strain on material was quite as serious as the drain on labour. Hundreds of engines and 20,000 wagons had been sent overseas, and the efficiency of the remaining rolling stock was greatly reduced. Not only was there abnormal wear and tear, due to the increase in heavy traffic, but railway workshops and artisan staff were largely engaged in the manufacture of munitions of war, and both labour and material for repairs were very short. Even the permanent-way on many lines showed signs of serious deterioration. Insulated vans were specially short—a very serious matter in connection with the diversions of meat cargoes—and there was a serious shortage of wagon sheets, as the Ministry of Food refused to release linseed oil for their manufacture. Yet the demands on the railways were greater than ever. Although the passenger services had been drastically reduced, the reductions were more than off-set by the increase in goods traffic, amounting on one line to 24 per cent. on the normal. All through 1917 there had been a steady growth in the heavy munitions traffic, the carriage of coal and other goods diverted from the coasting trade, and the requirements of the War Office for conveyance of troops, ammunition and stores. The Great Western Railway had run during the year 25,000 trains on Government account, the South-Eastern and Chatham Railway nearly 27,000. Moreover, the increasing use of the West Coast ports, the continual diversions of ships from one port to another, and the arrival of ships in convoy in large batches, all tended to render the distribution of the strain very unequal, with the result of frequent and serious blocks on the lines and at the terminals.

THE LIMITS OF DIVERSION

It was the railway difficulties above all which had proved the decisive factor in restricting the diversion of the London and East Coast traffic to the West Coast ports. The Committee under Colonel J. W. Pringle, appointed in October 1917 to consider this question, presented their final report on March 19th.[1] This Report, based on a full and careful analysis of the existing storage and transport facilities, dealt with the subject under three heads—Munitions Materials, Foodstuffs, and General Cargo.

As regards munitions materials, the Committee held that the diversion of ore and other materials used in the London and East Coast munitions factories was wholly impracticable. No large stocks could, in existing circumstances, be held at the blast furnaces or factories, and the railways were incapable of maintaining the necessary supplies, amounting to 84,000 tons a week.

Imports of foodstuffs averaged 69,000 tons a week for London and 18,000 tons for the North-Eastern ports. So far as the North-Eastern ports were concerned the Committee considered that all imports other than munitions could in an emergency be railed from Glasgow, Liverpool, and Manchester; but the problem of London was much more serious. To rail the whole 69,000 tons of foodstuffs from West Coast ports and Southampton would necessitate a daily service of 44 trains, and involve the provision of 140 engines and brake vans, 12,000 wagons, and 1,200 insulated vans. For the perishable portion of the traffic it would be necessary to build new rolling-stock, as only about 2,500 insulated vans were in existence and all these were already fully employed. The remaining rolling-stock could be taken from trains displaced by the food traffic; but this would seriously affect the running of munition workers' and ambulance trains. Further, the Port of London Authority could deal with the traffic only

[1] Members of the Committee: Colonel J. W. Pringle, R.E. (Chairman), Sir Joseph G. Broodbank (Chairman of the Dock and Warehouse Committee, Port of London Authority), Lieutenant-Colonel T. H. Hawkins, C.M.G. (Port and Transit Executive Committee), Mr. Frank Potter (General Manager, Great Western Railway), Sir George Saltmarsh (Po.t of London Authority, Director of the Baltic and Corn Exchange, Member of the Wheat Executive), Sir Robert Turnbull, M.V.O. (late General Manager, London and North-Western Railway), Mr. John Wardle (Ministry of Food), Mr. L. A. P. Warner (Director, Port Branch, Ministry of Shipping). Subsequently added: Mr. W. T. Watts (Ministry of Food), Mr. Howard Williams, C.B.E. (Ministry of Food); Mr. Wardle resigned his position at the Ministry of Food in December 1917, and consequently did not sign the report.

if 15 additional shunting engines were provided, new sidings laid down, a seven-day week worked, the labour supply increased, and the port closed entirely both to import and export trade. This total closure would involve railing to London about 41,000 tons weekly of raw materials, timber, petroleum, and general cargo, and to other ports some 5,000 to 10,000 tons a week, of goods hitherto exported from London. Large additional supplies of labour and equipment would also be necessary at the West Coast ports.

Taking into account the difficulty of providing labour and material, and the general dislocation involved, the Committee agreed unanimously that a total closing of the Port of London was impracticable. The utmost they considered possible was the diversion to West Coast ports of 12,000 tons weekly of food and general goods, and even this would require the provision of considerable additional accommodation, equipment, and labour, both at London and at the West Coast ports.

In view of the demands on man-power and railway transport arising from the German spring offensive and the consequent increase of American trooping to Great Britain, and having regard to the strain placed on the West Coast ports by the trooping convoys, and the absolute necessity for quick and regular turn-round of the vessels employed in trooping service, it was extremely fortunate that the great decrease in the Channel risk arising from the blocking of Zeebrugge and Ostend rendered it unnecessary to adopt diversion, even on the scale contemplated by the Committee. The Committee had, however, recommended that, to provide against the possibility of a temporary interruption of Channel traffic, not exceeding a fortnight, reserves of food, grain, and other essential foodstuffs and of petroleum products, sufficient to cover such period, should be accumulated at London and East Coast ports, and storage accommodation to contain such diverted cargoes as it might be necessary to discharge, kept vacant in the West Coast ports. The Port and Transit Committee accordingly took steps to carry out this precautionary measure.

Apart from the possibility of any sudden additional strain, it was difficult enough for the railways, at this period, to perform their ordinary distributive functions. But for the pooling of trucks which the Port and Transit

Committee had secured in 1916, it would have been impossible. This measure was further extended in March and April 1918, when the Railway Companies agreed to a more general system of pooling, and also entered into negotiations for further control over private trucks. As regards labour, considerable assistance was given by the men of the Transport Workers' Battalions. Their employment for this purpose had been agreed by the Government in April 1917, but although a considerable amount of work had been done, much of it at the request of the War Office and Ministry of Munitions, it was not until April 1918 that the War Office appointed representatives to the Local Committees formed to consider applications for railway work. From this time onwards the number of men employed in such work rapidly increased, and very valuable work was done, especially in loading trucks with ore and other heavy materials.

This, however, was not the only extension of the battalions' work. On March 27th, the Army Council, in accordance with a previous decision of the Government, issued an Instruction, authorising the increase of the strength to 15,000 men, and by the end of April that number had been raised. This increase was sanctioned partly on account of the extensive responsibilities now accepted by the Port and Transport Committee with regard to railway work, but it was also a part of the scheme that an additional battalion should be formed for special service on the canals.

It had now become a matter of urgent importance to relieve the railways as much as possible of traffic which could be handled by any other form of transport. A Road Transport Board had been appointed at the beginning of 1918, but though the use of motor lorries had been considerably extended during 1917, at Liverpool and elsewhere, the demands of the Armies for motor transport seriously restricted the relief which could be given in this way, and it was only by diverting traffic to barges and coasters that the strain on the railways could be appreciably relieved. The capacity of the inland waterways was now being developed by the Canal Control Committee, and boats were still available in considerable numbers; but skilled labour was very short. A new battalion for canal work was accordingly raised in May, and together with volunteers under the National Service Scheme, assisted the canals to relieve the railways of much distributive and local traffic.

All coastal tonnage was now under the control of the Home Trade Branch of the Ministry of Shipping. This Branch, originally formed in June 1917, under Mr. A. H. Read as Director and Mr. H. M. Macneal as Deputy, was organised in three sections. One of these, under the immediate supervision of the Director, looked after the regular cargo and passenger liners in the trade, both coastwise and cross-Channel, including the Highland and Islands service. These services were not greatly interfered with, but a weekly return was obtained from the owners showing the capacity and employment of their vessels, the amount and character of cargo carried, and future commitments; and directions were given, where necessary, as to priority of cargo. The section also arranged with the Shipping Department of the Royal Commission on Wheat Supplies for the transhipment of foodstuffs arriving from overseas, taking up general cargo coasters for this purpose when the railway and liner facilities were insufficient.

The two other sections, under the supervision of the Deputy Director, dealt with tramps and sailing tonnage in the traffic of the East Coast and North France, and the West Coast and Ireland respectively. The French coal trade, however, remained outside their province. The East Coast section was specially concerned with the London, East Coast, and South of England coal trade, the coal supply of the Channel Islands, the import of potatoes and tomatoes from those Islands, the trade to and from the Orkneys and Shetlands, and the distribution from the Thames of imported manganese ore, pyrites, and jute, as well as locally produced clay and cement. The West Coast Section dealt, in conjunction with the Director of Cross-Channel Transportation, with the carriage of coal to Ireland, and the import from Ireland of pit-wood, potatoes, oats, kelp, and other products. It supervised also the local traffic of the coast, including the Welsh limestone, and the Ramsay ore trade. In conjunction with the Requisitioning Branch it made arrangements for the allocation of tonnage to the Ministry of Food for the Stornoway herring trade, and for other Government services.

In its early developments, the control exercised by the

Branch was of a somewhat elastic character. Coasting steamers, other than those taken up for naval and military service, were not, generally speaking, requisitioned; but returns, similar to those obtained from the coasting lines, were obtained from all owners of vessels of 250 tons gross and upwards, and directions were issued as to the order of priority in which various classes of cargo were to be lifted. Particular care was exercised that no vessel should be allowed to move from port to port in ballast, and by co-operation with Requisitioning Branch, Collier Branch, and Norwegian Section, it proved possible to secure very considerable assistance in the carriage of coastwise cargoes, from ships other than those permanently employed in the coasting trade.

At the time when the Branch was formed, a large block of tonnage usually employed in the United Kingdom services had drifted into the French coal trade, where, despite the Freight Limitation Scheme, they were able to obtain higher rates than in the coasting services, and it became necessary to redirect such vessels into their original employment. By the beginning of 1918, however, coasting rates had risen above those in the French trade, and the Branch accordingly drew up, in consultation with representative owners, a schedule of rates covering all the principal commodities, and uniform, so far as possible, with those in the French trade. At the same time a system of ship licensing was introduced.[1]

Beyond this the Branch did not go. The threat of general requisition could be held *in terrorem* over the heads of owners who objected to the directions given by the Branch, but with very few exceptions the owners co-operated willingly and cordially in all measures taken to improve the efficiency of the services, and it was considered unwise to alienate them by recourse to stronger measures. The control exercised was, indeed, sufficiently close. The weekly returns enabled a watch to be kept on the movements of all liners, and the employment of tramps was controlled, not only by the licensing system, but by particular directions, when necessary, as to the cargo to be lifted on each voyage. If the liner returns showed that unessential cargo was being carried, instructions

---

[1] The Shipping Controller's power to license coasting voyages was acquired under Defence of the Realm Regulation 39DD, issued January 16th, 1918.

were given that it should be stopped. If a ship was not fully employed, instructions were given for her to be chartered to a line running in a congested trade. All delays in loading or discharging were strictly investigated.

The cross-Channel Irish traffic was now of particular importance, as owing to a large increase in the area under oats and potatoes, and increased cutting of pit-wood, the Irish produce available for export to the United Kingdom was estimated to be about a million tons above the normal. So far as it could not be carried by the regular services, the lifting of this surplus was arranged by the Director of Cross-Channel Services, in ships which had brought coal to Ireland.

In the coasting trade proper, the difficulty was not only to obtain tonnage, but to induce merchants to ship their goods by coaster, in view of the additional cost, as compared with the artificially restricted railway rates. It was, however, essential to relieve the railways of every possible ton of traffic, and both the Home Trade Branch and the Port and Transit Committee were ready to stretch their powers to the utmost for this purpose. Thus, in February 1918, the Port and Transit Committee induced the railway companies to refuse absolutely the carriage to Liverpool of cotton cargoes arriving in London, thus forcing this traffic on to the coastal service.

In the previous month the Committee had taken up the question of wood-pulp arriving from Norway for the London paper mills. The Ministry of Shipping were opposed to the practice of bringing direct to London vessels which must return to the Tyne to load coal for Norway, both on account of the loss of time, and because of the additional risk involved. The carriage of some 1,400 tons of pulp a week was, however, a serious strain on the railways, and the north-eastern ports were frequently congested by accumulations. After some investigation, a conference was held on March 6th, at which representatives of the Committee met those of the Ministry of Shipping (Home Trade Branch and Norwegian Section), the Railway Executive Committee, the Port of London Authority, and the paper manufacturers. At this conference it was decided that arrangements should be made, so far as possible, for the ships with pulp to come direct to London, on the understanding that the Port Authority and the manufacturers would make special arrangements

DIVERSIONS RAIL TO WATER 841

to deal with the traffic. In so far as it was necessary to land the cargoes at the northern ports, Home Trade Branch promised to provide as much coastal tonnage as possible for bringing it on to London.

On the following day, March 7th, a conference was held between the Port and Transit Committee, Home Trade Branch, and the representatives of the London railway companies, to consider the general question of the diversion of cargo from rail to coastal transport. At this Conference it was agreed that the companies should keep Home Trade Branch regularly informed of all goods they were unable to carry; that the Branch should then inform the companies what provision could be made for the carriage of such goods by the regular coasting services or by the allocation of tramp tonnage, and that the companies should thereupon refuse the carriage by rail of all cargoes for which coastal tonnage was available.

In April the West of England and Bristol Channel local Port and Transit Committee were able to arrange with Home Trade Branch, the Coal Controller, and the Railways, for the coal supply of certain areas to be confined exclusively to coasting traffic, except in special emergency. Both the Central Port and Transit Committee and Home Trade Branch were now pressing the diversion of traffic from the railways wherever possible, and during the three months ending May 31st, over 80,000 tons of munitions traffic alone were diverted, 10,000 tons to road, 67,000 tons to canal, and 3,000 tons coastwise. In June a Home Trade Transport Control Committee was set up, representing the Ministry of Shipping, the Port and Transit Committee, the Railway Executive Committee, and the Canal Control Committee. The object of this Committee was to co-ordinate all means of transport, both for the carriage of local traffic, and the distribution of imports from oversea, and District Committees were formed to carry out the detailed work. So successful were their efforts that, in July alone, they diverted 40,400 tons of cargo to canal, and 23,600 tons to coasting traffic. In addition Home Trade Branch itself, at the request of the Railway Clearing House, diverted to coasting traffic a further 13,000 tons. For the carriage of diverted cargoes they directed 17,400 dead-weight tons of itinerant shipping to assist the regular liners in the coasting trade.

Both in the general coasting and the Anglo-Irish trade

the total arrivals and departures of ships with cargo continued to fall away, for the losses of coasting tonnage were not, generally speaking, made good ; but, thanks to the restriction of unessential traffic and the care taken to provide tonnage for the essential trades and to ensure vessels sailing with full cargoes, the assistance given by coasters in the work of distribution was decidedly more effective than it had been in 1917. Together with the development of canal transport, it did a good deal to relieve the strain on the railways.

Apart from diversions to road, coasters, and barges, considerable relief was given to the railways by careful arrangements to avoid unnecessary haulage, and expedite delivery. In February, for instance, the Port and Transit Committee arranged with the London fruit importers to pool their facilities for dealing with fruit railed from the western ports, thus avoiding serious delays to trucks. Tea also had given considerable trouble. Practically the whole import was normally received in London, the headquarters of the trade ; but owing to convoy arrangements, about half was now going to Liverpool and Manchester. From these ports it was, at first, forwarded to London for blending and distribution, but towards the end of 1917 arrangements were made for a part of the northern consumption to be supplied from Liverpool and Manchester direct. Even so, a large amount required to be railed south, and in the opening months of 1918, caused serious congestion at Liverpool, owing to difficulty in dealing with the arrivals at the London end, and the consequent slowness with which cargoes were removed. The Port and Transit Committee took the matter up, and by co-operation between the Ministry of Food, the Customs, the Port of London Authority, and the railway companies, the difficulties were gradually overcome.

Generally speaking, the removal of goods from the quays was now much more prompt than at an earlier period of the war, largely as a result of the enforcement of penalty rents on both private traders and Government Departments. In their efforts to enforce, in this way, prompt removal of Government imports, the Port and Transit Committee were greatly assisted by the Treasury, who issued instructions that " the demand for penal rents should be taken as an indication of an administrative breakdown which requires immediate and strenuous efforts to rectify," and that every demand for penal rents should be reported "to some superior and responsible official who will be responsible for taking all practicable measures for reducing the block."

To this general improvement there was, however, one very serious exception. The Ministry of Food had bought, during the winter, very large quantities of bacon in the United States and Canada, and shipment of these purchases had been delayed by the block in United States ports, arising from severe weather and railway congestion. Thus the great bulk still remained to come forward in the spring of 1918, and the Ministry were still buying.

On March 14th the Ministry of Food informed the Port and Transit Executive Committee that about 47,000 tons of bacon was at sea on its way to the United Kingdom, and that these consignments were to be followed rapidly by shipments which might represent in the whole 400,000 tons. The Ministry added that a very considerable portion would consist of mild-cured bacon requiring, immediately on its arrival, either cold storage or further curing.

These imports were far in advance of anything yet experienced. The total import of bacon in 1913 had amounted to under 250,000 tons, and though imports had risen largely during the war, the total for 1917 was only 328,000 tons, the highest monthly import being in April 1918, when 49,000 tons was received. It was now evident that this figure would be greatly exceeded during the next few months of 1918, and the difficulty of dealing with such large arrivals was increased by the fact that practically the whole import was coming from North America and would require to be handled in the West Coast ports, whereas more than half the supply in 1913 had come from Denmark and Holland, and even in 1917 about 20 per cent. of the whole was received from those countries.

On receipt of this, the first notice of the abnormal imports expected, the Committee immediately communicated with the Ministry of Food, pointing out that the storage facilities in the ports were utterly inadequate to deal with such quantities, and that it would be impossible to use the quays or railway accommodation for the purpose of sorting and classifying the bacon, or to make retail deliveries by rail from the ports. They urged, therefore, that the bacon must be sent through "wholesale," immediately on discharge, to the districts in which it was to be consumed. To this the Ministry agreed on March 21st, at a conference with the Committee and the Port Branch of the Ministry of Shipping. The Committee further urged on the Ministry the importance of securing by cable the fullest possible information as to each shipment, so that they might be in a position to make arrangements, before the arrival of each ship, for the allocation and distribution of the cargo.

The actual imports in March amounted only to about 38,000 tons, but in April nearly 77,000 tons was received, and the May imports were on the same scale. Owing to the dislike of the Government to exposing food once landed in the country a second time to submarine risk, it was impossible to arrange for the distribution by coasting traffic of any part of these imports, and the strain on the railways was considerable. The chief difficulty, however, was not the provision of transport, but the clearing of the quays. On April 5th and again on April 30th, the Port and Transit Committee wrote to the Ministry of Food, reiterating the importance of taking delivery in bulk, and of issuing disposal instructions before, or immediately on discharge of the cargo, but it was some weeks before they were able to secure entire cessation of the attempt to take retail delivery from the ports, and at the beginning of May vessels were still arriving, and bacon being landed on the quays, before any instructions were received as to its ultimate destination. At Liverpool, Bristol, Glasgow, and Hull large quantities accumulated, awaiting disposal orders, with the result that, on the one hand, the flow of traffic was obstructed, and the turn-round of ships impeded, and, on the other hand, the bacon itself deteriorated.

Bacon was now strictly rationed, and the Ministry of Food explained their inability to remove the cargoes, partly by the reluctance of retailers to accept large consignments, through fear of stocks being left on their hands, partly by the fact that the cold storage capacity of the country was already fully utilised, and partly by their inability to issue allocation orders in advance, owing to difficulty in obtaining cable advice of the arrival of bacon ships. It was obvious, however, that the root of the trouble lay in the fact that the imports were altogether in excess of current requirements, and the Port and Transit Committee accordingly urged that steps should be taken both to restrict the imports and to increase the bacon ration, in order to restore the equilibrium between supply and demand. To both these steps the Ministry agreed early in May, and by the end of that month the measures taken had become effective; but by that time much damage had already been done.

So serious was the situation that, on May 10th, the Port and Transit Committee communicated with the Government recapitulating the whole history of the transaction and pointing out that the blocking of the ports by accumulations was of peculiar gravity at a time when, owing to the importance of American trooping, special efforts were being made to accelerate the turn-round of ships in the West Coast ports, and when tonnage and port facilities were being freely employed in forming the food reserves at East Coast ports recommended by the Traffic Diversion Committee. They further stated that only the unusual coldness of the weather during the past six weeks had saved a large proportion of the bacon from becoming absolutely unfit for human consumption prior to its removal from the quays. They urged, therefore, that the Government should take steps to limit the imports of the Departments, especially imports of perishable commodities, to the quantities which could be passed either into immediate consumption or into store, as and when the ships arrived.

As a result of the limitation of orders by the Ministry of Food, the June imports fell to 60,000 tons, and thanks to increased consumption and better arrangements for bulk delivery, the difficulties with regard to distribution had become less accentuated by the end of that month. In other respects, too, the position at the ports was fairly satisfactory. The work accomplished by the Port and Transit Executive Committee, the Port and Home Trade Branches of the Ministry of Shipping, the Liverpool Convoy Committee, and other bodies concerned with internal transport, was bearing fruit; except during the bacon rush the quays had been kept fairly free from accumulations of cargo; something had been done to relieve the strain on the railways. Generally speaking, the turn-round of ships, especially in the all-important trooping convoys, was much better than in 1917.

The effect of this improvement, combined with that of the better organisation of shipping already described, was to increase very considerably the annual carrying power of the available tonnage. During the six months, February to July inclusive, the average British tonnage actually available for foreign trade corresponded very closely with that available during the previous half-year, as economies effected in the employment of ships on naval and military service were set-off by the net loss of tonnage. Nevertheless, the entrances with cargo under the British flag increased by 650,000 tons net, or 7 per cent., and though the foreign entrances showed a still further decline, there was an increase of some 200,000 tons in the imports received, or, including oil-fuel, 300,000 tons.

Small as it was, this increase formed a very notable landmark in the history of seaborne trade during the war. It was the first time since January 1916 that the half-yearly total had not fallen below the figures for the preceding six months, and it was the more noteworthy in view of the immense reductions in imports anticipated at the beginning of the year. That these anticipations were so happily disappointed was due in part to the steady reduction in losses arising from the development and improvement of the convoy system, in part to the closer concentration of shipping on the shorter routes, but not least to the improvement in turn-round at home and abroad and the consequent increase in the annual carrying power of the ships.

Even this increase in carrying power was, as we shall see, barely sufficient for fulfilment of the increased demands on British shipping made by the Allied import programmes and American trooping; but before considering the situation as it developed during the late summer of 1918, it is necessary to trace the effect on the Enemy Powers of the events which had so profoundly modified the disposition of Allied shipping. In Germany, as well as in Great Britain, the problem of supplies had developed during the first half of 1918 on very different lines from those anticipated at the beginning of the year; but while this meant, for Great Britain, that gloomy anticipations had not been realised, it meant for Germany only the ultimate disappointment of exaggerated hopes.

CHAPTER XXII

REACTIONS OF THE RUSSIAN COLLAPSE
JANUARY—JULY 1918

IT was not only through the effect on imports of the American trooping programme that the interaction of the war at sea and the war on land was manifested during the spring and summer of 1918. The effects of the German offensive were felt at every turn. Drafts and reinforcements from Great Britain, immense quantities of stores and material to replace losses in the retreat, rolling stock and railway material for use in the development of the new front, had to be rushed out with the greatest possible speed. Thanks to the improvements effected in the cross-Channel transport service during 1917, and the institution of a railway ferry service in February 1918, the work was done with remarkable success and with little addition to the strain on tonnage; but the choking of the French railways made it necessary more and more to divert Italian coal to the long sea route, and the strain on man-power reacted seriously on the output of essential industries. The output of coal fell off as the result of the recruiting of miners, and with the War Office at their wits' end to fill up the depleted ranks, it proved impossible to procure the return of the skilled shipwrights and marine engineers for whom the Navy Controller had asked at the end of 1917.

Nor was this all. The German offensive itself was a direct result of the defection of Russia. An armistice between Russia and the Central Powers had been signed by the Bolshevik Government on December 15th, 1917, and though it was not until March 3rd that peace was finally signed at Brest-Litovsk, the Germans had been able for many weeks before that date to transfer troops from the Eastern to the Western front, and devote themselves, untroubled by any serious thought of Russian interference, to the preparation of their great stroke in the West.

Both in its causes and its effects the Russian débâcle illustrated the strength and the limitations of sea-power. Admitting the importance of the political elements in the Revolution, its fundamental cause must be sought largely in the economic situation. Owing to the German command of the Baltic and the closing of the Dardanelles, Russia had been unable, since the beginning of the war, to ship her surplus harvests, or receive any imports beyond those that could be forced through the narrow channels of trade provided by the White Sea, Vladivostok, and the Swedish transit route. This practically restricted all imports to the supply of urgent military requirements. Even for these the existing channels of trade were inadequate, and their distribution from the ports put a severe strain on the imperfect internal transport system. That system, further strained by military movements, progressively deteriorated, and the Western Allies could give little help in its improvement, shut off as they were from the Baltic and Black Sea ports. In the absence of imported fuel, coal for the Petrograd factories had to be brought from the Donetz basin, a thousand miles away, and this necessity, besides adding to the intolerable strain on the Russian railways, limited the development of those factories themselves. As a result, both of transport difficulties and of the pressure of military demands on the restricted output, the flow of manufactured goods from the industrial centre to the food-producing districts rapidly diminished, and the peasants, unable to obtain either imported goods or home manufactures in exchange for agricultural produce, were reluctant to accept paper money which was constantly depreciating, owing to the stoppage of exports and the effects of war expenditure, and for which they were now unable to obtain goods. Thus, although the production of food, even under war conditions, afforded a considerable surplus over the total requirements of the country, the industrial areas round Moscow and Petrograd found themselves short of food as well as of raw materials, while the agricultural population were unable to reap the fruits of their labour in a supply of the other necessities of life.[1]

---

[1] See, *inter alia*, the *Economic Survey of Certain Countries Specially Affected by the War at the Close of the Year* 1919, Department of Overseas Trade, 1920, pp. 110–11.

Actual shortage of imported goods, local shortages due to the failure of internal transport, fantastically high prices due both to shortage and to the financial consequences of the paralysis of the export trade, military failures arising from defective transport and defective supply—all contributed to bring about the Revolution, and to throw it, when it came, into the hands of the extremists. Had the Baltic been accessible to Allied shipping, had the Dardanelles been forced in 1915, it is at least possible that the Revolution would never have come, or that its worst consequences would have been averted.

No less far-reaching, and more easily separable, were the economic effects of the Revolution, both direct and indirect. The indirect effects, arising from the German offensive, undertaken as a consequence of the Russian breakdown, have already been indicated. The direct effects were almost as important. To the Central Powers peace with Russia came as a new lease of life in the economic as well as in the military sphere. Just as, in 1916–17, the conquest of Roumania had enabled them to struggle through the critical months preceding the gathering of the 1917 harvest, so now the defection of Russia from the Allied cause, enabled them to make good, temporarily, a deficit in their food supplies which might otherwise have been fatal. As with the Roumanian supplies in 1917, the total relief ultimately obtained was small in comparison with the extravagant hopes originally formed; but the gap between the 1917 and 1918 harvests was just bridged, and the hope of further relief, coupled with the military successes in the West, enabled the German and Austrian Governments to appeal once more to their peoples to hold out a little longer, in the expectation of ultimate victory.

In December 1917, when the armistice was concluded between the Bolshevik Government and the Central Powers, the Germans were already in possession of the greater part of Russian Poland and had advanced beyond Riga along the Baltic coast. From these quarters, however, no great quantity of foodstuffs could be wrung, and it was towards the Ukraine, the great wheat-producing district in the south-west, that all eyes in the Central Powers were turned. This district was no longer a part of Russia, so called. After the second Bolshevik revolution, a swift process of disintegration had set in, and province after province formed its own provisional

Government. On November 20th, 1917, the Ukrainian People's Republic was proclaimed; on the 28th the Esthonian local Diet declared its independence; on December 6th Finland followed suit. The Central Powers were quick to seize their opportunity and at once opened direct negotiations with the Ukrainian Government. On February 1st, 1918, they formally recognised the new Republic, and on February 9th they concluded with the Ukrainian Rada a treaty of peace, and a supplementary commercial treaty which provided for the supply by the Ukraine of about 1,000,000 tons of foodstuffs. Almost simultaneously the negotiations between the Central Powers and the Bolshevik Government broke down, owing to the refusal of the Germans to evacuate Courland and Lithuania, which had now become important sources of supply, though little grain was obtainable. On February 18th the German troops resumed hostilities and by the end of the month they had advanced along the Baltic coast as far as Reval and so secured a footing on the Gulf of Finland. Negotiations were resumed, and on March 3rd a treaty of peace was signed at Brest-Litovsk which left the whole of the Baltic provinces (Lithuania, Livonia, Courland, and Esthonia) in the possession of the Germans. Two days later a preliminary treaty of peace was signed by the fugitive Roumanian Government.

The first effect in Germany and Austria of the cessation of hostilities with Russia was an exaggerated optimism with regard to food supplies. At the beginning of 1918 the food situation in Germany was slightly better than in the corresponding period of the previous year. The rations themselves were somewhat above those of the dreadful winter of 1916–17, and including the supplementary ration issued to heavy workers, and the food passing by illicit trade (said to be 25 per cent. of the whole), the available supplies were sufficient to preserve life, though not to make good the previous physical deterioration, or to maintain the people in full vigour. In Austria, on the other hand, the conditions were worse than ever. Strikes, food riots, and peace demonstrations broke out during January in most of the chief industrial centres, and Vienna was on the brink of famine. Indeed, the Austrian Government were hampered during the course of the Brest-Litovsk negotiations, by the necessity of procuring food from Berlin, to avert actual starvation.

To Austria the prospect of supplies from the Ukraine promised deliverance from absolute disaster. To Germany it promised an amelioration of conditions not yet wholly insupportable. The Ukrainian Government had promised to deliver before the end of April, 300,000 tons of grain and considerable quantities of other foodstuffs. The military advantages derived from the collapse of Russia held out hopes of a speedy decision in the West, and even if those hopes should not be realised, the whole surplus production of the Ukraine, as well as of Roumania, would be available for 1918–19. A strong reaction set in against the pessimism which was growing on the German people; concealed hoards of foodstuffs came into the market, prices fell, and the Government maintained the official rations at a level higher than was justified by the existing stocks. At the same time they made every preparation to lift the Ukrainian grain, by rail, by steamer from Odessa, and by barges up the Danube.

This extreme optimism was short-lived. Transport of the Ukrainian supplies presented grave difficulties; it was the break-down of the transport system, more than anything else, which had led to the Russian collapse, and the German system was grievously strained. Finance also presented an awkward problem. The peasants refused to accept Russian, German, or Austrian currency, and it was not easy, in the state of the German industries, to provide the goods which they demanded by way of barter. Above all, the actual stocks of grain were much smaller than had been anticipated. The disorganisation caused by the Revolution, the confiscation of the large landed estates, the lack of skilled labour, good seed, and agricultural implements, had combined to reduce the harvest, and the peasants were loth to see grain which they might urgently require for their own consumption, despatched to Vienna or Berlin.

The Ukrainian Government was thus wholly unable to fulfil its promises, and the Germans were obliged to abandon the idea of obtaining supplies by voluntary purchase, and to undertake themselves the exploitation of the country. On March 2nd they occupied Kiev; on March 13th Odessa. On April 29th they proclaimed General Skoropadski, an ex-Russian officer, Hetman, and established a military dictatorship under German tutelage.

Their difficulties were far from over. Although they

devoted themselves with ruthless energy to the exploitation of the country, the Germans found the task of wringing supplies from a reluctant population more difficult than they had anticipated. In the first flush of their triumph, they had been lavish in their promises to neutrals, especially Sweden and Holland, of grain which would render those countries independent of the United States; but by the end of February the promised supplies had dwindled to nothing, and it soon became clear that the utmost for which the Central Powers could hope was a sufficiency of grain for their own consumption, to enable them to last out until the harvest. Meanwhile the German stocks had been depleted by increased consumption during the initial wave of optimism; the expected supplies which would alone have justified the maintenance of the rations had not been received; and it was necessary to afford some measure of relief to Austria, where the whole system of food administration had absolutely broken down. The natural result followed. On May 17th the German Food Control announced the reduction of the flour ration from 7 to $5\frac{1}{2}$ ounces, as from June 16th. This was the lowest level it had yet reached during the war, and the contrast between this reduction and the hoped-for increase, created bitter disappointment.

To make things worse, the outlook for the future was equally unsatisfactory. The Ukrainian peasants were disinclined to make efforts on behalf of their new masters; the standing crops in many places were destroyed in the course of local risings, and a prolonged drought had told heavily on the new harvest itself. Early reports from Roumania indicated the probability that the 1918 harvest would be an absolute failure, and it was clear that the amount of grain to be drawn from the conquered territories during 1918–19 was likely to be small.

Even apart from the shortage of breadstuffs, the food situation was now very bad. The only hopeful item was that it had proved possible to maintain the German potato ration at 7 lb. a week. The slaughter weight of cattle had now fallen to about 55 per cent., and of pigs to about 60 per cent. of the normal. Considerable assistance in maintaining the meat ration was afforded by the requisition of cattle in the occupied territories; but it was necessary to reduce still further the milk ration for children, and the supply of edible fats and fish was shorter than ever. The effect of the embargoes, following on the various agreements between the Allies and neutral States, had progressively reduced the imports of meat, bacon, and dairy produce from Holland and Scandinavia, until the total food supplies received from those countries was only a quarter of what it had been at the beginning of 1916. The general conditions among the urban population were appalling; the death-rate rose as steadily as the birth-rate fell, and it is not surprising that to the wide-spread, open evasion of the food regulations there was now added an outburst of crimes against property and person, more especially theft of food, which bore witness to the danger of a complete break-down of law and order in the near future.

So long, however, as the German armies in the West continued to advance, the military element remained in the ascendant. The Food Control was the target of constant attacks; but the hope of a favourable military decision was sufficient to buoy up the nation through the months preceding the harvest, and prevent the universal discontent from assuming the form of active opposition to the continuance of the war. In Austria the cry for peace was loud; but the very fact that Austria was now more and more dependent on German assistance in maintaining a bare minimum subsistence, rendered the Austrian Government a helpless tool of the Germans. Bitter as was the disappointment with regard to the Ukraine, even the scanty supplies received sufficed at least to prevent the actual defection of Austria, and to provide the German population with a ration they could be induced to accept so long as a hope of victory remained.

The success of the Western offensive, on which those hopes were based, was sufficient evidence that the energetic measures taken to scrape together every available scrap of copper, nickel, and other essential metals had, so far, sufficed to keep the munitions industries running. Poland and the Baltic Provinces were now being ruthlessly ransacked, and in addition to the requisitioning of metals, it was hoped ultimately to obtain from Russia and the Ukraine badly needed raw materials such as leather and flax.

The outlook for the war industries was not, however, satisfactory. Although much war material had been captured in the West in the shape of guns, machine-guns, and mortars, the booty had added little to the stocks of copper, brass, nickel, aluminium, and other metals, and against the possibility of supplies to be obtained from Russia had to be set a tightening of the blockade which cut off most of the materials hitherto obtained from Scandinavia.

Throughout the first quarter of 1917 the general Allied embargo on exports to Holland and Scandinavia had been maintained in all its severity. Norway and Denmark continued to draw their agreed coal supply from Great Britain, and shipments to Sweden had increased considerably as a result of the *modus vivendi* arrived at in January; but all other exports were absolutely at a standstill, and to Holland even the shipment of coal had entirely ceased by the end of March. As regards American exports to Scandinavia the only exceptions permitted were the agreed shipments of cereals to Norway, and those granted to Sweden under the *modus vivendi*. To Holland, as we have seen, a limited amount of wheat had been promised on March 21st, when Dutch shipping was requisitioned; but in all other respects the embargo was complete.

For all practical purposes, other than the avoidance of actual famine in Sweden and Norway, and the provision of a minimum supply of fuel, the four States affected by the embargo had now been without imports of any description since the autumn of 1916, with the exception of such scanty supplies as they could obtain from the Central Powers. Depleted as were their stocks, by the previous interruption of communications, the burden of isolation had become almost too great to be borne.[1]

[1] IMPORTS INTO SCANDINAVIA AND HOLLAND FROM ALL SOURCES OTHER THAN GERMANY (EXCLUSIVE OF COAL)

(In 1,000 tons)

	Quarterly average 1911-13, less Exports.	January-March 1918.
Corn and grain	1,223	35
Other foodstuffs	191	39
Oils, fats, and gums	200	9
Textiles and manufactures thereof	54	1
Metals and manufactures thereof	280	6
Other principal articles	226	4
	2,174	94

Norway was the least affected, as her imports had been less restricted prior to the general embargo, and the licensing of cereals, together with the maintenance of the coal supply, had considerably modified the effect of the embargo itself. Moreover, the Norwegian shipowners had no reason to be dissatisfied with the terms of the Tonnage Agreement, and the Fish Agreement, under which large shipments were made to Great Britain during the early months of 1918, was very lucrative for the fishing industry.[1] Nevertheless, Norway was the first of the four States to come to terms with the Associated Powers. Norwegian relations with the Allies had always been friendly, and though some of the outstanding questions proved difficult of adjustment, an agreement was eventually arrived at on terms extremely satisfactory to the Allies.

The United States had originally demanded the complete cessation of all exports to the enemy, of every description. This would have borne too hardly on Norwegian interests, to which some small imports from Germany were important, and it became necessary to accept a compromise. The Allies, like the Norwegians, were anxious for a settlement, as the Fish Agreement was running out and Great Britain could ill afford the expense of an arrangement, on similar terms, with regard to the 1918 catch. On April 30th, the Norwegian-American Agreement was signed. It provided for a complete stoppage of all exports to the Central Powers of nickel, molybdenum, mica, pyrites, chrome ore, and other articles of military importance, and of all food exports except 48,000 tons of fish and fish products. Exports of carbide, nitrates, iron ore, zinc, aluminium, and other commodities were drastically restricted, and it was specifically provided that no goods of any description should be exported to the Central Powers,

---

[1] The purchase of 185,000 metric tons of Norwegian herrings and other fish products under the 1916 scheme had cost £11,000,000. Under the Fish Agreement of 1916–17, 329,000 tons were purchased at a cost of £13,800,000. The net loss to the British Government was £5,320,000 under the old scheme and £5,270,000 under the Agreement. This loss was due in great part to the collapse of Russia, to whom a large proportion of the fish had been, or was to have been, sold. It must be remembered, however, in estimating the value of the Agreement to the Allies that, in addition to the 500,000 tons actually purchased, a very large amount was diverted from the enemy to approved markets. Of 250,000 tons of wet-salted fish produced in 1917, only 14,000 tons was purchased by Great Britain, yet only about 18,000 tons reached the enemy. The balance—over 200,000 tons—was exported, under the terms of the Agreement, to approved destinations.

which had been produced with the aid of materials supplied by the Allies or the United States. Finally, provision was made for the shipment of essential supplies to the Allies, in specified quantities, free of export tax. In return the embargo was lifted, and supplies guaranteed on a rationing basis, including 300,000 tons of breadstuffs and 200,000 tons of fodder.[1]

In the following month, May 1918, the prolonged dispute with Sweden was at last terminated. Even more than the Norwegian Agreement, the Swedish General Agreement represented a compromise between the extreme demands of the United States and neutral interests. The crux of the problem was the question of iron ore. It was the desire of the Associated Governments to put an end to this traffic, so vital to the enemy's supply of munitions, which had hitherto prevented any agreement being reached; but it had to be recognised that the situation in the Baltic prevented the Allies from interposing physical barriers to the traffic, and since the Swedes were ready to face any degree of privation rather than expose themselves to the retaliatory measures which might follow a total prohibition of export, it seemed better to accept the principle of limitation. Whether the embargo was maintained or lifted, the export of ore would go on, and meanwhile the Allies were deprived of the use of Swedish tonnage, which they urgently required. It was accordingly agreed that exports to the enemy should be limited to 3,500,000 tons a year, and that 2,000,000 tons should be purchased by the Allies.

In other respects the provisions of the Agreement were much more stringent. All exports to the enemy of most other ores and metals, of foodstuffs, and of textiles were definitely stopped, and those of wood-pulp, paper, carbide, and iron and steel were restricted to specified quantities.

[1] How stringently Norwegian trade with the Central Powers was restricted may be seen from the following figures, indicating, in thousands of metric tons, the agreed distribution of certain of the more important Norwegian products:

	Associated Powers.	Central Powers.
Iron ore	200	40
Pyrites	130	nil.
Nitrates and cyanamide	112	8
	10	—
Ferro-silicon	20	2
Carbide	30	10

ALLIED AGREEMENT WITH SWEDEN

Further, the Swedes agreed not only to prohibit all exports of articles produced from materials supplied by the Allies, but all exports of commodities similar to those imported from the Associated Powers. For instance, the export of paper yarn, or paper from which such yarn could be manufactured, was prohibited as a condition of the right to receive imports of textiles.

It was, however, the tonnage provisions of the Agreement which were of the greatest immediate importance. By these the Swedes agreed to charter to the Associated Powers for war-zone trade, 200,000 dead-weight tons of Swedish shipping, and for trade outside the war zone a block of tonnage of the same size. One-half the shipping in each class was to be chartered to the Inter-Allied Chartering Executive and one-half to the United States Chartering Committee, and it was provided that 50 per cent. of the ships were to be delivered in Allied ports within one month, 75 per cent. within six weeks, and the whole within two months of the signing of the Agreement. The remaining tonnage under the Swedish flag was to be left free for employment in the national interests, with the provision that a minimum of 100,000 tons dead-weight should be maintained in the Anglo-Swedish-French trade. In consideration of these undertakings, the North Sea Freight Regulations were suspended, and all restrictions on the bunkering of Swedish ships removed.

In addition to these provisions, the Agreement included the raising of an Allied loan in Sweden, which greatly facilitated the financing of imports from that country. The total advantages thus secured to the Allies were very considerable, and the only unsatisfactory feature of the Agreement was the large proportion of iron ore allocated to the Central Powers. It was probable, however, that the Germans had already accumulated stocks sufficient to see them through the campaign of 1918, and the positive and immediate benefits were too great to be thrown aside for the possibility that a more drastic restriction of the ore export might, later on, be achieved.

Although the general embargo had now been lifted in respect of both Norway and Sweden, it was still maintained against Holland and Denmark. The total breakdown of the tonnage negotiations with Holland, which led to the requisitioning of Dutch shipping, no less than the failure to obtain satisfactory assurances in respect of the sand and gravel traffic, put any agreement with the Netherlands Government out of the question for the time being. As regards Denmark, the chief difficulty was the inability of the Danish Government to give guarantees with regard to the export of horses and live cattle, a point on which the American Government strongly insisted. Both Holland and Denmark, therefore, continued to be practically cut off from overseas supplies other than those they could obtain from their own colonies or from neutral sources not controlled by the Allies, and the restricted shipments of coal permitted to go forward from Great Britain.

Norway and Sweden were now free to import, but both these countries and Switzerland were still strictly rationed, on a basis permitting only such imports as would suffice for the normal domestic consumption, without allowing any possible margin for re-export. In order to provide for still stricter and more scientific application of this principle, an Inter-Allied Rationing and Statistical Committee was formed in May, with the British War Trade Statistical Department as its secretariat.[1] In the same month the agreement with the Société Suisse de Surveillance was revised, with the object of still further restricting exports to the Central Powers, and the Icelandic Agreement was replaced by a new General Agreement, on similar lines, with the Associated Governments.

Meanwhile steps were taken to restrict so far as possible the advantages to be drawn by the enemy from the Russian collapse, and in particular to prevent the great accumulations of munitions and war material at Archangel and Vladivostok from falling into their hands.

The Russian summer programme of 1917, as we have seen, had been loyally fulfilled, so long as any spark of resistance to Germany remained, but on the fall of the Kerensky Government, the ships still in the White Sea were hurried away, the Naval Transport Officer left Archangel, and preparations for a winter programme to Murmansk were abandoned. The fact that no tonnage for the White Sea had to be allocated in 1918 was no small set-off to the disastrous consequences of the Russian defection. The transport of some two and a half million

---

[1] An Allied Blockade Committee had already been formed, in March 1918, for the purpose of co-ordinating the action of the Allied and Associated Powers.

tons of coal and general cargo to Russian ports had proved an almost unbearable strain in 1917; in 1918, with a still more pronounced tonnage deficit, its consequences must have been very grave. As it was, the ships formerly employed in the White Sea programme were set free for the carriage of cereals and other essential imports, or for employment in the French and Italian coal trade, where British tonnage was in greater and greater demand, owing to the decreased supply of neutral shipping.

Thanks to the measures taken to expedite sailings from Archangel, practically the whole of both the British and the Russian tonnage in the White Sea was brought away before the closing of navigation by ice. Of the ships locked in the Baltic all but seven had already escaped. Efforts were now made to bring these seven away; but they were unsuccessful. In April, when the Germans landed in Finland, three of the steamers were sunk to prevent their falling into the enemy's hands; the other four were seized by the Bolsheviks.

As between Russia and the Allies the situation was now somewhat complicated. The Allies had not recognised the Bolshevik Government, and were still hopeful of a counter-revolutionary movement. On the other hand, they were not formally at war with Russia, nor even with the Bolsheviks themselves; nor was Bolshevik Russia in alliance with the Central Powers. The German penetration into Russia had, however, proceeded so far, and German influence had become so strong, that it was impossible to feel any assurance that material which fell into Russian hands would not ultimately reach the enemy. It was, moreover, vitally important to prevent the Germans from forming, at Archangel and Murmansk, submarine bases outside the Northern Barrage. For these reasons the Allies decided on active measures to anticipate such contingencies. On April 5th British and Japanese marines landed at Vladivostok to protect the stores at that port from seizure, and under their protection a local provisional government was subsequently formed. It had been impossible to cling to Archangel, which was nearer to the centre of Bolshevik Power; but there were counter-revolutionary elements at that port and on the Murman Coast which the Allies hoped to use for the capture of the city and its vast accumulations of war material. On

May 24th General Poole arrived at Pechenga to organise the local forces. These forces were to be stiffened by Allied troops, and on June 23rd the British contingent of those troops arrived.[1]

The development of this North Russian Expeditionary Force was some slight set-off to the tonnage set free from Russian supply. The expedition, however, was on a small scale, and its transport and supply involved no heavy strain on shipping. Most of the troops were taken out by British steamers on American trooping service, as part of a triangular voyage, United States–United Kingdom–White Sea–United States; but the number of voyages required was small.[2] Moreover, the importing power of the ships was not wholly lost, as they brought, on their homeward voyages during 1918, nearly 35,000 tons of flax, two-thirds of which was received by the United Kingdom, together with a little timber and general cargo.

Meanwhile it had been necessary to decide as to the *status* of Russian ships. The owners of these were opposed to the Bolshevik revolution, and technically they were still Allied vessels. On the other hand, many of the crews were believed to be infected with Bolshevik doctrines, and it was impossible to rely on their services. The British Government accordingly decided to requisition the ships on terms arranged with the Russian Committee in London, which continued to function, and to run them under the British flag. In all, about fifty steamers were ultimately requisitioned. These included, not only colliers hitherto employed in the White Sea service, but ships on Allied charter, and more than a dozen good-sized liners of the Russian Volunteer Fleet and the Russian East Asiatic Company, engaged in the Pacific trade. The aggregate tonnage amounted to about 150,000 gross, and included the bulk of the available Russian shipping, outside the Baltic and Black Sea. A few ships with trustworthy crews continued, however, to run under the Russian flag between Japan and Vladivostok, and on various Allied services. Of the ships requisitioned, the

---

[1] There is a good analysis of the motives prompting the North Russian Expedition in a lecture on "The Dvina Campaign," by Captain F. Altham, C.B., R.N., in the *Journal of the Royal United Service Institution*, vol. lxvii, No. 470, May 1923.

[2] From June 1918 to October 1919, when the last troops were withdrawn, only forty-two outward voyages were made.

majority had been placed under British management in 1917; for the remainder Ship Management Branch appointed managers.[1]

Thus, by mid-summer of 1918, the effects of the Russian defection could, to a considerable extent, be discounted. The British tonnage heretofore employed in Russian supply was available for other services; Russian shipping outside the Baltic and Black Sea was brought completely under British and Allied control. The exploitation of the Ukraine had permitted the Central Powers to obtain food supplies just sufficient to enable them to struggle on until the harvest, and a certain amount of military and other stores was, no doubt, obtained by the enemy from the occupied territories; but against this was to be set the effect of the Norwegian and Swedish Agreements in closing avenues of supply hitherto open. Steps were being taken to secure the great accumulations of munitions and stores at Archangel and Vladivostok. Most important of all, it was now clear that the relief to the food situation in Germany and Austria was very limited, and that there was little prospect of any substantial supplies coming forward from the Ukraine in 1918–19. In these circumstances the enemy peoples could look forward to no real alleviation of their sufferings. The utmost for which they could hope was to hold out, and the length of time for which they could be induced to hold out was likely to depend mainly on the military situation. That situation had changed greatly in their favour as a result of the Russian collapse, but by May the momentum of the advance had spent itself, and June saw the Allies holding firm on their new line. During that month the Italians retrieved on the Piave the disaster of Caporetto, and in July an Allied counter-offensive in France drove the Germans back across the Marne. Meanwhile the submarines, which had already failed to fulfil their promise to bring Great Britain to her knees through starvation, had failed equally to interrupt the steady flow of American troops across the Atlantic, and it became more and more obvious that unless another great and successful effort

[1] Special difficulties arose with regard to Finnish ships. Finland being anti-Bolshevik, the owners claimed to be treated as neutrals, but the Finns were obliged to accept German assistance in clearing out the " Reds," and the position became somewhat anomalous. Eventually, terms were arranged, less favourable than neutral rates, but higher than the ordinary requisition terms.

could be made in 1918, the Central Powers were likely to sink into a permanent military inferiority. In such circumstances it was very doubtful whether their peoples would endure much longer the privations of the past two years.

CHAPTER XXIII

TROOPING AND IMPORTS
JULY—AUGUST 1918

BOTH at sea and on land the early summer of 1918 was the final turning point in the long struggle. The year had opened badly for the Allies. The defection of Russia had not only opened a serious gap in the cordon drawn around the Central Powers, but had permitted the enemy to mass their forces for an advance which threatened, in April, to carry the German flag to Paris on the one hand, to Calais and the Channel coast on the other. At the same time the new inshore tactics of the submarines had met with a measure of success which discounted, to no small extent, the protection afforded to Allied shipping by the system of ocean convoys. The flow of supplies had been seriously threatened at the very moment when the demand for carrying power was enormously increased by the reactions of military developments.

For some two months the tension had been acute; but by mid-summer it was considerably relaxed. On both the Western and the Southern front the enemy's hope of an immediate, decisive military victory had waned. Once more they were thrown back on the prospect of a war of exhaustion, in which it was now clear that the supplies to be obtained from Russia and the Ukraine would give them little assistance. Meanwhile the military strength of the Allies was growing steadily, through the transport to Europe of the American armies; the new tactics of the submarines had been successfully countered; and the effective carrying power of the available shipping had been greatly increased.

It was the increase in American trooping, above all else, which gave immediate importance to the improvement in turn-round at both British and American ports. Quick turn-round was essential not only to the rapid building up of a great American army in France, but to the ability of the Allies to maintain the stream of essential supplies, despite the allocation of so much space in British liners to the carriage of troops, and the absorption of all surplus American tonnage in the carriage of military stores.

Further, this increase in the annual carrying power of the ships coincided, happily, with the establishment of a definite ascendancy on the part of the defence over the attack. Greatly as the adoption of convoy had reduced the percentage of risk, the monthly wastage had long continued to exceed appreciably the replacement of shipping, and though the upward curve of destruction had been checked, there was still a danger that the cumulative deficit might reduce the available carrying power below the essential minimum, before an equilibrium between losses and replacements was attained.

This was no imaginary peril, for though the Germans had lost heavily in material during 1917, the losses had been made good by an intensified programme of new construction. At the beginning of 1918 they had more " front boats " in commission than in the submarines' " banner month," April 1917, and the number under construction was very large, even old battleships and cruisers of the High Seas Fleet having been broken up to supply steel.[1] Moreover, the newer types included boats capable of more distant and more prolonged cruises than the old.

Even so, the development of the defence had outstripped the attack. The establishment of the Rio convoys, and the reorganisation of the Atlantic system, brought up the average number of ships convoyed homewards, on ocean voyages, from about 150 every eight days in February and March to about 180 in June and July,[2] and there was now no considerable proportion either of the homeward or the outward traffic for which protection was not provided. The increased radius of action of the newer submarines had been met by the establishment of the Rio convoys for the South Atlantic trade,[3] and

[1] Capt. L. Perseus, *How Tirpitz Ruined the German Fleet*, translated in *Journal of the Royal United Services Institution*, August 1919.

[2] These figures include the North and South Atlantic, Mediterranean Through, and Gibraltar Convoys, and in June and July the American Store Convoy to Bay ports.

[3] The fast Rio Convoy was discontinued on the withdrawal of the two submarine cruisers sent out to attack the Plate trade; but the slower convoy was continued until the bulk of the Argentine wheat had been shipped. The last Rio convoy sailed on August 5th.

by moving farther west the rendezvous for the North Atlantic homeward convoys with their destroyer escort, and the point of dispersal for the outward trade. The inshore tactics of the smaller craft had been countered by the new escort arrangements in the Irish Sea, and by the blocking of Zeebrugge and Ostend. The development of the local convoy system in the Mediterranean closed the last serious gap in the defensive system. Moreover, the defence had now acquired a definite moral superiority. It was far more difficult for the Germans to replace the crews of the earlier submarines than to make good the loss of the submarines themselves. A large proportion of the crews lost during 1917 were highly trained and experienced men, with the prestige of successful cruises behind them. Their successors were inferior both in training and in morale, and were weighed down by the consciousness that, while the risks of the service continually increased, the probability of decisive results as steadily receded.

The result of this growing moral and material ascendency on the part of the defence was clearly to be seen in the return of losses. Against ships sailing in organised convoy the submarine was comparatively impotent, especially now that, with better organisation and greater experience in station-keeping, few vessels were exposed to attack through parting with their escort. The slower North Atlantic convoys still continued to suffer occasional losses; but the fast convoys from New York and Halifax homewards, from Liverpool and Southend outwards, were practically immune from loss, and no ship from Sierra Leone or Dakar had been sunk since January. The American trooping convoys to France direct were equally successful.

One new danger area had, indeed, been revealed at the beginning of June, when news was received that a submarine was operating off the American coast. So early as the end of April this vessel, U 151, was known to have left Germany for a long cruise, and during May reliable information was received as to her destination; but it was not until May 25th that she made her first prize in American waters, after laying mines off the entrance to Delaware Bay. In the course of a month's active cruise, she destroyed about a score of vessels, mostly American coasters and sailing craft; but though the operations gave rise to extravagant hopes in Germany, they had no effect either on the flow of trade or on the embarkation of American troops. It was impossible for the Germans to develop a really effective attack in American waters without unduly weakening their forces in the European approaches, and although it became known before the end of June that another submarine was on the way out, the American Admiralty refused to allow their attention to be diverted from their task of co-operation with the British Navy in ensuring the safety of the convoys through the permanent danger areas.[1]

In Home Waters the blocking of Zeebrugge and Ostend was followed, from May onwards, by a great reduction in the number of casualties in the English Channel. By June a similar decrease of submarine activity was visible in the Irish Sea and Bristol Channel. In the North Sea, the Methil Convoy had proved splendidly successful in reducing losses on the track to Norwegian ports; but during June a good many ships were sunk on the East Coast of Great Britain. Here the coastal traffic, ships dispersing from or on their way to join the Scandinavian Convoy, and vessels in the ocean trades, bound to or from the North-Eastern ports, were equally exposed to attack. A new system of East Coast convoys had recently been instituted for their protection; but the ships were mostly old and slow, and the ratio of loss was rather higher, at first, than in the majority of trades.

Apart from the losses in American Waters and on the East Coast, there was little cause for anything but congratulation. The approach areas had long been comparatively immune, and there were few casualties during 1918 in the Bay of Biscay or off the Spanish coast. This was important, as there was a tendency for a larger proportion of the ore supplies to be drawn from the North of Spain and less from the Mediterranean ports. Most of the Italian steamers in the coal and ore trade had been withdrawn from that to the cereal traffic, and their place had been taken by French ships which took out coal to Bay ports and returned with ore from Northern Spain.

To the Mediterranean coal and ore traffic, the improved system of local convoys had brought a great reduction of the risk. On the track between Gibraltar and Genoa, the rate of loss fell from an average of 5·4 steamers a month

[1] Admiral Sims, *The Victory at Sea*, Chapter X.

for the three months ending April 30th, to 1·6 for the three months ending July 31st. Taking the Spanish and Mediterranean ore trade as a whole, the percentage of cargoes lost at sea through war risks, or not shipped through sinking of the steamer on her outward voyage, was only 5 per cent. during the first six months of 1918, as against 8½ per cent. for the previous half-year.

The success of the measures taken to meet the submarine attack was the more gratifying as there was now no other serious menace to the transport of supplies. Since the return of the WOLF, the outer seas had been clear of surface raiders, and the mine peril in Home Waters was now inconsiderable. During the greater part of 1917 losses due to mines, though insignificant in comparison with the havoc that the submarines had wrought by more direct methods, had been heavier than in any previous period; but the number of craft available for minesweeping had increased, the methods of sweeping were improved, and the fitting of " Otter " and " Paravane " gear to both warships and merchantmen had assisted, to some extent, in reducing the danger. By the spring of 1918 the average monthly losses from this cause had greatly diminished, and the blocking of Zeebrugge and Ostend put an end to the activities of the submarine mine layers based on those ports. From April onwards, the casualties due to mines were very few.

Both in June and July the total destruction of British and foreign tonnage, in all areas, was less than in any previous month since the outbreak of unrestricted submarine warfare. For the three months ending July 31st the combined figures averaged 271,000 tons a month, 43,000 tons less than in the preceding quarter, and less by 60 per cent. than the average losses suffered during the first three months of unrestricted sinkings.

A mere reduction of the rate of loss, however, was not, as we have seen, a sufficient assurance against disaster. The most significant feature of the situation was that the progress of replacement had at last begun to keep pace with the wastage.

The execution of the shipbuilding programme was, it is true, hampered by all the old difficulties and, especially, by the shortage of steel and labour, which had been accentuated by the effects of the German spring offensive. The immense expenditure and loss of munitions and war material during March and April naturally increased the demands of the Ministry of Munitions which, in the circumstances, it was necessary to satisfy even at the expense of shipbuilding. The heavy losses of personnel and the necessity of filling the depleted ranks complicated all the arrangements for the supply of labour to the yards and led to a situation in which, at one and the same time, skilled workers were being released from the Army in compliance with the arrangements previously made, other workers were being withdrawn from the yards for military service under the revised schedule of protected occupations, and the Minister of National Service was called upon to make good such withdrawals from the depleted pool of general labour. Meanwhile, as had been foretold by the shipbuilders in October 1917, trouble had arisen with the shipbuilding Unions as to the use of prisoner-of-war and military labour in the National Yards, and in May 1918 the whole scheme of employing such labour was finally abandoned.

It is doubtful, indeed, whether, in the existing shortage of labour, sufficient skilled workers could, in any event, have been found to leaven a great mass of prisoner-of-war labour in the National Yards, without interfering unduly with the private establishments, and as the need for immediate delivery of tonnage was urgent, and the National Yards still required a great expenditure of money and labour before they could begin operations on a large scale, it would have been very doubtful policy to sacrifice, in their interests, the output of yards capable of giving prompt delivery. Such, at any rate, was the view of Lord Pirrie, who, on his advent to power, returned to a strict adherence to the priority promised to the private yards in respect of labour and material, and diverted to them a quantity of steel plates and sections previously allocated to the National Yards. At the same time he pressed on, so far as the supply of labour permitted, the policy of subsidised extensions, and hastened the release from Admiralty work of yards allocated to merchant shipbuilding. He was successful, too, in persuading the shipbuilding Unions to accept the general use of pneumatic riveting, which did much to provide compensation for the shortage of skilled workers.

Serious as were the obstacles to be overcome, and despite a considerable increase in the amount of repair work to be done, the output of the British shipyards during the spring and summer of 1918 rose well above the level of the previous year. This improvement was due, in part, to a change of policy with regard to the completion of ships already under construction when the standard programme was introduced. Hitherto the completion of many steamers building on private account had been postponed, even when they were in an advanced stage of construction, in order to concentrate the available labour on the building of standard ships. Among such vessels were, however, some eminently suitable for trooping, and in March it was decided to resume work on ships approaching completion, with the object of bringing them into service as rapidly as possible. In that month nine steamers were completed which had been under construction for eighteen months or over. In May nine ships which had been building for two years or more were brought into service, including two large liners laid down before the outbreak of war.

Ships laid down under the standard programme, too, were now coming on service in greater numbers. From May onwards, standard freighters and oilers were delivered at the rate of nearly a score a month, from British yards alone. In the same month, regular deliveries began under the Canadian steel programme, and in July the first wooden steamers were delivered from Canadian yards. Both steel and wood construction in Canada were now sufficiently advanced to ensure a small but steady stream of new tonnage, to supplement the efforts of the British builders.

From February to July inclusive, the ships completed monthly in British yards averaged over 140,000 tons gross, and the total gains, from all sources, very nearly balanced the losses from war and other causes.

This equilibrium between the losses and gains of British tonnage was due, in part, to the requisitioning of Dutch and Russian steamers, some of which had previously been employed in British or Allied interests; but there was, from May onwards, an actual net monthly addition to the world's tonnage, due mainly to the progress of the American shipbuilding programme. Completions under that programme, as under the British, fell considerably short of the original estimates, and the tonnage put into service by the United States during the first half of 1918 was little greater than the output of the British yards. In combination with that output, and with Japanese shipbuilding, it was sufficient, however, to provide a clear monthly surplus over the losses of ships under all flags.

As there was good reason to hope both for a further acceleration of output and a further diminution in the rate of loss, the outlook for the future was promising; but so far as the European Allies were concerned, the immediate position was still unsatisfactory. From Japan they could hope for no assistance. In March 1918 the United States Shipping Board had concluded an agreement with the Japanese Government, by which 150,000 tons dead-weight was rendered available for war-zone trade; but this, together with all other new tonnage built or acquired by the United States, was absorbed by the American military programme. Tonnage under the British, French, and Italian flags on July 31st was less by some 2 or $2\frac{1}{2}$ per cent. than at the beginning of the year, and even if replacements should, in the future, keep pace with losses, it must be a long time before they made good, to any appreciable extent, the destruction of tonnage during 1917. There was thus no hope that the shipping available for the cereal year 1918–19 would be equal to that available during the past twelve months.

Further, the proportion of ships off service for repairs had increased rather than diminished since the adoption of the convoy system. The effect of that system in reducing the number of ships hit by shell or torpedo, great as it was, was not so great as its effect in diminishing the number of ships actually sunk. For this there were two reasons. In the first place, submarines attacking a convoy were obliged to open fire at long range, with less certainty of hitting a vital spot; nor could they board a damaged vessel to finish her off by bombs. Moreover, a ship damaged while in convoy had consorts at hand to help in the work of salvage or to offer a tow, and special salvage tugs were despatched by the Admiralty to meet each homeward-bound convoy and bring in any injured vessels that could be kept afloat. In the second place, the convoy system, as we have seen, had driven the submarines to operate more and more inshore, where a damaged ship had a better chance of rescue, of making port under her own steam, or in the last resort, of running ashore, with

TONNAGE STILL INADEQUATE

the hope of subsequent salvage, than a ship attacked far out at sea.

Thus, while the tonnage sunk was now considerably less than one-half what it was before the introduction of convoy, the tonnage damaged by enemy action remained at about the same figure—an average of 100,000 tons a month.[1] The carrying power of damaged ships was not, indeed, permanently lost, but the average time during which ships were off service was about five months, a serious matter at the crisis of a war. Marine casualties, too, were on the increase, as a result of convoy conditions, sailing without lights, and postponement of repairs, and altogether over 8 per cent. of British steam tonnage was, in July 1918, undergoing repairs of a serious nature. For French and Italian shipping the proportion was still higher, as repairs were less rapidly executed, and for the three European Allies as a whole, it amounted to nearly $9\frac{1}{2}$ per cent.

It must be remembered, too, that the importing power of the available tonnage was reduced by the allocation of space on British liners to American trooping, and so far as ordinary imports were concerned, by the carriage of oil in double bottoms. The Allied Maritime Transport Council, at their second session, had urged strongly that an effort should be made to dispense with this use of double bottoms for oil-fuel, which now shut out about 50,000 tons of other imports monthly; but the United States were unable to spare any considerable amount of additional tanker tonnage for the service of the European Allies, and the Petroleum Conference reported that such savings as could be effected by rearrangement of routeing, would not in any way compensate for the relinquishment of the practice. As regards American trooping, the rate of embarkation for France and the United Kingdom had gone up by May to 250,000 and by July to 300,000 a month. In addition to the American tonnage employed,

[1] STEAMERS OF 500 TONS GROSS AND UP DAMAGED BY ENEMY ACTION
(In 1,000 tons gross)

Three months ended	British	Foreign	Total
April 1917	272	49	321
July 1917	242	55	297
October 1917	178	92	270
January 1918	233	57	290
April 1918	339	39	378
July 1918	212	41	253
October 1918	74	54	129

and the six Italian liners transferred earlier in the year, arrangements had now been made for a number of big French passenger steamers to be put into the service; yet the largest share of the work fell on British shipping, which carried more than half the troops embarked in May and June, and nearly two-thirds of those embarked in July. Although the liners employed carried goods as well as troops, it was estimated that their cargo capacity was reduced by 40 per cent., or $2\frac{1}{10}$ dead-weight tons per man, and for 519,000 American troops carried in British ships during the four months April to July inclusive, 1,000,000 tons of imports were shut out.

The enormous importance of the improvements in convoy organisation and turn-round achieved during the early months of 1918 can thus be seen. But for the increase in annual carrying power thus attained, it must have been absolutely impossible for British shipping to comply at once with the demands of France and Italy for additional assistance, and with the new demands imposed by the military situation. Had the average length of the round voyage remained what it was in the autumn of 1917, it must have been impossible, to whatever extent losses were reduced, to frame adequate import programmes for the cereal year 1918–19. Even as it was, the task was full of difficulty.

Since the April meeting of the Allied Maritime Transport Council considerable progress had been made with the formation of the Inter-Allied authorities to whom it had been decided to entrust the analysis and revision of import requirements. In addition to the previously existing Wheat Executive, Meat and Fats Executive, Nitrate Executive, and Petroleum Conference, Programme Committees were now formed, or in course of formation for Sugar; Oils and Oil-seeds; Hides, Leather, Skins, and Tanning Materials; Cotton and Cotton Textiles; Wool and Wool Products; Flax, Hemp, and Jute, and manufactures thereof; Coal and Coke; Paper; Tobacco and Matches; Horses and Mules; and Mechanical Transport. A Food Council, to co-ordinate the work of the Executives or Committees dealing with cereals, meat and fats, sugar, and oil-seeds, was formed by the Food Controllers of the Allies in July, and a Munitions Council was in course of formation, to which it was proposed to transfer the Mechanical Transport Committee, together with Committees to be formed for aircraft, chemicals, explosives, non-ferrous metals, and steel.

These bodies represented, as yet, only the European Allies. The United States Government was still considering the question of formal adherence to the scheme; but pending a decision, arrangements were made for American representatives to be informally associated with the various Executives and Committees, to facilitate co-operation. The majority of the Programme Committees, however, were occupied mainly with arranging the details of their procedure, and had been able to do little towards framing programmes for 1918–19.

In the meantime the more urgent of the Allies' requirements under the old programmes had been met with considerable success. In particular, the cereal position in France and Italy had been secured until the coming harvest. To effect this it had been necessary not only to economise space to the utmost by importing wheat, so far as possible in the form of flour,[1] but to restrict consumption in Great Britain, by dilution of the loaf, a higher percentage of extraction, increased import of concentrated farinaceous preparations, further restrictions on brewing, and economy in feeding-stuffs through slaughtering of cattle. In these ways, British imports of cereals for the six months February to July inclusive, were reduced by 1,700,000 tons, or nearly 33 per cent. on the figures for 1917. Thanks to this saving, it had been possible to direct to France and Italy since the beginning of April supplementary cereal cargoes amounting to 986,000 tons, and diversions on a still larger scale were being arranged for the following months.

As important as the supply of food was the supply of fuel. The disorganisation of the French railways by the German advance, and the consequent necessity of diverting an increasing proportion of the Italian supplies to the long-sea route, had gravely increased the strain on tonnage of the programme adopted during the spring; but British exports to Italy had now been raised to an average of nearly 400,000 tons a month, and despite the deficit in French coal, the total guaranteed supply of 600,000 tons

[1] For the six months February to July 1917, the United Kingdom imported wheat and wheat flour respectively in the proportion of approximately 100 to 9; during the same period of 1918 the bulk of the imports from North America was taken in the form of flour, and the total imports of flour were nearly equal to those of wheat,

a month was very nearly maintained. British shipments to France, on the other hand, fell short by about 300,000 tons a month of the agreed programme (1,740,000 tons). The difficulty here was not so much shortage of tonnage as diminished output in Great Britain, and the restricted capacity of the French ports.[1] It was, indeed, the capacity of the French ports which was the real limiting factor, and whatever tonnage might be allocated to the service, there was little hope of increasing the monthly export, owing to the inability of France to take effective delivery of a larger amount.

In addition to the cereal and fuel programmes, and the general services normally rendered to the Allies by British shipping, it had been necessary, since the last meeting of the Council, for the Allied Maritime Transport Executive to deal with a number of new demands. The Italian Government, as we have seen, had asked for the creation of a special strategic reserve of coal, outside the ordinary monthly programme. The military importance of such a reserve could not be disputed, and heavy as was the strain of the regular monthly shipments, the British Government agreed, in June, to provide an additional 150,000 tons for this purpose. By the end of the following month shipment of the greater part had already been effected or arranged.

Closely connected with the fuel problem was the French demand for the shipment of rolling-stock from the United States; for it was the shortage of rolling-stock in France which formed one of the main difficulties in the execution of the Italian coal programme. The allocation of French wagons to the British armies had been made good from Great Britain during 1917; but France was now obliged to find wagons for the use of the American as well as the British forces,[2] and it was of the utmost importance that she should be able to bring over large numbers of wagons and locomotives which had been purchased in America, but which she was unable to lift with the tonnage already under her control. This request, too, was met by the allocation of British tonnage, and by July 15th about 33,000 tons of rolling-stock and war material had been shipped.

---

[1] The effects of recruiting on output were accentuated in June by a short strike in the South Wales coalfield.

[2] So early as March 11,000 French wagons had been allocated to the American armies.

Other demands, met from British tonnage during the spring and early summer of 1918, included the diversion to France of about 47,000 tons of nitrates, the diversion to both France and Italy of several heavy cargoes of sugar, and the shipment of 70,000 tons of munitions from the United Kingdom to Italy. In view of these constant heavy calls, and of the difficulty of meeting, at short notice, emergency demands for cereal diversions to make good the French and Italian programmes, the Transport Executive decided in July to institute new regular services, under the Liner Requisition Scheme, between North America and French and Italian ports.[1] Such services could only be created by cutting down the liner tonnage in the trade of the United Kingdom itself, but even this was preferable to the dislocation caused by sudden demands which could often be met only by the diversion of liners carrying mixed cargoes.

A further sacrifice agreed to by the British representatives on the Executive, was the permission for withdrawal from the cereal programme to other Italian services of about 75,000 tons dead-weight of Italian shipping, a decision which increased proportionately the responsibility of Great Britain for making good the cereal deficit. Indeed, the only substantial demand for British assistance refused during the early summer of 1918, was an application by France for the shipment of 150,000 tons of oil-seeds, held over for consideration by the Programme Committee.

Heavy as was the burden already laid upon Great Britain, it was to Great Britain alone that the European Allies could look for the satisfaction of any further increase in their requirements ; for not only was all French and Italian tonnage already fully employed, but the bulk of the neutral tonnage under Allied control was already employed in their interests. The one substantial recent increase to such tonnage was that obtained under the Swedish agreement. The effect of this agreement was clearly seen in the fixtures of ships for the coal and ore traffic ; but it will be remembered that the use of one-half the tonnage obtained was hampered by a condition that it should not be employed in war-zone trade. The first call on such tonnage was accordingly given by the Allied Maritime Transport Executive to the Commission for Belgian Relief, whose

[1] About 66,000 tons dead-weight was allocated to France for August loading, and 52,000 tons to Italy.

requirements it went far to satisfy. Pending the actual fixture of Swedish ships, the assistance necessary to make good the deficit in the relief programme was provided in equal shares by the United States and Great Britain.

How deeply British shipping, in July 1918, was pledged to the service of the Allies will appear from a comparison of the proportions in which the various Powers contributed to, and drew from, the tonnage pool. The total steam shipping under the British, French, and Italian flags on July 31st amounted, exclusive of ships repairing or unemployed, to about 21,600,000 tons dead-weight, of which 27 per cent. was on naval or military service, and 13 per cent. was employed in the coasting and colonial trade, or in the import service of other Allies, including the United States, or neutrals.[1] In view of the increased American trooping programme, no reduction could be expected in the proportion on naval and military service, and the colonial trades had already been drastically combed, both by the French and British authorities.[2]

There remained available for employment in the import services of the three countries just under 13,000,000 tons dead-weight; but to this must be added 2,500,000 tons of shipping under other flags. The total tonnage available for fulfilment of the import programmes of the three countries was thus 15,500,000 tons. Of this 72 per cent. was British, 11 per cent. was French or Italian, and the remainder was about equally divided between neutral tonnage and tonnage contributed by the United States, or by other Allies, such as Japan, Belgium, Portugal, or Brazil.

Very different were the proportions in which the tonnage was allocated. Of the whole 15,500,000 tons, only 57 per cent. was in the import service of the United Kingdom, who contributed nearly three-quarters of the pool; 43 per cent. was in the service of France and Italy, who contributed less than one-eighth. Although 27 per cent. of British tonnage was on naval or military service, very little of the shipping provided by the United States and the minor Allies, or procured from neutrals, was claimed by Great Britain, and no less than 92 per cent. of the tonnage in the import service of the United Kingdom was

---

[1] Steamers of 500 tons gross or over, including tankers. Allowance made in estimating tonnage on military service for proportion of space sacrificed to American trooping in British liners.

[2] French shipping in colonial and inter-colonial service had been reduced from 92 steamers before the war, to 27.

under the British flag. On the other hand, British shipping provided 47 per cent. of the tonnage in French and Italian service, or nearly twice as much as was provided by French and Italian shipping.[1]

Thanks to the increase in the annual carrying power of the ships, Great Britain had been able to contribute thus largely to the supply of her Allies without making those wholesale reductions in the British import programme which had been contemplated towards the end of 1917, but there was clearly little margin left for further diversions. Moreover, the Allied Military Authorities were now pressing for the transport to Europe of every man that America could send, and a point would shortly be reached at which the supply requirements of the American troops in France would exceed the capacity of the available American tonnage. Hitherto, while British shipping had carried a large proportion of the troops, the shipment of military stores and supplies had been carried out entirely in tonnage owned or controlled by the United States; but it was now evident that the ultimate size of the American Army in France would depend not only on the provision of transport, but on the amount of tonnage which could be released from the import services of the European Allies for supply purposes.

It was the food, and above all the cereal requirements of the Allies which formed at once the largest and the most important factor in the import programmes, so far at any rate as the ocean trades were concerned, and on July 30th the Allied Maritime Transport Council wrote to the Food Council, emphasising the gravity of the position. In this letter the Transport Council pointed out that for each American soldier landed, about five tons of stores had to

[1] TONNAGE AVAILABLE FOR IMPORT SERVICES OF THE UNITED KINGDOM, FRANCE, AND ITALY

—	Total available.		In import service of United Kingdom.		In import service of France and Italy.	
	1,000 tons dead-weight.	%	1,000 tons dead-weight.	%	1,000 tons dead-weight.	%
British	11,198	72·2	8,060	91·5	3,138	46·8
French and Italian	1,776	11·4	86	0·9	1,690	25·2
American	341	2·2	123	1·4	218	3·3
Other Allies	985	6·4	270	3·1	715	10·7
Neutral	1,210	7·8	270	3·1	940	14·0
	15,510	100·0	8,809	100·0	6,701	100·0

be transported during the year, so that for every 5,000 tons saved on the imports programmes, 1,000 additional American troops could be maintained in France. They urged, therefore, that no consideration either of finance or of civilian comfort should be allowed to stand in the way of reducing the food programme to the lowest adequate level, drawing supplies from the nearest source, and obtaining them in the most concentrated form. As a basis, they suggested that the maximum limit of importation should be regulated by the record of total consumption during the last cereal year, so that any improvement of home production would enable the import programme to be reduced and tonnage to be released.

The importance of these suggestions lay in the fact that the harvest reports from all the three principal European Allies as well as from North America, the nearest source of supply, indicated the prospect of heavier crops than in 1917, and the Transport Council hoped to obtain, through a substantial reduction of cereal imports, especially from the more distant sources, additional tonnage for the military and munitions programmes.

To this proposition the Food Council were unable to agree. In their view, the restriction of imports on the basis of the previous year's consumption, would seriously endanger the morale of the Allied peoples, and they put forward as an alternative the employment for each nation of the same ship-ton-mileage as during the preceding year.

The actual food import programmes, as finally presented, amounted to 27,000,000 tons, or about 4,400,000 tons above the actual imports for 1917. Of this increase, military oats accounted for nearly 1,200,000 tons, and the balance was about equally divided between the requirements of the three countries. In forwarding this programme, the Food Council stated that they had not criticised the demand for military oats; but they considered the figures for breadstuff cereals (amounting to about 12,000,000 tons) to represent the minimum requirements which would enable the reserve stocks in the United Kingdom to be maintained, and adequate provision to be made for building up stocks in France and Italy. They stated further that these figures represented a very considerable reduction of the original British demand.

In view of the possibility that tonnage for the full programme might not be procurable, the Food Council had prepared a priority programme mounting to 18,500,000 tons. Within the agreed priority totals, each country was to be entitled to call on the tonnage immediately available for carriage of such commodities as it considered most urgent, subject to an equitable division of available supplies. The balance of the programme, 4,890,000 tons, exclusive of military oats, was to be carried out for each country in proportion to its claim on such further shipping as could be allocated.

Such was the position with regard to the food programme, when the Allied Maritime Transport Council met in London, on August 29th, for its third session. The net result was that, while the total shipping available, after allowing for all losses and gains, and for all additional special commitments, was less by about 2,000,000 tons dead-weight than at the beginning of the cereal year 1917–18, the Food Council were asking for increased imports to the extent of 3,200,000 tons, or 4,400,000, including military oats. The programmes for munitions and raw materials were not yet completed; but sufficient work had already been done by the Programme Committees to indicate that those programmes were not likely, in the aggregate, to be smaller than in the previous year.

There was thus already a deficit to be dealt with, apart from any other new requirements, and new requirements were not lacking to add to the difficulty of the situation. An urgent request was put forward by Italy for 74,000 tons of pig-iron from the United States, and 105,000 tons of coke and anthracite from Great Britain, for use in the munitions industries, and this request was backed by the Munitions Council. France required additional assistance in the carriage of steel and raw material. The Swiss Government represented that permission to charter neutral vessels had become worthless owing to the Allied control of neutral tonnage, and that, in all fairness, the Transport Council should accept direct responsibility for the allocation of tonnage to carry Switzerland's minimum requirements. Most important of all, the American Government were now putting forward a direct request for assistance in maintaining military supplies.

Of the total tonnage under the American flag, amounting on July 31st to about 6,000,000 tons dead-weight,[1] 89 per cent. was already in naval or military employment,

[1] Exclusive of ships repairing, etc.

and 5 per cent. in the service of the European Allies. The remainder was mostly employed in the import, coasting, and colonial trade of the United States; and the American Government, who had already taken steps to restrict imports,[1] could hold out no hopes of sufficient further tonnage being diverted to fulfil the requirements of the American armies. The military programme, as now approved by the President, allowed for eighty American divisions in France by June 30th, 1919, but this programme was subject to the allocation of British shipping to make good the deficit in army supplies. The extent of the assistance required had not yet been definitely formulated; but it was understood to amount to some 1,200,000 deadweight tons, falling away gradually as the ships under construction in the United States became available, to 200,000 tons in February 1919, after which American tonnage would be sufficient for the execution of the whole programme.

In these circumstances it was obvious that any decisions arrived at, with regard to the allocation of tonnage for the coming year, must necessarily be of a provisional character, subject to revision when the munitions and raw materials programmes were available, and the full extent of the American demand was known. The Council accordingly decided to proceed with the execution of the foodstuffs programme on the provisional basis of the priority figures, leaving a final decision until the tonnage situation had been more definitely ascertained. With regard to all other imports for civilian use, they decided that the actual total consumption of the previous year should be adopted as the maximum limit of the 1918–19 programmes, subject to adjustments in respect of any commodities of which the stocks in any of the Allied countries had been exhausted. This decision was communicated to the Programme Committees for their guidance.

With regard to the other special demands put forward, the Council decided to accept responsibility for the essential requirements of Switzerland, subject to a satisfactory settlement of any negotiations on other points with the Swiss Government, and to refer to the Executive the question of the new French and Italian demands.

[1] American food imports were reduced from 555,000 metric tons a month for 1917, to 510,000 tons a month for the ten months ending April 30th, 1918.

CHAPTER XXIV

MUNITIONS TAKE PRECEDENCE OF FOOD
AUGUST—SEPTEMBER 1918

DESPITE all that had been accomplished, the situation at the opening of the fifth year of war was full of anxiety for the Allies. Although shipping services had been organised with a single eye to the development of importing power and a total disregard of financial and commercial considerations, the import programmes still exceeded the capacity of the available tonnage, and over all future arrangements hung the shadow of the American demand for assistance in the carriage of military stores.

The gravity of this demand can best be appreciated by recalling the fact that, at the end of 1917, the European Allies had regarded the allocation of a large block of American tonnage to their service, as the only means by which their supplies could be assured. At an early date it had been necessary to abandon all hope of such assistance, and by the summer of 1918 the United States had become a debit rather than a credit item in the tonnage balance sheet ; for the services of such American ships as carried imports to Allied ports were far outweighed by the absorption of a large block of neutral tonnage on which the Allies had confidently reckoned, and the allocation to American trooping of liner space equivalent, in July and August, to the shutting out of some 400,000 tons of imports a month. Thanks to economies in the employment of British and Allied shipping, and to the great improvement in turn-round, this strain had been met without disaster ; but there was no margin in hand, and to divert anything like 1,200,000 tons dead-weight from the Allied import services must inevitably cause a severe, immediate crisis in respect of food or munitions supplies.

Fortunately, the original estimate of the assistance required proved to be exaggerated. There was no question, however, that the fulfilment of the American military programme depended upon the ability of the Allies to supplement, to some extent, the tonnage under the American flag, and without waiting for the final decision of the Transport Council, the Transport Executive obtained the consent of the British Government to the allocation of 200,000 dead-weight tons to the American supply service, for September and October loading. Meanwhile the whole question of American army supplies was taken into consideration by the Associated Governments, and arrangements were made for the supply of artillery and ammunition from France and Great Britain, which would reduce, to some extent, the need for Transatlantic transport.

Even so, the additional burden to be shouldered was heavy enough, and it was more than ever essential to secure the maximum economy in the use of carrying power. For this purpose the machinery provided by the Transport Executive proved very valuable, as it enabled national problems and particular demands to be viewed in their proper perspective, in relation to the requirements of the Allies as a whole, and facilitated the placing of British experience at the service of France and Italy.

The Executive had already, during the summer of 1918, effected several improvements in the organisation of shipping. For example, the effective carrying power of French tonnage had been increased by the withdrawal from the Atlantic trade of eleven small steamers ill-suited to that employment, and their formation into a bunkering fleet for the larger Atlantic ships under the French flag, which were thus relieved, to a considerable extent, from the necessity of coming to Bristol Channel ports. Again, the attention of the Tonnage Committee was called to the fact that certain neutral steamers allocated to the Wheat Commission had left American ports for France light of their marks, and arrangements were accordingly made with the French Government to ensure that all such ships should load a proportion of steel or other heavy cargo, to ensure the full use of their maximum carrying-power.

The question of turn-round in port was not neglected. Apart from the perennial troubles at the French northern ports, the congestion at Genoa and other Italian ports, and at Port Said, was causing serious delays to shipping, and at the third meeting of the Council, Sir Joseph Maclay called attention to the consequent waste of carrying power. Signor Villa, one of the Italian representatives, was able to give an assurance that his Government had already taken steps to improve the situation, by the use of military labour, and by the appointment of Special Commissioners to supervise the working of the ports. As regards Port Said, the main trouble was the large amount of French and Italian transhipment cargo awaiting removal. For some time past the French liners in the Pacific trade had discharged their cargoes from the Far East at Port Said, and returned from that port to the Pacific, leaving goods destined for France to be brought on by local traders. These were unable to keep pace with the arrivals, and about 70,000 tons of transhipment cargo had accumulated. The French Government had already arranged that vessels in the Salonika service should proceed on a triangular route, France–Salonika–Port Said–France, for the purpose of dealing with these accumulations. They now sent vessels from other Mediterranean ports to assist in the work, and with the object of preventing a recurrence of the congestion, agreed that the liners should cease the practice of discharging at Port Said and come on to Marseilles direct. Steps were also taken to improve the supply of labour and appliances at Port Said itself.

In Great Britain the condition of the ports was fairly satisfactory. The Liverpool Convoy Committee had been remarkably successful in procuring regularity of sailings, and the new Convoy Committee appointed for London had got to work with excellent results. The railways were still subject to a heavy strain; but during August the Home Trade Transport Control Committee diverted 95,000 tons of cargo from rail to water, and these large diversions greatly facilitated the clearing of the ports. Nevertheless, there was still much congestion. Although the imports of wheat and flour during the first half of the year were considerably below the normal, and were, indeed, below the estimated consumption, there was an appreciable increase in the stocks held at the ports. Bacon, sugar, and wool were also taking up an unusual amount of storage space, in spite of a strong consumers' demand. The Port and Transit Executive Committee accordingly communicated with each of the Government Departments concerned, with a view to procuring either a diminution in the volume of imports, or more energetic efforts to store goods back from the ports, and in particular, to take full advantage of retailers' and domestic storage capacity.

The chief anxiety at this period arose, however, from the

increasing frequency of labour troubles. It will be remembered that the demand of the coal heavers at Liverpool for facilities for men engaged on night work to obtain liquid refreshment outside licensed hours, had been shelved, owing to the opposition of the Liquor Control Board. The feeling of the men on the matter was very strong, and during July the coal heavers refused to work any overtime, unless they were allowed to finish the half night at 9 instead of 10 o'clock. To this the employers were unable to agree, as the working hours of the port were fixed by Awards under the Munitions of War Acts. In these circumstances it appeared probable that all night work would be stopped. The Port and Transit Committee accordingly took up the question with the Liquor Control Board direct, as the supreme importance of turning round vessels in the fast convoys rendered a prompt settlement imperative. In view of the heavy nature of the work and the long hours—the men frequently worked from 6 to 10 p.m. and then from 11 p.m. to 5 a.m.—the Committee considered the request to be perfectly reasonable. On August 6th a conference was held at Liverpool between representatives of the Employers' Association, the Unions, the Shipowners, the Ship Repairers, the Liverpool Co-Ordination Committee, the Port and Transit Committee, the Port Branch of the Ministry of Shipping, the Ministry of Food, and the Liquor Control Board; but no great progress was made towards a settlement. Further efforts were, however, made by the Port and Transit Committee, who were strongly backed by the Admiralty and Ministry of Shipping, and as the result of a second conference at Liverpool, the Liquor Control Board issued instructions, on August 26th, for certain specified licensed premises to supply beer on a ticket system, between the hours of 10 and 10.45 p.m., to coal heavers who had worked the first spell of a night-shift.

A serious crisis was thus averted; but throughout the summer the growth of labour unrest continued to cause constant anxiety on the part of those responsible for the flow of traffic. The majority of the disputes arose from the continuous increase in the cost of living, and the discrepancies which emerged in practice from the wage advances granted to meet it, under various agreements and awards. In all such disputes the Port and Transit Committee and the officials of the Transport Workers'

ACCELERATED DISCHARGE

Federation used their influence to secure a continuance of work, pending a settlement, and in this they were generally successful; but the increasing number of disputes and temporary stoppages in the transport industries augured badly for the future.

Despite these difficulties, the general improvement in turn-round was fully maintained, and notwithstanding the decrease in the total tonnage available, and the number of ships with cereal cargoes diverted to France and Italy, the total entrances during August and September were equal to those recorded in the previous year. Entrances under the British flag were, indeed, substantially larger. The weight of imports, even including oil-fuel, fell somewhat short of the 1917 figures, but this was due to the large proportion of space occupied on the Atlantic liners by American troops, and not to any failure in the shipping services.

In one notable respect the position had decidedly improved. As a result of the Swedish Agreement there had been an appreciable increase in the number of neutral ships fixed for ore cargoes from Spain and the Mediterranean; the losses in that trade had been reduced to less than $2\frac{1}{2}$ per cent.,[1] and the excellent work of the Transport Workers' Battalions had resulted in a general acceleration of discharge, which enabled quicker turn-round to be given to the ships. The imports from Narvik were also on the increase, thanks to the new organisation of the Scandinavian convoys, and the total imports of iron-ore for the first nine months of 1918 were over 300,000 tons greater than in the same period of the previous year. Despite an increasing consumption of munitions, adequate stocks were in hand, and there was no immediate anxiety with regard to future arrivals.

The cereal position also was free from immediate anxiety. The wheat imports from North America were still a long way below the normal, but heavy shipments from the Plate arrived during August and September, and owing to the measures taken to stimulate production, the home harvest of wheat and oats was far above the normal. Imports of barley and maize were small; but this resulted from the fixed policy of the Government in restricting brewing, and encouraging the slaughter of cattle, in order to economise shipping space. As the harvest reports from

[1] Including cargoes not lifted through sinking of the ships on the outward voyage.

North America and elsewhere were good, there were adequate supplies in sight; but there was no intention of utilising the increased British harvest either to improve the quality of the loaf or in any other way to encourage an increase in consumption. The Food Council had resolved on the adoption of a uniform standard of dilution for all the Allied countries, and the Shipping Controller strongly supported the decision of the Transport Council that any gain through increased production in any one country should be utilised, not for increasing the total supply of breadstuffs, but for the provision of surplus space, to be allocated to food, munitions, or raw materials as circumstances might require.

Meanwhile the diversions of cereal cargoes to France and Italy had increased in size, and amounted during August and September to 350,000 tons a month. Still larger diversions had been fixed for October, bringing up the total for the eight months, April to October inclusive, to nearly 2,100,000 tons. As the total British imports of wheat and flour for the first nine months of 1918 were only 2,850,000 tons, and imports of all cereals and pulses under 5,000,000, it will be seen that the obligations imposed on Great Britain by the agreement of November 1917 involved no small restriction of her own supplies. There was some reason to hope, however, that during the cereal year 1918–1919 the burden would be lightened, as the result of better harvests in the Allied countries.

The meat supplies both of the British and of the French and Italian armies had been maintained without even a temporary check, and the total quantity of imported meat available for British civilians was considerably larger than in either of the two previous years.[1] On the other

[1] SOURCES AND DISTRIBUTION OF MEAT SUPPLY 1918
(In 1,000 tons)

Sources		Distribution	
Plate and Patagonia	580·5	British Army	381·0
Australia	73·7	British Civilians	301·8
New Zealand	106·5	French Army	301·9
North America	285·1	Italian Army	148·8
South Africa	7·8		
Brazil	57·5		
Venezuela	6·7		
Madagascar	6·0		
China	9·7		
	1133·5		1133·5

Losses at sea, not included above, amounted to 11,400 tons.
Of the French supplies 79·7 per cent., and of the Italian 71·3 per cent., were carried in British ships.

hand, the home output had been reduced by the policy of early slaughter to economise feeding-stuffs, and the greater part of the imported meat allocated to civilians was American beef, which the Army would not touch and even civilians would not readily consume.

A more serious matter was the depletion of the Army stocks. Partly owing to the unwillingness of the War Office to take North American meat, and partly owing to the increasing demands of France and Italy, these had fallen from 50,000 tons in January to less than 12,000 tons at the end of August, and in order to ensure the continuance of regular deliveries to the troops it was urgently important to build up stocks, if possible, with meat acceptable to the War Office.

So long as the necessity for American trooping on a large scale continued, it was impossible to discontinue the use of insulated shipping in the North Atlantic trade; but towards the end of the summer, the refrigerated cargo available was much reduced, through the growth of American military requirements, and the effects of a drought, which compelled the slaughter of immature cattle. It thus became impossible to utilise fully the insulated space on steamers in the North Atlantic, and during the latter part of August and September, considerable readjustments were effected in the distribution of the ships. Four steamers were retransferred to the Plate, and four to the Australasian trade; but the main feature of the readjustment was the establishment of a new triangular service; from Liverpool to the Plate to load meat; from the Plate to New York to embark troops; and from New York to Liverpool, where both men and meat were landed. For this service ten large steamers hitherto employed in the North Atlantic were now allocated, in addition to sixteen ships in the Plate trade, which were capable of carrying troops. As the triangular voyage only occupied five days longer than the direct passage, under existing conditions, the net result of this arrangement was to increase considerably the meat-carrying power of the tonnage in the Plate trade, without appreciable interference with American trooping.

Thanks to this rearrangement of services, it was possible to make some progress in building up British army stocks, without detriment to the supply of the Allies. Even so, the efficiency of the Board of Trade organisation and the

Refrigerated Shipping Committee was tested to the full, for by this time the requirements of the French and Italian armies absorbed over 40 per cent. of the monthly shipments from all sources. Of the total amount shipped over 90 per cent. was carried under the British flag, for neither France nor Italy had been in a position to insulate further tonnage. It had even been necessary to provide assistance from British shipping in the feeding of the American armies, as few American vessels were fitted for the carriage of refrigerated produce.

Had it been possible to lift all the meat available in Australia and New Zealand as well as at the Plate, the problem of building up stocks, while maintaining supplies, could easily have been solved; but the number of insulated ships was limited, the claims of American trooping and the demand for wheat and munitions from the nearest source were imperative, and tonnage in the Australasian trade remained throughout the summer at a very low ebb. The requirements of the Eastern armies were duly met, and the opening, in August, of a new store at Port Said greatly facilitated the work of distribution. There was not, however, nearly enough tonnage in the United Kingdom services to lift the cargoes available. Practically the whole output of butter and cheese was shipped; but the accumulations of meat were still very large, especially in New Zealand.

The priority given to butter and cheese shipments was fully justified; for the effect of the embargoes had reduced the imports from Denmark and Holland to a very small proportion of the previous year's receipts, and despite the Food Controller's large purchases of butter in Argentina, and cheese in North America, the total imports of both commodities, to the end of September, were very considerably smaller than in 1917. As in Germany, so in Great Britain, though to a much smaller extent, the supply of fats was one of the chief anxieties of the Food Control.

The food situation as a whole was, of course, infinitely easier in Great Britain than in the enemy countries. Not only were the supplies available much larger and more varied, but the very fact that so large a proportion of the total supply consisted of imports rendered the control of consumption far more effective. A further very important difference was the fact that, owing to the larger supplies of cereals available, it had been possible in Great Britain to leave bread, the staple foodstuff, unrationed. Although consumption had been checked to some extent by the less palatable quality of the loaf, arising from dilution and a high percentage of extraction, it was still possible for the poorer classes to make up by increased bread purchases for any temporary decrease in the issue of rationed foods, or their inability to purchase more expensive foodstuffs.

Prices, in spite of the controls, and the subsidy which kept down artificially the cost of the loaf, were still rising. The *Economist* and *Statist* Index Numbers stood, in September 1918, about 140 per cent. higher than at the outbreak of war ; the *Labour Gazette* Index of retail prices showed an advance of 110 per cent., and the rise had been rather sharply graded during the summer months. The Board of Trade " Cost of Living " Index Number (which included rent) was just double that for July 1914, and had risen about twenty-five points since January 1918, mainly as the result of a sharp advance in the cost of fuel and light, and a still greater advance in the price of clothing. Owing to the decrease in cotton imports, and the large proportion of the woollen output devoted to military or export purposes, the cost of clothing was now nearly half as great again as at the beginning of the year, and nearly three times as great as before the war.

The effect of high prices, however, though they gave rise to much discontent, was mitigated by the advance in wages, and fell mainly on the professional class and people with small fixed incomes. Of actual scarcity there was little. The shortage of butter and sugar, the dilution of the loaf, and the bad quality of much of the meat and bacon, led to a good deal of discomfort and to some under-feeding, especially among those whose lack of aptitude, or of utensils, prevented them from taking full advantage of the substitute foods available ; but there was as yet no restriction of supplies in any way comparable to that suffered by the populations of the Central Powers.

France and Italy too had been preserved by the cereal diversions from the consequences of their harvest failures, and though there had been local and temporary shortages, they had been successfully made good. The supply of fuel, as important to those Powers as that of food, had been maintained, and the new British liner services from the United States gave promise of more regular fulfilment of their demands for rolling-stock and materials,

Neither in Great Britain nor in the Allied countries, however, were the stocks, whether of food or materials, large enough for any considerable further reduction in imports to be viewed without anxiety; nor was it possible for such reductions to be made without imposing restrictions on civilian consumption which would test severely the morale of the people. It was, therefore, of the first importance, to maintain imports during the cereal year 1918–19, at, or if possible above, the level of the past twelve months.

It was not now the question of the supplies available that caused the chief anxiety, for throughout the world, and especially in North America, the harvests were better than in 1917. The one great problem was the provision of carrying power.

The actual imports of the United Kingdom, France, and Italy, during the calendar year 1917, had amounted, exclusive of oil carried in tankers, to about 78,000,000 tons. The demands, for the cereal year 1918–19, of the Departments in each country responsible for supply, amounted to 76,700,000. As against this, the annual carrying power of the total tonnage (including neutrals) available for the import services, was estimated by the Transport Executive at 72,500,000. There was thus a deficit of over 4,000,000 tons to be faced, irrespective of any assistance given in the supply of the American armies.

This was the more serious inasmuch as the food programme had already been cut down by the Council, at its last meeting, from 23,400,000 to 18,500,000 tons, a reduction of over 20 per cent. Including military oats, and certain shipments outside the programme, made direct to the armies, or in vessels whose employment was governed by their outward cargo, it was necessary to allow 22,000,000 tons in all for foodstuffs and items such as oil-seeds, included in the food programme even when used for other purposes. This figure had been accepted in face of a statement by the British representatives on the Food Council that, in their view, the British proportion of the regular programme (10,500,000 tons) would be inadequate to the needs of the people.[1] It could, therefore, be regarded only as a minimum.

The munitions programme was not yet finally settled, but was understood to amount to 22,000,000 tons, including

[1] Corresponding imports for 1917–18 amounted to 13,800,000 tons.

the supply of French and British artillery and ammunition to the American forces. For the rest, the coal shipments to Italy were to be maintained at 600,000 tons a month; and shipments to France at 1,500,000 tons a month, the maximum quantity the French ports were capable of receiving. This brought up the total of coal for the year to 25,200,000 tons. For all other raw materials 7,500,000 tons was allowed. The detailed programmes were not yet complete, but this figure was based on the previous year's imports, and it was unlikely that it could be much reduced. Textile materials, leather, and tobacco (3,500,000 tons in all) were so largely used for military as well as civilian purposes, that further cuts were hardly possible, and the remaining 4,000,000 tons was made up of commodities, chiefly timber, pulp, and paper, brought in shipping whose outward employment could not be altered, since it was determined by the needs of France and Italy for fuel, or by agreements with neutrals.

This question of non-transferable tonnage seriously complicated the problem of dealing with the deficit. Shipments of coal from the United Kingdom to France and Italy, and cargoes of ore, timber, and other commodities brought to the United Kingdom by colliers returning from those countries or from Scandinavia, made up rather more than half of the total weight of imports to be lifted under the joint programmes. Deducting these and the shipments of oats and food direct to the armies, there remained only about 32,000,000 tons in respect of which adjustments could be made.

On this tonnage, munitions and munitions material had now the first claim. Heavy expenditure during the German spring offensive, and the Austrian offensive of the preceding winter, had reduced the stocks in France and Italy to a low ebb. The resumption of the offensive by the Allies during the summer involved a further heavy drain, and the Allied Munitions Council were now pressing for the largest possible import during the next six months.

Such was the position laid before the Allied Maritime Transport Council at their fourth session, in London, on September 30th, October 1st and 2nd, 1918. The first point to be settled was the assistance to be given to America, and after full explanation of the American position, the Council decided not only to confirm the allocation by the Executive of 200,000 tons dead-weight for October loading, but the further allocation of 300,000 tons during November and December, together with any further space that could be provided through the release of double bottoms. In return, Secretary Baker, who attended the session, pledged the United States Government to full co-operation in the work of the Council, and agreed that the American Government would table statements of tonnage and import programmes, and would be guided by the recommendations of the Council and the Programme Committees in the arrangement of import services and the disposition of shipping. Further, it was agreed that the assistance to be given in the supply of the American armies during the winter months should be repaid from April 1919 onwards, by the allocation of American tonnage, as the new ships became available, to the Allied import services.

On this understanding the Council decided, on the advice of the Executive, to authorise the import programmes on the basis of 72,500,000 tons. The food programme was to go forward on the basis already fixed. Imports of raw materials were to be kept as close as possible to the level of the previous year, and as the bulk of these were either required for military purposes or carried in non-transferable tonnage, the Munitions Council agreed to meet the 4,000,000-ton deficit by a provisional reduction of their programme to 18,000,000 tons. In order, however, to fulfil the demand for the largest possible shipments, October to March inclusive, the Transport Council gave instructions that munitions and army supplies should receive a general preference over food during those months, and that, in order to facilitate this priority, all Supply Departments should be asked to effect a gradual reduction of stocks until they approximated, towards the end of August 1919, to the quantities required for actual distribution.

This relegation of food to a secondary priority, coupled with a deliberate reduction of stocks, was in marked contrast to the policy by which the Allies had hitherto been guided. It was justified solely by confidence in the co-operation of the United States. By the summer of 1919 the results of the American shipbuilding programme should give a big surplus of tonnage over losses and army requirements combined, and the States would be able to place this surplus at the disposal of the European Allies.

At the same time there would be in North America, the nearest source, immense stocks of cereals, from which the supplies of the European Allies could be replenished during the latter half of 1919, and from which, even in the spring, emergency shipments could be made, if necessary.

In the meantime, the effect of large tonnage diversions to American army supply, coupled with a postponement of food to munitions in the priority order, could not but involve, for all the Allied peoples, sacrifices considerably greater than any they had previously made. The Transport Executive were accordingly instructed to prepare for publication by the French, British, Italian, and American Governments, a statement of the purposes for which those sacrifices were required, and an appeal to bear patiently severe, though temporary hardship, in order that the maximum number of American troops might be transported to France and fully equipped for the campaign of 1919.

CHAPTER XXV

THE LAST PHASE
SEPTEMBER—NOVEMBER 1918

No time was lost by the Allied Maritime Transport Executive in preparing to carry out the general decisions of the Council. By the middle of October, the Tonnage Committee had agreed with the Freight Committee of the Food Council a working programme to cover the first four months of the cereal year (September to December inclusive), adjustments in detail being made from time to time to meet fluctuations in the position. Progress on the munitions programme was not so rapid, as the Committee had not yet received full details of the French and Italian requirements for the six months October to March. It was known, however, that the French demands would show a very large increase, and the Executive anticipated great difficulty in meeting them, owing to the shortage of tonnage and the congestion of the French ports, whose ability to handle a greatly increased volume of heavy cargoes was extremely doubtful.

As regards tonnage, the Executive were able to make arrangements with the American Government, providing for a great economy of carrying power. The American army supplies programme included a very high proportion of light, measurement cargo, so that the ships became full long before they were down to their marks. On the other hand, the French munitions programme included a large proportion of heavy dead-weight cargo such as steel rails, which would bring the ships far below their marks if all space were filled. This was the sort of problem—solved automatically under commercial conditions—which was constantly arising in the use of requisitioned tonnage for the fulfilment of departmental demands. To solve such problems was one of the main functions of the Allied Maritime Transport Council, and the Executive now arranged with the American Government to increase the French steel loaded by them from 35,000 to 150,000 tons a month. They calculated that the improved stowage arising from this combination of dead-weight and measurement cargo gave a net saving of 50,000 tons a month, equivalent to the continuous employment of about 125,000 tons dead-weight of shipping in the North Atlantic.

In addition to this and other economies effected by the Transport Council, the Allied import services were now reaping the full benefit of the efforts made by the Convoy Committees at Liverpool, London, and New York, to reduce the time occupied by the round voyage in the Atlantic. The great majority of the liners in the New York fast convoy were now achieving a forty-day turn-round, but the improvement was by no means confined to these special vessels. Thanks to the co-operation of the Convoy Committees, the Ministry of Shipping, and the Admiralty, the time spent in loading or discharging, or awaiting escort, had been greatly reduced for steamers of all classes, both in British and American ports. The average stay of all liners in American ports had been cut down from $22\frac{1}{2}$ days in January to 14 days in September; for tramps the time had been reduced from $27\frac{1}{2}$ days to $16\frac{3}{4}$. Already the effect of improved organisation and quicker turn-round had falsified the anticipation of a disastrous reduction in British imports during 1918; it was not unreasonable to hope that the estimate of carrying power for the cereal year now beginning might also be exceeded.

It appeared likely, moreover, that the anticipated surplus to be yielded by the shipbuilding programmes would be increased, through a still further reduction in the rate of loss. The ascendancy gained by the defence over the attack on merchant shipping was still challenged, but it was successfully maintained, and tended, on the whole, to become more and more effective.

By the summer of 1918, the development of the convoy system had rendered the submarines comparatively powerless, except in distant waters where ships sailed without escort, or close inshore where coastal shipping and short-sea traders of low speed offered an easier target than the ocean convoys. By September, the new East Coast convoys had checked the renewed outbreak of activity in the North Sea; but during August a dozen steamers were sunk in the Irish Sea and Bristol Channel, and in September nearly double that number. The new escort arrangements, however, afforded efficient protection to the Liverpool trade, and most of the steamers sunk were comparatively small vessels.

In distant waters, the chief development was a renewal of submarine activity on the American coast, where, at one period of August, three submarines were operating simultaneously. Working up and down the coast from Cape Hatteras to Newfoundland, they sank a dozen steamers of various nationalities, the Diamond Shoal Light Vessel off Cape Hatteras, and a few sailing craft. In addition, they harried the British and American fishing fleets off the coast of Nova Scotia and the Newfoundland Banks.

Among the ships sunk off the American coast was one British steamer in an American store-ship convoy. These convoys, which ran, as will be remembered, direct from New York to Bay ports, had been reorganised at the beginning of August, and now ran at regular intervals of eight days, with the object of affording some relief to the Hampton Roads, Sydney, and New York slow convoys.[1] They had already lost one or two ships in the Atlantic, sunk by submarines on their way to, or returning from, the American coast; but this was the first casualty that had occurred in American waters. Its effect was small. The movements of submarines in American waters could usually be followed with sufficient accuracy to enable convoys to be deflected for the purpose of avoiding an attack,[2] and by now it had been proved that, even if a submarine were encountered, the attack need not be greatly dreaded. Even ships on their way to a port of assembly, or dispersed from an outward convoy, were formidable opponents to the raider, for all British and Allied steamers in the Atlantic trade were now armed, most of them heavily. Indeed, of six British steamers attacked in the West Atlantic during September, not one was sunk. The ships sunk in August were mostly engaged in coastwise traffic, and their fate had practically no effect

---

[1] With the object of affording still further relief to these convoys, the New York Bay Convoy was subsequently (in October) reduced to a speed of 8 knots, in order to absorb a larger proportion of the slower ships. From September 10th onwards, the organisation of the Bay Convoys was transferred from the British to the American authorities.

[2] Sims, *The Victory at Sea*, p. 271.

on the stream of troops and supplies flowing from American ports to France and Great Britain.

The one real danger arising from the presence of submarines in the West Atlantic was the extension of the mine peril. The minefields laid at various localities off the coast of the United States were, in general, quickly detected and cleared ; but it was suspected that the approaches to Halifax had been mined, and there sweeping was a difficult operation, owing to the depth of water and the weather conditions. In order to guard against this danger, which subsequently proved to be a real one, the Halifax–Channel convoys were transferred, at the beginning of September, to Quebec. The result was a heavy drop in the number of troops carried, as, owing to difficulties in connection with equipment, the United States War Department would only undertake to embark 6,000 men per month from that port. Hence the total embarkations of American troops fell off from 313,000 in August (of whom 199,000 were carried in British ships) to 228,000 in September (116,000 in British ships). On the other hand, ample cargo was available, and the importing capacity of the ships was utilised to the full.

Mainly owing to the operations of submarines in the Atlantic, the total destruction of tonnage in August was rather higher than in either of the two preceding months ; but in September the total losses of British and foreign shipping sank to 188,000 tons gross—much the lowest figure recorded since August 1916. It was under one-third of the monthly average during the first twelve months of the unrestricted submarine campaign, and less by 68,000 tons than the total for June 1918, the lowest previously recorded since the barred zone declaration.

It was noteworthy that in the Mediterranean, where the Otranto Mine Barrage was approaching completion, only ten steamers of 500 tons and upwards were sunk ; but the ascendancy of the defence was now everywhere manifest. As now improved, the convoy system not only gave very efficient protection to shipping, but provided for instant and effective retaliation. The coastal patrols, on the surface, under the water, and in the air, made the inshore work of the submarines very dangerous. The Northern Barrage took its silent toll of U-boats starting on or returning from a cruise. The enemy's losses increased rapidly, and the progressive diminution in the destruction of merchant tonnage may be attributed, in part at least, to a steady deterioration in the efficiency of the attack, due to the unbearable strain of the conditions in which alone that attack could now be carried on.

It was not, however, to the course of events at sea that all eyes were now turned, but to the progress of the struggle on the Western front, where the pendulum had swung back with startling rapidity and violence. Although the German offensive had been brought to a standstill in June, and the rapid increase in the number of American troops in France went far to ensure the ability of the Allies to hold their own on their new line, it was still doubtful whether they would venture to attack in their turn until 1919, when the training of a large proportion of the new American armies would be complete. Even the counter-attack on the Marne, which began on July 18th, might be regarded only as an attempt to improve the defensive position before the approach of winter.

Not for long did the suspense continue. The Allied High Command had resolved on a big throw for high stakes. The French successes were rapidly pushed; on August 8th the French and British made a breach of twenty miles in the German lines before Amiens; successive waves of attack were launched during the remainder of the month along the whole line from the Marne to the Flanders ridges, and by the beginning of September the Germans were in full retreat on the great series of prepared positions which they had constructed behind the lines held during the long period of trench warfare.

They were given no rest. On September 12th the American First Army attacked the St. Mihiel salient, on the Meuse. Before the month was out a Franco-American offensive on a broad front had begun in Champagne and Argonne, the British had broken into the Hindenburg line, and British, French, and Belgians were advancing side by side in Flanders. Meanwhile, the Central Powers had seen their battle-front in the South-Eastern theatres crumble into ruins; General Allenby had swept through Palestine, and an Allied offensive on the Salonika front had been crowned with such overwhelming success that, on September 27th, the Bulgarian Government was driven to ask for an armistice. With the signing of this on September 30th, Bulgaria passed out of the war.

All this is matter of military history, but the repercussion of these blows on the economic stability of the Central Powers was of decisive influence on the course of the war, and demands some little attention. The destruction of their hopes in the field affected profoundly both the ability and the will of the German and Austrian peoples to sustain the privations from which they had so long been suffering.

By August 1918 the immediate food crisis in Germany had been, for the moment, overcome. June and July, indeed, had been bad months. The flour ration was very low, and the quality of the bread supplied to the poorest classes was so bad that it possessed little or no nutritive value, even if it were not positively harmful.[1] Meat and milk were still more difficult to obtain than bread. In Bavaria the meat ration for adults was only 7 oz. a week, and in Berlin 8½ oz. To make matters worse, the Government were obliged on July 1st to reduce the potato ration —the last stand-by of the people—from 7 to 3 lb. per week per head, and even the reduced ration was often unprocurable.

Owing to the lateness of the harvest, and the delay in receipt of supplies from the Ukraine, it was not until the middle of August that the Government were able to raise the daily flour ration to 7 oz. per head. Nevertheless, the critical period before the harvest had once more been passed, and by the end of the month the general conditions were a little better than during June and July. Meat, indeed, was fast disappearing from the diet of the ordinary German household, and one week in every three was wholly meatless; but the potato supply had improved, and other vegetables were comparatively plentiful. With bread and potatoes secured in quantities just sufficient to maintain life, it was still possible to hold out.

But to hold out, under such conditions, hope was necessary. Although the actual shortage of food during 1917–18 had never, perhaps, been quite so acute as in the " turnip winter " of 1916–17, it had been bad enough. The total food supplies available for the civil population would, indeed, have sufficed for a ration of 3,000 calories per average man, or only 10 per cent. below the amount

[1] A sample loaf, said to be of the kind supplied to prisoners of war and the very poor, contained only a minute proportion of starch granules, a quantity of husks and bran of rye, barley, and possibly oats, a large quantity of bunt, several specimens of ergot of rye (a disease germ), and a residue of dust and dirt. There was no gluten present.

considered by the Allied Authorities as sufficient. But, as has already been pointed out, the utmost efforts of the Food Control were insufficient to ensure an equitable distribution. The producing class still consumed up to 4,000 calories per day, and the food available for the remainder of the population was reduced to an average of 2,000 calories per head, or 2,500 per " man." From this had to be provided the supplementary rations for the workers in munition factories and others engaged in heavy labour; and the food available on the ration cards, for the bulk of the urban population, did not exceed 1,500 to 1,600 calories per head, or 2,000 per " man "—less by one-third than the minimum essential to health. Nor was it possible for the majority to supplement the rations largely by additional purchases. Although it was estimated that about a quarter of all food released by the self-suppliers passed into illicit trade, the fantastic prices demanded for such articles as eggs and butter put them out of the reach of all but the wealthiest classes and the big manufacturing firms, some of whom purchased largely for the support of their workmen. Even so, the workers in important factories generally received a diet inadequate to the needs of men in regular employment.[1]

Apart from the restricted quantity of the food, its monotonous, unpalatable, and indigestible character, and in particular the terrible shortage of fats, deprived it of much of its nutritive value. The effects of a semi-starvation diet were aggravated by the shortage of beer, coffee, and tobacco, and above all by the want of adequate clothing. The various substitute fabrics woven out of nettles or paper had proved exceedingly unsatisfactory, and a large proportion of the population were miserably ill-equipped to withstand the cold of the approaching winter. In the industrial district of Westphalia it was reported, in September, that many of the women were without underclothes or stockings, and wore nothing but a thin blouse, skirt, and wooden shoes. Even among the middle class it was only with difficulty that sufficient clothing could be procured for the children, by cutting up old clothes or bed-covers.

These conditions, it must be remembered, had now been going on for a long time, and their effects were cumulative. To a population whose powers of resistance had been

[1] Cmd. 280.

undermined by two years of persistent underfeeding, each reduction in the rations, temporary or permanent, was a heavier blow both morally and physically than when, in 1916, they had been nerved to endurance by the hope of speedy victory. The spread of illicit trade, the increasing bitterness with which the Food Control was criticised, the constant recriminations between class and class and between State and State, the numberless thefts of food, and the outbreak of riots and semi-political strikes, all gave evidence of a deterioration in morale which showed that the breaking point was in sight.

It was for this reason that the flour ration had been raised again to a level which the situation did not really justify. The outlook for 1918–19 was very black. The German cereal harvest was a little better than that of 1917, but it was not much more than half as large as the average of 1912–13. The potato harvest, which had helped to save the situation in 1917, was only about two-thirds as large as in that year, or one-half of the normal.[1] The livestock were diminishing in numbers, and continued to deteriorate in condition.[2] Worst of all, there was little prospect of relief from across the frontiers.

Bitter as had been the disappointment with regard to supplies from the Ukraine, those supplies had made for Germany, and still more for Austria, just the difference between shortage and starvation; but the reports as to the Ukrainian harvest, coupled with the prevalence of agrarian disturbances, and the difficulties of transport and administration, gave very little hope of obtaining any substantial supplies in 1919. From Roumania nothing could be expected; the harvest had been one of the worst on record, and was wholly insufficient for the normal consumption even of Roumania itself.

Only in Turkey, Bulgaria, and Serbia was the harvest reported good, and whatever small relief might have been expected from the Balkans, was utterly cut off by the collapse of the Bulgarian resistance before the advance of the Allies. But the effects of the Bulgarian débâcle went further than this. With Bulgaria out of the war, the Allies were in a position to control the " Eastern Corridor " and to cut off not only supplies from Roumania, but those received, viâ Odessa and the Danube, from the Ukraine.

The importance of this threatened severance of com-

[1] Cmd. 280, p. 24.   [2] Ibid., pp. 24–5.

munications with the East lay as much in its influence on the supply of materials as in its effect on the supply of food. The shortage of mineral oils had already reached a point at which it became a source of serious embarrassment to the military authorities. The Galician output was falling off; the Roumanian output, in spite of all endeavours, had not yet recovered its normal volume.[1] So short were the supplies that the German Government were obliged to announce, in August, that the distribution of lighting oils during the coming winter would be at only one-quarter the rate of the previous year. Even after imposing the most drastic restrictions on civilian consumption, the supply of petrol and lubricants for military purposes gave rise to great anxiety. Army orders captured by the Allies in their advance bore impressive witness to the necessity for economy enforced on the German troops and the fears entertained by the High Command as to a grave petroleum crisis in the spring of 1919.

At one period the Germans had hoped to supplement the Galician and Roumanian supplies by oil from the Caucasus, but this hope was defeated in August by the British expedition to Baku. Now even the Roumanian supplies were threatened, and in view of the enormous importance of mineral oils to the air, submarine, and transport services, the consequences were incalculable.

Another result of the Allied advance in the East was to frustrate all hope of developing wool and cotton imports, through the Black Sea ports, from the Don district and the Caucasus, whence some small supplies had already been obtained. The importance of this lay in the fact that the shortage of textiles, which had reduced the civilian population to such straits, was already beginning to affect the armies. Hitherto the troops had been adequately clad, but the difficulty of clothing, as well as feeding them, continually increased, and the proportion of shoddy employed was already dangerously large. The hope of obtaining a large amount of clothing from Russia and Poland was defeated by the political chaos in Russia and by the difficulty of transport, and the blocking of the

[1]

Galician Output, in 1,000 metric tons.		Roumanian Output, in 1,000 metric tons.	
1913	1,087	1913	1,885
1917	902	1917	527
1918	679	1918	1,214

Eastern corridor now threatened to cut off the only available source of raw textiles.

In every direction the productive power of Germany was failing. Many factories were obliged to close down altogether, or to reduce hours of work, through lack of materials, or through the wearing out of machinery which could not be replaced. The deterioration of the transport system through shortage of skilled labour, absence of repair facilities, and want of lubricants, was more and more rapid; accidents on the railways were numerous, and long delays in delivery impeded not only commercial traffic but the distribution of food. The coal output was falling, owing to further combing-out of skilled workers, shortage of pit-props, and the effects of disease and underfeeding. Not only was a coal famine threatened in the winter, but the shortage of fuel affected the output of the iron and steel industries, which were still well supplied with ore, despite the reduction in Swedish shipments. More serious in its direct military effects was the shortage of other metals, such as copper, brass, bronze, nickel, and steel-hardening materials. Statues, busts, church bells, the roofs of the Bavarian royal palaces, the door-handles, knockers, and stair-rods of the Reichstag building were sent to the melting-pot; yet the supply was still inadequate for the needs of the armies, and the inferior quality of much of the ammunition used on the Western front proved that the time was not far distant when the enemy's fighting strength would be seriously crippled. Rubber, too, was now so short as to hamper the field telephone service, and no further supplies could be secured. Further, all hope of obtaining possession of the military stores accumulated at Archangel and Vladivostok had vanished during August, when Archangel was captured by the North Russian Expeditionary Force, and the Siberian port was secured by the landing of British and Japanese troops.

There was now no hope of any improvement in the economic position of the Central Powers. Even the German public would listen no longer to reports of an improved harvest, or promises of future supplies from Roumania or the Ukraine. It was evident that another year of war must bring not merely a continuation but an intensification of their sufferings. Further, it was evident that, apart from the failure of the submarines to prevent the building up of great American armies in

France, the military strength of Germany must steadily deteriorate as the result of an increasing shortage of petrol, lubricants, and munition materials. To a greater extent than ever before, the Central Powers were forced back on their own unaided resources, and it is exceedingly doubtful whether those resources could have carried them through another year's campaign.

Had the German High Command still been able to hold out the prospect of a military victory in the near future, the German people would, no doubt, have been capable of enduring for some time longer the privations to which they had become accustomed ; but the victories of the Allies in August and September had not only tightened their grip on German supplies, they had shaken the belief of the German people in the invincibility of their arms. The revelation that the American armies, whom they had been taught to believe existed only on paper, were already capable of taking their place in the line of battle and dealing staggering blows, was a terrible shock. The breaking of the line in the West, and the collapse of the South-Eastern front, not only destroyed the last hope of a German victory, but proclaimed the approach of the day when the tide of war would roll over the frontiers on to German soil. The motive for endurance was gone. Much might have been endured for the chance of a victory which would bring in its train a renewal of the supplies so urgently needed for the restoration of Germany's economic life ; but a people debilitated by hunger, cold, and disease, disillusioned, distrustful of their rulers, and without hope, were in no mood to rally for a desperate defence against overwhelming odds.

From the moment of the first successful Allied offensive, strikes, riots, " stop-the-war " demonstrations, and revolutionary propaganda became more and more prevalent ; but it was in Austria, as might have been expected, that the débâcle first became complete. Conditions in Austria-Hungary as regards food, clothing, and materials, reflected in an exaggerated form those existing in Germany. Continual struggles with Germany over the division of the spoils of conquered territories—struggles in which Austria, the weaker partner, invariably came off second-best—continual struggles between Austria proper and Hungary over food supplies, coal, and materials, continual recrimination between the diverse nationalities of the Empire, made the task of the Controls still more difficult than in Germany. Neither the collection nor the distribution of food approached efficiency, and it was said that about half the available supplies was absorbed into the illicit trade, where the fantastic prices extorted placed it beyond the reach of the majority of the people.[1]

Conditions were naturally at their worst in Vienna, where abdominal typhoid broke out with severity in July; but they were nearly as bad in Prague and other large industrial centres, and even in Hungary food was very short. The supply of meat had practically broken down throughout the whole of the Empire, and the position with regard to milk was almost equally bad. To add to the trouble, Austrian finances were in such an alarming state that the Government were compelled, in August, to take the extremely unpopular step of abolishing the bread subsidy, with the result that the price of a 3-lb. loaf in Vienna went up, at one bound, from $7\frac{1}{2}d.$ to $1s. 3\frac{1}{2}d.$

The moral breakdown arising from these conditions was naturally more complete in a polyglot Empire where a large proportion of the population was composed of subject nationalities, than among the comparatively homogeneous people of Germany, and it was accentuated by the suspicion, even among German-speaking Austrians, that they were being sacrificed and exploited, both politically and economically, by the predominant partner in the alliance. So early as July it was necessary to protect food trains on the railways by troops with machine guns; the countryside was infested with brigands—Czech and Slav " Green Guards," escaped Russian prisoners, discharged Austrian soldiers, and armed peasants; part of the Skoda arms factory was blown up by strikers, and even in the active army discipline was on the verge of dissolution.

Even before the Allied offensive, the symptoms of disintegration were so strong as to cause the utmost alarm in Germany; the success of that offensive gave the last blow to the tottering fabric. It was the strength and prestige of Germany and the dependence of the Austrian Government on their Allies, which had alone kept Austria so long in the war. Now that Germany herself was threatened with disaster, the bonds were loosened. In

[1] In July beef and butter were practically unprocurable in Vienna except by illicit trade. In that trade, beef fetched from 26 to 32 kronen, and butter from 65 to 72 kronen, per kilog.

addition to a rapid increase of lawlessness and brigandage, the subject peoples, thinking the day of deliverance at hand, began to stir. In Poland, in Czecho-Slovakia, in the Slav districts of the south, there were popular demonstrations, secret arming, and preparations for revolt. By the end of September the Empire was beginning to break up.

The prospective collapse of Austria, following on the defection of Bulgaria, was not without effect on the attitude of the German Government. So early as September 15th, the Austrian Government put forward to President Wilson a suggestion for an " unofficial " peace conference, and on the same day Germany made to Belgium proposals for a separate peace. Both proposals were promptly rejected, and the Allied advance was vigorously pushed. From this point events moved rapidly. By the first week in October the British had completely broken the Hindenburg line; on October 4th the Central Powers made definite proposals for an armistice. While negotiations as to the armistice terms went forward, the tide of the Allied advance flowed on. By October 19th the British and Belgians were in Ostend, Zeebrugge, and Lille; by the end of the month the Germans were falling back on the Meuse.

One result of the armistice negotiations was the practical suspension, from the middle of October, of submarine activity. But though this step was dictated by political considerations, it was impossible for the Germans to conceal, even from themselves, the fact that the submarine campaign had already definitely failed. From the very beginning of the ocean-convoy system, the rate of loss inflicted on ships in convoy had been small, and throughout 1918 it had steadily declined. The short-sea convoys had proved equally successful. Since the reorganisation of the Scandinavian Convoy at the beginning of 1918, the percentage of loss had dropped by more than one-half; in the French coal trade convoys not one sailing in a thousand now resulted in a casualty.

While the percentage of loss had fallen, the proportion of convoyed sailings had greatly increased. During the last few months of 1917 just over one-half the total traffic in the overseas trade of the United Kingdom was included in either the ocean or the short-sea convoys. The proportion had now risen to 90 per cent. Among the few ships which still ran without escort, the rate of loss was falling.

Even in the Mediterranean, where the difficulties to be overcome by the defence were greater than in any other area, the submarines now met with comparatively little success. During the first seven months of 1918 an average of 23 steamers of 500 tons gross and upwards had been sunk by submarines in that sea. In August the number was 13 only; in September it sank to 10. Of special importance was the great reduction in the risks of the Gibraltar–Genoa track, followed by the vital Italian coal trade.

On no route in any part of the world did the submarines, in October 1918, seriously threaten the flow of traffic. Yet the anxiety with which the tonnage situation was viewed by those responsible for the supply services of the Allies, had hardly diminished. The offensives so vigorously pursued in France, Palestine, and the Balkans had, in fact, added to the difficulties of the tonnage problem, as they involved an increase in the number of ships on military and naval service, with a consequent reduction in those available for the carriage of imports. Moreover, the effect of the allocation of British shipping to the American army supply service, was now being felt, and was likely to be felt with still greater severity during the next few months.

This reduction in available tonnage had not yet been allowed to affect the chief French and Italian services. Grain from North America was now coming forward freely, and the diversions of cereals in British, or British-controlled tonnage, amounted to 400,000 tons a month. The new liner services from the United States provided about 150,000 tons dead-weight monthly for munitions and general cargo. The shipments of coal to Italy were kept up to, or very near, the programme figures.[1] There

[1] EXECUTION OF ITALIAN COAL PROGRAMME
MARCH 15TH–NOVEMBER 14TH, 1918
(In 1,000 tons)

	Programme, 8 months.	Coal despatched.	Surplus or Deficiency.
Shipments of British coal by long Sea Route	1,200	2,208	+ 1008
British coal passing Italian Frontier	800	876	+ 76
French coal passing Italian Frontier	1,360	854	− 506
French coal on board at Mediterranean ports	1,440	820	− 620
TOTAL	4,800	4,758	− 42

Of the coal despatched, about 78,000 tons was lost at sea. The above figures are exclusive of the 150,000-ton strategic reserve.

was much difficulty in maintaining the French supplies, owing to the reduction of output in Great Britain, the effects of a railway strike in South Wales, and a lack of tonnage for the shallower French ports; but on the whole, colliers were supplied in sufficient numbers to carry as much as Great Britain could provide, or the receiving ports could handle.[1]

The total allocations to French and Italian services remained, during September and October, practically unchanged. Tonnage available for British imports, on the other hand, decreased during those months by 6 per cent. The most encouraging feature of the situation was that the Admiralty's reserve stocks of oil-fuel were now approaching the safety minimum, and there was, therefore, some prospect of being able to dispense with the use of double bottoms for the carriage of oil.

Any possible economy in the utilisation of shipping was, indeed, of the first importance, for all new American tonnage was absorbed by the military programme, and the British output, though improved, fell far short of the original expectations. The National Yards, from which so much had been hoped, were not yet in a position to affect the situation. The enormous scale on which they had been planned prevented concentration on the completion of the more advanced berths, and the difficulties with regard to prisoner-of-war labour struck at the very root of the scheme for fabricated shipbuilding. Hence, though a few fabricated ships had previously been laid down in private yards, it was not until October that the first three keels were laid at Chepstow. Even more complete had been the failure of a scheme for concrete shipbuilding adopted at the end of 1917. The idea of reinforced concrete construction was not altogether a new one, and it was hoped that its adoption for small craft such as tugs and sea-going barges, and even for colliers and oilers, would effect a large economy in steel and skilled labour. More skilled labour, however, proved to be necessary than had been anticipated, and the actual cost of construction was nearly twice the original estimate and much greater than for steel vessels of the same type. So slow was the rate

---

[1] The Provisional Programme for Coal to France was 1,740,000 tons a month. The actual shipments for the eight months, March to November inclusive, amounted to 10,925,500 tons, an average of 1,365,690 tons a month.

A FINAL CRISIS 409

of progress that, by the end of October 1918, only one 1,000-ton barge had been completed, though eight small yards had been built or adapted for the purpose, and 209 orders placed.

It was, however, on the building of ordinary steamers, especially standard freighters and oilers, that the bulk of the effort had been concentrated under Lord Pirrie's direction, and these were now being delivered in considerable numbers. Yet even in September, a third of the yards specifically allocated to mercantile construction were still occupied by Admiralty orders, and Lord Pirrie stated, in that month, that unless these were cleared by a reduction in the naval programme, and 76,000 additional workers secured, of whom half must be skilled, it would be impossible to attain the 3,000,000-ton level.[1]

The actual output for 1918, to anticipate a little, was 1,534,000 tons, as compared with the original estimate of 2,800,000, or the revised figure of 1,800,000 put forward in November 1917, and the average monthly deliveries during the autumn gave no hope of any great increase in the rate of construction. Apart from the British output, the only reliable source of new tonnage was the comparatively small Canadian programme, and control over neutral shipping had already reached practically its possible limit. In September, however, an agreement was concluded between the Associated Powers and Denmark, which provided not only for restrictions on Danish exports to Germany, but for an increase in the Danish tonnage available for war-zone trade.

Even so, the import programmes continued to show a large excess over the tonnage in sight for the winter of 1918–19, and owing to the urgency of munitions requirements, it was, as we have seen, on the food supply of the Allied countries that the burden of the deficit must fall. Proclamations exhorting the Allied peoples to bear patiently privations greater than any they had yet suffered, had been drafted by the Transport Executive. They were about to be issued when, on November 11th, the end of the long struggle came.

Since the opening of armistice negotiations, the enemy's resistance had been rapidly crumbling. On October 30th,

[1] The total increase in shipyard labour during the first nine months of 1918 had amounted to 28,000, of whom 20,000 were absorbed by naval construction and by naval and mercantile repairs, leaving only 8,000 for mercantile construction.

an armistice was signed with Turkey. On the following day the Austrian collapse found dramatic expression in an outbreak of revolution in Vienna and the assassination of Count Tisza. Even before this event the bonds of Imperial authority had been loosed. Czecho-Slovakia had already declared its independence; the Southern Slavs had, for some weeks, been organising under a national council; everywhere the Austro-Hungarian Empire was being resolved into its component parts.

Even now there is little doubt that Germany could have prolonged for many months a defensive struggle, had the army or the people retained any strong will to resist. That the will to resist was lacking is no matter for surprise. The victories of the Allies in the East and the consequent defection or collapse of Bulgaria, Turkey, and Austria, had not only left Germany without an ally, to face a world in arms; they had cut off the last hope of obtaining the supplies of food and materials which alone could bring about some alleviation of the internal position, or give reasonable hope of prolonging the war indefinitely.

It is not surprising that a people who had been sustaining existence for more than two years on a diet totally insufficient to maintain normal health and energy, a people among whom the diseases that spring from hunger, cold, and dirt were making rapid headway, collapsed under the strain. The effects of the Austrian débâcle, and of President Wilson's declaration that the Allies would treat with Germany only on the abandonment of the existing autocratic Government, speedily made themselves felt. On November 7th a Bavarian Republic was proclaimed. On November 9th a revolution broke out in Berlin, and the Imperial Chancellor announced the Emperor's intention to abdicate. On the 11th an armistice was signed.

The war at sea, as has already been said, had come practically to an end some three weeks before this date. During the second half of October a few ships were sunk by mines, or by submarines which had not received, or disregarded, the instructions of the Government, but they were very few. The British steamers *Surada* and *Murcia*, torpedoed without warning near Port Said, on November 2nd, were the last ships to be sunk in the world-war. The distinction of being the last ship to be attacked was reserved for the *Sarpedon*, missed by a torpedo in the Mediterranean, on November 7th.

CHAPTER XXVI

AFTER THE ARMISTICE

TECHNICALLY speaking, the armistice amounted only to a suspension of hostilities. It was not until June 28th, 1919, that the state of war between the Associated Powers and Germany was brought to an end by the Treaty of Versailles, and it was more than a year later before peace with Austria was formally concluded. So far, however, as concerned active operations between the principal belligerents, the war ended on November 11th, 1918. The terms of the armistice were too drastic, the collapse of the Central Powers was too complete, to permit any reasonable likelihood of the resumption of hostilities, whatever course the peace negotiations might take. The fleets and armies of the Allies remained on a war footing, the restrictions on the trade of the Central Powers were continued, with some modifications, as a precautionary measure and an instrument for the enforcement of demands; but the position of the Associated Powers was of such overwhelming strength that they were able to take, without waiting for the signature of the treaty, the preliminary steps in the transition from a war to a peace economy.

It is true that the effects of the war on seaborne trade did not cease either with the armistice or with the treaties. They are felt to-day and they are likely to be felt for many years, perhaps for generations, in every department of national life; but they have been so profoundly modified and accentuated by *post-bellum* developments that it is impossible to attempt in these pages any final analysis of the injury inflicted on the economic life of the world by four and a half years of destruction. All that can be done is to sum up, briefly, the direct effects of the war at sea on the position in which the principal belligerents were left at the end of the long struggle.

The outstanding feature of the situation was this: that the Allies were, and the Central Powers were not, able, if necessary, to continue the war for another year. That a complete break-down in the German supply both of foodstuffs and of essential materials was almost inevitable in the event of the war lasting far into 1919, we have already seen; but so much stress has been laid on the difficulties of the Allies with regard to tonnage and supplies, that it is necessary to say a few words with regard to their prospects, in the event of a prolongation of the struggle.

So far as Great Britain was concerned, the import position, which had so greatly deteriorated in 1917, had now been, to a great extent, stabilised. The total entrances of ships with cargoes at ports in the United Kingdom were almost exactly the same in 1918 as in the previous year. Those of foreign shipping fell away by about a million tons, but a considerable part of this difference was due to the substitution of British for Norwegian shipping in the North Sea, and to the fact that requisitioned Norwegian ships were placed under the British flag. For the rest, the decline was mainly accounted for by the increasing absorption of Allied and neutral tonnage in the service of France and Italy. The whole decrease was, however, practically wiped out by the increased entrances of British shipping, due to greater concentration and quicker turn-round.

Thanks to these economies in the use of British tonnage, the total volume of imports was only 5·7 per cent. less than in 1917. Even if oil-fuel on Admiralty account be excluded from the figures of both years, the decrease was slightly under 2,500,000 tons or 7·3 per cent., a much less serious decline than had been anticipated at the beginning of 1918.

Among the individual decreases the largest were in wheat and flour, roughly 1,000,000 tons, and in other cereals and pulses, about 900,000 tons. At first sight these are rather startling figures, but they are partly accounted for by the increased proportion of wheat taken in the form of flour, and the actual reduction was off-set by a large increase in the area under cultivation in the United Kingdom itself. With regard to other foodstuffs, the imports of meat and bacon, though they included much of doubtful quality, were considerably heavier than in 1917, and those of miscellaneous foodstuffs about the same.

Imports of the two bulkiest raw materials required for war purposes were both larger than in 1917; those of petroleum by over 1,000,000 tons, and those of iron-ore by 390,000. As against this there was a further cut of 500,000 tons in the supplies of timber, and a drastic reduction in the purchases of manufactured goods, and in the transit trade. Except where it was absolutely necessary to build up depleted stocks,[1] the restrictions in force during 1917 had been applied with increased stringency, and the import of many articles, such as clocks, cotton hosiery and textiles, leather gloves, hats, hardware, and ostrich feathers, had been practically wiped out. If certain articles of luxury, such as fancy goods and embroidery, were still permitted to come in, it was because their exchange value to the exporting countries outweighed the importance of the small amount of ship-space occupied.

The transit trade had been ruthlessly dealt with. Re-exports of cotton, jute, tin, rice, tea, coffee, cocoa, palm-oil, rubber, gums, spices, and many other products were either prohibited altogether, or reduced to a very small proportion of the 1917 total. The total saving in carrying power was considerable, but the effect on the exchanges was necessarily bad. Of still greater importance, however, was the reduction in imports of wool and cotton, amounting respectively to 100,000 and 60,000 tons. With a view to alleviating the effects of trooping on the American cotton shipments, the Ministry of Shipping had allocated additional space for Egyptian cotton, and re-exports were entirely prohibited, so that the total decrease in net supplies was only 13,000 tons, or about $1\frac{1}{2}$ per cent. on 1917 ; but even during 1917 the industry had been living on its stocks, and only the arrangements made by the Cotton Control Board to adjust the incidence of the shortage, averted widespread ruin and destitution. In the woollen industry, larger stocks were held, owing to the importance of the army demand, and though exports suffered from the reduction of supplies, which was due mainly to the depletion of the Australasian services, the general position of the industry was comparatively favourable.

It was, of course, the effect on the export trade which was the most serious aspect of this reduction in the imports of textile materials ; but this was only one phase of an all-round decline in exports during 1918. There was hardly a single important item of the export trade in which the volume of shipments was not well below the level of 1917,

[1] As, for example, jute, tea, and tobacco.

and whereas the combined value of exports and re-exports in that year had reached nearly 56 per cent. of the import values, this proportion dropped, in 1918, to barely 40 per cent.

What this meant to the country's power of economic recovery we shall have to consider later; but with the almost unlimited credit of the United States to draw on, it was still possible to finance inward shipments, and the imports received during 1918 had been at least sufficient to meet the essential requirements of the food supply and the war industries. The same may be said of France and Italy. Their essential requirements for cereals, munitions, and fuel had been fulfilled, though at heavy cost, and the arrangements made by the Allied Maritime Transport Council secured their fulfilment in 1919. For the maintenance of a volume of supplies greatly in excess of their actual purchasing power, all three countries would, in the future, have to pay a heavy price; but even under war conditions they were still in a position to satisfy their immediate needs.

It is true that, in the months immediately preceding the armistice, the Allied Governments had not been free from anxiety. Had the war continued beyond the winter, its strain must have been more severely felt than ever before, especially in Great Britain, which had hitherto suffered least of the European Allies. It is necessary, however, to emphasise the fact that this accentuation of the strain arose neither from lack of available supplies nor from a permanent shortage of importing power. It was deliberately accepted as the temporary price of overwhelming military superiority. When the Allied Maritime Transport Council decided to give munitions, during the winter of 1918–19, a priority over food, they did so in the certain knowledge that, by the spring, sufficient tonnage would be available to build up the depleted stocks and restore the balance of imports. So far as could be judged, the submarine menace had been definitely mastered. Already the current rate of replacement was keeping pace with losses, and it was reasonable to expect that the rate of loss would be still further reduced through the increasing efficiency of the convoy system and the effect of the mine barrages in the North Sea and the Straits of Otranto. By the spring, or at latest the early summer of 1919, the progress of the American shipbuilding programme, aided by the efforts of British yards, should give a supply of tonnage sufficient to meet in full, not only the needs of the armies, but the import requirements of the Allies. Should the position as regards food stocks become critical before that date, there were ample supplies of cereals in North America, and a large volume of tonnage in the Atlantic could be diverted from the military programme to the carriage of emergency shipments. Provided the morale of the Allied peoples held, their economic position was as assured as their military superiority.

Apart from this question of ability to continue the struggle, and apart also from those permanent effects of the war which we shall have hereafter to consider, there was a fundamental difference between the position of the two belligerent groups at the date of the armistice, which dominated the whole course of events during the period of transition from war to peace, and thus affected, to an incalculable extent, the ultimate capacity for recuperation displayed by the nations concerned. Not only were the Central Powers economically prostrate, they were unable, of their own strength, to take the first steps towards recovery. Their chief markets, their chief sources of supply, were in the possession or under the control of their enemies; their resources were mortgaged for fulfilment of the victors' demands; their shipping was in the power of the Allies, and even neutral tonnage was still barred from their ports. They were at the mercy of their enemies alike for permission to purchase and for the means of transport.

To the Allied and Associated Powers, on the contrary, the sea routes of the world and the markets of the world were alike open. They controlled by ownership, by hire or purchase, or by agreement, by far the greater proportion of the world's exportable surplus of food and materials, and by far the greater proportion of the world's disposable tonnage.

It is true that, under war conditions, the available tonnage had proved insufficient to maintain the stream of supplies at anything like its normal volume; but this arose not so much from an actual deficiency of shipping, as from the effect of the war on its employment. It was not because the submarines had reduced the available tonnage to a level inadequate to the essential demands of commerce, but because a third of the entire steam tonnage under the British, French, Italian, and American flags was on naval or military service, that the outlook, just before the cessation of hostilities, had given rise to anxiety.

On the signing of the armistice, the whole position was changed, and the Allies were free, without further regard to preparations for a spring campaign, to take advantage of their access to the sources of supply. The extent to which tonnage in naval and military service could be diverted to the carriage of food and raw materials was limited for some time by the necessity of maintaining large forces on a war footing, and by the repatriation of troops and prisoners; but, as already stated, the Allied Governments were sufficiently confident to take, without delay, the first steps towards economic restoration.

Owing partly to the necessity for repatriating the Allied armies and the difficulty of winding up the enormous commitments into which the Allied Governments had entered; partly to their fear of the effects of unrestricted competition in a world still short, as a whole, of supplies and tonnage, the control both of commodities and of shipping was only very gradually relaxed. The history of this period of transition, profoundly interesting and significant, lies outside the scope of these volumes; but for the sake of completeness and to make clear certain points in the subsequent analysis, it is necessary to refer very briefly to the immediate effects of the cessation of hostilities.

Even before the armistice was signed, the Allied Maritime Transport Executive had taken into consideration the extent to which the previously agreed import programme could be modified, and new instructions, to be carried into effect immediately the cessation of hostilities was officially announced, were sent out through the Ministry of Shipping and kindred Allied organisations. These instructions amounted to a complete reversal of the decision arrived at at the beginning of October, and shipments of munitions gave place to foodstuffs and the raw materials of industry.

No less prompt were the Admiralty in releasing commerce from the restrictions which it had been necessary, for its own safety, to impose upon it. Even in the unlikely event of a renewal of hostilities, that safety was now assured, for the terms of the armistice provided for the surrender to the Allies of the bulk of the German fleet, including every submarine then in existence, and for the disclosure of all areas in which mines had been laid. These terms were duly fulfilled, but the Admiralty did not wait for their fulfilment. On the very day the armistice was signed, they issued orders suspending the application of the convoy system. On that day independent sailings were resumed from the United Kingdom, and within a fortnight the last homeward-bound convoys had arrived at British ports.

Not only was British shipping thus released from the delays and restrictions incidental to the system of protection which had served it so well, it was relieved at the same time of the financial burden of insurance against the risks of loss. On November 11th the hull premium under the State scheme was reduced at one stroke from 140s. to 15s. per cent. for a ninety-one-day time policy, and to 2s. 6d. per cent. for a single voyage. For a voyage policy this was only the normal rate of insurance against the outbreak of war, current in 1914, and as the certainty of peace became stronger and the minefields were disclosed and swept up, the time premium was further reduced on January 11th, 1919, to 7s. 6d., and on February 6th to 5s. per cent.[1] Insurance of cargoes with the State Office had ceased on the termination of hostilities.

As a result of this virtual disappearance of war risk, the Ministry of Shipping reduced the freights on Government cargoes, as from December 15th, 1918, by approximately 50 per cent., and arrangements were made for a substantial reduction of commercial tariffs by the Liner Conferences. This was the more important as, from the date of the armistice, rapid progress was made by the Liner Requisition Committee in the redistribution of liner tonnage and the restoration of the normal services. Vessels which had been diverted from the Australasian, Far Eastern, and other trades to the North Atlantic were returned to their accustomed employment, and tonnage was thus provided not only for imports from the more distant countries, but for the exports of which those countries had so long been deprived. Pending the approaching release of their ships from requisition, the lines were instructed to give preference to shipments of foodstuffs and the more important materials required for restoring the normal economic life of the country; but in the North Atlantic trade a proportion of the space was

[1] Liverpool and London War Risks Insurance Association. Report for year ending February 19th, 1919, p. 17.

released to the lines, to be booked at their own discretion, with a view to reviving ordinary commercial intercourse.

In the disposition of tramp tonnage also, it was possible, now that the pressure of military demands had diminished, to pay greater regard to ordinary commercial considerations, and break up the concentration on the North Atlantic tracks. Immediately after the armistice, arrangements were made to send a large number of ships to Australian ports, to lift at least a portion of the enormous stocks of wheat held in the Commonwealth; another large block of tonnage was allocated to the Plate, with the object of increasing maize imports, and many sugar steamers were diverted from Cuba to Java and Mauritius.

The actual immediate effect of the armistice on the supply of tonnage was limited, as has been said, by the necessity of providing for repatriation and for maintaining, in the meantime, the immense forces on the Continent; but even before the end of November many steamers were released for commercial employment, by the diminution in shipments of stores and munitions to France. The cessation of American trooping and of the shipment of remounts not only released a large amount of liner space in the North Atlantic, but enabled the Allied Maritime Transport Executive to cancel at once the allocation of a large block of British tonnage to American military supply. In December the French steel service from the United States to France and Italy came to an end, together with the special liner services to those countries. In the same month the Chilean nitrate service was suspended, several of the cargoes on passage being diverted to Allied or neutral ports where fertilisers were in demand. The import of oil in double bottoms had been discontinued even before the armistice, and in December, owing to the great reduction in consumption arising from the cessation of hostilities and the discontinuance of convoy, the Admiralty made preparations for releasing the requisitioned tankers on naval service. At the same time, owing to the removal of war risk, neutral ships began to come in greater numbers on to the freight market, and were willing to accept considerably lower rates, especially for Mediterranean voyages.

Whether on military or commercial service the bulk of British and Allied tonnage was still, at the beginning of 1919, under the direct control of the State, but in February of that year the British, French, and American Governments alike began, in earnest, the process of setting free their ships from requisition. In that month the Liner Requisition Scheme was terminated by an agreement under which the lines received back their ships, subject to heavy commitments with regard to the carriage of Government cargo and passengers at limitation rates, from which they were not finally freed until August 1920. Fully requisitioned ships on naval and military service were released as fast as the requirements of the forces permitted, and those engaged in the transport of cereals and sugar were returned to their owners as the current charters ran off. On March 1st the Official Ore Broker ceased to charter, and on the same date the Ministry of Shipping ceased to be responsible for the French and Italian coal services.

It was not, however, considered advisable to withdraw at one step all control over the movements of shipping, and for the purpose of bridging the period of transition the Ship Licensing Committee was reconstituted, and entrusted with the task of directing, in consultation with the supply Departments, ships coming off requisition, into the trades where tonnage was most urgently needed. It was not until February 1920 that the licensing system was finally discontinued, and meanwhile the Government cargoes, which still formed a large proportion of the total imports, were carried at limitation freights. Further, by arrangement with the French and Italian Governments, the Licensing Committee were instructed to direct into the service of France and Italy, at rates not exceeding 25*s.* per ton dead-weight, for ordinary ocean-going steamers, as much British tonnage as was running in such employment on October 31st, 1918.

It was, of course, impossible for the Allied Governments, while releasing their own ships from requisition, to retain possession of the neutral ships which they had seized, and redelivery of the requisitioned Dutch steamers began in January 1919. In the same month Norway gave notice requiring redelivery of the ships requisitioned under the Norwegian Agreement. But perhaps the most important question with regard to tonnage, arising during the first few months after the armistice, was that of enemy shipping.

On October 28th, 1918, the Transport Executive had strongly recommended that a clause should be inserted in the armistice, providing for the immediate surrender of German shipping, against a guarantee of food supplies to Germany. Unfortunately this proposal was not adopted. It was not until the renewal of the armistice in January 1919 that provision was made, by the Trèves Agreement of January 17th, for the bulk of the ships to be handed over to the Allies, without prejudice to their subsequent disposal, in return for permission to import 200,000 tons of bread-stuffs and 70,000 tons of pork products.

Even then all was not plain sailing. The Germans were unwilling to deliver the ships until full guarantees for food supplies had been given, and the Allies were unwilling to give such guarantees until the difficult question of finance had been arranged. Further, the ambiguity of the Trèves Agreement led to prolonged wrangling with regard to the conditions on which the ships were to be taken over, the exceptions to be allowed, and the hire to be credited. It was not until the middle of March that matters were finally arranged, and meanwhile this great mass of shipping lay absolutely idle.

By this time the question had become a burning one. During the first few weeks after the armistice, more tonnage had been rendered available for commercial service than could readily be utilised, especially at British ports. The coal output was still lamentably insufficient, and during the first fortnight of December, over half a million tons of shipping was sent away in ballast. This state of things, however, was not of long duration. As the pressure of peace demands became effective, the surplus tonnage was rapidly absorbed. To these demands were added the requirements of European relief, both in enemy and liberated territories, and the repatriation of troops, prisoners, and refugees, and it was not long before the supply of tonnage again became inadequate to the demand.

It is true that there were now no war losses to offset the effects of new construction in Britain and America, and the available British tonnage had been increased during December and January, by the return of ships hitherto interned in German ports. On the other hand, though 76 per cent. of the yards allocated to mercantile construction in the United Kingdom had been cleared of naval work by the end of 1918,[1] the output was still limited by

[1] War Cabinet Report for 1918, p. 180.

labour difficulties. Moreover, the cessation of hostilities had been followed by a great increase in the number of ships under repair, owing to the necessity of reconditioning vessels released from Government service, and making good the postponement of repairs during the war. Delivery of these ships was delayed by strikes in the repairers' yards, and during the first three months of 1919 some 10 per cent. of the ocean-going tonnage under the British flag was thus off service. Further, labour troubles combined with the rush of imports which followed the armistice to reduce the annual carrying power of the ships, by producing acute congestion at the ports, and by March 1919 there was a shortage of tonnage comparable to the worst periods of the war.

Some relief, indeed, had been found in the requisitioning of Austrian steamers. These were much more easily dealt with than German shipping, as the bulk of the tonnage lay in Adriatic ports occupied by Italy. The total, in steamers of 500 tons gross and upwards, was less by about one-fourth than at the outbreak of war, when it amounted to just over 1,000,000 tons. Nearly 360,000 tons gross had been sunk, captured, seized in Allied ports, or transferred to foreign flags; but 97,000 tons of new shipping had been launched, and on December 31st, 1918, the total amounted to 753,000 tons, of which nearly 330,000 tons had been brought into service by March 1st, and was employed either in naval and military service or in European relief.

The acquisition of German tonnage was, however, a much more important matter. In steamers of 500 tons gross and upwards, it had amounted before the war to about 5,000,000 tons. Owing to the promptitude with which German ships had sought shelter, and their abstention from any attempt to carry on trade during the war, except with Baltic and Scandinavian ports, the total tonnage sunk through war and marine risks was only about 300,000 gross; but over 2,000,000 tons had been captured or seized by the Allies, and nearly 300,000 tons had been transferred to, or requisitioned by, neutral States.[1] On the other hand, about 625,000 tons of new shipping had been launched, and the total on December 31st, 1918, was roughly 3,000,000 tons, of which about 800,000 tons lay in neutral, and the remainder in German, ports.

[1] Including States which afterwards joined the Allies.

The disposal of this great block of tonnage was finally provided for by the Brussels Agreement of March 14th, 1919. By this agreement the Germans undertook to surrender to the Allies, on conditions which were now fully set out, and without prejudice to the final decision as to ownership, the whole of their steam fleet, with the exception of tankers, certain vessels engaged in supporting German forces in Eastern Germany, a proportion of the smaller cargo vessels (under 2,500 tons gross), and steamers under construction, requiring more than six months for completion. In all, about 2,000,000 tons was to be delivered. In return, the Allies agreed to supply as quickly as transportation could be arranged, the 270,000 tons of foodstuffs originally mentioned, and to permit the purchase by Germany of 370,000 tons of foodstuffs monthly up to September 1st. The carriage of such foodstuffs was to be a first charge on the employment of the German shipping surrendered.

Most of the German ships in neutral ports, even when not seriously damaged, required a considerable amount of reconditioning after their long period of enforced idleness, but those in German ports were in fairly good condition, and between March 21st, when the first ship left Germany, and the end of April, about 1,000,000 tons had been delivered. Rather more than half of this was on active service on May 1st, and the remainder repairing, refitting, or awaiting allocation. For purpose of management, the ships were divided among the Allies, but the employment of all ships was regulated by two main principles: passenger steamers were used exclusively for the repatriation of troops, prisoners, and refugees; cargo steamers were employed in priority for European, and mainly for German, relief.

Following the conclusion of the Brussels Agreement, and the delivery of German shipping, the Supreme Economic Council of the Allies, into which the Transport Council and the Food Council were absorbed, during April, proposed that all restrictions on German trade should be lifted; but this proposal was rejected by the Council of Four, and it was not until July 12th, a fortnight after the signing of the peace treaty, that the German ports were fully re-opened. The various agreements with neutral countries were, however, gradually relaxed, to enable Germany to obtain food from neutral as well as Allied sources up to the permitted total,[1] and to export goods in payment.

From May onwards, when the German tonnage was coming freely into service, the shipping situation was greatly eased, as not only was the burden of European relief lifted, in large measure, from the shoulders of the Allies, but the use of German passenger steamers for repatriation purposes set free a large block of liner tonnage. By June 1919 the British ocean-going tonnage available for the import services of the United Kingdom had risen to 9,340,000 dead-weight, against 6,700,000 in October 1918.

To Germany, unfortunately, the relief was less apparent. Large as was the tonnage now available for relief purposes, it was not so large as was required, and even greater than the difficulty of arranging tonnage, was the difficulty of arranging finance. The hire credited in respect of the steamers delivered was overbalanced by the cost of repairs and the freights on German cargoes, and Germany, as we have seen, and shall see, was in no condition either to pay her way by exports, or to negotiate extensive credits. The total food supplies received by September 1st amounted to considerably less than half the permitted total,[2] and a scheme for arranging the import of raw materials had hopelessly broken down.

[1] Fish from contiguous neutrals did not count against the ration.
[2] Food purchased through the British Government was supplied at cost price.

CHAPTER XXVII

THE LEGACY OF THE WAR

MORE than once in these volumes it has been necessary to emphasise the fact that the history of seaborne trade covers only one phase of the economic effects of the war. Had no submarine or raider ever issued from a German port, had Germany herself been free to trade with all neutral countries, the war must, nevertheless, have affected profoundly the economic position of the belligerents. It was impossible that so many millions should be called to arms from the plough, the workshop, and the desk; that so many thousands of factories should be diverted to the fulfilment of military requirements, without disastrous reactions on industry, commerce, and finance. Between the results of this diversion of effort, and the effects of the submarine campaign and economic pressure no hard-and-fast line can be drawn; for the two things were simultaneous and inter-related in their development. We have already seen, however, that there was a marked and suggestive contrast, at the end of the war, between the position of those countries which had preserved the use of their maritime communications and those which had been deprived of them. That contrast it is necessary to examine in rather greater detail.

How desperate was the economic condition of Germany at the date of the armistice, and how powerfully it had contributed to the collapse of the German resistance, we have already seen. Even graver in its significance was the cumulative effect of four and a half years of isolation on the country's power of recovery. It was not only that, as pointed out in the preceding chapter, Germany was dependent upon the victors for leave to resume commercial relations with the outside world; her capacity for production and exchange had received such wide and lasting injuries that, even had all restrictions been immediately removed, her recovery must have been slow and doubtful. The end of the war found the soil of Germany impoverished; the live stock diminished and deteriorated; the stocks of raw materials exhausted; the machinery of transport and production impaired; the people physically and morally enfeebled. Victory itself would have given no certain assurance against economic collapse, followed by social and political upheaval.

It has been repeatedly pointed out that, so far as the German food supply was concerned, the danger of interrupted communications lay not so much in the loss of that small proportion of foodstuffs for direct human consumption, procured from overseas, as in the cutting off of imported fertilisers and imported fodder. It was this which had been mainly responsible for the calamitous decrease in the home production of cereals, meat, and fats. The supply of agricultural labour had always been fairly adequate, men called to the Colours being replaced by voluntary labour and by prisoners of war, and owing to the impossibility of enforcing the rationing system strictly on self-suppliers, the strength and activity of the agricultural labourer had not been sapped, like that of the industrial worker, by malnutrition. Even when the demands of the war industries were at their highest, agricultural machinery, as a primary national necessity, had enjoyed a large measure of priority, and there is little evidence of any real shortage of plant or implements. The bad harvests of 1915, 1916, and 1917 were, no doubt, due in part to exceptionally unfavourable weather, but there can be no doubt that the chief cause of diminished production was the lack of artificial fertilisers, and the diminution in both the quantity and quality of animal manure, due to the reduction of herds and the scarcity of concentrated feeding-stuffs.

By 1918, the nitrogen available for agricultural purposes had been reduced by more than one-half, the supply of phosphoric acid by over 70 per cent. The works established during the war for the extraction of nitrogen from the air were capable, if fully utilised, of providing two and a half times the total amount used for all purposes before the war; but a great part of their output had been required for munitions, and owing to coal and labour difficulties, their full capacity had never been developed. In the months immediately following the armistice, these difficulties increased, and restricted the output of the works to about one-sixth of their potential capacity.

The effects on naturally poor soil of a shortage of manures are in a high degree cumulative, and by the end of 1918 the latent reserve of productivity built up by many years of intensive cultivation was approaching exhaustion. According to the experts who visited Germany in 1919, on behalf of the British Government, the productivity of the soil had declined by approximately 40 per cent. : " several years, and a large expenditure on concentrated foods and manures will be necessary before the productive state of the land can be brought to its previous figure." [1] Whether that expenditure could be carried out, whether Germany could provide the necessary exports, or arrange the necessary credits, to enable her to resume her imports of oil-cake, phosphate rock, and Chile saltpetre, depended on other factors of her economic position. How far she could develop the manufacture of air nitrates depended on the coal output and on labour and transport conditions.

In any event, some considerable time must elapse before either soil or live stock recovered from the effects of the war. The herds of cattle had decreased in numbers by about 18 per cent., and of pigs by no less than 60 per cent. The deterioration in quality was as serious as the reduction in numbers; in respect of cattle it was, indeed, the greater evil. In the summer of 1919, the British experts failed to discover a single first-grade beast in the Berlin slaughter houses. The whole supply consisted of inferior third- or fourth-grade carcasses, devoid of all fat. Moreover, not only was the number of cows giving milk reduced, but the yield of milk per cow had fallen by over 40 per cent., and the total output of milk in 1918 was only about half the normal.[2]

To build up the depleted stocks, both in numbers and condition, as well as to restore the land to its original fertility, must inevitably be a costly and lengthy business, even if it were possible at once to resume importation on a large scale; but apart from any restrictions imposed by the Allies, Germany was in no condition to obtain the necessary supplies. The effect of the war on German industries was as serious as its effect on the supply of food. Even where raw materials were available, the output

---

[1] Cmd. 280, pp. 11, 15, 18.   [2] *Ibid.*, pp. 19-20, 24-5.

had greatly diminished, owing to the shortage of skilled workers, the effects of malnutrition, the deterioration of plant, and the disorganisation of transport. The men who had been called to the Colours were now once more available ; but the other effects of the war were of a more lasting character. The coal mines, in particular, had deteriorated seriously owing to lack of pit-props and to postponement of repairs and extensions, and the output of coal had sunk to about two-thirds of the normal. The deterioration of the railways and rolling-stock impeded distribution of the coal produced. There was thus an acute shortage of fuel for industrial as well as for domestic purposes, which lasted long after the cessation of hostilities, and was in itself sufficient to cause the closing down of many factories for longer or shorter periods, and to prevent the majority from running full time.[1]

To shortage of fuel and deterioration of plant, there was added in most industries, an acute shortage of raw materials. Textiles, fibres, metals, rubber, leather, were all equally scarce ; in fact, with the exception of some small army stocks, Germany was stripped practically bare of all materials other than those produced within the country itself. The release of military stocks after the armistice did something to relieve the situation, but the amounts held were very small in comparison with the demands of industry, and very large imports were required to give adequate employment to the factories.[2]

Neither imports of food nor imports of raw materials could be obtained immediately after the armistice, save by the good-will of the Associated Powers ; but a more lasting obstacle to economic restoration was the difficulty of financing shipments. Accumulated stocks of manufactured goods were as scanty as the stocks of materials,[3] and Germany had very little to export. Moreover, the Allies retained a right of pre-emption over a large proportion of such goods as were available for shipment. Nor was it easy to arrange other methods of payment. The income annually derived before the war from shipping, banking, and insurance services rendered to foreigners, had been utterly cut off, and there was no prospect of such

---

[1] *Economic Survey of certain Countries specially affected by the War at the Close of the Year* 1919. Department of Overseas Trade, 1920, pp. 35-8, 45.
[2] *Ibid.*, p. 35.
[3] *Ibid.*, pp. 37-8, 39.

business being built up, for many years, to anything like its former proportions. The pick of the German securities in America, North and South, and in contiguous neutral countries, had been parted with during the war. Investments in Russia, Austria-Hungary, and the Balkans were now of little, if any, value. Of the total German investments abroad, amounting before the war to about £1,000,000,000, not more than £20,000,000 proved immediately available for the provision of credits. Gold to the amount of about £115,000,000 lay in the vaults of the Reichsbank, but this was subject to the demands of the Allies for reparations, and could not be unduly depleted without further depreciation of German credit.[1]

To add to the difficulties of the situation, the cost of all imports was enormously enhanced by the condition of the exchanges. By September 1918 the mark stood at a discount of from 42 to 48 per cent. in the contiguous neutral countries, and apart from the effects of revolution and defeat, it could not fail to fall still further when Germany obtained access to oversea markets. The character of German war finance, the enormous inflation of the currency, the effects of defeat and of political upheaval, all combined with the diminution of productive and exporting power, and the immensity of the import needs, to forbid any hope of an improvement in the rate of exchange. Over all attempts to obtain credits abroad hung the shadow of the peace negotiations, involving probable loss of territory, the payment of heavy reparations, and the surrender of German shipping.

A vicious circle was thus set up which imposed almost insuperable obstacles to the resumption of trade. It was impossible to restore the productivity of the soil and industries without obtaining large, immediate supplies of foodstuffs and raw materials; it was impossible to pay for such supplies until productivity had been restored.

Such was the immediate position. The outlook for the future was further darkened by the condition of the principal markets for German exports. Before the war over 40 per cent. in value of those exports went to the British Empire, France, Belgium, Italy, and the United States, over 20 per cent. to Austria-Hungary, Russia, and the Balkan States. Russia and Austria were now in a state

[1] About £50,000,000 was ultimately transferred to the Allies during the first six months of 1919 in payment for foodstuffs.

of political and economic chaos far worse than that of Germany herself, and shipments to the Associated Powers were likely to be earmarked for the payment of reparations, and not available for the building up of new credits. To all this must be added the effect of the long interruption of communications on the machinery of commerce and finance, the closing down of German businesses and agencies in Allied countries, and the destruction of German connections in many neutral States, by the operation of the Black Lists.

The prospect was thus sufficiently black to appal even a healthy and vigorous people, but behind all the adverse material conditions lay the effects of the war on the physique and mentality of the Germans themselves. The moral effects of defeat and revolution must, in any event, have hampered recovery. There can be no doubt that they were magnified enormously by the cumulative effects of three years' acute privation.

Among the civilian population of Germany the death-rate, in 1918, was 37 per cent. higher than before the war. For the four years, 1915 to 1918, the total number of civilian deaths exceeded by 760,000 the expectation of mortality based on *ante-bellum* statistics. Deaths directly traceable to starvation were comparatively few, but the statistics of tuberculosis, pneumonia, and similar diseases afford terrible proof of the extent to which the people's vitality and power of resistance had been diminished by cold, dirt, and hunger. To take a single instance, the rate of mortality arising in Prussia as a whole from tubercule of the lungs, was two and a half times as great at the end as it was at the beginning of the war.[1] Meanwhile the birth-rate had fallen by nearly one-half, and in the twelve months ending June 1918, the total deaths exceeded the total births by 885,000.[2]

It was not, however, only in the vital statistics that the effects of the war were shown, but in the general condition of the population. Among the food-producing classes there had been comparatively little suffering, and their physical energies remained unimpaired; but the condition of the consuming classes, forming two-thirds of the whole, was generally deplorable. A very large number had lost from 15 to 25 per cent. of their original

[1] Cmd. 280, p. 8.
[2] *Ibid.*, p. 9 and Appendix 22 (*a*). Figures by C. Döring, Copenhagen.

body-weight, and the effect was seen, not only in their decreased resistance to infectious disorders, but in diminished working capacity, and a weakening of moral fibre which formed one of the most formidable impediments to economic restoration. The people as a whole were listless, apathetic, and hopeless, and the constant evasions of food regulations during the war, had inevitably led to a lessening of respect for laws, which was accentuated by the disillusionment of defeat, and by the relaxation of authority which followed the revolution.[1]

Particularly serious were the effects of the war on the rising generation. Children born during the war were normal, in spite of the malnutrition of the mothers, but the condition of the mothers, and the shortage of cow's milk, seriously affected their growth. Although the total milk supply in 1918 was about half the normal, the distribution was very unequal. Self-suppliers, as usual, received far more than their share, and much was used for butter, which fetched high prices in illicit trade. The actual supply of milk to Berlin was about one-fifth of the normal, and most large centres of population were similarly affected. As a consequence of this, coupled with the general shortage of food, the mortality of children between the ages of two and six years was said to have risen 49 per cent. by the end of 1917. By 1918 the death-rate among children of school age had increased by 55 per cent. A very large proportion of the children were tuberculous, and the wide spread of rickets among all classes, not only weakened the resistance to infection, but produced much permanent deformity.[2]

Such was the condition in which Germany was left by the failure of her bid for world dominion, and as we have already seen, the worst effect of that condition was to paralyse the measures attempted for its relief. It is true that it was mainly the prolonged wrangle over the delivery of German shipping which postponed the first deliveries of food until the end of March, more than four months after the signing of the armistice; but it was the financial difficulty, above all else, which restricted so greatly the imports of foodstuffs under the Brussels Agreement, and for many months after the conclusion of peace continued to prohibit any extensive import of raw materials.

[1] Cmd. 280, pp. 10, 12, 15. *Economic Survey*, p. 45.
[2] Cmd. 280, pp. 9, 11, 15.

The financial difficulty itself was caused in large measure by the Allies' lien on such resources as Germany possessed, and by the effect on German credit of the vast, undefined claim for reparations; but even if this factor had been absent, the exhaustion both of the German resources and of the German people must have rendered the task of economic restoration one of superlative difficulty.

As it was, the total food supplies available during a great part of 1919 were somewhat smaller than in the last year of the war, and right down to the end of the year the supply of food and fuel was the one preoccupation of the people; only a small beginning had been made in the import of raw materials, and the foreign trade of the country was practically negligible.[1] The inevitable result was to accentuate and in large measure to stereotype the conditions existing at the armistice. What progress was subsequently made in the restoration of supplies and industry, and how that progress was affected by political developments, internal and external, and by the effect on German production and German credit of the Treaty of Versailles, lies outside the scope of this history. The final analysis of the effect of the war on the political, social, and economic life of Germany will not be made in this generation.

In Austria-Hungary all the conditions which had led to the collapse, and now hampered the recovery of Germany, were present in an exaggerated form, but they were less directly traceable to the effects of Allied pressure. The loss of imported materials and imported fertilisers was, indeed, serious, but the acute food shortage of the later period of the war was largely the result of defective transport and administrative weakness. It was, however, the loss of maritime communications which prevented this shortage from being made good, and contributed powerfully both to the breakdown of transport and to the appalling rise in prices that played so great a part in fanning the flames of discontent.

Over the whole area of South-Eastern Europe, Austria-Hungary, and the Balkans, the hopeless break-down of the transport system, the shortage and bad condition of locomotives and rolling-stock, presented one of the most serious obstacles to recovery. To this must be added the

[1] *Economic Survey*, pp. 35-45, *passim*.

widespread destruction of crops, live stock, and oil-wells, in the invasions of Galicia, Roumania, and Serbia, and the universal depreciation of the currency caused by the financial strain of the war. In producing both the transport and the financial break-down the loss of power to import or export by sea was a big factor; but any clear analysis of the position produced by the war itself is almost impossible, owing to the way in which the problem was complicated by the spread of revolution, the break-up of the Austrian Empire, the mutual jealousies of the liberated States, and the restrictions imposed on traffic by the new Governments. It must be said, however, that the conditions which favoured the outbreak of revolution, and which actuated, and to some extent justified the attitude of the Governments towards freedom of commerce, were themselves a legacy of the war, and were in large measure the results of suspended sea communications. Further, there was no factor more powerful in delaying the recovery of South-Eastern Europe than the collapse of Germany, its natural economic centre.

Much the same may be said of Russia, and of the new States carved out of the old Russian Empire. It is unnecessary to repeat here what has already been said with regard to the causes of the Russian revolution. When all allowance has been made for the social and political causes of unrest, it remains true that the economic conditions arising from the closing of the Baltic and Black Sea played a large, perhaps a preponderant, part in producing both the revolution itself and the peculiarly violent and destructive character that it ultimately assumed. Unhappily, the effect of the revolution was to accentuate the very conditions from which it took its origin. The failure of the Bolshevik Government to establish peaceful relations with the Western Powers led to continued commercial isolation, and the disintegration of the Empire into a number of independent and mutually hostile States, perpetuated the barriers which had arisen between the industrial centre and the food- and coal-producing districts.

To the condition of these countries, that of the Western Allies, whose oversea communications, though continually harassed, had never been definitely interrupted, presented a vivid contrast. Able, as they were, to obtain all through the war sufficient supplies to nourish their fighting strength and provide at least the bare essentials of civilian life, they emerged from it as victors, secure, at least comparatively, in the stability of their political and social fabric, and with unhampered access to the markets of the world. Even Belgium, prostrate as she had lain under the German occupation, had been fed from overseas, and now shared in the triumph of the Allies.

With regard to Belgium little need be said here. Her sufferings form an important chapter in the general economic history of the war, but they were the effect of the German occupation, not of the interruption of communications by operations at sea. When once the armies of occupation were removed, recovery was surprisingly rapid. The stocks of raw materials had, it is true, been consumed or requisitioned, and many of the factories had suffered much from the requisitioning of metals; but outside the narrow fighting zone in Flanders, the damage done was less serious than in North-Eastern France. By the end of 1919 the production of coal had almost reached the normal level, and both the re-equipment of the factories and the import of raw materials had made great progress, despite the drawback of high prices and labour unrest, from which Belgium suffered in common with all other countries.[1]

One very important factor in recuperation was the good physical condition of the people. Even during the period of unrestricted submarine warfare, ships chartered by the Commission for Belgian Relief had enjoyed a measure of immunity, and thanks to the energy displayed by the Commission, and the assistance latterly afforded by the Allied Maritime Transport Council, the population had received sufficient food to maintain them in health under the sedentary conditions of the war years. When, therefore, ample food supplies became available after the armistice, they were able to resume work with vigour little, if at all, impaired.[2]

The main direct effects of the war at sea were the depletion of Belgian tonnage, and the damage done to the ports by the German occupation and the British blocking expeditions. So far as shipping was concerned, the recovery was rapid, for though the war losses by enemy action

---

[1] *Economic Survey*, pp. 10–16.
[2] Cmd. 280, p. 7n, p. 10n, pp. 44–5. *Economic Survey*, p. 10. Salter, *Allied Shipping Control*, pp. 236–7.

amounted to 86,000 tons, or about a quarter of the tonnage owned before the war, the steam fleet had been raised, by July 1919, to within 10 per cent. of the *ante-bellum* total. The damage to the ports took longer to make good ; more than a year's work was necessary before Zeebrugge could be reopened to commerce ; and for a long period, a considerable part of the trade that formerly flowed through Antwerp continued to be conducted through Rotterdam.[1]

In considering the state of France, as well as of Belgium, it is necessary to distinguish between the effects of the war at sea and those of the German invasion on land. It was the devastation in the invaded areas which imposed the main physical obstacles to recuperation. The departments occupied, or partially occupied by the German armies during the war, comprised those in which the chief centres of mining and industrial activity were concentrated. Three-quarters of the annual output of coal, zinc, and sugar was derived from districts actually occupied by the enemy or brought under their fire ; in those districts stood three-quarters of the factories producing metallurgical products or machinery, about 80 per cent. of the spindles in the woollen, and 90 per cent. of those in the linen industry. Nor was the effect on production confined to the period of hostilities. Within a large proportion of the invaded areas the coal mines had been flooded ; the factories wrecked, either deliberately or in the course of operations ; railways, waterways, roads, bridges, tunnels, and buildings destroyed or damaged. Crops and orchards had been laid waste, and in the actual war zone the soil itself had been rendered temporarily unfit for cultivation.

To the ravages of war and the damage wantonly inflicted, must be added the effects of the terrible drain of the war on the man-power of France. Of the whole male population 61·5 per cent. had been mobilised, and the losses in killed and missing exceeded 1,880,000.[2] Almost equally important from the economic point of view, was the disorganisation of the internal transport system arising, not merely from the direct effects of the invasion, but from the redirection of the traffic, and the strain of supporting the British and American armies.

These were the main factors in a reduction of produc-

---

[1] See *Economic Survey*, p. 5.
[2] *Journal of the Royal United Service Institution*, lxvi, 465, February 1922, pp. 149–54.

tivity which was reflected by the fact that, in 1919, the area under wheat was less by 25 per cent. than before the war; the coal output was reduced by 50 per cent., and out of 1,820 industrial enterprises in the liberated regions, only 835 had recommenced work in October of that year.[1]

The effects of the invasion and those of the war at sea were, however, inextricably entangled. It was the destruction wrought by the German armies and the shortage of agricultural labour which, together with bad weather in 1917 and the great demand for military fodder, had rendered necessary cereal imports far above the normal level. It was the occupation of the chief coal- and iron-producing areas which had caused France to lean so heavily on Great Britain for fuel, and on the United States for steel and munitions. It was the reduction of native herds and the increased meat consumption of the troops which led to abnormal imports of meat and bacon.

In the net result France was, throughout the war, as dependent as Great Britain on oversea supplies. If the proportion of imported foodstuffs was smaller, the imports were none the less indispensable, and without coal, steel, and munitions from Great Britain and America, the resistance of the French armies must speedily have collapsed. Thanks to the success with which the sea routes were kept open, and to the immense assistance given by British shipping and by neutral shipping under British control, these essential needs were fulfilled in sufficient quantities to avert famine or military disaster; but the necessity for such enormous shipments of coal and munitions material involved the most rigorous restriction of all other imports, and the coal supplies themselves could be rendered adequate only by drastic regulation of industrial and domestic consumption.

This shortage of coal and other supplies must, no doubt, be attributed in part to the losses and delays caused by the submarine campaign; but in the main, the restriction, as well as the urgency of oversea supplies, is traceable rather to the effects of the invasion than to the course of the war at sea. Heavy as were the losses, acute as was the shortage of tonnage during the later stages of the war, sufficient shipping was generally procurable to carry as much cargo to French ports as those ports could handle.

The congestion of the ports was itself due, in part, to

[1] *Economic Survey*, pp. 18, 19.

the effect of the submarine campaign in dislocating traffic and diminishing coastwise activity; but the main factors in the problem were the strain of the increased coal shipments on the northern ports, the dislocation of internal transport, and the pressure of trooping and army supplies on the ports and railways. The military traffic of the British armies alone amounted, in 1917 and 1918, to imports at the rate of 9,000,000 tons a year, and to this were added in 1918 the ever-growing requirements of the American troops. For the assistance of the British and American armies a heavy price had to be paid.

It was, however, the financial effects of the French dependence on imported supplies which left the most lasting mark. All through the war, the f.o.b. prices of imports were continually rising, and on the greater part of these imports, freights swollen by war risks and shortage of tonnage, had to be paid to foreign shipowners or foreign Governments. Even before the war French shipping carried only 40 per cent. of the seaborne imports; but in 1918 practically all imports were seaborne, and well over 40 per cent. were carried in British ships alone.

The actual losses of French shipping by enemy action amounted to just under 900,000 tons gross, or nearly 39 per cent. of the 1914 total.[1] In addition 137,000 tons had been lost by marine risk. Very little of this loss had been made good by new construction in French yards, but a considerable proportion of the ocean-going steamers destroyed had been replaced by German vessels seized or captured, and purchases from the United Kingdom or from neutrals; so that, on October 31st, 1918, the ocean-going steam tonnage amounted to 1,436,000 gross, as against 1,600,000 before the war. After the armistice a considerable number of standard steamers were purchased from the British Government to supplement the output of the French yards, and by the end of June 1919, the total steam tonnage under the French flag was slightly greater than in the same month of 1914.

It is true that France remained largely dependent on foreign shipping; but we have seen that the assistance of a large block of British tonnage, at limitation rates, was secured for the transition period. With the exception of coal, the British output of which was inadequate to French

---

[1] A French estimate, which appears to include commissioned auxiliaries, gives the total loss as 961,000 tons (*Economic Survey*, p. 25)

requirements, there was no physical difficulty in procuring most of the raw materials and manufactured products required for economic restoration; but the general decline in productivity continued to restrict grievously the shipment of French goods in payment. Though far less serious, the position of France resembled, in many respects, that of her late adversary. The majority of her markets indeed were open, though Germany had taken over 12 per cent. of the exports before the war, and the collapse of Russia, in which country much French capital was invested, was a serious blow; but the dominating factor was the inability of France to pay by exports for the imports required, until the devastated areas were once more fully at work. In 1918 the value of exports had been little over one-fifth of the imports received, and even in 1919 it rose only to one-third. During the war the exchanges with Great Britain and the United States had been artificially stabilised by Government loans; but after the armistice these arrangements ceased, and with exports showing little improvement and import requirements as great as or greater than ever, the exchange value of the franc came down with a run. At the date of the armistice it stood at 25·95 to £1; by the end of 1918 it had fallen to 40·20.

With the effect of the reparations policy and of the acquisition, under the Treaty of Versailles, of territory rich in coal and iron, we are not here concerned. Even the very brief examination which has here been possible will show how serious was the position in which France was left as the direct result of the war itself. That position was due in the main to the results of the German invasion and of the immense military effort which it imposed on the French people; but it is incontestable that, by adding largely to the cost of imports, and hampering their distribution, shortage of tonnage did much to aggravate the evil.

It affected Italy even more directly. Italy had suffered comparatively little from invasion, and the drain on manpower, though severe, was lighter than in France; but Italy was normally more dependent than France on imported foodstuffs, and was almost wholly dependent on oversea supplies for fuel and raw materials. Moreover, it was in the Mediterranean that it had proved most difficult to check the activities of the submarines, and the war losses of Italian shipping, exclusive of commissioned vessels, amounted to 846,000 tons gross, or rather more than half the 1914 total. Although a considerable part of the loss had been made good by the seizure of enemy shipping, the ocean-going steam tonnage under the Italian flag on October 31st, 1918, was nearly 30 per cent. less than before the war.

Equally serious was the effect of the high Mediterranean risks on the employment of British and neutral tonnage in Italian trade. It was only with the greatest difficulty that the supply of munitions, and of fuel for military transport and the munitions industries, had been maintained. Not only had there been acute temporary food crises, but many important industries had been practically shut down, owing to the lack of coal and materials, all reserve stocks had been exhausted, and long after the cessation of hostilities the fuel famine was reflected in reduced railway services, restrictions on the consumption of gas, and factories on short-time.

In these circumstances Italy had been as little able as France to maintain her production for export, and the subsequent recovery of the export trade was hampered, not only by the shortage of coal and materials, but by the fact that some of the principal markets for Italian products, such as Germany, Austria-Hungary, and the Levant, had lost most of their purchasing power. Thus the proportion of export to import values, which had fallen to 21 per cent. in 1918, rose only to 37 per cent. in the first year of peace. Further, the two principal sources of revenue by which the trade balance was normally adjusted, had been shattered by the war. The tourist industry was at a standstill, and remittances by emigrants were greatly reduced owing to the return of reservists and their families. Even after the restoration of peace it was some time before conditions were sufficiently settled for the tourist traffic to revive, and emigration was hindered both by legislation in the United States, and by the disinclination of the returned reservists to go abroad a second time.[1]

The fall of the lira after the war was still more rapid than that of the franc, and in spite of bread subsidies estimated to cost £80,000,000 a year, the resulting increase in the cost of living, combined with war taxation, gave rise to a degree of social and industrial unrest which threatened seriously the political stability of the country. These difficulties were undoubtedly aggravated by other factors,

[1] *Economic Survey*, pp. 29, 30.

such as the uncertainty of the political situation in the Adriatic, which necessitated heavy military expenditure ; but the main roots of the trouble lay in the stagnation of industry due to shortage of coal and materials, and the enormous excess of imports over exports.

With regard to America and Japan little need be said. For both, the war had been a period of expanding trade and increasing tonnage. Immense as had been the contribution of the United States to the conduct of the war, and loyally as the American people had accepted restrictions on consumption in the interest of the Allies, they had suffered comparatively little from the war at sea, and the chief problems left to them as a legacy of the struggle were an exact converse of those presented to the European Allies : to find employment for the enormous fleet on the stocks at the date of the armistice, and to reconcile with their traditional commercial policy their transition from a debtor to a creditor nation. This, indeed, was no light task, but its implications lie outside our scope and we must turn to the direct effects of the war on the nation which had, of necessity, borne the lion's share of the burden involved in the maintenance of Allied supplies.

To deal first with the most direct effect of the war at sea, the total losses of British shipping by enemy action amounted, exclusive of commissioned vessels, to 7,760,000 tons gross, or nearly 37 per cent. of the tonnage under the British flag at the outbreak of war. After allowing both for war and marine losses and for all ships built or acquired, the gross steam tonnage on the Register of the United Kingdom itself was less by nearly 16 per cent. on December 31st, 1918, than at the end of 1913.[1]

In ocean-going steamers, the importance of which had been increased by the reduction, even after the conclusion of peace, in the proportion of continental traffic, the losses had been particularly heavy. Including ships on colonial register, they amounted to 42 per cent. of the 1914 tonnage, and the net reduction, on October 31st, 1918, was 18 per cent.[2] The actual reduction was, indeed, somewhat greater, as the returns for that date, while they exclude

---

[1] Cmd. 1246. Figures include steamers of all sizes.
[2] These percentages are based on returns which exclude Canadian steamers of ocean-going size employed on the Great Lakes, and other ships on Dominion or Colonial Register, not available for general trade.

British vessels in German ports, include a larger number of requisitioned neutrals subsequently released.

The shipbuilding capacity of the United Kingdom, on the other hand, had been decidedly increased. It is true that little was done after the war towards the development of the National Yards. These, with all other shipbuilding operations, were transferred after the armistice to the general direction of the Shipping Controller, who considered that the disadvantages attaching to the site, especially as regards labour supply and accommodation, rendered any large further expenditure imprudent. The Chepstow yard was accordingly completed on a greatly reduced scale and sold as a going concern, and the Beachley and Portbury yards were ultimately scrapped. The whole programme of concrete construction was also abandoned, the majority of the contracts being cancelled, the completed vessels sold, and the yards converted to other uses. There remained, however, the extensions to the private yards, and these represented, when sufficient steel and labour were available, a large addition to the previously existing plant. Even under war conditions, they had enabled a total output to be attained which, including naval construction, exceeded that for the record year of peace, however short it fell of war necessities.

It is true that many factors in the *post-bellum* situation tended to keep the level of output considerably below the maximum; but it is doubtful whether, after the surrender of German shipping had eased the stringency that arose in the spring of 1919, the recovery of British trade was ever really handicapped by lack of tonnage. Nothing indeed is more remarkable than the way in which the shipping of the world recovered from a war in which 12,850,000 tons gross had been destroyed by enemy action alone. By June 1919 the steam tonnage of the world was already greater than before the war, and by June 1920, not only the United States and Japan, but France and Italy had added largely to their mercantile fleets, while British tonnage approached very closely to its old level. This was due in part to the final transfer of the surrendered enemy shipping under the peace treaties; but most of the neutrals had also made good their losses. Holland had considerably increased her fleet, and even Norway, whose war losses (steam and sail) amounted to well over a million tons, had recovered her actual, though not her comparative position. Greece alone, whose political condition was unfavourable to recuperation, had fallen seriously behind.

The comparative position of the shipowning Powers had, indeed, been greatly altered. The Austrian flag had been eliminated, and the mercantile fleet of Germany dwindled, as a result of the peace, to less than a tenth of its former size. Great Britain still held the leading place, but with a reduced percentage of the total tonnage, and the United States was a much closer second than Germany had been before the war.

In the quality and efficiency of the ships Great Britain still held her own. The postponement of repairs had been common to all countries, and in contrast to many of the ships hastily constructed under the American Emergency Programme, most of those built during the war in the United Kingdom, or purchased in Canada and Japan, were well suited to the requirements of commerce.

The actual number of standard freighters and oilers completed in the United Kingdom down to the date of the armistice was 148, in addition to which 289 were on the stocks or fitting out, and contracts for many others had been placed. By December 31st, 1918, the completions had been raised to 181, with an aggregate tonnage of 804,000 gross, and 83 per cent. of the steamers then under construction were of standard type, including about 40 coasters, ranging from 360 to 2,000 tons dead-weight, and some 30 vessels which met, to some extent, the requirements of the liner trades.

Of the ships completed after the armistice, a considerable number were sold to France or Norway, in fulfilment of promised assistance, and others were transferred to neutral flags in replacement of requisitioned tonnage sunk on service. Many others were sold, while on the stocks, to British shipowners, and completed with or without modifications. All ships completed for the Controller, either before or after the armistice, were similarly disposed of, through a group of shipowners headed by Lord Inchcape and Sir Owen Phillips, and in disposing both of completed ships and those under construction, priority was given to the purchasers in approximate proportion to their war losses.

For the ordinary tramp trade the standard steamers were well suited. It is true that even the tramp owner normally builds his ships with a special view to economical working in trade of a particular class, and the standard steamers, built with rigid uniformity to a few very simple types, were not ideal ships for all trades. For average purposes, however, they compared very well with the ordinary freighter. They were sound, seaworthy ships of good speed for their class and of large cargo capacity, easy to handle, and economical to work. Indeed, since many of the ships lost during the war were old vessels, they were probably better, generally speaking, than the ships they replaced. On the other hand, the prohibition during the war, of transfers to foreign flags, involved the retention on the Register of a large number of old steamers which would normally have been sold to foreign owners and replaced by new tonnage.

For the liner trades, the standard steamers were not, generally speaking, suited, and the problem of liner replacement was serious, as the lines had been obliged, during the war, to make good their losses by acquiring a large amount of tonnage originally built for other purposes. The position had been eased by the modification of some of the later standard types, and by the priority given to vessels with insulated space, but as regards passenger and intermediate liners there was a big leeway to be made up. This was no light matter, for the cost of construction was enormously high, and the liner companies had benefited less than tramp owners from the boom in freights while tonnage was still, in part, free from requisition. The State Insurance Scheme had, indeed, gone very far to secure the financial position of shipowners ; but while that scheme as a whole had yielded a handsome profit to the State, the dissolution of the partnership between the State and the War Risks Associations had come at a time when the hull side of the scheme showed a heavy deficit, and the Liverpool and London War Risks and Excess Values Associations alone were obliged to make calls on their members to the extent of over £7,000,000 to make good their share of the loss.[1]

Upon the whole, however, British shipping was still able to provide for the requirements of British commerce, and to resume, in large measure, its old activities in the general carrying trade. Indeed, its greatest difficulties arose from the fact that the growth of the world's tonnage, during the period immediately succeeding the war, easily

[1] Report for year ending February 19th, 1919.

outstripped the recovery of the world's commerce, in which alone it could find employment.

With regard to the effect of the war on the food supply and industries of the United Kingdom much has already been said, and there is no room here for anything but the barest summary ; but a very brief analysis of the imports of 1918, as compared with those of 1913, will show how different was the situation of Great Britain from that of the enemy, or even the Allied, Powers.

The total volume of imports was reduced by about 19,380,000 tons, say 35·5 per cent. Of this decrease about one-third represented food, drink, and tobacco. In cereal imports alone the reduction amounted to 4,440,000 tons. This, however, was not all clear loss, for the greater proportion of flour to wheat imports represented a saving of 300,000 tons. Further, the increase in home production rendered it possible to reduce cereal imports without a corresponding decrease in the total available supplies. While the imports of wheat and flour, as wheat, were less by nearly 1,400,000 tons than in 1913, the 1918–19 harvest showed an increase of hard on a million tons on that of 1913–14, and the increased production of oats more than outweighed the decline in imports. Both the imports and the home production of barley were smaller than before the war ; but the weight of this reduction fell mainly on brewing and distilling. It combined, however, with the diminution in imports of maize and oilcake to reduce the output of home-grown meat, owing to the necessity of economising feeding-stuffs.

Imports of meat, bacon, and hams were actually a little larger than in 1913 ; but this, as we have seen, did not prevent a shortage of civilian supplies, owing to reduced home output and the enormous demands of the Army. Imports of fish were reduced only by 25,000 tons or about 14 per cent., but the total available supplies were much smaller than before the war. Owing partly to the dangers of the fisheries and partly to the requisitioning of trawlers for naval purposes, the weight of fish landed on the coasts of the United Kingdom fell away from 1,233,000 to 438,000 tons, and the diminution in the total supply, after deducting exports and re-exports, amounted to nearly one-third.[1]

Sugar imports had been greatly affected by the war,

[1] Figures exclusive of shellfish landed on coasts.

owing to the longer average distance from which supplies had to be brought, and the very large volume of tonnage required to maintain the shipments on the *ante-bellum* scale. It was impossible to make good, as with cereals, any part of the reduction in imports by home production, and the whole weight of the decrease had to fall on the consumer; but the shortage of tonnage rendered a heavy decrease inevitable, and by 1918 it amounted to 664,000 tons or 34 per cent. on the 1913 figures. Smaller in bulk, but even larger in proportion, were the reductions in shipments of eggs and dairy produce, which had been specially affected by the dangers of North Sea navigation and the friction with the Northern neutrals arising out of the blockade. In imports of eggs the reduction was 88 per cent., in margarine 80, in butter 61, and in cheese 45 per cent. These reductions were of special importance, inasmuch as half the eggs and margarine, two-thirds of the butter, and four-fifths of the cheese annually consumed before the war, came from overseas. The expansion of the margarine industry in Great Britain, however, did something to make good the loss of imported fats, and there was a considerable increase in the imports of condensed milk which partly compensated a reduction in home output due to restrictions on feeding-stuffs. Of somewhat less importance than the above were heavy reductions in the imports of fruit, vegetables, and other miscellaneous foodstuffs.

Turning to raw materials and manufactures, one of the most striking features is an increase of 3,300,000 tons in the imports of petroleum and of 420,000 tons in those of chemicals.[1] Both items were, of course, of special importance to the conduct of the war; but the heavy shipments of these essential commodities had to be paid for by large reductions in other directions. Of these reductions by far the most striking in actual bulk was that in the imports of timber which, together with paper and paper-making materials, was responsible for more than half the total decline in volume of imports. Of the other important decreases, the largest were in iron ore and scrap (994,000 tons), other ores and metals (549,000 tons), and manufactured iron and steel (1,883,000 tons). The reduction in imports of iron ore amounted to 13 per cent., and together with a decrease in the supply of native ore, was responsible

[1] Including nitrates.

for a decline in the total output of pig-iron from 10,250,000 to 9,100,000 tons.[1] As we have seen, the shortage of steel for mercantile shipbuilding was one of the main obstacles to the replacement of losses ; but by drastic restrictions on exports and civilian consumption, the enormous demands of the munitions industries were met in full.

In textile materials the reduction amounted to 786,000 tons ; but over 400,000 tons of this was made good by prohibition of re-exports. Including the home production of wool and flax, and the material obtained from imported sheepskins and woollen rags, the reduction on the 1913 figures, in the total supplies available during 1918 for the leading industries, was approximately as follows : cotton, 22 per cent. ; wool, 29 ; flax and tow, 63 ; jute, 8 per cent. The effect on the export trade was serious, but it will be evident that there was no such paralysis of industry as existed even in Allied, and still more in enemy, countries. While Germany was put to the greatest straits to clothe adequately even her first-line troops, Great Britain was still able to serve, though at greatly enhanced cost, the essential needs of the home market, and to produce a considerable surplus for export.

With regard to the remainder of the reductions, little need be said. They ranged over a wide field : leather, hides and skins, cutlery and hardware, electrical goods, and a long list of miscellaneous materials and manufactures. In the main, they represented the deliberate exclusion of luxury goods, and the restriction of civilian consumption, even of necessaries, to the essential minimum, in order to secure ship-space for the supply of food and military requirements.

Remembering that imports during the earlier years of the war had been larger—down to 1916 much larger—than in 1918, it is evident that at no time was the reduction of supplies sufficient to inflict vital injury on the economic life of the country. Periods of acute anxiety there had been, owing to depletion of stocks and uncertainty as to the future. Had losses continued at the same rate as in the spring of 1917, had the time occupied by the round voyage in the Atlantic continued to be what it was in the autumn of that year, there would have been a different tale to tell, and the gravity of the danger should not be

[1] It should be noted, however, that 1913 was an exceptional year. The average production for three years before the war was 9,850,000 tons.

forgotten because it was surmounted; but in the events which happened, the strain was never so great as to be intolerable. There were undoubtedly much hardship and more irritation. The shortage of meat, sugar, and butter, the bad quality of much of the meat and bacon released for civilian consumption, the unaccustomed restrictions on diet and habits, and the rise in the cost of living to about 140 per cent. above the 1914 figures, were not without their effect in contributing to war weariness, and to the widespread industrial unrest which became acute immediately after the armistice, and hampered the progress of economic recovery; but at their worst, the conditions never approached those in Germany, or even in other Allied countries.

There was, of course, much leeway to be made up. The output of coal had fallen off by 45,500,000 tons, or nearly 17 per cent. on the average for the three years preceding the war, and the whole working of the industry had been dislocated to an extent which forbade any immediate hope of recovering the old standard. Apart from the effect of shortage and consequent high prices on industry and the domestic consumer, this was a matter of grave significance in the foreign trade, as it was mainly on the coal exports that tramp shipping had been accustomed to rely for outward cargoes, and any diminution of those exports must inevitably be reflected in increased inward freights, forcing up the prices of imports, and hampering the competition of British shipping in the world's freight markets.

Almost equally serious was the condition of the ports and railways. Both permanent-way and rolling-stock had deteriorated seriously through overstrain and postponement of repairs, and both this, and the effects on coasting traffic of the artificially restricted railway rates, which were continued long after the armistice, rendered the distribution of imports a matter of extreme difficulty. That difficulty was increased by the large proportion of imports which, even after the armistice, continued to be rationed, and hence to be more slowly distributed from the ports. To the effects of port congestion, especially on the effective supply of foodstuffs, many of the main difficulties of the transition period may be attributed.

Again, the suspension of private building, due to restrictions on the import of materials, as well as to shortage of labour, was responsible for the acute housing shortage, which had such serious results on the social life of the nation. It would, indeed, be easy to multiply instances of industrial, commercial, and social dislocation, directly or indirectly due to war conditions.

Nevertheless, the productive power of the country as a whole was little impaired. The area under cultivation was larger than before the war, the reduction in live stock was comparatively small, and to an extent unparalleled by any other European belligerent, the main industries had been preserved as going concerns. The transition from war to peace presented many difficulties, but there was no such gulf to be bridged as in Germany, or even in France or Italy. It should be added that, of the chief internal obstacles to recovery, the reduction in the coal output was almost wholly, and the spread of industrial unrest very largely, the outcome of conditions only indirectly affected by the course of the war at sea.

Far more serious in its permanent results than any direct effect of the constriction of supplies, was the financial situation produced by the reduction of the export, and the redirection of both the export and the import trade. For these, the submarine campaign was, in large measure, responsible.

Both tendencies had shown themselves at an early stage of the war. In 1915, owing to the initial loss of markets, and general industrial and financial dislocation, the volume of all exports dropped heavily, and the proportion of export to import values fell off from about 83 per cent. in 1913, to 57 per cent. In 1916, while the volume of imports was somewhat reduced, that of exports showed a considerable expansion. The process of replacing recruited or diverted labour had made good progress ; trade had settled down into its new channels, and the cessation of German exports, coupled with reduced production in France and Italy, led to a strong demand for British goods in both Allied and neutral countries. It is true that the restrictions imposed for war purposes hampered the development of many branches of the export, and especially the re-export, traffic, and the effective demands of the Allies were limited both by tonnage difficulties in the coal trade, and by the receiving capacity of their ports. Nevertheless, in spite of steadily increasing military demands on labour and material, shipments of the main staple exports were on the up-grade, and the total proportion of export to import values rose to 64 per cent.

The direction of the trade, however, was changing. Shipments to France, Italy, and Russia amounted, in 1916, to 27·5 per cent. in value of the total exports and re-exports, as against 13·1 per cent. in 1913, and the necessity of supplying the urgent requirements of the Allies, led to the severe restriction of exports, especially of coal, to many neutral markets. Meanwhile, the proportion of imports drawn from North America had been steadily rising. The vast agricultural and manufacturing resources of the United States and Canada, convenience of shipment, convenience of credit, especially for Government purchases, all combined to make it natural to seek in North America the fulfilment of the new war demands, and the replacement of the supplies cut off by the closing of the Baltic and Black Sea, and the failure of the Australian harvest. From 18·4 in 1913, the proportion of imports (recorded values) drawn from the United States alone rose to 27·9 per cent. in 1915, and in 1916, when the tonnage problem began to affect the situation acutely, to 30·8 per cent.

Unfortunately, the demand for British products in the United States was comparatively small and exports to that country showed no comparable increase. By the beginning of 1917, as we have seen, the Treasury were at their wits' end to provide dollar credits. At this point came the entry of America into the war, by which the financial problem was temporarily solved. This development coincided alike with the acute shortage of tonnage produced by the extended submarine campaign, and with the wide extension of Government control over imports and shipping by which it was sought to meet it. From that moment, the term "seaborne trade" becomes almost a misnomer as applied to the process by which Great Britain and her European Allies were fed and equipped. It was no longer a question of free exchange of commodities in an open market, but of obtaining supplies, at any cost, from the nearest possible sources, on credits which mortgaged the future to meet the necessities of the present.

By 1918 shipments from the United States alone amounted to 39·2 per cent. in value of the total imports received, and though there were many commodities which the United States did not produce in sufficient quantities

THE BALANCE OF TRADE

for British requirements, the purchase of such commodities was concentrated with equal rigour on the nearest available source. Meanwhile, the total volume of exports and re-exports had greatly decreased, and an increasing proportion of the diminished shipments was devoted to supplying the essential needs of the Allies. Of the total import values only two-fifths was offset by exports and re-exports, and of those exports over 33 per cent. went to France and Italy alone, and represented, in the main, credits granted to the French and Italian Governments. On the other hand, owing to the restrictions on re-exports, the total shipments to the United States had fallen, even in nominal value, below the peace figures. While less than one-third of the exports to France and Italy was paid for by imports from those countries, the value of goods received from the United States was nineteen times as great as that of the British and foreign produce shipped in return.

Exactly how far the invisible exports by which the balance of trade was normally adjusted, had suffered from the effects of the war, it is difficult to estimate. The earnings of British shipping were certainly large; but it must be remembered that, not only were British ships withdrawn in large numbers from the inter-foreign trade, but a large proportion of the services rendered to foreigners during the later years of the war, were performed for the Allies at Blue Book or limitation rates. The actual charges made to the Allied Governments for the services of requisitioned tonnage were not on a strict basis of cost, but they were substantially below free market rates, and it must further be remembered that services for the Allies went to swell the total of their ultimate indebtedness, rather than to assist in redressing the balance of trade with the main sources of supply.

Other sources of revenue had been grievously reduced. The sale of foreign, chiefly American, securities had cut down by about 25 per cent. the annual income from investments abroad, and though the new indebtedness contracted in the United States and elsewhere was offset by loans made to the Allies, it was doubtful how far these loans could be regarded as recoverable. Further, the restriction of the transit and entrepôt trade involved a serious loss of commissions and intermediate profits.

This reduction of the entrepôt trade was mainly due to restrictions on imports and rearrangement of services arising from the shortage of tonnage. Down to 1916 the trade had been fairly well maintained, especially the re-exports to America of Egyptian cotton, and of wool, tin, rubber, and tropical products. It was the import restrictions of 1917 which struck the first heavy blow at the general re-export traffic, and the big further reduction in 1918 was the direct outcome of the accentuated Atlantic concentration, and consequent reduction of the inward tonnage available on the Eastern, Australasian, and African tracks.

The decline in exports of British produce and manufactures cannot so easily be attributed to any one cause. As we have seen, it set in early in the war, and there were other factors, besides the shortage of tonnage, which checked the subsequent recovery. By 1918 the Russian market had been wholly lost, and the friction with Scandinavia and Holland had culminated in the general embargo on shipments to those countries. This restriction of markets, however, is by no means sufficient to account for the whole, or even the greater part, of the decline.

How great that decline was, the figures for a few typical exports will show. Shipments of cotton piece-goods in 1918 were smaller than in 1913 by 48 per cent., of woollen and worsted tissues by 42, of silk broadstuffs and mixtures by 46, and of linen and jute piece-goods by 64 and 82 per cent. respectively. Exports of iron and steel had fallen off by 67, of machinery by 75, and of coal, coke, and patent fuel by 55 per cent. Among miscellaneous manufactures may be mentioned decreases varying from 67 to 84 per cent. in the exports of china and earthenware, plate glass, bottles, boots and shoes, cement, oilcloth, and paper, and the list could be almost indefinitely extended.

Except as regards coal, for which tonnage had been short from the first, owing to the number of colliers requisitioned for Admiralty purposes, very little of this decrease can be attributed directly to lack of shipping space. It is true that the decline in British exports to the Far East, to India, and to Australasia was proportionately greater than that in shipments to markets less affected by the redistribution of liner services ; but the difference between the shipments to these countries and their average share of exports, accounts only for a small proportion of the total reduction. Moreover, there were other causes at work to reduce the value of the more distant markets. Quite apart from actual shortage of outward tonnage, the length of the routes rendered high freights a serious obstacle to trade. It is noteworthy that, although the Indian services were never so severely treated as those to the Far East or Australasia, it was the exports of cotton piece-goods to India which show the most startling reduction, and much of this must be attributed to the financial effects of the war on the purchasing-power of the native population, and to the high cost of the British product. To a great extent British manufactures were displaced, especially as regards the coarser lines, by cheap Japanese goods; and while British exports to India were, even in nominal value, less by one-third in 1918 than in 1913, those from Japan were more than six times as great as in that year. The Indian output itself was also greatly expanded. Even had ample tonnage been available, much trade must have been lost.

It was by restricting the inward tonnage available from such important sources of raw material as Australasia for wool, India for jute, the Philippines for hemp, and China and Japan for silk, rather than by the reduction in outward tonnage for the less bulky manufactured article, that the Atlantic concentration struck its most severe blow at the export trade. A considerable reduction in exports there must have been in any event. By 1918, not only was the total number of persons, of both sexes and all ages, employed in industry, rather smaller than in 1914, but no less than 61·5 per cent. were employed on Government work. Even allowing for the priority, in the allocation of labour and material, given to the export trade over manufacture for the home market, the demands of the fighting services must have reduced largely the exportable surplus of many staple products.

Nevertheless, the effect of import restrictions can be very clearly traced. The drop in shipments of iron and steel was no doubt due mainly to the munitions demand, but had it been possible to maintain the imports of iron ore, pig-iron, and steel at the level of 1913, the exports need not have fallen off, as they did, by over two-thirds. Cotton is an instance still more to the point; the war demand on the cotton industry was comparatively small, and could be met by restrictions on civilian consumption. But, owing to the decrease in the allocation of space to imports of raw cotton, the output of the mills fell off in

1917 to about three-quarters, and in 1918 to about two-thirds, of the 1913 figures, and this decrease goes a very long way to account for the reduction in exports.

The export of woollens illustrates equally clearly the effect of the restrictions. Down to 1917 the net import of wool was on the average little below the peace level, and though the demands of the Army for clothing and blankets involved considerable restriction of civilian consumption, the total export of woollens during the whole of this period compared not unfavourably with 1913. It was not until 1918, when the supply of material was so drastically cut down, that exports showed a heavy decrease.[1] The figures for linen, jute, and leather goods tell the same story, and to the shortage of tonnage for imports, coupled with the war demands on output, the greater part of the general decline may fairly be attributed.

Reduced as it was, the volume of British exports during the war was yet considerable, and some part at least of the adverse balance had been made good by invisible exports and the sale of securities. To a far greater extent than France or Italy, Great Britain had been able to pay her way in goods and services, and the effect of this was seen after the war in the stability of sterling as compared with the continental currencies. This stability, however, was comparative only, and while the high premium on sterling in Paris, Rome, and Brussels restricted the ability of the Allied markets to absorb British exports, adverse exchanges in New York added greatly to the cost of imports.

Any discussion of the effect on industry and commerce after the war of the problems presented by Inter-Allied indebtedness and the fluctuations of the exchanges lies, of course, outside the scope of these volumes. Nevertheless it is necessary, in order to present any true picture of the effect of the war at sea, to emphasise the fact that, so far as Great Britain was concerned, the fundamental factors were the enormous surplus of imports over exports during the war years, and the redirection of both the import and the export trades, on lines dictated by war necessities rather than by commercial considerations. For this the military obligations incurred were primarily

[1] The effect of a reduction in imports of any material was, of course, to reduce exports of the manufactured product by a still larger proportion, owing to the necessity of keeping up army supplies to the previous level.

responsible, by diverting labour, material, and tonnage, in ever-increasing proportions, from commercial employment ; but the effect of this diversion was aggravated to an incalculable extent by the destruction of tonnage.

For Great Britain at any rate, the primary necessity of economic recovery was the speediest possible return to the natural flow of trade. Apart, however, from all *post-bellum* developments, there were many obstacles to this process, inherent in the actual situation at the cessation of hostilities. Germany, second only to India as a market for British exports, and second only to the United States as a source of supply, was wiped, temporarily, almost off the commercial map. The Austro-Hungarian Empire lay in ruins, and though the States created or aggrandised at its expense were in dire need of every kind of goods, the difficulty of financing shipments opposed an almost insuperable bar to any full satisfaction of their demands. With the greater part of Russia all commercial relations were suspended, and it was likely to be many years, in any event, before either the productive or the purchasing power of the late Empire was restored to its former maximum. Even the Allied countries, great as was their need of goods, were to a large extent restrained, by the condition of the exchanges, from making their demands effective.

The European neutrals, on the other hand, were both eager and able to resume the full current of trade which the war had so gravely interrupted. The Scandinavian States and Holland, in particular, had been drained of all accumulated stocks by the effect of the embargoes ; their financial position was far stronger than that of the late belligerents, and in the first year of peace their effective demand did something to make good the diminished purchasing-power of the other European markets.

In the more distant countries much ground had inevitably been lost. The reduction of British exports and the withdrawal of British shipping had presented Japan and the United States with opportunities for effective competition in India, the Far East, Australia, and South America, of which their comparatively abundant tonnage and expanding production had enabled them to take full advantage. Further, the actual purchasing-power of the great Indian market had been seriously impaired by the effects of interrupted communications, war taxation, and unrest. In particular, the area under cultivation fell off so greatly that, from October 1918, the export of wheat temporarily ceased.

Many of these conditions might reasonably be expected to be temporary only, and some make-weight was provided by the increase of trade with British West Africa, enriched by the demand for oil-seeds and kernels, whether for margarine or munitions purposes, and with Egypt, whence the imports of cotton, wool, cotton-seed, and onions had increased in relative importance, though not in actual volume.

Nothing, however, could fully compensate for the prostration of so large a part of the European continent. It was not only in the loss of markets that the effect was felt. The loss of the Russian supplies of wheat, oil, flax, hemp, and timber, of German and Austrian sugar, and of German manufactures, all tended to perpetuate the concentration of purchases on those sources of supply where the war had created so great an adverse balance of trade. Even when all restrictions on the freedom of commerce were removed, it was impossible that trade could resume a " normal " course while abnormal conditions continued to dominate so large a proportion of the economic world.

It would be idle, if not impertinent, to attempt in the few pages that remain, any general discussion of the deductions to be drawn from the record of this titanic conflict. It is impossible to drop the curtain, entirely without comment, on the record of events that have left their mark so deeply graven on the life of the world; but that comment must be confined to one or two points of outstanding significance.

In the first place, the course of the war emphasised beyond all precedent, and beyond all general expectation, the importance of maritime communications. The dependence of Great Britain on oversea supplies was an accepted axiom; but the extent to which that dependence was shared, at any rate under war conditions, by other nations, had hardly been sufficiently appreciated. That dependence was, however, the inevitable result of the economic developments of the century preceding the war, the increasing importance to industrial countries of raw materials and fuel, and the increasing tendency of such countries to rely on foreign sources to supplement their own production of foodstuffs. In Germany, where the process of industrialisation had been very rapid during recent years, it had been accompanied by an intensification of agricultural development ; but this agricultural development itself was based on large oversea supplies of artificial fertilisers and concentrated feeding-stuffs. Indeed, the extent to which the European food production depended on imported fodder and fertilisers was one of the lessons most clearly brought out by the war.

For all the belligerents alike, this dependence on oversea supplies was greatly accentuated by the character of the war itself. The development of naval and military material, and the direct demands of the fighting services on the products of industry, exceeded anything that had been known or anticipated, and those demands increased both directly and indirectly the importance of maritime communications ; directly, because no country produced in itself all the materials necessary to the arming and equipment of its forces ; indirectly, because the diversion of labour to the war industries, as well as to the fighting line, inevitably reacted on the home output, whether of food or of the civil industries. To France and Italy the freedom of overseas communications was as vital as to Great Britain herself, and though Germany's balance of agricultural and industrial strength fitted her to endure a prolonged period of isolation better than any other European Power, she was able to hold out for four and a half years only at the cost of a complete economic and social collapse, which was indeed precipitated by military defeat, but had already become inevitable. It must be remembered, too, that Germany was never completely isolated, for it proved impossible to stop the supplies of Swedish ore, and twice at least, by the invasion of Roumania and by the collapse of Russia, she was enabled to increase her food supplies at a moment of the acutest crisis. Further, her stocks of many materials necessary for war purposes, scanty as they were, had been built up, to some extent, during the first twelve or eighteen months of war, before the machinery of economic pressure became fully effective.

This leads us to the result of that development of communications which was emphasised in the introduction to the first volume, as the main new factor in the exercise of economic pressure. It had become necessary to block the passage of supplies not only through the enemy's own ports, but through every port with which he could communicate by rail, road, river, or canal. This inevitably meant wide-spread interference with neutral trade, and apart altogether from the legal aspect of the matter, it early became evident that the dependence of the belligerents themselves on supplies from neutral countries, rendered it impossible to ride rough-shod over neutral interests. It was necessary to proceed by negotiation and agreement as well as by decree. At first there seemed to be a possibility that the exercise of sea-power might be stultified by the new conditions that had arisen ; but if the belligerents were economically dependent on the neutrals, so were the neutrals on the belligerents, and there gradually arose round the Central Powers a network of agreements and undertakings, enforced by bunker regulations, embargoes on supplies, and financial restrictions, as well as by naval force, which, though no technical blockade was instituted, amounted to a more effective and drastic stoppage of enemy trade than naval force alone had ever secured.

The foundation on which the whole of this elaborate structure was reared was itself dual in character. In the first place, the Allies possessed a working command of the sea, enabling them to exercise such control of the trade routes as rendered evasion extremely difficult. The result of this was that, even in respect of traffic the contraband nature of which was technically doubtful, neutral merchants and shipowners were willing to make large concessions, rather than incur the delay and inconvenience arising from exercise by the Allies of their undoubted right of visit and search. In the second place, the Allies possessed from the first something approaching a practical monopoly of many supplies especially important to the only neutral Powers who were in a position to give substantial assistance in maintaining German trade. In particular, their control over the supplies of fuel—the primary essential of all industry and transport—gave them a lever the importance of which it is impossible to exaggerate. In the later stages of the war, after the intervention of the United States, the Allied and Associated Powers controlled, by original ownership, by purchase, or by agreement, so large a proportion of the world's supplies, tonnage, cables, and credit facilities, that they were able to back their demands by an extraordinary intensity of pressure. For this very reason, it is necessary to be cautious in drawing deductions for the future. The results achieved in 1914–18 were rendered possible by the exceptional strength, economic as well as military, of the belligerent groups. With the exception of the United States, all the leading industrial and commercial Powers were, from the first, participants in the struggle, and it must be remembered that the attitude both of the United States and of the minor neutrals, towards the measures taken by the Allies, was strongly coloured by the exceptional disregard of neutral interests that marked Germany's conduct of the war at sea.

In the events which happened, the effect of modern conditions proved to be not only to accentuate the importance of economic pressure, but to increase the stringency with which it could be applied by belligerents strong at sea and strong in their economic position. To Germany the exercise of this more drastic form of pressure was impossible, and she endeavoured to make good the loss, by employing ruthlessly a form of sporadic raiding which differed in no essential respect from the cruiser warfare of the past, but was at once more difficult to counter and infinitely more destructive of civilian lives and of neutral property. How nearly she attained her ends, and how she was ultimately frustrated, these pages have attempted to show.

It is for others to comment on the success or failure of the methods adopted to defend commerce against the submarine attack; but it may perhaps be emphasised that, in the frustration of that attack, the utilisation of shipping was as important as its defence. It was not only by war losses that the shortage of tonnage was produced, and but for economies in the employment of shipping, and the acceleration of turn-round, that shortage might well have been decisive, despite the gradual reduction in the rate of loss. It is, indeed, somewhat misleading to think of the problem of supply in terms of " tonnage." What governs the volume of supplies received is not tonnage but annual carrying power, and nothing was more clearly demonstrated by the war than the complexity of the factors which go to make up carrying power, and the danger of dealing singly with any one of them. Whether under private enterprise or State control, the carrying power of the ships depends, not only on the smooth working of the whole machinery of transport and distribution, but on its instantaneous response to the fluctuating demands of the commerce which it serves. It depends also on the regularity and elasticity of that commerce itself. The ships, the ports, the railways, the merchant's office, and the banker's counting-house are all cog-wheels in the one great machine, and a break-down or lack of co-ordination at any one point will clog the working of the whole. How difficult, and at the same time how necessary, it is to maintain this co-ordination and flexibility, even under the stress of war, we have learned by bitter experience.

In judging the achievements of all who shared, whether as officials or in their private capacity, the task of maintaining supplies, one thing must be remembered. The strain to which British commerce and shipping were subjected was beyond all previous experience. It was no new thing that Great Britain should keep the seas, should finance and supply her Allies, and should furnish a contingent in the field. That she should bear the main brunt of the war at sea and of the economic and industrial effort, while providing and equipping an army on the continental scale, was altogether without precedent. To the perplexities, and to the strain on the national resources arising from this immense expansion of the military effort, may be attributed, in large measure, the failure to maintain the shipbuilding output, to preserve the free flow of traffic through the ports, and to keep up the export trade. As the war went on and the intensity of the submarine attack increased, the consequences of these failures became manifest; at the same time there was a steady growth both in the military contribution itself and in the assistance required by the Allies from British industries and shipping. Finally a crisis was reached in the problem of British and Allied supplies, which could be surmounted only at a heavy sacrifice of economic strength, and then only by the financial assistance of the United States. Looking back, we can see that, had the extent of our resources and the demands upon them been more justly appreciated from the beginning of the war, had some measures been adopted earlier and others never adopted at all, the double burden imposed upon Great Britain might have been sustained with greater ease at the time and at less cost to the future. It is no little thing that it was sustained unflinchingly.

APPENDIX "A"

POWERS OF THE SHIPPING CONTROLLER

THE chief powers conferred on the Controller by Regulations under the Defence of the Realm Act were as follows :

Regulation 37C, 14 April, 1917. Empowers the Admiralty or the Shipping Controller, with the concurrence of the Board of Trade, to enforce equipment with safety apparatus and (by amendment of 21 December, 1917) dazzle painting.

Regulation 39*BBB*, 28 June, 1917, gives the Controller general powers over shipping and shipbuilding. As amended in November 1917 it read as follows :

(1) The Shipping Controller may make orders regulating, restricting or giving directions with respect to the nature of the trades in which ships are to be employed, the traffic to be carried therein, and the terms and conditions on which the traffic is to be carried, the ports at which cargo is to be loaded or discharged or passengers embarked or disembarked (including directions requiring ships to proceed to specified ports for the purpose of loading or unloading cargo or embarking or disembarking passengers), the ports at which consignees of cargo are to take delivery thereof, the rates (maxima or minima) to be charged for freight or hire of ships and the carriage of passengers, the form of bills of lading and passenger tickets, the building, repairing, equipping, refitting, converting or altering of any ship or vessel, the user of and the work to be done in or with any dock, shipyard, dry dock, or other accommodation adapted or capable of being adapted for building, repairing, equipping, or refitting ships or vessels (in this regulation included in the term " shipyard "), and any plant in or about the same, the priority and manner in which and the places at which orders or contracts for building, repairing, equipping, refitting, converting or altering ships or vessels are to be executed or any such work is to be done, and the payments to be made in respect thereof and other matters affecting shipping, where it appears to the Controller necessary or expedient to make any such order for the purpose of making shipping available for the needs of the country in such manner as to make the best use thereof having regard to the circumstances of the time or for providing and maintaining an efficient supply of shipping :

Provided that any order made under this regulation shall have effect subject to any regulations made or orders given under Regulations 37, 38 or 39 [relating to pilotage, etc.].

(2) Any order made under this regulation may contain such provisions as to entry, inspection of books and documents, or otherwise as may appear to the Controller necessary or expedient for the purposes of his duties.

(3) The Shipping Controller may by order requisition or require to be placed at his disposal, in order that they may be used in the manner best suited for the needs of the country, any ships, or any cargo space or passenger accommodation in any ships, or any rights under any charter, freight engagement, or similar contract affecting any ship, and require ships so requisitioned to be delivered to the Controller or any person or persons named by him at such times and at such places as the Controller may require, where it appears to the Controller necessary or expedient to make any such order for the purpose of making shipping available for the needs of the country in such manner as to make the best use thereof having regard to the circumstances of the time.

Such compensation shall be paid in respect of the use of a ship or cargo space or passenger accommodation requisitioned under this regulation and for services thereby occasioned as in default of agreement may be determined by the Board of Arbitration constituted under the Proclamation of the third day of August, nineteen hundred and fourteen, respecting the requisitioning of ships by the Admiralty.

(4) Any order made under this regulation affecting any ship may be served on the owner of the ship, and shall be deemed to be sufficiently served if sent by registered post addressed to the managing owner or other person to whom the management of the ship is entrusted by or on behalf of the owner at his registered address.

(5) Any order under this regulation may be made either so as to apply generally to all ships or shipyards or to apply to ships or shipyards belonging to any particular owner, or to ships or shipyards of any class or description, or so as to apply to any specified ship or shipyard, and any such order may direct that all contracts or any class or any special contract affected by the order shall be abrogated, or shall remain in force notwithstanding anything in the order, but subject to any exceptions or modifications for which provision may be made by the order.

(6) If the owner, master, or other person in charge of a ship or the occupier of a shipyard or any other person affected by an order under this regulation acts in contravention of or fails to comply with any provisions of the order, or aids or abets any other person, whether or not such other person is in the United Kingdom, in doing anything which if done in the United

Kingdom would be a contravention of any such provision, he shall be guilty of a summary offence against these regulations.

(7) The powers conferred by this regulation shall be in addition to and not in derogation of any prerogative right or other powers of His Majesty, and the Shipping Controller may make arrangements with any other Government department for the exercise by that department on behalf of the Shipping Controller of any of the powers of the Shipping Controller under this regulation, and where before the twenty-eighth day of June, nineteen hundred and seventeen, any ship or any cargo space or passenger accommodation in any ship or any rights under any charter, freight engagement, or similar contract affecting any ship has been requisitioned by the Shipping Controller this regulation shall, after that date, apply as if the same had been requisitioned in pursuance of this regulation.

Regulation 39C sets forth the powers of the Port and Transit Executive Committee and was first issued in February 1916. By an amendment of 28 June, 1917, the directions of the Committee are to be " subject to any instructions of the Shipping Controller."

Regulation 39CC, 16 February, 1917, prohibits the purchase of any ship, or (by amendment of 5 February 1918) of a controlling interest in any ship, without permission of the Controller.

Regulation 39CCC, 29 September, 1917, empowers the Controller to requisition buildings or property for the purpose of providing storage accommodation at ports.

Regulation 39D, 10 January, 1917, prohibits the chartering of any foreign ship, or the purchase of goods exceeding one thousand tons in weight on c.i.f. terms, without permission of the Board of Trade. An amendment of 16 January, 1918, substitutes the Shipping Controller as the licensing authority.

Regulation 39DD, 16 January, 1918, requires a licence to be obtained from the Shipping Controller in respect of

(a) All voyages whatsoever made by steamers of 500 tons gross and up or sailing vessels of 1,000 tons gross and up, registered in the United Kingdom.

(b) All voyages made by any British ship starting at a port in the United Kingdom.

(c) All voyages whether by British or foreign ships, in the coasting trade.

Regulation 39DDD, 5 February, 1918, requires all charters of a ship registered in the United Kingdom, and all charters of any ship effected in the United Kingdom, to contain a clause making the validity of the contract subject to the Controller's approval.

Regulation 39E, 6 February, 1917, modifies the regulations with regard to tonnage measurement in respect of certain alterations made by direction of the Controller.

APPENDIX "B"
NOTE ON STATISTICS

THE following tables and the statistical diagrams which accompany this volume have been prepared wth a view to illustrating the losses of shipping and the movement of trade throughout the whole period of the war. For reasons explained below, all figures of imports and exports during the war contain an element of approximation. It is believed, however, that the figures of total imports and of coal exports given in Tables VIII and X and in Diagrams 4, 5, and 11 are substantially more accurate than any yet published, and that the margin of possible error is too small to invalidate any deductions that may be drawn from a comparison of periods.

The main published sources for statistical analysis of the effect of the war on British trade are the monthly Board of Trade Returns, the Annual Statements of Trade and Navigation, and the Statistical Abstract for the United Kingdom.

These sources, however, are imperfect. In the first place, the returns for the war period do not give the total weight of imports, and owing to variations in the conversion factors employed, no two sets of estimates exactly agree.

In the second place, the returns for the period May 1915 to June 1917 inclusive, exclude imports of oil-fuel for Admiralty purposes, and the returns for August 1914 to June 1917 inclusive, exclude all other imports (other than foodstuffs) on Government account, and all Government exports. As will be seen from the notes to Table VIII, the oil-fuel figures have been obtained from the Petroleum Department of the Board of Trade. Figures of other Government imports for the first six months of 1917 are also available; for 1915 and 1916 it has been necessary to employ an estimate.

The figures of coal exports used in constructing Diagram 11 have been based on the assumption that all shipments on Admiralty account to France, Italy, and Russia are excluded from the Board of Trade Returns. It is possible that a few cargoes shipped to France and Italy may have been included with the commercial exports, but if so, the proportion was very small.

Similarly, certain ships carrying full cargoes on Government account were excluded from the navigation returns prior to

July 1917. It has been impossible to make any allowance for these; but it will be seen from the note to Table X, that they would probably make no appreciable difference so far as entrances are concerned.

The total import volumes in six-monthly periods (Table X and Diagram 5) have been based on official monthly figures for the years 1916, 1917 and 1918, corrected by adding a proportionate allowance for imports excluded from the Board of Trade Returns. For the previous periods a table given in the Report of the Liverpool Steamship Owners' Association for 1918 has been used as a basis, subject to certain adjustments rendered necessary by the fact that the conversion factors used by the Association gave a somewhat higher result than the official figures adopted in Table VIII.

It was hoped to include a table showing the employment of British shipping at various periods; but this intention had to be abandoned, owing to changes in the basis of classification adopted in the Transport Department and Ministry of Shipping returns. These changes were undoubtedly fully justified, as they ensured greater accuracy and facilitated the work of the Departments; but they render detailed comparison, over a long period, impossible. A table showing the employment of British, Allied and neutral shipping on October 31st, 1918, is here given (Table VII), and figures relating to earlier periods will be found in the text of this and the previous volumes.

APPENDIX "C"

LIST OF TABLES

I. (a) GROSS TONNAGE OF MERCHANT SHIPPING LOST THROUGH ENEMY ACTION, TO NOVEMBER 11TH, 1918: BRITISH AND WORLD TOTALS.

   (b) SUMMARY SHOWING CAUSES OF LOSS AND NATIONALITY OF FOREIGN VESSELS.

II. COMPARISON OF LOSSES AND SHIPBUILDING OUTPUT, TO OCTOBER 31ST, 1918.

III. TONNAGE GAINS AND LOSSES OF THE CHIEF ALLIED AND NEUTRAL POWERS, TO OCTOBER 31ST, 1918.

IV. STEAM TONNAGE OWNED BY THE CHIEF MARITIME POWERS IN JUNE 1914, 1919, 1920.

V. (a) BRITISH OCEAN-GOING TONNAGE AVAILABLE AT END OF EACH MONTH OF 1917 AND 1918.
   (b) EFFECT OF WAR ON BRITISH OCEAN-GOING TONNAGE TO OCTOBER 31ST, 1918.

VI. CONVOY SAILINGS AND LOSSES.

VII. (a) EMPLOYMENT OF ALLIED AND NEUTRAL TONNAGE ON OCTOBER 31ST, 1918.
    (b) TONNAGE IN NAVAL AND MILITARY SERVICE OF ALLIES, ON OCTOBER 31ST, 1918.
    (c) TONNAGE IN IMPORT SERVICE OF PRINCIPAL ALLIES, ON OCTOBER 31ST, 1918.

VIII. TOTAL VOLUME OF IMPORTS, 1913–18.

IX. ANALYSIS OF IMPORTS, 1913, 1917, 1918.

X. MOVEMENTS OF SHIPPING AND TRADE AT PORTS IN THE UNITED KINGDOM, IN SIX-MONTHLY PERIODS.

XI. IMPORT AND EXPORT VALUES, SHOWING DIRECTION OF TRADE.

TABLES

I (a)

GROSS TONNAGE OF MERCHANT SHIPPING LOST THROUGH ENEMY ACTION, TO NOVEMBER 11TH, 1918

N.B.—These figures exclude Commissioned Auxiliaries. The British figures include merchant vessels only; the world total includes British and foreign fishing vessels. The figures include steam and sailing vessels of all sizes.

	British.	World Total.		British.	World Total.
1914			**1917**		
August	40,254	62,767	January	153,666	368,521
September	88,219	98,378	February	313,486	540,006
October	77,805	87,917	March	353,478	593,841
November	8,888	19,413	April	545,282	881,027
December	26,035	44,197	May	352,289	596,629
			June	417,925	687,507
Total	241,201	312,672	July	364,858	557,988
			August	329,810	511,730
			September	196,212	351,748
1915			October	276,132	458,558
January	32,054	47,981	November	173,560	289,212
February	36,372	59,921	December	253,087	399,111
March	71,479	80,775			
April	22,453	55,725	Total	3,729,785	6,235,878
May	84,025	120,058			
June	83,198	131,428			
July	52,847	109,640			
August	148,464	185,866			
September	101,690	151,884			
October	54,156	88,534			
November	94,493	153,043	**1918**		
December	74,490	123,141	January	179,973	306,658
			February	226,896	318,957
Total	855,721	1,307,996	March	199,458	342,597
			April	215,543	278,719
			May	192,436	295,520
1916			June	162,990	255,587
January	62,288	81,259	July	165,449	260,967
February	75,860	117,547	August	145,721	283,815
March	99,089	167,097	September	136,859	187,881
April	141,193	191,667	October	59,229	118,559
May	64,521	129,175	November	10,195	17,682
June	36,976	108,855			
July	82,432	118,215	Total	1,694,749	2,666,942
August	43,354	162,744			
September	104,572	230,460	Grand Total	7,759,090	12,850,814
October	176,248	353,660			
November	168,809	311,508			
December	182,292	355,139			
Total	1,237,634	2,327,326			

APPENDIX "C"

I (b)

SUMMARY

SHOWING CAUSE OF LOSS AND NATIONALITY OF FOREIGN VESSELS

—	By Cruisers, tbds., etc.	By Submarines.	By Mines.	By Aircraft.	Total.
	Tons gross.	Tons gross.	Tons gross.	Tons gross.	Tons gross.
British, 1914	203,139	2,950	35,112	—	241,201
1915	29,685	748,914	77,122	—	855,721
1916	103,352	888,689	244,623	970	1,237,634
1917	100,693	3,325,534	296,616	6,942	3,729,785
1918	5,833	1,668,972	19,944	—	1,694,749
	442,702	6,635,059	673,417	7,912	7,759,090
British fishing vessels	5,637	57,583	8,545	—	71,765
Total British	448,339	6,692,642	681,962	7,912	7,830,855
French	52,905	812,309	34,144	—	899,358
Russian	5,041	160,960	17,082	—	183,083
Belgian	6,752	70,129	8,877	—	85,758
Japanese	6,557	108,648	4,971	—	120,176
Italian	6,016	803,092	37,280	—	846,388
Portuguese	—	94,946	—	—	94,946
Roumanian	—	3,688	285	—	3,973
American	8,428	364,200	24,431	—	397,059
Greek	724	334,408	10,384	—	345,516
Brazilian	—	25,464	—	—	25,464
Norwegian	15,172	1,043,077	122,067	—	1,180,316
Swedish	8,185	142,493	50,598	—	201,276
Danish	4,834	201,394	37,479	—	243,707
Dutch	5,584	131,948	74,310	127	211,969
Spanish	—	152,387	16,104	—	168,491
Peruvian	—	1,419	—	—	1,419
Argentine	—	4,275	—	—	4,275
Uruguayan	—	6,027	—	—	6,027
Persian	—	—	758	—	758
Total	568,537	11,153,506	1,120,732	8,039	12,850,814

Countries which joined the Allies are named in the order in which they entered the war.

Of the Russian losses 3,407 tons was incurred after Russia ceased to be an Ally.
" Roumanian " 285 " " " before Roumania entered the war.
" American " 55,665 " " " before the United States entered the war.
" Greek " 228,497 " " " before Greece entered the war.
" Brazilian " 13,946 " " " before Brazil entered the war.

N.B.—These figures, compiled from Admiralty Returns, are not guaranteed as complete in respect of foreign shipping. The figures of foreign shipping include fishing vessels.

TABLES

II
COMPARISON OF LOSSES AND SHIPBUILDING OUTPUT TO OCTOBER 31ST, 1918

Period.	British Empire.			United Kingdom.	World (excluding Enemy Countries).		
	Losses, War and Marine.	New Ships brought on to Register.	Output.	Output.	Losses, War and Marine.	Output.	Enemy Tonnage brought into Service.
	1,000 tons gross.	1,000 tons gross.	1,000 tons gross.	1,000 tons gross.	1,000 tons gross.	1,000 tons gross.	1,000 tons gross.
1914							
August and September	342*	154	253		428*	—	705
4th Quarter	155	330	422		281	—	28
	497	*484*	*675*		*709*	*1,013*	*733*
1915							
1st Quarter	216	246	266		320	—	9
2nd ,,	224	244	147		380	—	89
3rd ,,	356	156	145		530	—	5
4th ,,	307	176	93		494	—	2
	1,103	*822*	*651*		*1,724*	*1,202*	*105*
1916							
1st Quarter	325	93	96		524	—	245
2nd ,,	271	113	108		522	—	3
3rd ,,	284	118	125		592	—	194
4th ,,	618	220	213		1,159	—	—
	1,498	*544*	*542*		*2,797*	*1,688*	*442*
1917							
1st Quarter	912	326	246		1,619	587	—
2nd ,,	1,362	305	249		2,237	685	656
3rd ,,	953	287	248		1,494	675	339
4th ,,	783	389	420		1,273	991	116
	4,010	*1,307*	*1,163*		*6,623*	*2,938*	*1,111*
1918							
1st Quarter	697	329	320		1,143	870	1
2nd ,,	631	423	443		962	1,243	—
3rd ,,	512	477	411		916	1,384	—
October	84	144	136		178	511	—
	1,924	*1,373*	*1,310*		*3,199*	*4,008*	*1*
Total	9,032	4,530	4,342		15,053	10,849	2,392

* Includes ships interned in enemy ports.

N.B.—In the above table the second column, which represents new ships actually brought on to the Register in the United Kingdom and the Oversea Dominions and Colonies, is taken from a table in *Allied Shipping Control*, by Sir J. A. Salter. The remaining figures are from Cmd. 9221, *Merchant Tonnage and the Submarine*. "Enemy tonnage brought into service" is credited in the table to the quarter during which the ships were seized. In most instances they were not actually brought into service until a later date.

TONNAGE GAINS AND LOSSES OF THE CHIEF ALLIED AND NEUTRAL POWERS FROM THE OUTBREAK OF WAR TO OCTOBER 31ST, 1918

(In 1,000 tons gross)

—	British Empire.	France.	Russia.	Italy.	Japan.	United States (including Lakes).	Norway.	Sweden.	Denmark.	Holland.	Greece.	Spain.
July 1914	21,045	2,319	1,054	1,668	1,708	5,368	2,505	1,118	820	1,496	837	899
Add:												
New Construction .	4,765	155	—	209	970	3,643	213	110	132	556	—	35
Tonnage Captured, etc. .	717	72	—	242	11	732	—	—	—	—	—	—
Gains by transfer or Purchase .	1,197	75	63	30	33	706	46	19	6	6	45	8
	6,679	*302*	*63*	*481*	*1,014*	*5,081*	*259*	*129*	*138*	*562*	*45*	*43*
Deduct:												
War Losses .	7,748	907	184	853	121	389	1,177	202	240	200	338	167
Interned in Enemy Ports	184	5	11	—	—	—	—	—	—	—	—	—
Marine Losses	1,100	83	40	81	78	302	132	54	37	60	41	37
Transfers and Sales	731	53	162	1	138	194	210	16	61	548	14	1
	9,763	*1,048*	*397*	*935*	*337*	*885*	*1,519*	*272*	*338*	*808*	*393*	*205*
Oct. 31st, 1918	17,961	1,573	720	1,214	2,385	9,564	1,245	975	620	1,250	489	737
Net Gain or Loss	−3,084 −14.6%	−746 −32.2%	−334 −31.7%	−454 −27.2%	+677 +39.6%	+4,196 +78.2%	−1,260 −50.3%	−143 −12.8%	−200 −24.4%	−246 −16.4%	−348 −41.6%	−162 −18.0%

N.B.—This table represents the approximate position *at the Armistice*; that is to say, requisitioned neutrals are shown as transfers, although there was an obligation to return them after the war. A more correct picture of the final position is given in Table IV. There are a few trifling discrepancies between the war losses as shown in this table and the figures in Table I. Both are taken from Admiralty returns.

TABLES

IV

STEAM (AND MOTOR) TONNAGE OWNED BY THE CHIEF MARITIME POWERS IN JUNE 1914, 1919, 1920, AS SHOWN BY LLOYD'S REGISTER BOOK.

(To illustrate recovery from War Losses, and effect of Peace Treaties)

	June 1914.	June 1919.	June 1920.
	1,000 tons gross.	1,000 tons gross.	1,000 tons gross.
Great Britain	18,892	16,345	18,111
British Dominions and Colonies	1,632	1,863	2,032
British Empire	20,524	18,208	20,143
France	1,922	1,962	2,963
Italy	1,430	1,238	2,118
Russia	852	514	510
Belgium	341	306	410
Japan	1,708	2,325	2,996
United States	2,070	9,824	12,456
Brazil	308	493	475
Norway	1,957	1,597	1,980
Sweden	1,015	917	996
Denmark	770	631	719
Holland	1,472	1,574	1,773
Spain	884	709	937
Greece	821	291	497
Germany	5,135	3,247[1]	419
Austria	1,052	713[1]	—
Turkey	116	99	—
Total, including other countries	43,144	45,737	51,786[2]

[1] Includes all vessels which, at the date of the Armistice, had not been captured or requisitioned by other countries.

[2] The figures of ships whose flag was not recorded amounted to 1,275,000 tons, and included all ex-enemy vessels (of 1,600 tons gross and up), the allocation of which was not yet known.

N.B.—The figures are exclusive of American ships on the Great Lakes.

V (a)

BRITISH OCEAN-GOING TONNAGE
(Steamers of 1,600 G.R.T. and up)

AVAILABLE FOR WAR OR TRADE AT THE END OF EACH MONTH OF 1917 AND 1918

Month.	1,000 tons gross.	Net gain or loss. 1,000 tons gross.	Month.	1,000 tons gross.	Net gain or loss. 1,000 tons gross.
1917			**1918**		
January	16,591	—	January	14,547	− 33
February	16,464	− 127	February	14,414	− 133
March	16,291	− 173	March	14,425	+ 11
April	15,874	− 417	April	14,482	+ 57
May	15,664	− 210	May	14,448	− 34
June	15,412	− 252	June	14,413	− 35
July	15,209	− 203	July	14,417	+ 4
August	15,060	− 149	August	14,346	− 71
September	14,975	− 85	September	14,363	+ 17
October	14,827	− 148	October	14,407	+ 44
November	14,755	− 72	November	14,444	+ 37
December	14,580	− 175	December	14,626	+ 182

N.B.—The above figures are taken from Requisition Branch Returns and include tankers, prizes, vessels on Colonial Register, requisitioned neutrals under the British flag, and ships repairing, or launched and completing. They exclude ships interned in enemy ports, or locked up in the Black Sea or Baltic. Owing to the inclusion of ships launched and completing or under repair, they present an unduly favourable picture in 1918 as compared with 1917. It must be remembered also that they include many requisitioned neutrals and Russians previously trading in Allied interests.

V (b)

EFFECT OF WAR ON BRITISH OCEAN-GOING TONNAGE
(Steamers of 1,600 G.R.T. and up)

TO OCTOBER 31ST, 1918

	s.s.	Tons gross.	s.s.	Tons gross.	s.s.	Tons gross.
Tonnage in July 1914	—	—	—	—	4,068	17,516,876
Deduct :						
War Losses	1,764	7,379,986				
Interned in enemy ports or captured	46	153,067				
Marine Losses	248	917,997				
Transferred to foreign flags, etc.	248	998,463				
Locked in Baltic	2	2,462				
			2,308	9,451,975		
Add :						
Launched	890	4,170,601				
Transferred from foreign flags, etc.[1]	328	1,354,526				
Prizes	144	611,778				
Alterations to gross tonnage (net gain)	—	204,920				
			1,362	6,341,825		
Net Loss (17·7%)					946	3,110,150
Tonnage on October 31st, 1918					3,122	14,406,726

[1] Includes new ships built abroad.

VI

CONVOY LOSSES AND SAILINGS

Ocean Convoys—Homewards

Number of Convoys.	Direction.	Ships escorted safely.	Gross Tonnage.	Ships Sunk.			
				Torpedoed in Convoy.	Marine Perils.	Not in Convoy.	Total.
56	Halifax	556	6,678,512	2	1	1	4
63	Sydney	1,432	6,744,592	4	3	7	14
89	New York	1,619	9,690,581	7	4	5	16
24	Halifax-Channel	307	2,563,273	1	—	—	1
78	Hampton Roads	1,596	7,572,804	13	—	5	18
56	Sierra Leone	421	2,928,020	2	1	1	4
57	Dakar	596	2,507,040	3	—	2	5
119	Gibraltar	1,732	5,516,483	16	2	9	27
23	Med. Through	344	2,105,896	7	—	1	8
22	Rio	305	1,466,097	2	—	—	2
20	Bay	342	1,768,015	4	1	—	5
607	Total	9,250	49,541,313	61	12	31	104

Ocean Convoys—Outwards

Number of Convoys.	Direction.	Ships escorted safely.	Gross Tonnage.	Ships Sunk.			
				Torpedoed in Convoy.	Marine Perils.	Not in Convoy.	Total.
57	Falmouth	791	2,846,043	5	—	—	5
136	Devonport	1,715	10,057,339	6	—	3	9
113	Milford	2,652	9,961,655	8	2	2	12
29	Queenstown	209	954,503	—	—	—	—
85	Lamlash	954	5,169,290	8	1	—	9
8	Liverpool Special	22	246,650	1	—	—	1
39	Liverpool	319	2,917,763	7	—	—	7
25	Med. Through	304	1,868,601	5	1	—	6
10	Channel	93	777,459	—	—	—	—
12	Liverpool–Buncrana	103	616,364	—	—	—	—
13	Liverpool Fast	127	1,416,745	1	—	—	1
527	Total	7,289	36,832,412	41	4	5	50

SUMMARY

	Ships.	Gross Tonnage.	Percentage of Total.	
			Ships.	Tonnage.
Homewards:				
Escorted safely	9,250	49,541,313	98·89	98·97
Torpedoed in Convoy	61	305,643	0·65	0·61
Lost by Marine Perils	12	64,540	0·13	0·13
Lost while not in Convoy	31	145,633	0·33	0·29
Total Sailings	9,354	50,057,129	100·00	100·00
Outwards:				
Escorted safely	7,289	36,832,412	99·32	99·13
Torpedoed in Convoy	41	279,640	0·56	0·75
Lost by Marine Perils	4	17,819	0·06	0·05
Lost while not in Convoy	5	26,419	0·06	0·07
Total Sailings	7,339	37,156,290	100·00	100·00
Homewards and Outwards:				
Escorted safely	16,539	86,373,725	99·08	99·04
Torpedoed in Convoy	102	585,283	0·61	0·67
Lost by Marine Perils	16	82,359	0·09	0·09
Lost while not in Convoy	36	172,052	0·22	0·20
Total Sailings	16,693	87,213,419	100·00	100·00

N.B.—The above tables are taken from statistics prepared by the Convoy Section of the Ministry of Shipping. The sailings include all Convoys arrived or departed to November 23rd, 1918. The losses include one or two Armed Merchant Cruisers or Commissioned Escort Ships. Losses " Not in Convoy " include vessels sunk after dispersal, after being detached, or after dropping out of convoy through lack of speed or stress of weather.

SHORT SEA CONVOYS

	Sailings.	Losses in Convoy.	Percentage of Loss.
Scandinavian:			
Old System, April 28th, 1917–January 1918	3,423	40	1·17
New System, January 19th–November 25th, 1918	4,230	15	0·35
Coastal System:			
April 1st to December 31st, 1917 (Prior to Amalgamation with East Coast System)	3,304	2	0·06
East Coast:			
Old System, April 28th, 1917–January 15th, 1918	3,654	34	0·93
New System, January 16th–November 25th, 1918	16,102	35	0·22
French Coal Trade:			
(a) Penzance–Brest	10,292	36	
(b) Portland–Cherbourg	7,442	4	
(c) St. Helens or Portland–Havre	14,860	13	0·13
(d) Southend–Boulogne or Calais	6,758	—	
Total French Coal Trade	39,352	53	
Dutch Convoy	1,861	6	0·32
Mediterranean Local	10,464	127	1·21

N.B.—The above are taken from Admiralty sources. All casualties in the Dutch Convoy occurred prior to the adoption of close formation in June 1917.

VII (a)

EMPLOYMENT OF ALLIED AND NEUTRAL TONNAGE, OCTOBER 31ST, 1918

(Steamers of 500 G.R.T. and up)

	British.		French.		Italian.		American.		Other Allies.		Neutrals.	
	1,000 tons d.w.	%	1,000 tons d.w.	%	1,000 tons d.w.	%	1,000 tons d.w.	%	1,000 tons d.w.	%	1,000 tons d.w.	%
I. In Naval or Military Service of Allies, including American Trooping (a)	5,238 (b)	29·5	310	22·5	173	16·2	2,865	49·3	213	4·3	144	2·4
II. In Import Service of own Country	6,762	38·0	934	68·0	771	72·3	782	13·5	(included in IV)		(included in IV)	
III. In Import Service of other Principal Allies	3,262	18·4	60	4·4	24	2·3	297	5·1	1,077	21·9	1,744	29·0
IV. In other Merchant Service (Coasting, Colonial, Minor Allies, Neutrals)	2,512	14·1	54	3·9	57	5·4	1,513	26·1	2,518	51·0	3,004 (c)	49·9
V. Unemployed or Employment Unknown	—	—	16	1·2	41	3·8	351 (d)	6·0	1,127 (e)	22·8	1,129	18·7
Total Available	17,774	100·0	1,374	100·0	1,066	100·0	5,808	100·0	4,935	100·0	6,021	100·0
Repairing	1,385	—	256	—	126	—	185	—	101	—	137	—
Tankers (excluded above)	1,681	—	24	—	48	—	1,371	—	36	—	188	—
Grand Total	20,840	—	1,654	—	1,240	—	7,364	—	5,072	—	6,346	—

(a) Includes a very few ships in special Government service, such as cable-repairing.
(b) Includes allowance for space on Atlantic liners devoted to American trooping.
(c) Includes 8,000 tons in naval service of neutrals; and 21,000 tons in enemy service.
(d) Includes new ships completed but not yet allocated.
(e) Includes 525,000 tons Russian locked up in Black Sea and Baltic.

N.B.—The figures exclude certain American passenger steamers in coasting trade. The figures for some of the Minor Allies and Neutrals are estimates.

TABLES

SUMMARY

		1,000 tons d.w.	%
I.	In Naval or Military Service of Allies	8,943	24·2
II & III.	In Import Service of Four Principal Allies	15,713	42·5
IV.	In Other Merchant Service	9,658	26·1
V.	Unemployed or Employment Unknown	2,664	7·2
	Total Available	36,978	100·0
	Repairing	2,190	
	Tankers	3,348	
	Grand Total	42,516	

VII (b)

TONNAGE IN NAVAL AND MILITARY SERVICE OF ALLIES, OCTOBER 31ST, 1918

(Steamers of 500 G.R.T. and up, excluding tankers)

	1,000 tons d.w.	%
British	5,238	58·6
French	310	3·5
Italian	173	1·9
American	2,865	32·0
Other Allies	213	2·4
Neutrals[1]	144	1·6
	8,943	100·0

[1] Chiefly Swedish employed in carriage of American military stores.

VII (c)

TONNAGE IN IMPORT SERVICE OF PRINCIPAL ALLIES, OCTOBER 31ST, 1918

(Steamers of 500 G.R.T. and up, excluding tankers)

	United Kingdom.		France.		Italy.		Total, Principal European Allies.		United States.	
	1,000 tons d.w.	%	1,000 tons d.w.	%	1,000 tons d.w.	%	1,000 tons d.w.	%	1,000 tons d.w.	%
British .	6,762	90.8	1,546	45.4	1,556	51.6	9,864	71.1	160	8.7
French .	60	} 1.7	934	27.4	—	—	994	7.2	—	—
Italian .	19		5	} 3.8	771	25.6	795	5.7	—	—
American	45		124		128	4.2	297	2.1	782	42.3
Other Allies .	200	2.7	311	9.1	231	7.6	742	5.4	335	18.1
Neutral .	356	4.8	486	14.3	331	11.0	1,173	8.5	571	30.9
Total .	7,442	100.0	3,406	100.0	3,017	100.0	13,865	100.0	1,848	100.0

VIII

TOTAL VOLUME OF IMPORTS, 1913-18

	(a) Imports as in Board of Trade Returns.	(b) Government Imports not included in Returns.	(c) Oil Fuel not included in Returns.	Total.
	1,000 tons.	1,000 tons.	1,000 tons.	1,000 tons.
1913	54,548	—	—	54,548
1914	46,368	—	—	46,368
1915	45,470	600	527	46,597
1916	41,356	1,500	1,426	44,282
1917	33,957	2,070	1,257	37,284
1918	35,167	—	—	35,167

(a) From Board of Trade Memoranda and table in Report of the Chamber of Shipping of the United Kingdom 1919-20, " compiled from the Accounts of the Trade and Navigation of the United Kingdom and statement made in the House of Commons by Sir Auckland Geddes." Other estimates for 1913 give a total of over 56,000,000 tons.

(b) Estimate for 1915, 50,000 tons a month. Estimate for 1916, by Statistical Branch of Ministry of Shipping, 125,000 tons a month. Figures for first six months of 1917: $254 + 268 + 335 + 374 + 437 + 402 = 2,070$, from a Board of Trade Memorandum.

(c) Figures supplied by Petroleum Department of the Board of Trade.

APPENDIX "C"

IX
ANALYSIS OF IMPORTS, 1913, 1917, 1918

N.B.—These figures are by Statistical Branch, Ministry of Shipping, and it will be observed that the totals for all three years are rather higher than those shown in Table VIII.

	1913.	1917.	1918.	Increase or Decrease in 1918 on 1913.
	1,000 tons.	1,000 tons.	1,000 tons.	1,000 tons.
I. Food, Drink, and Tobacco:				
A. Wheat and Flour	5,893	5,288	4,220	− 1,673
Other Grains	3,370	3,430	2,619	− 2,751
B. Meat and Animals	1,178	986	1,269	+ 91
C. Other Food, Non-dutiable	2,838	1,369	1,317	− 1,521
" " Dutiable	2,783	1,968	1,913	− 870
D. Tobacco	74	22	81	+ 7
Total, Class I	18,136	13,063	11,419	− 6,717
II. Raw Materials:				
A. Coal, Coke, etc.	—	4	—	—
B. Iron Ore and Scrap	7,565	6,205	6,571	− 994
C. Other Ores	2,078	1,645	1,603	− 475
D. Wood and Timber	11,590	2,975	2,481	− 9,109
E. Cotton	970	736	665	− 305
F. Wool	433	360	201	− 232
G. Other Textiles	609	358	360	− 249
H. 1. Petroleum	1,849	4,085	5,152	+ 3,303
2. Oils, Seeds, and Fats	2,000	1,350	1,498	− 502
I. Hides and Skins	176	139	113	− 63
J. Paper-making Materials	1,229	446	439	− 790
K. Miscellaneous	2,237	868	867	− 1,370
Total, Class II	30,736	19,171	19,950	−10,786
III. Manufactures:				
A. Iron and Steel	2,220	681	337	− 1,883
B. Other Metals	633	752	559	− 74
C. Cutlery and Hardware	43	21	22	− 21
D. Electrical Goods	7	4	3	− 4
E. Machinery	104	81	80	− 24
F. Boats (new)	1	—	—	− 1
G. Wood Manufactures	142	38	52	− 90
H. Yarns and Fabrics	231	101	115	− 116
I. Apparel	10	3	2	− 8
J. Chemicals	586	954	1,006	+ 420
K. Leather	62	44	35	− 27
L. Earthenware and Glass	289	34	9	− 280
M. Paper	644	140	105	− 539
N. Carriages	35	21	25	− 10
O. Miscellaneous	2,118	2,743	1,763	− 335
Total, Class III	7,125	5,617	4,113	− 3,012
IV. Miscellaneous and Unclassified	38	224	111	+ 73
Grand Total	56,035	38,075	35,593	−20,442

TABLES

X

MOVEMENTS OF SHIPPING AND TRADE AT PORTS IN THE UNITED KINGDOM

Six months ended	Shipping entered with Cargoes.			Shipping Cleared with Cargoes.			Shipping arrived with Cargoes in the Coasting Trade.			Total Volume of Imports.
	British.	Foreign.	Total.	British.	Foreign.	Total.	Trade between Great Britain and Ireland.	General Coasting Trade.	Total.	
	1,000 tons net.	1,000 tons net.	1,000 tons net.	1,000 tons net.	1,000 tons net.	1,000 tons net.	1,000 tons net.	1,000 tons net.	1,000 tons net.	1,000 tons
January 31st, 1914	16,591	8,585	25,176	20,605	13,887	34,492	11,408	6,202	17,610	27,646
July 31st, 1914	16,142	8,205	24,347	20,278	13,702	33,980	11,866	7,778	19,644	24,130
January 31st, 1915	12,235	5,384	17,619	10,823	9,030	19,853	8,837	6,738	15,575	22,221
July 31st, 1915	11,642	5,436	17,078	10,519	9,759	20,278	7,986	6,379	14,365	22,821
January 31st, 1916	11,136	5,466	16,602	9,422	9,312	18,734	6,646	5,975	12,621	23,416
July 31st, 1916	9,899	5,110	15,009	8,829	9,334	18,163	5,811	5,413	11,224	22,634
January 31st, 1917	10,146	4,607	14,753	8,863	8,129	16,992	5,087	5,849	10,936	21,378
July 31st, 1917	9,584	2,154	11,738	8,273	4,353	12,626	4,836	5,179	10,015	19,497
January 31st, 1918	9,059	1,943	11,002	8,415	4,328	12,743	3,938	4,950	8,888	17,111
July 31st, 1918	9,717	1,748	11,465	7,448	3,914	11,362	3,702	4,710	8,412	17,458
January 31st, 1919	10,218	1,614	11,832	7,869	4,025	11,894	3,695	4,734	8,429	18,168

N.B.—Certain requisitioned ships carrying Government cargoes were excluded from the returns prior to July 1917. During the six months ended January 31st, 1918, the tonnage of ships that would have been excluded under the old system was: Entered 117,000 (113,000 British); Cleared 1,788,000 (1,652,000 British). During the six months ended July 31st, 1918, the figures were 26,000 and 1,715,000 respectively. No allowance has been made for such ships in previous periods, as it is impossible to find a reliable basis. This note applies also to Diagrams 1 and 2.

XI
IMPORT AND EXPORT VALUES
(In millions of £)
Showing Direction of Trade during War

	Imports from							Exports and Re-exports to					
	1913	1914	1915	1916	1917	1918		1913	1914	1915	1916	1917	1918
Germany	80·4	47·0	0·2	0·1	—	—		60·5	36·4	—	—	—	—
Austria-Hungary	7·7	4·4	—	—	—	—		5·8	3·4	—	—	—	—
Turkey and Turkey in Asia	5·4	4·2	1·3	0·9	0·5	0·7		8·0	6·0	0·5	0·5	0·9	1·8
Bulgaria	—	0·2	—	—	—	—		0·5	0·9	0·1	—	—	—
Roumania	2·0	3·2	1·6	1·3	0·3	—		2·0	2·0	0·5	—	0·7	—
Belgium	23·4	16·1	—	—	—	0·2		20·7	13·3	0·2	0·3	0·3	0·1
Total, principal trades cut off by War	118·9	75·1	3·1	2·3	0·8	0·9		97·5	62·0	1·3	0·8	1·9	1·9
Percentage of Grand Total	*15·4*	*10·7*	*0·3*	*0·2*	—	—		*15·4*	*11·8*	*0·1*	*0·1*	*0·1*	*0·1*
France	46·4	37·8	31·4	26·6	22·9	35·0		40·9	35·1	81·2	107·6	128·0	144·5
Italy	8·1	8·7	11·3	11·2	10·4	18·4		15·6	13·9	17·6	24·0	31·8	33·5
Russia	40·3	28·1	21·4	18·3	17·9	6·7		27·2	21·8	24·9	34·3	52·7	0·3
Total, Principal Allies	94·8	74·6	64·1	56·1	51·2	60·1		84·2	70·8	123·7	165·9	212·5	178·3
Percentage of Grant Total	*12·3*	*10·7*	*7·5*	*5·9*	*4·8*	*4·6*		*13·3*	*13·5*	*25·3*	*27·5*	*35·4*	*33·3*
Norway	7·4	7·7	13·7	16·7	18·4	23·7		6·7	7·2	9·4	12·3	9·3	5·6
Sweden	14·2	14·1	19·8	20·6	14·9	22·5		9·2	9·0	10·2	8·9	3·3	2·7
Denmark, Iceland, and Greenland	24·0	25·5	22·9	22·9	18·3	5·3		6·6	7·4	12·1	14·6	8·0	4·0
Holland	23·6	24·3	23·4	22·1	19·9	7·7		20·4	20·7	30·5	33·0	24·8	15·4
Total, Northern Neutrals	69·2	71·6	79·8	82·3	71·5	59·2		43·0	44·3	62·2	68·8	45·4	27·7
Percentage of Grand Total	*9·1*	*10·3*	*9·5*	*8·7*	*6·7*	*4·5*		*6·8*	*8·4*	*12·7*	*11·4*	*7·4*	*5·2*

TABLES

2.3	2.6	2.4	3.0	3.5	4.8	Channel Islands, Deep Sea Fisheries, and Northern Whale Fisheries	1.6	1.6	1.8	2.1	2.0	2.3
15.9	15.8	20.8	27.3	22.3	30.8	Spain and Canaries	10.5	8.5	8.7	11.5	5.7	4.2
3.1	3.3	4.1	5.4	3.9	9.8	Portugal, Azores, and Madeira	4.3	3.6	4.3	5.4	4.4	4.3
11.1	10.1	15.3	15.5	11.3	13.1	Switzerland	5.1	3.6	4.1	5.6	6.9	9.2
0.2	0.3	0.5	0.3	0.2	0.5	Gibraltar, Malta, and Cyprus	2.3	2.0	3.1	3.4	6.1	6.1
2.7	2.3	3.3	4.1	5.0	6.4	Algeria, Tunis, Tripoli, Morocco, and Spanish ports in North Africa	3.7	3.1	4.0	5.3	7.0	10.2
2.2	2.5	4.0	4.7	1.0	2.3	Greece, Crete, Serbia, and Montenegro	2.7	3.2	3.5	1.3	0.2	1.1
21.4	17.5	22.3	27.5	33.4	55.4	Egypt and Sudan	10.0	8.4	8.9	12.3	15.4	22.6
58.9	54.4	72.7	87.8	80.6	123.1	Total, Rest of Europe, and Mediterranean	40.2	34.0	38.4	46.9	47.7	60.0
7.7	*6.0*	*8.6*	*9.3*	*7.6*	*9.4*	*Percentage of Grand Total*	*6.3*	*6.4*	*7.8*	*7.8*	*7.8*	*11.2*
141.7	138.6	237.8	291.8	376.3	515.4	United States	59.5	64.0	56.5	64.5	60.1	26.8
30.5	31.5	41.0	58.5	84.4	124.4	Canada	27.3	20.5	16.0	21.6	17.8	14.9
1.0	0.9	1.2	1.9	0.8	0.9	Newfoundland and Bermudas	1.2	0.8	0.6	0.6	0.6	0.5
173.2	171.0	280.0	352.2	461.5	640.7	Total, N. America	88.0	85.3	73.1	86.7	78.5	42.2
22.3	*24.5*	*33.0*	*37.2*	*43.2*	*48.7*	*Percentage of Grand Total*	*13.9*	*16.2*	*15.1*	*14.4*	*12.9*	*7.9*
1.9	1.8	2.2	2.6	2.3	5.1	Mexico	2.5	0.7	0.3	0.4	0.9	1.1
2.2	2.4	2.5	1.8	1.1	0.4	Central America and Panama	2.0	1.4	0.9	1.3	1.5	1.1
2.1	2.4	4.1	5.1	6.2	8.1	British West Indies and Bahamas	2.8	2.8	2.3	2.5	2.2	1.8
4.0	4.7	8.5	13.4	18.2	22.9	Cuba, Porto Rico, and Foreign West Indies	3.6	2.8	3.1	3.4	2.7	2.4
10.2	11.3	17.3	22.9	27.8	36.5	Total, Central America and West Indies	10.9	7.7	6.6	7.6	7.3	6.4
1.3	*1.9*	*2.1*	*2.4*	*3.6*	*2.8*	*Percentage of Grand Total*	*1.7*	*1.5*	*1.3*	*1.3*	*1.0*	*1.2*

XI—continued
IMPORT AND EXPORT VALUES
(In millions of £)

Showing Direction of Trade during War

Imports from							Exports and Re-exports to					
1913	1914	1915	1916	1917	1918		1913	1914	1915	1916	1917	1918
1·6	1·3	1·5	0·4	0·6	0·5	Colombia and Venezuela	2·6	1·8	1·6	2·6	2·4	2·2
1·0	1·3	1·5	1·2	2·0	2·7	Guiana, British, French, and Dutch	0·9	0·9	0·9	0·9	0·9	0·8
10·0	8·0	8·3	9·0	10·0	8·8	Brazil	13·0	6·6	5·6	7·1	7·4	9·0
2·8	2·8	4·3	4·0	5·5	6·5	Uruguay and Paraguay	3·2	1·8	1·6	2·1	2·5	3·4
42·5	37·2	63·9	51·6	48·4	63·0	Argentina	23·4	15·1	12·1	14·6	13·3	17·7
11·3	10·7	14·9	19·3	20·5	31·1	Chile, Peru, Ecuador, and Bolivia	8·8	5·9	3·3	6·3	7·3	9·2
0·6	0·6	1·3	3·0	2·0	3·2	Falkland Is. and Southern Whale Fisheries	0·1	0·1	0·2	0·3	0·2	0·2
69·8	61·9	95·7	88·5	89·0	115·8	*Total, South America*	52·0	32·2	25·3	33·9	34·0	42·5
9·1	*9·0*	*11·3*	*9·3*	*8·4*	*8·8*	Percentage of Grand Total	*8·2*	*6·1*	*5·1*	*5·6*	*5·5*	*8·0*
5·2	6·0	9·6	12·0	14·9	19·2	British West Africa, St. Helena, and Ascension	7·3	7·4	6·4	8·0	7·9	8·1
1·4	1·3	3·2	5·2	5·4	3·4	Foreign West Africa and Belgian Congo	3·0	1·9	2·1	3·8	5·6	6·2
6·6	7·3	12·8	17·2	20·3	22·6	*Total, West Africa*	10·3	9·3	8·5	11·8	13·5	14·3
0·9	*1·6*	*1·6*	*1·8*	*1·9*	*1·7*	Percentage of Grand Total	*1·6*	*1·8*	*1·7*	*1·9*	*2·2*	*2·7*
12·5	11·1	11·5	12·3	12·1	12·9	British South Africa	25·0	21·2	20·6	25·9	20·9	24·0
1·0	1·0	1·1	1·3	2·2	2·9	British East Africa	1·4	1·2	1·1	1·9	1·9	2·5
0·3	1·3	4·0	2·7	1·9	3·7	Mauritius and Seychelles	0·6	0·5	0·8	1·0	0·6	0·5
0·8	1·0	1·6	1·9	1·9	3·7	Foreign East Africa, Madagascar, and Réunion	2·3	1·9	1·3	1·6	1·3	1·6
14·6	14·4	18·2	18·2	18·1	23·2	*Total, South and East Africa*	29·3	24·8	23·8	30·4	24·7	28·6
1·9	*2·5*	*2·2*	*1·9*	*1·7*	*1·8*	Percentage of Grand Total	*4·6*	*4·7*	*4·8*	*5·0*	*3·9*	*5·4*

TABLES

0.7	1.0	1.4	1.0	1.4	0.3	Persia, Aden, and Arabia	1.3	1.1	1.3	1.0	1.3	1.9
48.7	43.6	62.2	72.5	66.9	88.6	India, including Goa, Pondichery, etc.	71.9	63.9	47.0	54.4	60.7	49.6
7.8	8.1	12.2	10.7	10.2	11.5	Ceylon	4.3	3.0	2.1	2.9	2.2	2.0
57.2	52.7	75.8	84.2	78.5	100.4	*Total, Middle East*	77.5	68.0	50.4	58.3	64.2	53.5
7.7	*7.7*	*9.0*	*8.9*	*7.4*	*7.6*	*Percentage of Grand Total*	*12.2*	*12.8*	*11.9*	*9.7*	*13.8*	*10.0*
19.4	16.4	20.0	22.3	23.0	13.0	Straits Settlements and Federated Malay States	7.4	5.8	4.4	6.3	5.7	6.9
0.8	1.1	2.2	1.2	1.4	0.1	Siam and French Indo-China	1.5	1.2	1.1	2.2	1.9	2.5
4.0	13.3	14.7	19.2	17.8	9.7	Dutch East Indies, British Borneo, Papua, etc.	7.4	6.6	6.4	8.6	7.4	7.7
2.2	1.6	2.2	4.0	3.8	6.1	Philippines and Guam	1.0	0.8	0.6	0.5	0.5	0.6
4.7	4.7	7.0	8.3	8.5	9.7	China	15.0	13.1	8.6	10.9	10.7	11.9
0.7	0.6	0.9	1.0	1.5	1.4	Hong Kong	4.6	3.7	2.2	4.1	3.1	3.8
4.4	4.1	9.4	12.5	15.3	23.9	Japan and Korea	15.1	8.7	5.3	8.0	5.9	7.4
36.2	41.8	56.4	68.5	71.3	63.9	*Total, Far East*	52.0	39.9	28.6	40.6	35.2	40.8
4.7	*6.1*	*6.7*	*7.2*	*6.7*	*4.9*	*Percentage of Grand Total*	*8.2*	*7.6*	*5.8*	*6.7*	*5.7*	*7.6*
38.1	36.9	45.2	36.2	64.3	45.4	Australia	37.8	37.1	31.9	39.1	24.0	28.1
20.3	23.0	30.4	31.6	29.1	24.5	New Zealand	11.8	10.4	10.1	12.9	7.4	8.0
0.6	0.7	0.5	0.4	0.2	—	Pacific Islands	0.4	0.3	0.1	0.2	0.1	0.1
59.0	60.6	76.1	68.2	93.6	69.9	*Total, Australasia*	50.0	47.8	42.1	52.2	31.5	36.2
7.7	*8.8*	*8.0*	*7.2*	*8.8*	*5.3*	*Percentage of Grand Total*	*7.9*	*9.1*	*8.6*	*8.6*	*5.0*	*6.8*
768.7	696.6	851.9	948.5	1064.2	1316.1	*Grand Total*	634.8	526.2	483.9	603.8	596.8	532.4

N.B.—The above figures are exclusive of certain Imports and Exports on Government account prior to July 1917. If these figures were available they would tend to increase the percentage of Imports from North America and of Exports to Allied Countries during the earlier years of the war. This note applies also to Diagrams 6 and 7.

DIAGRAM SHEWING the NET TONNAGE of vessels entered with cargoes at ports in the UNITED KINGDOM for the SIX MONTHS ENDING

British tonnage......RED
Foreign tonnage....BLACK

PREPARED IN THE HISTORICAL SECTION OF THE COMMITTEE OF IMPERIAL DEFENCE

Ordnance Survey, 1923.

DIAGRAM SHEWING the NET TONNAGE of vessels cleared with cargoes at ports in the UNITED KINGDOM for the SIX MONTHS ENDING

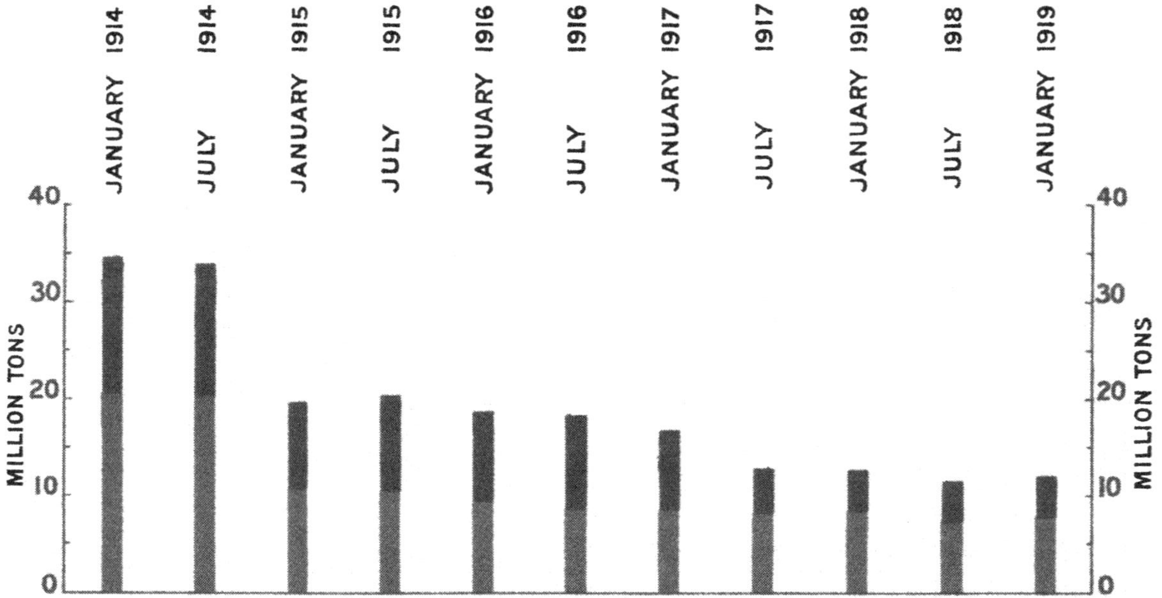

British tonnage......RED
Foreign tonnage....BLACK

PREPARED IN THE HISTORICAL SECTION OF THE COMMITTEE OF IMPERIAL DEFENCE

Ordnance Survey, 1923.

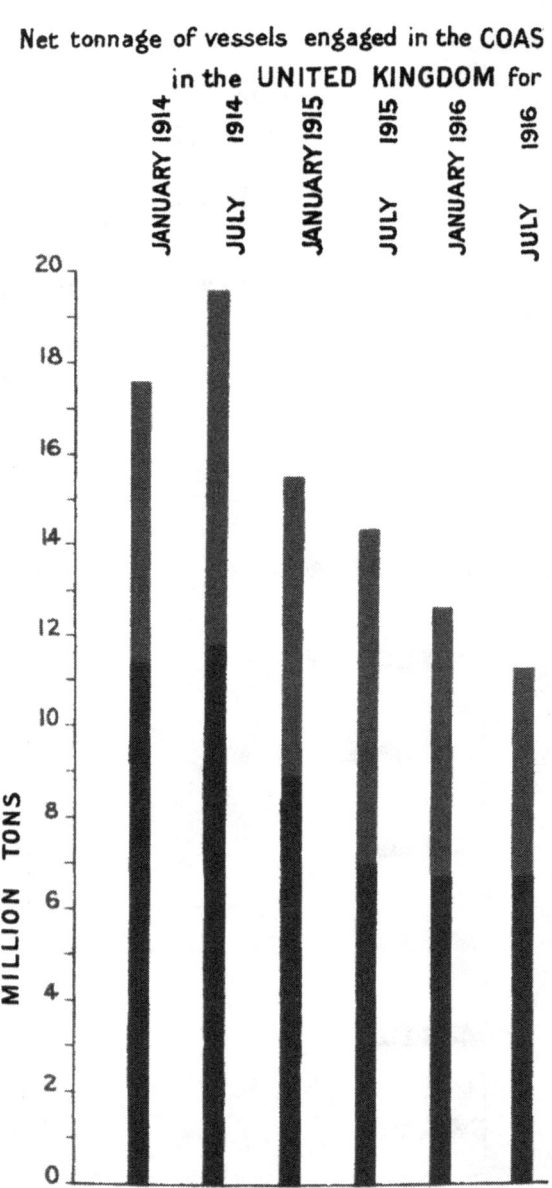

TING TRADE arrived with cargoes at ports
the SIX MONTHS ENDING

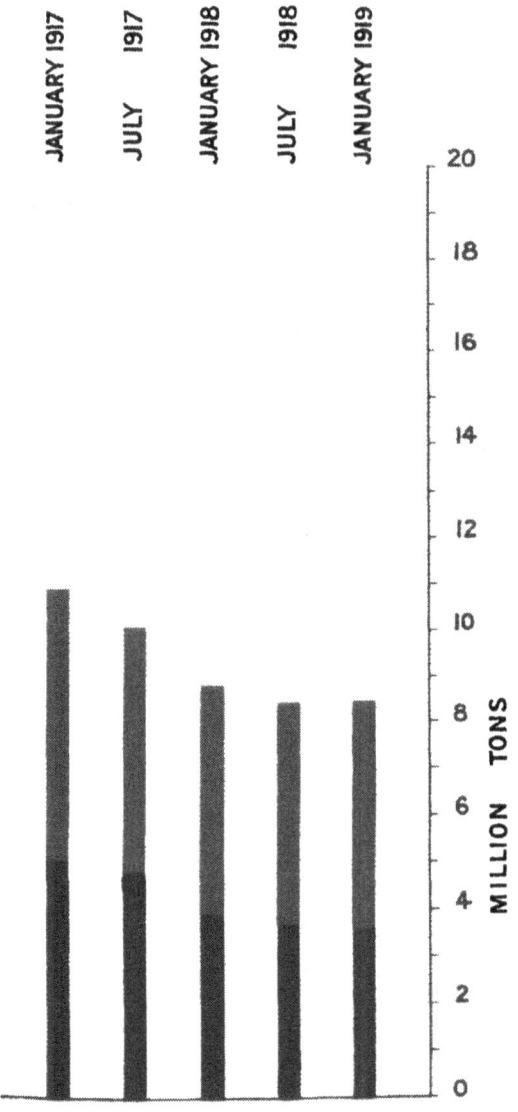

Trade...BLACK
iin and Ireland ... RED

ESTIMATED WEIGHT OF IMPORTS INTO THE UNITED KINGDOM
distinguishing Foodstuffs (shown in black)

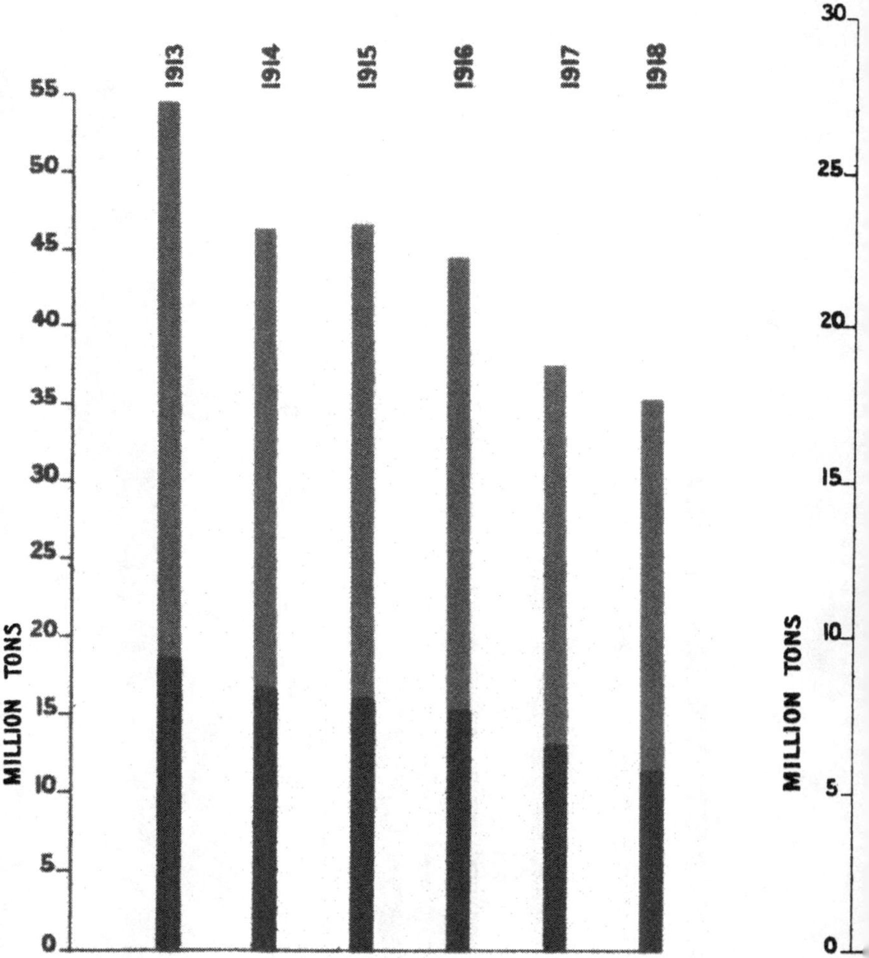

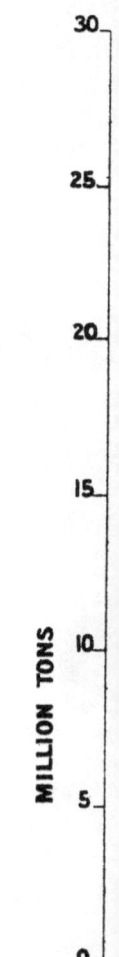

PREPARED IN THE HISTORICAL SECTION OF THE COMMITTE OF IMPERIAL DEFENCE.

ESTIMATED WEIGHT OF IMPORTS INTO THE UNITED KINGDOM
in six-monthly periods.

5

| JANUARY 1915 | " | JANUARY 1916 | " | JANUARY 1917 | " | JANUARY 1918 | " | JANUARY 1919 |

Ordnance Survey 1923

DIAGRAM SHEW
from the UNITED STATES and CANADA, and from FRAN
TOTAL IMPO

BLACK....UNITED STA
RED ....FRANCE, ITA

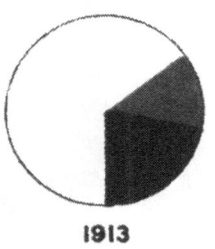 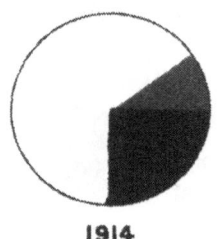 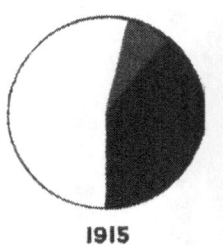

1913   1914   1915

DIAGRAM SHEW
from the UNITED STATES and CANADA, and from FRAN
TOTAL EXPO

BLACK....UNITED STA
RED ....FRANCE, ITA

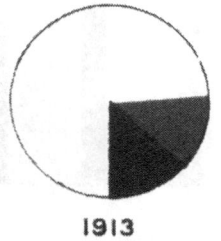 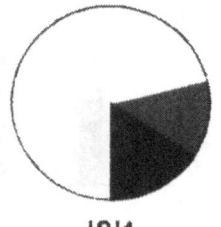 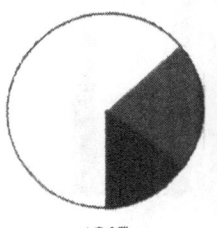

1913   1914   1915

PREPARED IN THE HISTORICAL SECTION OF THE COMMITTEE OF IMPERIAL DEFENCE

ING IMPORTS
CE, ITALY and RUSSIA respectively, as a proportion of the
RT VALUES.

TES and CANADA.
LY and RUSSIA.

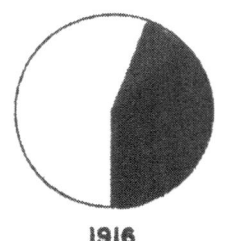
1916

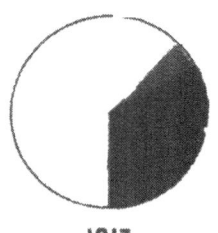
1917

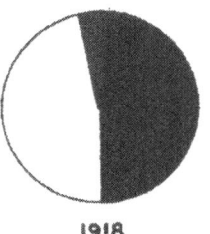
1918

ING EXPORTS
CE, ITALY and RUSSIA respectively, as a proportion of the
RT VALUES.

TES and CANADA.
,LY and RUSSIA.

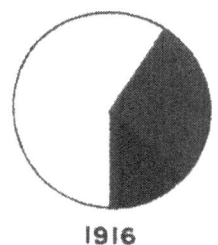
1916

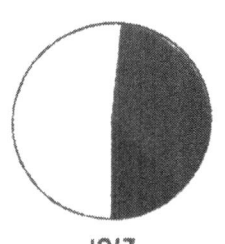
1917

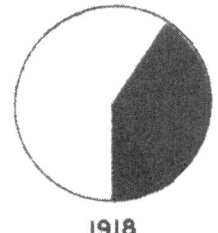
1918

Ordnance Survey 1923

8

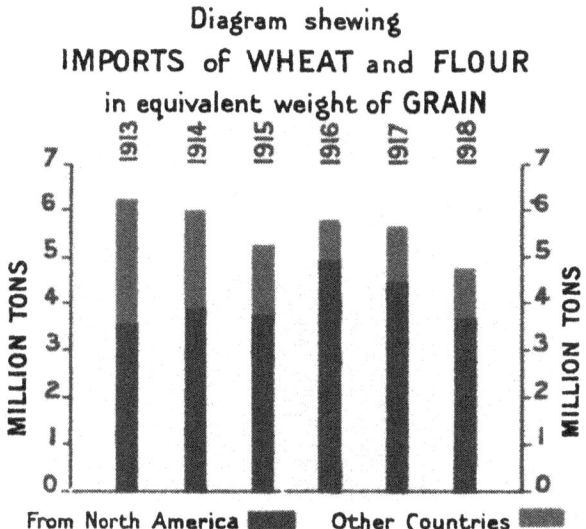

Ordnance Survey 1923

9

Diagram shewing
the TOTAL IMPORTS of IRON ORE quarterly

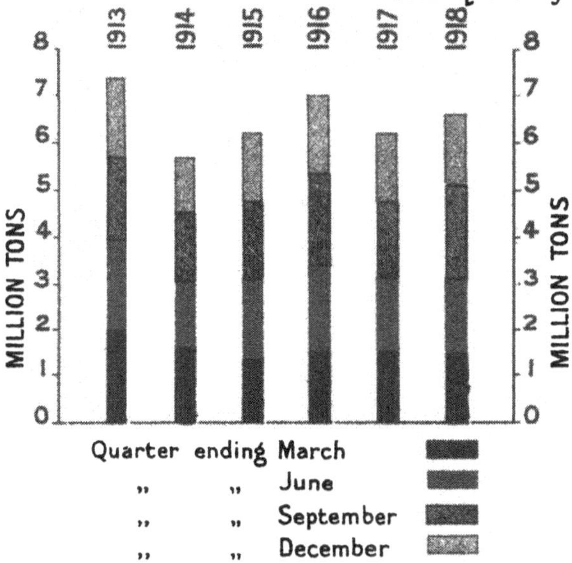
1913
1914
1915
1916
1917
1918
MILLION TONS
MILLION TONS
0
1
2
3
4
5
6
7
8
Quarter ending March
" " June
" " September
" " December

10

Diagram shewing
IMPORTS of IRON ORE in

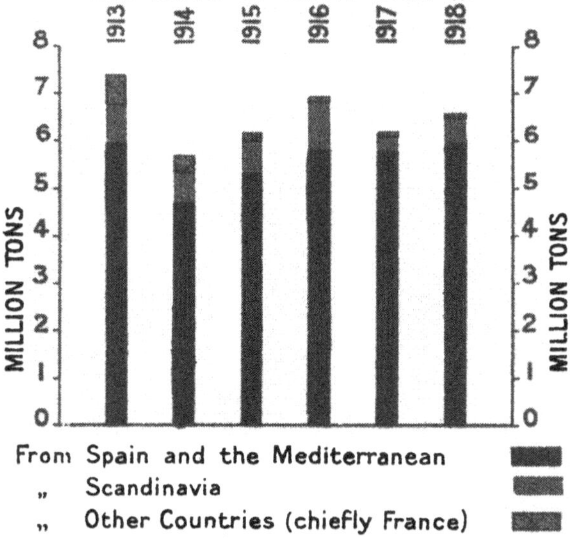
1913
1914
1915
1916
1917
1918
MILLION TONS
MILLION TONS
0
1
2
3
4
5
6
7
8
From Spain and the Mediterranean
" Scandinavia
" Other Countries (chiefly France)

PREPARED IN THE HISTORICAL SECTION OF THE COMMITTEE OF IMPERIAL DEFENCE

Ordnance Survey 1923

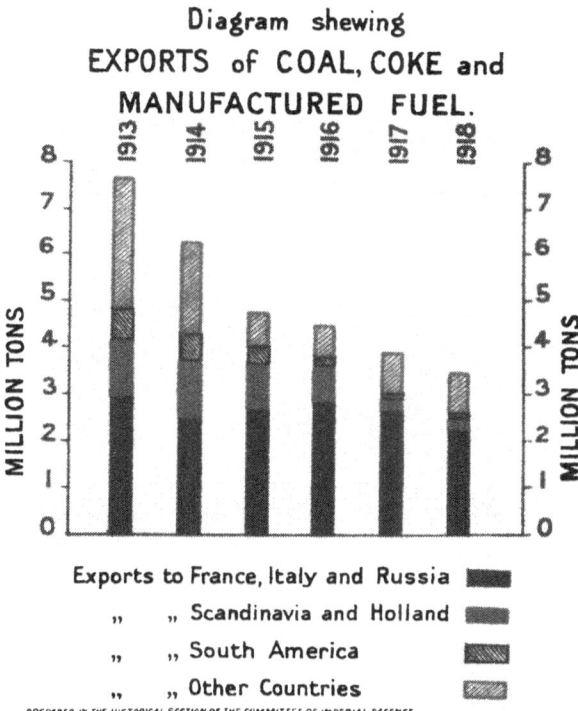

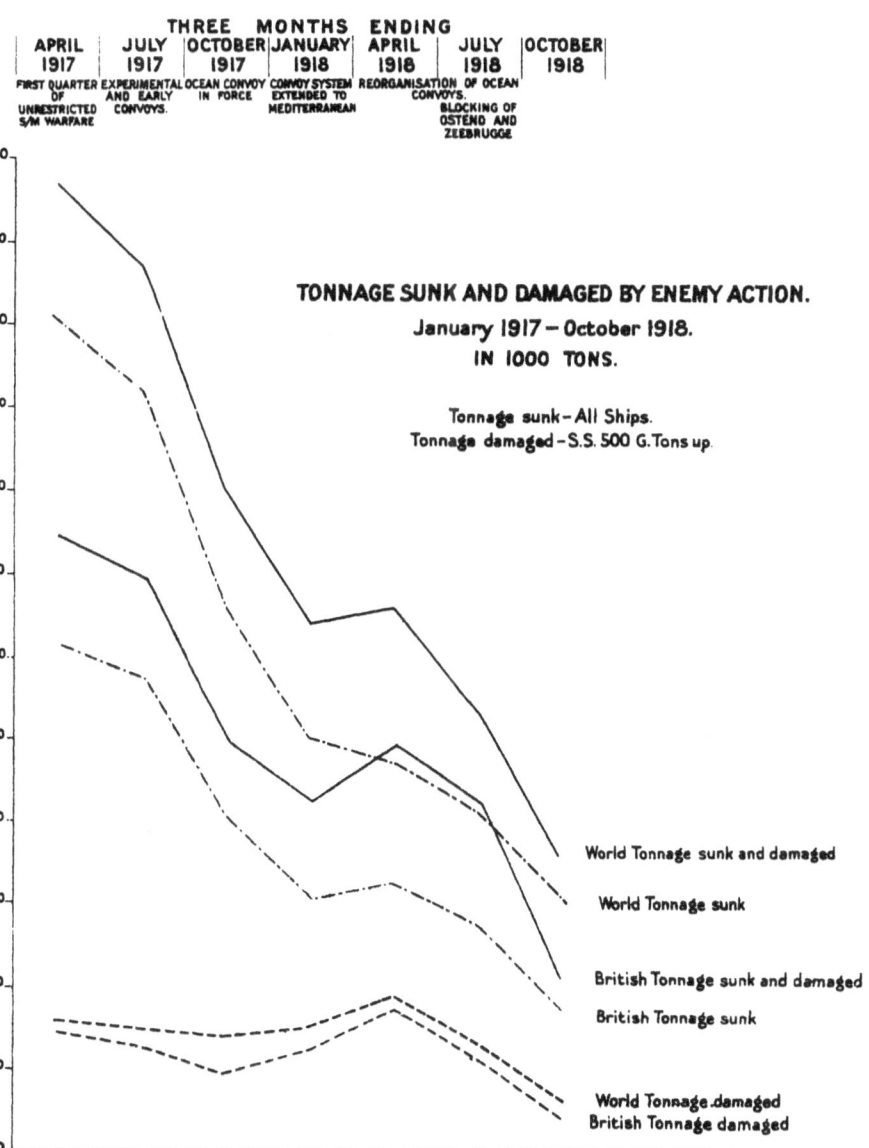

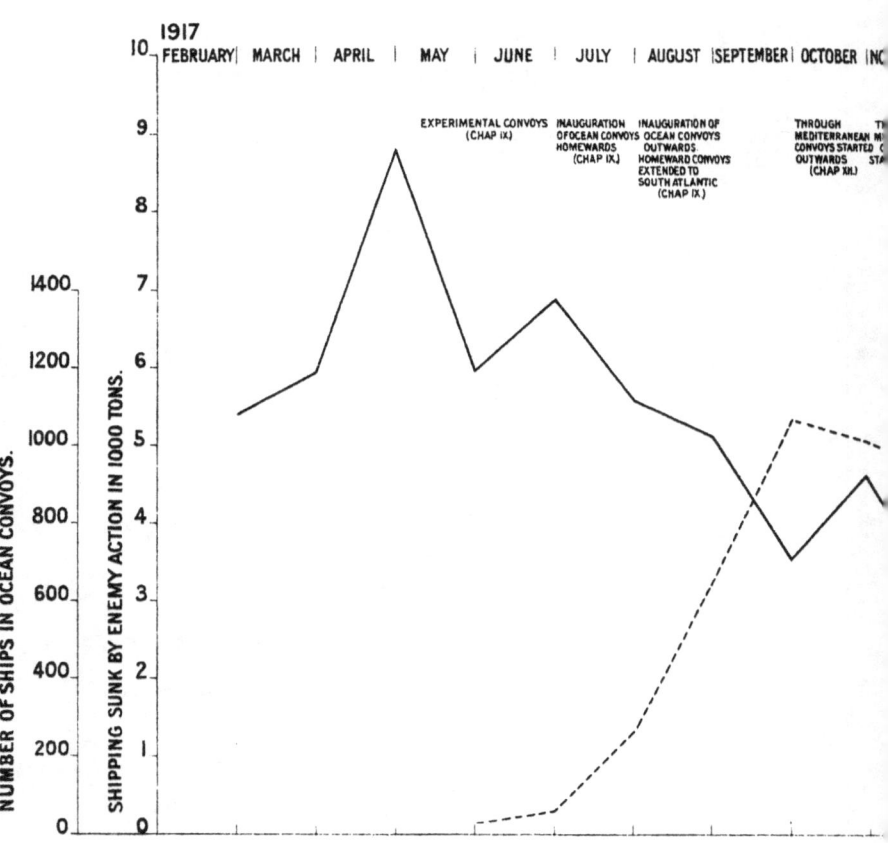

RECORD
ED SUBMARINE WARFARE.

LOST THROUGH ENEMY ACTION.
ED IN OCEAN CONVOYS.

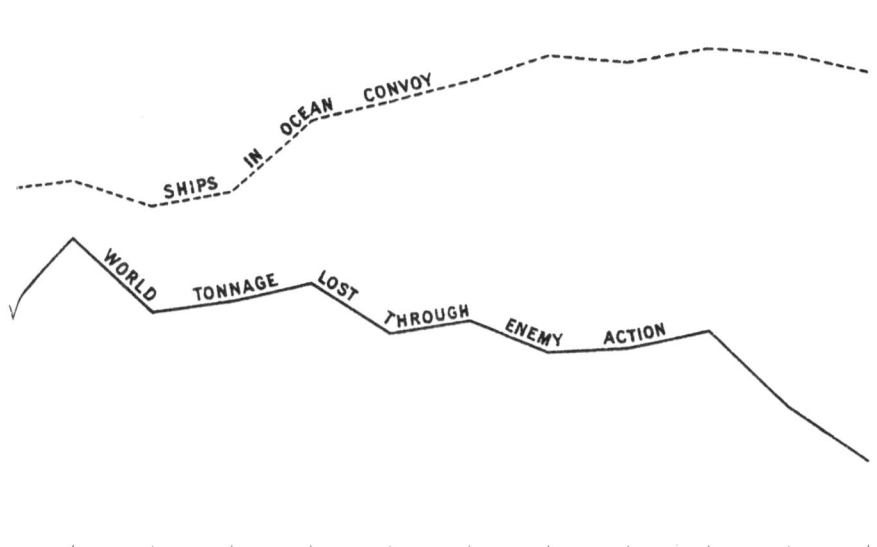

Ordnance Survey 1923

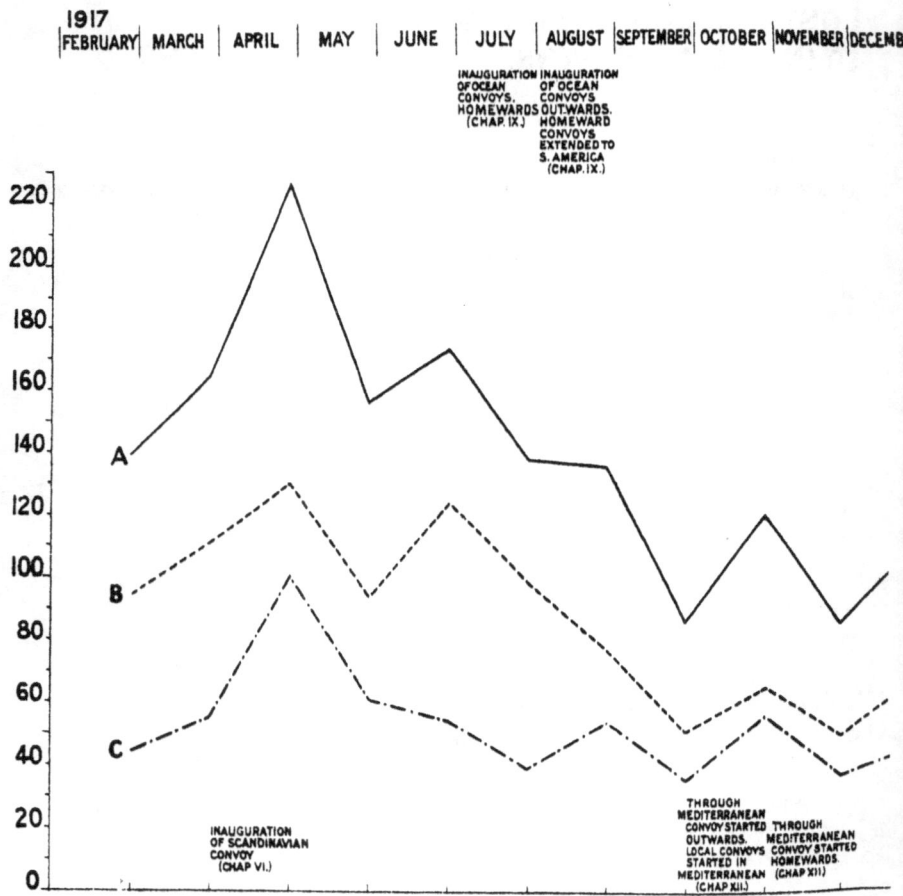

SUNK BY SUBMARINES.
ONVOY SYSTEM.

14

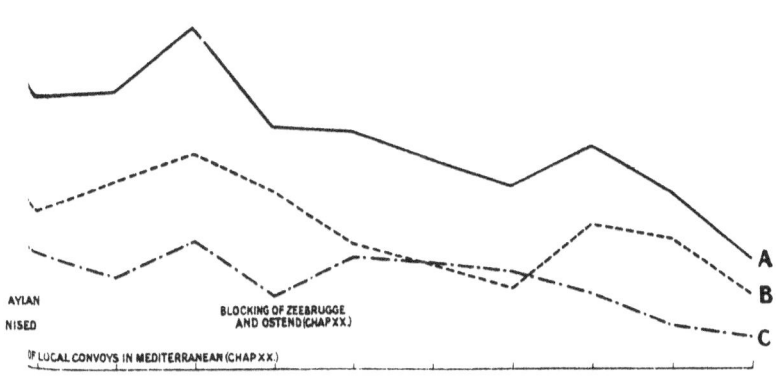

| JANUARY | FEBRUARY | MARCH | APRIL | MAY | JUNE | JULY | AUGUST | SEPTEMBER | OCTOBER |

REORGANISATION OF NORTH ATLANTIC CONVOYS HOMEWARDS (CHAP XX.)

INAUGURATION OF RIO CONVOYS (CHAP. XVIII.)

REORGANISATION OF NORTH ATLANTIC CONVOYS. OUTWARDS. (CHAP XX.)

AYLAN
NISED

BLOCKING OF ZEEBRUGGE AND OSTEND (CHAP XX.)

OF LOCAL CONVOYS IN MEDITERRANEAN (CHAP XX.)

A
B
C

SEA, BRISTOL CHANNEL, WEST COAST,
AR, BAY, AMERICAN COAST.

KNOWN.

Ordnance Survey 1923

INDEX

Abbreviations employed: A.M.C., Armed Merchant Cruiser; Cr. cruiser; L.cr., light cruiser; s/m, submarine; T.B.D., destroyer; s.s., steamer; s.v., sailing vessel; Br., British; D., Dutch; Dan., Danish; Fr., French; Ger., German; It., Italian; Jap., Japanese; Nor., Norwegian; Sp., Spanish; Sw., Swedish; U.S., American; A.M.T.C., Allied Maritime Transport Council; I.A.C.C., Inter-Allied Chartering Committee; M/S., Ministry of Shipping.

Abell, Mr. W. S., Technical Adviser to Shipping Controller, 8
ACHILLES, Br. Cr., sinks LEOPARD, 73
Addison, Rt. Hon. C., 17 n
Aden, Gulf of, mines in, 71
Admiralty, British, relations with M/S., 10–12; and convoys, 98–100, 129–41, 189–98, 314–15, 370, 384, 395; and merchant shipbuilding, 107–8; and oil fuel, 175–6; and bunkers, 194, 322; Trade Division of, 42–3, 69; Naval Stores Department of, 323
Adriatic Sea, s/m base in, 184
Agriculture, Board of, 62, 173
Agulhas, Cape, mines off, 71, 142
Alexandria, examination service at, 45; convoy assembly port, 184, 252
Allenby, General Sir Edmund, 398
Allied Maritime Transport Council and Executive, origins of, 240–6; organisation of, 293–4; work of, 296–9, 301, 302–6, 324, 330–1, 371–2, 373–80, 382–3, 386, 390–3, 394–5, 416, 419–20, 422
Allied Naval Conference, 30–2, 236, 240
Allies, increased demands for tonnage by, 30–2, 241–4, 247, 302–4, 374–5, 379–80; effect of import restrictions on, 58, 63; tonnage in the service of, 162, 376–7, 474–6; joint supply organisation of, 240, 245, 295–6, 372–3; British responsibilities to, 236–7. *See also* "Allied Maritime Transport Council," etc., and under countries

American Expeditionary Force, provision of tonnage for, 217, 243, 297, 301–2, 312, 363–4, 370–2, 377–8, 380, 381–2, 391–3, 397, 418; convoys for, 312–14, 316, 396–7
American Wheat Export Co., 169
Anderson, Mr. John, Secretary to M/S., 9, 241
Anderson, Sir Alan, Navy Controller, 205 n
Anderson, Sir Kenneth, and Liner Requisition, 67, 112, 116–17
Angary, Law of, 150, 300
Anglesea, s/ms off, 288
Aquitania, Br.s.s., 312
Archangel, port of, 238–9; withdrawal of ships from, 239, 358–9; war material at, 358–60, 403
Argentina, and s/m campaign, 41; British exchanges in, 121; prohibits export of wheat, 124; railway strikes in, 274, 284; British coal exports to, 323. *See also* "Plate, River, supplies from"
Asbestos, priority for, 122 n²
Asphalt, priority for, 126
Atlantic Ocean, concentration of shipping on, 68· 89, 92, 109, 114, 119, 126, 131, 144, 163, 170, 192, 248–9, 283, 285–7, 326–8, 418; convoys in North, 131, 134–5, 139–41, 191–2, 313–17, 365, 396–7; in South, 138–9, 290, 308–9; surface raiders in, 29, 68, 71–2, 289; s/m cruisers in, 138, 188, 307, 309, 364 n², 365–6, 396–7
Attolico, Professor, 294 n
Australia, export of wheat, 1, 20–1, 89, 109, 123–4, 172, 282–3, 321,

485

418; of meat and meat products, 122–3, 248, 274, 285–6, 327, 386 n, 388; of butter and cheese, 172, 388; shortage of tonnage for, 68, 85, 122–3, 126, 193, 248, 286–7, 326–7
Austria-Hungary, war with Greece, 155; with Siam, 217; economic conditions in, 178, 180–1, 349–53, 404–6, 431–2; shortage of coal. 38; of food, 38, 350, 352, 405; of fats, 233; financial position of, 231, 405; peace movement in, 353, 406; disintegration of, 405–6, 410
Auxiliary Patrol, 91
Avonmouth, port of, 193, 194 n
Azores, s/m activity off, 29–30, 188, 290 n

Babington-Smith, Sir Henry, Chairman of Imports Restriction Committee, 19
Bacon and hams, supplies of, 48, 123, 126 n², 172, 221–2, 227, 326, 343–5, 443; glut of, 343–5; German supplies of, 48, 221, 232, 353, 443
Bailhache, Mr. Justice, 250
Baker, Mr. Secretary, 392
Baku, British expedition to, 402
Balfour, Rt. Hon. A. J., mission to the United States, 104, 214
Ballast voyages, 120, 124, 267–8
Baltic Sea, closing of, 60, 238; ships held up in, 43, 46, 152
Bangkok, enemy ships at, 217
Barley, decline in imports of, 171, 320, 385, 443. *See also* "Brewing materials"
Baron Sternblad, Dan.s.s., Prize Court decision, 36–7
"Barred zones," 39–40, 290 n. *See also* "Submarine campaign"
Barry, port of, 193, 194 n
Bates, Sir Percy, Director Commercial Services, M/S., 241; re-organises M/S. in New York, 318
Batocki, Herr, German Food Controller, 37 n
Beachley, National shipyard at, 210, 440
Beans, priority for, 122
Beans, soya, control of neutral supplies, 223
Belgian Relief Commission, tonnage for, 27, 95, 260–2, 265, 303–4, 375–6; work of, 433
Belgium, economic condition of, 433–4

Bergen, produce ships at, 48
Bernstorff, Count von, 41
Bevan, Commodore G. P., at Archangel, 238
Beveridge, Mr. W. H., 19 n
Biscay, Bay of, s/ms in, 88; losses in, 182, 188, 366
Bizerta, convoy assembly port, 184, 186, 252
Black, Captain A. Stuart, 118 n
Black List, Ships, *see* "Bunker Control"
Black List, Statutory, 231
Black Sea, closing of, 238
Blaye, shipment of coals to Italy viâ, 161, 298
Blockade Committee, Allied, 358 n
Blockade, Ministry of, 36, 43, 222–3
Blue Book rates, 2, 77, 87, 109–12, 114; increased, 331 n
Bolivia, and s/m warfare, 41
Bolsheviks, *coup d'état*, 239; make peace with Central Powers, 347, 350; capture British ships, 359; Allied attitude to, 359, 432
Bombay, mines off, 142
Booth, Sir Alfred, Chairman of the North Atlantic Conference, 115–16, 139
Borate of lime, priority for, 124
Boyd, Mr. William, Deputy Director-General of M/S., in New York, 318
Brazil, and s/m warfare, 41; breaks off relations with Germany, 87, 101; war with Germany, 217; German coffee debt to, 101; export of rubber from, 124; of meat, 173, 276 n, 386 n; coal exports to, 323; enemy ships in, 87, 101–2, 217, 259
Bread, dilution of, 283–4, 373, 385; of German, 399 n; consumption of, 284, 389
Brest-Litovsk, Peace of, 347
Brewing materials, imports restricted, 61, 270, 373
Bristol Channel, losses in, 69, 90, 188, 251, 288, 396
Bristol, port of, 194 n, 198, 344
British and Argentine Meat Co., 173
British Corporation, 9
Brocklebank, Sir Aubrey, 117, 310
Brookbank, Sir Joseph G., 335 n
Brussels Agreement, 422
Bulgaria, war with Greece, 155; armistice with, 398
Buncrana, s/ms off, 147
Bunker Committee, 42, 157
Bunker control, 24, 28, 42, 45, 148, 150, 220; American, 224–5

INDEX 487

Bunker depôts, supply of, 124–5, 162, 194, 284, 321–3
Bunsen, Sir Maurice de, 17 n
Bureau Veritas, 9
Burgess, Mr. H. F., Director of Cross-Channel Services, 165
Burton, Lieut. G. E., R.N., 129 n
Butter, supplies of, 48, 172, 195–6, 221–2, 227, 286, 327, 388, 444; German supplies of, 37, 48, 222, 400, 430

Calthorpe, Vice-Admiral Hon. Sir S. A. Gough-, and Mediterranean Convoys, 184–5
Cambronne, Fr.s.v., captured by SEEADLER, 71
Canada, shipbuilding in, 81, 102, 216, 256, 369; M/S. organisation in, 169, 287. *See also* " North America, supplies from "
Canadian Pacific Railway Co., 169
Canal Control Committee, 254, 337, 341
Canals, use of, 167, 254, 337–8, 341–2, 383
Canary Islands, enemy ships in, 82
Canned goods, imports restricted, 61
Cape Town, mines off, 142
Capps, Admiral, President of the Emergency Fleet Corporation, 215
Carbide, supplies of, 227
Cardiff, port of, 194 n
Carter, Sir George, 9 n, 210
Catto, Mr. T. S., 168–9
Cecil, Lord Robert, British representative on A.M.T.C., 293 n
Cereals, diverted to France and Italy, 319, 373, 386, 389, 407; import programmes, 241–2, 247, 282, 319, 373, 378. *See also* " Barley," " Maize," " Oats," " Rice," " Wheat "
Cette, port of, 40
Channel, English, losses in, 69, 90, 163, 182, 188, 251, 288, 310, 336, 366
Channel Islands, trade with, 338
Chartering Committee and Executive, Inter-Allied, formed, 22–3; work of, 23–8, 52–4, 89, 94–5, 96, 153, 154–7, 161, 219, 225–6, 237, 260, 262, 306, 330–1, 357
Chartering, control of, 22–3; by U.S.A., 224–6
Cheese, supplies of, 124, 172, 195–6, 227, 286, 327, 388, 444
Chepstow, National shipyard at, 210, 408, 440

Chile, and s/m campaign, 41; nitrates from, 126, 248, 418; German ships in, 102
China, and s/m campaign, 41, breaks off relations with Germany, 83; reduction of British exports to, 120; beans from, 122; enemy ships in, 82–3, 102, 217, 259
" China Mutual *v.* Maclay," decision in, 249–50
Chrome ore, priority for, 122 n[1] and n[2]
Churchill, Mr. Winston, 281 n
" C.i.f." shipments, prohibition of Australian, 21; of all private, 23
City of Lucknow, Br.s.s., sunk, 252
Clan MacCorquodale, Br.s.s., sunk, 202
Clearances of shipping, 52–3, 156, 479
Clémentel, M., 241; French representative on A.M.T.C., 293 n
— Agreement, 22, 161, 236
Clothing, German shortage of, 38, 180, 400
Coal Controller, 341
Coal Exports Committee, 6, 50
Coal, output of, in U.K., 304, 321–2, 374, 420, 446; in France, 301; supply of, to France, 22, 28, 31, 50–4, 162, 280, 298, 301–2, 304, 373–4, 419; to Italy, 20, 22, 28, 31–2, 50–4, 68, 95, 125, 161, 236, 252, 280, 297–9, 301, 305, 373–4, 407, 419; to Russia, 33 n, 160–1, 238–9; to Norway. 47–8, 151, 154, 218–9, 227, 253, 354; to Sweden, 152, 227, 264, 354; to Denmark, 49, 153, 227, 354; to Holland, 50, 227, 265, 354; to Spain, 51, 153, 263; to S. America, 323; coastwise distribution of, 341; freights on, 26, 28, 52–4, 95, 151, 339; ex ports of, 38, 50, 152, 228, 230–1 403, 427. *See also* " Bunker control," " Bunker depôts "
Coasting traffic, war risks in, 146–7; decrease in, 164–5, 342; volume of, 479; s/m attacks on, 187, 251, 288, 395; control of, 338–40; traffic diverted to, 340–1, 383
Cocoa, restriction of imports, 61; priority for, 126; decline in re-exports, 278
Coffee, imports prohibited, 61, 124; decline in re-exports, 278; German shortage of, 65, 400

Colby, Mr. Bainbridge, 241
Collard, Brig.-General C. S., Deputy Controller of Auxiliary Shipbuilding, 204; and National Shipyards, 209–10
Collegian, Br.s.s., sunk, 186
Colliers, losses of, 252
Colombia, proposed export of meat from, 173 n
Colombo, mines off, 71
Colon, bunkering at, 324–5
Commercial Services Branch, M/S., work of, 119–20, 127, 271, 287; mineral section, 26 n; wheat section, 169 n, 236, 320; Norwegian section, 219, 253, 339–40
Commission Internationale de Ravitaillement, 10, 27, 241, 295
" Commissioned escort steamers," 137
Contraband, Orders in Council as to, 36, 44; stoppage of, 44–5, 233–4
" Controlled sailings," system of, 99–100, 148
Convoy Committee, Admiralty, 129–31, 134–5, 141
—, Liverpool, 198–9, 288, 315–17, 345, 383, 395
—, London, 314, 383, 395
—, New York, 317, 395
Convoys, Ocean, proposals for and objections to, 97–100, 128–30, 132–4; experimental, 129–30; inauguration of North American, 131, 134–5; of Gibraltar, 134; of Mid-Atlantic, 138–9; of Outwards, 141; of Mediterranean Through, 184–6; of Rio, 290, 308–9; organisation and working of, 129–30, 134–42, 184–6, 189, 198–9, 202–3, 252, 288, 307–10, 313–17, 325, 364, 370, 396–7, 406, 472; losses in, 130, 137, 147, 186, 189, 202, 252, 309, 310, 365–7, 396, 472–3; effect on losses, 158, 182, 187–9, 203, 250–1, 272–3, 309, 364–6, 370–1, 395–7; on carrying-power, 159, 184–5, 190–3, 318–9, 345, 372; discontinued, 417
—, Short Sea, Dutch, 99, 141 n, 473; French Coal Trade, 99, 149, 189, 252, 473; Scandinavian, 99, 149, 186–7, 189, 252–4, 366, 473; Mediterranean Local, 183–6, 252, 288, 310–12, 365, 366–7, 407, 473; East Coast, 366, 395, 473
Cook Straits, mines in, 142
Copper, priority for, 122, 122 n², 124; German shortage of, 65, 179–80, 353, 403
Cotton Control Board, 175, 196, 200, 271, 319, 413
Cotton Industry, effects of war on, 174–5, 242, 271, 278, 319, 450–2
Cotton, supplies of, 20, 124, 125, 170, 174–5, 196, 242, 270–1, 319, 413, 445
Cramp, Mr. C. T., 201 n
Crespi, Signor, Italian representative on A.M.T.C., 293 n
Cross-Channel transport, improvement of, 162, 347; volume of, 436
Cuba, and s/m campaign, 41; war with Germany, 101 n; enemy ships in, 101
Cumberland, Br.s.s., mined, 142
" Cunard Contracts," *see* " Ship purchase "
Cunard S.S. Co., 12, 81, 153, 170 n
Curzon of Kedleston, Lord, resigns chairmanship of Shipping Control Committee, 8; Chairman of Imports Restriction Committees, 17 n, 281 n

Dairy produce, struggle over, 48–50, 179, 221–3, 353; priority for, 123. *See also* " Butter," " Cheese," " Eggs," " Milk "
Dakar, convoy assembly port, 138; bunkering at, 322
Dassen Island, mines off, 71
Davis, Mr. C. T., 19 n
Defensively armed merchantmen, 35, 50, 72, 96, 154, 396
Denman, Mr., Chairman of the American Shipping Board, 214–15
Denmark, and s/m campaign, 41; dairy produce from, 48, 50, 172, 221–3, 227, 388; fodder and fertilisers to, 43, 46, 48–9, 151, 179; cut off, 223, 227, 229, 232; coal to, 49, 153, 227, 354; agricultural agreement with, 48, 179; tonnage agreement with, 153; German trade with, 48, 179, 221–3, 232, 409; general embargo on exports to, 224, 226–7, 354, 358; general agreement with, 409
DEUTSCHLAND, Ger. s/m cr., 138
Devonport, convoy assembly port, 142, 252
Diamond Shoal L.V., sunk by s/m, 396
Dock Allotment Committees, 107
Dohna-Schlodien, Count zu, 29, 72

INDEX

Donetz, coal mines, 238
Duff, Rear-Admiral, A. L., and convoy system, 133–4, 136, 137
Dumayne, Sir Frederick, 20 n
Duncan, Mr. A. K., 9 n
DUNDEE, Br. armed boarding steamer, 73

East African Expedition, tonnage for, 89, 162
Economist, The, Index Number, 389
EDINBURGH CASTLE, Br. A.M.C., 72
Eggs, supplies of, 48, 227, 444; German supplies of, 48, 221–2, 400
Egypt, tonnage and meat supplies for, 162, 248, 274, 285–6
Elderton, Mr. W. P., Statistical Adviser to M/S., 10
Ellerman, Sir John, 133
Ellerman-Wilson Lines, 161, 219
Elliot, Capt. F. B., 14
Embargoes, system of, 220–9, 233–4, 263–6, 354–8
EMDEN, Ger. L. cr., 29, 72
Emergency Fleet Corporation, formed, 103; work of, 214–15
Enthoven, Mr. R. E., 19 n
Entrances of shipping, 52–3, 85, 93, 156, 170–1, 192–3, 346, 385, 410, 479
Esplen, Mr. James, Technical Adviser to M/S. in North America, 81
Esplen, Mr. John, Director of Overseas Ship Purchase, 8, 79, 80, 102–3
Excess Profits Duty, applied to shipping, 2, 114
Excess Value Associations, 145–6, 442
Exchanges, condition of British, 58, 86, 111, 118, 121–2, 177, 414, 448, 452; of French, 437; of Italian, 438; of German, 231–2, 428; of Austrian, 231–2
Export Priority Committee, 121
Exports, volume of, 276–9, 413–14, 447–54; effect of import restrictions on, 18, 58–9, 277, 413, 451; effect of liner requisition on, 120–1, 176, 276–7, 451; embargoes on, 226–9, 263–4, 277, 354–8; redistribution of, 279–80, 447–54, 480–3

Falmouth, convoy assembly port, 141
Farewell, Cape, mines off, 142
Fastnet, losses in approach to the, 69 n, 91–2, 109, 182, 188

Fats, German shortage of, 179, 221, 233, 352, 400; Austrian, 233; British, 388
Faulkner, Lieut. M., R.N.V.R., 169; Chairman of New York Convoy Committee, 317
Fertilisers, German shortage of, 38, 425–6; Allied control of, 43, 46, 48–50, 151, 179, 223, 227, 229, 232, 425–6; decline in exports of, 278; European dependence on imported supplies, 455
Fielding, Mr. C. W., 19 n
Finch & Co., Messrs., 210
Findlay, Sir M. de C., 151
Finland, Germans land in, 359; Allied relations with, 361 n
Fisher, Captain T., R.N., 43 n, 318
Fishing fleets, Dutch laid up, 233; Br. and U.S. attacked by s/ms, 396
Fish, supplies of, 123, 172, 195, 355, 443; German supplies of, 37, 179, 233, 352, 355 n
Flax, supplies of, 196, 360, 445
Fletcher, Commander Sir Lionel, R.N.R., and refrigerated shipping, 14; on liner requisition, 67, 112
Flour, *see* "Wheat"
Fodder, German shortage of, 37, 179, 425–6; Allied control of neutral imports of, 43, 46, 48, 50, 222–3, 264–5; European dependence on imported supplies of, 455
Food, British and Allied supplies of, 57, 65, 172, 193–6, 388–90; German shortage of, 37–8, 64–5, 177–9, 221, 352–3, 367, 399–400; Austrian, 38, 350, 352, 405; Inter-Allied agreement as to supply of, 238. *See also* under separate commodities
Food Council, Inter-Allied, formed, 372; programme of, 377–80, 390–2
Food, Ministry of, 10, 14; tonnage requirements of, 88, 123, 125, 160, 282, 338; meat purchases by, 195; and distribution of food imports, 342–5
Forth, Firth of, as convoy base, 254
Fountain, Mr. H., 19 n
France, supply of railway material to, 20, 164, 304, 374; of coal, 22, 28, 52–4, 95, 162, 279, 298, 301–2, 304–5, 374, 391, 408; of steel and oats, 161–2, 236–7, 320; of wheat, 202, 236, 283, 320–1; of

meat, 236, 274, 386 n, 388; of steel, 237, 379, 394–5; of sugar, 296, 375; of nitrate, munitions, etc., 304, 375, 407; cereals diverted to, 319, 373, 386, 389, 407; timber cutting in, 60, 171; shipbuilding in, 79 n; harvest failure in, 177, 235, 241, 247; coal output in, 301–2; dislocation of railways in, 301, 374; pit-props from, 269; general situation and import requirements of, 30–1, 242–3, 279–80, 302–3; effects of war on, 434–7; tonnage in service of, 89, 161–2, 376–7, 419. *See also* above, under commodities, and under "Allied Maritime Transport Council," "Allies, joint supply organisation of," "Chartering Committee, Inter-Allied"

Freight Limitation Schemes, objections to, 2–3
—, coal, 6, 26, 28, 52–4, 95, 339
—, coasting trade, 339
—, North Sea, 45, 47, 219
—, post armistice, 419

Freights, rise in, 1, 28, 52–4, 95; on coal, 28, 52, 151; on ore, 52; on timber, 151; fall in, 417

Fruit, Spanish decrees as to export of, 51, 263; imports restricted, 61; increased from Spain, 263; decline in import of, 86, 171, 286, 444; distribution of imports, 342

Fuller, Sir J. Bampfylde, Director of Timber Supplies, 60

Furness, Withy & Co., Messrs., 23–5, 150 n, 169, 192, 330

Gabo Island, mines off, 142
Galicia, mineral oil from, 230, 402 n
Geddes, Sir Eric, Navy Controller, 108, 204; and transport reforms, 162, 311; First Lord of the Admiralty, 205 n
Genoa, M/S. representative at, 311; congestion at, 382
George, Right Hon. D. Lloyd, 1
Germany, decides on "unrestricted s/m warfare," 35–6, 39; makes new enemies thereby, 41, 55, 83, 101, 155, 217; general economic conditions in, 36–8, 64–5, 177–81, 229–33, 349–54, 399–404, 415; imports of, 37, 48, 179, 221–2, 229, 232–3, 353, 355, 356; exports, 38, 50, 152, 228–9, 230–1, 264, 352; measures to restrict trade of, 36–7, 44–5, 179, 220–34, 354–8; shortage of food in, 37–8, 64–5, 177–9, 221, 232, 350–3, 399–401; of textiles and clothing, 38, 180, 400, 402; of metals and war material, 65, 179–80, 353–4; of soap, 65; of rubber, 180, 403; of oil, 180, 230, 402; supplies from Roumania, 177–8, 180, 230, 352, 401; from Russia, 349–50, 353; from Ukraine, 350–3, 361, 399, 401; deterioration of transport in, 180, 230, 351, 403; disease and mortality in, 178–9, 353; breakdown of morale in, 401, 403–4, 410; armistice with, 406, 410; post-armistice relations with, 421–3; effects of war on, 424–31

Gibbs, Messrs. Anthony, 325
Gibraltar, examination service at, 45; convoy assembly port, 129, 134, 252; M/S. representative at, 311
Glasgow, port of, 166, 193, 194 n, 344
Glass, imports prohibited, 59
Glover, Mr. Ernest, Director of Ship Management Branch M/S., 15
Godfrey, Lieut.-Commander, R.N., 184
Goethals, General, President of the Emergency Fleet Corporation, 214–15
Gosling, Mr. Harry, relations with Port and Transit Committee, 200–1
Great Britain, effect of the war on economic position of, 56–65, 177, 277–9, 388–9, 412–15, 439–54. *See also* under "Imports," "Shipping," etc.
Greece, political situation in, 24, 25 n, 154–5; supply of cereals to, 155; shipping agreement with, 24–5
Greek Ship Scheme, started, 24–5; working of, 94, 155
Gun-cotton, priority for, 122 n²
Guthrie, Sir Connop, head of shipping organisation in New York, 169, 317, 318

Halifax, examination service at, 45, 152, 234 n; convoy assembly port, 139–40, 397; munitions explosion at, 284 n
Hampton Roads, convoy assembly port, 129, 134

INDEX

Harland & Wolff, Messrs., 211, 291
Harris, Rt. Hon. F. Leverton, Chairman, Neutral Tonnage Committee, 43 n
Harris, Sir Arthur, M/S. representative in Canada, 169 n
Harwich, naval base at, 94, 99
Hatteras, Cape, s/ms. off, 396
Hawkins, Lieut.-Col. T. H., 335 n
Healdton, U.S.s.s., sunk, 55
Hemp, supplies of, 122, 196
Henderson, Captain R. G. H., R.N., and convoy system, 100, 129–30, 133, 136, 198, 311
Henderson, Mr. F. N., 9 n
Henderson, Mr. H. D., Secretary, Cotton Control Board, 175; cited, 175 n, 271 n, 319 n
Hides, priority for, 122; shortage of tonnage for, 248, 286
Hill, Sir Norman, on restriction of imports, 17 n, 19, 65; on protection of shipping, 132–3; Chairman of Port and Transit Committee, 199 n, 201
Hipwood, Mr. C., Chairman, International Shipping Committee, 23; member Neutral Tonnage Committee, 43 n
Holland, and s/m campaign, 41, 49–50; trade with, 50, 176, 196, 227, 265, 354, 388; coal to, 50, 227, 265, 354; agricultural agreement with, 37, 45, 50, 172, 179, 228–9; German trade with, 37–8, 50, 179, 228–9, 299; unneutral sand and gravel traffic, 228, 300, 358; control of shipping by, 45; embargo on exports to, 224, 228–9, 265–6, 300, 354 n, 357–8; fishing fleets laid up, 233; *modus vivendi* with, proposed, 266, 291, 299; shipping requisitioned by Allies, 299–300
Holmden, Mr. O. G., Director of the Inter-Allied Chartering Executive, 23
Holt, Messrs. A., & Co., 150 n
Holt, Mr. R. D., 249–50
Home-grown Timber Committee, 60
Home Trade Branch, M/S., formed, 165; work of, 288, 338–42, 345
Home Trade Transport Control Committee, formed, 341; work of, 383
Honolulu, enemy ships in, 83
Horses, German imports of, 222
House, Colonel, 241
Hudson Maru, Jap.s.s., arrives in Pernambuco with prisoners, 30

Hughes, Mr. T. Harrison, Chairman, Liverpool Convoy Committee, 198
Hull, port of, 194 n, 320, 344
Hurley, Mr. Edward N., Chairman, American Shipping Board, 215

Iceland, agreement with, 358
Igotz Mendi, Sp.s.s., captured by WOLF, 289 n
Illingworth Committee, 70–1, 166
Illingworth, Mr. Percy, Chairman, Committee on Railway Facilities, 70
ILTIS, Ger. raider, ex *Turitella*, lays mines, 72
Imperial Munitions Board, 81
Import Priority Lists, 119–23, 124–5, 127, 241, 248, 269
— Restrictions Cabinet, or " Curzon " Committee formed, 17; members, 17 n; work of, 58
— Cabinet, or " Milner " Committee formed, 241; members, 281 n; work of, 281–2
—, Inter-departmental, or " Babington-Smith " Committee formed, 19; members, 19 n; work of, 57–9, 93
Imports, volume of, 17, 57, 65–6, 86, 93, 170–7, 193–7, 269, 346, 412–13, 443–6, 447–54, 477–9; programme of British, 57–8, 65–7, 93, 197, 242, 281–2, 296; of British and Allied, 241–3, 296–7, 302–3, 305, 377, 390–3, 416; Inter-Allied control of, 241,245–6; restriction of, 9, 17–20, 32, 57–64, 86, 170–1, 174, 197, 269, 270 n, 281–2; drawn from nearest sources, 118–20, 183, 282, 480–3. *See also* under commodities
Inchcape, Lord, Chairman of the North Atlantic Conference, 117; on protection of shipping, 133; resigns from Port and Transit Committee, 199 n; on replacement of liner tonnage, 211; and disposal of standard ships, 441
India, rice from, 122n, 320; wheat from, 283, 321; trade with U.S.A., 120, 125; withdrawal of tonnage from trade with, 121, 126, 248, 257, 277, 451; jute from, 451; decline in exports to, 277, 451
Indian Ocean, German raiders in, 72, 142–3
Insulated ships, losses of, 173, 272–3. *See also* " Meat," " Refrigerated Shipping Committee "

International Shipping Committee, formed, 32; failure of, 236
Ireland, ports of, 69; trade with, 288, 338–40
Irish Sea, losses in, 69, 90, 188, 251, 288, 395
Iron and steel, imports of, 271, 444; exports of, 278, 450
Iron ore, supplies of and tonnage for, 20, 22, 50–1, 88, 151, 153–4, 156, 174, 227, 253, 271–2, 366–7, 385, 413, 444; coal-ore agreement with Italy, 22, 95, 271; Spanish decrees *re* loading of, 51, 263; German supplies of, 229, 356–7, 403; official ore broker, 26 n, 419
Italy, supply of coal to, 20, 22, 28, 52–4, 95, 161, 236, 252, 279, 297–9, 305,373–4, 379, 391, 407; of wheat, 161, 202, 236, 283, 320–1; of steel and oats, 161–2, 236–7, 320; of meat, 236, 275, 386 n, 388; of sugar, 296, 375; of munitions, 375, 407; of pig iron, 379; cereals diverted to, 319, 373, 386, 389, 407; shipbuilding in, 79; harvest failure in, 177, 235, 241, 247; coal ore agreement with 22, 95, 271; general situation and import requirements of, 31, 242–3, 279–80, 303; effects of war on, 437–8; tonnage in service of, 161–2, 376–7, 419. *See also* above, under commodities, and under "Allied Maritime Transport Council," "Allies, joint supply organisation of," "Chartering Committee, Inter-Allied"

Jams, priority for, 122
Japan, shipping boom in, 81; shipbuilding in, 81, 103, 370; M/S. purchase of shipping from, 81, 216, 256; naval assistance from, 87; reduction of British exports to, 120; beans from, 122; expedition to Vladivostok, 359; shipping agreement with U.S.A., 370; effects of war on, 439
Java, British exchanges in, 121; sugar from, 248, 418; export of fertilisers to, 278
Jellicoe of Scapa, Viscount, Chairman of Committee on Atlantic Concentration, 119; views on convoy system, 131, 133; cited, 99 n, 119 n, 129 n, 149 n

Jones, Captain Clement, 9, 281 n
Jute, imports restricted, 62; priority for, 122 n¹; supplies of, 170–1, 196, 270, 445, 451; re-exports of, 278, 413; exports of piece goods, 278, 450

Karana, Br.s.s., sunk, 202
KARLSRUHE, Ger. L.cr., achievements of, 72
Kaye, Mr. S. H., 14
Kemball-Cook, Mr. B. A., and carriage of oil in double-bottoms, 176
Kem, rate of discharge at, 239
Kerensky, M., 237–9
Kerr, Mr. A. C., 9 n
Kerr, Mr. E. J., 169
Kershaw, Mr. L. J., 19 n
Keynes, Mr. J. M., 19 n
Kim, Nor.s.s., prize court decision, 36
Kogrund Passage closed, 46
— Agreement, 152, 155, 159
Kohistan, Br.s.s., sunk, 202
Korniloff, General, 238
Knatchbull-Hugessen, Mr. H. M., 43 n
Kristiansand, fire at nickel factory, 179

Labour, displacement of, 277, 451
Labour Gazette, The, Index Number, 389
Labour Party, and nationalisation of shipping, 2
Laconia, Br.s.s., sunk, 55
Lamlash, convoy assembly port, 141
Lamport & Holt, Messrs., 126
Lard, priority for, 126 n²; German shortage of, 232
Lead, priority for, 122, 125
Leather, imports restricted, 62, 445; German shortage of, 180
Leeuwin, Cape, WOLF operating off, 142
LEOPARD, Ger. raider, ex *Yarrowdale*, activities of, 73
Lerwick, convoy assembly port, 99, 154, 253–4
Leslie, Mr. Norman, member of Admiralty Convoy Committee, 129 n; head of Convoy Section, M/S., 136
Lever, Mr. S. H., 17 n
Lewis, Sir Frederick, report on shipping in War Office service, 34; member Liner Requisition Committee, 117, 118 n

INDEX

Linen, decline in exports of, 278, 450
Liner Requisition Committee, formed, 117; work of, 117, 120–3, 126, 249, 417
Liner Requisition Scheme, proposed, 67–8; difficulties of, 109–11; negotiated with shipowners, 112–17, 144–6, 249–50; organisation and working of, 117–27, 247–9, 287, 375; termination of, 419. *See also* "Exports," "Import Priority Lists," "Atlantic Ocean, concentration on," "Shipping, diversion of"
Linseed, import of, 321
Liquor Control Board, 333, 384
Lithgow, Lieut.-Col., Director of Merchant Shipbuilding, 205
Liverpool and London War Risks Association, 192, 417 n, 442
Liverpool, port of, 9, 167, 201, 333, 337, 342, 344, 384; meat imports, 194; wheat imports, 199; strain on, 201–2; convoy assembly port, 309; convoy organisation at, 185, 198–9. *See also* "Convoy committees"
Liverpool Steam Ship Owners' Association, 17, 198
Livestock, Danish slaughtering of, 48, 179; British, 195, 275, 373, 385; condition of German, 37–8, 352, 426. *See also* "Meat"
Living, cost of, in Russia, 238; in Great Britain, 389, 446
—, standard of, 58
Llewellyn-Smith, Sir H., 19 n
Lloyds Register, 9
Lodge, Mr. T., Assistant Secretary to M/S., 9
London, port of, 163, 164, 342; meat imports, 194; wheat imports, 199; paper imports, 340–1; supply of, through West Coast ports, 335–6. *See also* "Convoy committees"
Long, Mr. Walter, 281 n
Longden, Captain H. W., R.N., 129 n
Loucheur, M., French representative on A.M.T.C., 293 n
Ludendorff, General, cited, 35 n
Lunham & Moore, Messrs, 168
Lundy Island, s/ms off, 288
Lyons, Gulf of, traffic in, 183, 252

Machinery, decline in exports of, 450
Maclay, Sir Joseph P., Shipping Controller, 1, 8, 17 n, 281 n, 293 n, 382, 386; powers of, 6–7, 133, 339 and Appendix I; and shipbuilding, 8, 57, 75–82, 104–8, 205, 209; and ports, 70, 166. *See also* "Shipping, Ministry of"
Macneal, Mr. H. M., Deputy Director of Home Trade Branch M/S., 338
Macrosty, Mr. H. W., and meat supplies, 14, 196
Magnesite, priority for, 122 n[1]
Maize, imports of, 20, 172, 272, 278, 320, 385, 418, 443; world crop of, 235, 283; decline in re-exports of, 278
Malay Peninsula, tin and rubber from, 122
Malta, convoy assembly port, 183–4; M/S. Intelligence Section at, 184; M/S. representative at, 311
Man, Isle of, s/ms off, 288
Manchester, port of, 193, 194 n
Manganese, priority for, 122 n[1]; German shortage of, 180
Manistry, Fleet-Paymaster, H. W. E., R.N., Organising Manager of Convoys, 129, 136
Man-power, shortage of, 208
Manufactured goods, imports restricted, 62, 413; exports, 227, 279, 450
Margarine, supplies of, 50, 125, 196, 222–3, 227, 265, 444
Marker, Mr. E. H. S., 19 n
Marr, Mr. James, 9 n
Marseilles, convoy assembly port, 184
MARY ROSE, Br. T.B.D., sunk, 187
Mathwins, Messrs., 160
Mattox, Mr. W. C., cited, 82 n, 215 n
Mauretania, Br.s.s., 312
Mauritius, sugar from, 248, 418
Meat, British and Allied Supplies of, 123–4, 172–3, 193–5, 194 n, 272–5, 285–6, 325–7, 386–8, 412, 443; shortage of, 173, 195, 275; re-exports of, 275; shipment of meat by-products, 248, 286; sources and distribution of, 276 n, 386 n; German supplies of, 37–9, 48, 222, 352. *See also* "Insulated ships," "Livestock," "Refrigerated Shipping Committee"
Meat and Fats Executive, Inter-Allied, 195, 245, 255
Mediterranean Sea, losses in, 24, 52, 90, 161, 182, 187–8, 251, 397,

494 INDEX

407; protection for ships in, 30, 397; iron ore from, 88, 174, 366; convoys in, 182–6, 202, 250, 252, 288, 307, 310–2, 366–7, 407; shipping organisation in, 311

Mercantile Marine, and convoy system, 130, 134, 136–7, 189

Merchant Shipbuilding Advisory Committee, formed, 8; members, 9 n; work of, 75, 106, 204

Merchant Shipping Acts, 13

Mersey, river, s/ms off, 288

Mesopotamia expedition, tonnage and supplies for, 162, 285

Methil, convoy assembly port, 254

Milford, convoy assembly port, 141

Military Sea Transport Branch, M/S., 287, 320

Milk, supplies of, 172, 227, 444; German supplies of, 37, 65, 221–2, 352, 430

Milner, Lord, Chairman of Imports Restriction Committee, 281

Minefields, Ger., laid by WOLF, 71–2, 142; by U 151, 365; by s/ms, 397; casualties from, 71, 142, 289, 367; protection against, 367

Miners, recruitment of, 304, 322

MOEWE, Ger. raider, activities of, 29, 68, 71–2, 173 n

Molybdenite, priority for, 122 n³

Molybdenum, German shortage of, 180

Money, Sir Leo Chiozza, Parliamentary Secretary to M/S., 8; Chairman, Tonnage Priority Committee, 10, 66; member Imports Restriction Committee, 19 n; Restriction of Enemy Supplies Committee, 36 n; on Atlantic concentration, 133

Monnet, M. Jean, 241; member Allied Maritime Transport Executive, 294 n

Montevideo, German ships at, 102; bunkering at, 323

Montmorency, Mr. H. A. de, 10

Munitions Council, Inter-Allied, formed, 372; programme, 390–1; priority for programme, 392, 414–5, 416

Munitions, Ministry of, 10, 26 n; steel for, 107; labour for, 164; organisation in U.S.A., 168, 170; tonnage requirements of, 18, 20, 68, 88–9, 90, 125, 127, 160, 175, 282

Munitions of War Acts, 2

Murmansk, winter programme to, 1916–17, 32; 1917–18 programme abandoned, 238–9

Narvik, iron ore from, 88, 154, 174, 253, 385

National Maritime Board, 329 n

National Service, Director of, 71, 332, 368

National Union of Railwaymen, 167, 201 n

Naval Sea Transport Branch, M/S., collier section, 323, 339

"Navicert" System, 45

Nelson, H. and W., Messrs., 194

Neutral Tonnage Committee, formed, 43; members, 43 n

Neutral Tonnage Conference, 219 n

Newcastle, congestion at, 167

Newfoundland, s/ms off, 396

New Ministers and Secretaries Act, 6–7

Newport News, *see* "Hampton Roads"

New York, M/S. organisation at, 168–70, 237, 287, 317–8; congestion at, 284; convoy assembly port, 134, 313. *See also* "Convoy Committee"

New Zealand, export of meat and meat products, 248, 274, 285–6, 327, 386 n, 388; surplus stocks of, 274, 286, 327; cheese and butter from, 196, 326–7, 388; financial crisis in, 327; withdrawal of tonnage from trade with, 68, 85, 122–3, 126, 193, 248, 286–7, 326–7; minefields off, 142

—, Union Steam Ship Co. of, 123–4

Nickel, German shortage of, 179–80

Nitrates Executive, Inter-Allied, 295

Nitrates, supplies of, 68, 88–90, 124, 324–5, 418; to France, 304, 375; German shortage of, 425–6. *See also* "Fertilisers"

North America, principal source of supplies, 119, 131, 448; wheat and cereals from, 21, 123, 163, 168, 172, 193, 272, 282–4, 321, 385, 393, 407; meat from, 193, 195, 274, 285, 326, 387; munitions from, 90; butter and cheese from, 172, 196, 286; bacon from, 343; s/ms off, 365–6, 396. *See also* "Canada," "U.S.A.," "North Atlantic"

North Atlantic Allocation Committee, 118

INDEX 495

North Atlantic Conference, 114-18, 130, 139-40
North Channel, s/ms in, 288
Northern Barrage, 397
North Russian Expeditionary Force, 360
North Sea, s/ms in, 90, 187, 188, 366; convoys in, 99, 141 n, 149, 186-7, 189, 252-4, 366, 395; neutral traffic in, 233-4
Norway, and s/m campaign, 41; coal to, 47-8, 151, 154, 218-19, 227, 253, 354; German trade with, 179, 228; embargo on exports to, 224, 227-8, 354 n, 355; lifted, 356; Fish Agreement with, 37, 47, 172, 179, 227, 355; shipping agreement with, 153-4; general agreement with, 355-6, 356 n
Norwegian Shipowners' Association, 151
— Victualling Commission, 151

Oats, supplies of, 172, 272, 320, 443; stocks of, 193, 284; world crops of, 235; import programme, 378
Odessa, German supplies from, 351
Oil fuel, shortage of, 175-6; shipment in double-bottoms, 176, 196, 243, 305, 318-19, 371, 418; reserve built up, 408
Oil seeds, priority for, 122 n[1], 125; control of neutral supplies of, 223, 265
Oils, mineral, shortage of, 196; imports of, 413, 444; German supplies of, 180, 230, 402. *See also* " Oil Fuel," " Tankers "
Olympic, Br.s.s., 312
Onions, priority for, 125
Orkney Islands, forces of, 99; trade of, 338
Orlando, Onorevole Salvatore, Italian representative on A.M.T.C., 293 n[2]
Ostend, blocking of, 309-10; Allied occupation of, 406
Otaki, Br.s.s., captured by MOEWE, 72
Otranto Barrage, 30, 184, 310, 397
" Otter " gear, 367

Pacific Ocean, Ger. raiders in, 142-3
Palestine, expedition to, 398
Panama, and s/m campaign, 41; enemy ships in, 101; declares war on Germany, 101 n
Panama Canal, 308, 325
Paper and materials, imports restricted, 59; decline in imports of, 86, 171, 444; supplies of, 196, 227; exports, 278; coastwise distribution of, 340-1
Parana, Braz.s.s., sunk, 87
" Paravanes," 367
Paris, Conference at, 241, 244
Paris-Lyons-Marseilles Railway, 31
PARTRIDGE, Br. T.B.D., sunk, 253
Pas de Calais coal mines, output of, 301, 304
Pass of Balmaha, *see* SEEADLER
Patagonia, meat from, 172
" Patrolled routes," in Mediterranean, 30, 183; in Home Waters 90-1, 97, 100
Paxton, Messrs., 21
PELLEW, Br. T.B.D., damaged, 253
" Penalty rents," 70, 342-3
Penzance, convoy assembly port, 99
Pera, Br.s.s., sunk, 186
Perim, convoy assembly port, 185
Persian Gulf, withdrawal of ships from, 33; berthing facilities in, 162
Peru, and s/m campaign, 41; severs relations with Germany, 217; enemy ships in, 102, 217, 259
Petroleum, *see* " Oils, mineral "
Petroleum Conference, 296, 371
Philippines, hemp from, 122
Phillips, Sir Owen, and disposal of standard ships, 441
Phosphate, priority for, 125
Pirrie, Lord, Controller-General of Merchant Shipbuilding, 291, 368
Pit-props, decline in import of, 269. *See also* " Timber "
Plate, River, meat from, 123-4, 173, 272-4, 326-7, 387-8; Quebracho extract from, 124; wheat from, 124, 172, 284, 321, 385; butter from, 327, 388; maize from, 418
Plymouth, congestion at, 164
Ponta Delagada, bombarded by s/m, 138
Poole, Major-General F. C., 360
Port and Transit Executive Committee, work of, 1, 6, 12-13, 18-19, 69-70, 163, 165-8, 194, 199-202, 254, 332-7, 340-5, 383-5; relations with M/S., 13, 168
Port Branch, M/S., formed, 168; work of, 344-5, 384
Portbury, site for National Shipyards, 210, 440
Port Kembla, Br.s.s., mined, 142
Port Said, convoy assembly port,

183–4, 186; M/S. representative at, 311; congestion at, 382–3
Ports, congestion of British, 19, 70, 163–8, 199–202, 253, 342–5, 383, 421, 446; of North American, 19, 168–9, 284; of South African, 185; of French, 374, 382, 394, 435; of Italian, 382–3; labour supply at, 71, 89, 166–7, 200–1, 332–4, 384–5; proposed diversion of trade to Irish, 69–70; diversions from East to West Coast, 70, 163–5, 193–4, 201–2, 288, 334–6; effect of convoys on turn-round at, 97–8, 190; of convoy reorganisation, 318–19; improved turn-round at, 167, 345–6, 372, 385. *See also* " Convoy committees," " Illingworth Committee," " Penalty rents," " Railways," " Traffic Diversion Committee," " Transport Workers' Battalions "
Potatoes, German supplies of, 37–8, 352; proposed export of, 230
Potter, Mr. Frank, 335 n
Prices, *see* " Living, cost of "
Princess Melita, Br.s.s., refused entry into Dutch port, 50
Pringle, Colonel J. W., Chairman of Traffic Diversion Committee, 201, 335 n
Prize Courts, decisions of British, 36
Prize Regulations, German, 35
Prizes and interned ships, management of, 328
Programme Committees, Inter-Allied, 305, 372
" Protected sailings," 99
Pyrites, supply of, 227

Quebec, convoy assembly port, 397
Quebracho, priority for, 124
Queenstown, convoy assembly port, 141, 252

Rabbits, " hook-skinned," 286; shut out, 327
Raiders, surface, German policy with regard to, 73, 144, 289–90
Railway Executive Committee, 165, 167, 168, 254, 340–1
Railways, capacity of British, 69–70, 335–6; shortage of trucks on, 70, 164, 167, 202, 334; pooling of trucks on, 71, 165, 337; pressure on, 164, 202, 334; shortage of labour on, 334, 337; diversion of traffic from 337–8;

340–2, 383; effects of war on, 446; provision of rolling stock for French, 20, 164, 304, 374; dislocation of North American, 168–9, 284; of German, 180, 230, 351, 403, 427; of South African, 185, 324; of Siberian, 239; of French, 301, 374, 434; of European, 431
Railways, Joint Committee on, 165
Rationing and Statistical Committee, Inter-Allied, 358
Read, Mr. A. H., Director of Home Trade Branch, M/S., 165
Re-exports effect of import restrictions on, 62, 177, 277–8, 413, 449–50
Refrigerated Shipping Committee, formed, 14; work of, 124 n, 193–5, 236, 248, 274, 285, 326, 388
Reiss, Mr. C., 117
Requisitioning, of shipping, " universal," 4, 109; of insulated space, 13–14; of liner space, 18, 20, 33, 88; of ships on Colonial Register, 283 n. *See also* " Liner Requisition Scheme," "Shipping"
Requisitioning Branch, M/S., work of, 15, 32–3, 67–9, 87, 160, 338–9; liner section, 117; card index, 128–9, 184, 236 n; convoy section, 136; intelligence section at Malta, 184
Restriction of Enemy Supplies Committee, 36
Reval, Germans in, 350
Rhondda, Lord, 281 n
Rice, supplies of, 122 n[1], 270, 320
Richborough, port of, 204, 207
Riga, Germans in, 238
Rio de Janeiro, news of SEEADLER reaches, 71; meat from, 173; hides from, 248; convoy assembly port, 290, 308–9
Road Transport Board, 337
Robinson, Lieut.-Col. Sir Thomas, Chairman, Refrigerated Shipping Committee, 14 n, 196
Rome, M/S. representative at, 170 n
Roumania, occupation of, 38; effect of, 180–1; German and Austrian supplies of grain from, 177–8; of mineral oils, 180, 230; makes peace with Central Powers, 350; failure of the harvest in, 352, 401
ROXBURGH, Br. Cr., 130
Royden, Sir Thomas, 43 n; mission to U.S.A., 214; M/S. representative at Washington, 318

INDEX

Rubber, priority for, 122, 124; German shortage of, 180, 403
Rublee, Hon. George, American representative on A.M.T.C., 294 n
Ruddock, Mr. T. E., head of Norwegian section M/S., 219
Russia, supplies to, 32–3, 160–1, 238–9; wheat from, 89, 90; overland route to, 151; supervision of U.S. shipments to, 168; revolution in, 86–7, 160, 231, 237–9; economic conditions in, 238–9, 348–9, 432; collapse of, 347–50, 361; Allied expeditions to, 359–60
Russian Government Committee, 160–1
Russian Purchases Committee, 168

Sailing trade, SEEADLER attacks, 29, 71; convoys for, 99
St. Davids, Lord, Chairman of Committee on Port Development, 70
St. George's Channel, losses in, 90
St. Helens, convoy assembly port, 99
St. Theodore, Br.s.s., captured by MOEWE, 29, 72
Salonika, overland route to, 163; expedition to, 162, 274, 285; Allied offensive from, 398
Salter, Sir J. A., 19 n; mission to U.S.A., 214; and Inter-Allied shipping organisation, 241; Secretary to A.M.T.C., 293 n; Chairman of the Allied Maritime Transport Executive, 294 n; cited, 128 n, 306 n², 467
Saltmarsh, Sir George, 335 n
Saltpetre, priority for, 122 n¹
Sandbags, priority for, 122 n¹
Sanders, Mr. C. J. O., Director of Shipbuilding Work, 8
Sanderson, Mr. Oswald, 311
Scilly Islands, Dutch ships sunk off, 49; losses in approach to, 69 n, 182, 188
Scrutton, Mr. J. Herbert, Chairman, London Convoy Committee, 314
SEEA·LER, Ger. raider, ex-*Pass of Balmaha*, activities of, 29, 71; wreck of, 143; achievements of, 144
Sexton, Mr. James, 201 n
Shetland Islands, forces of, 99; trade of, 338
Shipbuilders, co-operation with M/S., 9; circular to, 209; deputation to the Prime Minister, 210
Shipbuilding, control of, 8–9, 76–7; transferred to Admiralty, 108, 204–6; to Lord Pirrie, 290–1; Shipping Controller's programme, 57, 79, 106; Navy Controller's, 205–6, 213; progress of, 57, 74–5, 84, 106, 207, 255–6, 290, 368–9, 409, 420, 441–2, 467; shortage of labour and steel for, 77–8, 106–7, 206–9, 256, 367–8, 409, 420; standard types, 75–6, 104–6, 211–3, 441–2; concrete, 408–9; increased facilities for, 440; in France and Italy, 32; in Japan, 80–1, 256; in U.S.A., 80, 214–15, 243–4, 369–70, 392; of world, 467; in enemy countries, 421. *See also* "Ship purchase," "Ship repairs," "Shipyards"
" Ship-for-ship " policy, 44, 48, 50–1, 93–4, 150–1, 156, 159
Ship Licensing Committee, 1, 6, 9, 12, 18, 419
Ship Management Branch, M/S., formed, 15; work of, 15, 328–30, 361
Shipowners, profits of, 2; attitude to liner requisition, 68, 113–7, 144–6; to convoys, 130, 133, 136–7, 189; *post-bellum* position of, 442
Shipping, Mercantile, British, problem of control of, 1–6; proportion requisitioned, 4–5, 32–3, 68–9, 85, 87–8, 110–1; concentrated on shorter routes, 33, 68, 89, 92, 109, 126 n, 131, 144, 163, 170–1, 192, 193, 248–9, 285, 287; 325–8, 412; in naval and military service, 34, 68, 89, 162–3; general employment of, 87, 376–7, 474–6; proportion in service of Allies, 162, 376–7, 474–6; decontrol of, 417–19; losses of, 56, 85, 91–3, 96, 130–1, 132, 137, 147 n, 158, 182–3, 187–8, 203, 251, 255, 288, 439, 465–8; damaged, 78, 92, 132, 159, 255, 370–1; effects of war on, 439–43, 468–71. *See also* " Clearances," " Convoys," " Entrances," " Defensively armed merchantmen," " Liner Requisition Scheme," " Requisitioning," " Shipping, Ministry of," " Tonnage "
—, Allied, losses of, 28, 56, 91, 158 n, 257, 365, 371, 466, 468; employment and control of, 95–6, 257–8, 376–7, 474–6; of Fr. and It., 30–1, 236, 302, 372, 375, 382–3; of Jap., 155, 243, 370; of U.S., 103, 176, 243, 302, 370,

379–80; requisitioning of Russian, 360–1; effect of war on, 468–9; on Belg., 433–4; on Fr., 436; on It., 437–8; on Jap. and U.S., 439
—, Mercantile, Enemy, laid up abroad, 82; seizures of and negotiations for, 82–3, 87, 89, 101–2, 216–17, 246, 258 n, 259; delivery of, under Armistice, 419–23; under Peace Treaty, 440
—, Neutral, withdrawn from Allied trade, 22, 86, 148, 156; effect of s/m campaign on supply of, 39–55, 93–5, 148–52, 155–7, 171, 259–61, 299; negotiations and agreements for use of, 24–5, 46, 48, 49, 51, 151, 152–4, 156, 217–19, 263–6, 357, 375–6, 409; requisitioning of, 49, 150, 154, 218, 299–300; admitted to convoy, 148–9; U.S.A. and, 156–7, 219, 224–6, 243, 261–2; Paris resolution on, 245–6; in Allied service, 377 n, 474–6; after Armistice, 418, 419; losses of, 22, 28, 54–5, 91–4, 149, 158, 260, 466, 468; effects of war on, 440, 468–9; fixtures and allocation of, *see* "Chartering Committee, Inter-Allied"
— of the World, losses of, 56, 91, 158, 188, 203, 251, 255, 288, 367, 371 n, 397, 440, 465–7; recovery of, 440–1, 469
Shipping and Coal Co-ordinating Committee, 323
Shipping Board, American, 82, 103, 215–17, 225; Chartering Committee of, 224, 357; relations with I.A.C.C., 225–6, 262
Shipping, Chamber of, 134, 331 n
Shipping Control Committee, 1, 4, 5–6, 8, 9, 10, 12, 18, 33–4, 65, 106, 205
Shipping Control Committee, American, 318
Shipping Controller, *see* "Maclay, Sir Joseph"
"Shipping Control Officers," 184, 311
Shipping, Ministry of, organised, 7–16; development of, 26, 117, 136, 160–1, 165, 168–9, 170, 184, 311, 317–19, 329–30; work of, 57, 87–9, 100, 113–30, 144–6, 184–5, 189, 194, 198, 237, 241, 253, 281, 314–15, 322, 331 n, 384, 395, 417, 419. *See also* "Commercial Services Branch," "Home Trade Branch," "Military Sea Transport Branch," "Naval Sea Transport Branch," "Port Branch," "Requisitioning Branch," "Ship Management Branch," "Statistical Branch"
Ship purchase, control of, 8, 80, 103; programme and progress, 102, 237, 256; from European neutrals, 79–80, 102; from Canada, 81, 84, 102, 216, 256, 369; from Japan, 81, 84, 102–3, 216, 256; from U.S.A., 81–2, 84, 102–4, 213–16
Ship Purchase Committee, Inter-Allied, 103, 237
Ship repairs, control of, 79; increase in, 78, 370–1, 421; efforts to accelerate, 107
Shipyards, National, proposed, 209; approved, 210; attitude of shipbuilders to, 210; progress of, 368, 408, 440
—, private, extensions to, 209, 368, 440
Siam, war with Germany and Austria, 217
Sierra Leone, convoy assembly port, 139; bunkering at, 322
Silk, imports of, 63; exports of manufactured, 450
Skoropadski, General, 351
Soap, German shortage of, 65
Société Suisse de Surveillance Économique, 358
South Africa, trade with, 122; meat from, 172, 195, 274, 285; dislocation of railways in, 185, 324; coal to Colombo, 322; to S. American, 324
South America, meat and meat products from, 195, 248, 285; supply of bunker depôts in, 323–4; shortage of coal, 323–5. *See also* under countries
Southampton, port of, 194
South Atlantic, activities of raiders in, 71; minefields in, 72; concentration of shipping in, 287, 327–8
Southend, convoy assembly port, 99
South-Western Approach, s/ms in, 67. *See also* "Fastnet," "Scilly Islands"
Spain, and s/m warfare, 41; agreements with shipowners, 153; commercial agreement with, 51, 156, 263; "10%" and "33%," orders, 51, 156, 263; iron ore from, 51, 156, 174, 271, 366; fruit from, 51, 63, 156, 263;

INDEX 499

coal exports to, 51, 263; control of shipping, 263
Sparkes, Mr. T. Ashley, agent of Cunard Co. in New York, 81; Director-General of M/S. in New York, 318
Standard Oil Co., 42
"Standard" ships, merits and defects of, 75–6, 441–2; disposal of, 441. *See also* "Shipbuilding"
Stanley, Sir Albert, 17 n, 281 n
State Insurance Scheme, premiums raised, 56–7, 92, 146; reduced, 417; revision of, 145–6; winding up of, 442
Statist, The, Index Number, 389
Statistical Branch, M/S., formed, 10; work of, 65–7, 93, 197, 241
Steel, shortage of, for shipbuilding, 77–8, 106–7, 206–7, 367–8; supplies to France and Italy, 161–2, 236–7, 320, 379, 394–5; Japanese shortage of, 103, 256; German output and exports of, 38, 229
Stevens, Hon. Raymond B., American representative on A.M.T.C., 293 n
Stewart, Mr. W. A., Head of Minerals Section, M/S., 26 n
Stones and slates, imports restricted, 59; decline in imports, 171
STRONGBOW, Br. T.B.D., sunk, 187
Submarine campaign, "unrestricted," 35, 39–40; neutral protests, 41; measures to counter, 42–5; grave menace of, 56–7, 85, 91–3, 131–2; increased range and efficiency of, 69, 96, 138; delays caused by, 158–9, 183–5; German exaggeration regarding, 177; effect on bunkering, 322; attacks on colliers, 28, 252; on Dutch ships, 49–50; on American, 55; on terminal waters, 69; on approach areas, 90–1, 92, 131; on outward traffic, 141; on meat ships, 173, 272–3; on tankers, 175; on inshore tracks, 187, 251, 288–9, 307, 370, 395–6; by s/m cruisers, 138, 188, 307, 309, 364 n³; off American coast, 365–6, 396–7; checked by convoys, 158, 182, 187–9, 203, 251, 308–9, 366–7, 370–1, 395; by blocking of bases, 309–10, 365; failure to disturb American trooping, 361; ascendency of defence, 364–5, 397–8, 407; suspended, 406, 410. *See also*

"Convoys," "Patrolled routes," "Shipping, losses of"
Suez route, reopened, 184–5, 308
Sugar Executive, Inter-Allied, 245
Sugar, supplies of, 124, 126, 173, 248, 271, 443–4; to France and Italy, 375
Sugar Supplies, Royal Commission on, 200, 295
Sulphur, priority for, 125
Supreme Economic Council, 422
Supreme War Council, 297, 301–2
Swansea, bunkering at, 194
Sweden, and s/m campaign, 41; German trade with, 38, 152, 179, 227, 264; munitions from, 151, 227; coal to, 152, 227, 229, 264, 354; friction with, 46–7, 151–2, 229; embargoes on supplies to, 152, 224, 226–7, 229, 264, 354; Kogrund agreement with, 152; *modus vivendi* with, 264, 354; general agreement with, 356–7
Switzerland, provision of tonnage for, 27, 379–80; and s/m campaign, 40, 41; German trade with, 231
Sydney, Cape Breton, convoy assembly port, 131, 134, 140

Tallow, priority for, 122, 286
Tankers, losses of, 175; requisitioned by U.S.A., 216 n; standard, 212–13; U.S.A. asked to provide, 243, 371; decontrolled, 418
Tea, imports restricted, 61; priority for, 122 n¹; decline in imports of, 171; in re-exports of, 278; distribution of imports, 342
"Temporary release," discontinued, 4
Tenth Cruiser Squadron, broken up, 234
Textile Exports Committee, 121–2
Textile materials, German shortage of, 38, 180, 229
Thomas, Mr. J. H., 201 n
Thompson, Mr. W. Rowan, 9 n
Thomson, Mr. Graeme, Director of Transports and Shipping, 11; member, imports Restriction Committee, 19 n; reorganises M/S. in New York, 318
Tillett, Mr. Ben, 201 n
Timber, imports restricted, 59–60, 282; decline in imports of, 86, 170–1, 269–70, 413, 444; increased production of, in Great

Britain, 60, 171, 196; in France, 60, 86, 171; economy in use of, 60, 171; supply of, 196, 227, 254; proposed shipment from Sweden in rafts, 171 n; War Office requirements of 175
Timber Supply Department, 10, 60
Tin, priority for, 122
Tobacco, imports restricted, 59; decline in imports, 171; German shortage of, 400
Tonnage Priority Committee, formed, 10; work of, 10, 66–7, 88, 119, 160, 241, 269, 281
Tonnage, shortage of, 1, 17–20; 32–3, 57, 65–9, 74, 85, 87–90, 93, 131, 158–63, 192–3, 197, 240–6, 255–7, 259, 267–8, 281–2, 296–7, 302–5, 370, 378–80, 381, 390–3, 407, 409, 415–16; for cereals, 19–21, 88, 241–2, 247, 283–4, 319–20; for coal and ore, 22, 28, 30–2, 52–4, 94–5, 161, 297–9, 301, 322; for munitions, 88, 390–3; for meat, 173, 248, 285–6, 327, 388; for sugar, 173–4; economies in use of, 34, 68–9, 160-1, 162–3, 183, 237, 286, 302, 382–3, 394–5; improvement in tonnage position, 177, 319, 345–6, 363–4, 372, 385; Inter-Allied agreement as to, 236–46; position after armistice, 420–3
Tory Island, losses in approach to, 91, 182, 188
Trade, adverse balance of, 177, 280, 447
Trade, Board of, relations with M/S., 7, 13–14, 122–3, 204; and import restrictions and priorities, 9–10, 18–19, 66; and meat supplies, 13–14, 195, 236, 274, 295, 327, 387; and other food supplies, 172, 195–6; and cotton, 175, 271; and control of chartering, 23; and ports, 200–1; Index Number, 389
Trade, Seaborne, *see* "Clearances," "Entrances," "Exports," "Imports," "Shipping," and under countries and commodities
Traffic Diversion Committee, 201, 288, 335–6
Transfer Restrictions Regulations 214
Transport Department, *see* "Ministry of Shipping," "Admiralty"
Transport Workers' Battalions, 70–1, 89, 165–7, 200–1, 254, 315–16, 332–3, 337

Transport Workers' Federation, 200, 201 n, 333, 384
Trawlers, use of armed, for patrol work, 30, 133, 137; for escort, 137
Treasury, 10; difficulties in financing Government purchases, 120–1, 177; on "Penalty rents," 342–3
Tr$^\cdot$ves Agreement, 420
Tuffill, Paymaster Lieut.-Commander H. B., R.D., R.N.R., 201 n
Tufton, Hon. C. H., 19 n
Turitella, Br.s.s., captured by WOLF, *see* ILTIS
Turkey, war with Greece, 155; armistice with, 410
Turnbull, Sir Robert, 335 n
Turnips, German consumption of, 37
Turn-round of shipping, effect of convoys on, 159, 190–3; of convoy reorganisation on, 313–19, 345; in North Sea, 253–4; importance of improvement in, 346, 372, 385. *See also* "Ports"
Tyser, Mr. W. P., 118 n

U 151, Ger.s/m, 365
U 155, Ger.s/m, *see* DEUTSCHLAND
Ukraine, supplies to Central Powers from, 349–53, 399, 401
Underwood, Commander T. H., R.N.V.R., 69
United States, and s/m campaign, 39–41; declares war, 55, 101 n; British credit in, 5, 86, 121, 122, 177, 414, 448; shipbuilding in, 80, 103, 214–15, 243–4, 369–70, 392; and "Cunard Contracts," 81–2, 103–4, 273–6; control of shipping by, 82, 103, 215; enemy ships in, 82–3, 101, 216–17; naval assistance from, 100, 129, 133, 137; British missions to, 104, 214, 318; and Japanese shipping, 155, 370; and neutral shipping, 156–7, 219, 224–6, 243, 261–2, 299; M S. organisation in, 168–70, 317–18; proposed tonnage a^{c}si·tance from, 176, 243–4, 297, 302–3; control of exports by, 223–5; of bunkers, 224–5, 324; and embargoes, 223–5, 227–9, 355–8; and Inter-Allied organisations, 293, 294 n² and n³, 373, 392; tonnage assistance to, 379–80, 381–2, 391–2; food imports of, 380 n; effects of war on, 439. *See also* "American

INDEX

Expeditionary Force," "North America, supplies from"
Uruguay, and s/m campaign, 41; breaks off relations with Germany, 217; coal exports to, 323; enemy ships in, 102, 217, 217 n, 259
Ushant, s/ms off, 28; patrols off, 30

Vaterland, ex-Ger.s.s., 83
Vegetables, imports restricted, 61; decline in imports, 171, 444
Venizelos, M., 155
Versailles, Treaty of, 411, 431, 437
Vienna, distress in, 233, 405
Vigilancia, U.S.s.s., sunk, 55
Villa, Signor, Italian representative on Allied Maritime Transport Executive, 293 n, 382-3
VINDICTIVE, Br. L.cr., 309
Vladivostok, port of, 160, 239, 240; Allies land at, 359, 403

Wachtfels, Ger.s.s., *see* WOLF
Wairuna, Br.s.s., captured, 143
War Cabinet, on import restrictions, 58; on port development, 70; on convoys, 100, 131-2; on Atlantic concentration, 119; on control of meat purchases, 195
Wardle, Mr. John, 335 n
War King, Br.s.s., 216
Warner, Mr. L. A. P., Director of Port Branch, M/S., 168, 335 n
War Office, shipping in service of, 34; labour supply, 71, 107, 207; and meat supplies, 173; timber shipments for, 175; and port congestion, 200
War Purchases and Finance, Inter-Allied Council for, 295, 305
War Queen, Br.s.s., 216
War risks, on neutrals, 22, 48-9, 52, 153-4. *See also* "State Insurance Scheme"
War Risks Associations, 145-7, 417
War Shamrock, Br.s.s., first standard ship, 211
War Trade Advisory Committee, 36
War Trade Statistical Department, 358
Warwick, Mr. C. W., 117
Watson, Sir Alfred, Statistical Adviser to M/S., 10
Wattle bark, priority for, 122 n²
Watts, Mr. W. T., 335 n
Webb, Captain Richard, R.N., Director of Trade Division, Admiralty, 133
Welborn, Mr. G. C., official ore broker, 26 n

Wemyss, Rear-Admiral Sir Rosslyn E., and Mediterranean convoys, 183-4
Wheat, British and Allied supplies of, 20-1, 88-90, 123-4, 172, 193, 202, 235-6, 271-2, 282-5, 319-21, 373, 385-6, 412, 443; stocks of, 88, 193, 284-5; storage and distribution of, 168, 199, 202, 320, 338; increased proportion taken as flour, 283, 319, 373 n; world shortage of, 235; increased production of, in U.K., 271, 285; German shortage of, 64, 177-8, 350-2, 399, 401
Wheat Executive, provision of tonnage for, 24, 26-7, 32, 162; work of, 155, 236, 295, 304, 320
Wheat Supplies, Royal Commission on, agents of, 21, 169-70; purchases of, 21-2; relations with Port and Transit Committee, 168, 200; work of, 172, 236, 295, 338
White, Mr. F., 14 n
Whitehead, Captain F. A., R.N., 130; Director of Mercantile Movements, Admiralty, 136
White Sea, 1917 programme arranged, 32-3, 87; effect on tonnage, 68, 88-9; carried out, 160-1, 238-9; 1918 programme abandoned, 358-9; ships escape from, 359
Wilde, Commander J. S., R.N., 129 n
Williams, Mr. Howard, 335 n
Williams, Mr. Robert, 201 n
Wills, Messrs., 21
Wilson, President, 41, 55, 406
Wines and spirits, import restricted, 61; decline in imports of, 171
Wintour, Mr. F. W., 19 n
WOLF, Ger. raider, ex-*Wachtfels*, activities of, 72, 142-3, 173 n, 289; achievements of, 289 n
Wolfram, priority for, 122 n²; German shortage of, 180
Wood, *see* "Timber"
Woollen industry, effect of war on, 278, 400, 413, 450, 452
Wool, supply of, 20, 122, 174, 196, 413, 445

Yarrowdale, Br.s.s., captured, 29; becomes Ger. raider, 73. *See also* LEOPARD

Zeebrugge, naval raid on, 309-10; reopening of, 434

www.ingramcontent.com/pod-product-compliance
Lightning Source LLC
Chambersburg PA
CBHW031152020526
44117CB00042B/242